The

DIVAN

of

HAFIZ

دیوان حافظ

Edition of Complete Poetry

Persian - English

Translated By:

Henry Wilberforce Clarke

Created by:

Hamid Eslamian

The Divan of Hafiz

Published by Persian Learning Center

Web: www.persianbell.com

Email: info@persianbell.com

ISBN: 978-1-63620-901-2

WWW.PERSIANBELL.COM

... So Much More Online!

✓ FREE Farsi Lessons

✓ More Farsi Learning Books!

✓ Persian Lessons

✓ Online Farsi Tutors

For a PDF Version of This Book

Please Visit www.persianbell.com

گر همچو من افتاده‌ی این دام شوی ای بس که خراب باده و جام شوی

ما عاشق و رند و مست و عالم سوزیم با ما منشین اگر نه بدنام شوی

If like me, you too fall in this trip,

Hold the wine and cup upon your lap.

We are the lovers, burning our tracks,

Join us if you can put up with the crap.

Shamsuddin Mohammad Hafiz Shirazi (1320–1389), the great lyric Persian poet is known for his ghazals. He has published about 500 ghazals and 42 Rubaiyees. The most popular Persian book, Divan-e Hafez, is a pinnacle of Persian literature and is to be found in the homes of most Iranian people, who learn his poems by heart and still use them as proverbs and sayings. Hafiz's poems of intimate divine love spread through the East in his lifetime, then into the West. Adaptations, imitations, and translations of Divan-e Hafez exist in all major languages.

The translation appearing in this book is by Henry Wilberforce Clarke (1840 - 1905). All Hafez's ghazals are provided in this bilingual book in Persian and English languages. This book can be useful for Persian and English language speakers and enjoyable for poetry lovers of any age.

Divan-e Hafiz is a precious learning resource for Persian language learners or Persian literature students. Not only will poems improve your Persian language, but they'll help your understanding of Persian culture and literature. Students will have ample opportunities to enrich their Persian learning experience and extend a range of language abilities through exploring these ghazals and poems.

Ghazal /Ode (غزل)

Ghazals are a type of poetry that follows a structured form with specific rules for meter, rhyme, and refrain. This poetic form originated in Arabic literature and later spread to Persian, Urdu, and other languages. Ghazals are known for their lyrical and melodic qualities and are often set to music.

Ghazals commonly explore themes of love, longing, loss, and spirituality and may incorporate religious or mystical concepts, metaphors, and symbolism. The convention of the "beloved" as a figure of desire and unattainable love is also often employed in ghazals.

This is a love poem, consisting of from five to fifteen verses: any meter except the ruba'i meters may be used; the same rhyme goes through the whole poem; the first hemistich of the first verse rhymes with the second hemistich of the same verse. The poem must be finished, without defects in rhyme, and pure in language, all obsolete words, or vulgar expressions being avoided. Each verse must convey a complete thought. The verses are strung like pearls on a thread, which makes them a necklace, the value whereof lies in the value of each pearl, not in the thread. The parts are:

مطلع (matla') the beginning,

مقطع (makta') end.

In the makta' the poet introduces his takhallus (تخلص). The takhallus is the name that the poet assumes. It is taken:

a) from the name of the Ruler of the time, or from the Patron.

b) from his occupation.

c) from his own name.

d) from his birthplace.

Throughout the centuries, many famous poets have written ghazals, including Rumi, Hafiz, Mirza Ghalib, and Faiz Ahmed Faiz. Today, the ghazal remains a popular and influential form of poetry in numerous cultures and languages.

©ONTENTS

الف THE LETTER ALIF..9

ب THE LETTER BĀ...22

ت THE LETTER TĀ...24

ث THE LETTER SĀ...95

ج THE LETTER JIM..96

ح THE LETTER HĀ...97

خ THE LETTER KHĀ...98

د THE LETTER DĀL..99

ر THE LETTER RĀ..225

ز THE LETTER ZĀ..238

س THE LETTER SIN...246

ش THE LETTER SHIN...251

ع THE LETTER ÀIN...269

غ THE LETTER GHÀIN...272

ف THE LETTER FĀ...273

ق THE LETTER GHĀF..274

ک THE LETTER KĀF..277

ل THE LETTER LĀM..280

م THE LETTER MIM..287

ن THE LETTER NŪN..353

و THE LETTER WĀW...373

ه THE LETTER HĀ..383

ى THE LETTER YĀ..394

الف
The Letter Alif

غزل ۱ ⓞⓓⓔ ①

أَلا یا اَیُّها السّاقی اَدِر کأساً و ناوِلها

Ho! O Saki[1], pass around and offer the bowl (of love for God)

که عشق آسان نمود اول ولی افتاد مشکل‌ها

For (the burden of) love (for God) at first (on the day of covenant) appeared easy, but (now) difficulties have occurred.

به بوی نافه‌ای کاخر صبا زان طره بگشاید

By reason of the perfume (hope) of the musk-pod, that, at the end (of night), the breeze displayeth from that (knotted) fore-locked

ز تاب جعد مشکینش چه خون افتاد در دل‌ها

From the twist of its musky (dark, fragrant) curl, what blood (of grief) befell the hearts (of the lovers of God)! that forelock,

مرا در منزل جانان چه امن عیش چون هر دم

In the stage (this world) of the (true) Beloved, mine what ease and pleasure, when momently,

جرس فریاد می‌دارد که بربندید محمل‌ها

The (loud) bell (of the call of death) giveth voice, saying: "Bind ye up the chattels of existence!"

به می سجاده رنگین کن گرت پیر مغان گوید

With wine, becolour the prayer-mat if the Pir[2] of the Magians[3] (the perfect murshid) bid thee;

که سالک بی‌خبر نبود ز راه و رسم منزل‌ها

For of the way and usage of the stages (to God) not without knowledge is the holy traveler (the perfect murshid).

شب تاریک و بیم موج و گردابی چنین هایل

The dark night, (of the world) and the fear of the wave, (of grief) and the whirlpool so fearful (the time of death).

کجا دانند حال ما سبکباران ساحل‌ها

The light-burdened ones of the shore, (ancestors who have passed the flood of death) how know they our state?

همه کارم ز خود کامی به بدنامی کشید آخر

By following my own fancy (in hastening to union with God), me (only) to ill fame all my work brought:

نهان کی ماند آن رازی کز او سازند محفل‌ها

Secret, how remaineth that great mystery (of love) whereof (great) assemblies speak?

حضوری گر همی‌خواهی از او غایب مشو حافظ

Hafez! if thou desire the presence (union with God Most High) from Him be not absent:

متی ما تلق من تهوی دع الدنیا و اهملها

When thou visitest thy Beloved, abandon the world; and let it go.

1-Tapster
2-A Muslim saint or holy man

3-Fire worshipper

غزل ۲ ⓞⓓⓔ ②

صلاح کار کجا و من خراب کجا

The rectitude of work, where? and I ruined (wanting in rectitude) where?

ببین تفاوت ره کز کجاست تا به کجا

Behold the distance of the Path, from where (rectitude) to (ruin) where?

دلم ز صومعه بگرفت و خرقه سالوس

My heart wearied of the cloister, and of the patched garment of hypocrisy:

کجاست دیر مغان و شراب ناب کجا

The Magians[1] cloister (the circle of the murshid;) where? the pure wine of the love of God where?

چه نسبت است به رندی صلاح و تقوا را

With profligacy (the being severed from friend and stranger), what connections have rectitude and piety (hypocrisy)?

سماع وعظ کجا نغمه رباب کجا

The hearing of the exhortation (that affecteth not the heart) where? The melody of the stringed instrument (the murshid) where?

ز روی دوست دل دشمنان چه دریابد

From the Friend's (luminous) face, what gaineth the dark heart of enemies?

چراغ مرده کجا شمع آفتاب کجا

The dead (extinguished) lamp, where? The candle of the resplendent resplendent sun, where?

چو کحل بینش ما خاک آستان شماست

The dust of Thy threshold is like the kuhl of our vision:

کجا رویم بفرما از این جناب کجا

Where go we? Order. Hence, where?

مبین به سیب زنخدان که چاه در راه است

Look not at the apple (dimple) of the chin; for in the path is a (great) pit:

کجا همیروی ای دل بدین شتاب کجا

O heart! where goest thou? With this haste, to amend where?

بشد که یاد خوشش باد روزگار وصال

He is gone! To him, (the true beloved or the murshid) be the time of union a pleasant memory.

خود ان کرشمه کجا و آن عتاب کجا

Gone is that (tender) glance, where? and that reproof, where?

قرارو خواب زحافظ طمع مدار ای دوست

O friend! from Hafez seek neither ease nor patience:

قرار چیست صبوری کدام و خواب کجا

Ease, what? Patience, what? Sleep, where?

غزل ۳ ⓞⓓⓔ ③

اگر آن ترک شیرازی به دست آرد دل ما را

If that Bold One (the true Beloved) of Shiraz gain our heart,

به خال هندویش بخشم سمرقند و بخارا را

For His dark mole, I will give Samarkand and Bukhara[2] (both worlds).

1-Fire worshipper   2-To give importance Hafiz to the beloved

بده ساقی می باقی که در جنت نخواهی یافت

Saki![1] give the wine (of divine love) remaining (from the people of religion); for, in Paradise, thou wilt not have

کنار آب رکن آباد و گلگشت مصلا را

The bank of the water of the Ruknabad[2] (the lover's weeping eye) nor the rose of the garden of Musalla[3] (the lover's heart).

فغان کاین لولیان شوخ شیرین کار شهرآشوب

Alas! These saucy dainty ones (lovely women) sweet of work, the torment of the city,

چنان بردند صبر از دل که ترکان خوان یغما را

Take patience from the heart even as the men of Turkistan (take) the tray of plunder.

ز عشق ناتمام ما جمال یار مستغنی است

The beauty of the Beloved (God) is in no need of our imperfect love:

به آب و رنگ و خال و خط چه حاجت روی زیبا را

Of luster, and color, and mole and tricked line (of eyebrow), what need hath the lovely face?

من از آن حسن روزافزون که یوسف داشت دانستم

By reason of that beauty, daily increasing that Yusof [4] (the absolute Existence, the real Beloved, God) h ad, I (the first day) know

که عشق از پرده عصمت برون آرد زلیخا را

That Love for Him would bring Zulaikha[5] (us, things possible) forth from the screen of chastity (the pure existence of God).

اگر دشنام فرمایی و گر نفرین دعا گویم

(O murshid!) Thou (to amend my work) spakest ill of me; and I am happy. God Most High forgive thee thou spakest well

جواب تلخ می‌زیبد لب لعل شکرخا را

The bitter reply suiteth the ruby lip, sugar-eating.

نصیحت گوش کن جانا که از جان دوست‌تر دارند

O Soul! Hear the counsel (of the Murshid)., for, dearer than the soul

جوانان سعادتمند پند پیر دانا را

Hold happy youths the counsel of the wise old man

حدیث از مطرب و می گو و راز دهر کمتر جو

The tale of minstrel and of wine (of Love) utter; little seek the mystery of time;

که کس نگشود و نگشاید به حکمت این معما را

For this mystery, none solved by skill (thought and knowledge); and shall not solve.

غزل گفتی و در سفتی بیا و خوش بخوان حافظ

Thou utteredest a ghazal[6]; and threadedest pearls (of verse). Hafez! come and sweetly sing

که بر نظم تو افشاند فلک عقد ثریا را

That, on thy verse, the sky may scatter (in thanks) the cluster of the Pleiades.

1-Tapster
2-An area in Shiraz
3-An area in Shiraz

4-Name of a prophet
5-Lover Yusof
6-Sonnet

غزل ۴ ⓄⒹⒺ ④

صبا به لطف بگو آن غزال رعنا را
O breeze! with softness speak to the beautiful fawn (the murshid),

که سر به کوه و بیابان تو داده‌ای ما را
Saying: Thou hast given to us desire for the mountain and the desert (the hardship and pain of separation).

شکرفروش که عمرش دراز باد چرا
The sugar-seller (the murshid, seller of the sugar of Divine knowledge), whose life be long! why?

تفقدی نکند طوطی شکرخا را
Maketh he no inquiry of the welfare of the parrot (Hafiz, the disciple) sugar of devouring?

غرور حسنت اجازت مگر نداد ای گل
O rose (murshid, beautiful as the rose)! perhaps the pride of beauty hath not given thee permission

که پرسشی نکنی عندلیب شیدا را
That thou makest no inquiry as to the state (full of grief, void of hypocrisy) of the distraught nightingale (Hafiz)

به خلق و لطف توان کرد صید اهل نظر
By beauty of disposition, people of vision one can captivate:

به بند و دام نگیرند مرغ دانا را
Not by snare and net, take they the wise bird.

ندانم از چه سبب رنگ آشنایی نیست
I know not why the color of constancy, they have not

سهی قدان سیه چشم ماه سیما را
Those straight of stature, dark of eye, moon of face (the prophets in the garden of the shar').

چو با حبیب نشینی و باده پیمایی
When thou sittest with the beloved; and drinkest wine,

به یاد دار محبان بادپیما را
Bring to mind the beloved ones, wind-measuring.

جز این قدر نتوان گفت در جمال تو عیب
Of defect in thy beauty, one cannot speak save to this degree

که وضع مهر و وفا نیست روی زیبا را
That the way of love and of constancy belongeth not to the lovely face.

در آسمان نه عجب گر به گفته حافظ
On the sky, what if, of Hafez's utterances

سرود زهره به رقص آورد مسیحا را
Zuhra's[1] singing should bring to dancing the Masiha (Christ).

غزل ۵ ⓄⒹⒺ ⑤

دل می‌رود ز دستم صاحب دلان خدا را
For God's sake (come to my cry (relief). O pious ones (murshids of the age)!! forth from the hand (of control), goeth my heart (in perturbation). For God's sake (come to my cry and aid me):

دردا که راز پنهان خواهد شد آشکارا
O the pain that the hidden mystery (of love) should be disclosed.

1-Refers to the planet Venus, the symbol of the beloved

کشتی شکستگانیم ای باد شرطه برخیز

We are boat-stranded ones! O fair breeze (the murshid; or divine love)! arise:

باشد که بازبینیم دیدار آشنا را

It may be that, again, we may behold the face of the Beloved (God).

ده روزه مهر گردون افسانه است و افسون

For the (short) space of ten days, the sphere's favor is magic and sorcery (entrancing):

نیکی به جای یاران فرصت شمار یارا

O friend! regard as booty, goodness in friends (companions, disciples).

در حلقه گل و مل خوش خواند دوش بلبل

Last night in the assembly of the rose and of wine (the banquet of taste, of desire, of glories, of splendour, of love for God), the bulbul[1] (murshid) sweetly sang:

هات الصبوح هبوا یا ایها السکارا

O Saki! give wine: O intoxicated ones! come to life!

ای صاحب کرامت شکرانه سلامت

O generous one! in thanks for thy own safety

روزی تفقدی کن درویش بی‌نوا را

One day, make inquiry of the welfare of the foodless dervish.

آسایش دو گیتی تفسیر این دو حرف است

The ease of two worlds (this and the next) is the explanation of these two words:

با دوستان مروت با دشمنان مدارا

With friends, kindness; with enemies, courtesy.

در کوی نیک نامی ما را گذر ندادند

In the street of good name (outward rectitude), they gave us no admission:

گر تو نمی‌پسندی تغییر کن قضا را

If thou approve not, change our Fate.

آن تلخ وش که صوفی ام الخباثش خواند

That (true wine of the love of God, which is like to thee) bitter wine, which the Sufi[2] (Muhammad) called "The mother of iniquities,"

اشهی لنا و احلی من قبله العذارا

To us, is more pleasant and more sweet than the kisses of virgins.

هنگام تنگدستی در عیش کوش و مستی

In the time of straitedness, strive in pleasure and in intoxication:

کاین کیمیای هستی قارون کند گدا را

For, this elixir of existence maketh the beggar (rich as) Karun[3].

سرکش مشو که چون شمع از غیرتت بسوزد

Don't rebel, due to defiance thou burnt like candle

دلبر که در کف او موم است سنگ خارا

Darling in whose hands granite is like wax soft

آیینه سکندر جام می است بنگر

The cup of wine (the heart filled with recollection of God) is Sikandar's mirror. Behold

تا بر تو عرضه دارد احوال ملک دارا

So that it may show thee the state of Dara's kingdom[4] (the soul).

1-Nightingale
2-A Muslim saint or holy man Pietist

3-Korah, The rich man of the time of Prophet Moses
4-Reminder; the great defeat is from the Sikandar

خوبان پارسی گو بخشندگان عمرند

Life-givers, are the lovely ones, Persian-prattling:

ساقی بده بشارت رندان پارسا را

O Saki[1]! this news gives to the old men of Fars (Persia).

حافظ به خود نپوشید این خرقه می آلود

Of himself, Hafez put not on this patched, wine-stained garment (of poverty)

ای شیخ پاکدامن معذور دار ما را

O Shaikh[2], pure of sins! hold us excused.

غزل ۶ ⓄⒹⒺ ⓖ ODE 6

به ملازمان سلطان که رساند این دعا را

To the Sultan's attendants, who will convey this prayer

که به شکر پادشاهی ز نظر مران گدا را

In thanks for sovereignty, away from sight drive not the beggar?"

ز رقیب دیوسیرت به خدای خود پناهم

From the watcher (imperious lust), demon of nature, I take shelter in my God

مگر آن شهاب ثاقب مددی دهد خدا را

Perchance that gleaming light (God's bounty and grace) may, for God's sake, give a little aid.

مژه سیاهت ار کرد به خون ما اشارت

If Thy dark eye-lash (arrow-like) made for our blood,

ز فریب او بیندیش و غلط مکن نگارا

O Idol! think of its deceit (in blood-shedding); and make no mistake (lest Thou suffer regret for my blood).

دل عالمی بسوزی چو عذار برفروزی

When (by Thy splendour) Thou enkindlest thy face, Thou consumest a world,

تو از این چه سود داری که نمی‌کنی مدارا

From this, what profit hast Thou that Thou doest no kindness

همه شب در این امیدم که نسیم صبحگاهی

All night (all my life), in this hope I am that the breeze of dawn (the angel of death),

به پیام آشنایان بنوازد آشنا را

With the message of lovers (giving release by death from the world's tumult), will cherish (me) the lover.

چه قیامت است جانا که به عاشقان نمودی

O Beloved! what is the tumult that to lovers thou displayedest?

دل و جان فدای رویت بنما عذار ما را

Thy face like the gleaming moon, Thy stature like the heart-ravishing cypress?

به خدا که جرعه‌ای ده تو به حافظ سحرخیز

O Murshed![3] to the lover Hafez morning-rismg, give thou, for God's sake, a draught, (of wine of love),

که دعای صبحگاهی اثری کند شما را

May his prayer of the morning-time avail thee

غزل ۷ ODE 7

صوفی بیا که آینه صافیست جام را

O Sufi[1] (outwardly pure, inwardly impure)! come; for bright is the mirror of the cup
(the heart of the perfect murshid):

تا بنگری صفای می لعل فام را

That thou mayst see the brightness of the wine of ruby hue (or experience the
intoxication of the wine of the love of God).

راز درون پرده ز رندان مست پرس

Of profligates intoxicated (with excess of love for God) as the mystery (unutterable
and hidden) within the veil;

کاین حال نیست زاهد عالی مقام را

For, this state (wherein they utter mysteries) is not the Zahed's[2], lofty of degree.

عنقا شکار کس نشود دام بازچین

The Anka[3] (God's pure existence) is the prey of none. Up-pluck thy snare:

کان جا همیشه باد به دست است دام را

For, here ever, in the hand of the snare, is (only) wind (vain thought).

در بزم دور یک دو قدح درکش و برو

At time's banquet, enjoy one or two cups (moments of union with the true
Beloved); and go (to eternity):

یعنی طمع مدار وصال دوام را

(Here) Verily desire not perpetual union (for 'tis vain).

ای دل شباب رفت و نچیدی گلی ز عیش

O heart! youth's vigor hath departed; and, from life, thou hast not plucked a
single rose (of true love, or of divine grace):

پیرانه سر مکن هنری ننگ و نام را

Elderly of head, show skill (in permanence) of name and fame (in
supplication and lamentation to God).

در عیش نقد کوش که چون آبخور نماند

(Whilst thou art in the world) Strive in the pleasure (of zikr va[4] filer) of the
present. As, when no water remained,

آدم بهشت روضه دارالسلام را

"Adam let go the garden of the house of safety (Paradise)."

ما را بر آستان تو بس حق خدمت است

On our part, at thy threshold, many are thy rights of service.

ای خواجه بازبین به ترحم غلام را

O Sir! again, in pity, look upon thy slave (who, at least, hath not quitted thy threshold).

حافظ مرید جام می است ای صبا برو

The disciple of the cup of Jamshid is Hafez. O breeze, go:

وز بنده بندگی برسان شیخ جام را

And give salutation from the slave to the Shaikh of Jam[5].

1-A Muslim saint or holy man Pietist   4-And
2-Pietist   5-Cup
3-Phoenix

غزل ۸ ODE ⑧ 🕉️

ساقیا برخیز و درده جام را
O Saki[1]! (murshid) arise; and give the cup (of wine of desired):
خاک بر سر کن غم ایام را
Strew dust on the head of the grief of time.

ساغر می بر کفم نه تا ز بر
In my palm, place the cup of wine so that, from my breast,
برکشم این دلق ازرق فام را
I may pluck off this patched garment of blue color.

گر چه بدنامیست نزد عاقلان
Although in the opinion of the (apparently) wise, ill-fame is ours,
ما نمی‌خواهیم ننگ و نام را
Not name nor fame, do we (distraught with love for God) desire.

باده درده چند از این باد غرور
Give wine! with this wind of pride, how long,
خاک بر سر نفس نافرجام را
Dust on the head of useless desire?

دود آه سینه نالان من
The smoke of the sigh of my burning heart
سوخت این افسردگان خام را
Consumed these immature ones (hypocrites; fathers of lust).

محرم راز دل شیدای خود
Of the secret (of love) of my distraught heart, a friend,
کس نمی‌بینم ز خاص و عام را
Among high and low, none, I see.

با دلارامی مرا خاطر خوش است
Glad is my heart with a heart's ease (a lovely one),
کز دلم یک باره برد آرام را
Who, from my heart, once took ease.

ننگرد دیگر به سرو اندر چمن
At the cypress in the sward, again looketh not
هر که دید آن سرو سیم اندام را
That one, who beheld that cypress of silvern limb.

صبر کن حافظ به سختی روز و شب
Hafez! day and night, be patient, in adversity:
عاقبت روزی بیابی کام را
So that, in the end, thou mayst, one day, gain thy desire.

1-Tapster

غزل ۹ ⓄⒹⒺ 9

رونق عهد شباب است دگر بستان را
The splendor of youth's time (the murshid's assembly) again belongeth to the garden (the holy traveller's existence);

می‌رسد مژده گل بلبل خوش الحان را
The glad tidings of divine glories of the rose (the Beloved) reacheth the bulbul[1] the lover sweet of song.

ای صبا گر به جوانان چمن بازرسی
O breeze! if again thou reach the youths of the meadow, (the murshid's disciples)

خدمت ما برسان سرو و گل و ریحان را
Convey our service (of prayer) to the cypress, the rose, and the sweet basil (the murshid's disciples).

گر چنین جلوه کند مغبچه باده فروش
If the young Magian, (the khalifa, showing the true Path) wine-seller, display such splendor, of explanation

خاکروب در میخانه کنم مژگان را
(In thanks) I will make my eye-lash the dust-sweep er of the door of the wine-house (his dwelling).

ای که بر مه کشی از عنبر سارا چوگان
O thou that drawest, over the moon (of thy face), the polo of purest ambergris, (the black tress)

مضطرب حال مگردان من سرگردان را
(by concealing thy grace) Make not distraught of state, me of revolving head.

ترسم این قوم که بر دردکشان می‌خندند
This crowd that laugheth (and carpeth) at those (lovers of God) drinking the wine-dregs (of the wine of the love of God), I fear?

در سر کار خرابات کنند ایمان را
They will, in the end, ruin their Faith.

یار مردان خدا باش که در کشتی نوح
Be the friend of the men of God; for, in Noah's ark (the existence of the people of God),

هست خاکی که به آبی نخرد طوفان را
Was a little dust (humbleness), that purchased not the deluge (the empire of the world) for a drop of water.

برو از خانه گردون به در و نان مطلب
Forth from the house of the sphere, go; and bread, seek not.

کان سیه کاسه در آخر بکشد مهمان را
For, in the end, this dark cup (of avarice) slayeth the guest.

هر که را خوابگه آخر مشتی خاک است
To him, whose last sleeping-place is with two handfuls of earth, (the grave)

گو چه حاجت که به افلاک کشی ایوان را
Say "Thine what need to exalt the turrets to the sky?"

ماه کنعانی من مسند مصر آن تو شد
My moon of Kan'an! (my soul) the throne of Egypt (the rank of perfection the world of souls) is thine:

وقت آن است که بدرود کنی زندان را
The time is that (time) when thou shouldst did farewell to the prison (of the body, or of the world)

1-Nightingale

ملک آزادگی و کنج قناعت گنجیست

Not (even) one mystery of the mysteries of the (Absolute) existence mayest thou
know, If head bewildered of the circle of possibility, thou be

که به شمشیر میسر نشود سلطان را

The land of liberty, and the corner of contentment is a treasure, That, by the sword,
the Sultan cannot attain

حافظا می خور و رندی کن و خوش باش ولی

Hafez! drink wine (of love); practice profligacy (the concealing of secrets) and be
happy (grieve not and grieved be not); but

دام تزویر مکن چون دگران قرآن را

Like others, make not the Kuran[1] the snare of deceit.

غزل ۱۰ ⓄⒹⒺ ⓵⓪

دوش از مسجد سوی میخانه آمد پیر ما

Last night (the first day of Eternity without beginning) from the Masjed[2] (the place where the soul is
separate from the body) towards the wine tavern (the stage of truth and love) our Pir[3] (Muhammad) came:

چیست یاران طریقت بعد از این تدبیر ما

O friends of the Path! after this, (lapse of time, and this departure) what is our plan?

ما مریدان روی سوی قبله چون آریم چون

How may we, disciples, turn to the Ka'ba[4], (the Masjid), when

روی سوی خانه خمار دارد پیر ما

Our Pir (Muhammad) hath his face towards the house of the Vintner (the stage of Truth and Love).

در خرابات طریقت ما به هم منزل شویم

In the Fire-worshipper's Tavern (the stage of Truth and Love) we also shall be lodging;

کاین چنین رفته‌ست در عهد ازل تقدیر ما

For, in the Covenant of eternity without beginning, even so was our destiny.

عقل اگر داند که دل دربند زلفش چون خوش است

in the bond of His (the Beloved's) tress, how happy is the Heart! If Wisdom knows,

عاقلان دیوانه گردند از پی زنجیر ما

In pursuit of our tress chain, the wise will become distraught.

روی خوبت آیتی از لطف بر ما کشف کرد

By its grace, Thy beautiful face explained to us a verse of the Kuran:

زان زمان جز لطف و خوبی نیست در تفسیر ما

For that reason, in our explanation, is naught save grace and beauty.

با دل سنگینت آیا هیچ درگیرد شبی

A single night, against Thy stony heart, ever effecteth aught

آه آتشناک و سوز سینه شبگیر ما

Our sigh, fire-raining (supplicating God) and the burning of our heart in the night-time?

تیر آه ما ز گردون بگذرد حافظ خموش

Beyond the sphere passeth the arrow of our sigh. Hafez! silence.

رحم کن بر جان خود خود پرهیز کن از تیر ما

Show compassion to thy soul; avoid the arrow of ours.

1-Quran
2-Mosque

3-A Muslim saint ascetic and mystic
4-Muslims turn at prayer.

غزل ۱۱ ⓄⒹⒺ ⑪

ساقی به نور باده برافروز جام ما

Saki (murshid)! with the light of wine (divine love), up-kindle the cup of the heart) of ours.

مطرب بگو که کار جهان شد به کام ما

Minstrel! (Murshid) speak, saying: "The world's work hath gone agreeably to the desire of ours."

ما در پیاله عکس رخ یار دیدهایم

In the cup, (of the heart), we have beheld the reflection of the face of the Beloved (God)

ای بیخبر ز لذت شرب مدام ما

O thou void of knowledge of the joy of the perpetual wine-drinking of ours.

هرگز نمیرد آن که دلش زنده شد به عشق

Never dieth that one, whose heart is alive with (true) love (to God):

ثبت است بر جریده عالم دوام ما

On the world's record, is written the everlasting existence of ours.

چندان بود کرشمه و ناز سهی قدان

The coy glance and the grace of those straight of stature (illusory beloved ones) (is only) till

کاید به جلوه سرو صنوبرخرام ما

With grace, moving like a lofty pine-tree, cometh the cypress of (the true Beloved) ours.

ای باد اگر به گلشن احباب بگذری

O breeze! if thou pass by the rose-bed of beloved ones,

زنهار عرضه ده بر جانان پیام ما

Take care! present to the beloved (the murshid) the message of ours.

گو نام ما ز یاد به عمدا چه میبری

(O breeze!) From thy memory, our name why purposely takest thou?

خود آید آن که یاد نیاری ز نام ما

Itself (forgetfulness) cometh, when (after death) cometh no recollection of ours.

مستی به چشم شاهد دلبند ما خوش است

To the eye of our heart-binding beloved (the murshid) pleasing is intoxication

زان رو سپردهاند به مستی زمام ما

For that reason, to intoxication they (Fate and Destiny) have given the rein of ours.

ترسم که صرفهای نبرد روز بازخواست

On the day of up-rising (the resurrection), I fear, a profit taketh not

نان حلال شیخ ز آب حرام ما

The lawful bread (piety) of the Shaikh, more than the unlawful water wine of love) of ours.

حافظ ز دیده دانه اشکی همیفشان

Hafez! from thy eye, keep shedding a teardrop;

باشد که مرغ وصل کند قصد دام ما

It may be, that the bird of union may attempt the snare of ours.

دریای اخضر فلک و کشتی هلال

The green (blue) sea of sky, and the bark of the new moon (the mysteries of the sphere)

هستند غرق نعمت حاجی قوام ما

Are immersed in the favor of Haji Kivam[1] (the murshid) of ours.

1-Hafiz's close friend

غزل ۱۲ ÔDE ①②

ای فروغ ماه حسن از روی رخشان شما

O (true Beloved)! the splendor of the moon-beauty (the illusory beloved is) from the illumined face of Thine!

آب روی خوبی از چاه زنخدان شما

The luster of beauteousness from the chin-dimple of Thine!

عزم دیدار تو دارد جان بر لب آمده

My soul at the lip (ready to depart in death) desireth the sight of Thee:

بازگردد یا برآید چیست فرمان شما

Back it goeth; forth, it cometh; what order is Thine? '

کس به دور نرگست طرفی نبست از عافیت

By the revolution of Thy eye, none obtained a portion of enjoyment:

به که نفروشند مستوری به مستان شما

Best, that they sell the veil of chastity to the intoxicated ones of Thine.

بخت خواب آلود ما بیدار خواهد شد مگر

Our sleep-stained fortune will, perchance, become vigilant,

زان که زد بر دیده آبی روی رخشان شما

On that account that a little water on its eye, expressed that gleaming face of Thine.

با صبا همراه بفرست از رخت گلدسته‌ای

Along with the wind, send from Thy cheek a handful of roses

بو که بویی بشنویم از خاک بستان شما

It may be that I may perceive a perfume from the dust of the rose garden of Thine.

عمرتان باد و مراد ای ساقیان بزم جم

O Saki's of the banquet of Jam, long be your life; desire.,

گر چه جام ما نشد پر می به دوران شما

Although our cup be not full of wine at the circulation of yours.

دل خرابی می‌کند دلدار را آگه کنید

My heart worketh desolation. Inform the heart-possessor:

زینهار ای دوستان جان من و جان شما

Verily, O friends, I swear by soul of mine and soul of Thine.

کی دهد دست این غرض یا رب که همدستان شوند

O Lord! when these desires (of union with Thee), that are our companions appear,

خاطر مجموع ما زلف پریشان شما

Collected will be the heart of ours; and dishevelled the tress of Thine.

دور دار از خاک و خون دامن چو بر ما بگذری

When by us, Thou passest, from dust (the illusory lover) and from blood (the true lover) keep far thy skirt:

کاندر این ره کشته بسیارند قربان شما

For, on this Path (of love) many a one (a pretender) hath become a sacrifice of Thine.

ای صبا با ساکنان شهر یزد از ما بگو

O breeze! from us to the dwellers of Yazd say:

کای سر حق ناشناسان گوی چوگان شما

The head of those not recognizing truths the polo ball of yours.

گر چه دوریم از بساط قرب همت دور نیست

From the plain of propinquity, though we be far, not far is desire:

بنده شاه شماییم و ثناخوان شما

The slave of your King we are, and the praise-utterer of yours.

ای شهنشاه بلنداختر خدا را همتی

O King of Kings, lofty of star! for God's sake, a blessing,

تا ببوسم همچو اختر خاک ایوان شما

That, like the sky, I may kiss the dust of the court of yours.

می‌کند حافظ دعایی بشنو آمینی بگو

Hafez uttereth a prayer. Listen: say an amin!

روزی ما باد لعل شکرافشان شما

Be my daily food the lips sugar-scattering of Thine.

◈◉⟩⟨◉◈

The Letter Bā ب

ⓄⒹⒺ ①③   غزل ۱۳

می‌دمد صبح و کله بست سحاب
The morning (of ecstatic state) blossometh; and the cloud bindeth a veil (obscuring the sun of truth):

الصبوح الصبوح یا اصحاب
O companions! the morning cup! the morning cup!

می‌چکد ژاله بر رخ لاله
(From the trickling cloud) The hail (of death) droppeth on the face of the tulip (people of the world):

المدام المدام یا احباب
O companions! the wine! (Of love) the wine! (Of love)

می‌وزد از چمن نسیم بهشت
From the sward (the society of the murshid) bloweth the breeze of Paradise (God's blessing):

هان بنوشید دم به دم می ناب
Then, ever drink pure wine (ask for God's blessing).

تخت زمرد زده است گل به چمن
In the sward, the rose (the murshid) causing bounty to arrive hath fixed its emerald throne:

راح چون لعل آتشین دریاب
Get wine (ruddy and fiery) like the fiery ruby!

در میخانه بسته‌اند دگر
Again, they have closed the door (of manifestations) of the tavern (the heart and the brain):

افتتح یا مفتح الابواب
O Opener of doors! (God)! open!

لب و دندانت را حقوق نمک
Right of salt, thy ruby lip

هست بر جان و سینه‌های کباب
Hath against the wound of roast-hearts (that have gathered salt from my lip)

این چنین موسمی عجب باشد
At such a time, 'tis wonderful

که ببندند میکده به شتاب
That hastily they close the tavern.

بر رخ ساقی پری پیکر
O cheers to the glamorous Saki

همچو حافظ بنوش باده ناب
Like Hafez drink pure wine, then.

ⓄⒹⒺ ①④   غزل ۱۴

گفتم ای سلطان خوبان رحم کن بر این غریب
(To the true Beloved) I said: "O Sultan of lovely ones! show pity to this poor stranger."

گفت در دنبال دل ره گم کند مسکین غریب
He said: "In the desire of his own heart, loseth his way the wretched stranger."

گفتمش مگذر زمانی گفت معذورم بدار

To Him, I said: "Pass awhile with me." He replied: "Hold me excused."

خانه پروردی چه تاب آرد غم چندین غریب

A home (delicately) nurtured one, what care beareth he for such griefs of the poor stranger?

خفته بر سنجاب شاهی نازنینی را چه غم

To the gently nurtured one, asleep on the royal ermine, what grief,

گر ز خار و خاره سازد بستر و بالین غریب

If, should make the couch of thorn; and, the pillow of the hard stone, the poor stranger.

ای که در زنجیر زلفت جای چندین آشناست

O thou in the chain of whose tress, are the souls of so many lovers,

خوش فتاد آن خال مشکین بر رخ رنگین غریب

Happily, fell that musky mole, on thy colored cheek, so strange.

می‌نماید عکس می در رنگ روی مه وشت

In the color of the moon-like face, appeareth the reflection of wine (of love or of unity):

همچو برگ ارغوان بر صفحه نسرین غریب

Like the leaf of the (ruddy) Arghavan[1] on the surface of the wild red rose, strange

بس غریب افتاده است آن مور خط گرد رخت

Strangely hath fallen that ant-line the down around thy face:

گر چه نبود در نگارستان خط مشکین غریب

Yet, in the picture gallery (of Arzhang) the musky line of shading is not strange.

گفتم ای شام غریبان طره شبرنگ تو

I said: "O thou tress of night-hue, (the attraction of grace) the evening shelter of the stranger!

در سحرگاهان حذر کن چون بنالد این غریب

"In the morning time, beware, if his need bewail this stranger."

گفت حافظ آشنایان در مقام حیرتند

He said: "Hafez!, (At my beauty) friends are in the stage of astonishment:"

دور نبود گر نشیند خسته و مسکین غریب

"Far (from wonder) it is not, if shattered and wretched sitteth the stranger."

❖◉❖◉❖

1-Name of a flower

ت
The Letter Tā

غزل ۱۵ ⓄⒹⒺ ①⑤

ای شاهد قدسی که کشد بند نقابت

O chaste beloved! Who draweth the fastening of the veil of thee?

و ای مرغ بهشتی که دهد دانه و آبت

O (lovely) bird of Paradise! grain and water, who giveth thee?

خوابم بشد از دیده در این فکر جگرسوز

Went sleep from my eye in this liver-consuming thought

کاغوش که شد منزل آسایش و خوابت

Whose bosom is the dwelling and sleeping place of thee

درویش نمی‌پرسی و ترسم که نباشد

The dervish, thou askest not! and I fear that there is

اندیشه آمرزش و پروای ثوابت

Neither thought of his forgiveness, nor care for his punishment, to thee.

راه دل عشاق زد آن چشم خماری

That eye of intoxication struck (and made restless) the path of the lover's heart:

پیداست از این شیوه که مست است شرابت

From this way, 'tis manifest that wine is intoxicated of thee.

تیری که زدی بر دلم از غمزه خطا رفت

The great arrow of a glance that, at my heart, thou castedest, missed:

تا باز چه اندیشه کند رای صوابت

Let us see what designeth the good judgement of thee.

هر ناله و فریاد که کردم نشنیدی

The wail and plaint that I made, all thou heardest not:

پیداست نگارا که بلند است جنابت

O idol! 'tis manifest that lofty is the station of thee.

دور است سر آب از این بادیه هش دار

In this desert, of divine knowledge the water poolstage of purpose is far. Keep sense,

تا غول بیابان نفریبد به سرابت

So that the creatures one outwardly good inwardly bad of the desert, may not, with the mirage, deceive thee

تا در ره پیری به چه آیین روی ای دل

O heart! while in the path of old age, by what way goest thou?

باری به غلط صرف شد ایام شبابت

In mistake, all at once, became expended the season of youth of thee.

ای قصر دل افروز که منزلگه انسی

O thou heart-kindling palace that art the dwelling of affection,

یا رب مکناد آفت ایام خرابت

O Lord! ruined, let not the calamity of time make thee

حافظ نه غلامیست که از خواجه گریزد

Hafez is not a slave who fleeth from his master,

صلحی کن و بازآ که خرابم ز عتابت

Show a little kindness; come back; for I am ruined through reproach of thee.

غزل ۱۶ ⓄⒹⒺ ①⑥

خمی که ابروی شوخ تو در کمان انداخت

The great curve that, into the bow, (of thy eye-brow), thy told eye-brow cast,

به قصد جان من زار ناتوان انداخت

In design of the blood of me, miserable, powerless, it cast.

نبود نقش دو عالم که رنگ الفت بود

Not the picture (of existence) of the two worlds was, when was the color of love:

زمانه طرح محبت نه این زمان انداخت

Not at this time, Love's foundation, did Time cast.

به یک کرشمه که نرگس به خودفروشی کرد

With one glance, in boasting, that the Narcissus made

فریب چشم تو صد فتنه در جهان انداخت

A hundred calamities into the world, thy eye's deceit cast.

شراب خورده و خوی کرده می‌روی به چمن

Wine drunk, sweat expressed (I know not) when thou when thou wentest to the sward (and broughtest it to this state):

که آب روی تو آتش در ارغوان انداخت

(But, I see) That fire into the ruddy Arghavan, thy sweat cast.

به بزمگاه چمن دوش مست بگذشتم

Me, drunken passing the lawn yard

چو از دهان توام غنچه در گمان انداخت

The bud of Thy lips made me think, last night

بنفشه طره مفتول خود گره می‌زد

The violet fastened up (arranged) her lovely twisted tresses:

صبا حکایت زلف تو در میان انداخت

Before the assembly, the tale of Thy (still more lovely tress), the wind cast.

ز شرم آن که به روی تو نسبتش کردم

Through shame of that one who likened it (the lily) to thy face,

سمن به دست صبا خاک در دهان انداخت

Dust into her own mouth, by the hand of the wind, the lily cast.

من از ورع می و مطرب ندیدمی زین پیش

Through (having chosen) austerity, I should never have seen the wine cup or the minstrel.

هوای مغبچگانم در این و آن انداخت

(What shall I do) (Me) Into this and into that, desire for young Magians cast.

کنون به آب می لعل خرقه می‌شویم

Now, with water of ruby wine, I wash my religious garment:

نصیبه ازل از خود نمی‌توان انداخت

From one's self, the lot (of the ruby wine) of eternity without beginning one cannot cast.

مگر گشایش حافظ در این خرابی بود

Perchance in this disastrous state, was the opening (of the work) of Hafez,

که بخشش ازلش در می مغان انداخت

Whom, into the wine of Magians[1], (consuming with the fire of divine love) the destiny of eternity without beginning cast.

1-They were originally a tribe of the Medes to whom the position of clergy belonged exclusively

جهان به کام من اکنون شود که دور زمان

Now, the world becometh to my desire. For time's revolution

مرا به بندگی خواجه جهان انداخت

Me, into the service of the Khwaja[1] of the world, cast.

غزل ۱۷   ODE 17

سینه از آتش دل در غم جانانه بسوخت

From the fire (of love) of my heart, my chest in grief for the Beloved consumed.

آتشی بود در این خانه که کاشانه بسوخت

In this house (of the heart), was (such) a fire, that the house consumed.

تنم از واسطه دوری دلبر بگداخت

From the farness of the Heart-Ravisher, my body melted waned:

جانم از آتش مهر رخ جانانه بسوخت

From Love's fire for the Beloved's face, my soul consumed.

سوز دل بین که ز بس آتش اشکم دل شمع

Behold the heart's burning! For, from the great fire of my tears, the candle's heart (wick),

دوش بر من ز سر مهر چو پروانه بسوخت

Last night, from Love's desire, like the moth, consumed.

آشنایی نه غریب است که دلسوز من است

Strange it is not that the Friends are heart-consuming (for me):

چون من از خویش برفتم دل بیگانه بسوخت

When out of myself (distraught), I went (even), the stranger's heart consumed.

خرقه زهد مرا آب خرابات ببرد

The water of the tavern took my religious garment of austerity:

خانه عقل مرا آتش میخانه بسوخت

My house of reason, the fire of the tavern consumed.

چون پیاله دلم از توبه که کردم بشکست

As the cup of my heart broke from the repentance that I made,

همچو لاله جگرم بی می و خمخانه بسوخت

(So) my liver, like a wine flagon, without wine and the tavern, consumed.

ماجرا کم کن و بازآ که مرا مردم چشم

O Admonisher! make little talk; come back (and be not my prohibitor of love's Path). For, the man of my eye

خرقه از سر به درآورد و به شکرانه بسوخت

Plucked from off my head, the religious garmen (of m odesty); and, in thanks (for the acquisition of love), consumed.

ترک افسانه بگو حافظ و می نوش دمی

Hafez! Abandon idle talk (of outward worshippers); and, awhile, drink wine (of love):

که نخفتیم شب و شمع به افسانه بسوخت

For (by reason of such profitless talk), last night, we slept not; and, with this idle talk, the candle (of my life) consumed.

1-Eunuch, dignitary, vizier, boss, host

غزل ۱۸ ⓄⒹⒺ ①⑧

ساقیا آمدن عید مبارک بادت
O Saki! (Murshid) be the coming of the 'Id time of love's manifestations auspicious to thee

وان مواعید که کردی مرواد از یادت
And these promises (that at the beginning of the mystic state) thou madest, let them not go from thy memory.

در شگفتم که در این مدت ایام فراق
In astonishment, I am that, at this period of time of separation,

برگرفتی ز حریفان دل و دل می‌دادت
Thou tookest up thy heart from the companions; (lovers of God) and he (the lover) gave thee his heart.

برسان بندگی دختر رزگو به درآی
Cause the attendance of the daughter of the vine (wine) to reach (to the true Beloved) Say (From the bond of repute, and of name, of outward worshipping, of solitariness and of moroseness) come out:

که دم و همت ما کرد ز بند آزادت
For the breath of resolution of us (lovers) hath made thee free of the bond.

شادی مجلسیان در قدم و مقدم توست
In the foot of thy (happy) arrival, is the joy of the people of the assembly

جای غم باد مر آن دل که نخواهد شادت
Griefs place be every heart that joy wisheth thee not!

شکر ایزد که ز تاراج خزان رخنه نیافت
Thanks to God that from this autumnal wind, no injury received

بوستان سمن و سرو و گل و شمشادت
Thy garden of the jasmine, of the cypress, of the rose, and of the tox-tree.

چشم بد دور کز آن تفرقه‌ات بازآورد
Far, the evil eye! For, from that separation, happily brought back

طالع نامور و دولت مادرزادت
Thee, renowned fortune and mother-born luck.

حافظ از دست مده دولت این کشتی نوح
Hafez! From the hand, surrender not association with this Ark of Noah[1] (the perfect Murshid):

ور نه طوفان حوادث ببرد بنیادت
If not, thy foundation the deluge of vicissitudes (of the world) will take

غزل ۱۹ ⓄⒹⒺ ①⑨

ای نسیم سحر آرامگه یار کجاست
O fragrant morning breeze! (the Angel of Death) the Beloved's rest-place is where?

منزل آن مه عاشق کش عیار کجاست
The dwelling of that Moon, Lover-slayer, Sorcerer, is where?

شب تار است و ره وادی ایمن در پیش
Dark is the night; (the world) and in front, the path of the Valley of Aiman (the desert of the Path):

آتش طور کجا موعد دیدار کجاست
The fire of God's (splendour from the olive bush) of Toor where? The time and the place of promise of beholding is where?

1-The metaphor of the brave king

هر که آمد به جهان نقش خرابی دارد
Whoever came to this (effacing) this world hath the mark of ruin the effacement by death, of this borrowed existence:

در خرابات بگویید که هشیار کجاست
In the tavern, (the world) ask ye saying: "The sensible one is where?"

آن کس است اهل بشارت که اشارت داند
One of glad tidings is he who knoweth the sign:

نکته‌ها هست بسی محرم اسرار کجاست
Many are the subtleties. The confidant of mysteries is where?

هر سر موی مرا با تو هزاران کار است
Every hair-tip of mine hath a thousand bits of work with Thee:

ما کجاییم و ملامت گر بی‌کار کجاست
We, are where? And the reproacher, void (knowledge) of work, is where?

بازپرسید ز گیسوی شکن در شکنش
The lover, shattered with pain of grief of separation from thee, consumed:

کاین دل غمزده سرگشته گرفتار کجاست
Thou theyself asked not, saying: "That lover, grief suffering, is where?"

عقل دیوانه شد آن سلسله مشکین کو
Reason hath become distraught: that (musky) dark tress, where?

دل ز ما گوشه گرفت ابروی دلدار کجاست
(Apart) From us, the heart hath taken the corner (of retirement): the eye-brow of the heart-possessor – is where

ساق و مطرب و می جمله مهیاست ولی
The cup, and the minstrel, and the rose, all are ready.

عیش بی یار مهیا نشود یار کجاست
But, ease without the Beloved is not attainable. The Beloved is where?

حافظ از باد خزان در چمن دهر مرنج
Hafez! grieve not of (cruel) the autumn wind (which bloweth) in the sward of the world:

فکر معقول بفرما گل بی خار کجاست
Exercise reasonable thought. The rose (time) without the thorn (the autumn wind) is where?

غزل ۲۰ ⓞⒹⒺ ②ⓞ

روزه یک سو شد و عید آمد و دل‌ها برخاست
The fast (the time of austerity and of inward purity) a side hath gone; and the Eid[1] (the time of manifestations, of glory of God's qualities, of tumult of love, and of the light of the heart) hath come; and hearts have risen (in tumult):

می ز خمخانه به جوش آمد و می باید خواست
In the wine-house (of the heart), the wine (of love) hath come into tumult; and it is necessary to ask (for the Murshid).

نوبه زهدفروشان گران جان بگذشت
The season of (hypocritical) austerity boasters, weighty of life, hath passed:

وقت رندی و طرب کردن رندان پیداست
Hath risen, the time of gladness and of joy-making of profligates.

1-A holy day

چه ملامت بود آن را که چنین باده خورد

Him, who like us drinketh the cup, what reproach reacheth?

این چه عیب است بدین بی‌خردی وین چه خطاست

In regard to the profligate lover, neither is defect, nor is fault.

باده نوشی که در او روی و ریایی نبود

That wine-drinker (profligate) in whom is neither the double face, nor hypocrisy

بهتر از زهدفروشی که در او روی و ریاست

Is better than an austerity-boaster, in whom is the face of hypocrisy.

ما نه رندان ریاییم و حریفان نفاق

We are neither hypocritical profligates, nor the companions of hypocrisy:

آن که او عالم سر است بدین حال گواست

Witness to this state is He, who "is the Knower-of-hearts."

فرض ایزد بگذاریم و به کس بد نکنیم

The ordinances of God, we perform; and do evil to none:

وان چه گویند روا نیست نگوییم رواست

Whatever they say is "unlawful," we say not "it is lawful."

چه شود گر من و تو چند قدح باده خوریم

What mattereth it-if thou and I drink some goblets of wine?

باده از خون رزان است نه از خون شماست

Wine is of the blood of grapes; it is not of your blood.

این چه عیب است کز آن عیب خلل خواهد بود

This (wine – drinking) is not the defect that, from this defect, injury will be:

ور بود نیز چه شد مردم بی‌عیب کجاست

And if it be the defect, what matter? The man without defect is where?

غزل ۲۱ ⓄⒹⒺ ②①

دل و دینم شد و دلبر به ملامت برخاست

Went heart and faith; and the Heart-Ravisher god with reproach arose,

گفت با ما منشین کز تو سلامت برخاست

And said: "Sit not with me; for, from thee, safety hath risen.

که شنیدی که در این بزم دمی خوش بنشست

Of whom heardest thou, who at this banquet (of the world), hath awhile sat happy:

که نه در آخر صحبت به ندامت برخاست

Who, at the end of the companionship, not in remorse hath risen.

شمع اگر زان لب خندان به زبان لافی زد

If, with its tongue (wick), the candle expressed a boast of that laughing face

پیش عشاق تو شب‌ها به غرامت برخاست

In fine (for that boast), nights before thy lovers, it (burning) hath risen.

در چمن باد بهاری ز کنار گل و سرو

In the sward, from the border of the rose and the cypress, the spring breeze,

به هواداری آن عارض و قامت برخاست

In longing for that cheek and stature of Thine, hath risen.

مست بگذشتی و از خلوتیان ملکوت

Intoxicated, Thou passedest by, and from the Khilvatis[1] of angels

به تماشای تو آشوب قیامت برخاست

The tumult of resurrection at the sight of Thee hath risen.

پیش رفتار تو پا برنگرفت از خجلت

Before thy (graceful) gait, from shame its foot uplifted not,

سرو سرکش که به ناز از قد و قامت برخاست

The head-extending (lofty) cypress that, with grace of stature and of form, hath risen.

حافظ این خرقه بینداز مگر جان بری

Hafez! cast off this religious garment (of hypocrisy). Perchance thou mayst take thy life:

کاتش از خرقه سالوس و کرامت برخاست

For, from the religious garment of hypocrisy and of miracle, fire (wherein thou mayst be consumed) hath risen.

غزل ۲۲ ⓄⒹⒺ ②②

چو بشنوی سخن اهل دل مگو که خطاست

O Heart-ravisher! thou art not a speech-recognizer. Here, the fault is:

سخن شناس نه‌ای جان من خطا این جاست

When thou hearest the speech of people of heart speak not saying: "A fault it is."

سرم به دنیی و عقبی فرو نمی‌آید

Neither to this world, nor to the next world, boweth my head (filled with great ideas)

تبارک الله از این فتنه‌ها که در سر ماست

Blessed be God! for this tumult that, in our head, is.

در اندرون من خسته دل ندانم کیست

Within this shattered heart, I know not who is.

که من خموشم و او در فغان و در غوغاست

For, I am silent; and in clamour and tumult, it (my heart, in which is the true Beloved) is.

دلم ز پرده برون شد کجایی ای مطرب

Forth from the screen, went my heart. O Minstrel! where art thou?

بنال هان که از این پرده کار ما به نواست

Ho! sing. For, on account of this note, in melody, our work is.

مرا به کار جهان هرگز التفات نبود

To the world's work, never was 'attention mine;

رخ تو در نظر من چنین خوشش آراست

In my sight, Thy face its happy adorner thus is.

نخفته‌ام ز خیالی که می‌پزد دل من

From a (crude) fancy that I mature, nights I have not slept:

خمار صدشبه دارم شرابخانه کجاست

Wine-sickness of a hundred nights, I have: the wine-house, where is?

چنین که صومعه آلوده شد ز خون دلم

With my heart's blood, thus it is that the cloister became stained:

گرم به باده بشویید حق به دست شماست

If ye wash me in (ruddy) wine, lawful at your hand it is?

1-Solitude

از آن به دیر مغانم عزیز می‌دارند

In the cloister of the Magians, me dear they hold for the reason

که آتشی که نمیرد همیشه در دل ماست

That, in our heart, a fire that dieth not ever is.

چه ساز بود که در پرده می‌زد آن مطرب

What was the melody that last night, the minstrel played?

که رفت عمر و هنوزم دماغ پر ز هواست

Life passed; and yet, full of that melody, my brain is?

ندای عشق تو دیشب در اندرون دادند

Last night, within my heart, the announcement of love for Thee, they gave

فضای سینه حافظ هنوز پر ز صداست

Yet, with desire, full of that voice, the plain of my heart is?

غزل ۲۳ ⓄⒹⒺ ②③

خیال روی تو در هر طریق همره ماست

In every path of Islam, the image of Thy face fellow traveler of ours is.

نسیم موی تو پیوند جان آگه ماست

Ever, the perfume of Thy hair, the soul-informer of ours is.

به رغم مدعیانی که منع عشق کنند

In grief of those claimants, who forbid love,

جمال چهره تو حجت موجه ماست

The beauty of Thy face, the approved argument of ours is.

ببین که سیب زنخدان تو چه می‌گوید

Behold, what saith the apple of Thy chin!

هزار یوسف مصری فتاده در چه ماست

"Many a Yusuf of Egypt fallen into the pit, of ours is."

اگر به زلف دراز تو دست ما نرسد

If to our hand reach not Thy long tress,

گناه بخت پریشان و دست کوته ماست

The sin of the perturbed fortune, and of the short-hand of ours is.

به حاجب در خلوت سرای خاص بگو

To the chamberlain (Iblis full of fraud) of the door of the private chamber, say:

فلان ز گوشه نشینان خاک درگه ماست

"Of those corner-sitting, a certain one (though through grief yellow of face like straw), the dust of the court of Ours is.

به صورت از نظر ما اگر چه محجوب است

Although, apparently, He is veiled from our sight,

همیشه در نظر خاطر مرفه ماست

He, ever, in the sight of the tranquil heart, of ours is.

اگر به سالی حافظ دری زند بگشای

(O Iblis) If, as a beggar, Hafez knock at that door (whereof thou art chamberlain), open:

که سال‌هاست که مشتاق روی چون مه ماست

For, it is years since he, desirous of the moon-like face of Ours was.

غزل ۲۴ ⓄⒹⒺ ②④

مطلب طاعت و پیمان و صلاح از من مست
From me intoxicated, is the desire of devotion and of covenant, and of rectitude.
که به پیمانه کشی شهره شدم روز الست
For, in Eternity without beginning, I became renowned for wine-drinking.

من همان دم که وضو ساختم از چشمه عشق
The very moment when, with the fountain of Love (the state of a Lover), I performed ablution, (in the heart's pure blood and from its tablet effaced all exterior to God)
چارتکبیر زدم یک سره بر هر چه که هست
I expressed completely on all that is, four Laudations, Allah Akbar![1]

می بده تا دهمت آگهی از سر قضا
Give wine that I may give thee news of the mystery of Fate:
که به روی که شدم عاشق و از بوی که مست
By whose face, I became a Lover; and by whose perfume, intoxicated

کمر کوه کم است از کمر مور این جا
Here, (in God's sight) less than the ants' (slender) waist is the waist of the (great) mountain (of Sin):
ناامید از در رحمت مشو ای باده پرست
O wine-worshipper! Be not hopeless of the door of God's mercy.

بجز آن نرگس مستانه که چشمش مرساد
Save that intoxicated eye the (evil) eye reach him not!
زیر این طارم فیروزه کسی خوش ننشست
None state happy beneath this turquoise vault (of Heaven).

جان فدای دهنش باد که در باغ نظر
Be my soul the ransom of Thy mouth! For, in the garden of vision,
چمن آرای جهان خوشتر از این غنچه نبست
The Parterre-arrayer (the Creator) of the World established no rose-bud more sweet than this rose-bud.

حافظ از دولت عشق تو سلیمانی شد
Through the fortune of Love for thee, Hafez became a Soleiman (in grandeur) [2]:
یعنی از وصل تواش نیست بجز باد به دست
That is of Union with thee, he hath naught in hand save wind.

غزل ۲۵ ⓄⒹⒺ ②⑤

شکفته شد گل حمرا و گشت بلبل مست
Blossomed is the red rose; and intoxicated is the nightingale.
صلای سرخوشی ای صوفیان باده پرست
(And given is) The invitation to merriment O Lovers, wine-worshipping!

اساس توبه که در محکمی چو سنگ نمود
The foundation of penitence that, firm as a rock, appeared,
ببین که جام زجاجی چه طرفه‌اش بشکست
How the crystal cup (of wine) hath shattered it, behold!

1-It is a term used by Hafez to place more emphasis on turning her back on everything

2-Name of a prophet

بیار باده که در بارگاه استغنا

Bring wine! for, in the Court of the Independent One (God),

چه پاسبان و چه سلطان چه هوشیار و چه مست

Whether the (humble) shepherd or the (lofty) Sultan; whether sensible or insensible (what matter)

از این رباط دودر چون ضرورت است رحیل

Since there is necessity for departing from this Inn of two doors (this world, one door of birth, the other door of death).

رواق و طاق معیشت چه سربلند و چه پست

The gallery and the arch the mode of thy living, whether lofty (in ease) or low (in calamity) (what matter)

مقام عیش میسر نمی‌شود بی‌رنج

Unattainable, is the place of ease without toil:

بلی به حکم بلا بسته‌اند عهد الست

Yes: with the decree of calamity they (Fate and Destiny) established the "day of Alast."[1]

به هست و نیست مرنجان ضمیر و خوش می‌باش

Grieve neither at existence nor at non-existence: Be thy mind, happy.

که نیستیست سرانجام هر کمال که هست

For the end of every perfection that is-is non-existence.

شکوه آصفی و اسب باد و منطق طیر

The pomp of being an Asaf[2], the wind-steed, and the language of birds

به باد رفت و از او خواجه هیچ طرف نبست

(All) Went to the wind (of destruction); and from them, the Khwaja obtained no profit.

به بال و پر مرو از ره که تیر پرتابی

With the wing (of wealth) and the feather (of rank)

go not (in pride) from the Path (and be not fascinated with thy own frail life). For, the arrow far flying

هوا گرفت زمانی ولی به خاک نشست

Keepeth (loftily), the air awhile; but, at last, lieth low in the dust.

زبان کلک تو حافظ چه شکر آن گوید

Hafez! What thanks, uttereth the tongue of thy (eloquent) reed for the reason that

که گفته سخنت می‌برند دست به دست

They take (in joy) the utterance of its speech from hand to hand?

غزل ۲۶ ⓞⓓⓔ ②⑥

زلف آشفته و خوی کرده و خندان لب و مست

(The Beloved) Tress dishevelled; sweat expressed; lip laughing; intoxicated.

پیرهن چاک و غزل خوان و صراحی در دست

Garment rent; song-singing; goblet in His hand;

نرگسش عربده جوی و لبش افسوس کنان

Eye, contest-seeking; lip lamenting

نیم شب دوش به بالین من آمد بنشست

Came, at midnight, last night, to my pillow (and there); sate.

1-The day that God made sea and land   2-Suleiman's minister

سر فراگوش من آورد به آواز حزین
To my ear, He brought His head; and in a low soft voice,

گفت ای عاشق دیرینه من خوابت هست
Said: "O my distraught Lover! sleep is thine" (sleep hath overcome thee).

عاشقی را که چنین باده شبگیر دهند
That Aref[1] (lover), to whom they give wine like this, night-watching

کافر عشق بود گر نشود باده پرست
Is infidel to love, if he be not wine-worshipper.

برو ای زاهد و بر دردکشان خرده مگیر
O Zahed[2]! go seize not a small matter against the drinkers of wine-dregs

که ندادند جز این تحفه به ما روز الست
For, save this gift (of dregs), naught did they give us on the day of Alast.

آن چه او ریخت به پیمانه ما نوشیدیم
Of whatever, He god poured into our cup, we have drunk good or bad;

اگر از خمر بهشت است وگر باده مست
Whether it be of the wine of Paradise, or of the cup of intoxication.

خنده جام می و زلف گره گیر نگار
The laughter (mantling foam) of the cup of wine, and the knot-seizing tress of the Beloved

ای بسا توبه که چون توبه حافظ بشکست
O many a repentance, hath it shattered like the repentance of Hafez

غزل ۲۷ ⓞⓓⓔ ②⑦

در دیر مغان آمد یارم قدحی در دست
Into the Magian's cloister, came my Friend a goblet in His hand:

مست از می و میخواران از نرگس مستش مست
With wine intoxicated, He with his eye intoxicated the wine-dirnkers.

در نعل سمند او شکل مه نو پیدا
In His steed's hoof, appeared the form of the new moon

وز قد بلند او بالای صنوبر پست
From His lofty stature, low, the stature of the lofty cypress.

آخر به چه گویم هست از خود خبرم چون نیست
Well, wherefore, shall I say: "Existence" (is mine) when no knowledge of myself is mine?

وز بهر چه گویم نیست با وی نظرم چون هست
Wherefore shall I say: "Non-existence" (is mine) when my expectation is to be with Him (God)?

شمع دل دمسازم بنشست چو او برخاست
When He arose (to depart), (light of the) candle of the heart of friends went out (in non – existence):

و افغان ز نظربازان برخاست چو او بنشست
When He sat down, (entered the hidden) the spectators' clamour (through loss of Him, and farness from Him) arose.

گر غالیه خوش بو شد در گیسوی او پیچید
If noisome civet became fragrant, it was associated with His tress:

ور وسمه کمانکش گشت در ابروی او پیوست
If indigo became a bowman, it was associated with His (curved) eye-brow.

بازآی که بازآید عمر شده حافظ
(O true Beloved) Come back that Hafez's spent life may come back:

هر چند که ناید باز تیری که بشد از شست
Although the arrow that hath sped from the aim (of the bowman) cometh not back.

غزل ۲۸ ⓄⒹⒺ ②⑧

به جان خواجه و حق قدیم و عهد درست
By the Khwaja's[1] soul, and by ancient right, and by true covenant,

که مونس دم صبحم دعای دولت توست
(I swear) That, at the breath of dawn, prayer for thy welfare is my (sole) companion.

سرشک من که ز طوفان نوح دست برد
My tears, that surpass Noah's (great) deluge,

ز لوح سینه نیارست نقش مهر تو شست
Have not washed the picture of Thy love from the heart's tablet.

بکن معامله‌ای وین دل شکسته بخر
Strike the bargain; purchase this shattered heart,

که با شکستگی ارزد به صد هزار درست
That, despite its shattered state, is worth many an unshattered (heart).

زبان مور به آصف دراز گشت و رواست
Against (the great) Asaf[2], (the soul) the tongue of the (weak) the ant (lust) became long in reproach; and, it is lawful:

که خواجه خاتم جم یاوه کرد و بازنجست
For, the Khwaja (the soul in the human body) lost the seal (of divine knowledge) of Jam[3] (God); and, sought not (for it).

دلا طمع مبر از لطف بی‌نهایت دوست
O heart! of the endless kindness of the Friend hope, sever not:

چو لاف عشق زدی سر بباز چابک و چست
When thou boastest of love, quickly and instantly play (stake) thy head.

به صدق کوش که خورشید زاید از نفست
Be honest and see the sun comes out of thy breath

که از دروغ سیه روی گشت صبح نخست
At the outset, the liar was disgraced.

شدم ز دست تو شیدای کوه و دشت و هنوز
(O Beloved) By Thy hand, I became distraught for the mountain and the plain:

نمی‌کنی به ترحم نطاق سلسله سست
(Yet to give me freedom) in pity Thou loosest not my waist-chain.

مرنج حافظ و از دلبران حفاظ مجوی
Hafez! grieve not! and constancy from heart-ravishers seek not:

گناه باغ چه باشد چو این گیاه نرست
The crime of the garden, what is it, when this grass hath not sprung.

1-Eunuch, dignitary, vizier, boss, host
2-Suleiman's minister

3-Suleiman

غزل ۲۹ ⓄⒹⒺ ㉙

ما را ز خیال تو چه پروای شراب است

With fancy for (perpetual union with) for Thee, what desire for wine Love is ours?

خم گو سر خود گیر که خمخانه خراب است

To the jar (the Murshid possessed of truths and of divine knowledge) say: "Take thy head depart; for the jar-house is ruined."

گر خمر بهشت است بریزید که بی دوست

(Even) If it be the wine of Paradise, spill it. For without the Friend (God),

هر شربت عذبم که دهی عین عذاب است

Every draft of sweet water that thou givest is the very essence of torment.

افسوس که شد دلبر و در دیده گریان

Alas! The Heart-Ravisher nath departed, and in the weeping eye

تحریر خیال خط او نقش بر آب است

The picturing of the fancy of a letter from Him is (only) the picture on water (quick of decline, calamitous to the seeker).

بیدار شو ای دیده که ایمن نتوان بود

O eye! be vigilant. For, one cannot be safe (on the couch of ignorance),

زین سیل دمادم که در این منزل خواب است

From this lasting torrent (of vicissitudes) that occurreth in the stage of sleep (this world).

معشوق عیان می‌گذرد بر تو ولیکن

The Beloved One (God) openly passeth, by thee; but

اغیار همی‌بیند از آن بسته نقاب است

Keepeth seeing strangers. On that account, the Beloved is veil-bound.

گل بر رخ رنگین تو تا لطف عرق دید

Since the (ruddy) rose beheld the grace of sweet (latest beauty) on thy colored cheek,

در آتش شوق از غم دل غرق گلاب است

In envy's fire, through the heart's grief, it is immersed in rose-water.

سبز است در و دشت بیا تا نگذاریم

The world around is green and so green,

دست از سر آبی که جهان جمله سراب است

But the world is only a mirage.

در کنج دماغم مطلب جای نصیحت

In the corner of my brain, seek no place of counsel:

کاین گوشه پر از زمزمه چنگ و رباب است

For this (brain)-cell is full of the hum of the harp and of the ribab[1].

حافظ چه شد ار عاشق و رند است و نظرباز

If Hafez be lover, or profligate, or glance-player, what then

بس طور عجب لازم ایام شباب است

In the time of youth, many a strange way is necessary

1- Rebec, psaltery, Robab (Girl's name)

غزل ۳۰ ⓄⒹⒺ ③⓪

زلفت هزار دل به یکی تار مو ببست

With a single hair (delight) of its, a thousand hearts, the tress (the world) bound, (kept back from truth and thought of the future world)

راه هزار چاره گر از چار سو ببست

The path of a thousand remedies (men of learning and of heart) bound.

تا عاشقان به بوی نسیمش دهند جان

So that all may give their soul to the perfume of the great breeze,

بگشود نافه‌ای و در آرزو ببست

He opened the musk-pod; and, the door of desire bound.

شیدا از آن شدم که نگارم چو ماه نو

Distraught, I became on that account that, my Beloved, like the (crescent) new moon

ابرو نمود و جلوه گری کرد و رو ببست

His eye-brow, displayed; gracefully moved; and His face bound.

ساق به چند رنگ می اندر پیاله ریخت

The Saki[1] (Fate) poured, into the cup, (the traveller's heart) the wine of love many colors:

این نقش‌ها نگر که چه خوش در کدو ببست

These pictures, (of creation and of glories of God) behold how beautifully in the wine-vessel (the traveller's heart), he bound.

یا رب چه غمزه کرد صراحی که خون خم

O Lord! What glance of sorcery made the long-necked goglet (Muhammad), that the blood of the jar?

با نعره‌های قلقلش اندر گلو ببست

Notwithstanding the sweet sounds of its guggling, its (long) throat (in silence) bound.

مطرب چه پرده ساخت که در پرده سماع

In the circle of sama'[2], what note played the minstrel that

بر اهل وجد و حال در های و هو ببست

On the people of wajd[3] (ecstasy) and of hal (mystical state), the door of lowly matters (ha and hu!) he bound?

حافظ هر آن که عشق نورزید و وصل خواست

Hafez! Who practiced not love; and union (with God) desired

احرام طوف کعبه دل بی وضو ببست

Without (necessary) ablution, the Ihram of the Tawaf[4] of the Ka'ba[5], bound

غزل ۳۱ ⓄⒹⒺ ③①

آن شب قدری که گویند اهل خلوت امشب است

What men of our closed circle call "the Night of Power" to-night is.

یا رب این تاثیر دولت در کدامین کوکب است

O Lord! from what constellation, (is it that) this effect of fortune is?

1-Tapster
2-Hearing, Singing
3- Joy and understanding

4-To circumambulate, to go round
5-Center-point, chief aim

تا به گیسوی تو دست ناسزایان کم رسد

In order that the hand of those unfit (outward worshippers) may rarely reach Thy trees, Thy tress
(the Path of God)

هر دلی از حلقه‌ای در ذکر یارب یارب است

Every (lover's) heart, in the circle (of the world) engaged in the zikr of O Lord O Lord is

کشته چاه زنخدان توام کز هر طرف

(O Beloved) I am one slain by Thy chin-dimple. For, from every side

صد هزارش گردن جان زیر طوق غبغب است

Beneath Thy chin-dimple, many a neck of souls is.

شهسوار من که مه آیینه دار روی اوست

My horseman, the mirror-holder of whose face is the moon,

تاج خورشید بلندش خاک نعل مرکب است

The crown of the lofty sun, the dust of the hoof of his steed is.

عکس خوی بر عارضش بین کفتاب گرم رو

Behold the reflection of sweat on His (the Beloved's) cheek! For the sun, ardent of face.

در هوای آن عرق تا هست هر روزش تب است

As long as it is, (day) daily in desire of this sweat, ardent is.

من نخواهم کرد ترک لعل یار و جام می

I will not abandon the ruby lip of the Beloved, nor the wine-cup,

زاهدان معذور داریدم که اینم مذهب است

Zaheds[1]! hold me excused: for, my religious order, this is.

اندر آن ساعت که بر پشت صبا بندند زین

In that cavalcade when they fasten the saddle on the back of the wind,

با سلیمان چون برانم من که مورم مرکب است

With (the great) Sulaiman[2], how may proceed I, whose steed the (feeble) ant is

آن که ناوک بر دل من زیر چشمی می‌زند

Who (from) beneath his eye winking dischargeth an arrow at my heart,

قوت جان حافظش در خنده زیر لب است

In the (covert)

smile beneath His lip the life-sustenance of me Hafez is.

آب حیوانش ز منقار بلاغت می‌چکد

The water of life trickleth from the beak pen of my eloquence.

زاغ کلک من به نام ایزد چه عالی مشرب است

In God's name! what a lofty drinker the black crow of my pen is!

غزل ۳۲ ⓄⒹⒺ ③②

خدا چو صورت ابروی دلگشای تو بست

When the form of thy heart alluring eye-brow, God established.

گشاد کار من اندر کرشمه‌های تو بست

In thy glances, the solving of my work, He established.

1-Pietist   2-Name of a prophet

مرا و سرو چمن را به خاک راه نشاند

From my heart and the heart of the bird of the sward. He took ease,

زمانه تا قصب نرگس قبای تو بست

When, in the morn, the heart of both in lament for thee, He established.

ز کار ما و دل غنچه صد گره بگشود

From our work, and from the heart of the rose-bud, a hundred knots (of difficulties) it (the breeze of the rose) loosed,

نسیم گل چو دل اندر پی هوای تو بست

When, in desire of thee, its own heart the breeze of the rose established.

مرا به بند تو دوران چرخ راضی کرد

With Thy bond, the sphere's revolution made me content:

ولی چه سود که سررشته در رضای تو بست

But, what profit, when, the end of the thread in Thy will, it (the sphere's revolution) established.

چو نافه بر دل مسکین من گره مفکن

On my wretched heart, cast not a knot like the (twisted) musk-pod.

که عهد با سر زلف گره گشای تو بست

For, with Thy tress, knot-loosening, a covenant it (my heart) established.

تو خود وصال دگر بودی ای نسیم وصال

O breeze of union! thou thyself wast another life (like life without fidelity):

خطا نگر که دل امید در وفای تو بست

Behold my (heart's) fault that, hope in fidelity to Thee, my heart established.

ز دست جور تو گفتم ز شهر خواهم رفت

(O beloved) I said: "On account of thy violence, I shall depart from the city:"

به خنده گفت که حافظ برو که پای تو بست

Laughing, the beloved spake saying: "Hafez! go Thy foot, (of dwelling here) who established?"

غزل ۳۳ ⓄⒹⒺ ③③

خلوت گزیده را به تماشا چه حاجت است

To him that hath chosen solitude, of the spectacle is what need?

چون کوی دوست هست به صحرا چه حاجت است

When the street of the Beloved is, (at hand) of the desert is what need?

جانا به حاجتی که تو را هست با خدا

O Soul! By the need of God that is thine,

کخر دمی بپرس که ما را چه حاجت است

At last, a moment, ask, saying: "Ours is what need?"

ای پادشاه حسن خدا را بسوختیم

O sovereign of beauty! (by the need of Thee that is mine) For God's sake, I consumed.

آخر سال کن که گدا را چه حاجت است

At last ask, saying: The beggar's, is what need?

ارباب حاجتیم و زبان سال نیست

We are the Lords of need, and (ours) is no tongue to question:

در حضرت کریم تمنا چه حاجت است

In the presence of the Merciful One, (God) petitioning is what need?

محتاج قصه نیست گرت قصد خون ماست

If intention be Thine against our life, there is no need of pretence:

چون رخت از آن توست به یغما چه حاجت است

When the chattels are Thine, of plunder, is what need?

جام جهان نماست ضمیر منیر دوست

The cup, world-displaying is the luminous mind of the Friend (God):

اظهار احتیاج خود آن جا چه حاجت است

Then, of the revealing of my own necessity is what need?

آن شد که بار منت ملاح بردمی

Past is that time when I used to bear the burden of favor of the Sailor (the Murshid):

گوهر چو دست داد به دریا چه حاجت است

When the jewel (of divine knowledge) appeared, of the Ocean (of Love) is what need?

ای مدعی برو که مرا با تو کار نیست

O beggar-lover! when the soul-giving lip of the Beloved

احباب حاضرند به اعدا چه حاجت است

Knoweth thee, petitioning for an allowance is what need?

ای عاشق گدا چو لب روح بخش یار

O pretender! go I have naught with thee:

می‌داندت وظیفه تقاضا چه حاجت است

Dear friends are present. Of enemies is what need?

حافظ تو ختم کن که هنر خود عیان شود

Hafez! End thy verse: for skill itself becometh clear:

با مدعی نزاع و محاکا چه حاجت است

Disputation and contention with the pretender is what need?

غزل ۳۴ ⓄⒹⒺ ③④

رواق منظر چشم من آشیانه توست

(O true Beloved) The chamber of vision of my eye is the dwelling of Thine:

کرم نما و فرود آ که خانه خانۀ توست

Show courtesy, and alight, for this house is the House of Thine.

به لطف خال و خط از عارفان ربودی دل

By the grace of mole and of down (Thy creations). Thou scratchedest the heart of Arefs[1] (lovers of God):

لطیفه‌های عجب زیر دام و دانه توست

Wondrous, are the subtleties beneath the snare of the grain (the down of the mole) of Thine.

دلت به وصل گل ای بلبل صبا خوش باد

O nightingale! (the perfect murshid) glad of heart be, in union with the rosethe true Beloved.

که در چمن همه گلبانگ عاشقانه توست

For, in the sward (the world), the amorous warbling the melody of utterance of divine truths all is thine.

علاج ضعف دل ما به لب حوالت کن

To Thy (ruby) lip, the stream of divine grace entrust the remedy for our feeble (resourceless) heart.

که این مفرح یاقوت در خزانه توست

For exhilarating is the ruby-medicine, the talk of the perfect murshid in the treasury (of liberality) of Thine.

1-Mystic

به تن مقصرم از دولت ملازمتت

In body, unworthy of Thy service am I;

ولی خلاصه جان خاک آستانه توست

But my soul, its essence is the dust of the threshold of Thine.

من آن نیم که دهم نقد دل به هر شوخی

Not that one am I to give my heart's coin to every impudent one:

در خزانه به مهر تو و نشانه توست

(Closed) is the treasure door with the seal of Thine, and the mark of Thine.

تو خود چه لعبتی ای شهسوار شیرین کار

O horseman, excellent of work! (Murshid) what a magician indeed thou art,

که توسنی چو فلک رام تازیانه توست

That an impetuous steed, (Shaitan or imperious) lust like the (ever – revolving) sky, is obedient to the whip (of command) of thine.

چه جای من که بلغزد سپهر شعبده باز

My place, what? When (even) the sky, the juggler, staggereth

از این حیل که در انبانه بهانه توست

At the sorceries that are in the store-house of pastime of the storehouse of pastime of Thine.

سرود مجلست اکنون فلک به رقص آرد

Now, the melody of Thy assembly bringeth the sky to dancing;

که شعر حافظ شیرین سخن ترانه توست

For, the verse of Hafez, sweet of speech, is the melody of Thine.

غزل ۳۵ ⓞⒹⒺ ③⑤

برو به کار خود ای واعظ این چه فریادست

O admonisher! Go about thy own work: what is this tumult? (That thou hast raised)

مرا فتاد دل از ره تو را چه افتادست

From the hand, my heart hath fallen (in love): what hath befallen thee? that thou makest this absurd tumult and easiest the seed of wheat upon the barren soil)

میان او که خدا آفریده است از هیچ

The connection with Him, which God out of naught hath created

دقیقهایست که هیچ آفریده نگشادست

Is a subtlety which no created being hath solved.

به کام تا نرساند مرا لبش چون نای

So long as His lip causeth me not to reach my desire (and kisseth me not), like the reed, (which, being played, kisseth the lip).

نصیحت همه عالم به گوش من بادست

In my ear, the counsel of the whole world is like wind (that cometh, goeth, and nowhere settleth).

گدای کوی تو از هشت خلد مستغنیست

Independent of the eight ab odes of Paradise is the beggar of Thy street:

اسیر عشق تو از هر دو عالم آزادست

Free of both worlds is Thy bound captive.

اگر چه مستی عشقم خراب کرد ولی

Although love's intoxication hath received me (made me senseless); yet,

اساس هستی من زان خراب آبادست

By that (very) intoxication, the foundation of own existence is prosperous.

دلا منال ز بیداد و جور یار که یار
O heart! bewail not of the injustice of Thy beloved's violence. For, the Beloved

تو را نصیب همین کرد و این از آن دادست
Hath thus advised thee: and this is justice (being reproof for the sake of admonition).

برو فسانه مخوان و فسون مدم حافظ
Hafez! Go; utter no tale; breathe no majestic verse,

کز این فسانه و افسون مرا بسی یادست
For I remember many a one of these wondrous conceits and magic verses.

غزل ۳۶ ⓞⒹⒺ ③⑥

تا سر زلف تو در دست نسیم افتادست
Since thy trees tip, into the power of the breeze, fell,

دل سودازده از غصه دو نیم افتادست
My distraught heart, into two pieces on account of grief, fell

چشم جادوی تو خود عین سواد سحر است
In the midst of the dark morning, (morning – twilight) is is thy eye of sorcery:

لیکن این هست که این نسخه سقیم افتادست
This is the degree, where to this prescription, ineffective fell (became).

در خم زلف تو آن خال سیه دانی چیست
That mole in the curve of thy tress knowest thou what it is?

نقطه دوده که در حلقه جیم افتادست
(It is) a dot of ink, that, in the curve of Jim fell.

زلف مشکین تو در گلشن فردوس عذار
In the rose-bed of the garden of thy cheek, thy musky tress,

چیست طاووس که در باغ نعیم افتادست
What is it? A peacock, that, in the garden of delights, (Paradise) fell.

دل من در هوس روی تو ای مونس جان
O Friend of my soul! In desire of thy perfume, my heart,

خاک راهیست که در دست نسیم افتادست
Behind (following) the wind, as road-dust, fell.

همچو گرد این تن خاکی نتواند برخاست
Like the dust, this dusty body cannot rise

از سر کوی تو زان رو که عظیم افتادست
From the head of thy street since it severely (fatally) fell.

سایه قد تو بر قالبم ای عیسی دم
O thou of Isa (life – giving) breath! the shade of thy cypress stature on my body,

عکس روحیست که بر عظم رمیم افتادست
Is the reflection of a soul, that, on the rotten bone, fell.

آن که جز کعبه مقامش نبد از یاد لبت
(O Beloved) in memory of Thy lip, that one, whose place is none save the Ka'ba[1],

بر در میکده دیدم که مقیم افتادست
I saw that, (the fate of being) a dweller, at the Tavern-door, him befell.

1-Muslims turn at prayer. Center-point, chief aim

حافظ گمشده را با غمت ای یار عزیز
O dear soul! With grief for thee, to Hafez heart-lost

اتحادیست که در عهد قدیم افتادست
Is a great friendship that, in the ancient covenant, fell.

غزل ۳۷ ⓄⒹⒺ ③⑦

بیا که قصر امل سخت سست بنیادست
Come! For most unstable is the foundation of the Palace of Hope (the body), relying for permanency on external worship:

بیار باده که بنیاد عمر بر بادست
Bring the cup (of God's love); for the foundation of Life (of the soul) is (swiftly departing) on the (swift) wind

غلام همت آنم که زیر چرخ کبود
Beneath the azure vault, I am that slave of resolution, who

ز هر چه رنگ تعلق پذیرد آزادست
Is free from whatever taketh color of attachment.

چه گویمت که به میخانه دوش مست و خراب
What shall I tell thee? Last night, in the wine-tavern, completely (the stage of Truth) completely intoxicated

سروش عالم غیبم چه مژده‌ها دادست
Me, Jibrail of the invisible world gave tidings how glad,

که ای بلندنظر شاهباز سدره نشین
Saying: "O Falcon of lofty visions sitting on the Sidra tree (of lofty degree)

نشیمن تو نه این کنج محنت آبادست
"Not thy nest. is this corner (of the world) full of woe?

تو را ز کنگره عرش می‌زنند صفیر
"From highest Heaven's pinnacle, they utter a cry for thee that with it, thou art fascinated:

ندانمت که در این دامگه چه افتادست
"In this snare-place (the World), I know not what (Fortune) hath befallen thee."

نصیحتی کنمت یاد گیر و در عمل آر
Counsel, I proffer thee: take it to mind: bring it into action:

که این حدیث ز پیر طریقتم یادست
For, from the Pir[1] of Tarikat[2] (the Path), I recollect this matter.

غم جهان مخور و پند من مبر از یاد
Suffer not grief for the World: take not my counsel from thy mind:

که این لطیفه عشقم ز ره روی یادست
For, from a wayfarer, I recollect this sweet saying

رضا به داده بده وز جبین گره بگشای
"Give contentment to that (God) given; unloose the frown from thy forehead:

که بر من و تو در اختیار نگشادست
"For, the door of choice is not open to me and thee."

1-A Muslim saint or holy man, Pietist   2-Principle, Sufism, religious way

مجو درستی عهد از جهان سست نهاد

From the world of unstable nature, seek hot uprightness of covenant:

که این عجوز عروس هزاردامادست

For, this old woman is the bride of a thousand Lovers.

نشان عهد و وفا نیست در تبسم گل

In the smile of the rose, is no trace of the covenant of fidelity:

بنال بلبل بی دل که جای فریادست

O nightingale-lover; beware; for it is the place of wail.

حسد چه می‌بری ای سست نظم بر حافظ

O languid verse! wherefore bearest thou envy towards Hafez?

قبول خاطر و لطف سخن خدادادست

God-given are the acceptance of the hear; and the grace of speech

غزل ۳۸ ⓄⒹⒺ ③⑧

بی مهر رخت روز مرا نور نماندست

Without the sun of Thy cheek, light for my day, hath remained not

وز عمر مرا جز شب دیجور نماندست

And of my life, save the blackest night, aught hath remained not.

هنگام وداع تو ز بس گریه که کردم

At the time of farewell to Thee, from much weeping that I made,

دور از رخ تو چشم مرا نور نماندست

Far (be it) from Thy face! to my eye, light hath remained not.

می‌رفت خیال تو ز چشم من و می‌گفت

From my eye, Thy image departed; and said:

هیهات از این گوشه که معمور نماندست

"Alas, inhabited, (by My image) this corner of thy eye hath remained not."

وصل تو اجل را ز سرم دور همی‌داشت

(In non-existence, in the world of spirits) union with Thee kept thought of death from my head:

از دولت هجر تو کنون دور نماندست

Now (in this world), from the (ill)-fortune of separation from Thee, far, it (death) hath remained not.

نزدیک شد آن دم که رقیب تو بگوید

Near is that moment when the watcher (Shaitan) shall say:

دور از رخت این خسته رنجور نماندست

Far (be he), from thy door! "That abandoned shattered one hath remained not."

صبر است مرا چاره هجران تو لیکن

For me, patience is the remedy for separation from Thee. But

چون صبر توان کرد که مقدور نماندست

How can one exercise patience when power hath remained not?

در هجر تو گر چشم مرا آب روان است

In separation from Thee, if to my eye no water (tear) remained,

گو خون جگر ریز که معذور نماندست

Say: "Spill the blood of the liver; for excuse hath remained not."

حافظ ز غم از گریه نپرداخت به خنده

Through grief and weeping, Hafez engaged not in laughter,

ماتم زده را داعیه سور نماندست

To the grief-stricken one, desire for the feast, hath remained not

غزل ۳۹ ⓄⒹⒺ ③⑨

باغ مرا چه حاجت سرو و صنوبر است

(Of) the cypress and the pine (the apparent Murshid), what need hath my garden (of apparent existence that, in the fresh spring of intoxication and of youth, is all beflowered)?

شمشاد خانه پرور ما از که کمتر است

Our (lofty) box-tree (the true, perfect, love-experienced, Murshid) nurtured (in the shade), is less than who?

ای نازنین پسر تو چه مذهب گرفته‌ای

O beloved youth (the admonisher, love forbidding)! What religion hast thou adopted,

کت خون ما حلالتر از شیر مادر است

Where in our blood is more lawful to thee than mother's milk?

چون نقش غم ز دور ببینی شراب خواه

Since, from afar, thou seest the picture (effects) of grief (sown in the world by the gardener, Fate drink (wine of love):

تشخیص کرده‌ایم و مداوا مقرر است

The diagnosis, we have made: certain is the cure.

از آستان پیر مغان سر چرا کشیم

(Forth) from the threshold of the Pir of (wine-sellers), why draw I (my) head?

دولت در آن سرا و گشایش در آن در است

In this (his head), is fortune; in this (his) door, (tranquility).

یک قصه بیش نیست غم عشق وین عجب

Love's pain is (but) one tale-no more Wonderful is this

کز هر زبان که می‌شنوم نامکرر است

That from every one (lover) whom I hear, (the tale) is not repeated (but uttered differently)

دی وعده داد وصلم و در سر شراب داشت

Last night, (the day of covenant He the true Beloved, God) gave promise (of union); and, in (His) head, had the wine (of intoxication of Lovers):

امروز تا چه گوید و بازش چه در سر است

To-day, (this upspringing place of elemental water, the world, the place of woe, of self-seeing and of egotism let us see) what He saith; in (His) head is what.

شیراز و آب رکنی و این باد خوش نسیم

Shiraz (Hafiz's existence) and the water of Ruknabad[1], (love, life – giving) and the breeze of pleasant air, (the soul's breathings)

عیبش مکن که خال رخ هفت کشور است

(Them), contemn not; for (though contemptible they are the lustre of) adornment of they are the luster of adornment of seven territories (of the world).

فرق است از آب خضر که ظلمات جای او است

From the water (of life love, giving eternal life) of Khizr[2], whose place is the Land of Darkness, man's elemental existence it is far

تا آب ما که منبعش الله اکبر است

Up to our water, whose fountain is Allah-u Akbar[3].

1-An area in Shiraz

2-Name of a prophet

3- Name of a hill in Shiraz

ما آبروی فقر و قناعت نمی‌بریم
We take (spill) not the honor of poverty and (of) contentment:
با پادشه بگوی که روزی مقدر است
To the king, speak (saying): Daily victuals are destined (by the Provider, God).

حافظ چه طرفه شاخ نباتیست کلک تو
Hafez! how strange, the twig of candy is thy reed,
کش میوه دلپذیرتر از شهد و شکر است
Whose fruit (verse) is more heart-pleasing than honey and sugar.

غزل ۴۰ ⓄⒹⒺ ④⓪

المنه لله که در میکده باز است
Thanks be to God that the door of the wine-tavern open, is.
زان رو که مرا بر در او روی نیاز است
In such a way that, my face of supplication upon its door is.

خم‌ها همه در جوش و خروشند ز مستی
Through intoxication, all in tumult and shout are the jars (the seekers of God);
وان می که در آن جاست حقیقت نه مجاز است
And that wine that in that place (the threshold of the Murshid) true is, not illusory, is

از وی همه مستی و غرور است و تکبر
From Him, intoxication, and (tumult), and pride: all is.
وز ما همه بیچارگی و عجز و نیاز است
From us, helplessness, and weakness, and supplication all is.

رازی که بر غیر نگفتیم و نگوییم
The mystery that to the people I uttered not, and shall not utter:
با دوست بگوییم که او محرم راز است
To the Friend, I shall utter; for confidant of the mystery He is.

شرح شکن زلف خم اندر خم جانان
The twist of the tress, curl within curl, the explanation
کوته نتوان کرد که این قصه دراز است
One cannot shorten; for long this story is.

بار دل مجنون و خم طره لیلی
The load of Majnun's[1] heart; and the curl of Laila's[2] tress
رخساره محمود و کف پای ایاز است
The cheek Of Mahmud (of Ghuzni) and the sole of the foot of Ayaz is.

بردوخته‌ام دیده چو باز از همه عالم
Like the hawk, I have stitched up my eye from all the world:
تا دیده من بر رخ زیبای تو باز است
Since, on Thy adorned cheek, my eye open is.

در کعبه کوی تو هر آن کس که بیاید
Whoever entereth the Ka'ba of Thy street,
از قبله ابروی تو در عین نماز است
Through the Kibla[3] of Thy eye-brow (arch) in the very act of prayer is.

1-A lover
2-A lover

3-Direction to Mohammadans turn which in praying

ای مجلسیان سوز دل حافظ مسکین
O people of the assembly (Murshids)! the consuming of the heart of poor Hafez
از شمع بپرسید که در سوز و گداز است
Ask ye the candle that, in burning and melting is.

غزل ۴۱ ⓄⒹⒺ ④①

اگر چه باده فرح بخش و باد گل‌بیز است
Though wine (love) is joy exciting! and the breeze (the Murshid) rose-enslaving,
به بانگ چنگ مخور می که محتسب تیز است
(Openly) Drink not wine (of love) to the sound of the harp (the holy traveller's utterances of love's mysteries). For bold the Muhtaseb[1] (the law of Muhammad) is.

صراحی ای و حریفی گرت به چنگ افتد
If to thy grasp fall a flagon (ecstasy and rapture) and a Companion (the true Beloved),
به عقل نوش که ایام فتنه انگیز است
Drink with reason; for the season, (fraught with) calamity is.

در آستین مرقع پیاله پنهان کن
(O holy Traveller) Conceal the cup (of thy existence) in the sleeve of the tattered garment (of the);
که همچو چشم صراحی زمانه خون‌ریز است
For, like the wine-flagon's (ruddy) eye, time is blood-shedding.

به آب دیده بشوییم خرقه‌ها از می
With the color of wine, (some of the mysteries and stages of love) we cleanse the religious garments (the existence of the holy traveller) with (penitential) tears:
که موسم ورع و روزگار پرهیز است
For, the season of austerity, and the time of piety it is.

مجوی عیش خوش از دور بازگون سپهر
From the revolution of the inverted sphere, seek no sweet pleasure.
که صاف این سر خم جمله دردی آمیز است
For all mixed with dregs the pure (substance) of this head of the wine jar is.

سپهر برشده پرویزنیست خون افشان
The up-lifted sky! Is it not the sieve Is it not the sieve blood-splattering,
که ریزه‌اش سر کسری و تاج پرویز است
Whose scattering, the head of Kasra and the crown of Parviz is?

عراق و فارس گرفتی به شعر خوش حافظ
O Hafez! (with thy sweet verse) thou hast captivated Iraq and Persia.
بیا که نوبت بغداد و وقت تبریز است
Come. For the turn (of capture) of Baghdad, and the time of Tabriz is.

غزل ۴۲ ⓄⒹⒺ ④②

حال دل با تو گفتنم هوس است
(O Beloved) to utter to thee the state of my heart is my desire:
خبر دل شنفتنم هوس است
To hear news of my heart (by way of counsel and advice) is my desire.

1-Sheriff

طمع خام بین که قصه فاش
Behold the crude desire—how the well-known tale (of love)
از رقیبان نهفتنم هوس است
To conceal from the watchers (hypocrites or devils) is my desire

شب قدری چنین عزیز و شریف
A night of power (the twenty-seventh night of the Ramazân) like this, precious and holy,
با تو تا روز خفتنم هوس است
To sleep with thee till day, is my desire.

وه که دردانه‌ای چنین نازک
Alas! the unique pearl (mysteries of divine knowledge) so tender
در شب تار سفتنم هوس است
To pierce (understand) in the dark night, (the world) is my desire.

ای صبا امشبم مدد فرمای
O breeze (Murshid)! tonight (in this world) give help and make me honoured by union with the true Beloved,
که سحرگه شکفتنم هوس است
For, in the morning time, (in the next world) to blossom is my desire.

از برای شرف به نوک مژه
For exaltation's sake, with the point of the eye-lash
خاک راه تو رفتنم هوس است
To sweep the dust of the Path (of love) is my desire

همچو حافظ به رغم مدعیان
In abhorrence of the (false) claimants, like Hafez
شعر رندانه گفتنم هوس است
To utter profligate verse is my desire.

غزل ۴۳ ⓄⒹⒺ ④③

صحن بستان ذوق بخش و صحبت یاران خوش است
The court of the garden (the world) is joy-giving (producing manifestations of Love's glories); and the society of friends (the soul and the body that intervene between the seeker and the Sought), pleasant;
وقت گل خوش باد کز وی وقت میخواران خوش است
Pleasant, be the time of the rose (the Murshid), whereby the time of wine-drinkers (lovers of God) is pleasant.

از صبا هر دم مشام جان ما خوش می‌شود
From the morning breeze, momently our soul's perfume is pleasant.
آری آری طیب انفاس هواداران خوش است
Yes, yes. The perfume of desire-possessing spirits is pleasant.

ناگشوده گل نقاب آهنگ رحلت ساز کرد
The rose (the Murshid), veil unlifted prepared to depart (to the next world):
ناله کن ای بلبل که گلبانگ دل افکاران خوش است
O nightingale (holy Traveller) bewail; for the plaint of heart-wounded ones is pleasant.

مرغ خوشخوان را بشارت باد کاندر راه عشق
To the night-singing bird, be the good news that, in Love's path,
دوست را با ناله شب‌های بیداران خوش است
To the Friend (God), the vigilant one, weeping at night for sin is pleasant.

نیست در بازار عالم خوشدلی ور زان که هست
In the world's market, is no happy-heartiness. If there be

شیوه رندی و خوش باشی عیاران خوش است
The way of profligacy and of happy-being of hypocrites is pleasant.

از زبان سوسن آزادهام آمد به گوش
From the tongue of the Lily, came to my ear this noble speech,

کاندر این دیر کهن کار سبکباران خوش است
In the old cloister, (this world) the work of those light of burden is pleasant."

حافظا ترک جهان گفتن طریق خوشدلیست
Hafez! Abandoning the world is the path of happy heartiness.

تا نپنداری که احوال جهان داران خوش است
So long as thou thinkest not that the circumstance of World-Possessors (Kings) is pleasant.

غزل ۴۴ ⓞⒹⒺ ④④

کنون که بر کف گل جام باده صاف است
Now that in the palm of the rose (the holy traveller), is the cup of pure wine borrowed worldly existence,

به صد هزار زبان بلبلش در اوصاف است
In it praise, is the nightingale (the flattering Friend) with a hundred thousand tongues.

بخواه دفتر اشعار و راه صحرا گیر
Seek the book of verse (truths and subtleties) and make way to the desert (choose solitude):

چه وقت مدرسه و بحث کشف کشاف است
(Tis the time of justice) what time is this for the College, and the argument of the Kashf-i-Kashshaf?

فقیه مدرسه دی مست بود و فتوی داد
Yesterday, the Head of the College was intoxicated; and gave decision,

که می حرام ولی به ز مال اوقاف است
Saying: "Wine is unlawful, but (is) better than the property of legacies. (Obtained by fraud)"

به درد و صاف تو را حکم نیست خوش درکش
(O Slave) no order is thine for the dregs, (bad) or for the pure (good): Drink happily (be content);

که هر چه ساق ما کرد عین الطاف است
For, whatever our Saki (Fate and Destiny) did is the essence of grace and source of justice.

ببر ز خلق و چو عنقا قیاس کار بگیر
Pluck up thy attachments to the people: take note of the work (of solitude) from the Anka[1]

که صیت گوشه نشینان ز قاف تا قاف است
(that liveth in solitude) ;For, the clamour of those sitting in solitude is from Kaf to Kaf[2].

حدیث مدعیان و خیال همکاران
The tale of claimants (outward worshippers) and the mean fancy of thy fellow-workers,

همان حکایت زردوز و بوریاباف است
Resemble the tale of the gold-stitcher and the mat-weaver.

خموش حافظ و این نکتههای چون زر سرخ
Hafez! silence: and these subtleties like (pure) red gold,

نگاه دار که قلاب شهر صراف است
Keep. For the false coiner of the city is the Banker.

1-Phoenix   2-Used to express the maximum distance

غزل ۴۵ ⓄⒹⒺ ④⑤

در این زمانه رفیقی که خالی از خلل است

At this time (full of iniquity), a friend, who is free from defect (of insincerity, and in whose society is joy),

صراحی می ناب و سفینه غزل است

Is the goblet of pure wine, (the glorious Kuran from whose companionship, one can momently snatch delight) and the song-book (Divine knowledge, whose reading perpetually is full of pleasure)

جریده رو که گذرگاه عافیت تنگ است

Go alone (free from all attachments); for the highway of safety (love) is narrow (full of thorns and of stones):

پیاله گیر که عمر عزیز بی‌بدل است

Seize (quickly) the cup (love's attraction); for dear life is without exchangereturneth not and permitteth not the traveller to make good the omission of the past.

نه من ز بی عملی در جهان ملولم و بس

In the world, not I alone am distressed from being without work

ملالت علما هم ز علم بی عمل است

From learning without doing, is the grief of the learned.

به چشم عقل در این رهگذار پرآشوب

In this thoroughfare full of tumult, to reason's eye,

جهان و کار جهان بی‌ثبات و بی‌محل است

The World and the world's work is without permanency and without place.

بگیر طره مه چهره‌ای و قصه مخوان

Seize the tress of the one of moon face (the true Beloved), and utter not the tale;

که سعد و نحس ز تأثیر زهره و زحل است

For fortune and misfortune are the effects of Venus and of Saturn.

دلم امید فراوان به وصل روی تو داشت

Great hope of union with thee, had my heart.

ولی اجل به ره عمر رهزن امل است

But, on life's path, death is hope's robber.

به هیچ دور نخواهند یافت هشیارش

At no time, will they find him sensible:

چنین که حافظ ما مست باده ازل است

For this reason, that Hafez is intoxicated with the cup of eternity without beginning

غزل ۴۶ ⓄⒹⒺ ④⑥

گل در بر و می در کف و معشوق به کام است

(When) the rose is in the bosom; wine in the hand; and the Beloved to my desire,

سلطان جهانم به چنین روز غلام است

On such a day, the world's Sultan is my slave.

گو شمع میارید در این جمع که امشب

Say: Into this assembly, bring ye no candle for to-night.

در مجلس ما ماه رخ دوست تمام است

In our assembly, the moon of the Friend's face is full.

در مذهب ما باده حلال است ولیکن

In our order, (of profligates) the wine-cup is lawful; but,

بی روی تو ای سرو گل اندام حرام است

O Cypress, rose of body! without thy face (presence), unlawful.

گوشم همه بر قول نی و نغمه چنگ است

My ear is all (intent) on the voice of the reed; and, the melody of the harp (the instruction of the Murshid):

چشمم همه بر لعل لب و گردش جام است

My eye is all (intent) on Thy ruby lip, and on the circulation of the cup (the manifestations of glories of God in the night season).

در مجلس ما عطر میامیز که ما را

In our assembly, of lovers mix not 'itr (Perfume); for our soul,

هر لحظه ز گیسوی تو خوش بوی مشام است

Every moment, receiveth perfume from the fragrance of the tip of Thy tress.

از چاشنی قند مگو هیچ و ز شکر

Say ye naught of the sweetness of candy and sugar; (the delights of the world)

زان رو که مرا از لب شیرین تو کام است

For my desire is for Thy sweet lip. (the sweet stream of Divine grace, the source of endless delight)

تا گنج غمت در دل ویرانه مقیم است

From the time when the treasure of grief for Thee was dweller in my ruined heart,

همواره مرا کوی خرابات مقام است

The corner of the tavern is ever my ab ode.

از ننگ چه گویی که مرا نام ز ننگ است

Of shame, why speakest thou? For from shame is my name (renown):

وز نام چه پرسی که مرا ننگ ز نام است

Of name (renown), why askest thou? For from name (renown) is my shame.

میخواره و سرگشته و رندیم و نظرباز

Wine-drinker, distraught of head, profligate, and glance-player I am:

وان کس که چو ما نیست در این شهر کدام است

In this city, who is that one who is not like this?

با محتسبم عیب مگویید که او نیز

To the Muhtaseb, utter not my crime; for he also

پیوسته چو ما در طلب عیش مدام است

Is ever like me in desire of the drinkers of wine.

حافظ منشین بی می و معشوق زمانی

Hafez! sit not a moment without wine, and the Beloved

کایام گل و یاسمن و عید صیام است

Tis the season of the rose, and of the Jasmine, and of the celebration of fasting!

غزل ۴۷ ⓄⒹⒺ ④⑦ ODE 47

به کوی میکده هر سالکی که ره دانست

In the Street of the tavern (the stage of love and divine knowledge), every holy traveler, that knew the Path

دری دگر زدن اندیشه تبه دانست

The knocking at another door, the source of ruin knew.

زمانه افسر رندی نداد جز به کسی

The diadem of profligacy, Time gave to none save to that one

که سرفرازی عالم در این کله دانست

Who, exaltation of the world (to be) in this cup (of profligacy), knew.

بر آستانه میخانه هر که یافت رهی

To the threshold of the tavern, whoever found a Path,

ز فیض جام می اسرار خانقه دانست

The mysteries of the cloister (the stage of Abids) from the bounty of the cup of wine (of love) knew.

هر آن که راز دو عالم ز خط ساغر خواند

From the Saki's line (of instruction of love), who ever read the mystery of both worlds,

رموز جام جم از نقش خاک ره دانست

The mysteries of Jamshid's cup with (equal to) the pictures of the (worthless) the road-dust knew.

ورای طاعت دیوانگان ز ما مطلب

Seek not from us aught save the (sincere) the devotion of the distraught (perfect lovers)

که شیخ مذهب ما عاقلی گنه دانست

For the being wise, a sin, the Shaikh[1] of our religious order knew.

دلم ز نرگس ساقی امان نخواست به جان

From the eye of the Saki[2] (the true Beloved, God), my heart desired not safety for life;

چراکه شیوه آن ترک دل سیه دانست

For the way of that Bold One (God), black of heart, my heart knew.

ز جور کوکب طالع سحرگهان چشمم

From the violence of (oppression) of the constellation of nativity, my eye in the mornings

چنان گریست که ناهید دید و مه دانست

So wept, that Nahid (Venus) beheld, and the moon knew.

حدیث حافظ و ساغر که می‌زند پنهان

The tale of Hafez and the cup which he secretly drinketh

چه جای محتسب و شحنه پادشه دانست

What room for the Muhtaseb[3] and the watchman? The king knew.

بلندمرتبه شاهی که نه رواق سپهر

A king of lofty rank is that one who, the nine halls of the sky

نمونه‌ای ز خم طاق بارگه دانست

The form of the curve of the arch of his court, knew

غزل ۴۸ ⓄⒹⒺ ④⑧ ODE 48

صوفی از پرتو می راز نهانی دانست

From the wine's sparkle, (the glories of Love for God) the Arif knew the hidden mystery:

گوهر هر کس از این لعل توانی دانست

Every one's essence, (of capability) by this ruby the ruddy wine of Love thou canst know.

قدر مجموعه گل مرغ سحر داند و بس

Only the bird of the morning (the nightingale) knoweth the value of the rose bud:

که نه هر کو ورق خواند معانی دانست

For, not everyone that read a page, the meaning knew.

1-A leader in a Muslim community   3-Sheriff
2-Tapster

عرضه کردم دو جهان بر دل کارافتاده

To my work-stricken heart, I offered (this and the next worlds).Them it accepted not.

بجز از عشق تو باقی همه فانی دانست

Save love for Thee, the rest all effacement, it (my heart) knew.

آن شد اکنون که ز ابنای عوام اندیشم

Passed hath that time, when I thought of (the talk of) the people. Now (what fear) since

محتسب نیز در این عیش نهانی دانست

Of this my secret pleasure, the Muhtaseb knew.

دلبر آسایش ما مصلحت وقت ندید

The Heart-Ravisher (God) regarded not our ease, (union with Him) time's business (in this world)

ور نه از جانب ما دل نگرانی دانست

If not, on our part, the heart-expectation (and the complete desire), He knew.

سنگ و گل را کند از یمن نظر لعل و عقیق

The stone and the clay, the ruby and the cornelian, maketh with auspicious glance

هر که قدر نفس باد یمانی دانست

Whoever the value of the breath of the breeze of Yaman (time of leisure) knew

ای که از دفتر عقل آیت عشق آموزی

O thou that learnest Love's verse from Reason's book!

ترسم این نکته به تحقیق ندانی دانست

I fear (that, notwithstanding thy labour) this subtlety by investigation, thou wilt not know.

می بیاور که ننازد به گل باغ جهان

Bring wine! (of love) for of the rose of the world's garden (pleasure and ease), boasteth not.

هر که غارتگری باد خزانی دانست

He who, the robbery of the autumn-wind, (death) knew.

حافظ این گوهر منظوم که از طبع انگیخت

This versified jewel of verse that, from his mind, he evoked, Hafez

ز اثر تربیت آصف ثانی دانست

The effect of the instruction of Asef[1] the second, knew.

غزل ۴۹ ⓄⒹⒺ ④⑨ ODE 49

روضه خلد برین خلوت درویشان است

The garden of lofty Paradise is the retreat of Dervishes:

مایه محتشمی خدمت درویشان است

Grandeur's source is the service of Dervishes.

گنج عزلت که طلسمات عجایب دارد

The treasure of retirement that hath the tilisms of wonders,

فتح آن در نظر رحمت درویشان است

Their revealing is in the mercy-glance of Dervishes.

قصر فردوس که رضوانش به دربانی رفت

The palace of paradise, for the door guarding of which, Rizvan[2] went

منظری از چمن نزهت درویشان است

Is only a spectacle-place of the sward of pleasure of Dervishes.

1-Touranshah's minister   2-Heaven

آن چه زر می‌شود از پرتو آن قلب سیاه
By whose ray, the dull alloy becometh gold, that
کیمیاییست که در صحبت درویشان است
Is an alchemy that is in the society of Dervishes.

آن که پیشش بنهد تاج تکبر خورشید
Before whom the lofty Sun layeth (in such submission) his crown of glory,
کبریاییست که در حشمت درویشان است
Is a glory that is in the grandeur of Dervishes.

دولتی را که نباشد غم از آسیب زوال
That great fortune, whereof is no grief through the torment of decay,
بی تکلف بشنو دولت درویشان است
Hear-ceremony aside,-is the fortune of Dervishes.

خسروان قبله حاجات جهانند ولی
Khusraus[1] are the Kibla[2] of our needs, and of prayer but,
سببش بندگی حضرت درویشان است
The cause is their service of the majesty of Dervishes.

روی مقصود که شاهان به دعا می‌طلبند
The form of the object that the Kings of the world seek,
مظهرش آینه طلعت درویشان است
Its reflection is the mirror of the appearance of Dervishes.

از کران تا به کران لشکر ظلم است ولی
From pole to pole, is the army of tyranny; but
از ازل تا به ابد فرصت درویشان است
From eternity without beginning to eternity without end is the victory of Dervishes.

ای توانگر مفروش این همه نخوت که تو را
O potent one! Boast not all this pomp: for thy
سر و زر در کنف همت درویشان است
Head (life) and gold are in the keeping of the blessing of Dervishes!

گنج قارون که فرو می‌شود از قهر هنوز
Karun's[3] treasure that, from the wrath (of Musa) 1, yet descendeth (into the earth).
خوانده باشی که هم از غیرت درویشان است
That also, thou wilt have read, is from the wrath of Dervishes.

من غلام نظر آصف عهدم کو را
I am the slave of the glance of the Asef[4] of the age who
صورت خواجگی و سیرت درویشان است
Hath the form of mastership and of mind of Dervishes.

حافظ ار آب حیات ازلی می‌خواهی
Hafez! be here with respect. For sovereignty and country,
منبعش خاک در خلوت درویشان است
All are from the service of the majesty of Dervishes.

1-Kings
2-Temple
3-Korah, The rich man of the time of Prophet Moses
4-Touranshah's minister

غزل ۵۰   ⓞⓓⓔ ⑤ⓞ

به دام زلف تو دل مبتلای خویشتن است
In the snare of Thy tress, my heart entangled of itself is.

بکش به غمزه که اینش سزای خویشتن است
Slay with a glance; for to it (the heart), punishment of itself is

گرت ز دست برآید مراد خاطر ما
If from Thy hand issue our heart's desire,

به دست باش که خیری به جای خویشتن است
Be (ready) at hand: for goodness in place of itself is.

به جانت ای بت شیرین دهن که همچون شمع
O sweet idol! by Thy soul (I swear) that like a candle,

شبان تیره مرادم فنای خویشتن است
In dark nights my desire, effacement of myself is.

چو رای عشق زدی با تو گفتم ای بلبل
O nightingale! when thou expressedest opinion of love, to thee, I said

مکن که آن گل خندان برای خویشتن است
"Do not (express an opinion); for that rose (the beloved), self-going, for the sake of itself is."

به مشک چین و چگل نیست بوی گل محتاج
The perfume of the rose is in no need of the musk of Chin and of Chigal:

که نافه‌هاش ز بند قبای خویشتن است
For, its pods of musk (sweet fragrance) from the fastenings (leaves) of the coat of itself is

مرو به خانه ارباب بی‌مروت دهر
Go not to the house of the Lords void of liberality of the age;

که گنج عافیتت در سرای خویشتن است
For the corner of ease in the dwelling of one's self is.

بسوخت حافظ و در شرط عشقبازی او
Hafez consumed; and (so consumed) in the condition of love and of life stakin

هنوز بر سر عهد و وفای خویشتن است
Yet, at the head of covenant and of fidelity of himself is

غزل ۵۱   ⓞⓓⓔ ⑤①

لعل سیراب به خون تشنه لب یار من است
The fresh ruby, thirsty for blood the ruby lip of the Beloved of mine is

وز پی دیدن او دادن جان کار من است
Yet for seeing Him (God), life-surrendering the work of mine is.

شرم از آن چشم سیه بادش و مژگان دراز
Of that dark eye and long eyelash (of the true Beloved), shame be his,

هر که دل بردن او دید و در انکار من است
Who beheld His heart ravishingness (and yet); in reproach (of conduct) of mine is

ساروان رخت به دروازه مبر کان سر کو
O Camel-driver! (Fate) to the door, take not my chattels. (of borrowed existence) For that street-end

شاهراهیست که منزلگه دلدار من است
Is a highway, where the lodging of the heart-possessor of mine is.

بنده طالع خویشم که در این قحط وفا
I am the slave of my own fortune; for, in this (time of) scarcity of fidelity,
عشق آن لولی سرمست خریدار من است
Love for that intoxicated idol (the world) the purchaser of mine is.

طبله عطر گل و زلف عبیرافشانش
The platter of Perfume of rose, and its casket ambergris diffusing (man – fascinating)
فیض یک شمه ز بوی خوش عطار من است
A little favor of the pleasant perfume of the Perfumer of mine is.

باغبان همچو نسیمم ز در خویش مران
O Gardener! (God, the Creator) drive me not away like the wind (portionless) from the door of the garden of existence
کب گلزار تو از اشک چو گلنار من است
For the water (of dominion and of creation) of Thy rose-bed, like the (ruddy) pomegranate, with the (bloody) tears of mine is.

شربت قند و گلاب از لب یارم فرمود
From my Friend's lip, the draft of candy and of rose-water, ordered.
نرگس او که طبیب دل بیمار من است
His narcissus (eye) that the physician of the sick heart of mine is.

آن که در طرز غزل نکته به حافظ آموخت
I am the decoration of the ghazal, He who taught subtlety to Hafez,
یار شیرین سخن نادره گفتار من است
Sweet of speech, lustrous of talk, the Friend of mine is.

غزل ۵۲ ⓄⒹⒺ ⑤②

روزگاریست که سودای بتان دین من است
'Tis a (long) time since the passion for idols was my faith:
غم این کار نشاط دل غمگین من است
The pain of this work, the joy of the sorrowful heart of mine is.

دیدن روی تو را دیده جان بین باید
For beholding Thy ruby (lip), the soul-seeing eye is necessary:
وین کجا مرتبه چشم جهان بین من است
Where this rank for the world-seeing eye of mine is.

یار من باش که زیب فلک و زینت دهر
Be my friend. For the day's decoration and time's advancement,
از مه روی تو و اشک چو پروین من است
From the moon-face of Thine and from the Pleiade ode like tears of mine is.

تا مرا عشق تو تعلیم سخن گفتن کرد
Since Thy love gave me instruction in speech-uttering,
خلق را ورد زبان مدحت و تحسین من است
The practice of the people's tongue, the praise and the glory of mine is.

دولت فقر خدایا به من ارزانی دار
O God! keep for me the lot of poverty
کاین کرامت سبب حشمت و تمکین من است
For this blessing, the cause of pomp and of power of mine is.

واعظ شحنه شناس این عظمت گو مفروش

O admonisher, ruler-recognizer! display no pride

زان که منزلگه سلطان دل مسکین من است

For the lodging of the Sultan, (the One God) the wretched heart of mine is.

یا رب این کعبه مقصود تماشاگه کیست

O Lord! that Ka'ba[1] of (my) object is whose place of entertainment,

که مغیلان طریقش گل و نسرین من است

The mighty thorn of whose Path, the rose and the wild rose of mine is.

حافظ از حشمت پرویز دگر قصه مخوان

Hafez! utter not again the tale of the pomp of (khusrau) Parviz,

که لبش جرعه کش خسرو شیرین من است

Whose lip, the draft-drinker of the sweet Khosro of mine is.

غزل ۵۳   ⓞⓓⓔ ⑤③

منم که گوشه میخانه خانقاه من است

Such a one am I that the tavern-corner is the cloister of mine:

دعای پیر مغان ورد صبحگاه من است

The prayer from the Pir of wine – sellers is the morning task of mine.

گرم ترانه چنگ صبوح نیست چه باک

Although the melody of the harp of the morning be not mine, what fear?

نوای من به سحر آه عذرخواه من است

At morning-time (the resurrection) my cry is the excuse-utterer of mine.

ز پادشاه و گدا فارغم بحمدالله

Of the king and of the beggar, I am free. Al hamdu-l'illah (God be praised)!

گدای خاک در دوست پادشاه من است

The beggar of the dust of the Friend's door is king of mine!

غرض ز مسجد و میخانه‌ام وصال شماست

(O true Beloved) through the tavern and the Masjed[2], my desire is union with Thee:

جز این خیال ندارم خدا گواه من است

Save this, no fancy have I. God is the witness of mine!

مگر به تیغ اجل خیمه برکنم ور نی

Perchance, with death's sword, I may up-pluck the tent. (of life) If not,

رمیدن از در دولت نه رسم و راه من است

Shunning the door of fortune (the true Beloved) is not the custom of mine.

از آن زمان که بر این آستان نهادم روی

From that time when, on that threshold of Thine, I placed my face,

فراز مسند خورشید تکیه گاه من است

The sun's lofty throne was the pillow-place of mine.

گناه اگر چه نبود اختیار ما حافظ

Hafez! though sin be not our choice,

تو در طریق ادب باش و گو گناه من است

Strive in the way of manners; and say: "The sin is of mine."

1-Muslims turn at prayer.   2-Mosque

غزل ۵۴ ODE 54

ز گریه مردم چشمم نشسته در خون است
(O true Beloved) from (much) weeping, the pupil of my eye seated in blood (of grief) is,

ببین که در طلبت حال مردمان چون است
(From this) Behold the state of men in search of Thee, how it is.

به یاد لعل تو و چشم مست میگونت
To the memory of Thy ruby (lip) and wine-like (ruddy) intoxicated eye,

ز جام غم می لعلی که می‌خورم خون است
From griefs cup, the wine of that ruby that I drink, blood is.

ز مشرق سر کو آفتاب طلعت تو
From the east of the head of the street, the sun of Thy countenance,

اگر طلوع کند طالعم همایون است
If it rise, my fortune auspicious is.

حکایت لب شیرین کلام فرهاد است
The tale of Shirin's lip, Farhad's talk is;

شکنج طره لیلی مقام مجنون است
The twist of Laila's tress, Majnun's dwelling is.

دلم بجو که قدت همچو سرو دلجوی است
(O Beloved) Seek my heart. For thy stature, (lofty), like the cypress is heart-seeking (and agreeable).

سخن بگو که کلامت لطیف و موزون است
Utter speech. For thy speech gracious and weighed is.

ز دور باده به جان راحتی رسان ساقی
O Saki[1]! From the circulation of the cup, cause a little mercy to reach my soul:

که رنج خاطرم از جور دور گردون است
For, from the grief of the sphere's revolution, the heart's sorrow is.

از آن دمی که ز چشمم برفت رود عزیز
From that time when, from my grasp, went the precious musical chord (the true Beloved),

کنار دامن من همچو رود جیحون است
Like the river Jeyhun, (through much weeping) my skirt's border is.

چگونه شاد شود اندرون غمگینم
Gladsome, how may my sorrowful heart become

به اختیار که از اختیار بیرون است
By the power (God) that beyond my power is?

ز بیخودی طلب یار می‌کند حافظ
Through distraughtness, Hafez seeketh for the true Beloved:

چو مفلسی که طلبکار گنج قارون است
Like 'an indigent one, who a seeker of Qarun's[2] treasure is

غزل ۵۵ ODE 55

خم زلف تو دام کفر و دین است
The curve of Thy tress is the snare of infidelity and of Faith (Islam):

ز کارستان او یک شمه این است
This matter is a little from His work-shop.

1-Tapster   2-Korah, The rich man of the time of Prophet Moses

جمالت معجز حسن است لیکن
Thy beauty is the miracle of beauty. But

حدیث غمزهات سحر مبین است
The tale of Thy glance is clear magic.

ز چشم شوخ تو جان کی توان برد
(In safety) How can one take one's life from Thy bold eye,

که دایم با کمان اندر کمین است
That ever is in ambuscade with the bow?

بر آن چشم سیه صد آفرین باد
Be a hundred (shouts of) Afarin! on that dark eye,

که در عاشق کشی سحرآفرین است
Which, in lover-slaying is the creator of magic.

عجب علمیست علم هیت عشق
A wonderful science is the science of love's form:

که چرخ هشتمش هفتم زمین است
For the (lofty) seventh sky is the low seventh land.

تو پنداری که بدگو رفت و جان برد
Thou thinkest not that the evil-speaker departed (in death), and took his life (in safety):

حسابش با کرام الکاتبین است
(In error, thou art) His account is with the two noble recorders.

مشو حافظ ز کید زلفش ایمن
Hafez! be not secure from the snare of His tress.

که دل برد و کنون دربند دین است
That taketh the heart; and is now in fancy (of taking away) religion.

غزل ۵۶ ⓄⒹⒺ ⑤⑥

دل سراپرده محبت اوست
The heart is the chamber (comprehender) of love of His:

دیده آیینه دار طلعت اوست
The eye is the mirror-holder (displayer) of the form of His.

من که سر درنیاورم به دو کون
I, who incline not to the two worlds (this and the next),

گردنم زیر بار منت اوست
My neck is beneath the burden of favor of His.

تو و طوبی و ما و قامت یار
(O Zahid) Thou and the Tuba1 tree; and we and the form of the (true) Beloved;

فکر هر کس به قدر همت اوست
Every one's thought (of arrangement of affairs) is to the limit of ambition of His.

گر من آلوده دامنم چه عجب
If I be soiled of skirt, what loss?

همه عالم گواه عصمت اوست
For the whole world is the evidence of the innocence of His.

1-The name of a tree in heaven

من که باشم در آن حرم که صبا
I, who am in that holy place, where the breeze
پرده دار حریم حرمت اوست
Is the screen-holder (door – keeper) of the fold of the dignity of His.

بی خیالش مباد منظر چشم
Without His image, be not the vision of thy eye:
زان که این گوشه جای خلوت اوست
For the reason that this corner (of the eye) is the special chamber of His

هر گل نو که شد چمن آرای
Every new rose (seeker) that became sward-adorner
ز اثر رنگ و بوی صحبت اوست
Is the mark of the colour and the perfume of His

دور مجنون گذشت و نوبت ماست
Passed the time of Majnun; the distraught lover and our turn it is:
هر کسی پنج روز نوبت اوست
Every one, a space of five days is the term of His.

ملکت عاشقی و گنج طرب
The realm of being a lover (of God); and the corner of joy,
هر چه دارم ز یمن همت اوست
All I have is from the favor of the fortune of His.

من و دل گر فدا شدیم چه باک
If I and my heart become ransom (for the beloved) what fear
غرض اندر میان سلامت اوست
The object in view is the safety of his

فقر ظاهر مبین که حافظ را
Regard not his (Hafiz's) external poverty. For Hafez's
سینه گنجینه محبت اوست
Heart is the treasury of the love of His

غزل ۵۷ ⓄⒹⒺ ⑤⑦

آن سیه چرده که شیرینی عالم با اوست
This blackish (beautiful) one (Muhammad) all the sweetness (goodness, laudable qualities, external beauty, internal excellence) of the world is with him
چشم میگون لب خندان دل خرم با اوست
The fair eye, the laughing lip, the joyous heart (each) is with Him.

گر چه شیرین دهنان پادشهانند ولی
Although those sweet of mouth (other prophets) are Sovereigns, yet
او سلیمان زمان است که خاتم با اوست
He (Muhammad) is the Soleiman of the age; for the sealof prophecy is with Him.

روی خوب است و کمال هنر و دامن پاک
He (Muhammad) is fair of face, perfect in skill, pure of sin;
لاجرم همت پاکان دو عالم با اوست
Verily the spirit of the Pure Ones of the two worlds is with Him.

خال مشکین که بدان عارض گندمگون است
The musky (dark) mole that is on that wheat-hued fair face

سر آن دانه که شد رهزن آدم با اوست
The mystery of that grain, (of wheat) that became the highway robber of Adam, is with it.

دلبرم عزم سفر کرد خدا را یاران
My heart-ravisher hath set out on a journey. O friends! for God's sake,

چه کنم با دل مجروح که مرهم با اوست
What shall I do with my wounded heart; for plaister (of remedy) is with him

با که این نکته توان گفت که آن سنگین دل
With whom, (of men void of divine knowledge) can one discuss this matter, that that stoney-hearted One the true Beloved

کشت ما را و دم عیسی مریم با اوست
Slew us; and (yet) the (life – giving) the breath of Isa (son) of Maryam is with Him.

حافظ از معتقدان است گرامی دارش
Hafez is of the believers. Hold him dear.

زان که بخشایش بس روح مکرم با اوست
For the forgiveness of many a noble soul is with Him.

غزل ۵۸ ⓄⒹⒺ ⑤⑧

سر ارادت ما و آستان حضرت دوست
(Together are) the head of our desire, and the threshold of the Mighty Friend (God):

که هر چه بر سر ما می‌رود ارادت اوست
For, whatever (of good, or of bad) passeth over our head is His will.

نظیر دوست ندیدم اگر چه از مه و مهر
My Friend's equal, I have not seen; although the (gleaming) of the moon and of the shining sun,

نهادم آینه‌ها در مقابل رخ دوست
The mirrors opposite to the Friend's face I placed.

صبا ز حال دل تنگ ما چه شرح دهد
Of our straitened heart, giveth the breeze what news,

که چون شکنج ورق‌های غنچه تو بر توست
That, like the folding of the leaves of the rosebud, tightly folded it (the heart) is.

نه من سبوکش این دیر رندسوزم و بس
Not alone, am I a wine-drinker (a lover) of this cloister, profligate consuming (the wine tavern, the stage of love):

بسا سرا که در این کارخانه سنگ و سبوست
O many a (great) head in this workshop is (only) the dust of the pitcher!

مگر تو شانه زدی زلف عنبرافشان را
Verily, Thou combedest Thy tress, ambergri ode scattering,

که باد غالیه سا گشت و خاک عنبربوست
Since that the breeze became like civet; and the dust, beperfumed with ambergris.

نثار روی تو هر برگ گل که در چمن است
The sprinkling of Thy face, (be) every rose-leaf that is in the sward:

فدای قد تو هر سروبن که بر لب جوست
The ransom of Thy lofty form, (be) every cypress that is on the river-bank.

زبان ناطقه در وصف شوق نالان است
In the description of His Love, (even) the tongue of speech is dumb:

چه جای کلک بریده زبان بیهده گوست
What room for the (feeble) reed, split of tongue, folly uttering?

رخ تو در دلم آمد مراد خواهم یافت
(Of happy omen) thy face came into my heart: my desire I shall gain:

چراکه حال نکو در قفای فال نکوست
For, after the happy omen, is the happy state.

نه این زمان دل حافظ در آتش هوس است
Not, at this time, is Hafez's heart in the fire of search (of love):

که داغدار ازل همچو لاله خودروست
For, in Eternity without beginning, it was the possessor of the mark (of love) like the self-growing wild tulip (of Shiraz)

غزل ۵۹ ⓞⓓⓔ ⑤⑨

دارم امید عاطفتی از جانب دوست
Of a great favor from the threshold of the Friend (God), hope mine is.

کردم جنایتی و امیدم به عفو اوست
A great sin I have done; of His pardon hope mine, is.

دانم که بگذرد ز سر جرم من که او
I know that He will pass by (forgive) my sin; for

گر چه پریوش است ولیکن فرشته خوست
Although, Pari-like (vengeful and omnipotent) He is, of angel-nature (merciful and compassionate) He is,

چندان گریستم که هر کس که برگذشت
To such a degree, I wept that everyone who passed (by me)

در اشک ما چو دید روان گفت کاین چه جوست
When he beheld running the pearl of our tears, spake saying: "This stream what is?

هیچ است آن دهان و نبینم از او نشان
That (small) mouth, no trace whereof I see, is naught:

موی است آن میان و ندانم که آن چه موست
That waist is only a hair (in slenderness); and I know not what that hair is.

دارم عجب ز نقش خیالش که چون نرفت
(O true Beloved) at the picture of Thy (peerless) form, I wonder saying: How goeth it not

از دیده‌ام که دم به دمش کار شست و شوست
From my eye, whose work, momently, washing and washing (with the stream of tears) is.

بی گفت و گوی زلف تو دل را همی کشد
Speechless, Thy tress (the attraction of divine grace) draweth my heart:

با زلف دلکش تو که را روی گفت و گوست
Against Thy heart-alluring tress, the way of speech whose is?

عمریست تا ز زلف تو بویی شنیده‌ام
A (long) lifetime it is since we perceived the perfume of Thy tress

زان بوی در مشام دل من هنوز بوست
Yet in the perfume-place of my heart, the perfume of that (great) perfume is.

حافظ بد است حال پریشان تو ولی
Hafez! bad is thy distraught state; but
بر بوی زلف یار پریشانیت نکوست
Good, to the memory of the Friend's tress thy distraught state is.

غزل ۶۰ ⓞⓓⓔ 60

آن پیک نامور که رسید از دیار دوست
That envoy, (Jibra.il) who arrived from the country of the Friend the Court of the Eternal.
آورد حرز جان ز خط مشکبار دوست
And brought the amulet of life (against Shaitan's deceit) from the dark writing (the glorious Kuran) of the Friend.

خوش می‌دهد نشان جلال و جمال یار
Pleasantly, giveth trace of the Friend's grandeur and grace:
خوش می‌کند حکایت عز و وقار دوست
Pleasantly, maketh mention of the glory and the greatness of the Friend.

دل دادمش به مژده و خجلت همی‌برم
For his glad tidings, I gave him my heart; and, I bear shame
زین نقد قلب خویش که کردم نثار دوست
Of this little wealth of my heart wherewith I bescattered the Friend.

شکر خدا که از مدد بخت کارساز
Thanks to God that, by the aid of concordant Fortune,
بر حسب آرزوست همه کار و بار دوست
All my work is to the desire of the Friend

سیر سپهر و دور قمر را چه اختیار
Of the Sphere's procession (through space) and of the Moon's revolution, what power?
در گردشند بر حسب اختیار دوست
I progression, they were by the power of the Friend.

گر باد فتنه هر دو جهان را به هم زند
If calamity's Wind dash together (and destroy) the two worlds (this and the next),
ما و چراغ چشم و ره انتظار دوست
(Together are) We, and the light of the eye, and the path of expectation (of arrival of) the Friend.

کحل الجواهری به من آر ای نسیم صبح
O morning breeze! Bring me the bejewelled kuhl,
زان خاک نیکبخت که شد رهگذار دوست
From that happy dust that was the thoroughfare of the Friend.

ماییم و آستانه عشق و سر نیاز
(Together are) we, and the Friend's threshold, and our head of supplication
تا خواب خوش که را برد اندر کنار دوست
Let us see for whom is sweet sleep in the bosom of-the Friend

دشمن به قصد حافظ اگر دم زند چه باک
If in design (of the life of) Hafez, the enemy speak-what fear?
منت خدای را که نیم شرمسار دوست
Thanks to God that I am not ashamed of the Friend.

غزل ۶۱ ⓄⒹⒺ ⓋⒶ

صبا اگر گذری افتدت به کشور دوست
O Breeze! If thy path should chance by the Land of the Friend.

بیار نفحه‌ای از گیسوی معنبر دوست
Bring a fragrant waft of air from the beperfumed tress of the Friend.

به جان او که به شکرانه جان برافشانم
By this soul (I swear) that, in thanks, I will surrender my Life (for thee)

اگر به سوی من آری پیامی از بر دوست
If thou bring to me a message from the Friend.

وگر چنان که در آن حضرتت نباشد بار
And, if, even so, in that Presence, (difficult of approach) no access be thine

برای دیده بیاور غباری از در دوست
Bring a little dust (as collyrium) for my eye from the door of the Friend.

من گدا و تمنای وصل او هیهات
I, The beggar, where? The longing desire for union with Him, where? alas!

مگر به خواب ببینم خیال منظر دوست
Perchance, in sleep, I may behold the form of the aspect of the Friend.

دل صنوبریم همچو بید لرزان است
My pine cone-like heart is trembling like the willow,

ز حسرت قد و بالای چون صنوبر دوست
In envy of the form and the pine-like stature of the Friend.

اگر چه دوست به چیزی نمی‌خرد ما را
Although, the Friend purchase us not for even a small thing,

به عالمی نفروشیم مویی از سر دوست
For a whole world, we sell not a single hair from the head of the Friend.

چه باشد ار شود از بند غم دلش آزاد
If his (Hafiz's) heart be free from the bond of grief, what then?

چو هست حافظ مسکین غلام و چاکر دوست
When poor Hafez is the slave and servant of the Friend.

غزل ۶۲ ⓄⒹⒺ ⓋⒷ

مرحبا ای پیک مشتاقان بده پیغام دوست
Welcome! O Messenger of the Longing Ones give the message of the Friend.

تا کنم جان از سر رغبت فدای نام دوست
That, with the essence of pleasure, I may make my soul a sacrifice for the Friend.

واله و شیداست دایم همچو بلبل در قفس
Wailing and lamenting perpetually is like the nightingale in the cage:

طوطی طبعم ز عشق شکر و بادام دوست
Of parrot-nature am I through love of sugar (the lip) and of the almond (the eye) of the Friend.

زلف او دام است و خالش دانه آن دام و من
His tress is the snare; the grain of that snare, his mole; and I,

بر امید دانه‌ای افتاده‌ام در دام دوست
In hope of that grain, have fallen into the snare of the Friend

سر ز مستی برنگیرد تا به صبح روز حشر

Till the morning of the day of assembling (the judgment – day), through intoxication, raiseth not his hand.

هر که چون من در ازل یک جرعه خورد از جام دوست

Whoever, in Eternity without beginning, drinketh like me a draught (of Love) from the cup of the Friend

بس نگویم شمه‌ای از شرح شوق خود از آنک

(Even) a little by way of explanation of my own desire, I uttered not on that account

دردسر باشد نمودن بیش از این ابرام دوست

It is head-pain to show more than this importunity to the Friend

گر دهد دستم کشم در دیده همچون توتیا

Into my eye, I put as collyrium, if it be gained,

خاک راهی کان مشرف گردد از اقدام دوست

The dust of the precious path that becometh honored by the footstep of the Friend

میل من سوی وصال و قصد او سوی فراق

My inclination, towards Union; and His towards separation:

ترک کام خود گرفتم تا برآید کام دوست

(Helpless) I abandoned my own desire that there might issue the desire of the Friend.

حافظ اندر درد او می‌سوز و بی‌درمان بساز

Hafez! In grief for Him, continue to consume; remediless, be content.

زان که درمانی ندارد درد بی‌آرام دوست

on that account, that no remedy hath the restless pain of the Friend

غزل ۶۳ ۞ ODE 63 ۞

روی تو کس ندید و هزارت رقیب هست

Thy face, none hath seen; and (yet) a thousand watchers are Thine,

در غنچه‌ای هنوز و صدت عندلیب هست

Still (hidden) in the (folded) rosebud, Thine many a nightingale is.

گر آمدم به کوی تو چندان غریب نیست

Not so strange is it if to Thy street came

چون من در آن دیار هزاران غریب هست

I, since in this country many a stranger (traveller) is.

در عشق خانقاه و خرابات فرق نیست

In love, the cloister (islâm) and the tavern (other religions) are not different:

هر جا که هست پرتو روی حبیب هست

Wherever, they are, the ray of the true Beloved's face is

آن جا که کار صومعه را جلوه می‌دهند

There, where they give splendor to the work of the cloister,

ناقوس دیر راهب و نام صلیب هست

The bell of the Christian monk's cloister associated with the name of the cross is.

عاشق که شد که یار به حالش نظر نکرد

Lover, who became, at whose state the true Beloved gazed not?

ای خواجه درد نیست وگرنه طبیب هست

O Sir! (the truth is) there is no pain. Otherwise, the Physician (God) is.

فریاد حافظ این همه آخر به هرزه نیست

In short, all this lament of Hafez is not in vain:

هم قصه‌ای غریب و حدیثی عجیب هست

Both a strange story and a wonderful tale, it is

غزل ۶۴ ⓄⒹⒺ 64

اگر چه عرض هنر پیش یار بی‌ادبیست

Since the presentation of skill before the Beloved disrespect, is

زبان خموش ولیکن دهان پر از عربیست

The tongue, silent; yet, the mouth full (of eloquence) Arabia is.

پری نهفته رخ و دیو در کرشمه حسن

The Pari (the Beloved) concealed her face; and the Div (desires of Lust) engaged in the glance of beauty.

بسوخت دیده ز حیرت که این چه بوالعجبیست

Through amazement, Reason consumed, saying: "What Father of Wonders (that every fair one, for whom the concealing of the face is proper, maketh glance, and giveth herself airs) this is!"

در این چمن گل بی خار کس نچید آری

In this parterre, (the world) none plucked the rose without the thorn.

چراغ مصطفوی با شرار بولهبیست

So the (glorious) lamp of Mustafa[1] (the soul) with the horrid flames of Abu Lahab[2] imperious Lust is.

سبب مپرس که چرخ از چه سفله پرور شد

The reason, ask not why the cherisher of the mean, became the sphere,

که کام بخشی او را بهانه بی سببیست

Whose design of giving, pretence without reason is.

به نیم جو نخرم طاق خانقاه و رباط

For half a barley-corn, I purchase not the arch of the monastery and of the inn (the place of worship of Abids, outward worshippers and of austerity of Zahids, sitting in the prayer – niche):

مراکه مصطبه ایوان و پای خم طنبیست

Because for me, the tavern (the stage of love and of divine knowledge) is the palace; and the foot of the jar (the perfect Murshid, possessor of mysteries) the pavilion (the lofty building and impregnable shelter) is

جمال دختر رز نور چشم ماست مگر

The beauty of the Daughter of the grape (love) is the light of our eye. Perchance

که در نقاب زجاجی و پرده عنبیست

In the veil of (white) glass, (the perfect Murshid) and in the screen of the (red) grape (the perfect Murshid) it is.

هزار عقل و ادب داشتم من ای خواجه

O Sir a thousand reasons and manners, I had

کنون که مست خرابم صلاح بی‌ادبیست

Now, that I am intoxicated and ruined, (this my state, due to the) invitation of one void of manners is

بیار می که چو حافظ هزارم استظهار

Bring wine; for, as (is the way of) Hafez, the asking God for aid always

به گریه سحری و نیاز نیم شبیست

In weeping in the morning-time, and in supplication at midnight is

---

1-It is one of the titles of the Prophet of Islam   2-It is the nickname of the Prophet's uncle

غزل ۶۵ ⓄⒹⒺ ⑥⑤

خوشتر ز عیش و صحبت و باغ و بهار چیست
More pleasant than the pleasure (the manifestations of glories of the Absolute One, God) and the enjoyment of the garden and the spring (the world, adorned with trees and flowers) is what?

ساقی کجاست گو سبب انتظار چیست
Where is the Saki (the Murshid) Say: "The cause of our waiting is what?

هر وقت خوش که دست دهد مغتنم شمار
Every pleasant moment that appeareth, reckon plunder;

کس را وقوف نیست که انجام کار چیست
Delay is to none. For the end of work is what?

پیوند عمر بسته به موییست هوش دار
The fetter of life is bound by a single hair: keep sense:

غمخوار خویش باش غم روزگار چیست
Be thy own grief-devourer. Time's grief is what?

معنی آب زندگی و روضه ارم
The meaning of the Water-of-Life and the garden of Iram (Paradise)

جز طرف جویبار و می خوشگوار چیست
Save the bank of the rivulet and the wine (of love, the cause of eternal life) pleasant-tasting is what?

مستور و مست هر دو چو از یک قبیله‌اند
The austere one (the Abid, or the Zahid) and the intoxicated one (the profligate) both are of one family:

ما دل به عشوه که دهیم اختیار چیست
To whose glance, shall we give our heart? choice is what?

راز درون پرده چه داند فلک خموش
The secret within the screen, what knoweth the silent sky?

ای مدعی نزاع تو با پرده دار چیست
O pretender! (philosopher) thy contention with the screen-holder the revolving sky is what?

سهو و خطای بنده گرش اعتبار نیست
If the esteeming rightly (in pardon) the forgetfulness and the negligence of the slave be not His (and every one hath a stage for minute enquiry),

معنی عفو و رحمت آمرزگار چیست
The meaning of the Omnipotent's pardon and mercy is what?

زاهد شراب کوثر و حافظ پیاله خواست
The Zahed[1] desired the wine of Kousar[2]; and Hafez, the cup (of love):

تا در میانه خواسته کردگار چیست
Let us see between these two, the choice of the Omnipotent is what?

غزل ۶۶ ⓄⒹⒺ ⑥⑥

بنال بلبل اگر با منت سر یاریست
O (distraught) nightingale! (illusory lover) bewail if, the desire of being a lover with me, thine is.

که ما دو عاشق زاریم و کار ما زاریست
For, we two are, weeping lovers; and our work, weeping is.

1-Pietist　　　　　2-Springhead

در آن زمین که نسیمی وزد ز طره دوست

In that land (the holy traveller's ab ode) where bloweth the fragrant breeze from the (true) Beloved's tress, (divine attraction)

چه جای دم زدن نافه‌های تاتاریست

For boasting of the fragrant the musk-pods of Tatar, what room is.

بیار باده که رنگین کنیم جامه زرق

Bring the wine, (of love) where with we may becolour the garment of hypocrisy (borrowed, illusory, centreless existence);

که مست جام غروریم و نام هشیاریست

For, we are intoxicated with the cup of pride; and (with us only) the name of sensibleness is.

خیال زلف تو پختن نه کار هر خامیست

To devise the fancy for Thy tress, is not the work of immature ones:

که زیر سلسله رفتن طریق عیاریست

To go beneath the (suspended) chain, (of death) the way of a bold one is.

لطیفه‌ایست نهانی که عشق از او خیزد

Wherefrom love ariseth, is a hidden subtlety,

که نام آن نه لب لعل و خط زنگاریست

Whose name neither the ruby lip, nor the auburn hair is.

جمال شخص نه چشم است و زلف و عارض و خال

The person's beauty is not the eye, nor the tress, nor the cheek, nor the mole;

هزار نکته در این کار و بار دلداریست

In this matter many a thousand subtlety, heart-possessing is.

قلندران حقیقت به نیم جو نخرند

For half a barleycorn Kalandars[1] of the Path purchase not,

قبای اطلس آن کس که از هنر عاریست

The satin coat (of worldly rank) of that one who void of skill (and spirituality) is.

بر آستان تو مشکل توان رسید آری

To Thy threshold, (the sky of joyousness) one can reach only with difficulty. Yes

عروج بر فلک سروری به دشواریست

With difficulty, the ascent to the sky of joyousness is.

سحر کرشمه چشمت به خواب می‌دیدم

In the morning, in a dream, I beheld the glance of union with Him:

زهی مراتب خوابی که به ز بیداریست

Oh excellent! when the stage of sleeping better than (the stage of) waking is.

دلش به ناله میازار و ختم کن حافظ

Hafez! vex not His heart with weeping and conclude:

که رستگاری جاوید در کم آزاریست

For, in little injuring, everlasting safety is.

1-Released from bondage

غزل ۶۷ ⓄⒹⒺ ⓺⓻

يا رب اين شمع دل افروز ز كاشانه كيست

O Lord! that candle, (the beloved) night-illuminating, (by her resplendent beauty) from the house of whom is?

جان ما سوخت بپرسيد كه جانانه كيست

Our soul hath consumed. Ask ye, saying: "She, the beloved, of whom is?"

حاليا خانه برانداز دل و دين من است

Now, the up-setter of my heart and of my religion, she is:

تا در آغوش كه می‌خسبد و همخانه كيست

Let us see: she the fellow-sleeper of whom is; the fellow-lodger of whom is:

باده لعل لبش كز لب من دور مباد

The ruby-wine of her lip, from my lip, far be it not!

راح روح كه و پيمان ده پيمانه كيست

The wine of the soul of whom is? The cup-giver of the cup of whom is?

دولت صحبت آن شمع سعادت پرتو

The Fortune of the society of that candle of happy ray, '

بازپرسيد خدا را كه به پروانه كيست

Again, for God's sake, ask ye saying: "For the moth of whom is?"

می‌دهد هر كسش افسونی و معلوم نشد

For (to win) her, everyone deviseth a great spell. Yet known it is not,

كه دل نازك او مايل افسانه كيست

Her tender heart, inclined to the tale (of Love) of whom is.

يا رب آن شاهوش ماه رخ زهره جبين

O Lord! that one, king-like, moon of face, Venus of forehead,

در يكتای كه و گوهر يك دانه كيست

The inestimable pearl of whom; and the incomparable jewel of whom is?

گفتم آه از دل ديوانه حافظ بی تو

(To the beloved) I said "Without thee, sigh coir.eth from the distraught heart of Hafez:"

زير لب خنده زنان گفت كه ديوانه كيست

Under the lip, (covertly) laughing, she spake, saying: He distraught of whom is?"

غزل ۶۸ ⓄⒹⒺ ⓺⓼

ماهم اين هفته برون رفت و به چشمم ساليست

From the city, my moon (the beloved) went went this week; to my eye (by reason of pain of separation) a year it is:

حال هجران تو چه دانی كه چه مشكل حاليست

The state of separation what knowest thou how difficult the state is?

مردم ديده ز لطف رخ او در رخ او

From the grace of her cheek, in her cheek, the pupil of my eye

عكس خود ديد گمان برد كه مشكين خاليست

Beheld its own reflection; and imagined that (on the Beloved's cheek) a musky (dark) mole it is.

می‌چکد شیر هنوز از لب همچون شکرش

Milk (so youthful is my beloved) yet droppeth from her lip like sugar,

گر چه در شیوه گری هر مژه‌اش قتالیست

Although, in glancing, her every eyelash a slaughterer is

ای که انگشت نمایی به کرم در همه شهر

O thou that art in the city the pointing-stock for generosity,

وه که در کار غریبان عجبت اهمالیست

Alas! in the work of (caring for) strangers, wonderful thy negligence is

بعد از اینم نبود شائبه در جوهر فرد

After this, no doubt is mine in respect of (the existence) of the incomparable jewel;

که دهان تو در این نکته خوش استدلالیست

For, on that point, thy mouth (by its exceeding smallness and freshness) a sweet proof is.

مژده دادند که بر ما گذری خواهی کرد

Glad tidings, they (Fate and Destiny or a party of lovers of God) gave that thou wilt pass by us (may God's grace be thy companion)

نیت خیر مگردان که مبارک فالیست

Change not thy good resolve; for a happy omen it is.

کوه اندوه فراقت به چه حالت بکشد

By what art, doth the mountain of grief of separation draw

حافظ خسته که از ناله تنش چون نالیست

Shattered Hafez, who, through the weeping of his body, like a reed is.

غزل ۶۹ ⓄⒹⒺ 69

کس نیست که افتاده آن زلف دوتا نیست

Who is not fallen into that doubled tress is none;

در رهگذر کیست که دامی ز بلا نیست

In whose path is it, that a snare of calamity is none

چون چشم تو دل می‌برد از گوشه نشینان

Since from the corner-sitters Thy eye ravished my heart:

همراه تو بودن گنه از جانب ما نیست

To be thy train, a sin on our part is none.

روی تو مگر آینه لطف الهیست

Perchance, thy face is the mirror of divine light

حقا که چنین است و در این روی و ریا نیست

O God! (I swear) that thus it is and, in this, dissimulation and hypocrisy is none.

نرگس طلبد شیوه چشم تو زهی چشم

The narcissus seeketh the way of thy eye, O excellent eye

مسکین خبرش از سر و در دیده حیا نیست

To the wretched (narcissus) news of its mystery; and, in its eye, light is none.

از بهر خدا زلف مپیرای که ما را

For God's sake, adorn not thy tress; for ours,

شب نیست که صد عربده با باد صبا نیست

Is no night when, with the morning wind, many a conflict is none.

بازآی که بی روی تو ای شمع دل افروز

O candle, heart-kindling! com bake: for, without Thy face,

در بزم حریفان اثر نور و صفا نیست

At the banquet of companions, the effect of light and of purity is none.

تیمار غریبان اثر ذکر جمیل است

The consoling of travellers is the cause of excellent mention;

جانا مگر این قاعده در شهر شما نیست

O soul! in your city, this rule is none.

دی می‌شد و گفتم صنما عهد به جای آر

Last night, He went; and I said: "O idol! fulfill Thy covenant:"

گفتا غلطی خواجه در این عهد وفا نیست

He said: "O Khwaja! thou art in error: fidelity in this covenant is none.

گر پیر مغان مرشد من شد چه تفاوت

If the Pir[1] of the Magians become my Murshid[2] what difference?

در هیچ سری نیست که سری ز خدا نیست

There is no head, in which a mystery of God is none.

عاشق چه کند گر نکشد بار ملامت

If he suffers not the arrow of reproach, what doeth the lover?

با هیچ دلاور سپر تیر قضا نیست

With any warrior, the shield against the arrow of destiny is none.

در صومعه زاهد و در خلوت صوفی

In the cloister of the Zahed[3]; and in the chamber of the Sufi[4]

جز گوشه ابروی تو محراب دعا نیست

Save the corner of Thy eye-brow, the arch of prayer is none

ای چنگ فروبرده به خون دل حافظ

O thiu that hast lowered thy claw for the blood of Hafiz's heart

فکرت مگر از غیرت قرآن و خدا نیست

Perchance, thought of the plunder of the Quran of God (that is in Hafiz's heart), thine is none.

غزل ۷۰ ⓄⒹⒺ ⑦⓪

مردم دیده ما جز به رخت ناظر نیست

A gazer save upon Thy face, the pupil of our eye is not.

دل سرگشته ما غیر تو را ذاکر نیست

A remembrancer save of Thee, our overturned heart is not.

اشکم احرام طواف حرمت می‌بندد

My tear bindeth the Ihram of the Tawaf of Thy sacred enclosure.

گر چه از خون دل ریش دمی طاهر نیست

Although pure blood of the blood of my wounded heart, it (my tear) is not.

1-A Muslim saint or holy man, Pietist
2-Guru

3-Pietist
4-A Muslim ascetic and mystic

بسته دام و قفس باد چو مرغ وحشی
Be bound in the snare of the cage like the wild bird
طایر سدره اگر در طلبت طایر نیست
If, flying in search of Thee, the bird of Sidrah (Jibra, il) is not

عاشق مفلس اگر قلب دلش کرد نثار
If the poor lover scattered the counterfeit coin of his heart, (accept it)
مکنش عیب که بر نقد روان قادر نیست
Censure him not, for potent as to current coin he is not.

عاقبت دست بدان سرو بلندش برسد
In the end, to that lofty cypress, reacheth the hand of him,
هر که را در طلبت همت او قاصر نیست
Whose spirit in search of Thee, defective is not.

از روان بخشی عیسی نزنم دم هرگز
Before Thee, I boast not of Isa's[1] life-giving;
زان که در روح فزایی چو لبت ماهر نیست
For like Thy lip, in soul-refreshing, expert he ('Isa) is not.

من که در آتش سودای تو آهی نزنم
I who, in passion's fire for Thee, express no sigh,
کی توان گفت که بر داغ دلم صابر نیست
How can one say: "As to the stains (of love) my heart, patient He is not."

روز اول که سر زلف تو دیدم گفتم
The first day, (day of Alast) when I beheld Thy tres ode tip I spake,
که پریشانی این سلسله را آخر نیست
Saying: "End to this chain's confusion is not."

سر پیوند تو تنها نه دل حافظ راست
The desire of union with Thee alone, to Hafez's heart is not:
کیست آن کش سر پیوند تو در خاطر نیست
Who is he in whose heart desire of union with Thee is not

غزل ۷۱   ⓄⒹⒺ ⑦①

زاهد ظاهرپرست از حال ما آگاه نیست
The Zahed[2], outward worshipper! Of our state, (his) knowledge is none
در حق ما هر چه گوید جای هیچ اکراه نیست
In respect of us, whatever he saith, (in it) room for abhorrence is none.

در طریقت هر چه پیش سالک آید خیر اوست
In (the stage of) Tarikat[3], the Path whatever befalleth the holy Traveler is his welfare:
در صراط مستقیم ای دل کسی گمراه نیست
O heart! In the straight highway, (which is the nature of Tarikat) road lost is none.

تا چه بازی رخ نماید بیدقی خواهیم راند
That we may see how the game turneth, a pawn, I will move.
عرصه شطرنج رندان را مجال شاه نیست
The power of Shah (check – mate) to the chess board of profligates is none.

1-Name of a prophet
2-Pietist

3-Principle, Sufism, religious way

چیست این سقف بلند ساده بسیارنقش

What is this lofty roof, (the sky) smooth, with many pictures (clouds, celestial bodies)?

زین معما هیچ دانا در جهان آگاه نیست

In the world, acquainted with this mystery, Sage there is none.

این چه استغناست یا رب وین چه قادر حکمت است

O Lord! Who is this independent One? What is this powerful creed?

کاین همه زخم نهان هست و مجال آه نیست

For this is all internal (painful) wound; but power of heaving a sigh is none.

صاحب دیوان ما گویی نمی‌داند حساب

Thou mayst say: "The Lord of the Secretariat (the Beloved) knoweth not the account:

کاندر این طغرا نشان حسبه لله نیست

For, in this imperial signature, (love – play) trace of "Hasbatanu-li-llah"[1] is none.

هر که خواهد گو بیا و هر چه خواهد گو بگو

Whoever wisheth, (love) say: "Come:" Whoever wisheth, (love) say: "Speak:"

کبر و ناز و حاجب و دربان بدین درگاه نیست

In this Court (of the true Beloved) is neither arrogance nor haughtiness; chamberlain, or door-keeper, is none.

بر در میخانه رفتن کار یک رنگان بود

To go to the Tavern-door (the stage of divine knowledge, and of Love) is the work of those of one color:

خودفروشان را به کوی می فروشان راه نیست

For the Self-sellers, path. (Of admission) into the street of the Wine-Sellers, ('Arifs and Lovers), "is none."

هر چه هست از قامت ناساز بی اندام ماست

Whatever unfitness there is, is by reason of our unfit, formless form:

ور نه تشریف تو بر بالای کس کوتاه نیست

If not, on a person's stature, thy dress of honor, short is none.

بنده پیر خراباتم که لطفش دایم است

I am the slave of the Pir[2] of the tavern, (the perfect Murshid) whose favor is constant:

ور نه لطف شیخ و زاهد گاه هست و گاه نیست

If not, the favor of the Shaikh[3] and of the Zahed[4], is sometimes; and, sometimes is none.

حافظ ار بر صدر ننشیند ز عالی مشربیست

If, through lofty spirit, Hafez sit not on the chief seat, (what matter)

عاشق دردی کش اندربند مال و جاه نیست

The Lover, dregs of wine (of Love) drinking drinking, in the bond of property
and of rank is none.

غزل ٧٢ ⓄⒹⒺ ⑦② ODE 72

راهیست راه عشق که هیچش کناره نیست

Love's path is Path whereof the shore is none:

آن جا جز آن که جان بسپارند چاره نیست

And there, unless they surrender their soul, remedy is none.

1-Written to the left of government decrees, the letter
indicated the letter was legal.
2-A Muslim saint or holy man, Pietist

3-A leader in a Muslim community
4-Pietist

هر گه که دل به عشق دهی خوش دمی بود

Every moment that to love thou givest thy heart is a happy moment,

در کار خیر حاجت هیچ استخاره نیست

In the right work, need of praying to God to be directed aright is none.

ما را ز منع عقل مترسان و می بیار

With reason's prohibition, (of wine) affright us not; and bring wine:

کان شحنه در ولایت ما هیچ کاره نیست

In our Land, the work of the watchman, (reason) work is none.

از چشم خود بپرس که ما را که می‌کشد

Ask thou thy own eye "Who draweth us?"

جانا گناه طالع و جرم ستاره نیست

O soul! the sin of fortune and the crime of the star is none.

او را به چشم پاک توان دید چون هلال

Him, (the true Beloved) one can see with the pure eye like hardly visible the crescent moon:

هر دیده جای جلوه آن ماه پاره نیست

The place of splendor of that moon-fragment, every eye is not.

فرصت شمر طریقه رندی که این نشان

Reckon as plunder the path of profligacy. For this track,

چون راه گنج بر همه کس آشکاره نیست

Like the path to the (hidden) treasure, evident to everyone is not.

نگرفت در تو گریه حافظ به هیچ رو

In no way, Hafez's weeping affected thee

حیران آن دلم که کم از سنگ خاره نیست

Astonishment (is) mine at that heart, which less hard than the (hard) stone is not.

غزل ۷۳ ⓄⒹⒺ ⑦③

روشن از پرتو رویت نظری نیست که نیست

(O true Beloved) From the ray of Thy face, luminous a glance is not. that is not:

منت خاک درت بر بصری نیست که نیست

The favor of (collyrium) of the dust of Thy door, on an eye is not, that is not.

ناظر روی تو صاحب نظرانند آری

Those possessed of sight (the prophets who, with the inward eye, behold the real beauty of God), are the spectator of Thy face. Yes:

سر گیسوی تو در هیچ سری نیست که نیست

The desire of Thy tress, in any, a desire is not, that is not.

اشک غماز من ار سرخ برآمد چه عجب

If through my grief for Thee, my tear issue red (bloody), what wonder?

خجل از کرده خود پرده دری نیست که نیست

Ashamed of that done by himself, a screen-holder is not that is not.

تا به دامن ننشیند ز نسیمش گردی

(O Beloved) so that on Thy skirt, a little dust may not settle,

سیل خیز از نظرم رهگذری نیست که نیست

The torrent of tears from my vision, a great pathway is not that is not

تا دم از شام سر زلف تو هر جا نزنند

So that, everywhere, itthe breeze, the acquainted Murshid may not boast of the evening of Thy tres ode tip, the time of ecstasy of attraction of God's grace

با صبا گفت و شنیدم سحری نیست که نیست

Conversation with (the breeze, the acquainted Murshid) mine mine a morning is nor that is not.

من از این طالع شوریده برنجم ور نی

Of this distraught fortune, I grieve and if not,

بهره مند از سر کویت دگری نیست که نیست

Apportioned from the head of Thy street, another is not, that is not.

از حیای لب شیرین تو ای چشمه نوش

O sweet fountain! from the m odesty of Thy sweet lip, the stream of divine grace

غرق آب و عرق اکنون شکری نیست که نیست

Now, steeped in water and sweat, (of toil of search) a piece of sugar (the illusory beloved) is not, that is not.

مصلحت نیست که از پرده برون افتد راز

No good counsel is it that the mystery should fall out of the screen

ور نه در مجلس رندان خبری نیست که نیست

And, if not, in the assembly of profligates, a piece of news (of both worlds) is not that is not.

شیر در بادیه عشق تو روباه شود

In the desert of love for Thee, the (noble) lion becometh (through fear) the crafty the fox:

آه از این راه که در وی خطری نیست که نیست

Alas, this Path! wherein a danger is not that is not.

آب چشمم که بر او منت خاک در توست

The water of my eye, whereon is the favor (collyrium) of the dust of Thy door

زیر صد منت او خاک دری نیست که نیست

Under a hundred favors of His. the dust of a door is not that is not.

از وجودم قدری نام و نشان هست که هست

From the head of Thy street, I cannot go a step:

ور نه از ضعف در آن جا اثری نیست که نیست

And, if not, in the heart of the heart-bereft, a journey is not that is not.

غیر از این نکته که حافظ ز تو ناخشنود است

Save this subtlety that Hafez is not pleased with thee,

در سراپای وجودت هنری نیست که نیست

Wholly, in thy existence, a skill is not, that is not.

غزل ۷۴ 🔟 🔒🇪 7️⃣4️⃣

حاصل کارگه کون و مکان این همه نیست

The produce of the workshop of existence and dwelling (the whole world) all this is naught.

باده پیش آر که اسباب جهان این همه نیست

Bring wine (of the love of God). For the goods of the world all this is naught.

از دل و جان شرف صحبت جانان غرض است

The desire of the heart and of the exalted soul is the society of the Beloved:

غرض این است وگرنه دل و جان این همه نیست

All that is (my desire); and, if not (gained), heart and soul, all this is naught.

منت سدره و طوبی ز پی سایه مکش

For the sake of shade, endure not the favor (even) of the (great) Sidra and the (great) the Tuba tree

که چو خوش بنگری ای سرو روان این همه نیست

For, O moving cypress, when well thou lookest, all this is naught.

دولت آن است که بی خون دل آید به کنار

Fortune is that which, without the heart's blood, cometh to the bosom:

ور نه با سعی و عمل باغ جنان این همه نیست

And, if not, the garden of the Beloved gained with effort and toil all this is naught.

پنج روزی که در این مرحله مهلت داری

A space of five days (it is) that thou hast in this stage of favor;

خوش بیاسای زمانی که زمان این همه نیست

Rest pleasantly awhile. For Time all this is naught.

بر لب بحر فنا منتظریم ای ساقی

O Saki[1]! We are waiting on the shore of the ocean of death

فرصتی دان که ز لب تا به دهان این همه نیست

Regard (it) again. For from lip to mouth all this is naught.

زاهد ایمن مشو از بازی غیرت زنهار

Zahed![2] beware; be not secure of the sport of pride

که ره از صومعه تا دیر مغان این همه نیست

For the path from the cloister to the temp le of the Magians, all this is naught.

دردمندی من سوخته زار و نزار

Wailing and weeping (have) consumed me sorrowful:

ظاهرا حاجت تقریر و بیان این همه نیست

The need of narrating and of explaining apparently all this is naught.

نام حافظ رقم نیک پذیرفت ولی

The name of Hafez accepted the writing of honor (in the whole world);

پیش رندان رقم سود و زیان این همه نیست

But, in the opinion of profligates, the writing of profit and of loss all this is naught

غزل ۷۵ ⓄⒹⒺ ⑦⑤

خواب آن نرگس فتان تو بی چیزی نیست

The sleep of that thy seducing eye without something is not

تاب آن زلف پریشان تو بی چیزی نیست

The curl of that thy dishevelled tress, without something is not.

از لبت شیر روان بود که من می‌گفتم

Running from thy lip, was milk (in infancy) when I spake,

این شکر گرد نمکدان تو بی چیزی نیست

(Saying):This sugar round about thy salt-pan (mouth) without something is not

جان درازی تو بادا که یقین می‌دانم

Be thy lifelong; for well I know

در کمان ناوک مژگان تو بی چیزی نیست

The arrow of thy eye-lash in the bow, without something is not.

1-Tapster   2-Pietist

مبتلایی به غم محنت و اندوه فراق

With the grief, the pain, the sorrow of separation, thou art distressed

ای دل این ناله و افغان تو بی چیزی نیست

O heart this thy wailing and lamenting without something is not.

دوش باد از سر کویش به گلستان بگذشت

Last night, from the head of his street, the wind passed to the rose-garden

ای گل این چاک گریبان تو بی چیزی نیست

O rose this rent of thy collar, without something is not

درد عشق ار چه دل از خلق نهان می‌دارد

Although the heart keepeth love's pain secret from the people,

حافظ این دیده گریان تو بی چیزی نیست

Hafiz This weeping eye without something is not.

غزل ۷۶ ⓄⒹⒺ ⑦⑥

جز آستان توام در جهان پناهی نیست

Save Thy threshold, my shelter in the world is none.

سر مرا بجز این در حواله گاهی نیست

Save this door, my fortres ode place is none.

عدو چو تیغ کشد من سپر بیندازم

When the enemy (Iblis, full of fraud, man – seducing) draweth the sword, we cast the shield in flight

که تیغ ما بجز از ناله‌ای و آهی نیست

For save weeping and wailing, our sword is none:

چرا ز کوی خرابات روی برتابم

From the tavern-street, why turn I away my face?

کز این به هم به جهان هیچ رسم و راهی نیست

For better than this, in the world, my way and path is none.

زمانه گر بزند آتشم به خرمن عمر

If, into the harvest of my life, Time cast fire (and consume it)

بگو بسوز که بر من به برگ کاهی نیست

Say: "Consume; (it) for, equal to a little blade of grass, in my opinion, it life is none."

غلام نرگس جماش آن سهی سروم

I am the slave of the saucy eye of that straight stature,

که از شراب غرورش به کس نگاهی نیست

From whose wine of pride, at any one, glance is none.

مباش در پی آزار و هر چه خواهی کن

Be not in the pursuit of injury: do whatever (else) thou desirest:

که در شریعت ما غیر از این گناهی نیست

For in our Shariat[1], save this, a sin is none.

عنان کشیده رو ای پادشاه کشور حسن

O King of the dominion of beauty! go (impetuously) rein drawn:

که نیست بر سر راهی که دادخواهی نیست

For at the head of a street, is it not a justice-seeker is none?

1-Religion

چنین که از همه سو دام راه می‌بینم
Thus it is, that, in every direction, I behold the snare of the Path:
به از حمایت زلفش مرا پناهی نیست
Save the shelter of His tress, my shelter is none

خزینه دل حافظ به زلف و خال مده
To the (black) tress and the dark mole give not the treasure of the heart of Hafez;
که کارهای چنین حد هر سیاهی نیست
For (to do) deeds like these, the power of every b lack one (the black tress and dark mole) is none.

غزل ٧٧ ODE 77

بلبلی برگ گلی خوش رنگ در منقار داشت
A nightingale had a rose-leaf, pleasant of hue in his beak
و اندر آن برگ و نوا خوش ناله‌های زار داشت
And, on that leaf and pleasant food, bitter lamentation held.

گفتمش در عین وصل این ناله و فریاد چیست
To him, I said: "In the very time of union (with the beloved) wherefore is this lament and cry?"
گفت ما را جلوه معشوق در این کار داشت
He said: "In this work (of lament), me the beloved's beauty held."

یار اگر ننشست با ما نیست جای اعتراض
If the true Beloved sate not with us (beggars), room for complaint is none;
پادشاهی کامران بود از گدایی عار داشت
King, prosperous was He; shame of beggars, He held.

در نمی‌گیرد نیاز و ناز ما با حسن دوست
Our supplication and entreaty affect not the Friend possessed of beauty,
خرم آن کز نازنینان بخت برخوردار داشت
Happy he, who from beloved ones, the fortune of prosperity held.

خیز تا بر کلک آن نقاش جان افشان کنیم
Arise! (from carelessness) so that on the reed of that Painter, (God) we may scatter our soul;
کاین همه نقش عجب در گردش پرگار داشت
For, all this wonderful picture, in the revolution of His compass, Lie held

گر مرید راه عشقی فکر بدنامی مکن
If thou be a disciple of love's Path, defame not:
شیخ صنعان خرقه رهن خانه خمار داشت
Pawned at the vintner's house, his religious garment Shaikh[1] San'an (held).

وقت آن شیرین قلندر خوش که در اطوار سیر
Happy, the time of that gentle Kalandar[2] (Shaikh San'an) who, in the paths of wandering,
ذکر تسبیح ملک در حلقه زنار داشت
Mention of the rosary of the King (God), in the girdle of the Zunnar[3], held.

چشم حافظ زیر بام آن قصر آن حوری سرشت
Below the roof of the palace of that beloved of Hun-nature, the eye of Hafez
شیوه جنات تجری تحتها الانهار داشت
The way of paradise, beneath which streams are flowing, held

1-A leader in a Muslim community
2-The Shaikh of San'an

3-A string which Christians hang cross around their necks,
Christian's or Jew's girdle distinguishing him from a Muslim

غزل ۷۸ ⓄⒹⒺ ⑦⑧

دیدی که یار جز سر جور و ستم نداشت
Thou sawest that, save the desire of violence and of tyranny, my beloved aught had not

بشکست عهد و ز غم ما هیچ غم نداشت
He shattered the covenant; and, on account of our grief, grief (at the shattering) had not.

یا رب مگیرش ار چه دل چون کبوترم
O Lord! (as guilty) take him not. Although my heart, like the pigeon, flying in love to Thee

افکند و کشت و عزت صید حرم نداشت
He cast down and slew; and respect for the prey of the sacred enclosure had not.

بر من جفا ز بخت من آمد وگرنه یار
Against me, on account of my (ill)-fortune, came this violence (on the Beloved's part). If not the Beloved,

حاشا که رسم لطف و طریق کرم نداشت
Save the way of courtesy and the path of liberality, aught had not.

با این همه هر آن که نه خواری کشید از او
With all this, (violence) everyone who endured from Him no contempt,

هر جا که رفت هیچ کسش محترم نداشت
Everywhere he went, him honored any one had not

ساقی بیار باده و با محتسب بگو
Saki! bring wine; say to the Muhtaseb[1]:

انکار ما مکن که چنین جام جم نداشت
Deny us not. For such a cup (even) Jamshid had not."

هر راهرو که ره به حریم درش نبرد
Every way-farer (holy traveller or lover of God) who took not the path to the sacred enclosure of His door,

مسکین برید وادی و ره در حرم نداشت
Unhappy, traveled the valley (of love) yet; yet, the path to the sacred enclosure had not.

حافظ ببر تو گوی فصاحت که مدعی
Hafez! do thou take the ball of eloquence. For the claimant,

هیچش هنر نبود و خبر نیز هم نداشت
His was no skill at all; and any information, he had not.

غزل ۷۹ ⓄⒹⒺ ⑦⑨

کنون که می‌دمد از بوستان نسیم بهشت
Now, that the fragrant breeze of Paradise bloweth from the rose garden.

من و شراب فرح بخش و یار حورسرشت
(Together are) I and the wine, joy-giving and the Beloved angel.

گدا چرا نزند لاف سلطنت امروز
To-day, why boasteth not the beggar of empire?

که خیمه سایه ابر است و بزمگه لب کشت
For his (lofty) pavilion is the Cloud's shade; and his banquet place, the field's (wide) border

---

1-Sheriff

چمن حکایت اردیبهشت می‌گوید
The sward (the Murshid) uttereth the tale (of glories) of the (spring month) Urdibihisht

نه عاقل است که نسیه خرید و نقد بهشت
No Aref[1] is he, who purchased a loan. (the hope of tomorrow) and let go cash (divine glories here)

به می عمارت دل کن که این جهان خراب
With wine (of divine love) make (prosperous) the building of the heart. For this evil world

بر آن سر است که از خاک ما بسازد خشت
Is bent on that it may make a brick of our dust (in the grave).

وفا مجوی ز دشمن که پرتوی ندهد
From the enemy, (this world) seek not fidelity. For, a feeble ray it giveth not,

چو شمع صومعه افروزی از چراغ کنشت
When thou kindliest the candle of the cloister (of the Muslim) from the lamp of the church (of the Kafir).

مکن به نامه سیاهی ملامت من مست
(O Zahid) For recorded (open) blackness, (of sin) reproach not me intoxicated:

که آگه است که تقدیر بر سرش چه نوشت
Who knoweth what Fate (in Eternity without beginning) hath written on his (fore) – head?

قدم دریغ مدار از جنازه حافظ
From the bier of Hafez, keep not back thy foot:

که گر چه غرق گناه است می‌رود به بهشت
For though he be immersed in sin, he goeth to paradise

غزل ۸۰ ⓞⓓⓔ ⑧⓪

عیب رندان مکن ای زاهد پاکیزه سرشت
O Zahed[2], pure of nature! censure not the profligates;

که گناه دگران بر تو نخواهند نوشت
For, against thee, they will not record another's crime.

من اگر نیکم و گر بد تو برو خود را باش
If I be good, (I am for myself) or if I be bad (I am for myself). Go thou be thyself about thy work:

هر کسی آن درود عاقبت کار که کشت
In the end, everyone reapeth that work that (at this time) he sowed.

همه کس طالب یارند چه هشیار و چه مست
Every one, whether sensible (sober) or insensible, is the seeker of the (true) Beloved:

همه جا خانه عشق است چه مسجد چه کنشت
Every place, whether the Masjed (of Islam) or the church, (of the Kafir) is the house of love.

سر تسلیم من و خشت در میکده‌ها
(Together are) My head of submission and the brick of the Tavern-door:

مدعی گر نکند فهم سخن گو سر و خشت
If the complainant understand not this speech, say: Thy head and brick (beat together)

ناامیدم مکن از سابقه لطف ازل
Of the former kindness (established in) in eternity without beginning, make me not hopeless:

تو پس پرده چه دانی که که خوب است و که زشت
What knowest thou, behind the screen who is good, who is bad?

1-Mystic   2-Pietist

نه من از پرده تقوا به درافتادم و بس

From the cell of piety, not only I fell out:

پدرم نیز بهشت ابد از دست بهشت

My father (Adam) also let go from his hand Paradise of Eternity without end.

حافظا روز اجل گر به کف آری جامی

O Hafez! If, on the day of death, thou bring a cup (of Love).

یک سر از کوی خرابات برندت به بهشت

Immediately, they will take thee from the street of the tavern to Paradise.

غزل ۸۱ ⓄⒹⒺ ⑧① ODE 81

صبحدم مرغ چمن با گل نوخاسته گفت

At dawn, the bird of the sward (the necessarily existent One, God) spake to the rose (faithful men in the state of being beloved):

نازکم کن که در این باغ بسی چون تو شکفت

"Display less disdain; for, in this garden (the world) many a one like thee hath blossomed."

گل بخندید که از راست نرنجیم ولی

The rose laughed saying: "We grieve not at the truth; but

هیچ عاشق سخن سخت به معشوق نگفت

No lover spoke a harsh word to the beloved."

گر طمع داری از آن جام مرصع می لعل

If thou desire ruby wine (the mystery of haklkat) from that begemmed cup the Murshid,

ای بسا در که به نوک مژهات باید سفت

O many the pearl (the tear) that it is necessary for thee to pierce with the point of thy eyelash.

تا ابد بوی محبت به مشامش نرسد

To eternity without end, the perfume of (divine) love reacheth not the perfume place of him

هر که خاک در میخانه به رخساره نرفت

Who, with his face, swept not the dust of the door of the tavern (the stage of love and of divine knowledge).

در گلستان ارم دوش چو از لطف هوا

Last night, in the Paradise, when from the bounty of the air,

زلف سنبل به نسیم سحری میآشفت

The tress of the hyacinth was disturbed by the morning breeze,

گفتم ای مسند جم جام جهان بینت کو

I said: "O throne of Jamshid! thy cup world-displaying, where?"

گفت افسوس که آن دولت بیدار بخفت

It said: "Alas! wakeful fortune slept."

سخن عشق نه آن است که آید به زبان

Not that which cometh to the tongue is the talk of love:

ساقیا می ده و کوتاه کن این گفت و شنفت

O Saki! (Murshid) give wine; make short this uttering and hearing of love.

اشک حافظ خرد و صبر به دریا انداخت

Into the sea, the tear of Hafez hath (so great is his weeping) cast wisdom and patience:

چه کند سوز غم عشق نیارست نهفت

What shall he do (Neither choice, nor power in his) The consuming of love's grief, he cannot conceal (and other remedy, he knoweth not).

غزل ۸۲ ⓄⒹⒺ ⑧②

آن ترک پری چهره که دوش از بر ما رفت
That Bold One of Angel-face (the true Beloved) who, last night, by me passed,

آیا چه خطا دید که از راه خطا رفت
What sin saw He that, by way of sin, He passed?

تا رفت مرا از نظر آن چشم جهان بین
Since from my sight, went that world-seeing eye,

کس واقف ما نیست که از دیده چه‌ها رفت
None knoweth what tears from my eye have passed.

بر شمع نرفت از گذر آتش دل دوش
Last night from the passing of the heart s fire to the candle passed not

آن دود که از سوز جگر بر سر ما رفت
That smoke (sigh) that, to our head, from the liver's consuming passed.

دور از رخ تو دم به دم از گوشه چشمم
(Being) Far from His face, momently, from the fountain of my eye,

سیلاب سرشک آمد و طوفان بلا رفت
A torrent of tears came; and the deluge of calamity passed

از پای فتادیم چو آمد غم هجران
From our feet, we fell when separation's grief came:

در درد بمردیم چو از دست دوا رفت
In grief we remained when from the hand, the remedy union with Thee passed.

دل گفت وصالش به دعا باز توان یافت
The heart said: "With prayer, one can again obtain (union with Him) passed."

عمریست که عمرم همه در کار دعا رفت
Tis a life-time since my life all in the work of prayer passed.

احرام چه بندیم چو آن قبله نه این جاست
Wherefore do I bind (put) on the pilgrim-robe, (of the true Beloved) for that Ka'ba[1] is not here?

در سعی چه کوشیم چو از مروه صفا رفت
In effort, wherefore do I strive since from (mount) Marvah, (mount) Safa[2] he hath passed?

دی گفت طبیب از سر حسرت چو مرا دید
Yesterday, with the essence of the pity, when he beheld me, the physician said:

هیهات که رنج تو ز قانون شفا رفت
"Alas! beyond the rules of cure, thy grief hath passed."

ای دوست به پرسیدن حافظ قدمی نه
O friend! for asking Hafez (how he fareth) plant thy foot (to visit him)

زان پیش که گویند که از دار فنا رفت
Before that time when they shall speak saying: From the frail house (this world) he hath passed.

1-Muslims turn at prayer.

2- Safa and Marwa are two small hills, in Mecca, Saudi Arabia,

غزل ۸۳ ⓞⓓⓔ ⑧③

گر ز دست زلف مشکینت خطایی رفت رفت
(O true Beloved) If from the hand of Thy musky tress, a fault passed, it passed:

ور ز هندوی شما بر ما جفایی رفت رفت
And, if against us from Thy dark mole, an act of tyranny passed, it passed.

برق عشق ار خرمن پشمینه پوشی سوخت سوخت
If, the harvest of one wool-clad, (the Sufi) Love's lightning consumed, it consumed:

جور شاه کامران گر بر گدایی رفت رفت
If, against a beggar, the violence of the prosperous king passed, it passed.

در طریقت رنجش خاطر نباشد می بیار
In Tarikat[1], (love's path) is no grief of heart. Bring wine of love:

هر کدورت را که بینی چون صفایی رفت رفت
Every (former) impurity (of thy heart) that thou seest, when, (into us) purity passed, it passed.

عشقبازی را تحمل باید ای دل پای دار
O heart! keep firm of foot. For love-playing, endurance is necessary:

گر ملالی بود بود و گر خطایی رفت رفت
If a vexatious matter was, it was; if a tyrannous matter passed, it passed.

گر دلی از غمزه دلدار باری برد برد
If, from the Heart-possessor's glance, a load a heart bore, it bore:

ور میان جان و جانان ماجرایی رفت رفت
(If) between the soul (the lover of God) and the true Beloved (God) a matter passed, it passed.

از سخن چینان ملالت‌ها پدید آمد ولی
From carpers, reproaches appear; but,

گر میان همنشینان ناسزایی رفت رفت
If, among fellow-sitters, aught unfit passed, it passed.

عیب حافظ گو مکن واعظ که رفت از خانقاه
O admonisher! say: "Censure not Hafez who hath gone from the cloister."

پای آزادی چه بندی گر به جایی رفت رفت
How bindest thou the foot of a free one? If to a place he passed, he passed.

غزل ۸۴ ⓞⓓⓔ ⑧④

ساقی بیار باده که ماه صیام رفت
O Saki[2]! (Murshid) bring wine; for the fasting month (the Ramazan) hath passed.

درده قدح که موسم ناموس و نام رفت
Give the goblet; for the season of name and fame hath passed.

وقت عزیز رفت بیا تا قضا کنیم
Dear time hath passed. Come; let us repeat the omitted prayers

عمری که بی حضور صراحی و جام رفت
Of a long life that without the presence of a goblet and of the cup (the Murshid) hath passed.

1-Principle, Sufism, religious way   2-Tapster

مستم کن آن چنان که ندانم ز بیخودی

(O perfect Murshid with the wine of divine love) Make me intoxicated even so that from selflessness I shall not know,

در عرصه خیال که آمد کدام رفت

In the plain of imagination, who hath come, who hath passed.

بر بوی آن که جرعه جامت به ما رسد

In the smell (hope) that a draught of Thy cup may reach us,

در مصطبه دعای تو هر صبح و شام رفت

In the inn, (place of worship) every morning and evening, prayer to Thee hath passed.

دل را که مرده بود حیاتی به جان رسید

To the heart that was dead, a great life reached the soul,

تا بویی از نسیم می‌اش در مشام رفت

Since into its (the heart's) perfume-place a perfume, (of wine of love) from Thy breeze, hath passed.

زاهد غرور داشت سلامت نبرد راه

The Zahed[1] had pride; (of his devotion) took not the path to safety:

رند از ره نیاز به دارالسلام رفت

By the path of supplication, the Profligate (the holy traveller) to the House of Safety (Paradise) hath passed

نقد دلی که بود مرا صرف باده شد

The cash of the heart that was mine became expended in wine:

قلب سیاه بود از آن در حرام رفت

It was counterfeit coin. Therefore, into the unlawful it hath passed.

در تاب توبه چند توان سوخت همچو عود

Like aloe-wood, how long can one consume in the torment of repentance?

می ده که عمر در سر سودای خام رفت

Give wine. For life in the essence of raw madness hath passed.

دیگر مکن نصیحت حافظ که ره نیافت

(O admonisher) again counsel not Hafez; for the path of austerity, found not,

گمگشته‌ای که باده نابش به کام رفت

A lost one, (in love's path) to whose palate the sweet wine of love hath passed.

غزل ۸۵ ⓄⒹⒺ 🔔 85 🔔

شربتی از لب لعلش نچشیدیم و برفت

From His lip of ruby, a (single) draft we tasted not; and He departed:

روی مه پیکر او سیر ندیدیم و برفت

His face, moon of form, we beheld not to our fill; and He departed.

گویی از صحبت ما نیک به تنگ آمده بود

Thou mayst say: "By our society, He hath become greatly straitened."

بار بربست و به گردش نرسیدیم و برفت

His chattels, (thus quickly) He bound up: about him, we arrived not, and He departed.

1-Pietist

بس که ما فاتحه و حرز یمانی خواندیم

Many the Fatiha[1] and the Harz[2]-i-Yamani that we recited:

وز پی اش سوره اخلاص دمیدیم و برفت

After that, we murmured the wholeheartedness, and He departed.

عشوه دادند که بر ما گذری خواهی کرد

A glance, He gave saying: "From the street of desire (love), I depart not:"

دیدی آخر که چنین عشوه خریدیم و برفت

Thou sawest how, at last, we purchased the glance, and He departed.

شد چمان در چمن حسن و لطافت لیکن

Proudly moving, He went into the sward of beauty and of grace. But

در گلستان وصالش نچمیدیم و برفت

In the rose garden of union with (Him), we moved not, and He departed.

همچو حافظ همه شب ناله و زاری کردیم

All night, weeping and wailing, we did like Hafez:

کای دریغا به وداعش نرسیدیم و برفت

For alas! forbidding Him farewell, we arrived not, and He departed.

غزل ۸۶ ⓄⒹⒺ ⑧⑥

ساقی بیا که یار ز رخ پرده برگرفت

Saki[3]! (Murshid) come; for the true Beloved God hath taken up the veil

کار چراغ خلوتیان باز درگرفت

The work of the lamp (love's glory) of the Khilvatis[4] again kindled.

آن شمع سرگرفته دگر چهره برفروخت

That candle head uplifted (the true Beloved's) face again enkindled its face,

وین پیر سالخورده جوانی ز سر گرفت

And youth from his head, this Pir[5] years endured (love) took

آن عشوه داد عشق که مفتی ز ره برفت

The true Beloved gave that glance, such that piety departed from the path,

وان لطف کرد دوست که دشمن حذر گرفت

And the Friend exercised that kindness, that the enemy caution took.

زنهار از آن عبارت شیرین دلفریب

From the sweet and heart-ravishing example, (I seek) shelter:

گویی که پسته تو سخن در شکر گرفت

Thou mayst say "Thy mouth speech into sugar took."

بار غمی که خاطر ما خسته کرده بود

The load of that great grief (the state of kabz) that had wounded our heart,

عیسی دمی خدا بفرستاد و برگرفت

God sent one of Isa[6]-breath: (a Murshid) the load of grief up, he took.

هر سروقد که بر مه و خور حسن میفروخت

Every cypress stature, (beloved) that boasted beauty over the sun and the moon,

چون تو درآمدی پی کاری دگر گرفت

When Thou camest, the pursuit of other work took.

1-The beginning or introductory part
2-Enclosure
3-Tapster

4-Solitude
5-A Muslim saint or holy man, Pietist
6-Name of a prophet

زین قصه هفت گنبد افلاک پرصداست

Full of clamour of this tale, are the seven vaults of the sky.

کوته نظر ببین که سخن مختصر گرفت

Behold the short-sighted one who, the tale (to be) short, took!

حافظ تو این سخن ز که آموختی که بخت

Hafez! from whom hast thou learned this prayer, that the beloved

تعویذ کرد شعر تو را و به زر گرفت

Made thy verse an amulet; and it, into gold, took.

غزل ۸۷ ⓄⒹⒺ ⑧⑦

حسنت به اتفاق ملاحت جهان گرفت

By concord with darkish beauty, the world Thy beauty took.

آری به اتفاق جهان می‌توان گرفت

Yes; by concord, the world one can take.

افشای راز خلوتیان خواست کرد شمع

The revealing of the mysteries of the Khilvatis[1], the candle wished to make:

شکر خدا که سر دلش در زبان گرفت

Thanks to God! that its tongue (the candle's wick) the, the heart's desire kindled.

زین آتش نهفته که در سینه من است

From out of this (great) concealed fire (of mysteries and divine knowledge) that is in my chest,

خورشید شعله‌ایست که در آسمان گرفت

(Only) a flame is the (great) sun that the sky, kindled.

می‌خواست گل که دم زند از رنگ و بوی دوست

The rose (the Arif) wished to boast of the color and the perfume of the Friend (God):

از غیرت صبا نفسش در دهان گرفت

In jealousy of it, its breath, in its mouth the breeze (of love) took.

آسوده بر کنار چو پرگار می‌شدم

Rested apart (from the world), I was like the compass:

دوران چو نقطه عاقبتم در میان گرفت

At last, me, into the center, like a point, Time took.

آن روز شوق ساغر می خرمنم بسوخت

Desire of the cup of wine consumed my harvest that day,

کتش ز عکس عارض ساقی در آن گرفت

When, from the reflection of the Saki's cheek, fire kindled.

خواهم شدن به کوی مغان آستین فشان

To the street of the Magians (the abode of love and of divine knowledge), I wish to go, shaking my sleeve,

زین فتنه‌ها که دامن آخرزمان گرفت

Of these calamities, that, the skirt of time's end took.

می خور که هر که آخر کار جهان بدید

Drink wine. For, whoever, at the end of work, beheld the world,

از غم سبک برآمد و رطل گران گرفت

From grief, came forth light; and, the heavy cup of wine, took.

1-Solitude

بر برگ گل به خون شقایق نوشته‌اند

With the blood of tulips, on the rose-leaf, they have written

کان کس که پخته شد می چون ارغوان گرفت

Saying: (Red) "Wine like the ruddy Arghavan[1] that one, who became mature, took."

حافظ چو آب لطف ز نظم تو می‌چکد

Hafez! like water, grace trickleth from thy verse:

حاسد چگونه نکته تواند بر آن گرفت

On it, nice distinction, the envious one how took.

غزل ۸۸ ⓄⒹⒺ ⑧⑧

شنیده‌ام سخنی خوش که پیر کنعان گفت

I heard a pleasant speech that the old man of Kan'an[2] (the Murshid) uttered:

فراق یار نه آن می کند که بتوان گفت

Separation from (want of acquisition of divine knowledge of) the true Beloved (God) maketh not that which can be uttered."

حدیث هول قیامت که گفت واعظ شهر

The tale of terror of the resurrection day, which the city-admonisher uttered?

کنایتیست که از روزگار هجران گفت

Is (only) a hint, which, of the time of separation, he uttered

نشان یار سفرکرده از که پرسم باز

Of whom, may I ask the trace of the Beloved, many a journey made, (the absolute existence, God?

که هر چه گفت برید صبا پریشان گفت

For whatever the wind's messenger the man learned and excellent uttered, confusedly he uttered).

فغان که آن مه نامهربان مهرگسل

Alas! that unkind moon, the Friend's enemy,

به ترک صحبت یاران خود چه آسان گفت

For the abandoning the society of his own lovers, (words) how easily he uttere

من و مقام رضا بعد از این و شکر رقیب

After this (together are) I and the stage of contentment, and thanks to my rival:

که دل به درد تو خو کرد و ترک درمان گفت

For accustomed to pain by thee, my heart hath become; and the abandonment of remedy uttered

غم کهن به می سالخورده دفع کنید

With wine of many years, repel ye the old grief of the heart:

که تخم خوشدلی این است پیر دهقان گفت

For, the seed of happy-heartedness is this. It, the Pir of the village uttered.

گره به باد مزن گر چه بر مراد رود

Fix not a knot on the wind (rely not on the world) though, on thy object, it favorably blow,

که این سخن به مثل باد با سلیمان گفت

For to Soleiman this speech, as a proverb, the wind, uttered

به مهلتی که سپهرت دهد ز راه مرو

For a frivolous excuse that the sky may give thee, go not from the Path

تو را که گفت که این زال ترک دستان گفت

Who told thee, that, the abandoning of tales, this old woman (the sky) uttered.

1-Flower   2-Ancient regions in southern Syria

مزن ز چون و چرا دم که بنده مقبل

As to "how and why," express no breath. For the happy slave

قبول کرد به جان هر سخن که جانان گفت

Accepteth with soul every word that the Sultan (God) uttered.

که گفت حافظ از اندیشه تو آمد باز

From thought of thee, who said Hafez hath come back'

من این نگفته‌ام آن کس که گفت بهتان گفت

This, I have not said. He who uttered it, calumny uttered.

غزل ۸۹ ⓄⒹⒺ ⑧⑨

یا رب سببی ساز که یارم به سلامت

O Lord! devise a means, whereby in safety my Beloved

بازآید و برهاندم از بند ملامت

May come back and release me from the claw of reproach.

خاک ره آن یار سفرکرده بیارید

Bring ye the dust of the Path of that traveled Beloved (the necessarily existent One)

تا چشم جهان بین کنمش جای اقامت

That I may make my world-seeing eye His sojourn-place.

فریاد که از شش جهتم راه ببستند

Justice! For, they have barred my Path on six sides

آن خال و خط و زلف و رخ و عارض و قامت

(By the power of) That mole, beard, tress, face, cheek, and stature.

امروز که در دست توام مرحمتی کن

To-day, when I am in thy hand, show a little mercy

فردا که شوم خاک چه سود اشک ندامت

To-morrow, when I become clay, (in the grave) what profit are tears of repentance?

ای آن که به تقریر و بیان دم زنی از عشق

O thou that of love expressest breath in relating and explaining,

ما با تو نداریم سخن خیر و سلامت

With thee no word have we save this "Prosperity and safety be thine!"

درویش مکن ناله ز شمشیر احبا

Dervish! Lament not of the sword of friends;

کاین طایفه از کشته ستانند غرامت

For this band (of friends) taketh the blood-price for the slain.

در خرقه زن آتش که خم ابروی ساقی

Set fire to the religious garment; for the curve of the Saki's eye-brow

بر می‌شکند گوشه محراب امامت

Shattereth the corner of the prayer-arch of the service of the Imam.

حاشا که من از جور و جفای تو بنالم

God forbid that of thy violence and tyranny I should bewail:

بیداد لطیفان همه لطف است و کرامت

The injustice of dainty ones is all daintiness and goodness.

کوته نکند بحث سر زلف تو حافظ

The (long) argument of thy tres ode tip, Hafez shorteneth not:

پیوسته شد این سلسله تا روز قیامت

This chain (of argument) is joined (extended) to the day of resurrection

غزل ۹۰ ⓄⒹⒺ ⑨⓪

ای هدهد صبا به سبا می‌فرستمت

O lapwing of the east wind! (the Murshid) to Saba[1], (the land of the true Be – loved) I send thee:

بنگر که از کجا به کجا می‌فرستمت

Behold from where (the dense, impure, world) to where (the light, pure, world) I send thee

حیف است طایری چو تو در خاکدان غم

Alas! a (glorious) bird like thee in the dust-heap of grief:

زین جا به آشیان وفا می‌فرستمت

Hence to the nest of fidelity, (the land of the true Beloved) I send thee.

در راه عشق مرحله قرب و بعد نیست

In love's Path, is no stage of nearness or of farness:

می‌بینمت عیان و دعا می‌فرستمت

(Hence, true Beloved) I clearly see Thee; and prayer, I send Thee.

هر صبح و شام قافله‌ای از دعای خیر

Every morning and evening, the Kafila[2] of prayer for Thy welfare,

در صحبت شمال و صبا می‌فرستمت

In company with the (cool) north and the east wind, I send Thee

تا لشکر غمت نکند ملک دل خراب

So long as grief 's army ruineth not the heart's country,

جان عزیز خود به نوا می‌فرستمت

Words and   odes, (of mine) with melody and modulation, I send thee.

ای غایب از نظر که شدی همنشین دل

O Fellow-sitter of my heart! Thou that becomest hidden from sight,

می‌گویمت دعا و ثنا می‌فرستمت

Prayer, I utter for Thee; praise, I send Thee.

در روی خود تفرج صنع خدای کن

The creation of God, behold (with joy) in thy own face (the mirror, God displaying);

کآیینه خدای نما می‌فرستمت

For (since thou art careless of the Creator) the mirror, God-displaying, I send thee.

تا مطربان ز شوق منت آگهی دهند

So that the minstrels inform thee of my desire,

قول و غزل به ساز و نوا می‌فرستمت

Words and sonnet (ghazal), overwhelmed with melody and harmony, I send thee.

ساق بیا که هاتف غیبم به مژده گفت

Saki! come; for the invisible messenger uttered to me glad tidings,

با درد صبر کن که دوا می‌فرستمت

In pain, exercise patience; for the remedy of union, (with the true Beloved) I send Thee."

1-Name of a city in Yemen   2-Convoy

حافظ سرود مجلس ما ذکر خیر توست
Hafez! the song of our assembly is the mention of thy welfare
بشتاب هان که اسب و قبا می‌فرستمت
Make haste. (come quickly) a horse and a coat, I send Thee

غزل ۹۱ ÔDÊ ⑨①

ای غایب از نظر به خدا می‌سپارمت
O (beloved) hidden from my sight! to God, I entrust, thee.
جانم بسوختی و به دل دوست دارمت
(In pain of separation) Thou consumedest my soul; yet with heart, friend I hold thee.
تا دامن کفن نکشم زیر پای خاک
So long as I trail not the skirt of my shroud beneath the foot of the dust (of the grave),
باور مکن که دست ز دامن بدارمت
Believe not, I will keep hand from off the skirt of thee.
محراب ابرویت بنما تا سحرگهی
Display the prayer-arch of thy eye-brow, that, in the morning-time,
دست دعا برآرم و در گردن آرمت
(In excuse) I may bring forth my hand of prayer and bring it upon the neck of thee.
گر بایدم شدن سوی هاروت بابلی
If it be necessary for me to go to Harut[1] of Babil,
صد گونه جادویی بکنم تا بیارمت
A hundred kinds of sorcery (learned from him) I will evoke to bring thee.
خواهم که پیش میرمت ای بی‌وفا طبیب
O faithless physician! (the beloved) I wish to die before thee.
بیمار بازپرس که در انتظارمت
Ask the sick; for I am in expectation of thee
صد جوی آب بسته‌ام از دیده بر کنار
(In exceeding love for thee) I have, in my bosom, established a hundred streams of (tear) from my eye
بر بوی تخم مهر که در دل بکارمت
In the hope that I may sow love's seed in the heart of thee
خونم بریخت و از غم عشقم خلاص داد
(The beloved) Spilled my blood and released me from grief of separation,
منت پذیر غمزه خنجر گذارمت
Thank-profferer, I am for the dagger-working glance of thee.
می‌گریم و مرادم از این سیل اشکبار
I weep and, from this tear, torrent raining, my hope
تخم محبت است که در دل بکارمت
Is that love's seed, I may plant in the heart of thee.
بارم ده از کرم سوی خود تا به سوز دل
Of thy grace, give me access to thy self so that, with heart-consuming
در پای دم به دم گهر از دیده بارمت
The jewel (the tear) of the eye, I may momently rain upon the feet of thee.

1-Name of an angel

حافظ شراب و شاهد و رندی نه وضع توست

Hafez! wine, (love) and the mistress, (the beloved) and profligacy the fearless, careless state
are not contrary to thy way of life:

فی الجمله می‌کنی و فرو می‌گذارمت

(Thus) Wholly thou doest; and (since thou exceedest not) I pardon thee.

غزل ۹۲ ⓄⒹⒺ ⑨②

میر من خوش می‌روی کاندر سر و پا میرمت

My Lord! sweetly, Thou goest in so much that in Thee, head to foot (altogether) I die

خوش خرامان شو که پیش قد رعنا میرمت

My Bold One sweetly, Thou movest before Thee, I die.

گفته بودی کی بمیری پیش من تعجیل چیست

Thou saidest Before me, when wilt thou die Why is haste

خوش تقاضا می‌کنی پیش تقاضا میرمت

A sweet demand, Thou makest. (Even) before Thy demand I die.

عاشق و مخمور و مهجورم بت ساقی کجاست

The lover, separated and intoxicated, I am The idol, Saki, where is he

گو که بخرامد که پیش سروبالا میرمت

Say Proudly move for before Thy beautiful form, I die.

آن که عمری شد که تا بیمارم از سودای او

O Beloved through separation from whom, an age hath passed, so that I may die,

گو نگاهی کن که پیش چشم شهلا میرمت

Make say only one glance so that, before thy dark gray eye, I die.

گفته لعل لبم هم درد بخشد هم دوا

Thou hast said My ruby lip giveth pain and also the remedy

گاه پیش درد و گه پیش مداوا میرمت

Sometimes before the pain and sometimes before the remedy, I die.

خوش خرامان می‌روی چشم بد از روی تو دور

Sweetly moving, Thou goest. Far, the evil eye from Thy face

دارم اندر سر خیال آن که در پا میرمت

In my head, I have a fancy that, at Thy feet, I die.

گر چه جای حافظ اندر خلوت وصل تو نیست

Although, the place of Hafiz is not in the private chamber of union with Thee,

ای همه جای تو خوش پیش همه جا میرمت

O Thou (that hast) all places happy, before all Thy places, I die.

غزل ۹۳ ⓄⒹⒺ ⑨③

چه لطف بود که ناگاه رشحه قلمت

What kindness it was when, suddenly, the dropping (of ink) of thy pen

حقوق خدمت ما عرضه کرد بر کرمت

Represented the obligations of our service according to the goodness of thee.

به نوک خامه رقم کرده‌ای سلام مرا

To me, salutation thou hast written with the nib of the pen:

که کارخانه دوران مباد بی رقمت

Be not the work of Time's house without the writing of thee

نگویم از من بی‌دل به سهو کردی یاد

I say not in mistake, thou recollectedest me, heart bereft:

که در حساب خرد نیست سهو بر قلمت

For, in wisdom's account, mistake lieth not in the pen of thee

مرا ذلیل مگردان به شکر این نعمت

Despicable, make me not in thanks for this (divine) favor

که داشت دولت سرمد عزیز و محترمت

That lasting Fortune, dear and honored, held thee.

بیا که با سر زلفت قرار خواهم کرد

Come. For, by thy tres ode tip, I will vow

که گر سرم برود برندارم از قدمت

'That (even) if my head goeth, (from my body) I will not uplift it from the feet of thee.

ز حال ما دلت آگه شود مگر وقتی

Of the state of us, (slain) thy heart may become acquainted; only but at the time,

که لاله بردمد از خاک کشتگان غمت

When the tulip blossometh from the dust of those slain of grief for thee.

روان تشنه ما را به جرعه‌ای دریاب

O beloved With a draught, assist the soul of us thirsty

چو می‌دهند زلال خضر ز جام جمت

When, from the cup, (of Jamshid) the limpid water (of life) of Khizr[1] they give thee.

همیشه وقت تو ای عیسی صبا خوش باد

O Isa[2]-breeze! happy ever be all thy time

که جان حافظ دلخسته زنده شد به دمت

For alive became the heart-broken soul of Hafez by the breath of Thee.

غزل ۹۴ ⓄⒹⒺ ⑨④

زان یار دلنوازم شکریست با شکایت

On account of that heart-cherishing beloved, thanks (mixed) with complaint are mine (and, verily, this is wonderful):

گر نکته دان عشقی بشنو تو این حکایت

If thou be a subtlety-understander of love list well to this tale.

بی مزد بود و منت هر خدمتی که کردم

Rewardless was and thankless every service that I rendered:

یا رب مباد کس را مخدوم بی عنایت

O Lord! void of kindness let none be the served one (master).

رندان تشنه لب را آبی نمی‌دهد کس

To profligates, thirsty of lip, none giveth (even) a little water:

گویی ولی شناسان رفتند از این ولایت

Thou mayest say: "Those recognizing holy men have departed from this land."

در زلف چون کمندش ای دل مپیچ کان جا

O heart! In His tres ode like noose, twist not, (and from its fancy come out); For, there,

سرها بریده بینی بی جرم و بی جنایت

Thou seest severed heads, crimeless, guiltless.

1-Name of prophet   2-Name of prophet

چشمت به غمزه ما را خون خورد و می‌پسندی
With a glance, Thy eye drank our blood; and Thou approvest:

جانا روا نباشد خون ریز را حمایت
o Soul! (of mine) lawful is not protection to the blood-shedder.

در این شب سیاهم گم گشت راه مقصود
In this dark night, (the world) lost to me became the path of my purpose (knowledge of the true Beloved):

از گوشه‌ای برون آی ای ای کوکب هدایت
O Star of guidance! (the Murshid, perfect and excellent) come forth from the corner.

از هر طرف که رفتم جز وحشتم نیفزود
From every direction, where I went naught increased to me save terror.

زنهار از این بیابان وین راه بی‌نهایت
Beware of this desert, and of this endless Path.

ای آفتاب خوبان می‌جوشد اندرونم
O sun of lovely ones my heart consumeth

یک ساعتم بگنجان در سایه عنایت
Contain me, a moment, in the shade of thy protection.

این راه را نهایت صورت کجا توان بست
Of this Path, (of love) the end openeth no form

کش صد هزار منزل بیش است در بدایت
For, in its beginning, are a hundred thousand stages (and) more.

هر چند بردی آبم روی از درت نتابم
Although, thou snatchedest my honor (and madest me despicable), I turn not my face from Thy door:

جور از حبیب خوشتر کز مدعی رعایت
More pleasant is violence from the Beloved, than from the enemy, courtesy.

عشقت رسد به فریاد ار خود به سان حافظ
To thy complaint, love reacheth, if like Hafez

قرآن ز بر بخوانی در چارده روایت
Thou recite (by heart) the Kuran[1] with the fourteen traditions

غزل ۹۵ ⓄⒹⒺ ⑨⑤

مدامم مست می‌دارد نسیم جعد گیسویت
Ever intoxicated keepeth me the waft of air of the tres ode curl of Thine.

خرابم می‌کند هر دم فریب چشم جادویت
Momently ruined maketh me the deceit of the eye of sorcery of Thine.

پس از چندین شکیبایی شبی یا رب توان دیدن
O Lord! after such patience, one can see a night

که شمع دیده افروزیم در محراب ابرویت
Whereon, we may kindle the candle of our eye in the prayer-arch of the eyebrow of Thine

سواد لوح بینش را عزیز از بهر آن دارم
The black tablet of vision, I hold dear for the sake

که جان را نسخه‌ای باشد ز لوح خال هندویت
That to the soul, it is a book of the picture of the dark mole of Thine.

1-Quran

تو گر خواهی که جاویدان جهان یک سر بیارایی

If Thou wish perpetually to adorn the world altogether

صبا را گو که بردارد زمانی برقع از رویت

Tell the breeze that it should uplift awhile the veil from the face of Thine.

و گر رسم فنا خواهی که از عالم براندازی

And if Thou wish to cast out from the world the custom of effacement.

برافشان تا فروریزد هزاران جان ز هر مویت

(O true Beloved) Scatter (Thy tress) that it may shed thousands of souls from every hair of Thine.

من و باد صبا مسکین دو سرگردان بی‌حاصل

(Wretched), I and the morning breeze; two heads, revolving without profit:

من از افسون چشمت مست و او از بوی گیسویت

Intoxicated, I, from the sorcery of the eye of Thine; it, from the perfume of the tress of Thine.

زهی همت که حافظ راست از دنی و از عقبی

O excellent! the spirit that Hafez hath of this world and of the next world

نیاید هیچ در چشمش بجز خاک سر کویت

Naught cometh into his eye, save the dust of the head of the street of Thine.

〈◉〉〈◉〉

ث
The Letter Sā

غزل ۹۶ ⓄⒹⒺ ⑨⑥

درد ما را نیست درمان الغیاث
For our pain, is no remedy, Justice

هجر ما را نیست پایان الغیاث
For our separation is no end, Justice

دین و دل بردند و قصد جان کنند
Religion and the heart, they ravish and make design upon our

الغیاث از جور خوبان الغیاث
Justice against the tyranny of lovely ones, Justice

در بهای بوسه‌ای جانی طلب
As the price of a kiss, the demand of a life,

می‌کنند این دلستانان الغیاث
These heart-ravishers make, Justice

خون ما خوردند این کافردلان
These of Kafir-heart drink our blood

ای مسلمانان چه درمان الغیاث
Muslims what remedy Justice

همچو حافظ روز و شب بی خویشتن
Day and night, self-less, like Hafiz

گشته‌ام سوزان و گریان الغیاث
Weeping and consuming (with grief) I have gone, Justice

❖◉❖❖◉❖

ج
The Letter Jim

غزل ۹۷ ⓄⒹⒺ 9⑦

تویی که بر سر خوبان کشوری چون تاج

From all the heart-ravishers, it is fit that thou (Muhammad) shouldest take tribute

سزد اگر همه دلبران دهندت باج

For, over all lovely ones (prophets) thou, crown-like, art chief

دو چشم شوخ تو برهم زده خطا و حبش

Thy two intoxicated eyes, the tumult of all Turkistan

به چین زلف تو ماچین و هند داده خراج

To the curl of thy tress, Machin and Chin have givent ribute.

بیاض روی تو روشن چو عارض رخ روز

The whiteness (of mercy) of thy face appeared more luminous than the face of day

سواد زلف سیاه تو هست ظلمت داج

The darkness (of vengeance) thy tress, more dark than the darkness of dark night

دهان شهد تو داده رواج آب خضر

To The water (of life) of Khizr[1], thy small mouth hath given permanency

لب چو قند تو برد از نبات مصر رواج

Over the sugar of Egypt, thy candy-like lip hath taken currency.

از این مرض به حقیقت شفا نخواهم یافت

In truth, from this disease (of love for, and of separation from, thee) where shall I find recovery

که از تو درد دل ای جان نمی‌رسد به علاج

If From thee, my heart-pain reacheth no remedy.

چرا همی‌شکنی جان من ز سنگ دلی

O my soul from stone-heartedness, why shatterest thou

دل ضعیف که باشد به نازکی چو زجاج

The feeble heart which, through feebleness, is (fragile) like crystal

لب تو خضر و دهان تو آب حیوان است

Thy hair is (ever fresh like) Khizr and thy mouth, the water of life

قد تو سرو و میان موی و بر به هیت عاج

Thy stature, the cypress thy waist, a hair and thy chest, like (lustrous) ivory.

فتاد در دل حافظ هوای چون تو شهی

In the head of Hafiz, the desire of a sovereign like thee hath fallen

کمینه ذره خاک در تو بودی کاج

Would to Heaven he (Hafiz) Were the humble slave of the dust of thy door

◉ ◉

1-Name of a prophet

ح
The Letter Hā

غزل ۹۸ ⓄⒹⒺ ⑨⑧

اگر به مذهب تو خون عاشق است مباح

If, in thy religious order, the (shedding of the) blood the lover is lawful (to us it is lawful)

صلاح ما همه آن است کان تو راست صلاح

Our rectitude is all that which is thy rectitude.

سواد زلف سیاه تو جاعل الظلمات

The black (hue) of thy hair (is) the explanation of the Bringer forth of the darkness.

بیاض روی چو ماه تو فالق الاصباح

The white (hue) of thy face, the manifestation of the Splitter of the morning.

ز چین زلف کمندت کسی نیافت خلاص

Escape from the grasp of thy tress noose, none gained

از آن کمانچه ابرو و تیر چشم نجاح

Nor freedom from the little bow of thy eye-brow, and from the arrow of thy eye.

ز دیده‌ام شده یک چشمه در کنار روان

From thy eye into the bosom, went flowing a (raging) stream,

که آشنا نکند در میان آن ملاح

In the midst whereof, the sailor swimmeth not.

لب چو آب حیات تو هست قوت جان

Thy lip, like the water of life, is the power of the soul

وجود خاکی ما را از اوست ذکر رواح

From him, our dusty existence is the taste of wine

بداد لعل لبت بوسه‌ای به صد زاری

With a hundred, stratagems the ruby of thy lip gave me no kiss

گرفت کام دلم ز او به صد هزار الحاح

With a hundred thousand solicitations, my heart gained no desire from him.

دعای جان تو ورد زبان مشتاقان

A prayer for thy soul be the morning-prayer of the tongue of Hafiz

همیشه تا که بود متصل مسا و صباح

Be ever continual till evening and morning

صلاح و توبه و تقوی ز ما مجو حافظ

(O Zahid) ever Seek not from me rectitude, or penitence, or piety

ز رند و عاشق و مجنون کسی نیافت صلاح

From the profligate, and the lover, and the distraught, none sought perseverance in good.

◈◉◈◈◉◈

خ
The Letter Khā

غزل ۹۹ ⓄⒹⒺ ⑨⑨

دل من در هوای روی فرخ
My heart, in desire of the face of Farrukh[1],

بود آشفته همچون موی فرخ
Is in confusion like the (dishevelled) hair of Farrukh.

بجز هندوی زلفش هیچ کس نیست
Save the (black) Hindu (slave) of his tress, is none,

که برخوردار شد از روی فرخ
That enjoyed prosperity from the face of Farrukh.

سیاهی نیکبخت است آن که دایم
The. Black (tress) of good fortune is that which ever

بود همراز و هم زانوی فرخ
Is the fellow-traveller and the fellow knee-sitter of Farruk

شود چون بید لرزان سرو آزاد
Like the trembling aspen, becometh the cypress of the garden,

اگر بیند قد دلجوی فرخ
If it see the heart-alluring stature of Farrukh.

بده ساقی شراب ارغوانی
O Saki! give wine of Arghavan[2] hue

به یاد نرگس جادوی فرخ
To the memory of the eye of sorcery of Farrukh.

دوتا شد قامتم همچون کمانی
Bent like a bow, became my stature

ز غم پیوسته چون ابروی فرخ
From grief continuous as the eye-brow of Farrukh.

نسیم مشک تاتاری خجل کرد
The breeze of the musk of Tatar, ashamed made

شمیم زلف عنبربوی فرخ
The perfume of the tress of ambergris of Farrukh.

اگر میل دل هر کس به جایست
If to a place, be the inclination of any one's heart,

بود میل دل من سوی فرخ
The inclination of my heart is towards (the grace) of Farrukh.

غلام همت آنم که باشد
I am the slave of resolution of that one who is

چو حافظ بنده و هندوی فرخ
Like Hafez, the attendant of the black (tress) of Farrukh.

⟨◉⟩⟨◉⟩

1-One of the martial of Hafez's time   2-Amethyst, or purple

د
The Letter Dāl

غزل ۱۰۰ ⓄⒹⒺ ①⓪⓪

دی پیر می فروش که ذکرش به خیر باد
Yesterday, the Pir[1], the wine-seller whose mention be for good!

گفتا شراب نوش و غم دل ببر ز یاد
Said: "Drink wine; and, from recollection, take the heart's grief."

گفتم به باد می‌دهدم باده نام و ننگ
I said: "To the wind, wine giveth my name and fame:"

گفتا قبول کن سخن و هر چه باد باد
He said: "Accept the word: be whatever be."

سود و زیان و مایه چو خواهد شدن ز دست
Since, from thy hand, will go profit and loss and capital,

از بهر این معامله غمگین مباش و شاد
Say: "For this matter, neither noyous nor joyous be!

بادت به دست باشد اگر دل نهی به هیچ
In thy hand is only wind, if thou place thy heart on any (perishing) thing:

در معرضی که تخت سلیمان رود به باد
In a meeting-place (the world) where to the wind, (even) Soleiman's[2] throne goeth.

حافظ گرت ز پند حکیمان ملالت است
Hafez! if thine be vexation on account of the counsel of the sages,

کوته کنیم قصه که عمرت دراز باد
Let us make short the tale, saying: "Long life be thine!"

غزل ۱۰۱ ⓄⒹⒺ ①⓪①

شراب و عیش نهان چیست کار بی‌بنیاد
Wine and hidden pleasure, (love) what are they? Baseless work.

زدیم بر صف رندان و هر چه بادا باد
On the ranks of (our own) profligates (the murshids) we dashed (and joined them). What is fit to be-be!

گره ز دل بگشا و از سپهر یاد مکن
Unloose the heart's knot; (of thought and of hesitation) and, think not of the sky:

که فکر هیچ مهندس چنین گره نگشاد
For such a knot, the thought of no geometrician hath loosed.

ز انقلاب زمانه عجب مدار که چرخ
At Time's changes, wonder not. For the sphere

از این فسانه هزاران هزار دارد یاد
Recollecteth many a thousand talesof sorcery of this kind.

1-A Muslim saint or holy man, Pietist   2-Name of prophet

قدح به شرط ادب گیر زان که ترکیبش
With respect (learning and knowledge), take the goblet. For its composition
ز کاسه سر جمشید و بهمن است و قباد
Is of the (dust of the) skull of Jamshid, of Bahman, and of Kubad[1].

که آگه است که کاووس و کی کجا رفتند
Where Kawoos[2] and Kay[3] went, who is informed?
که واقف است که چون رفت تخت جم بر باد
How Jamshid's throne went to the wind (of destruction) who is informed?

ز حسرت لب شیرین هنوز می‌بینم
From passion for Shirin's lip, yet I see
که لاله می‌دمد از خون دیده فرهاد
That, from the blood of Farhad's eye, the tulip blossometh.

مگر که لاله بدانست بی‌وفایی دهر
Perchance the tulip knew Time's unfaithfulness:
که تا بزاد و بشد جام می ز کف ننهاد
For, since she was torn and become, from out of her hand she hath not placed the cup of wine.

بیا بیا که زمانی ز می خراب شویم
Come! come! so that, awhile, with wine (of love) ruined (effaced and non – existent) we may become:
مگر رسیم به گنجی در این خراب آباد
Perchance, (by means of love) to that great fortune (union with the true Beloved) we may, (in the stage of effacement) in this ruined place (the world, the field of the first, and the last, world) reach.

نمی‌دهند اجازت مرا به سیر و سفر
For wandering and journeying, me, permission give not
نسیم باد مصلا و آب رکن آباد
The breeze of Musalla's[4] dust, and the water of Roknabad.

قدح مگیر چو حافظ مگر به ناله چنگ
Like Hafez take not the cup save to the sound of the harp:
که بسته‌اند بر ابریشم طرب دل شاد
For, to the silk (cord) of joy, they have bound the glad heart.

غزل ۱۰۲ ⓄⒹⒺ ①⓪②

دوش آگهی ز یار سفرکرده داد باد
Last night, the news of the beloved, journey-made, gave the wind:
من نیز دل به باد دهم هر چه باد باد
To the wind, I also give my heart. Whatever it be-be.

کارم بدان رسید که همراز خود کنم
To that, (limit) my work (turn) reached that, my confidant I make
هر شام برق لامع و هر بامداد باد
Every evening the flashing lightning; and, every morning, the wind.

1-Three Iranian Kings

2-Shahnameh characters

3-Kay Kawad or Kay Qobad, the father of Kay Kawoos

4-Praying place

در چین طره تو دل بی حفاظ من

In the curl of thy tress, my heart void of protection,

هرگز نگفت مسکن مالوف یاد باد

Ever said not: "Of my accustomed abode, recollection be."

امروز قدر پند عزیزان شناختم

To-day, I recognized the value of the counsel of those dear:

یا رب روان ناصح ما از تو شاد باد

O Lord! joyous by Thee, the soul of our adviser be.

خون شد دلم به یاد تو هر گه که در چمن

In memory of thee, blood become my heart, whenever, in the sward,

بند قبای غنچه گل می‌گشاد باد

The fastening of the rose-bud's coat, loosed the wind.

از دست رفته بود وجود ضعیف من

From my hand, had gone my feeble existence:

صبحم به بوی وصل تو جان بازداد باد

In the morning, by the perfume of thy tress, gave back life, the wind.

حافظ نهاد نیک تو کامت برآورد

Hafez! thy desire, thy good disposition bringeth forth:

جان‌ها فدای مردم نیکونهاد باد

The ransom of the man of good disposition, souls be.

غزل ۱۰۳ ⓄⒹⒺ ①⓪③

روز وصل دوستداران یاد باد

The day of union of friends remember:

یاد باد آن روزگاران یاد باد

Those times, remember, remember!

کامم از تلخی غم چون زهر گشت

From the bitterness of grief (of separation from the beloved) my palate hath become (bitter) like poison:

بانگ نوش شادخواران یاد باد

The tumult of the drinking of (bumpers) of wine-drinkers, remember!

گر چه یاران فارغند از یاد من

Although free of recollection of me, are friends

از من ایشان را هزاران یاد باد

Them, on my part a thousand times, remember!

مبتلا گشتم در این بند و بلا

Entangled, I am in this bond of calamity:

کوشش آن حق گزاران یاد باد

The endeavor of those upright ones, remember!

گر چه صد رود است در چشمم مدام

Although in my eye, are a hundred streams

زنده رود باغ کاران یاد باد

The Zende-rud[1] of gardeners, remember!

1-The name of a river

راز حافظ بعد از این ناگفته ماند

(Mystery-keeper, none) after this, the mystery of Hafez un-uttered remaineth:

ای دریغا رازداران یاد باد

Alas! the (passed) mystery-keepers, remember!

ⓞⓓⓔ ⓵⓪⓸ غزل ۱۰۴

جمالت آفتاب هر نظر باد

The sun of every vision, thy beauty be

ز خوبی روی خوبت خوبتر باد

More beautiful than the beauty, (of face of other lovely ones) Thy beautiful face be.

همای زلف شاهین شهپرت را

Of the Homa[1] of Thy tress, (which is) the falcon of long-wing feather

دل شاهان عالم زیر پر باد

Beneath the wing, the heart of the kings of the world be!

کسی کو بسته زلفت نباشد

To Thy tress, that one who is not attracted:

چو زلفت درهم و زیر و زبر باد

Like Thy tress, tossed and confused be.

دلی کو عاشق رویت نباشد

Of Thy face, that heart that is not the lover,

همیشه غرقه در خون جگر باد

In liver-blood, ever drowned be

بتا چون غمزه‌ات ناوک فشاند

O idol! When Thy glance casteth the arrow

دل مجروح من پیشش سپر باد

Before it, (the arrow) my wounded heart, the shield be.

چو لعل شکرینت بوسه بخشد

When Thy sugary ruby (lip) giveth the kiss

مذاق جان من ز او پرشکر باد

From it, the taste of my life, full of sugar be.

مرا از توست هر دم تازه عشقی

Momently mine, is a great fresh love for Thee:

تو را هر ساعتی حسنی دگر باد

Hourly, Thine another great (attraction of) beauty be!

به جان مشتاق روی توست حافظ

With soul, Hafez is desirous of Thy face.

تو را در حال مشتاقان نظر باد

On the state of desirous ones, Thy glance be

1-Is a mythical bird of Iranian legends and fable

غزل ۱۰۵ ⓄⒹⒺ ①⓪⑤

صوفی ار باده به اندازه خورد نوشش باد
If, to limit, (of his capacity) the Sufi (the outward worshipper) drink wine (of love) to him, sweet may it be!

ور نه اندیشه این کار فراموشش باد
If not, the thought of this work (of love) of his, forgotten be!

آن که یک جرعه می از دست تواند دادن
That one who can give up a single draft of wine (of sensual pleasure),

دست با شاهد مقصود در آغوشش باد
With the Beloved of his desire his hand in his bosom, be.

پیر ما گفت خطا بر قلم صنع نرفت
Said our Pir: "On the Creator's pen, passed no error:"

آفرین بر نظر پاک خطاپوشش باد
On his (the Pir's) pure sight, error-covering, afarin be!

گر چه از کبر سخن با من درویش نگفت
Although, through pride, he uttered no word to me, the poor dervish;

جان فدای شکرین پسته خاموشش باد
A ransom for His sweet, silent, pistachio nut, my life be!

چشمم از آینه داران خط و خالش گشت
Of (the number of) mirror-holders of his (the beloved's) line (of down) and mole, my eye became:

لبم از بوسه ربایان بر و دوشش باد
(Of the number of) the kiss snatchers (of his the beloved's) bosom and back, my lip be.

نرگس مست نوازش کن مردم دارش
The intoxicated narcissus, ('the beloved's eye), favor-doer, ma n-preserver;

خون عاشق به قدح گر بخورد نوشش باد
If it (the narcissus) drink lover's blood in a goblet, to it sweet may it be!

به غلامی تو مشهور جهان شد حافظ
Hafez! in thy service, the world became famous:

حلقه بندگی زلف تو در گوشش باد
In its ear, the ring of service of thy tress, be!

غزل ۱۰۶ ⓄⒹⒺ ①⓪⑥

تنت به ناز طبیبان نیازمند مباد
In need of the physician's care, thy body be not.

وجود نازکت آزرده گزند مباد
Vexed by injury, thy tender existence be not!

سلامت همه آفاق در سلامت توست
The safety of all horizons (the whole world) is in thy safety.

به هیچ عارضه شخص تو دردمند مباد
By any accident, sorrowful thy person be not!

جمال صورت و معنی ز امن صحت توست
(O perfect murshid) the beauty of the outward and of the inward is from the prosperity of thy well-being:

که ظاهرت دژم و باطنت نژند مباد
Outwardly anguished, inwardly afflicted, thou be not!

در این چمن چو درآید خزان به یغمایی

In this sward, when autumn entereth upon plundering

رهش به سرو سهی قامت بلند مباد

To the straight cypress of lofty stature, its path be not!

در آن بساط که حسن تو جلوه آغازد

In that place where thy beauty beginneth splendor,

مجال طعنه بدبین و بدپسند مباد

The power of reproach of the ill-seer and of the ill-approver be not!

هر آن که روی چو ماهت به چشم بد بیند

Everyone, who, with the evil eye, beholdeth thy moon-like face,

بر آتش تو بجز جان او سپند مباد

Save rue-casting on the fire of grief (for thee), his life be not

شفا ز گفته شکرفشان حافظ جوی

From the sugar-scattering utterance, of Hafez seek recovery,

که حاجتت به علاج گلاب و قند مباد

So that need of the remedy of rose-water and of candy, thine be not.

غزل ۱۰۷ ⓄⒹⒺ ①⓪⑦

حسن تو همیشه در فزون باد

Ever increasing, Thy beauty be!

رویت همه ساله لاله گون باد

All years, tulip-hued, Thy face be.

اندر سر ما خیال عشقت

In my head, the image of Thy love,

هر روز که باد در فزون باد

Every day that is, increasing be.

هر سرو که در چمن درآید

Every cypress that, in the sward, cometh up, (lofty and separate)

در خدمت قامتت نگون باد

Before the (straight and erect) (alif) of Thy stature, like the nun be!

چشمی که نه فتنه تو باشد

That eye that is not bewitched by Thee,

چون گوهر اشک غرق خون باد

Out of (from) the jewel of tears, (go and) in a sea of blood be!

چشم تو ز بهر دلربایی

For heart-ravishing, Thy eye

در کردن سحر ذوفنون باد

In practicing sorcery, sorcery-possessed be!

هر جا که دلیست در غم تو

Wherever in grief (of love) for Thee, is a heart,

بی صبر و قرار و بی سکون باد

Without patience, or rest; and without quietude, let it be.

قد همه دلبران عالم
The stature of all the heart-ravishers of the world,
پیش الف قدت چو نون باد
In service of Thy form, like the (curved) nun be,!

هر دل که ز عشق توست خالی
He who in separation from Thee is not content,
از حلقه وصل تو برون باد
Out of the circle of union with Thee, be.

لعل تو که هست جان حافظ
Thy ruby (lip) that is the soul of Hafez,
دور از لب مردمان دون باد
From the lip of every mean and base one, far be.

غزل ۱۰۸ ⓄⒹⒺ ①⓪⑧

خسروا گوی فلک در خم چوگان تو باد
O Khusrau! the ball of the sky in the curve of the polo of thine be:
ساحت کون و مکان عرصه میدان تو باد
The place of existence and of dwelling (the universe) the space of the plain of thine be!

زلف خاتون ظفر شیفته پرچم توست
The tress of the Lady of Victory is enamored with thy standard-tassel:
دیده فتح ابد عاشق جولان تو باد
The eye of eternity without end, the lover of the galloping (of attack) of thine be!

ای که انشا عطارد صفت شوکت توست
O thou (that art such a one) that the writing of Mercury is the description of thy pomp!
عقل کل چاکر طغراکش دیوان تو باد
Reason of all (Jibra.il) the Toghra-writer of the book of record of thine be!

طیره جلوه طوبی قد چون سرو تو شد
Thy cypress like stature became the shame of the splendor of the Tuba[1],
غیرت خلد برین ساحت بستان تو باد
The envy of lofty paradise, the plain of the hall of thine be.

نه به تنها حیوانات و نباتات و جماد
Not alone animals and vegetation and things inorganic;
هر چه در عالم امر است به فرمان تو باد
Whatever is in the world of order, under the order of thine be.

غزل ۱۰۹ ⓄⒹⒺ ①⓪⑨

دیر است که دلدار پیامی نفرستاد
'Tis a long time; and the Heart-possessor (God) a message sent not;
ننوشت سلامی و کلامی نفرستاد
A letter, wrote not; and a salutation, sent not

1-The name of a tree in heaven

صد نامه فرستادم و آن شاه سواران
A hundred letters, I sent; and that sovereign of horsemen
پیکی ندوانید و سلامی نفرستاد
A messenger hastened not; and a message sent not.

سوی من وحشی صفت عقل رمیده
To me, like a wild beast, reason affrighted,
آهوروشی کبک خرامی نفرستاد
One, deer of gait, partridge of strut, (messenger) He (the heart – possessor) He sent not.

دانست که خواهد شدنم مرغ دل از دست
(He the true Beloved) knew that (through separation from Him) the bird of my heart would
go from my hand, (would die)
و از آن خط چون سلسله دامی نفرستاد
Yet, of that chain-like hair, a snare, He sent not.

فریاد که آن ساق شکرلب سرمست
Complaint! that Saki (the true Beloved) sweet of lip, intoxicated,
دانست که مخمورم و جامی نفرستاد
Knew that I was wine-sick; and a cup of wine, sent not.

چندان که زدم لاف کرامات و مقامات
As long as I boasted of excellences and of the stages of divine knowledge,
هیچم خبر از هیچ مقامی نفرستاد
To me, any news of any stage (of divine knowledge), He sent not.

حافظ به ادب باش که واخواست نباشد
Hafez! be with respect. For appeal is none:
گر شاه پیامی به غلامی نفرستاد
If a message to a humble slave, the King sent not.

غزل ۱۱۰ ⓄⒹⒺ ①①Ⓞ

پیرانه سرم عشق جوانی به سر افتاد
Elderly of head, into my head youthful love, hath fallen:
وان راز که در دل بنهفتم به درافتاد
And that mystery (of love) that, in the heart, I concealed, out hath fallen.

از راه نظر مرغ دلم گشت هواگیر
From vision's path, the bird of my heart went soaring.
ای دیده نگه کن که به دام که درافتاد
O eye! (of my heart) behold into whose snare, it (the bird of the heart) hath fallen.

دردا که از آن آهوی مشکین سیه چشم
O sorrow! that, for that musky deer, dark of eye,
چون نافه بسی خون دلم در جگر افتاد
Like the musk-pod, much heart's blood, into my liver, hath fallen.

از رهگذر خاک سر کوی شما بود
From the thoroughfare of the (gracious) dust of the head of your street, is
هر نافه که در دست نسیم سحر افتاد
Every musk-pod that in the hand of the morning-breeze, hath fallen

مژگان تو تا تیغ جهان گیر برآورد
Since thy eye-lashes drew forth the sword, world-seizing,

بس کشته دل زنده که بر یک دگر افتاد
Many a slain one, heart-alive (the true lover it is) that, on each other, hath fallen.

بس تجربه کردیم در این دیر مکافات
In this house of retribution the upspringing of the world,

با دردکشان هر که درافتاد برافتاد
With the dreg-drunkards, holy men whoever in strife fell, out in wretchedness hath fallen.

گر جان بدهد سنگ سیه سنگ لعل نگردد
If the (valueless) black stone give (its own) life, it becometh not valuable the ruby:

با طینت اصلی چه کند بدگهر افتاد
What may it do? With its original (ill) nature, it, (the state of) ill-nature hath befallen.

حافظ که سر زلف بتان دست کشش بود
Hafez whose (happy) hand hath the tress of idols,

بس طرفه حریفیست کش اکنون به سر افتاد
Into his head, a very powerful rival is it (the tress) that hath fallen.

غزل ۱۱۱ ⓞⒹⒺ ⓲⓲⓲

عکس روی تو چو در آینه جام افتاد
(O true Beloved) When, into the mirror of the cup (of love), the reflection of Thy face fell,

عارف از خنده می در طمع خام افتاد
From the laughter of wine (love's glory), into the crude desire of (drinking) the cup, the Aref fell.

حسن روی تو به یک جلوه که در آینه کرد
With that splendor that in the mirror, (of the ruby) the beauty of Thy face made,

این همه نقش در آیینه اوهام افتاد
All this picture (of created beings that are illusory) into the mirror of fancy fell

این همه عکس می و نقش نگارین که نمود
All this reflection of wine (sensual love) and varied picture (brutal love) that have appeared

یک فروغ رخ ساقیست که در جام افتاد
Is (only) a splendor of the face of the Saki (God) that, into cup (of our heart and into things possible) fell.

غیرت عشق زبان همه خاصان ببرید
The jealousy of (true) love severed (and made dumb) the tongue of all the great ones (of love the Arifs):

کز کجا سر غمش در دهن عام افتاد
(Then) Into the mouth of the common people, the mystery of grief for Him, how fell?

من ز مسجد به خرابات نه خود افتادم
from the masjed to the tavern, I fell not of myself

اینم از عهد ازل حاصل فرجام افتاد
From the covenant of eternity without beginn ing, to me this result of the end (tavern – haunting) fell.

چه کند کز پی دوران نرود چون پرگار
(When), like the compass, for the sake of revolution, he moveth not, what may he do

هر که در دایره گردش ایام افتاد
Who in the circle of time's revolution fell?

در خم زلف تو آویخت دل از چاه زنخ
(After coming out) From the pit of (dimple) Thy chin, in the curl of Thy tress, my heart clung:

آه کز چاه برون آمد و در دام افتاد
Alas. forth from the pit, it came; and into the snare, fell.

آن شد ای خواجه که در صومعه بازم بینی
O Khwajeh! passed hath that time when thou sawest me in the cloister;

کار ما با رخ ساقی و لب جام افتاد
(Now) With the lace of the Said and the lip of the cup, my work fell.

زیر شمشیر غمش رقص کنان باید رفت
Beneath the sword of grief for Him, it is proper to go dancing (in joy)

کان که شد کشته او نیک سرانجام افتاد
For, that one who was slain of Him, his end happy fell.

هر دمش با من دلسوخته لطفی دگر است
Every moment, another kindness to me of consumed heart is His:

این گدا بین که چه شایسته انعام افتاد
Behold, how fit for reward, this beggar fell

صوفیان جمله حریفند و نظرباز ولی
The Sufis, all, are lovers and glance (of love)-players; but

زین میان حافظ دلسوخته بدنام افتاد
From the midst, to bad name, heart-consumed Hafez fell.

غزل ۱۱۲ ⓄⒹⒺ ①①② ODE 112

آن که رخسار تو را رنگ گل و نسرین داد
Who, to thy cheek, the hue of the (red) rose and of the wild (white) rose gave,

صبر و آرام تواند به من مسکین داد
To me, miserable, patience and ease, can give.

وان که گیسوی تو را رسم تطاول آموخت
Who taught thy tress the habit of being long,

هم تواند کرمش داد من غمگین داد
To me, grief-stricken, the gift of His liberality, can also give.

من همان روز ز فرهاد طمع ببریدم
Hope of Farhad, (that he would live) I severed that very day

که عنان دل شیدا به لب شیرین داد
When, to Shirin's lip, the rein of his distraught heart, he gave.

گنج زر گر نبود کنج قناعت باقیست
If (mine) be not that treasure of gold, contentment is left:

آن که آن داد به شاهان به گدایان این داد
Who, to kings that (treasure) gave, to beggars this (contentment) gave.

خوش عروسیست جهان از ره صورت لیکن
A fine bride, outwardly, is the world. But

هر که پیوست بدو عمر خودش کاوین داد
Who joined himself to her, (the world) his own life (as) the dowry gave.

بعد از این دست من و دامن سرو و لب جوی
After this, (together are) My hand and my skirt; the cypress and the marge of the stream,

خاصه اکنون که صبا مژده فروردین داد
Especially, now, that, glad tidings of (the coming of) February, the wind gave.

در کف غصه دوران دل حافظ خون شد
In the hand of grief for Time, Hafez's heart became blood:

از فراق رخت ای خواجه قوام الدین داد
O Khwajeh Kavam ud Din![1] for separation from thy face, justice!

غزل ۱۱۳ ⓄⒹⒺ ①①③

بنفشه دوش به گل گفت و خوش نشانی داد
Last night, to the rose, the violet spake; and a sweet trace gave,

که تاب من به جهان طره فلانی داد
Saying: "In the world, me, torment a certain one's tress gave."

دلم خزانه اسرار بود و دست قضا
The store of mysteries, was my heart; and, (so that it might reveal naught) the hand of Fate

درش ببست و کلیدش به دلستانی داد
Closed its door; and its key to that heart-ravisher (the true Beloved)-gave.

شکسته وار به درگاهت آمدم که طبیب
To Thy court, like one shattered, I came. For, the physician, (the Murshid)

به مومیایی لطف توام نشانی داد
Me, a trace to the electuary of Thy grace gave.

تنش درست و دلش شاد باد و خاطر خوش
By me, miserable, He passed; and to the watchers, said:

که دست دادش و یاری ناتوانی داد
Alas! What a soul my slain lover gave.

برو معالجه خود کن ای نصیحتگو
O counsel utterer! (wine – forbidder) go, devise thy own remedy:

شراب و شاهد شیرین که را زیانی داد
Loss to whom, (is it that) wine and the sweet mistress gave.

گذشت بر من مسکین و با رقیبان گفت
By me miserable, He passed and told to my opponents:

دریغ حافظ مسکین من چه جانی داد
What a pity! my Hafez how miserable life he gave."

غزل ۱۱۴ ⓄⒹⒺ ①①④

همای اوج سعادت به دام ما افتد
(O true Beloved) The Homa of the height of felicity to the snare of ours falleth.

اگر تو را گذری بر مقام ما افتد
If, Thy passing to the dwelling of ours falleth.

1-Abu Ishaq's minister

حباب وار براندازم از نشاط کلاه
Like the (up – rising) bubble, up I cast my cap with joy,
اگر ز روی تو عکسی به جام ما افتد
If a reflection of Thy face into the cup of ours falleth.

شبی که ماه مراد از افق شود طالع
A night when the moon of desire ariseth from the horizon
بود که پرتو نوری به بام ما افتد
It may be that the ray of that light (of the moon) on the roof of ours falleth.

به بارگاه تو چون باد را نباشد بار
When the path of dust-kissing of this door is not (even) for kings,
کی اتفاق مجال سلام ما افتد
How, the favor of an answer to the salutation of ours falleth?

چو جان فدای لبش شد خیال می‌بستم
When my life became the sacrifice for Thy lip I established the fancy
که قطره‌ای ز زلالش به کام ما افتد
That a drop of its limpid water to the palate of ours falleth.

خیال زلف تو گفتا که جان وسیله مساز
The fancy! Thy tress spake saying: "O Lover! make not (thy) life the means (of thy desire);
کز این شکار فراوان به دام ما افتد
"For, of this kind, many a prey into the snare of ours falleth."

به ناامیدی از این در مرو بزن فالی
From this door, go not in hopelessness. Strike an omen:
بود که قرعه دولت به نام ما افتد
It may be that the die of fortune to the name of ours falleth.

ز خاک کوی تو هر گه که دم زند حافظ
Whenever Hafez boasteth of the dust of Thy "street,"
نسیم گلشن جان در مشام ما افتد
Thy breeze of the rose-bed of the soul into the perfume-place of ours falleth.

غزل ۱۱۵   ⓄⒹⒺ ①①⑤

درخت دوستی بنشان که کام دل به بار آرد
Plant the tree of friendship, that, to fruit, the heart's desire bringeth:
نهال دشمنی برکن که رنج بی‌شمار آرد
Up-pluck the bush of enmity, that countless troubles bringeth.

چو مهمان خراباتی به عزت باش با رندان
When thou art the guest of the tavern, (of love) with profligates (holy travellers) be with respect:
که درد سر کشی جانا گرت مستی خمار آرد
For, O beloved, if thou be (only) a dreg-drinker, the intoxication, of wine-sickness, (of the love for God) (even) this (dreg) this bringeth

شب صحبت غنیمت دان که بعد از روزگار ما
The night of society, (with beloved ones) reckon plunder. For, after our time
بسی گردش کند گردون بسی لیل و نهار آرد
The sphere many a revolution maketh; many a night (winter) and day (spring) bringeth.

عماری دار لیلی را که مهد ماه در حکم است

Leyla's litter-keeper, in whose order is the moon's cradle,

خدا را در دل اندازش که بر مجنون گذار آرد

O God! into his heart cast (the wish) that, passing by (the ab ode of) Majnun, he may cause.

بهار عمر خواه ای دل وگرنه این چمن هر سال

O heart! desire the spring season. If not, every year, this sward (the world)

چو نسرین صد گل آرد بار و چون بلبل هزار آرد

A hundred beautiful roses. like the wild rose, and a thousand (birds) like the nightingale bringeth.

خدا را چون دل ریشم قراری بست با زلفت

Since, with Thy tress, my wounded heart hath established a covenant, for God's sake,

بفرما لعل نوشین را که زودش باقرار آرد

Order Thy sweet ruby (lip) that to rest, its the heart's state, it may bring.

در این باغ از خدا خواهد دگر پیرانه سر حافظ

In this garden, (the world) Hafez, gray of head, asketh God

نشیند بر لب جوبی و سروی در کنار آرد

That, by the marge of the stream, he may sit; and into his embrace, a cypress may bring.

غزل ۱۱۶   ⒪ⒹⒺ ①①⑥

کسی که حسن و خط دوست در نظر دارد

That one that, in his vision, the beauty of the line (of beard) of the true the (true) Beloved hath;

محقق است که او حاصل بصر دارد

Certain it is that the acquisition of vision he hath

چو خامه در ره فرمان او سر طاعت

Like the reed, on the writing of His order, the head of obedience,

نهاده‌ایم مگر او به تیغ بردارد

We have placed. Perchance, with His sword, (our head from the body) uplifted He hath.

کسی به وصل تو چون شمع یافت پروانه

In union with Thee, like the candle found the order that one

که زیر تیغ تو هر دم سری دگر دارد

Who, beneath Thy sword, momently another head hath.

به پای بوس تو دست کسی رسید که او

Attained to foot-kissing, the hand of that one, who

چو آستانه بدین در همیشه سر دارد

Ever his head, like the threshold, on this door, hath.

ز زهد خشک ملولم کجاست باده ناب

I am vexed with dry austerity. Bring pure wine:

که بوی باده مدامم دماغ تر دارد

For, my brain ever fresh, wine's perfume keepeth.

ز باده هیچت اگر نیست این نه بس که تو را

If from wine, thine is no good quality, is not this enough that, thee,

دمی ز وسوسه عقل بی‌خبر دارد

A moment, without news of the temptation of reason, it (wine) keepeth?

کسی که از ره تقوا قدم برون ننهاد

That one, who planted not his foot outside the door of piety,

به عزم میکده اکنون ره سفر دارد

Now, (since all are engaged in wine – drinking) with the intention of visiting the wine-house, desire for travel, hath

دل شکسته حافظ به خاک خواهد برد

To the dust, (of the grave) Hafez's shattered heart will take with itself

چو لاله داغ هوایی که بر جگر دارد

The stain of desire (of love for the true Beloved) that. like the (streaked) tulip, on the liver, it hath.

غزل ۱۱۷ ⓄⒹⒺ ①①⑦

دل ما به دور رویت ز چمن فراغ دارد

At the time of (beholding) His face (which is better than the sward), retirement from the sward, our heart hath:

که چو سرو پایبند است و چو لاله داغ دارد

For, like the cypress, foot-binding it is; and like the (streaked) tulip, stain it hath.

سر ما فرونیاید به کمان ابروی کس

To the bow of any one's eye-brow, our head descendeth not;

که درون گوشه گیران ز جهان فراغ دارد

For, retirement from the world, the heart of corner-takers (lovers of God) hath.

ز بنفشه تاب دارم که ز زلف او زند دم

Torment on account of the (dark) violet, I have: because it boasteth of (equality with, or love for) His (dark) tress

تو سیاه کم بها بین که چه در دماغ دارد

Behold thou what (conceit) in the brain, the black slave (violet) of little value hath.

به چمن خرام و بنگر بر تخت گل که لاله

(O true Beloved) Saunter into the sward; and gaze at the rose's throne. For the tulip

به ندیم شاه ماند که به کف ایاغ دارد

Resembleth the King's servant, that, in the hand, a cup hath.

شب ظلمت و بیابان به کجا توان رسیدن

In the night of darkness (the world) and in the desert, (of its vicissitudes) where can one arrive,

مگر آن که شمع رویت به رهم چراغ دارد

Unless, in my path, the lamp, of (manifestations of glories) the (luminous) candle of His face hath?

من و شمع صبحگاهی سزد ار به هم بگرییم

I and the candle of the morning, 'tis fit if went together:

که بسوختیم و از ما بت ما فراغ دارد

For, (in love for the Beloved) we consumed; and (no solicitude for) us, our idol hath.

سزدم چو ابر بهمن که بر این چمن بگریم

Tis fit that, in this sward, I should weep like the (winter) cloud of January

طرب آشیان بلبل بنگر که زاغ دارد

The joy of the bulbul[1]'s nest, be hold the (filthy) crow hath.

1-Nightingale

سر درس عشق دارد دل دردمند حافظ
Desire for love's lesson, hath Hafez's sorrowful heart:

که نه خاطر تماشا نه هوای باغ دارد
For neither desire for the spectacle, nor desire for the garden, (the heart) hath

غزل ۱۱۸ 🔘🔘🔘 ODE 118 🔘🔘🔘

آن کس که به دست جام دارد
That one (the murshid) who, in his hand the cup (of divine knowledge) hath.

سلطانی جم مدام دارد
Ever the sovereignty of Jamshid[1] hath.

آبی که خضر حیات از او یافت
That water, wherein Khizr[2] obtained life

در میکده جو که جام دارد
Seek in the wine-house; for, (life) the cup hath.

سررشته جان به جام بگذار
Pass life's thread into the cup;

کاین رشته از او نظام دارد
Wherein, order, (of life) this thread hath.

ما و می و زاهدان و تقوا
(Together are) We and wine, and Zaheds[3] and piety,

تا یار سر کدام دارد
Let us see desire for whom the (true) Beloved hath.

بیرون ز لب تو ساقیا نیست
O Saki[4]! without thy tress, there is naught,

در دور کسی که کام دارد
In the time of that one, who desire hath.

نرگس همه شیوه‌های مستی
All the ways of intoxication, the narcissus,

از چشم خوشت به وام دارد
From thy pleasant eye, loaned hath.

ذکر رخ و زلف تو دلم را
The mention of thy face and tress, to my heart,

وردیست که صبح و شام دارد
Is a great pain that, morning and evening, it (the heart) hath.

بر سینه ریش دردمندان
On the wounded hearts of the sorrowful,

لعلت نمکی تمام دارد
Complete saltiness, (effective towards healing) thy lip hath.

در چاه ذقن چو حافظ ای جان
O Soul! in the pit of the chin, like Hafez,

حسن تو دو صد غلام دارد
Two hundred slaves, thy beauty hath

1-King   3-Pietist
2 -Name of a prophet   4-Tapster

غزل ۱۱۹   ODE 119

دلی که غیب نمای است و جام جم دارد
That heart that is the hidden-displayer; and that the cup of Jamshid[1] hath,

ز خاتمی که دمی گم شود چه غم دارد
For a seal ring, (of Sulaiman) that awhile became lost, what grief (is it that) it hath?

به خط و خال گدایان مده خزینه دل
To the beard or to the mole, of beggars (outward lovers, who, before the true Beloved, are like beggars) give not the heart's treasure:

به دست شاهوشی ده که محترم دارد
Give to the hand of a king-like one, who it precious hath (holdeth).

نه هر درخت تحمل کند جفای خزان
Not every tree endureth the violence of autumn:

غلام همت سروم که این قدم دارد
The slave of resolution of the cypress, I am, who this foot (of endurance) hath

رسید موسم آن کز طرب چو نرگس مست
Hath arrived that season, when from joy like the intoxicated narcissus,

نهد به پای قدح هر که شش درم دارد
He placeth (it) at the goblet's foot, (as price for wine) who six derhams hath.

زر از بهای می اکنون چو گل دریغ مدار
Now, like the rose hold not back gold for the price of wine:

که عقل کل به صدت عیب متهم دارد
For, suspicion of thee, by a hundred defects, absolute reason (Jibrail or the Light of prophecy) hath.

ز سر غیب کس آگاه نیست قصه مخوان
With the hidden mystery, none is acquainted: utter not the tale (of the forbidders of wine):

کدام محرم دل ره در این حرم دارد
The path into this sacred enclosure, what confidant (friend) of the heart hath.

دلم که لاف تجرد زدی کنون صد شغل
My heart that used to boast of solitude, now a hundred occupations,

به بوی زلف تو با باد صبحدم دارد
With the morning breeze. on account of the perfume of Thy tress hath.

مراد دل ز که پرسم که نیست دلداری
The heart's desire-of whom may I seek? Since there is no heart-possessor,

که جلوه نظر و شیوه کرم دارد
Who, splendor of sight, and habit of liberality, hath.

ز جیب خرقه حافظ چه طرف بتوان بست
From the pocket of Hafez's religious garment, what profit can one gain?

که صمد طلبیدیم و او صنم دارد.
For (from him) we seek the eternal; and (his own work with) a beloved he hath.

1-King

غزل ۱۲۰ ⓄⒹⒺ ①②⓪

بتی دارم که گرد گل ز سنبل سایه بان دارد
I have an idol that, the canopy of the hyacinth around the rose hath:

بهار عارضش خطی به خون ارغوان دارد
A line in the blood of the Arghavan[1], the spring of his cheek hath

غبار خط بپوشانید خورشید رخش یا رب
O Lord! the dust of the line (of the beard) covered the sun of his face:

بقای جاودانش ده که حسن جاودان دارد
Give him everlasting life, who everlasting beauty hath.

چو عاشق می‌شدم گفتم که بردم گوهر مقصود
When I became lover,(of God) I spake saying: "I have carried off the jewel of my desire (union with God)

ندانستم که این دریا چه موج خون فشان دارد
I knew not what (tumultuous), blood-scattering, waves, this sea (of unity) hath

ز چشمت جان نشاید برد کز هر سو که می‌بینم
From his eye, it is not fit to take the soul. For, from every direction, I see

کمین از گوشه‌ای کرده‌ست و تیر اندر کمان دارد
Of the corner, he hath made the ambush; and the arrow in the bow hath.

چو دام طره افشاند ز گرد خاطر عشاق
When from around lovers' heart, He loosed the snare of the tress,

به غماز صبا گوید که راز ما نهان دارد
To the informer of the wind, He speaketh saying: "Secret, our mystery, he hath."

بیفشان جرعه‌ای بر خاک و حال اهل دل بشنو
On the dust, scatter the draught; and behold the state of people of rank:

که از جمشید و کیخسرو فراوان داستان دارد
For, of Jamshid, of Kay Khosro[2], a thousand tales, it the (dust) hath.

چو در رویت بخندد گل مشو در دامش ای بلبل
O nightingale! when in thy face the rose laugheth, be not in her snare

که بر گل اعتمادی نیست گر حسن جهان دارد
For, on the rose, is no reliance, say, (even if) the world's beauty, it hath.

خدا را داد من بستان از او ای شحنه مجلس
O watchman of the assembly! for God's sake, take my justice from him (do me justice):

که می با دیگری خورده‌ست و با من سر گران دارد
For, with others, (he) hath drunk wine; and with me, a heavy head hath.

به فتراک ار همی‌بندی خدا را زود صیدم کن
If thou bind me to the saddle-strap, for God's sake, quickly make me prey:

که آفت‌هاست در تاخیر و طالب را زیان دارد
For, in delay are calamities; and the seeker's loss, it (delay) hath.

ز سروقد دلجویت مکن محروم چشمم را
Make not excluded my eye from the cypress of thy heart-seeking stature:

بدین سرچشمه‌اش بنشان که خوش آبی روان دارد
Plant in this its fountain-head; for pleasant running water, it hath.

1-Flower   2-King

ز خوف هجرم ایمن کن اگر امید آن داری

From the fear of separation, make me safe, if thou have hope of it,

که از چشم بداندیشان خدایت در امان دارد

Saying: "In safety from the eye of ill-thinkers, thee, God hath."

چه عذر بخت خود گویم که آن عیار شهرآشوب

To my own fortune, what excuse may I utter? For that knave, city-upsetting

به تلخی کشت حافظ را و شکر در دهان دارد

Slew Hafez with bitterness; and, in his mouth, sugar hath.

غزل ۱۲۱ ⓄⒹⒺ ①②①

هر آن کو خاطر مجموع و یار نازنین دارد

Everyone, who, his heart collected and the beloved acceptable hath,

سعادت همدم او گشت و دولت همنشین دارد

Happiness became his fellow-companion; and fortune, his fellow-sitter, he hath.

حریم عشق را درگه بسی بالاتر از عقل است

Much more lofty than reason is the court of the fold of love:

کسی آن آستان بوسد که جان در آستین دارد

That threshold, that one kisseth who, his life in his sleeve, hath.

دهان تنگ شیرینش مگر ملک سلیمان است

(O beloved) Thy small sweet mouth is perchance Soleiman's1 seal;

که نقش خاتم لعلش جهان زیر نگین دارد

For, the world beneath the seal-stone, the picture of the seal of its ruby (lip) hath.

لب لعل و خط مشکین چو آنش هست و اینش هست

The ruby lip and the musky hair, when His is that (the lip) and His is this, (the hair (

بنازم دلبر خود را که حسنش آن و این دارد

Of my Heart-ravisher, I boast; because this and that, His beauty hath.

به خواری منگر ای منعم ضعیفان و نحیفان را

O opulent one! with contempt, regard not the weak and the poor:

که صدر مجلس عشرت گدای رهنشین دارد

For, the chief seat of honor, the Fakir (poor), the road-sitter hath.

چو بر روی زمین باشی توانایی غنیمت دان

When thou art on the surface of the land (yet living) regard powerfulness plunder (take profit of it be not careless):

که دوران ناتوانی‌ها بسی زیر زمین دارد

For, beneath the surface of the land, (in the grave) many a non-powerful one Time hath.

بلاگردان جان و تن دعای مستمندان است

The turner (aside) of calamity from the soul and the body, is the prayer of the poor:

که بیند خیر از آن خرمن که ننگ از خوشه چین دارد

Who experienceth good, who, from that harvest, shame of the poor corn-gleaner hath?

صبا از عشق من رمزی بگو با آن شه خوبان

O breeze! utter a secret of my love to the sovereign of the lovely ones,

که صد جمشید و کیخسرو غلام کمترین دارد

Who, as the meanest slave, a hundred (mighty) Jamshids and Kay-Khosros2 hath.

1-Name of a prophet   2-Two Iranian kings

وگر گوید نمی‌خواهم چو حافظ عاشق مفلس

If he (the beloved) say: "A poor lover like Hafez I desire not:"

بگوییدش که سلطانی گدایی همنشین دارد

Speak ye to him, saying: "Imperial sway, the beggar, road-sitter hath."

غزل ۱۲۲ ⓄⒹⒺ ①②②

هر آن که جانب اهل خدا نگه دارد

(O true Beloved) everyone, who regardeth the people of fidelity (lovers of God)

خداش در همه حال از بلا نگه دارد

Him, in every state, from calamity God preserveth.

حدیث دوست نگویم مگر به حضرت دوست

Save in the Friend's presence, I utter not the tale of the Friend;

که آشنا سخن آشنا نگه دارد

For the speech of the friend, the friend preserveth.

دلا معاش چنان کن که گر بلغزد پای

O heart! so, live that, if thy foot slip in fault,

فرشته‌ات به دو دست دعا نگه دارد

With both hands in prayer, thee the angel may preserve.

گرت هواست که معشوق نگسلد پیمان

If desire be thine that the (true) Beloved should not (by severing asunder attachments to thee) break the covenant,

نگاه دار سر رشته تا نگه دارد

Keep (with respect) the end of the cord, so that (the covenant) He may preserve.

صبا بر آن سر زلف ار دل مرا بینی

O breeze! If thou see my heart on that tres ode tip,

ز روی لطف بگویش که جا نگه دارد

By way of kindness, speak to it; (the heart) that its own place it may preserve.

چو گفتمش که دلم را نگاه دار چه گفت

When I spake to him, saying: Preserve my heart how (well) he said

ز دست بنده چه خیزد خدا نگه دارد

What ariseth from the slave's hand, God preserveth

سر و زر و دل و جانم فدای آن یاری

My head, and gold, and heart, and soul a ransom for that true Beloved.

که حق صحبت مهر و وفا نگه دارد

Who the right of society of love and of fidelity preserveth.

غبار راه راهگذارت کجاست تا حافظ

Where is the dust of Thy path, that it Hafez

به یادگار نسیم صبا نگه دارد

In recollection of the work of the fragrant air of the wind, may preserve.

غزل ۱۲۳ ⓄⒹⒺ ①②③

مطرب عشق عجب ساز و نوایی دارد
Wonderful harmony and great melody, my minstrel of love hath:
نقش هر نغمه که زد راه به جایی دارد
Every picture of the hidden (divine knowledge) that he striketh, path to place hath.

عالم از ناله عشاق مبادا خالی
Void of the wailing of lovers, be not the world:
که خوش آهنگ و فرح بخش هوایی دارد
For a note, pleasant of melody and joy-giving, it hath.

پیر دردی کش ما گر چه ندارد زر و زور
Although neither gold, nor force, hath our Pir, dreg-drinking,
خوش عطابخش و خطاپوش خدایی دارد
Happily, a God sin-forgiving, error-covering, he hath.

محترم دار دلم کاین مگس قندپرست
(O true Beloved) Keep my heart great. For this sugar-worshipping fly, (the heart)
تا هواخواه تو شد فر همایی دارد
Since Thy desire it became, the pomp of the (auspicious) Huma hath.

از عدالت نبود دور گرش پرسد حال
Far from justice it is not, if of his state inquireth
پادشاهی که به همسایه گدایی دارد
That King, (the true Beloved) who, in his neighborhood, a beggar (me) hath

اشک خونین بنمودم به طبیبان گفتند
To the physicians, I showed my bloody tears. They said:
درد عشق است و جگرسوز دوایی دارد
'Tis love's pain; and the remedy, (for it) "the burning of the liver hath."

ستم از غمزه میاموز که در مذهب عشق
The tyranny of the glance, learn not. For, in love's order,
هر عمل اجری و هر کرده جزایی دارد
Every work, a reward; and every deed, a requital hath.

نغز گفت آن بت ترسابچه باده پرست
That idol of the young Christian, the wine-seller, well said:
شادی روی کسی خور که صفایی دارد
"Enjoy the joy of that person's face, that purity, hath."

خسروا حافظ درگاه نشین فاتحه خواند
O King! Hafez, a sitter of thy court, reciteth the fatiha;
و از زبان تو تمنای دعایی دارد
And, from thy tongue, the desire of a prayer halt.

غزل ۱۲۴ ⓄⒹⒺ ①②④

آن که از سنبل او غالیه تابی دارد
That one, from whose (fragrant) hyacinth lock, a great torment, (of jealousy) ambergris hath.
باز با دلشدگان ناز و عتابی دارد
Again, with those heart-gone, (lovers) grace and reproach hath.

از سر کشته خود می‌گذری همچون باد

By the head of his own slain one, (the lover) He (the Beloved) passeth (swiftly) like the wind

چه توان کرد که عمر است و شتابی دارد

What can one do? For, He is (like swift) life and swiftness (of departing) it (life) hath.

ماه خورشید نمایش ز پس پرده زلف

From behind the screen of His tress, the moon, displaying (the brilliancy of) the sun,

آفتابیست که در پیش سحابی دارد

Is a great sun that, in front, a cloud hath.

چشم من کرد به هر گوشه روان سیل سرشک

In every corner, my eye made flowing a torrent of tears,

تا سهی سرو تو را تازه‌تر آبی دارد

So that, with a great (quantity of) water, freshness, Thy straight cypress hath.

غمزه شوخ تو خونم به خطا می‌ریزد

In error, Thy bold glance sheddeth my blood;

فرصتش باد که خوش فکر صوابی دارد

Be its opportunity (to do so); for a very correct judgment it hath.

آب حیوان اگر این است که دارد لب دوست

If that be the water of life, that the lip of my Beloved hath,

روشن است این که خضر بهره سرابی دارد

Clear this is that (only) a share of the mirage, (not of the water of life) Khizr[1] hath.

چشم مخمور تو دارد ز دلم قصد جگر

On account of my heart, Thy intoxicated eye desireth my liver (life):

ترک مست است مگر میل کبابی دارد

The Bold one is intoxicated. Perchance, inclination for a piece of roast meat (my liver), He hath.

جان بیمار مرا نیست ز تو روی سال

The path of questioning Thee is not my sick soul's:

ای خوش آن خسته که از دوست جوابی دارد

Happy that shattered one (the lover) who, an answer from the Beloved, hath.

کی کند سوی دل خسته حافظ نظری

Towards Hafez's wounded heart, when a glance casteth

چشم مستش که به هر گوشه خرابی دارد

Thy intoxicated eye, that, in every corner, a ruined one (a lover) hath.

غزل ۱۲۵ ⓄⒹⒺ ①②⑤

شاهد آن نیست که مویی و میانی دارد

That one is not the beloved, who hath (only) a hair and a waist:

بنده طلعت آن باش که آنی دارد

Be the slave of the form of that one (Muhammad) who, ravishingness to the highest degree, hath.

شیوه حور و پری گر چه لطیف است ولی

Although the way of the angels is pleasant, yet

خوبی آن است و لطافت که فلانی دارد

That is loveliness and gracefulness that a certain one (my beloved) hath.

1-Name of a prophet

چشمه چشم مرا ای گل خندان دریاب

O laughing rose! (the beloved) discover the fountain of my eye,

که به امید تو خوش آب روانی دارد

That, in hope of thee, a torrent of sweet water hath.

گوی خوبی که برد از تو که خورشید آن جا

From thee, who taketh the ball of beauty, when (even) the (refulgent) sun here

نه سواریست که در دست عنانی دارد

Is not a horseman, that in his hand, a rein (of choice) hath?

دل نشان شد سخنم تا تو قبولش کردی

Heart-sitting (quieting) became my speech since thou acceptedest it:

آری آری سخن عشق نشانی دارد

Yes, yes; an impression, love's speech hath

خم ابروی تو در صنعت تیراندازی

In the craft of arrow-casting, (archery) the curve of thy eye-brow (is so impetuous that)

برده از دست هر آن کس که کمانی دارد

It taketh (a bow) from everyone who, a bow hath

در ره عشق نشد کس به یقین محرم راز

In love's path, none with certainty became the confidant of the mystery:

هر کسی بر حسب فکر گمانی دارد

According to his understanding, everyone an idea hath.

با خرابات نشینان ز کرامات ملاف

With the tavern-haunters, boast not of generosity:

هر سخن وقتی و هر نکته مکانی دارد

Every word, a time; every subtlety, a place hath.

مرغ زیرک نزند در چمنش پرده سرای

The wise bird (the lover, sincere in love's claim) goeth not, song-singing, in its sward of beauty,

هر بهاری که به دنباله خزانی دارد

Every spring (beloved) in whose rear, an autumn (of effacement) hath.

مدعی گو لغز و نکته به حافظ مفروش

To the claimant, say: "To Hafez, boast not thy jest and subtlety:"

کلک ما نیز زبانی و بیانی دارد

A tongue and an explanation our reed also hath.

غزل ۱۲۶   ⓄⒹⒺ ①②⑥

جان بی جمال جانان میل جهان ندارد

Without the (true) Beloved's beauty, inclination for the world, my soul hath not:

هر کس که این ندارد حقا که آن ندارد

O God, (I swear) everyone who this (the Beloved's beauty) hath not, that (the soul) hath not.

با هیچ کس نشانی زان دلستان ندیدم

A trace of that Heart-Ravisher, with none, I beheld:

یا من خبر ندارم یا او نشان ندارد

No news of him, have I: He, a trace hath not.

هر شبنمی در این ره صد بحر آتشین است

In this path of love, every drop of night dew (sin) is a hundred fiery waves:

دردا که این معما شرح و بیان ندارد

Alas! explanation, or revelation, this subtlety (of love) hath not.

سرمنزل فراغت نتوان ز دست دادن

From the hand, one cannot give the stage of contentment.

ای ساروان فروکش کاین ره کران ندارد

O camel-driver! (of the East) lower, (the chattels of thy existence and stay) for this path (of the desert of avarice) limit hath not.

چنگ خمیده قامت می‌خواندت به عشرت

The harp, bent of form, calleth thee to joy:

بشنو که پند پیران هیچت زیان ندارد

Hearken: for any injury to thee, the counsel of old men hath not.

ای دل طریق رندی از محتسب بیاموز

O heart, from the Mohtaseb[1], learn profligacy

مست است و در حق او کس این گمان ندارد

Intoxicated , he is ; yet of him this suspicion (of intoxication) any one hath not .

احوال گنج قارون کایام داد بر باد

The circumstances of the treasure of Qarun[2] which, to the wind of destruction Time gave.

در گوش دل فروخوان تا زر نهان ندارد

Utter ye to (the rose-bud the miser) so that its gold, hidden, it have not

گر خود رقیب شمع است اسرار از او بپوشان

If the companion himself be the candle, from him conceal mysteries:

کان شوخ سربریده بند زبان ندارد

For that bold one, head severed, ligature (bridle) on his tongue, hath not.

کس در جهان ندارد یک بنده همچو حافظ

A slave like Hafiz, anyone in the world hath not.

زیرا که چون تو شاهی کس در جهان ندارد

For, a king like thee, anyone in the world hath not

غزل ۱۲۷ ⓄⒹⒺ ①②⑦

روشنی طلعت تو ماه ندارد

The luminosity of Thy face, the (resplendent) moon halt not:

پیش تو گل رونق گیاه ندارد

In comparison with Thee, the glory of (common) grass, the (splendid) rose hath not.

گوشه ابروی توست منزل جانم

The corner of Thy eye-brow is my soul's dwelling:

خوشتر از این گوشه پادشاه ندارد

More happy than this corner, the king hath not

تا چه کند با رخ تو دود دل من

With Thy (mirror – like) face, my heart's smoke-let us see-what it will do:

آینه دانی که تاب آه ندارد

Thou knowest-the mirror that power of (resisting) the (blight of the) sigh, it hath not.

1-Sheriff   2-Korah, The rich man of the time of Prophet Moses

شوخی نرگس نگر که پیش تو بشکفت
Behold the boldness of the narcissus, that blossometh before thee

چشم دریده ادب نگاه ندارد
Manners, one rent of eye (shameless) hath not.

دیدم و آن چشم دل سیه که تو داری
O beloved I have seen that eye of black heart that Thou hast,

جانب هیچ آشنا نگاه ندارد
A glance towards any friend, it hath not.

رطل گرانم ده ای مرید خرابات
O disciple of the tavern give me the heavy rotl[1]

شادی شیخی که خانقاه ندارد
The joy of a shaikh, that the cloister hath not.

خون خور و خامش نشین که آن دل نازک
Devour thy blood and sit silent. For that tender heart (of my beloved)

طاقت فریاد دادخواه ندارد
The power of (remedying) the complaint of the justice-seeker, hath (not).

گو برو و آستین به خون جگر شوی
Say: "Go; and wash thy sleeve in liver-blood:

هر که در این آستانه راه ندارد
Whoever, a path, in this threshold, of (the tavern) hath not."

نی من تنها کشم تطاول زلفت
Not I alone, drew the length of Thy tress:

کیست که او داغ آن سیاه ندارد
Who is there, who, the stain of this black tress, hath not.

حافظ اگر سجده تو کرد مکن عیب
If Hafez worshipped Thee, censure not: O idol

کافر عشق ای صنم گناه ندارد
The infidel to love, crime hath not.

غزل ۱۲۸ ⓞⓓⓔ ①②⑧

نیست در شهر نگاری که دل ما ببرد
In this city is no idol that, our heart, taketh:

بختم ار یار شود رختم از این جا ببرد
If fortune be my friend, hence my chattels, it (fortune) taketh.

کو حریفی کش سرمست که پیش کرمش
Where is a companion, disdainful and intoxicated, before whose generosity,

عاشق سوخته دل نام تمنا ببرد
The mention of his desire, the heart-consumed lover taketh?

باغبانا ز خزان بی خبرت می بینم
O gardener! (outward worshipper) careless of the autumn, (the resurrection, day) I behold thee:

آه از آن روز که بادت گل رعنا ببرد
Alas! that day when thy beautiful rose (of desire) the wind of death taketh.

1-Pound, large cup or goblet

رهزن دهر نخفتهست مشو ایمن از او

Time's highwayman (Shaitan) hath not slept. Of him, be not secure,

اگر امروز نبردهست که فردا ببرد

If thee, he hath not taken today. For, to-morrow, thee he taketh.

در خیال این همه لعبت به هوس میبازم

In fancy, I play all this idol (verse) in this desire,

بو که صاحب نظری نام تماشا ببرد

Possibly, the mention of the spectacle (of verse) a master of vision taketh.

علم و فضلی که به چل سال دلم جمع آورد

The science and the eloquence that, in forty years, my heart acquired;

ترسم آن نرگس مستانه به یغما ببرد

I fear that, as plunder, that intoxicated narcissus (the sorcery of the beloved's eye) taketh.

بانگ گاوی چه صدا بازدهد عشوه مخر

With miracle, sorcery maketh not equality. Safe be:

سامری کیست که دست از ید بیضا ببرد

Who is Samiri[1] that, from the white hand (of Musa) superiority he taketh

جام مینایی می سد ره تنگ دلیست

The obstacle of the heart-straitened one's path is the crystal-glass of wine:

منه از دست که سیل غمت از جا ببرد

From thy hand, put it not, lest from thy place, thee griefs torrent take.

راه عشق ار چه کمینگاه کمانداران است

Although Love's path is the ambush-place of bowmen,

هر که دانسته رود صرفه ز اعدا ببرد

Knowing, whoever goeth, profit from enemies taketh.

حافظ ار جان طلبد غمزه مستانه یار

Hafez! if the beloved's intoxicated eye seeks thy life,

خانه از غیر بپرداز و بهل تا ببرد

Clear out the house (of the heart) of life and let it go, so that (it thy life) it *the beloved's eye) may take.

غزل ۱۲۹ ⓄⒹⒺ ①②⑨

اگر نه باده غم دل ز یاد ما ببرد

If, the heart's grief from our memory, the cup (of love for God) do not take

نهیب حادثه بنیاد ما ز جا ببرد

The foundation of our work, the anxiety of the vicissitudes (of time) will take.

اگر نه عقل به مستی فروکشد لنگر

And if, in its intoxication, reason drag not its anchor,

چگونه کشتی از این ورطه بلا ببرد

From this whirlpool of calamity, (the world) the bark how will it take.

فغان که با همه کس غایبانه باخت فلک

Alas! with everyone the sky treacherously played:

که کس نبود که دستی از این دغا ببرد

Superiority over this treachery, is none who will take.

1-A person who made a calf in the absence of Prophet Moses
and encouraged the Hebrews to worship it

گذار بر ظلمات است خضر راهی کو

The path is by the darkness: (the land of darkness) where is the Khizr[1] of the road?

مباد کتش محرومی آب ما ببرد

Let it not be that, our honor, the fire of disappointment should take.

دل ضعیفم از آن می‌کشد به طرف چمن

Towards the sward, the feeble heart draweth me for the reason,

که جان ز مرگ به بیماری صبا ببرد

That, by the sickness of the morning breeze, my soul from death it may take.

طبیب عشق منم باده ده که این معجون

I am love's physician. Drink wine. (of love for God) For this confection,

فراغت آرد و اندیشه خطا ببرد

Bringeth relief, and the thought of danger taketh.

بسوخت حافظ و کس حال او به یار نگفت

Hafez consumed; and, to the Friend none told his state;

مگر نسیم پیامی خدای را ببرد

perchance, for God's sake, a message, the morning breeze will take.

غزل ۱۳۰ ⓞⒹⒺ ①③⓪

سحر بلبل حکایت با صبا کرد

In the morning, the nightingale (Hafiz) told a tale to the east wind, (the Murshid)

که عشق روی گل با ما چه‌ها کرد

Saying: (O wind thou sawest) for us what (calamities) love for the face of the rose (the true Beloved) made.

از آن رنگ رخم خون در دل افتاد

For that colour of face, He (God) cast into my heart the blood (of grief)

و از آن گلشن به خارم مبتلا کرد

And from this rose-bed (eternity without beginning) entangled in the thorn (of the world with a thousand afflictions) me made.

غلام همت آن نازنینم

I am the slave of resolution of that graceful one, (the true Beloved)

که کار خیر بی روی و ریا کرد

Who, without dissimulation and hypocrisy, the work of liberality made.

من از بیگانگان دیگر ننالم

Of strangers, ever I bewail not;

که با من هر چه کرد آن آشنا کرد

For whatever He made that Friend (God) made.

گر از سلطان طمع کردم خطا بود

If of the Soltan[2], I formed expectation, a fault it was:

ور از دلبر وفا جستم جفا کرد

If of the Heart-Ravisher, I sought fidelity, tyranny He made

1-Name of a prophet   2-King

خوشش باد آن نسیم صبحگاهی
Be that breeze of the morning pleasant to Him

که درد شب نشینان را دوا کرد
who, the remedy for the grief of the night's sitters (watchers) made.

نقاب گل کشید و زلف سنبل
If (the breeze) drew aside the veil of the rose (the true Beloved) and the tress of the hyacinth (glories of manifestations)

گره بند قبای غنچه وا کرد
The knot of the coat of the rose-bud (the patient traveller's heart) loose it made.

به هر سو بلبل عاشق در افغان
In every direction the lover nightingale (the skilled holy traveller or the abstinent Zahid) in lament:

تنعم از میان باد صبا کرد
In the midst, joy, (of union with the true Beloved) the morning breeze (the eternal lover and fearless profligate) made.

بشارت بر به کوی می فروشان
To the Street of the wine-sellers, the glad tidings take

که حافظ توبه از زهد ریا کرد
That repentance of austerity (and of) hypocrisy, Hafez hath made.

وفا از خواجگان شهر با من
On the part of the respected ones of the city, fidelity to me,

کمال دولت و دین بوالوفا کرد
The perfection of faith and of fortune, the Father of Fidelity made.

غزل ۱۳۱ ⓄⒹⒺ ①③①

بیا که ترک فلک خوان روزه غارت کرد
Come; for plunder of the tray of fasting, the Turk of the sky (Mars) hath made:

هلال عید به دور قدح اشارت کرد
Hint at the circulation of the cup, the new crescent moon hath made.

ثواب روزه و حج قبول آن کس برد
The reward of fasting and the pilgrimage of acceptance, took that one

که خاک میکده عشق را زیارت کرد
Who, to the dust of the wine-house of love, pilgrimage made.

مقام اصلی ما گوشه خرابات است
Our true dwelling is the corner of the tavern:

خداش خیر دهاد آن که این عمارت کرد
God give good to him, who this edifice made.

بهای باده چون لعل چیست جوهر عقل
What is the price of wine (of love) like the ruby? (It is) the jewel of reason:

بیا که سود کسی برد کاین تجارت کرد
Come; for profit took that one who, this barter made.

نماز در خم آن ابروان محرابی
In the curve of those eye-brows of prayer-arch fashion, prayer

کسی کند که به خون جگر طهارت کرد
That one maketh, who, in blood-water, pure (his heart) made.

فغان که نرگس جماش شیخ شهر امروز

Alas! to-day, the bold eye of the city Sheikh[1],

نظر به دردکشان از سر حقارت کرد

At the dreg-drinkers, glance with utter contempt, made.

به روی یار نظر کن ز دیده منت دار

Look at the lover's face and beg your eyes,

که کار دیده نظر از سر بصارت کرد

Because eyes can see deep through the view, made.

حدیث عشق ز حافظ شنو نه از واعظ

Hear love's tale from Hafez not from the admonisher, (against love)

اگر چه صنعت بسیار در عبارت کرد

Although, in example, much art he made

غزل ۱۳۲   ⓞⒹⒺ ⑴⑶⑵

به آب روشن می عارف طهارت کرد

(On the day of eternity without beginning) with the luminous liquid of wine, (of love and of divine knowledge) an Aref[2] purification (of his heart from every pollution) made,

علی الصباح که میخانه را زیارت کرد

Early in the morning when, to the wine-house, visit he made.

همین که ساغر زرین خور نهان گردید

As soon as the golden cup of the sun became hidden,

هلال عید به دور قدح اشارت کرد

Hint at the circulation of the cup, the new crescent moon of the Eid (the manifestations of the glories of existence) made

خوشا نماز و نیاز کسی که از سر درد

Be blessed prayers of the one who feels the pain,

به آب دیده و خون جگر طهارت کرد

And the one who with tears and heart's blood, purification made.

امام خواجه که بودش سر نماز دراز

The Imam, a khwajeh[3], whose desire was long prayers,

به خون دختر رز خرقه را قصارت کرد

In the blood of the daughter of the grape, (wine) cleansing of the religious garment mad

دلم ز حلقه زلفش به جان خرید آشوب

With soul, from the curl of His tress, my heart purchased tumult:

چه سود دید ندانم که این تجارت کرد

I know not what profit experienced he who this barter made.

اگر امام جماعت طلب کند امروز

If the Imam of the prayers sends for me today,

خبر دهید که حافظ به می طهارت کرد

Tell him that Hafez with wine today, purification made.

1-A leader in a Muslim community
2-Mystic

3-Eunuch, dignitary

غزل ۱۳۳ ⓄⒹⒺ ①③③

صوفی نهاد دام و سر حقه باز کرد

The Sufi[1] (outward worshipper and hypocrite) laid the snare; (of deceit) and open,
the cover of his box, of (sorcery) made.

بنیاد مکر با فلک حقه باز کرد

With (against) the sky sorcery-playing, the structure of deceit, he made.

بازی چرخ بشکندش بیضه در کلاه

The sport of the sphere shattereth the egg in his cap (and dishonoureth him):

زیرا که عرض شعبده با اهل راز کرد

Because, with (against) one of mystery, the presentments of sorcery, he made.

ساقی بیا که شاهد رعنای صوفیان

Saki! come. For the handsome friend of the Sufis[2]

دیگر به جلوه آمد و آغاز ناز کرد

Again, gracefully, came; and the beginning of blandishment made.

این مطرب از کجاست که ساز عراق ساخت

Whence is this minstrel who made the melody of Iraq;

و آهنگ بازگشت به راه حجاز کرد

And the resolution of turning back from the path of Hejaz[3] made?

ای دل بیا که ما به پناه خدا رویم

O heart! come; let us go to the shelter of God,

زان چه آستین کوته و دست دراز کرد

From whatever, the one, (Sufi) short of sleeve, long of hand, made.

صنعت مکن که هر که محبت نه راست باخت

Do no trick. (of deceit) For, whoever, truly played not love,

عشقش به روی دل در معنی فراز کرد

Open, on the face of (his) heart, the door of reality, (trouble love) made.

فردا که پیشگاه حقیقت شود پدید

Tomorrow, when the vestibule of truth (the judgment day) becometh revealed,

شرمنده ره روی که عمل بر مجاز کرد

Ashamed (will be) the way-farer, (of this world) who, illusory work (in desire and lust) made.

ای کبک خوش خرام کجا می‌روی بایست

O partridge, pleasant strutter! where goest thou? Stand!

غره مشو که گربه زاهد نماز کرد

Be not proud, that prayer (purification for evilness) the Abid's cat (imperious lust) made.

حافظ مکن ملامت رندان که در ازل

Hafez! reproach not profligates. For, in eternity without beginning,

ما را خدا ز زهد ریا بی‌نیاز کرد

Me, independent of austerity (and) of hypocrisy, God made.

1-A Muslim ascetic and mystic

2-A Muslim ascetic and mystic

3-A land in western Saudi Arabia

غزل ۱۳۴ ⓄⒹⒺ ①③④

بلبلی خون دلی خورد و گلی حاصل کرد

A nightingale (Hafiz) drank the blood of the liver, (in grief) and gained a rose (a son):

باد غیرت به صدش خار پریشان دل کرد

With a hundred thorns, perturbed his heart, the wind of, envy made.

طوطی ای را به خیال شکری دل خوش بود

In the desire of a piece of sugar, (a son) glad was the heart of the parrot (Hafiz);

ناگهش سیل فنا نقش امل باطل کرد

Suddenly, vain the picture of hope, (the son) decay's torrent made.

قره العین من آن میوه دل یادش باد

(Ever) be his memory my eye's cool luster, that fruit of my heart!

که چه آسان بشد و کار مرا مشکل کرد

That easy went; (in death) and hard my work of life made.

ساروان بار من افتاد خدا را مددی

O camel-driver; (perfect Murshid) my load (of grief) hath fallen. For God's sake, a little help!

که امید کرمم همره این محمل کرد

For me, fellow-traveler with this litter, (the holy traveller) hope of (thy) kindness made.

روی خاکی و نم چشم مرا خوار مدار

Hold not contemptible my dusty face and watery (weeping) eye:

چرخ فیروزه طربخانه از این کهگل کرد

Of this straw mixed clay, our hall of joy, the azure sphere hath made.

آه و فریاد که از چشم حسود مه چرخ

Sigh and lamentation that, through the envious eye of the sphere's moon,

در لحد ماه کمان ابروی من منزل کرد

His dwelling in the niche of the tomb, the moon of bow-like eye-brow (the son) hath made.

نزدی شاه رخ و فوت شد امکان حافظ

Hafez! Shah-rokh[1], (castle) thou didst not; and the time of opportunity hath departed.

چه کنم بازی ایام مرا غافل کرد

What shall I do? Me careless, Time's sport hath made.

⟨◉⟩⟨◉⟩

غزل ۱۳۵ ⓄⒹⒺ ①③⑤

چو باد عزم سر کوی یار خواهم کرد

Like the (swift) wind, resolution of (going to) the head of the (true) Beloved's street, I will make:

نفس به بوی خوشش مشکبار خواهم کرد

By His pleasant perfume, my own breath, musk-raining, I will make.

به هرزه بی می و معشوق عمر می‌گذرد

In folly, without wine and the (true) Beloved, my life passeth:

بطالتم بس از امروز کار خواهم کرد

Idleness, mine. After today, work (in love for Him) I will make.

1-Motion in the game of chess (castle)

هر آبروی که اندوختم ز دانش و دین

Every (drop of) water of His face that, by knowledge and faith, I collected,

نثار خاک ره آن نگار خواهم کرد

The scattering of (on) the dust of the path of that idol, (God) I will make.

چو شمع صبحدمم شد ز مهر او روشن

Like the (wasting) candle of the morning through love for the true Beloved, it became evident to me,

که عمر در سر این کار و بار خواهم کرد

That, in desire of this matter, (of His love) my life, I shall make.

به یاد چشم تو خود را خراب خواهم ساخت

In memory of Thy eye, myself ruined I will make:

بنای عهد قدیم استوار خواهم کرد

The foundation of the ancient covenant, strong I will make.

صبا کجاست که این جان خون گرفته چو گل

Where is the breeze? (the angel of death) for this life, blood gathered, like the (ruddy, opening) rose,

فدای نکهت گیسوی یار خواهم کرد

A sacrifice for the perfume of the (true) Beloved's tress, I will make.

نفاق و زرق نبخشد صفای دل حافظ

Hafez! hypocrisy and dissimulation give not purity of heart:

طریق رندی و عشق اختیار خواهم کرد

Choice of the path of profligacy and of love, I will make.

غزل ۱۳۶   ⓞⒹⒺ ①③⑥

دست در حلقه آن زلف دوتا نتوان کرد

Into the curve of that doubled tress, the hand one cannot put:

تکیه بر عهد تو و باد صبا نتوان کرد

(O true Beloved) Reliance on Thy covenant and the morning breeze, one cannot make.

آن چه سعی است من اندر طلبت بنمایم

Whatever is (due to) effort, I do in search of Thee:

این قدر هست که تغییر قضا نتوان کرد

This is the extent that alteration of Fate, one cannot make.

دامن دوست به صد خون دل افتاد به دست

With a hundred (draughts) of the heart's blood the (true) Beloved's skirt fell to my hand:

به فسوسی که کند خصم رها نتوان کرد

For the great reproach that the enemy maketh, release (of the true Beloved's skirt) one cannot make.

عارضش را به مثل ماه فلک نتوان گفت

One cannot call His (the true Beloved's) cheek-for instance the moon of the sky:

نسبت دوست به هر بی سر و پا نتوان کرد

Likening of the (true) Beloved to every headless and footless one-one cannot make.

سروبالای من آن گه که درآید به سماع

That moment when my lofty cypress (the true Beloved) cometh into the (assembly of) Sama[1]

چه محل جامه جان را که قبا نتوان کرد

What place is it where the soul's garment, rent one cannot make?

1-Dance

نظر پاک تواند رخ جانان دیدن

Only one of pure vision can behold the (true) Beloved's face:

که در آیینه نظر جز به صفا نتوان کرد

For save with purity in the mirror, glance one cannot make.

مشکل عشق نه در حوصله دانش ماست

The difficulty of love is not in (according to) the capacity of our knowledge:

حل این نکته بدین فکر خطا نتوان کرد

With this thought, the loosening of this subtlety, (of love) mistake one cannot make.

غیرتم کشت که محبوب جهانی لیکن

Jealousy became mine that Thou art the Beloved of the world. But (what can I do)

روز و شب عربده با خلق خدا نتوان کرد

Day and night, conflict with the creatures of God, one cannot make.

من چه گویم که تو را نازکی طبع لطیف

What shall I say? For delicacy of gentle disposition, thine

تا به حدیست که آهسته دعا نتوان کرد

Is to such a degree that, slowly, a prayer one cannot make.

بجز ابروی تو محراب دل حافظ نیست

Save Thy eye-brow, naught is the prayer-arch of Hafez's heart:

طاعت غیر تو در مذهب ما نتوان کرد

In our religious order, save to Thee, devotion one cannot make.

غزل ۱۳۷ ⓞⒹⒺ ①③⑦

دل از من برد و روی از من نهان کرد

My heart from me, He took; concealed from me, His face, Lie made:

خدا را با که این بازی توان کرد

For God's sake! With whom can this sport be made?

شب تنهاییم در قصد جان بود

The night of solitariness was in design upon my soul:

خیالش لطف‌های بی‌کران کرد

Endless favors, (upon my soul so that I remained alive) the thought of Him made.

چرا چون لاله خونین دل نباشم

Like the variegated tulip, why am I not bloody of heart,

که با ما نرگس او سرگران کرد

Since with me, the heavy head, His eye made

که را گویم که با این درد جان سوز

With this soul-consuming pain, how may I speak, saying:

طبیبم قصد جان ناتوان کرد

Design upon my powerless soul, the Physician (God) made

بدان سان سوخت چون شمعم که بر من

As a candle (consumeth itself) He (the true Beloved) consumed me in such a way that, on me,

صراحی گریه و بربط فغان کرد

The flagon, weeping; and the stringed instrument, clamour made.

صبا گر چاره داری وقت وقت است

O wind! if thou have the remedy, this (very) time is the time (of remedy):

که درد اشتیاقم قصد جان کرد

For, design upon my soul, the pain of desire made.

میان مهربانان کی توان گفت

Among kind ones, how can one speak,

که یار ما چنین گفت و چنان کرد

Saying: "Like this my (true) Beloved spake; like that (arrangement) made."

عدو با جان حافظ آن نکردی

Against the life of Hafez, the enemy would not have made that (ill – doing)

که تیر چشم آن ابروکمان کرد

That the arrow of the eye of that eye-brow bow made.

غزل ۱۳۸ ⓄⒹⒺ ①③⑧

یاد باد آن که ز ما وقت سفر یاد نکرد

Memory be of that one, who, at the time of journeying memory of us made not:

به وداعی دل غمدیده ما شاد نکرد

Who, by farewell, joyous our grief-stricken heart made not.

آن جوان بخت که می‌زد رقم خیر و قبول

That one of youthful fortune, that dashed the writing of good acceptance,

بنده پیر ندانم ز چه آزاد نکرد

I know not why the old slave, free he made not.

کاغذین جامه به خوناب بشویم که فلک

The papery garment, we wash in bloody water. For, the sky,

رهنمونیم به پای علم داد نکرد

My guidance to the standard of justice, made not.

دل به امید صدایی که مگر در تو رسد

In the hope that perchance a great cry may reach Thee, the heart

ناله‌ها کرد در این کوه که فرهاد نکرد

Made in this (desert) mountain, cries that Farhad[1] made not.

سایه تا بازگرفتی ز چمن مرغ سحر

Since the bird of the sward had taken its shadow from the sward,

آشیان در شکن طره شمشاد نکرد

Its nest in the curl of the tress of the box-tree, it made not.

شاید ار پیک صبا از تو بیاموزد کار

If from Thee, the footman of the east wind will learn work (it is) possible:

زان که چالاکتر از این حرکت باد نکرد

For movement, swifter than this, the wind made not.

کلک مشاطه صنعش نکشد نقش مراد

The reed of the attirer of nature draweth not the picture of desire of him

هر که اقرار بدین حسن خداداد نکرد

Who as to this beauty, God-given, confession made not

1-Farhad and his lover (Shirin) in a romantic poem

مطربا پرده بگردان و بزن راه عراق
O Minstrel! change the note, and strike the path, of Iraq;

که بدین راه بشد یار و ز ما یاد نکرد
For, in this path, the (true) Beloved went; and of us recollection made not.

غزل یات عراقیست سرود حافظ
The ghazals[1] of Iraq are the songs of Hafez:

که شنید این ره دلسوز که فریاد نکرد
This heart-consuming path, who heard, who lamentation made not

غزل ۱۳۹ ⓞⓓⓔ ①③⑨

رو بر رهش نهادم و بر من گذر نکرد
On her (the beloved's) path, I laid my face; and by me passing, she made not.

صد لطف چشم داشتم و یک نظر نکرد
I hoped for a hundred kindnesses; yet one glance, (of kindness) she made not.

سیل سرشک ما ز دلش کین به درنبرد
Malice from her heart, the torrent of our tears, took not.

در سنگ خاره قطره باران اثر نکرد
Impression on the hard stone, the rain-drop made not

یا رب تو آن جوان دلاور نگاه دار
O Lord! Preserve (from the calamity of time) that young saucy one (the beloved):

کز تیر آه گوشه نشینان حذر نکرد
For caution, against the arrow of the sigh of those sitting in the corner, (of retirement) she made not.

ماهی و مرغ دوش ز افغان من نخفت
Last night, from my lamenting, neither fish nor fowl slept

وان شوخ دیده بین که سر از خواب برنکرد
But behold that one of saucy eye (the beloved) who, raised from sleep, her head made not

می‌خواستم که میرمش اندر قدم چو شمع
Like the (wasting) candle, I desired to die at her feet

او خود گذر به ما چو نسیم سحر نکرد
Like the morning breeze, passing by us, she made not

جانا کدام سنگ‌دل بی‌کفایتیست
O soul! without sufficiency, stone of heart, is what person,

کو پیش زخم تیغ تو جان را سپر نکرد
Who, the shield before the wound of thy arrow, himself made not.

کلک زبان بریده حافظ در انجمن
O saucy one! behold the bird of my heart, wing and feather consumed:

با کس نگفت راز تو تا ترک سر نکرد
Yet go out of my head the crude madness of being a lover, it made not.

1-Sonnet

غزل ۱۴۰ ⓄⒹⒺ ①④⓪

دلبر برفت و دلشدگان را خبر نکرد

The Heart-Ravisher (God) departed; and hint (thereof) to those heart-gone (the lovers) made not:

یاد حریف شهر و رفیق سفر نکرد

Of the companion of the city; and of the friend of the journey, recollection He made not

یا بخت من طریق مروت فروگذاشت

Either, my fortune abandoned the path of love;

یا او به شاهراه طریقت گذر نکرد

Or He, (the Heart – Ravisher) by the highway of Tarikat[1], journeying made not.

گفتم مگر به گریه دلش مهربان کنم

I said: "Perchance, by weeping, I may make His heart kind."

چون سخت بود در دل سنگش اثر نکرد

Impression on the hard stone, (true Beloved's heart) the drops of rain, my tears made not.

شوخی مکن که مرغ دل بیقرار من

Although, through grief, the wing and the feather of my heart became broken,

سودای دام عاشقی از سر به در نکرد

Go out of my head, the crude madness of being a lover it made not.

هر کس که دید روی تو بوسید چشم من

(O true Beloved) everyone kissed Thy face who saw my weeping eye!

کاری که کرد دیده من بی نظر نکرد

Without value, the work that our (weeping) eye did, it made not.

من ایستاده تا کنمش جان فدا چو شمع

I standing, like the candle, to make my life a sacrifice for Him:

او خود گذر به ما چو نسیم سحر نکرد

Like the morning-breeze, passing by me, He made not.

غزل ۱۴۱ ⓄⒹⒺ ①④①

دیدی ای دل که غم عشق دگربار چه کرد

O heart! the grief of love, again, thou sawest what it did,

چون بشد دلبر و با یار وفادار چه کرد

When the heart-ravisher went; and with the beloved, fidelity-observing, what it did.

آه از آن نرگس جادو که چه بازی انگیخت

Alas! what play, (and calamities) that narcissus, the sorcerer, excited:

آه از آن مست که با مردم هشیار چه کرد

Alas! with men of sense (in making them senseless) that intoxicated, eye what it did.

اشک من رنگ شفق یافت ز بیمهری یار

From the mercilessness of the beloved, my tears gained the colour of (ruddy) twilight:

طالع بیشفقت بین که در این کار چه کرد

In this work, (of love) behold my compassionless fortune what it did.

1-Principle, Sufism, religious way

برق از منزل لیلی بدرخشید سحر

In the morning from Leyla's dwelling, lightning flashed;

وه که با خرمن مجنون دل افگار چه کرد

Alas! with the harvest (of existence) of Majnun, heart-rent what it did.

ساقیا جام می‌ام ده که نگارنده غیب

O Saki! (Murshid) give me a cup of wine. (that I may drink of divine knowledge; and, in His love, make myself non-existent). For the hidden writer (God)

نیست معلوم که در پرده اسرار چه کرد

None knoweth in the revolution of the compass, what He did.

آن که پرنقش زد این دایره مینایی

That one (God) who expressed this azure vault (the sky) on the picture

کس ندانست که در گردش پرگار چه کرد

In the screen of mysteries, evident it is not what He did.

فکر عشق آتش غم در دل حافظ زد و سوخت

Into Hafez's heart, the thought of love struck the fire of grief; and consumed it;

یار دیرینه ببینید که با یار چه کرد

With the lover, behold ye the ancient Friend (God) what He did.

غزل ۱۴۲   ⓄⒹⒺ ①④②

دوستان دختر رز توبه ز مستوری کرد

Friends! repentance of veiledness, the daughter of the vine love made:

شد سوی محتسب و کار به دستوری کرد

To the Mohtaseb reason, love's forbidder she[1] she went; and by God's permission the work of loosening the knot from the feet of holy travellers made.

آمد از پرده به مجلس عرقش پاک کنید

From out of the veil to the public assembly she love came. Make ye yourselves pure of sweat of the toil of separation from her,

تا نگویند حریفان که چرا دوری کرد

So that to the companions, the accursed envious ones, full of fraud ye may speak saying: "Wherefore is it that farness from us she made?"

مژدگانی بده ای دل که دگر مطرب عشق

O heart! give the glad tidings that, again, love's minstrel

راه مستانه زد و چاره مخموری کرد

Expressed the intoxicated path of song, and the remedy of the intoxicated made.

نه به هفت آب که رنگش به صد آتش نرود

Not with seven waters, nay not with a hundred fires, goeth its color,

آن چه با خرقه زاهد می انگوری کرد

Which, upon the Sufi's[2] dress, the wine of the grape made.

غنچه گلبن وصلم ز نسیمش بشکفت

From the clay of my nature and the breeze of the beloved, the blossom blossomed:

مرغ خوشخوان طرب از برگ گل سوری کرد

From the leaf of the beautiful, red, odoriferous rose, joy, the night singing bird the Bulbul made.

1-Sheriff   2-A Muslim ascetic and mystic

حافظ افتادگی از دست مده زان که حسود

Hafez! From the hand surrender not humbleness. For the reason that the envious one,

عرض و مال و دل و دین در سر مغروری کرد

In the desire way of pride, reputation, and wealth, and heart, and faith made.

غزل ۱۴۳ ⓄⒹⒺ ①④③

سال‌ها دل طلب جام جم از ما می‌کرد

Search for the cup of Jamshid[1] (divine knowledge) from me, (zahid and 'abid) years my heart made.

وان چه خود داشت ز بیگانه تمنا می‌کرد

And for what it (the cup) possessed, from a stranger, entreaty made.

گوهری کز صدف کون و مکان بیرون است

A jewel the (true Beloved) that is beyond the shell of existence and of time,

طلب از گمشدگان لب دریا می‌کرد

From those lost on the shore of the sea, (of unity) search it (my heart) made.

مشکل خویش بر پیر مغان بردم دوش

Last night, I took my difficulty to the Pir of the Magians[2] (the Murshid)

کو به تایید نظر حل معما می‌کرد

Who, by strengthening of sight, the solving of sublety made.

دیدمش خرم و خندان قدح باده به دست

Him, happy, laughing, wine-goblet in hand, I saw:

و اندر آن آینه صد گونه تماشا می‌کرد

And in the mirror, (of the goblet) a hundred kinds of views (mysteries of divine knowledge) he made.

گفتم این جام جهان بین به تو کی داد حکیم

I said: "When gave the All-wise this cup world-viewing to thee?"

گفت آن روز که این گنبد مینا می‌کرد

He said: "On that day, when the azure dome (of heaven) He made."

بی دلی در همه احوال خدا با او بود

One heart bereft (the lover of God) with him, in all states, is God

او نمی‌دیدش و از دور خدا را می‌کرد

(But) he beheld Him not, and from afar (the cry) For God's sake (be my helper) made.

این همه شعبده خویش که می‌کرد این جا

All those sorceries that (in the stage of love and of divine knowledge) reason here made

سامری پیش عصا و ید بیضا می‌کرد

Sameri[3] had the cane but the white hands of Moses, seekest made.

گفت آن یار کز او گشت سر دار بلند

He said: "That friend, (Husain Mansur Hallaj) by whom lofty became the head of the gibbet,

جرمش این بود که اسرار هویدا می‌کرد

"His crime was this that clear, the mysteries (of the sky), he made."

فیض روح القدس ار باز مدد فرماید

If, again, the bounty of the Holy Spirit (Jibrail) give aid,

دیگران هم بکنند آن چه مسیحا می‌کرد

Others also may make those, (miracles) which the Jesus (restorer of the dead to life) made.

1-King
2-Fire worshipper

3-A person who made a calf in the absence of Prophet Moses and encouraged the Hebrews to worship it

گفتمش سلسله زلف بتان از پی چیست

I said to him: (O beloved) "The chain-like tress of idols (beloved ones) is for the sake of what'?"

گفت حافظ گلهای از دل شیدا می کرد

He said: (With the chain of the tress, bind him, for, of the long dark night of separation or) "Of his own distraught heart, Hafez complaint made."

غزل ۱۴۴ ⓄⒹⒺ ①④④

به سر جام جم آن گه نظر توانی کرد

At the head of Jamshid's[1] cup, at that time thy glance, thou canst make,

که خاک میکده کحل بصر توانی کرد

When the dust of the wine-house, the collyrium of thy eye, thou canst make.

مباش بی می و مطرب که زیر طاق سپهر

Without wine and the minstrel, be not beneath the sky's arch. (this world For),

بدین ترانه غم از دل به در توانی کرد

Within melody, grief from out of thy heart (depart) thou canst make.

گل مراد تو آن گه که نقاب بگشاید

The rose of thy object openeth the veil at that time,

که خدمتش چو نسیم سحر توانی کرد

When, like the morning breeze, its service thou canst make.

گدایی در میخانه طرفه اکسیریست

Beggary in the tavern is the wonderful elixir,

گر این عمل بکنی خاک زر توانی کرد

If thou do this work, stone (into) gold, thou canst make.

به عزم مرحله عشق پیش نه قدمی

Advance a step for traveling to love's stage,

که سودها کنی ار این سفر توانی کرد

For, profits, thou mayst make if this journey thou canst make.

تو کز سرای طبیعت نمی‌روی بیرون

Thou that goest not forth from the house of nature (the body)

کجا به کوی طریقت گذر توانی کرد

How passage to the street of Tarikat[2], (is it that) thou canst make.

جمال یار ندارد نقاب و پرده ولی

Neither veil nor screen, hath the beauty of the true Beloved. But

غبار ره بنشان تا نظر توانی کرد

Lay aside the dust of the path (of thy existence) so that glance (at the true Beloved) thou canst make.

بیا که چاره ذوق حضور و نظم امور

Come. For, the remedy of the delight, and of the presence, (of love and) of the presence (of the true Beloved) and of the order of affairs,

به فیض بخشی اهل نظر توانی کرد

By the bounty-giving of one possess ed of vision thou canst make.

ولی تو تا لب معشوق و جام می خواهی

But as long as thou desirest the lip of the (illusory) beloved (woman) and the cup of (morning) wine,

طمع مدار که کار دگر توانی کرد

Think not that other work, thou canst make.

1-King   2-Principle, Sufism, religious way

دلا ز نور هدایت گر آگهی یابی
O heart! if thou gain knowledge of the light of austerity,

چو شمع خنده زنان ترک سر توانی کرد
Abandoning of life, like the laughing (consuming) candle thou canst make.

گر این نصیحت شاهانه بشنوی حافظ
Hafez! if thou hear this royal counsel,

به شاهراه حقیقت گذر توانی کرد
Passage to the highway of Hakikat[1] thou canst make.

غزل ۱۴۵ ⓄⒹⒺ ①④⑤

چه مستیست ندانم که رو به ما آورد
I know not what is the intoxication that to us its face hath brought:

که بود ساقی و این باده از کجا آورد
Who is the cup-bearer? This wine, whence hath he brought?

تو نیز باده به چنگ آر و راه صحرا گیر
To thy hand, bring thou also the cup; take the path to the desert (and strive in pleasure);

که مرغ نغمه سرا ساز خوش نوا آورد
For, the sweet melody of song, the melody-warbling bird hath brought.

دلا چو غنچه شکایت ز کار بسته مکن
O heart! complain not of thy work (fortune) enfolded like the rosebud:

که باد صبح نسیم گره گشا آورد
For the knot-loosening breeze, (the Murshid) the morning wind hath brought.

رسیدن گل و نسرین به خیر و خوبی باد
With welcome and happiness, be the arriving of the rose and of the wild rose;

بنفشه شاد و کش آمد سمن صفا آورد
The violet, glad and beautiful, hath come; (and) purity, the pure lily hath brought

صبا به خوش خبری هدهد سلیمان است
With glad tidings, the breeze is the lapwing of Soleiman[2]

که مژده طرب از گلشن سبا آورد
That, from the rose-bed of Saba[3], (the street of the true Beloved) tidings of joy brought.

علاج ضعف دل ما کرشمه ساقیست
The Saki[4]'s smile is our feeble heart's remedy;

برآر سر که طبیب آمد و دوا آورد
Bring forth thy hand. For the physician hath come; and the remedy, hath brought.

مرید پیر مغانم ز من مرنج ای شیخ
O Sheikh[5]! Of me, grieve not (that) I am the disciple of the Pir of the Magians[6] (the Murshid)

چراکه وعده تو کردی و او به جا آورد
For, (wine) thou promisedest; (on the day of resurrection) and (thy promise) he (the Murshid) to place hath brought.

1-Truth
2-Name of prophet
3-Name of a city in Yemen

4-Tapster
5-Fire worshipper
6-The perfect mystic man,

به تنگ چشمی آن ترک لشکری نازم

I boast of the narrow-eyedness of that warrior bold one,

که حمله بر من درویش یک قبا آورد

Who, on me the (poor) dervish of (only) one coat, assault brought.

فلک غلامی حافظ کنون به طوع کند

Now with submission, the sky doeth Hafez's service;

که التجا به در دولت شما آورد

Because refuge to the door of your fortune, he hath brought.

غزل ۱۴۶ ⓄⒹⒺ ①④⑥

صبا وقت سحر بویی ز زلف یار می‌آورد

At morning time, a perfume from the (true) Beloved's tress, the breeze (the fragrant murshid whereby the traveller's heart blossometh) brought:

دل شوریده ما را به بو در کار می‌آورد

Into action, our heart distraught for Thee brought

من آن شکل صنوبر را ز باغ دیده برکندم

(When my heart heeded not the murshid, and turned to sensuality) From the garden of the chest, I up-plucked that pine-branch (the heart intent on evil).

که هر گل کز غمش بشکفت محنت بار می‌آورد

From grief for which, every rose that blossomed, (only) the labor-load (of the thorn) brought.

فروغ ماه می‌دیدم ز بام قصر او روشن

From the roof of his palace, I beheld the moon's splendor (the Beloved's face),

که رو از شرم آن خورشید در دیوار می‌آورد

From shame of which, its face to the wall, the (resplendent) sun brought.

ز بیم غارت عشقش دل پرخون رها کردم

From fear of the plunder of His eye, I released my bloody (sinful) heart;

ولی می‌ریخت خون و ره بدان هنجار می‌آورد

But (at the time of turning back) it (my heart, weeping blood, spilled blood) on the path. In this way, (it the heart it His eye) brought.

به قول مطرب و ساق برون رفتم گه و بی‌گه

In season and out of season, forth to the voice of the minstrel and of the Saki I went:

کز آن راه گران قاصد خبر دشوار می‌آورد

For, with difficulty, on account of the heavy road, news, the messenger brought.

سراسر بخشش جانان طریق لطف و احسان بود

The way of graciousness and of kindness, altogether is the gift of the true Beloved:

اگر تسبیح می‌فرمود اگر زنار می‌آورد

Whether the Muslim rosary He ordered; or, the Christian cord, He brought.

عفاالله چین ابرویش اگر چه ناتوانم کرد

May God pardon the frown of his eye-brow, although powerless it made me;

به عشوه هم پیامی بر سر بیمار می‌آورد

Perchance In grace, to me sick, a message, (from the true Beloved) it brought.

عجب می‌داشتم دیشب ز حافظ جام و پیمانه

Last night, I wondered at Hafez's cup and goblet:

ولی منعش نمی‌کردم که صوفی وار می‌آورد

But, I argued not. For them, like a Sufi, (in exceeding delight and desire) he brought.

غزل ۱۴۷ ⓄⒹⒺ ①④⑦

نسیم باد صبا دوشم آگهی آورد

Last night, news to me the messenger of the morning wind brought,

که روز محنت و غم رو به کوتهی آورد

Saying: "To shortness, (ending) its face, the day of labor and of grief hath brought."

به مطربان صبوحی دهیم جامه چاک

To the minstrels of the morning cup, new raiment, we give

بدین نوید که باد سحرگهی آورد

For this news that the morning wind brought.

بیا بیا که تو حور بهشت را رضوان

Come! come! For thee, the Angel of Paradise, Rezvan[1],

در این جهان ز برای دل رهی آورد

A slave to this world, for the sake of thy heart, hath brought.

همی‌رویم به شیراز با عنایت بخت

Verily, to Shiraz, we will go with the favor of the friend (Shah Mansur)

زهی رفیق که بختم به همرهی آورد

O excellent friend who, as my fellow-traveler, fortune, brought.

به جبر خاطر ما کوش کاین کلاه نمد

Strive with the strength of our heart. For this (darvish) cap of felt,

بسا شکست که با افسر شهی آورد

Many is the shattering that, upon the kingly diadem, it hath brought.

چه ناله‌ها که رسید از دلم به خرمن ماه

From my heart to the palace (halo) of the moon (Shah Mansur) what wailings (they were) that reached

چو یاد عارض آن ماه خرگهی آورد

When, memory of the cheek of that regal moon, it (the heart) brought.

رساند رایت منصور بر فلک حافظ

Hafez may cause his standard of victory to reach the sky,

که التجا به جناب شهنشهی آورد

When, his refuge to the court of the great King, (Shah Mansur) he brought.

غزل ۱۴۸ ⓄⒹⒺ ①④⑧

یارم چو قدح به دست گیرد

When my (true) Beloved the wine-cup in hand taketh,

بازار بتان شکست گیرد

(Through His resplendent beauty) The market of idols, (lovely ones) disaster taketh.

هر کس که بدید چشم او گفت

Everyone, who beheld His (intoxicated) eye said:

کو محتسبی که مست گیرد

Where a Mohtaseb[2], who the intoxicated taketh?"

1-Guardian Angel of Heaven   2-Sheriff

در بحر فتاده‌ام چو ماهی

Like a fish, I have fallen into the sea, (of tears)

تا یار مرا به شست گیرد

So that, me, by the hook, the (true) Beloved taketh.

در پاش فتاده‌ام به زاری

In lamentation, at His feet, I have fallen

آیا بود آن که دست گیرد

In the hope that me, by the hand, (the true Beloved) taketh.

خرم دل آن که همچو حافظ

Happy the heart of that one who, like Hafez,

جامی ز می الست گیرد

A cup of the wine of Alast[1], taketh.

غزل ۱۴۹   ⓄⒹⒺ ①④⑨

دلم جز مهر مه رویان طریقی بر نمی‌گیرد

Save the love of those moon of face, a path my heart taketh not:

ز هر در می‌دهم پندش ولیکن در نمی‌گیرد

To it, (the heart) in every way, I give counsel; but it kindleth not.

خدا را ای نصیحتگو حدیث ساغر و می گو

O counsel-utterer! or God's sake, utter the tale of (the Saki's writing and abandon counsel – uttering):

که نقشی در خیال ما از این خوشتر نمی‌گیرد

For, a picture more beautiful than this, our imagination, taketh not.

بیا ای ساقی گلرخ بیاور باده رنگین

Come O beautiful Saki! Bring colorful cup.

که فکری در درون ما از این بهتر نمی‌گیرد

For a thought inside us, taketh better than this not.

صراحی می‌کشم پنهان و مردم دفتر انگارند

Secretly, I drink a goblet of (wine); and, men think it a book:

عجب گر آتش این زرق در دفتر نمی‌گیرد

Wonderful if the book, this hypocrisy's tire kindleth not.

من این دلق مرقع را بخواهم سوختن روزی

One day, I shall burn this gilded (hypocritical) dervish garment,

که پیر می فروشانش به جامی بر نمی‌گیرد

Which, for a single cup, the Pir of the wine-sellers taketh not.

از آن رو هست یاران را صفاها با می لعلش

The pure-players (lovers of God) have purities with wine, for the reason

که غیر از راستی نقشی در آن جوهر نمی‌گیرد

That in this jewel, save truthfulness a picture taketh not.

سر و چشمی چنین دلکش تو گویی چشم از او بردوز

The head and the eye of (the counsel – utterer) with all this goodness Yet
thou mayest say Take off thy eye from him (and to him go not)

برو کاین وعظ بی‌معنی مرا در سر نمی‌گیرد

Go for in my head, this meaningless counsel-taketh not.

1-The day when God made his covenant

نصیحتگوی رندان را که با حکم قضا جنگ است

The counsel-utterer of profligates, who hath war with God's decree

دلش بس تنگ می‌بینم مگر ساغر نمی‌گیرد

His heart, I see much straitened: perhaps, the cup he taketh not.

میان گریه می‌خندم که چون شمع اندر این مجلس

In the midst of weeping, I laugh. Because, like the candle in this assembly,

زبان آتشینم هست لیکن در نمی‌گیرد

The fiery tongue is mine; but (it, the tongue) it (the fire) kindleth not.

چه خوش صید دلم کردی بنازم چشم مستت را

How happily Thou madest prey of my heart! Of Thy intoxicated eye, I boast:

که کس مرغان وحشی را از این خوشتر نمی‌گیرد

For, better than this, the wild birds, a person taketh not.

سخن در احتیاج ما و استغنای معشوق است

In respect of our need and of the independence of the true Beloved, is speech

چه سود افسونگری ای دل که در دلبر نمی‌گیرد

O heart! what profit sorcery, when in the Heart-Ravisher, it taketh not.

من آن آیینه را روزی به دست آرم سکندروار

One day, like Sekandar[1], I shall bring to hand that (doll) mirror (of the heart),

اگر می‌گیرد این آتش زمانی ور نمی‌گیرد

If, (even) this (great) fire (love for God) seize it, for a moment, it (the mirror) kindleth not.

خدا را رحمی ای منعم که درویش سر کویت

O Benefactor! (the true Beloved) for God's sake, a little pity. For, the dervish of the head of Thy Street

دری دیگر نمی‌داند رهی دیگر نمی‌گیرد

Knoweth not another door; another Path, taketh not.

بدین شعر تر شیرین ز شاهنشه عجب دارم

For this verse, fresh (and) sweet, I wonder the King of kings

که سر تا پای حافظ را چرا در زر نمی‌گیرد

Why, Hafez, head to foot in gold, he taketh not.

غزل ۱۵۰ ⓄⒹⒺ ①⑤⓪

ساقی ار باده از این دست به جام اندازد

If the Saki[2] (the true Beloved) wine into the cup, in this way cast

عارفان را همه در شرب مدام اندازد

All the Arefs[3] into (the way of) ever (wine) drinking, He will cast.

ور چنین زیر خم زلف نهد دانه خال

If thus, beneath the curve of the tress, He place the grain of the mole

ای بسا مرغ خرد را که به دام اندازد

O many a bird of wisdom, that, into the net, it will cast!

ای خوشا دولت آن مست که در پای حریف

Happy the state of that intoxicated one, who (from exceeding intoxication) at the foot of the rival,

سر و دستار نداند که کدام اندازد

Head or turban, knoweth not which off he will cast.

1-He was the king of Macedonia in ancient Greece   3-Mystic

2-Tapster

زاهد خام که انکار می و جام کند

(In desire persistence) of denial, the Zahed[1] immature of nature (remaineth):

پخته گردد چو نظر بر می خام اندازد

Mature, he becometh when on the wine of the cup, his glance he casteth.

روز در کسب هنر کوش که می خوردن روز

By day, strive in the acquisition of skill. For wine-drinking by day,

دل چون آینه در زنگ ظلام اندازد

The heart (bright) like the mirror, into the blight of darkness, casteth.

آن زمان وقت می صبح فروغ است که شب

The time of wine of morning-splendour is that time when night,

گرد خرگاه افق پرده شام اندازد

The evening's screen around the tent of the horizon, casteth.

باده با محتسب شهر ننوشی زنهار

Take care drink not wine (of love) with the city-Mohtaseb[2] (reason):

بخورد باده‌ات و سنگ به جام اندازد

Thy wine he drinketh; and, into the cup the stone (of calumny), he casteth.

حافظا سر ز کله گوشه خورشید برآر

O Hafiz (with the great cup), a corner of the sun, bring forth thy head (in splendour)

بختت ار قرعه بدان ماه تمام اندازد

If the dice for that full moon (the true Beloved) fortune casteth.

غزل ۱۵۱ ⓄⒹⒺ ①⑤①

دمی با غم به سر بردن جهان یک سر نمی‌ارزد

A world altogether, to pass life a single moment in grief is not worth:

به می بفروش دلق ما کز این بهتر نمی‌ارزد

For wine, sell our ragged religious garment; for more than this it is not worth.

به کوی می فروشانش به جامی بر نمی‌گیرند

In the wine-seller's street, for a single cup of wine, they take it (the prayer mat of piety) not up:

زهی سجاده تقوا که یک ساغر نمی‌ارزد

O excellent prayer-mat of piety, that, a single cup of wine is not worth.

رقیبم سرزنش‌ها کرد کز این به آب رخ برتاب

The watcher reproached me saying: "Turn away thy face from this door (of the true Beloved):"

چه افتاد این سر ما را که خاک در نمی‌ارزد

To this our head, what happened that (even) the dust of the door, it is not worth.

شکوه تاج سلطانی که بیم جان در او درج است

The pomp of the imperial crown, in whose grandeur is fear of life,

کلاهی دلکش است اما به ترک سر نمی‌ارزد

Is verily a heart-alluring crown; but the abandoning of one's head life, it is not worth.

چه آسان می‌نمود اول غم دریا به بوی سود

At first, in hope of profit, very easy the toil of the sea appeared:

غلط کردم که این طوفان به صد گوهر نمی‌ارزد

I uttered a mistake. Because, a hundred jewels, (hopes of union with the true Beloved) this great deluge full of dangers is not worth.

1-Pietist   2-Sheriff

تو را آن به که روی خود ز مشتاقان بپوشانی

For thee, that best that from the desirous ones thou cover thy face,

که شادی جهان گیری غم لشکر نمی‌ارزد

Because, the grief of an army, the joyousness of world-seizing is not worth.

چو حافظ در قناعت کوش و از دنیی دون بگذر

Like Hafez, strive in contentment; and let go the mean world:

که یک جو منت دونان دو صد من زر نمی‌ارزد

Because two hundred "mans" of gold, one grain of the favor of the mean is not worth.

غزل ۱۵۲ ⓞⓓⓔ ①⑤②

در ازل پرتو حسنت ز تجلی دم زد

(O true Beloved) in eternity without beginning, (the day of misak) of glory, the splendor-ray of Thy beauty boasted.

عشق پیدا شد و آتش به همه عالم زد

Revealed became love; and, upon all the world, fire dashed.

جلوه‌ای کرد رخت دید ملک عشق نداشت

(O absolute existence) Thy face displayed splendour; (and) beheld (that) the angel had no (capacity for) love;

عین آتش شد از این غیرت و بر آدم زد

From this (exceeding) jealousy, it became the essence of fire; and upon Adam[1] dashed.

عقل می‌خواست کز آن شعله چراغ افروزد

From that torch, (of love) reason wished to kindle its lamp,

برق غیرت بدرخشید و جهان برهم زد

Jealousy's lightning flashed; and in confusion, the world dashed.

مدعی خواست که آید به تماشاگه راز

The adversary (Shaitan) sought to come to the spectacle-place of the mystery (of love)

دست غیب آمد و بر سینه نامحرم زد

The invisible hand (of God) came; and, at the heart of the excluded one, (Shaitan) dashed.

دیگران قرعه قسمت همه بر عیش زدند

Others, all on ease, dashed the dice of partition fate:

دل غمدیده ما بود که هم بر غم زد

Our grief-experienced heart it was that also, on grief (the dice of fate) cast.

جان علوی هوس چاه زنخدان تو داشت

The desire of Thy chin's dimple (Thy mysteries) possessed the lofty soul:

دست در حلقه آن زلف خم اندر خم زد

At the ring of that tress, curl within curl, hand, he dashed.

حافظ آن روز طربنامه عشق تو نوشت

The joy-book of love for Thee, Hafez wrote on that day,

که قلم بر سر اسباب دل خرم زد

When, on the head of the chattels of his joyous heart, the reed, (of cancellation) he dashed

---

1-Human

غزل ۱۵۳ 🛑 ODE 🛑 153 🛑

سحر چون خسرو خاور علم بر کوهساران زد

In the morning when, his standard on the mountainous lands, the Khosro of the east[1] (the rising sun) pitched,

به دست مرحمت یارم در امیدواران زد

With the hand of mercy, the door of hopeful ones, my beloved beat;

چو پیش صبح روشن شد که حال مهر گردون چیست

Before morning, when it became manifest what is the (inconstant) state of the sphere's love

برآمد خنده خوش بر غرور کامگاران زد

It (the morning) ascended; (and), on the pride of potentates, a sweet laugh expressed.

نگارم دوش در مجلس به عزم رقص چون برخاست

Last night, when with the intention of dancing, my idol stood up,

گره بگشود از ابرو و بر دلهای یاران زد

From the tress, she unloosed the knot; and on the hearts of beloved ones beat.

من از رنگ صلاح آن دم به خون دل بشستم دست

From (goodness and) the color of rectitude, (and piety) that moment, I washed my hand in the heart's blood:

که چشم باده پیمایش صلا بر هوشیاران زد

When His (the beloved's) eye, wine-measuring, to the sensible ones, invitation (for drinking wine) expressed.

کدام آهن دلش آموخت این آیین عیاری

This usage of deceit, what iron taught Him (the true Beloved),

کز اول چون برون آمد ره شب زنده داران زد

That when from (his own house) He came out, those keeping awake at night, (the 'abids, and the zahids) He first attacked.

خیال شهسواری پخت و شد ناگه دل مسکین

The idea of horsemen my wretched heart matured; and (near to them) went:

خداوندا نگه دارش که بر قلب سواران زد

O Lord! preserve it, for, on the center of the horsemen, it dashed.

در آب و رنگ رخسارش چه جان دادیم و خون خوردیم

In the luster and color of his cheek, what soul we gave: and what blood (of grief) we drank:

چو نقشش دست داد اول رقم بر جان سپاران زد

When His picture first appeared, on those soul-surrendering the writing of (effacement) he expressed.

منش با خرقه پشمین کجا اندر کمند آرم

By the woollen Khirka[2], how into the noose (of my power) may I bring Him,

زره مویی که مژگانش ره خنجرگزاران زد

A hair-clad one whose eye-lash, those dagger-thrusting attacked.

شهنشاه مظفر فر شجاع ملک و دین منصور

The great king, Muzaffar of pomp, the braver y of the kingdom, and the faith of Mansur

که جود بی‌دریغش خنده بر ابر بهاران زد

Whose (exceeding) liberality without hesitation, laughter, against the (generous) spring-cloud, expressed.

1-Sun   2-Cloak

از آن ساعت که جام می به دست او مشرف شد
From that moment when, by his hand, the cup of wine became honored,
زمانه ساغر شادی به یاد میگساران زد
In memory of its wine-drinkers, the cup of joyousness, time drained.

ز شمشیر سرافشانش ظفر آن روز بدرخشید
With his head-cleaving sword, gleamed victory that day.
که چون خورشید انجم سوز تنها بر هزاران زد
When, like the star-consuming sun, on thousands, alone he dashed.

دوام عمر و ملک او بخواه از لطف حق ای دل
(Hafez)! from God's grace, ask for his (Shah Mansur's) lasting life and kingdom.
که چرخ این سکه دولت به دور روزگاران زد
For, in the time of the people, this coin of fortune, the sphere struck.

نظر بر قرعه توفیق و یمن دولت شاه است
On the die of grace, and the felicity of the King's fortune, my glance is:
بده کام دل حافظ که فال بختیاران زد
(O beloved) Give the desire of the heart of Hafez who, the omen of the fortunate, struck.

غزل ۱۵۴ ⓞⒹⒺ ①⑤④

راهی بزن که آهی بر ساز آن توان زد
(O Minstrel) Play a note, at the melody whereof, a great sigh, (of rapture from the body) one can cast:
شعری بخوان که با او رطل گران توان زد
Utter a verse, whereby the heavy cup of wine (on the earth) one can cast.

بر آستان جانان گر سر توان نهادن
If at the (true) Beloved's threshold, one can lay one's head,
گلبانگ سربلندی بر آسمان توان زد
To the sky, the shout of loftiness, one can cast.

قد خمیده ما سهلت نماید اما
(In Thy sight) wretched appeareth our bent stature:
بر چشم دشمنان تیر از این کمان توان زد
To the eyes of (Thy) enemies, the arrow from this (our) bow, one can cast.

در خانقه نگنجد اسرار عشقبازی
Not contained in the cloisters are the mysteries of love-play (and of intoxication)
جام می مغانه هم با مغان توان زد
(For only) with Magians, the cup of Magian[1] wine one can cast.

درویش را نباشد برگ سرای سلطان
The victuals of the king's palace are not for the Dervish:
ماییم و کهنه دلقی کتش در آن توان زد
Old and ragged-clad are we upon whom fire one can cast.

اهل نظر دو عالم در یک نظر ببازند
In (exchange for) one glance (of the true Beloved's), men of vision stake two worlds,
عشق است و داو اول بر نقد جان توان زد
'Tis love; and, on life's cast, the first stake, one can cast.

1-They were originally a tribe of the Medes to whom the position of clergy belonged exclusively

گر دولت وصالت خواهد دری گشودن

If fortune should open the door of union with Him,

سرها بدین تخیل بر آستان توان زد

In this vain (fancy), on the threshold, many a head one can cast.

عشق و شباب و رندی مجموعه مراد است

The sum total of our desire is love, youth, and profligacy:

چون جمع شد معانی گوی بیان توان زد

When (luminous) the senses become (like) the (luminous) candle, the ball of explanation, one can cast.

شد رهزن سلامت زلف تو وین عجب نیست

(O true Beloved) the highwayman of safety became Thy tress. This is no wonder.

گر راه زن تو باشی صد کاروان توان زد

If Thou be highwayman, a hundred Karvans one can waylay.

حافظ به حق قرآن کز شید و زرق بازآی

Hafez! by the truth of the Kuran[1] I (swear) saying: From fraud and deceit come out:

باشد که گوی عیشی در این جهان توان زد

"It may be, that (if so thou do) the ball of (fortune with the sincere ones) one can cast.

غزل ۱۵۵ ⓄⒹⒺ ①⑤⑤

اگر روم ز پی اش فتنه‌ها برانگیزد

If after Him, I go, He up stirreth calamity (saying wherefore comest thou after me):

ور از طلب بنشینم به کینه برخیزد

And if I sit (abstaining) from search, in wrath, He ariseth.

و گر به رهگذری یک دم از وفاداری

And, if, through desire, a moment on a highway,

چو گرد در پی اش افتم چو باد بگریزد

I fall, like the dust at his foot, like the (swift) wind, He fleeth.

وگر کنم طلب نیم بوسه صد افسوس

And, if I desire (only) half a kiss, a hundred reproaches,

ز حقه دهنش چون شکر فروریزد

Like sugar, from the small round box of his (small) mouth, He out poureth.

من آن فریب که در نرگس تو می‌بینم

That deceit, that I behold in thy eye,

بس آب روی که با خاک ره برآمیزد

Many a reputation (it is) that, even with the dust of the path, it spilleth.

فراز و شیب بیابان عشق دام بلاست

The acclivity and declivity of love's desert is calamity's snare:

کجاست شیردلی کز بلا نپرهیزد

A lion-hearted one is where, who not calamity shunneth?

تو عمر خواه و صبوری که چرخ شعبده باز

Ask thou for (long) life and a great patience; (because then thou wilt see) that the sphere, sorcery-practising,

هزار بازی از این طرفه‌تر برانگیزد

A thousand tricks more strange than this, evoketh

1-Quran

بر آستانه تسلیم سر بنه حافظ

Hafez! place thy head on the threshold of submission:

که گر ستیزه کنی روزگار بستیزد

For if thou make contention, with thee, Time contendeth.

غزل ۱۵۶ ⓄⒹⒺ ①⑤⑥

به حسن و خلق و وفا کس به یار ما نرسد

To our friend, (Muhammad) in beauty (of) disposition and (of) fidelity, one reacheth not

تو را در این سخن انکار کار ما نرسد

In this matter, to thee, denial of our work reacheth not.

اگر چه حسن فروشان به جلوه آمده‌اند

Although, into splendor, have come beauty-boasters, (the prophets, the leaders of the people, the guides of the path)

کسی به حسن و ملاحت به یار ما نرسد

To our beloved (Muhammad, whose beauty was the world's boast) in beauty and grace, one reacheth not.

به حق صحبت دیرین که هیچ محرم راز

By the right of ancient society (I swear) that any mystery confidant

به یار یک جهت حق گزار ما نرسد

To our friend, of one way, (sincere) thank-offering, reacheth not.

هزار نقش برآید ز کلک صنع و یکی

From the Creator's reed, issue a thousand pictures: and one

به دلپذیری نقش نگار ما نرسد

To (the degree of) approval of the picture of our idol (Muhammad) reacheth not.

هزار نقد به بازار کانات آرند

To the market of created beings, they (Fate and Destiny) bring a thousand coins:

یکی به سکه صاحب عیار ما نرسد

To the die of our master of assay, one (coin) reaeheth not.

دریغ قافله عمر کان چنان رفتند

Alas! the Kafila (Convoy) of life (manifestations of glories) passed in such a way,

که گردشان به هوای دیار ما نرسد

That, to the air of our (far distant) country, its dust reacheth not.

دلا ز رنج حسودان مرنج و واثق باش

O heart! grieve not of the reproach of the envious; and be firm

که بد به خاطر امیدوار ما نرسد

For, to our hopeful heart, evil reacheth not.

چنان بزی که اگر خاک ره شوی کس را

So live that if thou (die and) become the dust of the path, to someone,

غبار خاطری از ره گذار ما نرسد

From our way (of life) a particle of dust of grief of the heart reach not.

بسوخت حافظ و ترسم که شرح قصه او

Hafez consumed; and I fear that the explanation of his tale

به سمع پادشه کامگار ما نرسد

To the ear of the powerful King reacheth not.

غزل ۱۵۷ ⓄⒹⒺ ①⑤⑦

هر که را با خط سبزت سر سودا باشد
Desire of passion for Thy fresh down to whomsoever, shall be:

پای از این دایره بیرون ننهد تا باشد
Forth from the circle (of passion) he planteth not his foot, so long as he shall be.

من چو از خاک لحد لاله صفت برخیزم
When, tulip-like, I arise from the dust of the tomb,

داغ سودای توام سر سویدا باشد
The stain of passion for Thee, (the secret of the black spot of my heart shall be).

تو خود ای گوهر یک دانه کجایی آخر
O priceless jewel! (the true Beloved) Till when, holdest thou lawful,

کز غمت دیده مردم همه دریا باشد
For, from (Thy image), my eye like a river shall be.

از بن هر مژهام آب روان است بیا
(O true Beloved) From the root of every eye-lash of mine, water (of tears) is flowing. Come:

اگرت میل لب جوی و تماشا باشد
If, for bank of the stream and for the view, Thy inclination shall be.

چون گل و می دمی از پرده برون آی و درآ
Like my heart, forth from the screen a moment come; and come, (to meet me)

که دگرباره ملاقات نه پیدا باشد
For, (my time being ended) again (my meeting with Thee) not manifest, shall be.

ظل ممدود خم زلف توام بر سر باد
On my head, be the prolonged shadow of Thy tress.

کاندر این سایه قرار دل شیدا باشد
For, my time being ended in that shadow, rest to the distraught heart shall be.

چشمت از ناز به حافظ نکند میل آری
Through disdain, Thy eye inclineth not to Hafez. Yes,

سرگرانی صفت نرگس رعنا باشد
The quality of the variegated narcissus, (the Beloved's eye) haughtiness shall be.

غزل ۱۵۸ ⓄⒹⒺ ①⑤⑧

من و انکار شراب این چه حکایت باشد
I and refusal of wine! What a tale this is!

غالبا این قدرم عقل و کفایت باشد
Doubtless, this degree of reason (that I abandon not wine, is) mine; and sufficient it is.

تا به غایت ره میخانه نمیدانستم
Up to the last, I knew not the path to the wine-house:

ور نه مستوری ما تا به چه غایت باشد
If not, to what an extent our austerity is.

زاهد و عجب و نماز و من و مستی و نیاز

(Together are) the Zahed[1], and haughtiness, and prayer; and I, and intoxication, and supplication:

تا تو را خود ز میان با که عنایت باشد

Let us see, with whom of these, (two) thy favor indeed is.

زاهد ار راه به رندی نبرد معذور است

If the Zahed take not the path to profligacy, he is excused,

عشق کاریست که موقوف هدایت باشد

Love is a work, that dependent on the guidance (of God) is.

من که شبها ره تقوا زدهام با دف و چنگ

I, who nights, with the drum and the harp, have dashed down (acted contrary-wise to) the path of piety

این زمان سر به ره آرم چه حکایت باشد

I, suddenly, bring my head to the path! of piety What a tale this is!

بنده پیر مغانم که ز جهلم برهاند

I am the slave of the Pir of the Magians[2], the (murshid perfect and excellent) who releaseth me from ignorance (of divine knowledge),

پیر ما هر چه کند عین عنایت باشد

Whatever our Pir[3] doeth, the essence of friendly assistance is.

دوش از این غصه نخفتم که رفیقی میگفت

Last night, I slept not on account of this thought that a sage uttered:

حافظ ار مست بود جای شکایت باشد

If Hafez be intoxicated, room for complaint is."

غزل ۱۵۹ ⓞⓓⓔ ①⑤⑨

نقد صوفی نه همه صافی بیغش باشد

Not all purity without alloy is the coat of the Sufi[4],

ای بسا خرقه که مستوجب آتش باشد

O many a Khirka[5], that is worthy of the fire!

صوفی ما که ز ورد سحری مست شدی

Our Sufi, who, with the morning reading, used to become intoxicated (with love for God),

شامگاهش نگران باش که سرخوش باشد

At evening time, behold him; for merry of head (with wine) is he.

خوش بود گر محک تجربه آید به میان

Happy it is, if the touch-stone of experience come into use,

تا سیه روی شود هر که در او غش باشد

So that black of face becometh everyone, in whom is alloy.

خط ساقی گر از این گونه زند نقش بر آب

If, in this way, the Saki[6]'s down maketh the (vanishing) picture on water,

ای بسا رخ که به خونابه منقش باشد

O many a face that colored with (tears of) blood will be!

1-Pietist
2-The perfect mystic man,
3-A Muslim saint or holy man, Pietist
4-Fire worshipper
5-Cloak
6-Tapster

ناز پرورد تنعم نبرد راه به دوست
The daintily nurtured in affluence took not the path to the Friend:
عاشقی شیوه رندان بلاکش باشد
The being a lover (of God) is the way of profligates, calamity enduring.

غم دنیی دنی چند خوری باده بخور
Grief for this mean world, how long sufferest thou? Drink wine:
حیف باشد دل دانا که مشوش باشد
Pity it is that the sage's heart is perturbed.

دلق و سجاده حافظ ببرد باده فروش
(In exchange) the ragged garment and the prayer-mat of Hafez, the wine-seller will take,
گر شرابش ز کف ساقی مه وش باشد
If, from the hand of that moon-like Saki, there is wine.

غزل ۱۶۰ ⓄⒹⒺ ①⑥⓪

خوش است خلوت اگر یار یار من باشد
Pleasant is Khalvat[1], if my beloved, the (true) Beloved shall be
نه من بسوزم و او شمع انجمن باشد
Not (pleasant) if I consume and the candle of (another) assembly, He shall be

من آن نگین سلیمان به هیچ نستانم
As naught, I take (regard) Sulaiman's seal-ring (the world's power),
که گاه گاه بر او دست اهرمن باشد
On which, sometimes, Ahriman's hand shall be.

روا مدار خدایا که در حریم وصال
O God! hold it not lawful that, in the sacred enclosure of union
رقیب محرم و حرمان نصیب من باشد
The watcher, included (as friend) and my lot, excluded shall be.

همای گو مفکن سایه شرف هرگز
To the Homa, say: "Cast not thy auspicious shadow
در آن دیار که طوطی کم از زغن باشد
On that land where the (noble) parrot less than the (mean) kite shall be."

بیان شوق چه حاجت که سوز آتش دل
What need of the description of (love's) desire, when the explanation of the heart's fire,
توان شناخت ز سوزی که در سخن باشد
One can recognize from the burning which in speech may be.

هوای کوی تو از سر نمی‌رود آری
From our head, the desire for Thy street goeth not,
غریب را دل سرگشته با وطن باشد
With his native land, the stranger's distraught heart shall be.

به سان سوسن اگر ده زبان شود حافظ
If like the lily, ten tongues be Hafez's,
چو غنچه پیش تواش مهر بر دهن باشد
Before Thee, like the (folded) rose-bud, on his mouth, the seal (of silence) shall be

---

1-Solitude

غزل ۱۶۱ ⓄⒹⒺ ①⑥①

کی شعر تر انگیزد خاطر که حزین باشد
How a (lustrous) verse exciteth afresh the heart that is sorrowful! (through love for, and through the stain of, the world and from search after lust)

یک نکته از این معنی گفتیم و همین باشد
A subtlety out of this book, we uttered; and (enough) is this very subtlety.

از لعل تو گر یابم انگشتری زنهار
(O beloved)! if, from thy ruby (lip) I gain a ring of protection,

صد ملک سلیمانم در زیر نگین باشد
Beneath the order of my seal-ring, will be a hundred countries of Soleiman[1].

غمناک نباید بود از طعن حسود ای دل
O heart! on account of the calumny of the envious, it is not proper to be sorrowful:

شاید که چو وابینی خیر تو در این باشد
When thou lookest well (and arrives at the truth of the matter) it is possible that, in this, is thy good.

هر کو نکند فهمی زین کلک خیال انگیز
Who understandeth not this (my) reed, image (loftily) raising (of God)

نقشش به حرام ار به خود صورتگر چین باشد
Let his form, move not, (let him die, even) if he himself be the (celebrated) painter of China.

جام می و خون دل هر یک به کسی دادند
The cup of wine (of ease) and the blood of the heart (of grief) each, they (Fate and Destiny) gave to each one:

در دایره قسمت اوضاع چنین باشد
In the action of destiny's circle, thus it is. (to one grief, to another ease)

در کار گلاب و گل حکم ازلی این بود
In the matter of rose-water and of the rose, the decree of eternity without beginning was this:

کاین شاهد بازاری وان پرده نشین باشد
"That (the rose) should be the lovely one of the bazar (the harlot); and that this (the rose – water) should be the sitter behind the veil." (the chaste one)

آن نیست که حافظ را رندی بشد از خاطر
(Possible) It is not that from Hafez's heart profligacy should pepart:

کاین سابقه پیشین تا روز پسین باشد
For, till the last of time will be that custom of first of time.

غزل ۱۶۲ ⓄⒹⒺ ①⑥②

خوش آمد گل وز آن خوشتر نباشد
Happy came the rose; and more happy than that aught is not.

که در دستت بجز ساغر نباشد
For, in thy hand, save the cup (of wine) aught is not.

زمان خوشدلی دریاب و در یاب
Gain, gain, the time of happy heartedness (leisure):

که دایم در صدف گوهر نباشد
For, in the shell, ever the jewel (wine in the cup, or concordant time) is not.

1-Name of a prophet

غنیمت دان و می خور در گلستان
Reckon (the season) plunder; and, in the rose-garden, drink wine:
که گل تا هفته دیگر نباشد
For (even) till another week, the rose is not.

ایا پرلعل کرده جام زرین
O thou that hast made full of ruby thy golden cup,
ببخشا بر کسی کش زر نباشد
(In thanks to God) Give to that one, to whom gold is not.

بیا ای شیخ و از خمخانه ما
O Sheikh[1]! come into our wine-jar house
شرابی خور که در کوثر نباشد
Drink a wine that in (the paradise-spring of) Kousar[2] is not.

بشوی اوراق اگر همدرس مایی
If, our fellow student, thou remain, wash white the leaves;
که علم عشق در دفتر نباشد
For, (inscribed) in the book, love's art is not.

ز من بنیوش و دل در شاهدی بند
Hear me. Fix thy heart on a mistress,
که حسنش بسته زیور نباشد
Whose beauty bound up with ornaments (of jewels) is not.

شرابی بی خمارم بخش یا رب
O Lord! give me a wine without mixing, (un – alloyed)
که با وی هیچ درد سر نباشد
Wherewith any head-pain is none.

من از جان بنده سلطان اویسم
With soul, I am the slave of the Soltan Uvays[3],
اگر چه یادش از چاکر نباشد
Although of (me) the servant, his recollection is none.

به تاج عالم آرایش که خورشید
By this crown, world-adorning, (I swear) that the sun
چنین زیبنده افسر نباشد
Like this, an adorner of the diadem is not.

کسی گیرد خطا بر نظم حافظ
On Hafez's soul, taketh exception that one
که هیچش لطف در گوهر نباشد
In whose essence, any grace is none.

غزل ۱۶۳ ⓄⒹⒺ ①⑥③

گل بی رخ یار خوش نباشد
Without the beloved's face, the rose is not pleasant.
بی باده بهار خوش نباشد
Without wine, spring is not pleasant.

1-A leader in a Muslim community   3-king
2-Kowsar pond is the source of refreshing water in paradise

طرف چمن و طواف بستان

The border of the sward and the air of the garden

بی لاله عذار خوش نباشد

Without the (beloved of) tulip cheek is not pleasant.

رقصیدن سرو و حالت گل

The dancing of the cypress, and the rapture of the rose,

بی صوت هزار خوش نباشد

Without the one thousand songs is not pleasant.

با یار شکرلب گل اندام

With the beloved, sugar of lip, rose of body,

بی بوس و کنار خوش نباشد

(To be) Without kiss and embrace is not pleasant.

هر نقش که دست عقل بندد

Every picture that reason's hand depicteth,

جز نقش نگار خوش نباشد

Save the picture of (the living beauteous) the idol is not pleasant.

جان نقد محقر است حافظ

Hafez! the soul is (but) a despicable coin:

از بهر نثار خوش نباشد

For scattering, (on the true Beloved) it is not pleasant.

غزل ۱۶۴   ⓄⒹⒺ ①⑥④

نفس باد صبا مشک فشان خواهد شد

Musk-diffusing, the breath of the morning breeze shall be:

عالم پیر دگرباره جوان خواهد شد

Again the world old (by autumn and winter) young shall be.

ارغوان جام عقیقی به سمن خواهد داد

To the (white) lily, the (ruddy) Arghavan[1] shall give the (red) cornelian cup

چشم نرگس به شقایق نگران خواهد شد

Glancing at the anemones, the eye of the narcissus shall be.

این تطاول که کشید از غم هجران بلبل

This tyranny that, from the grief of separation, the nightingale endured

تا سراپرده گل نعره زنان خواهد شد

In the rose's pavilion, clamour-making, shall be.

گر ز مسجد به خرابات شدم خرده مگیر

If from the Masjed[2] (outward worship) to the tavern (of truth) I go, carp not:

مجلس وعظ دراز است و زمان خواهد شد

Long is the assembly of admonition; (of the Zahid) and (short) the time (of life) shall be.

ای دل ار عشرت امروز به فردا فکنی

O heart! if to-morrow thou cast (postpone) the joy of to-day,

مایه نقد بقا را که ضمان خواهد شد

Surety for the capital of cash of permanency, (till to – morrow) who shall be?

1-Flower   2-Mosque

ماه شعبان منه از دست قدح کاین خورشید

In the month Shaban[1], put not the goblet from thy hand. For this sun,

از نظر تا شب عید رمضان خواهد شد

(Only) Till the night of the 'Id of Ramazan[2] out of sight, shall be.

گل عزیز است غنیمت شمریدش صحبت

Precious is the rose; its society reckon plunder.

که به باغ آمد از این راه و از آن خواهد شد

For in this way to the garden it came; and, (quickly) in that way shall go.

مطربا مجلس انس است غزل خوان و سرود

O minstrel! the assembly of associate friends, it is singing the ghazal and the ode:

چند گویی که چنین رفت و چنان خواهد شد

How long sayest thou: (This moment) "Passed like this; and like that shall be."

حافظ از بهر تو آمد سوی اقلیم وجود

(From the clime of non – existence) to the clime of existence, came Hafez for thy sake:

قدمی نه به وداعش که روان خواهد شد

Plant thy foot for farewell to him; for (quickly in death) passing he shall be.

غزل ۱۶۵ ⓞⓓⓔ ①⑥⑤

مرا مهر سیه چشمان ز سر بیرون نخواهد شد

As for me, out of my head, love for those dark of eye will not go:

قضای آسمان است این و دیگرگون نخواهد شد

This is the sky's decree; and other way, it will not be.

رقیب آزارها فرمود و جای آشتی نگذاشت

The watcher tormented, and abandoned not the place of peace:

مگر آه سحرخیزان سوی گردون نخواهد شد

Perchance, moving towards the sphere, the sigh of morning-risers will not be.

مرا روز ازل کاری بجز رندی نفرمودند

On the day of eternity without beginning, they (Fate and Destiny) ordered me no work save profligacy;

هر آن قسمت که آن جا رفت از آن افزون نخواهد شد

Every partition (of destiny) that here (on the day of eternity) passed, (less or) more than it, will not be.

خدا را محتسب ما را به فریاد دف و نی بخش

O Mohtaseb! for God's sake, pardon us for the clamour of drum and of reed,

که ساز شرع از این افسانه بی‌قانون نخواهد شد

For, with this idle tale without canon, the requirements of the shara will not be.

مجال من همین باشد که پنهان عشق او ورزم

This is my power that, secretly, I practice love for Him:

کنار و بوس و آغوشش چه گویم چون نخواهد شد

The bosom, the kiss, (and) the embrace, of these, how shall I speak, since (mine) they will not be

شراب لعل و جای امن و یار مهربان ساقی

The ruby-wine, and the place of safety, and the Saki, kind friend, (all are present)

دلا کی به شود کارت اگر اکنون نخواهد شد

O heart! better, when becometh thy work (of repentance by turning to pleasure and ease) if now it will not be?

1-The eighth lunar month   2-The ninth lunar month

مشوی ای دیده نقش غم ز لوح سینه حافظ
O eye! (with thy weeping) wash not grief's picture from the tablet of Hafez's heart:
که زخم تیغ دلدار است و رنگ خون نخواهد شد
For it (the picture) is the Heart-Possessor's sword-wound; and (with washing) the blood-color will not go.

غزل ۱۶۶ ⓄⒹⒺ ①⑥⑥

روز هجران و شب فرقت یار آخر شد
"The day of separation from, and the night of disunion with, the (true) Beloved is ended:"
زدم این فال و گذشت اختر و کار آخر شد
This omen, I cast; the star (of happy omen) passed; and the work of grief is ended.

آن همه ناز و تنعم که خزان میفرمود
All that grace and beauty, (of snare) that autumn (the world) displayed,
عاقبت در قدم باد بهار آخر شد
At last, at the foot of the (arrival of) spring-breeze, (the murshid) is ended.

شکر ایزد که به اقبال کله گوشه گل
Thanks to God that, by the fortune of the cap-corner of the (rose),
نخوت باد دی و شوکت خار آخر شد
The pomp of December's wind and the majesty of the thorn is ended.

صبح امید که بد معتکف پرده غیب
To the morning of hope, that was a worshipper of the hidden screen,
گو برون آی که کار شب تار آخر شد
Say: "Come forth. For the work of the dark night (of hopelessness) is ended."

آن پریشانی شبهای دراز و غم دل
That agitation of long nights and the heart's grief,
همه در سایه گیسوی نگار آخر شد
All, in the shade of the idol's tress, is ended.

باورم نیست ز بدعهدی ایام هنوز
I still cannot believe in the bad promises of the days,
قصه غصه که در دولت یار آخر شد
The story of sorrow that with the idol's coming, ended.

ساقیا لطف نمودی قدحت پری باد
O Saki[1]! thou showedest kindness. Be thy goblet full wine!
که به تدبیر تو تشویش خمار آخر شد
For, by thy deliberation, the disquietude of wine-sickness is ended.

در شمار ار چه نیاورد کسی حافظ را
Although, into reckoning (saying: Hath he all this truth) no one bringeth Hafez,
شکر کان محنت بیحد و شمار آخر شد
Thanks that that labor, without limit and reckoning, is ended

---
1-Tapster

غزل ۱۶۷ ⓞⒹⒺ ①⑥⑦

ستاره‌ای بدرخشید و ماه مجلس شد

The star (Muhammad) gleamed; and the moon of the assembly (of the world) became:

دل رمیده ما را رفیق و مونس شد

Of our affrighted heart, the consoler and comforter became.

نگار من که به مکتب نرفت و خط ننوشت

My idol, (Muhammad) who to school went not; and writing wrote not:

به غمزه مسله آموز صد مدرس شد

With a glance, the precept-teacher of a hundred schools became.

به بوی او دل بیمار عاشقان چو صبا

By His (the true Beloved's) perfume, the sick heart of lovers (of God) like the (swift) breeze,

فدای عارض نسرین و چشم نرگس شد

For the cheek of the wild rose, and for the (dark) eye of the narcissus, a ransom became.

به صدر مصطبه‌ام می‌نشاند اکنون دوست

Now, in the chief seat of the inn. the Beloved placeth us:

گدای شهر نگه کن که میر مجلس شد

Behold the city-beggar who, the chief of the assembly became!

خیال آب خضر بست و جام اسکندر

Fancy established the water of Khizr[1], and the cup of Kay Khosro[2]:

به جرعه نوشی سلطان ابوالفوارس شد

With one sweet draught, the Soltan Abul-Farwaris, it (the fancy) became.

طربسرای محبت کنون شود معمور

Now, became prosperous the joy of the palace of love:

که طاق ابروی یار منش مهندس شد

When, its geometrician, the arch of my beloved's eye-brow became.

لب از ترشح می پاک کن برای خدا

(Hafiz) Make pure thy lip of the excess of wine for God's sake:

که خاطرم به هزاران گنه موسوس شد

For, with thousands of sins, a mutterer to itself, my heart became.

کرشمه تو شرابی به عاشقان پیمود

(O Beloved) to lovers, thy glance poured such a draught of wine,

که علم بی‌خبر افتاد و عقل بی‌حس شد

That senseless fell their science; void of understanding, their, reason became.

چو زر عزیز وجود است نظم من آری

Like the precious gold of existence, is my verse. Yes:

قبول دولتیان کیمیای این مس شد

The alchemy of this copper, the acceptance of the wealthy became.

ز راه میکده یاران عنان بگردانید

Friends; from the path of the wine-house, turn the rein:

چراکه حافظ از این راه رفت و مفلس شد

For, by this path went Hafez; and poor became.

1-Name of a prophet   2-King

غزل ۱۶۸ ⓄⒹⒺ ①⑥⑧

گداخت جان که شود کار دل تمام و نشد

(In the wish) that my heart's work should be ended, my soul melted; and it became not (acquired)

بسوختیم در این آرزوی خام و نشد

In this immature wish, I consumed; and it (the wish) became not (acquired).

به لابه گفت شبی میر مجلس تو شوم

With reproach, the Chief of thy Assembly said to me: "One night, I go (to thy Assembly):"

شدم به رغبت خویشش کمین غلام و نشد

According to his wish, I became the least of His slaves; and it (my desire) became not (acquired)

پیام داد که خواهم نشست با رندان

He (the true Beloved) gave the message saying: "I will sit with profligates"

بشد به رندی و دردی کشیم نام و نشد

(In the hope of His society) Reputation for profligacy and dreg-drinking became mine; and it (my hope) became not (acquired).

رواست در بر اگر می‌طپد کبوتر دل

If the pigeon of my heart flutter, it is lawful

که دید در ره خود تاب و پیچ دام و نشد

For, in its path, it be held the twist and turn of the snare but it (freedom) became not (acquired)

بدان هوس که به مستی ببوسم آن لب لعل

In that desire that, in intoxication, I may kiss that ruby lip, (of the true Beloved)

چه خون که در دلم افتاد همچو جام و نشد

What blood (of grief it was) that, into my heart like a cup, fell; and it (the lip – kissing) became not (acquired)

به کوی عشق منه بی‌دلیل راه قدم

In Love's street, plant not thy foot without the road-guide (the murshid);

که من به خویش نمودم صد اهتمام و نشد

For, I, of myself, made a hundred efforts; and it (my desire) became not (acquired).

فغان که در طلب گنج نامه مقصود

In search of the treasure-mandate of my purpose, justice! For,

شدم خراب جهانی ز غم تمام و نشد

I became one altogether ruined in the world; and it (the mandate) became not (acquired)

دریغ و درد که در جست و جوی گنج حضور

In search of the cash treasure (of the true Beloved's) of the presence,

بسی شدم به گدایی بر کرام و نشد

To the generous, much in beggary I wandered; and it (the Beloved's presence) became not (acquired).

هزار حیله برانگیخت حافظ از سر فکر

Out of thought's desire, Hafez evoked a thousand desires,

در آن هوس که شود آن نگار رام و نشد

In the desire that that companion (the true Beloved) may become obedient to him and it (his desire) became not (acquired)

غزل ۱۶۹   ⓄⒹⒺ ①⑥⑨

یاری اندر کس نمی‌بینیم یاران را چه شد

Friendship in none, I perceive. To friends what hath happened?

دوستی کی آخر آمد دوستداران را چه شد

Friendship ended when? To friends what hath happened?

آب حیوان تیره گون شد خضر فرخ پی کجاست

Black of hue became (the limpid, gleaming) the water of life. Khizr[1], auspicious of foot, is where?

خون چکید از شاخ گل باد بهاران را چه شد

From (its own roseate color, the rose hath changed).To the spring-breeze what hath happened?

کس نمی‌گوید که یاری داشت حق دوستی

None saith: "A friend preserved the right of friendship."

حق شناسان را چه حال افتاد یاران را چه شد

Those right-understanding, what state hath be fallen? To friends what hath happened?

لعلی از کان مروت برنیامد سال‌هاست

Years it is since no ruby came from the mine of manliness:

تابش خورشید و سعی باد و باران را چه شد

To the sun's heat, to the wind's effort, to the rains, what hath happened?

شهر یاران بود و خاک مهربانان این دیار

This land was "the city of friends" and "the dust of kind ones"

مهربانی کی سر آمد شهریاران را چه شد

Friendship, how ended? To the city friends, what hath happened?

گوی توفیق و کرامت در میان افکنده‌اند

Into the midst, the ball of grace and of liberality, they (Fate and Destiny) have cast:

کس به میدان در نمی‌آید سواران را چه شد

In the plain (to take up the ball) none appeareth. To the horsemen (the seekers of God that they keep back from happiness and from liberality) what hath happened?

صد هزاران گل شکفت و بانگ مرغی برنخاست

Many a rose (a created being) hath blossomed; no cry of a bird hath risen:

عندلیبان را چه پیش آمد هزاران را چه شد

To the nightingales, (lovers of God) what hath chanced? To those of a thousand notes (lovers of God) what hath happened

زهره سازی خوش نمی‌سازد مگر عودش بسوخت

No sweet melody, maketh Zohre[2] (the murshid). Perchance, she hath consumed her lute (tongue):

کس ندارد ذوق مستی میگساران را چه شد

Intoxication, none desireth. To the wine-drinkers, what hath happened?

حافظ اسرار الهی کس نمی‌داند خموش

Hafez! Divine mysteries, none knoweth. Silence!

از که می‌پرسی که دور روزگاران را چه شد

Of whom, askest thou saying: "To the state of Time's revolution, what hath happened?"

1-Name of prophet   2-"Venus" is known as the goddess of dance and music

غزل ۱۷۰ ⓄⒹⒺ ①⑦Ⓞ

زاهد خلوت نشین دوش به میخانه شد
Last night, to the wine-house, (the Arif, the comprehender of truths) Zahed[1], sitting in khalwat[2], went:

از سر پیمان برفت با سر پیمانه شد
From the head of his covenant, he departed; (and) to the head of the cup, went.

صوفی مجلس که دی جام و قدح می‌شکست
Yesterday, the distraught Sufi[3] who broke the cup and the goblet:

باز به یک جرعه می عاقل و فرزانه شد
Yester-night, by one draught of wine, (of love) wise and learned became.

شاهد عهد شباب آمده بودش به خواب
To him, in dream, the mistress of youth's time had come:

باز به پیرانه سر عاشق و دیوانه شد
With elderly head, lover and distraught he became.

مغبچه‌ای می‌گذشت راه زن دین و دل
A young Magian, the highwayman of truth and of heart, passed:

در پی آن آشنا از همه بیگانه شد
In pursuit of that Friend, (God) a stranger to all else, he became.

آتش رخسار گل خرمن بلبل بسوخت
The (ruddy) fire of the cheek of the rose consumed the nightingale's harvest (of existence):

چهره خندان شمع آفت پروانه شد
The moth's calamity, the laughing face (the burning wick) of the candle, became.

گریه شام و سحر شکر که ضایع نگشت
Evening and morning, our weeping-thanks that it was not lost:

قطره باران ما گوهر یک دانه شد
A peerless jewel, a drop of our raining (weeping) became.

نرگس ساق بخواند آیت افسونگری
The narcissus (the perfect beauty of) the Saki[4] uttered a spell of sorcery:

حلقه اوراد ما مجلس افسانه شد
The assembly of sorcery, the circle of our religious readings became.

منزل حافظ کنون بارگه پادشاست
Now the stage of Hafez is the banquet-place of Kings (for).

دل بر دلدار رفت جان بر جانانه شد
To the Heart-possessor (God) his heart went to the true Beloved, his soul I went.

غزل ۱۷۱ ⓄⒹⒺ ①⑦①

دوش از جناب آصف پیک بشارت آمد
Last night (in the time of Muhammad) a messenger of news from His Highness Asaf[5] (the murshid) came.

کز حضرت سلیمان عشرت اشارت آمد
From His Highness Soleiman[6], (the true Beloved) the order of joy came.

1- Pietist
2- Reclusion, solitude
3-A Muslim ascetic and mystic
4-Tapster
5-Suleiman's minister
6-Name of a prophet

خاک وجود ما را از آب دیده گل کن

With water of the wine, make clay of the dust of our existence:

ویرانسرای دل را گاه عمارت آمد

To the heart's desolate mansion, the time of building came.

این شرح بی‌نهایت کز زلف یار گفتند

This endless explanation of the true Beloved's beauty, that they (men of knowledge) uttered,

حرفیست از هزاران کاندر عبارت آمد

Is only a word out of thousands, that, into example, came.

عیبم بپوش زنهار ای خرقه می آلود

O thou wine-stained of garment! Take care; conceal my defect:

کان پاک پاکدامن بهر زیارت آمد

For, to visit me, that one pure of skirt (the true Beloved) came.

امروز جای هر کس پیدا شود ز خوبان

The place (rank) of every one of the lovely ones (the beloved ones) becometh known to-day,

کان ماه مجلس افروز اندر صدارت آمد

When, to the chief seat, that moon, assembly-adorning, came.

بر تخت جم که تاجش معراج آسمان است

On the throne of Jam, whose crown is the (lofty) sun's ladder of ascen

همت نگر که موری با آن حقارت آمد

Behold the spirit! Notwithstanding (all) this contemptibility, a (feeble) ant (man) came.

از چشم شوخش ای دل ایمان خود نگه دار

O heart! Keep thyself safe from His bold eye;

کان جادوی کمانکش بر عزم غارت آمد

Because, for plunder, that sorcerer, (the eye) the archer, came.

آلوده‌ای تو حافظ فیضی ز شاه درخواه

Hafez! Stained, (with sin) thou art. Ask a favor of the king (the murshid);

کان عنصر سماحت بهر طهارت آمد

For, for purification, (of the sin – stained) that foundation of liberality (the murshid) came.

دریاست مجلس او دریاب وقت و در یاب

The King's assembly is a sea. Discover the time of pearl-gaining:

هان ای زیان رسیده وقت تجارت آمد

Ho! O loss stricken one! The time of barter and profit hath come.

غزل ۱۷۲ 🕉️🕉️🕉️ ODE 🕉️🕉️🕉️

عشق تو نهال حیرت آمد

Love for Thee, the plant of perturbation became

وصل تو کمال حیرت آمد

Union with Thee, the perfection (height) of perturbation became.

بس غرقه حال وصل کخر

In the sea of union, (is) many a drowned one who, at last,

هم بر سر حال حیرت آمد

With a head in the state of perturbation became.

یک دل بنما که در ره او
Show me one heart, in whose path,

بر چهره نه خال حیرت آمد
On the face, no mole (dark spot) of perturbation came.

نه وصل بماند و نه واصل
Remaineth neither union nor the uniter:

آن جا که خیال حیرت آمد
There, where the imagination of perturbation came.

از هر طرفی که گوش کردم
From every side, whereto I applied my ear,

آواز سال حیرت آمد
The sound of the question of perturbation came.

شد منهزم از کمال عزت
Was destroyed and brought down the one,

آن را که جلال حیرت آمد
For whom the glory of perturbation became

سر تا قدم وجود حافظ
Head to foot, Hafez's existence,

در عشق نهال حیرت آمد
In love, the plant of perturbation became

غزل ۱۷۳ ⊙ⒹⒺ ①⑦③

در نمازم خم ابروی تو با یاد آمد
When, in prayer, to me recollection of the curve of Thy eye-brow came.

حالتی رفت که محراب به فریاد آمد
(Over me such) a state passed that, into lament, the prayer-arch came.

از من اکنون طمع صبر و دل و هوش مدار
Now from me expect neither patience nor the heart of sense;

کان تحمل که تو دیدی همه بر باد آمد
For that patience, that (before) thou sawest, to the wind all came.

باده صافی شد و مرغان چمن مست شدند
Clear, became the wine: and intoxicated, became the birds of the sward:

موسم عاشقی و کار به بنیاد آمد
The season of being a lover; and to foundation, the work came

بوی بهبود ز اوضاع جهان می‌شنوم
From the world's quarters, I perceive welfare's perfume:

شادی آورد گل و باد صبا شاد آمد
Gladness, the rose brought; and joyous the morning breeze came.

ای عروس هنر از بخت شکایت منما
O bride of skill! (he holy traveller) Complain not of fortune (for that time, whereof thou complainest, hath passed):

حجله حسن بیارای که داماد آمد
Adorn the chamber of beauty. (thy own existence) for the bridegroom, skill understanding, is came.

دلفریبان نباتی همه زیور بستند
The flowery heart-allurers (the rose, the hyacinth, the sweet basil) all put on Jewels (of flowers):

دلبر ماست که با حسن خداداد آمد
Our heart-ravisher, who is with beauty God-given, came.

زیر بارند درختان که تعلق دارند
Beneath their load, are the trees, (persons) that have attachment (to the world):

ای خوشا سرو که از بار غم آزاد آمد
O happy the (free) cypress, (persons) who tree from grief's bond, came

مطرب از گفته حافظ غزل ی نغز بخوان
Minstrel! Of Hafez's utterance, utter a sweet ghazal[1].

تا بگویم که ز عهد طربم یاد آمد
So that I may speak, saying "Recollection of Time s Joy mine became."

غزل ۱۷۴ ⓄⒹⒺ ①⑦④

مژده ای دل که دگر باد صبا بازآمد
O heart! glad tidings that the morning breeze hath come back,

هدهد خوش خبر از طرف سبا بازآمد
From the quarters of Saba[2] (the land of Queen Balkis) the lapwing of good news hath come back.

برکش ای مرغ سحر نغمه داوودی باز
O bird of the morning! (the bulbul, or the dove) Prolong the melody of Dawood:

که سلیمان گل از باد هوا بازآمد
For from the quarter of the air, the So leiman of the rose hath come back.

عارفی کو که کند فهم زبان سوسن
(In the world) where is an Aref[3] who understandeth the lily's tongue?

تا بپرسد که چرا رفت و چرا بازآمد
That he may inquire: Why she went; and why she hath come back.

مردمی کرد و کرم لطف خداداد به من
Fortune, God-given, showed me manliness and kindness.

کان بت ماه رخ از راه وفا بازآمد
(In that for God's sake), the idol (of stone heart the beloved) hath come back.

لاله بوی می نوشین بشنید از دم صبح
From morn's breath, the tulip hath perceived the perfume of sweet wine:

داغ دل بود به امید دوا بازآمد
Hers was the heart's stain; streak in hope of remedy she hath come back.

چشم من در ره این قافله راه بماند
In rear of that Kafila[4], my (eye drew much water):

تا به گوش دلم آواز درا بازآمد
Since to my heart's ear, the sound of the bell hath come back.

گر چه حافظ در رنجش زد و پیمان بشکست
Although Hafez beat the door of offence and broke his covenant, (with the true Beloved)

لطف او بین که به لطف از در ما بازآمد
Behold His grace that, in peace, from our door, He (our excuse accepting) hath come back.

1-Sonnet
2-Urban name in Yemen

3-Mystic
4-Convoy

غزل ۱۷۵ ⓄⒹⒺ ①⑦⑤

صبا به تهنیت پیر می فروش آمد
For the congratulation of the Pir[1], wine-seller, (Muhammad) the morning-breeze (Jibrail) came

که موسم طرب و عیش و ناز و نوش آمد
Saying: "The season of joy, and of pleasure, and of freshness, and of sweet ness is came.

هوا مسیح نفس گشت و باد نافه گشای
The air became Jesus' breath, and the dust, musk-diffusing:

درخت سبز شد و مرغ در خروش آمد
Green, the tree became; and into song the bird came.

تنور لاله چنان برفروخت باد بهار
The oven (of beauty and of splendour) of the tulip the spring-breeze enkindled to such a degree, '

که غنچه غرق عرق گشت و گل به جوش آمد
That, immersed in sweat (of the rose – water) bud became; and into agitation, the rose came.

به گوش هوش نیوش از من و به عشرت کوش
With the ear of sense, listen to me; and for ease, strive:

که این سخن سحر از هاتفم به گوش آمد
For, to my ear, from an invisible messenger, this matter of the morning came.

ز فکر تفرقه بازآی تا شوی مجموع
From the thought of separation, come out, (from thy own heart) so that collected (of heart) thou mayst be,

به حکم آن که چو شد اهرمن سروش آمد
Since when Ahriman went, Surosh (Jibra, il) came.

ز مرغ صبح ندانم که سوسن آزاد
From the bird of the morning, (the Bulbul, the murshid) I know not the noble lily, (the Arif (

چه گوش کرد که با ده زبان خموش آمد
What (sorrowful matter) it heard, that, notwithstanding its ten tongues, silent it became.

چه جای صحبت نامحرم است مجلس انس
The assembly of affection is the place of society of the excluded what!

سر پیاله بپوشان که خرقه پوش آمد
Cover the mouth of the cup; for the Khirka[2]-wearer (the Zahid) is came.

ز خانقاه به میخانه می‌رود حافظ
From the cloister to the wine-house, Hafez goeth:

مگر ز مستی زهد ریا به هوش آمد
Perchance, (from) the intoxication of austerity (and of) hypocrisy to sense he is came.

غزل ۱۷۶ ⓄⒹⒺ ①⑦⑥

سحرم دولت بیدار به بالین آمد
In the morning, to my pillow, vigilant fortune came:

گفت برخیز که آن خسرو شیرین آمد
(And) said: (From sleep) Arise! For that thy dear Khosro[3] (the true Beloved) hath come.

1-A Muslim saint or holy man, Pietist
2-Cloak

3-Lover

قدحی درکش و سرخوش به تماشا بخرام

"A goblet drink; (and), for seeing Him, merry of head, go:

تا ببینی که نگارت به چه آیین آمد

"That thou mayst see in what fashion, thy idol hath come.

مژدگانی بده ای خلوتی نافه گشای

O Khilvati, musk-pod opener! Give the glad tidings

که ز صحرای ختن آهوی مشکین آمد

"That, from the desert of Khotan, (from afar) a musky deer (the true Beloved).

گریه آبی به رخ سوختگان بازآورد

To the (yellow) cheek of those consumed (with love in separation from Thee my bloody) weeping hath brought back a great ruddy lustre

ناله فریادرس عاشق مسکین آمد

"Weeping, the helper of the (yellow – cheeked) wretched lover hath come."

مرغ دل باز هوادار کمان ابرویست

Again desirous of the eye-brow bow is the bird of my heart:

ای کبوتر نگران باش که شاهین آمد

O pigeon! Be expectant. For the falcon hath come.

ساقیا می بده و غم مخور از دشمن و دوست

O Saki! Give wine; suffer no grief on account of the enemy or of the (true) Beloved:

که به کام دل ما آن بشد و این آمد

For, to our heart's desire, that (the enemy) hath gone; and this (the true Beloved) hath come.

رسم بدعهدی ایام چو دید ابر بهار

When, the spring-cloud beheld Time's bad faith,

گریه‌اش بر سمن و سنبل و نسرین آمد

On the lily and the hyacinth and the rose, its weeping came.

چون صبا گفته حافظ بشنید از بلبل

When, from the nightingale, the morning breeze heard Hafez's utterance,

عنبرافشان به تماشای ریاحین آمد

At the spectacle of the sweet basil, ambergris scattering, it (the breeze) came.

غزل ۱۷۷　ⓄⒹⒺ ①⑦⑦

نه هر که چهره برافروخت دلبری داند

Not every beloved (ofle) that up-kindleth his face the work of a heart-ravisher knoweth.

نه هر که آینه سازد سکندری داند

Not everyone who maketh the mirror, (of Sikandar) the work of a Eskandar knoweth.

نه هر که طرف کله کج نهاد و تند نشست

Not everyone who slantwise placed his cap and sat severe

کلاه داری و آیین سروری داند

The work of a crown-possessor, and the usage of a Ruler knoweth.

تو بندگی چو گدایان به شرط مزد مکن

Like the beggars, do not thou service for wages:

که دوست خود روش بنده پروری داند

For the way of slave-cherishing, the Friend Himself knoweth.

غلام همت آن رند عافیت سوزم

I am the slave of resolution of that profligate, safety-consuming, (the Murshid or the perfect Arif)

که در گدا صفتی کیمیاگری داند

Who, in beggar quality, the work of an alchemist (causing others to reach perfection) knoweth.

وفا و عهد نکو باشد ار بیاموزی

Good are fidelity (promise – fulfilling) and covenant, if thou wilt learn:

وگرنه هر که تو بینی ستمگری داند

If not, everyone thou seest, the work of a tyrant knoweth.

بباختم دل دیوانه و ندانستم

My distraught heart, I staked; and knew not

که آدمی بچه‌ای شیوه پری داند

That one born of man, the way of a Pari[1] knoweth

هزار نکته باریکتر ز مو این جاست

Here, finer than a hair, are a thousand (subtle) points:

نه هر که سر بتراشد قلندری داند

Not everyone who shaveth his head the work of a Kalandar knoweth.

مدار نقطه بینش ز خال توست مرا

(O beloved) the centre of the point of my vision is thy mole;

که قدر گوهر یک دانه جوهری داند

For the value of the incomparable jewel, the jeweler knoweth.

به قد و چهره هر آن کس که شاه خوبان شد

In stature and face, everyone who became the king of the lovely ones (Arifs)

جهان بگیرد اگر دادگستری داند

Taketh the world, if the work of a justice-dispenser, he knoweth.

ز شعر دلکش حافظ کسی بود آگاه

Acquainted with Hafez's heart-alluring verse, becometh that one,

که لطف طبع و سخن گفتن دری داند

Who, the grace of disposition, and the utterance of Dari[2] knoweth.

غزل ۱۷۸ ⓄⒹⒺ ①⑦⑧

هر که شد محرم دل در حرم یار بماند

Whoever became the confidant of his own he art, in the sacred fold of the (true) Beloved remained

وان که این کار ندانست در انکار بماند

He, who knew not this matter, in ignorance remained.

اگر از پرده برون شد دل من عیب مکن

If, forth from the screen, went my heart (abandoning outward reputation and choosing evilness) censure not:

شکر ایزد که نه در پرده پندار بماند

Thanks to God, that not, in the screen of thought (self-worshipping and pride), it remained.

1-Angels, a legendary creature that is very beautiful on hand.   2-Is a kind of dialect from the Persian language

صوفیان واستدند از گرو می همه رخت

Out from pawn for wine, the Sufis (holy travellers) took their Khirka[1]:

دلق ما بود که در خانه خمار بماند

Our dervish-habit, it was that, in the vintner's house, remained.

محتسب شیخ شد و فسق خود از یاد ببرد

Mohtaseb[2] became Sheikh[3] and forgot his own sin.

قصه ماست که در هر سر بازار بماند

Our tale is that which, at the head of every market, remained.

هر می لعل کز آن دست بلورین ستدیم

Every red wine that, from that crystal (pure) hand (of the murshid) I took,

آب حسرت شد و در چشم گهربار بماند

Became the water of regret; and, in my eye, the jewel of (rain) tear remained.

جز دل من کز ازل تا به ابد عاشق رفت

Save my heart, that, from eternity without beginning to eternity without end, proceeded Thy lover,

جاودان کس نشنیدیم که در کار بماند

I have heard of none, whoever in the work (of being Thy lover) remained.

گشت بیمار که چون چشم تو گردد نرگس

That, like Thy eye, it might become, the narcissus became sick (with futile effort):

شیوه تو نشدش حاصل و بیمار بماند

Its (Thy eye's) habit was not gained by it and, sick with futile effort it remained.

از صدای سخن عشق ندیدم خوشتر

More pleasant than the sound of love's speech, naught I heard:

یادگاری که در این گنبد دوار بماند

(Twas) a great token, that, in this revolving dome remained.

داشتم دلقی و صد عیب مرا می‌پوشید

A dervish garment, I had; and it concealed a hundred faults:

خرقه رهن می و مطرب شد و زنار بماند

For wine and the minstrel, the Khirka [4]was pawned; and the mystical cord (of a hundred faults) remained.

بر جمال تو چنان صورت چین حیران شد

The Chinese painter became astonished of Your face,

که حدیثش همه جا در در و دیوار بماند

Such that its story on very door and wall, remained.

به تماشاگه زلفش دل حافظ روزی

One day, to the spectacle-place of Thy tress, Hafez's heart

شد که بازآید و جاوید گرفتار بماند

Went (with the intention) that (after seeing Thy tress) it would return but, ever, captive (to Thy tress), it-remained.

1-Cloak

2-Sheriff

3-A leader in a Muslim community

4-Cloak

غزل ۱۷۹ ⓞⒹⒺ ①⑦⑨

رسید مژده که ایام غم نخواهد ماند
Arrived the glad tidings that grief's time shall not remain:
چنان نماند چنین نیز هم نخواهد ماند
Like that (joy's time) remained not; like this (grief's time) shall not remain.

من ار چه در نظر یار خاکسار شدم
Although, (by the ill-speaking of the watcher) I am, in the Beloved's sight, become dusty and despicable;
رقیب نیز چنین محترم نخواهد ماند
Honored like this, the watcher shall not remain.

چو پرده دار به شمشیر می‌زند همه را
Since the veil-holder (door – keeper) striketh all with the sword,
کسی مقیم حریم حرم نخواهد ماند
Dweller of the sacred territory, a person shall not remain.

چه جای شکر و شکایت ز نقش نیک و بد است
Of (regarding) the picture, good or bad, is what room for thanks or for lament
چو بر صحیفه هستی رقم نخواهد ماند
When, on the page of existence, the writing (of the decree) shall not remain?

سرود مجلس جمشید گفته‌اند این بود
The song of Jamshid's assembly, they have said, was this:
که جام باده بیاور که جم نخواهد ماند
"Bring the cup of wine; for Jam (Jamshid) shall not remain."

غنیمتی شمر ای شمع وصل پروانه
O candle! reckon union with the moth a great gain;
که این معامله تا صبحدم نخواهد ماند
For (even) till dawn, this commerce shall not remain.

توانگرا دل درویش خود به دست آور
O powerful one! Bring to thy hand (and help) the dervish's heart:
که مخزن زر و گنج درم نخواهد ماند
For the treasure of gold, and the treasure of derham shall not remain.

بدین رواق زبرجد نوشته‌اند به زر
In gold, on this mansion of chrysolite, they have written
که جز نکویی اهل کرم نخواهد ماند
"Save the goodness of people of lib erality, aught shall not remain."

ز مهربانی جانان طمع مبر حافظ
Hafez! Sever not desire for the (true) Beloved's favor:
که نقش جور و نشان ستم نخواهد ماند
For the picture of violence and the mark of tyranny shall not remain

غزل ۱۸۰ ⓞⒹⒺ ①⑧⓪

ای پسته تو خنده زده بر حدیث قند
O thou whose pistachio, (mouth) laugheth at the tale of candy!
مشتاقم از برای خدا یک شکر بخند
(Of thy laughter) I am desirous. For God's sake, one sweet smile, smile

طوبی ز قامت تو نیارد که دم زند

(Equality) with thy stature, (even) the (lofty) Tuba (tree of paradise) cannot boast

زین قصه بگذرم که سخن می‌شود بلند

By this tale, I pass. For long, becometh the matter.

خواهی که برنخیزدت از دیده رود خون

Thou wishest not that a river of blood should gush from thy eye?

دل در وفای صحبت رود کسان مبند

On the constancy of society of rosy ones, bind not thy heart.

گر جلوه می‌نمایی و گر طعنه می‌زنی

If sullenness thou display; or if reproach, thou make,

ما نیستیم معتقد شیخ خودپسند

The allied friend of the man, self-approving, we are not

ز آشفتگی حال من آگاه کی شود

(Of) the perturbation of my state, acquainted how becometh

آن را که دل نگشت گرفتار این کمند

That one, whose heart captive to this noose became not?

بازار شوق گرم شد آن سروقد کجاست

Brisk is the market of desire. Where is that candle-face (the beloved)?

تا جان خود بر آتش رویش کنم سپند

So that, on the ruddy fire of his face, soul (and heart), I may make rue (may scatter).

جایی که یار ما به شکرخنده دم زند

Where my (resplendent) beloved, with sweet smile, breatheth,

ای پسته کیستی تو خدا را به خود مخند

O pistachio who art thou For God's sake, to thyself, laugh not (for there, no splendour is thine)

حافظ چو ترک غمزه ترکان نمی‌کنی

Hafez! The glance (with eye-brow and with eye) of the saucy ones, thou abandonest not:

دانی کجاست جای تو خوارزم یا خجند

Knowest thou where thy place is Khwarazm[1], or Khojand[2]?

غزل ۱۸۱ ⓄⒹⒺ ①⑧① ODE 181

بعد از این دست من و دامن آن سرو بلند

After this (together are) my hand and the skirt of that lofty cypress (the Prince of Khujand)

که به بالای چمان از بن و بیخم برکند

Who, with a moving stature, plucked me up from root and branch (of the household)

حاجت مطرب و می نیست تو برقع بگشا

Need of the minstrel and of wine is none Lift thou the veil

که به رقص آوردم آتش رویت چو سپند

That the fire of thy (resplendent) face may bring me, like rue, to dancing.

هیچ رویی نشود آینه حجله بخت

No face becometh the mirror of fortune's (glorious) face,

مگر آن روی که مالند در آن سم سمند

Save that face, which they rub on the hoof of the bay steed (of the beloved)

1-A district in the Amu Darya (Oxus)　　　2-A great city in Turkmenistan

گفتم اسرار غمت هر چه بود گو می‌باش

I said The secret of thy grief, whatever it is, say be

صبر از این بیش ندارم چه کنم تا کی و چند

More than this, no patience have I. What shall I do till when, how long (shall I exercise patience)?

مکش آن آهوی مشکین مرا ای صیاد

O hunter death slay not that musky deer the beloved

شرم از آن چشم سیه دار و مبندش به کمند

Have shame of that dark eye and, in the noose, bind him not.

من خاکی که از این در نتوانم برخاست

I, dusty, who, from this door (of separation from the Beloved) cannot rise

از کجا بوسه زنم بر لب آن قصر بلند

How may I plant a kiss on the lip of that lofty palace

باز مستان دل از آن گیسوی مشکین حافظ

Hafiz Take not again the heart from that musky tress,

زان که دیوانه همان به که بود اندر بند

For the reason that the distraught one is verily best when he is in bonds.

غزل ۱۸۲ ⓞⓓⓔ ①⑧②

حسب حالی ننوشتی و شد ایامی چند

Thou wrotest not the account of thy state; and, passed sometime:

محرمی کو که فرستم به تو پیغامی چند

Where a confidant so that to thee, I may send some message?

ما بدان مقصد عالی نتوانیم رسید

(O Murshid) to this lofty desire (acquisition of union with the true Beloved) we cannot attain

هم مگر پیش نهد لطف شما گامی چند

Unless your favor advanceth (us) some paces.

چون می از خم به سبو رفت و گل افکند نقاب

Since from the jar, wine hath gone into the flagon; and the rose hath cast its veil,

فرصت عیش نگه دار و بزن جامی چند

Preserve the opportunity of ease; and drink some cups (of wine).

قند آمیخته با گل نه علاج دل ماست

Candy mixed with the rose, (rose – conserve) is not the remedy for our sick heart:

بوسه‌ای چند برآمیز به دشنامی چند

Some kisses mix with some abuse.

زاهد از کوچه رندان به سلامت بگذر

O Zahed1! Pass from the circle of profligates to safety:

تا خرابت نکند صحبت بدنامی چند

Lest ruined make thee, the society of some ill of fame.

عیب می جمله چو گفتی هنرش نیز بگو

The defect of wine, all thou toldest; its profit also tell us:

نفی حکمت مکن از بهر دل عامی چند

Negation of (God's) skill make not for the sake of the heart of some people.

1-Pietist

ای گدایان خرابات خدا یار شماست
O beggars of the tavern! God is your Friend,

چشم انعام مدارید ز انعامی چند
Have no eye of (expectation of) favor from some animals.

پیر میخانه چه خوش گفت به دردی کش خویش
To his dreg-drinker, how well spake the Pir[1] of the wine-house,

که مگو حال دل سوخته با خامی چند
Saying: "Utter not the state of the consumed heart to some immature ones."

حافظ از شوق رخ مهر فروغ تو بسوخت
From desire of thy face, love-kindling (that hath the sun's splendour) Hafez consumed:

کامگارا نظری کن سوی ناکامی چند
O one whose desire is fulfilled! Cast a glance towards one some desire unfulfilled.

غزل ۱۸۳ ⓞⒹⒺ ①⑧③

دوش وقت سحر از غصه نجاتم دادند
Last night, at morning time, me freedom from grief, they (Fate and Destiny) gave

واندر آن ظلمت شب آب حیاتم دادند
And, in that darkness of night, me the water-of-life they gave.

بیخود از شعشعه پرتو ذاتم کردند
Through the effulgence of the ray of His essence, me senseless, (and full of love for Him) they made:

باده از جام تجلی صفاتم دادند
(In the world) from the cup of splendor of His qualities, me wine they gave.

چه مبارک سحری بود و چه فرخنده شبی
It was a morning, how auspicious! And a moment how joyous!

آن شب قدر که این تازه براتم دادند
That "Night-of Power" when me, this new command, (as to wine) they gave:

بعد از این روی من و آینه وصف جمال
After this (together are) my face and the mirror of the glory of Beauty

که در آن جا خبر از جلوه ذاتم دادند
For in it, (me) news of His splendor they gave.

من اگر کامروا گشتم و خوشدل چه عجب
If I became desire-gainer and happy of heart, what wonder?

مستحق بودم و اینها به زکاتم دادند
Deserving, I was; and me, these as alms they gave.

هاتف آن روز به من مژده این دولت داد
That day, me glad tidings of this fortune the invisible messenger gave:

که بدان جور و جفا صبر و ثباتم دادند
That in respect to that violence and tyranny, me, patience and endurance they gave.

این همه شهد و شکر کز سخنم می‌ریزد
All this honey and sugar that from my speech poureth

اجر صبریست کز آن شاخ نباتم دادند
Is the reward of great patience, for which me, Shakh-i-Nabat they gave.

1-A Muslim saint or holy man, Pietist

همت حافظ و انفاس سحرخیزان بود

The blessing of Hafez and the breathings (of prayer) of morning-risers (Abids) it was

که ز بند غم ایام نجاتم دادند

That me, freedom from the bond of Time's grief they gave.

غزل ۱۸۴ ⓄⒹⒺ ①⑧④

دوش دیدم که ملایک در میخانه زدند

Last night (in the hidden world) I saw that the angels beat (at) the door of the tavern, (the world of love)

گل آدم بسرشتند و به پیمانه زدند

(Whence they brought out moulds of love) the clay of Adam, they shaped and into the mould, (of love) they cast.

ساکنان حرم ستر و عفاف ملکوت

The dwellers of the sacred fold of the veiling and of the abstaining (from what is forbidden) of the angels,

با من راه نشین باده مستانه زدند

On me, dust-sitter, (holy traveller) the intoxicating wine (of divine knowledge) cast.

آسمان بار امانت نتوانست کشید

The load of deposit (of love and of divine knowledge) the (lofty) sky could not endure

قرعه کار به نام من دیوانه زدند

In the name of helpless me, the dice of the work, (of deposit of love) they cast.

جنگ هفتاد و دو ملت همه را عذر بنه

The wrangle of seventy-two sects, establish excuse for all

چون ندیدند حقیقت ره افسانه زدند

When truth, they saw not, the door of feeble they beat.

شکر ایزد که میان من و او صلح افتاد

Thanks to God, between me and Him, peace chanced,

صوفیان رقص کنان ساغر شکرانه زدند

(On account of this peace) the cup of thankfulness, the angels, dancing, cast.

آتش آن نیست که از شعله او خندد شمع

Not fire is that, whereat the candle's flame laugheth:

آتش آن است که در خرمن پروانه زدند

Fire is that, wherein the moth's harvest (body) they cast.

کس چو حافظ نگشاد از رخ اندیشه نقاب

From off thought's face, none hath drawn the veil as Hafez (hath)

تا سر زلف سخن را به قلم شانه زدند

Since (the time when) the tress-tip, (the brides of) speech combed.

غزل ۱۸۵ ⓄⒹⒺ ①⑧⑤

نقدها را بود آیا که عیاری گیرند

Of coins, (of hearts) is it that they (Fate and Destiny) examination take

تا همه صومعه داران پی کاری گیرند

So that, (the path) after their own work, all the cloister-holders (Abids of outward worship) take?

مصلحت دید من آن است که یاران همه کار

In my sight, the counsel is that all work, friends

بگذارند و خم طره یاری گیرند

Should let go; and, the curl of the tress of a friend (God or the murshid) take.

خوش گرفتند حریفان سر زلف ساقی

The tip of the Saki's[1] tress, happily the companions take:

گر فلکشان بگذارد که قراری گیرند

If the sky permit them, a little rest they take.

قوت بازوی پرهیز به خوبان مفروش

To lovely ones, boast not of the strength of thy arm of chastity:

که در این خیل حصاری به سواری گیرند

For, among this tribe, (of lovely ones) with a single mounted one, a fortress, (of chastity) they take.

یا رب این بچه ترکان چه دلیرند به خون

O Lord! How bold for blood are these young bold ones;

که به تیر مژه هر لحظه شکاری گیرند

For, momently, with the arrow of the eyelash, a great prey, they take.

رقص بر شعر تر و ناله نی خوش باشد

To sweet song, and to the reed's voice sweet is the dance:

خاصه رقصی که در آن دست نگاری گیرند

Especially, that dance wherein, a (lovely) idol's hand, they take.

حافظ ابنای زمان را غم مسکینان نیست

Hafez! No grief for the wretched have the sons of Time:

زین میان گر بتوان به که کناری گیرند

A path aside from the midst of them (the Amirs) if possible (it is) best that they (the wretched ones) take.

غزل ۱۸۶ ⓄⒹⒺ ①⑧⑥

گر می فروش حاجت رندان روا کند

If lawful the need of profligates, the wine-seller maketh,

ایزد گنه ببخشد و دفع بلا کند

His sin, God forgiveth; and, repelling of calamity maketh.

ساقی به جام عدل بده باده تا گدا

Saki! Give wine in the cup of justice, so that the beggar

غیرت نیاورد که جهان پربلا کند

Gather not jealousy (such) that, the world full of calamity, he maketh.

حقا کز این غمان برسد مژده امان

O God! The glad tidings of safety from these griefs (the calamities of Shaitan's deceit) may arrive,

گر سالکی به عهد امانت وفا کند

If, fidelity in the covenant of trust, (that, in eternity without beginning, he made with Thee) the holy traveller maketh.

1-Tapster

گر رنج پیش آید و گر راحت ای حکیم

Sage! If before thee come sorrow or ease,

نسبت مکن به غیر که اینها خدا کند

Ascribe not to other; (than God) for these, God maketh.

در کارخانهای که ره عقل و فضل نیست

In the workshop, wherein is no path to reason and excellence,

فهم ضعیف رای فضولی چرا کند

An arrogant judgment, why (is it that) weak imagination maketh?

مطرب بساز پرده که کس بی اجل نمرد

Minstrel! Thy lyre, play: "Without death, none died."

وان کو نه این ترانه سراید خطا کند

This melody, who chanteth not, mistake maketh.

ما را که درد عشق و بلای خمار کشت

Since love's pain is ours, and the calamity of wine-sickness,

یا وصل دوست یا می صافی دوا کند

(Its remedy) either the ruby (lip) of the beloved, or the pure wine maketh.

جان رفت در سر می و حافظ به عشق سوخت

In the desire of wine, life passed; and in love Hafez consumed:

عیسی دمی کجاست که احیای ما کند

Where is one of Isa-breath[1] (life - giving) that our reviving maketh

غزل ۱۸۷ ⓄⒹⒺ ①⑧⑦

دلا بسوز که سوز تو کارها بکند

O heart! Consume. For deeds (of God) thy consuming maketh:

نیاز نیم شبی دفع صد بلا بکند

The repelling of a hundred calamities, the midnight supplication maketh.

عتاب یار پری چهره عاشقانه بکش

The reproach of the (true) Beloved, Angel of face, endure like a lover:

که یک کرشمه تلافی صد جفا بکند

Because, compensation for a hundred (acts) of tyranny, one glance maketh.

ز ملک تا ملکوتش حجاب بردارند

The screen from this world to the world of angels they rend for him,

هر آن که خدمت جام جهان نما بکند

Who, the service of the cup, world-displaying, maketh.

طبیب عشق مسیحادم است و مشفق لیک

Of Jesus breath (and) compassionate, is the physician of love; the murshid but,

چو درد در تو نبیند که را دوا بکند

When, in thee, he seeth no pain, to whom is it that remedy he maketh.

تو با خدای خود انداز کار و دل خوش دار

Upon thy God, cast thou the work; keep happy of heart:

که رحم اگر نکند مدعی خدا بکند

For if mercy, the adversary maketh not; (mercy) God maketh.

1-It means to raise the dead like Jesus with her or his soul

ز بخت خفته ملولم بود که بیداری

Through sleeping fortune, I am vexed. It may be that vigilance

به وقت فاتحه صبح یک دعا بکند

A prayer, at the time of opening of morning, maketh.

بسوخت حافظ و بویی به زلف یار نبرد

Hafez consumed; and took not the perfume of the (true) Beloved's tress:

مگر دلالت این دولتش صبا بکند

Perchance, the guide of this fortune of his, the wind maketh.

غزل ۱۸۸ ⓄⒹⒺ ①⑧⑧

مرا به رندی و عشق آن فضول عیب کند

For profligacy and love, my censure that foolish one maketh;

که اعتراض بر اسرار علم غیب کند

Who, on the mysteries of men of hidden (divine) knowledge, criticism maketh.

کمال سر محبت ببین نه نقص گناه

(In the lover of God) Behold the perfection of love's mystery, not sin's defect:

که هر که بی‌هنر افتد نظر به عیب کند

For, whoever skill-less is, glance at the defect of man maketh.

ز عطر حور بهشت آن نفس برآید بوی

From the perfume of the angel of paradise, perfume ascendeth at that time

که خاک میکده ما عبیر جیب کند

When, the dust of our wine-house the perfume of her collar, she maketh.

چنان زند ره اسلام غمزه ساق

The Saki's glance so struck the path of Islam,

که اجتناب ز صهبا مگر صهیب کند

That, perchance, shunning of the red morning wine, Suhaib[1] maketh.

کلید گنج سعادت قبول اهل دل است

The key of the treasure of happiness is the acceptance of one of heart:

مباد آن که در این نکته شک و ریب کند

Be it not that, doubt or suspicion, in this matter, any one maketh.

شبان وادی ایمن گهی رسد به مراد

To his desire reacheth the shepherd (Musa) of the Wadi of safety[2] at that time

که چند سال به جان خدمت شعیب کند

When (as shepherd) some years, with soul, the service of Shuayb[3], (Jethro) he maketh.

ز دیده خون بچکاند فسانه حافظ

Blood from the eye, Hafez's tale causeth to drop,

چو یاد وقت زمان شباب و شیب کند

When of youth's time and of the time of old age, recollection, he maketh.

1-One of the companions of the Holy Prophet who was known as a pious ascetic

2-An allusion to Prophet Moses who was a shepherd in the desert

3-Name of a prophet

غزل ۱۸۹ ⓄⒹⒺ ①⑧⑨

طایر دولت اگر باز گذاری بکند

If again passing, (by me) the bird of fortune shall make.

یار بازآید و با وصل قراری بکند

Again the (true) Beloved shall come; and contentment with union (with me) shall make.

دیده را دستگه در و گهر گر چه نماند

Although, to the eye remaineth no power of (producing) the pearl or the jewel, (to scatter on the true Beloved when He cometh)

بخورد خونی و تدبیر نثاری بکند

It shall devour a great quantity of blood, and the design of a great scattering (of that blood) shall make.

دوش گفتم بکند لعل لبش چاره من

Last night, (to my heart) I said: "Maketh the ruby of His lip my remedy?"

هاتف غیب ندا داد که آری بکند

Voice, gave the invisible messenger saying: "Yes! it maketh."

کس نیارد بر او دم زند از قصه ما

To Him, of our tale (of love) none can utter;

مگرش باد صبا گوش گذاری بکند

Perchance, its reporting the morning breeze maketh.

داده‌ام باز نظر را به تذروی پرواز

To the hawk (the murshid) of my own sight, I have given flight at the partridge (the true Beloved)

بازخواند مگرش نقش و شکاری بکند

Perchance, it (the partridge) may recall my (good) fortune; and a great prey may make.

شهر خالیست ز عشاق بود کز طرفی

Void is the city of lovers; it may be that from a quarter,

مردی از خویش برون آید و کاری بکند

Out from himself, a man cometh; and a work maketh.

کو کریمی که ز بزم طربش غمزده‌ای

Where a generous one, from whose banquet of joy, the grief-stricken one

جرعه‌ای درکشد و دفع خماری بکند

Drinketh a draft; and the repelling of wine-sickness maketh?

یا وفا یا خبر وصل تو یا مرگ رقیب

Either fidelity; or the news of union with Thee; or the death of the watcher:

بود آیا که فلک زین دو سه کاری بکند

Of these, (one), two, (or) three, deeds the sphere's (sport) maketh.

حافظا گر نروی از در او هم روزی

Hafez! If, even a day, from His door, thou go not,

گذری بر سرت از گوشه کناری بکند

From a corner of a quarter, passing by thy head, He maketh

غزل ۱۹۰ ⚙️ ODE ⚙️ 190

کلک مشکین تو روزی که ز ما یاد کند

One day, when recollection of us thy musky reed maketh,

ببرد اجر دو صد بنده که آزاد کند

It (the reed) will take reward: Two hundred slaves that free, it maketh_

قاصد منزل سلمی که سلامت بادش

The messenger of Her Highness Salma[1]-to whom be safety

چه شود گر به سلامی دل ما شاد کند

What is it if, with a (kind) salutation, our heart joyous, she maketh?

امتحان کن که بسی گنج مرادت بدهند

Examine this: "Many a treasure of desire will they give thee,

گر خرابی چو مرا لطف تو آباد کند

"If prosperous, one ruined like me, thy favor maketh."

یا رب اندر دل آن خسرو شیرین انداز

O Lord! Into the heart of that Khosro Shirin[2] (Sultan Uvays) cast (the thought)

که به رحمت گذری بر سر فرهاد کند

That, a passing in mercy, by Farhad, he maketh.

شاه را به بود از طاعت صدساله و زهد

For the king-, than a hundred years of piety and of austerity, better is

قدر یک ساعته عمری که در او داد کند

A Life to the extent of only an hour, where injustice, he maketh.

حالیا عشوه ناز تو ز بنیادم برد

Now, me from foundation, love's glance for thee hath taken:

تا دگرباره حکیمانه چه بنیاد کند

Let us see, again, what thy sage-like thought maketh.

گوهر پاک تو از مدحت ما مستغنیست

Independent of our praise is thy pure essence

فکر مشاطه چه با حسن خداداد کند

With beauty God-given, thought of the attirer, who maketh?

ره نبردیم به مقصود خود اندر شیراز

Into Shiraz we traveled not to our desire,

خرم آن روز که حافظ ره بغداد کند

Joyful the day, when (in the service of Sultan Uvays) way to Baghdad[3], Hafez maketh.

غزل ۱۹۱ ⚙️ ODE ⚙️ 191

آن کیست کز روی کرم با ما وفاداری کند

Who is that one, who, by way of manliness, fidelity with me will make;

بر جای بدکاری چو من یک دم نکوکاری کند

(Who) in respect of an ill-doer like me, once a good deed will make?

1-Like Lily or Shirin

2-like Lili and Majnoun

3-Is the largest city and capital of Iraq

اول به بانگ نای و نی آرد به دل پیغام وی

First, to the sound of the harp and of the reed, (me), His (the true Beloved's) message, he will bring:

وان گه به یک پیمانه می با من وفاداری کند

Then, with a measure of wine, fidelity with me, he will make.

دلبر که جان فرسود از او کام دلم نگشود از او

The Heart-ravisher, for whom my soul withered; by whom, the desire of my heart opened not:

نومید نتوان بود از او باشد که دلداری کند

Of Him, one cannot be hopeless. Perchance, loving kindness, He may make.

گفتم گره نگشوده‌ام زان طره تا من بوده‌ام

I said "So long as I have been, (Thy lover) I have not loosed a knot from that (thy) tress:"

گفتا منش فرموده‌ام تا با تو طراری کند

He said: "I have ordered it. (the tress) with thee, readiness (in having its knots unloosed) it shall make."

پشمینه پوش تندخو از عشق نشنیده‌است بو

(O Murshid) the wool-wearer, sullen of disposition (the hypocrite, captive to lust, in whom love hath no part) hath not perceived love's perfume

از مستیش رمزی بگو تا ترک هشیاری کند

Of (its) loves intoxication, utter a hint, that, abandonment of sensibleness (and the choosing of the intoxication of love) he may make.

چون من گدای بی‌نشان مشکل بود یاری چنان

A beggar, void of mark, like me! A Friend (God) like that was difficult to obtain:

سلطان کجا عیش نهان با رند بازاری کند

Hidden pleasure with the common bazar-haunter, where doth the (great) Soltan make?

زان طره پرپیچ و خم سهل است اگر بینم ستم

Tis easy if, from that tress, full of twist and turn, I experience tyranny:

از بند و زنجیرش چه غم هر کس که عیاری کند

Of its bond and chain, what grief is that one's, who, coming and going, may make?

شد لشکر غم بی عدد از بخت می‌خواهم مدد

Countless, became grief's army. From fortune, I seek aid.

تا فخر دین عبدالصمد باشد که غمخواری کند

Until, perchance, consolation Fakhru-d-Din Abdu- ode Samad[1] may make.

با چشم پرنیرنگ او حافظ مکن آهنگ او

Hafez! With this (the Beloved's) eye full of sorcery, attempt Him not:

کان طره شبرنگ او بسیار طراری کند

For that tress of night hue of His many a deceit shall make.

غزل ۱۹۲ ⓄⒹⒺ ①⑨②

سرو چمان من چرا میل چمن نمی‌کند

Inclination for the sward, the cypress of my sward, (the Beloved) wberefore maketh not?

همدم گل نمی‌شود یاد سمن نمی‌کند

The fellow-companion of the rose, (wherefore) becometh not? Memory of the lily (wherefore) maketh not?

1-One of the scholars of Hafez's time

دی گله‌ای ز طره‌اش کردم و از سر فسوس

(To the Beloved) I complained last night of (the tyranny of) His tress.By way of regret

گفت که این سیاه کج گوش به من نمی‌کند

He spake saying To me, the ear (of attention) this black curly (tress) maketh not.

تا دل هرزه گرد من رفت به چین زلف او

Until, into the curl of His tress, went my foolish heart,

زان سفر دراز خود عزم وطن نمی‌کند

On account of that long Journey, (to the next world) the resolution of (visiting its) native land,
(it my heart of) itself maketh not.

پیش کمان ابرویش لابه همی‌کنم ولی

Submissiveness, before the bow of His eye-brow, I keep displaying; but,

گوش کشیده است از آن گوش به من نمی‌کند

Ear-drawn it is. Therefore, for me, the ear, (of attention) He maketh not.

با همه عطف دامنت آیدم از صبا عجب

Notwithstanding all this perfume of Thy skirt, in respect of (the wind), wonder cometh to me,

کز گذر تو خاک را مشک ختن نمی‌کند

That, by Thy passing, the dust, the musk of Khotan[1], it (the wind) maketh not.

چون ز نسیم می‌شود زلف بنفشه پرشکن

When with the wind, the (dark) violet tress becometh full of twist:

وه که دلم چه یاد از آن عهدشکن نمی‌کند

Alas! Of that time of curl, (of Thy tress) what recollection is it that my heart maketh not.

دل به امید روی او همدم جان نمی‌شود

(O true Beloved) In hope of union with Thee, the fellow-companion of the soul, my heart is not:

جان به هوای کوی او خدمت تن نمی‌کند

In desire of Thy street, the service of the body, my soul maketh not.

ساقی سیم ساق من گر همه درد می‌دهد

If my Saki[2] (the true Beloved) of silver leg giveth naught but dregs, (poison)

کیست که تن چو جام می جمله دهن نمی‌کند

The body all mouth, like the wine-cup, who is there that maketh not.

دستخوش جفا مکن آب رخم که فیض ابر

Against my honour, exercise no Tyranny for the bounty of the cloud

بی مدد سرشک من در عدن نمی‌کند

Without the aid of my tears, the pearl of' And maketh not

کشته غمزه تو شد حافظ ناشنیده پند

Not listening to counsel, (heart given to Thee) Hafez was slain by Thy glance:

تیغ سزاست هر که را درد سخن نمی‌کند

Fit is the sword (destruction) for him, who the comprehension of speech (of counsel) maketh not.

غزل ۱۹۳ ⓄⒹⒺ ①⑨③

در نظربازی ما بی‌خبران حیرانند

Astonished at our glance-playing, (in love's path) those voids of vision (the men of shara') are:

من چنینم که نمودم دگر ایشان دانند

As I appeared (infidel, or lover of God) so I am; the rest, they know.

1-A special perfume made from the navel of a deer   2-Tapster

عاقلان نقطه پرگار وجودند ولی

The sages are the center of the compass of existence; but

عشق داند که در این دایره سرگردانند

Love knoweth that, in this circle, (of love) they head-revolving (their learning in love's path being useless) are.

جلوه گاه رخ او دیده من تنها نیست

Not alone is my eye the splendor-place of His cheek:

ماه و خورشید همین آینه می گردانند

Revolving this very mirror, the sun and the moon are.

عهد ما با لب شیرین دهنان بست خدا

With the lip of those sweet of mouth, God established my covenant (of service):

ما همه بنده و این قوم خداوندانند

We all slaves; (are) and these lords are.

مفلسانیم و هوای می و مطرب داریم

Poor (having only the woollen religious garment) are we; and desire for wine and for the minstrel, we have:

آه اگر خرقه پشمین به گرو نستانند

Also! If, in pledge, the woolen Khirka[1] they take not.

وصل خورشید به شبپره اعمی نرسد

The union of the sun (the true Beloved) reacheth not to the blind bat (common persons):

که در آن آینه صاحب نظران حیرانند

For, in this mirror (even) those of vision astonished are

لاف عشق و گله از یار زهی لاف دروغ

(To make) Boast of love; and lament of (the tyranny of) the beloved-O excellent the boast of falsehood!

عشقبازان چنین مستحق هجرانند

Deserving of separation, love-player-like these are.

مگرم چشم سیاه تو بیاموزد کار

(O beloved) Perchance Thy dark intoxicated eye will teach me (abstinent) the work (of intoxication)

ور نه مستوری و مستی همه کس نتوانند

If not, capable of (combining) abstinence and intoxication, not all are.

گر به نزهتگه ارواح برد بوی تو باد

If to the pleasure-place (the world) of souls, the wind carry Thy perfume,

عقل و جان گوهر هستی به نثار افشانند

In scattering, (for thee) the jewel of their existence, reason and soul scatter.

زاهد ار رندی حافظ نکند فهم چه شد

Zahed[2]! If Hafez practice not profligacy, what fear? Know

دیو بگریزد از آن قوم که قرآن خوانند

"From that tribe that readeth the Quran, the demon fleeth."

گر شوند آگه از اندیشه ما مغبچگان

If the young Magians become acquainted with our ill-thought,

بعد از این خرقه صوفی به گرو نستانند

After this, in pledge, the Sufi's Khirka they take not (and from him flee).

1-Cloak   2 -Pietist

غزل ۱۹۴ ⓄⒹⒺ ①⑨④

سمن بویان غبار غم چو بنشینند بنشانند
Those of lily perfume cause grief's dust to sit when they sit:

پری رویان قرار از دل چو بستیزند بستانند
Patience from the heart, those of Angel-face take when they strive.

به فتراک جفا دل‌ها چو بربندند بربندند
To the saddle-strap of tyranny, hearts they bind when they bind:

ز زلف عنبرین جان‌ها چو بگشایند بفشانند
From the ambergris be perfumed tress, soul s they scatter, when they scatter.

به عمری یک نفس با ما چو بنشینند برخیزند
In a life-time, with us a moment, they rise, when they sit,

نهال شوق در خاطر چو برخیزند بنشانند
In the heart, the plant of desire they plant, when they rise up.

سرشک گوشه گیران را چو دریابند در یابند
The tear of the corner-takers lovers they find, when they find:

رخ مهر از سحرخیزان نگردانند اگر دانند
(From) the love of morning-risers, the face (from love of them) they turn not, if (when) they know.

ز چشمم لعل رمانی چو می‌خندند می‌بارند
(From) my eye, the pomegranate-like ruby (bloody tears) they rain, when they laugh:

ز رویم راز پنهانی چو می‌بینند می‌خوانند
From my face, the hidden mystery, they read, when they look.

دوای درد عاشق را کسی کو سهل پندارد
The one who thought that the remedy for lover is simple:

ز فکر آنان که در تدبیر درمانند در مانند
Out of sight of those sages who consider treatment, be.

چو منصور از مراد آنان که بردارند بر دارند
Those who like Mansur[1] are on the gibbet, take up that desire of remedy:

بدین درگاه حافظ را چو می‌خوانند می‌رانند
To this court, (of God) they call Hafez when they cause him to die.

در این حضرت چو مشتاقان نیاز آرند ناز آرند
In that presence, the desirous ones bring grace, when they bring supplication:

که با این درد اگر دربند درمانند درمانند
For, if in thought of remedy they are, distressed with this pain, they are.

غزل ۱۹۵ ⓄⒹⒺ ①⑨⑤

غلام نرگس مست تو تاجدارانند
The slave of thy intoxicated eye, crown-possessors are:

خراب باده لعل تو هوشیارانند
Undone with the wine of Thy ruby lip, sensible ones are.

1-Hussein Ibn Mansour Hallaj, the famous mystic of the
fourth century AH

تو را صبا و مرا آب دیده شد غماز

(O true Beloved) For Thee, the wind (bearing news to men, and far and near thy perfume) and for me the water (tear) of the eye (declaring me to be a lover) became informers:

وگر نه عاشق و معشوق رازدارانند

If not, mystery-keepers (of each other) the lover and the Beloved are.

ز زیر زلف دوتا چون گذر کنی بنگر

When Thou passest, (supon the Path) glance: Beneath Thy two tresses,

که از یمین و یسارت چه سوگوارانند

From right and left, how restless they are.

گذار کن چو صبا بر بنفشه زار و ببین

(O true Beloved) Like the wind, pass over the violet-bed. Behold,

که از تطاول زلفت چه بی‌قرارانند

From the tyranny of thy tress, how sorrowful they are!

نصیب ماست بهشت ای خداشناس برو

O God-recognizer? Our portion is paradise. Go:

که مستحق کرامت گناهکارانند

For deserving of mercy, sinners are.

نه من بر آن گل عارض غزل سرایم و بس

To that rose cheek (of Thine) not alone do I sing the love song:

که عندلیب تو از هر طرف هزارانند

For, on every side, Thy nightingales (lovers) a thousand are.

تو دستگیر شو ای خضر بی خجسته که من

O Khizr[1] of auspicious foot! (the Murshid perfect and excellent) Be thou my handseizer. For I

پیاده می‌روم و همرهان سوارانند

Travel on foot; (and) my fellow-travelers. (Arifs) on horseback are

بیا به میکده و چهره ارغوانی کن

To the wine-house, go; and (with wine) make ruddy thy face:

مرو به صومعه کان جا سیاه کارانند

To the cloister, go not: for there, dark of deed, they are.

خلاص حافظ از آن زلف تابدار مباد

(O true Beloved) Free of that twist-possessing tress, Hafez be not:

که بستگان کمند تو رستگارانند

For, free, (from evilness, from grief, and from attachment to any one) those bound to Thy girdle are.

غزل ۱۹۶   ÔDÉ ①⑨⑥

آنان که خاک را به نظر کیمیا کنند

Those (Mursheds[2]), who, (from exceeding firmness) with their glance alchemy of the dust (of the traveller's existence) make,

آیا بود که گوشه چشمی به ما کنند

At us, eye-cornering, (oblique glancing) do they make?

دردم نهفته به ز طبیبان مدعی

My pain concealed from the claimant's physician, best:

باشد که از خزانه غیبم دوا کنند

It may be that, its remedy from the treasury of the hidden, they (Fate and Destiny) make.

1-Name of the prophet   2-Guru

معشوق چون نقاب ز رخ در نمی‌کشد
Since the (true) Beloved up lifteth not the veil from His face,

هر کس حکایتی به تصور چرا کنند
Why doth everyone, in imagination, a tale make?

چون حسن عاقبت نه به رندی و زاهدیست
Since (they carried not away) the beauty of ease; and austerity is,

آن به که کار خود به عنایت رها کنند
That best that, as a favor, release of their own work, they make.

بی معرفت مباش که در من یزید عشق
Be not without divine knowledge; for in excess of love:

اهل نظر معامله با آشنا کنند
Bargains with the friend, people of vision make.

حالی درون پرده بسی فتنه می‌رود
Now, within the screen, many a calamity goeth:

تا آن زمان که پرده برافتد چه‌ها کنند
At that time when the screen falleth down, let us see what they make.

گر سنگ از این حدیث بنالد عجب مدار
If of this tale the stone bewail, hold it not wonderful;

صاحب دلان حکایت دل خوش ادا کنند
Utterance of the tale of the happy heart, those of heart make

می خور که صد گناه ز اغیار در حجاب
Drink wine. For, within the screen, a hundred crimes on the part of strangers

بهتر ز طاعتی که به روی و ریا کنند
Better than a devotion which, with dissimulation and hypocrisy, they make.

پیراهنی که آید از او بوی یوسفم
The garment (of faith and of divine knowledge) wherefrom cometh the perfume of Yusef[1]
(God, great and glorious)

ترسم برادران غیورش قبا کنند
It, I fear, the proud brothers (Shaitans) rent make.

بگذر به کوی میکده تا زمره حضور
Pass to the street of the tavern since the present crowd,

اوقات خود ز بهر تو صرف دعا کنند
For the sake of thee only, at their own times, prayer make.

پنهان ز حاسدان به خودم خوان که منعمان
Secretly (from) the envious ones, call me to thyself For, the affluentones

خیر نهان برای رضای خدا کنند
For God's sake, much secret good make.

حافظ دوام وصل میسر نمی‌شود
Hafez! Union (with the true Beloved) is ever unattainable:

شاهان کم التفات به حال گدا کنند
God forbid! To the beggar's state, less attention they should make.

1-Name of a prophet

غزل ۱۹۷ ⓄⒹⒺ ①⑨⑦

شاهدان گر دلبری زین سان کنند

If, in this way, heart-ravishingness, lovely ones make,

زاهدان را رخنه در ایمان کنند

In the faith of Zahed1s, breaches, they will make.

هر کجا آن شاخ نرگس بشکفد

Wherever that branch of the narcissus (the true Beloved) blossometh (entereth upon manifestations of glories)

گلرخانش دیده نرگسدان کنند

Its narcissus holder, their own eye, those of rose-cheek (illusory beloved ones) make.

ای جوان سروقد گویی ببر

O youth, cypress of stature! Strike the bail,

پیش از آن کز قامتت چوگان کنند

Before that time when, of thy stature, the polo they make.

عاشقان را بر سر خود حکم نیست

Over their own head, (life) lovers have no command:

هر چه فرمان تو باشد آن کنند

Whatever be Thy order, that they make.

پیش چشمم کمتر است از قطره‌ای

In my eye, less than a drop are

این حکایت‌ها که از طوفان کنند

Those tales that of (Noh's great) deluge, they make.

یار ما چون گیرد آغاز سماع

When our beloved (the Murshid) beginneth, sama2,

قدسیان بر عرش دست افشان کنند

Hand waving, (and dancing) the holy ones of the ninth Heaven make.

مردم چشمم به خون آغشته شد

Immersed in blood (from much weeping on account of Thy tyranny) became the pupil of my eye

در کجا این ظلم بر انسان کنند

This tyranny against man, where (in what religious order) do they make?

خوش برآ با غصه‌ای دل کاهل راز

O heart, careless of mystery! Forth from grief, come happy:

عیش خوش در بوته هجران کنند

In the crucible of separation, pleasant ease they make.

سر مکش حافظ ز آه نیم شب

Hafez! Draw not forth thy head from the midnight sigh,

تا چو صبحت آینه رخشان کنند

So that, gleaming like the morning, the mirror (of thy heart) they may make.

1-Pietist   2-It means hearing every pleasant song

غزل ۱۹۸ ÓDE 198

گفتم کی ام دهان و لبت کامران کنند

I said: (O Beloved) "Me, prosperous, Thy mouth and lip, when do they make?"

گفتا به چشم هر چه تو گویی چنان کنند

He said: "By my eye (I swear that) whatever thou sayest even so do they make."

گفتم خراج مصر طلب می‌کند لبت

I said: "Thy lip (from exceeding sweetness) demandeth tribute of Egypt (sugar):"

گفتا در این معامله کمتر زیان کنند

He said: "In this matter, loss they seldom make."

گفتم به نقطه دهنت خود که برد راه

I said: "To the point of Thy mouth, who taketh the way?"

گفت این حکایتیست که با نکته دان کنند

He said "This Is a tale that (only) to the subtlety-knower, (the perfect Arif) they make."

گفتم صنم پرست مشو با صمد نشین

I said: "In the society of the lofty-sitter, be not idol worshipper?"

گفتا به کوی عشق هم این و هم آن کنند

He said: "In love's street, also this and also that (talk) they make"

گفتم هوای میکده غم می‌برد ز دل

I said: "The desire of the wine-house taketh grief from the heart."

گفتا خوش آن کسان که دلی شادمان کنند

He said: "Happy, those who joyous a single heart make."

گفتم شراب و خرقه نه آیین مذهب است

I said: (Drinking) "Wine and (putting on) the religious garment, are they not the ordinances of the religious order?

گفت این عمل به مذهب پیر مغان کنند

He said: "In the religious order of the Pir of the Magians, this work (of wine and of the garment) they make."

گفتم ز لعل نوش لبان پیر را چه سود

I said "From the sweet ruby of thy lips, what profit the old is?"

گفتا به بوسه شکرینش جوان کنند

He said: "Him, with a sweet kiss, young they make."

گفتم که خواجه کی به سر حجله می‌رود

I said "To the chamber (of pleasure) when goeth the Khwajeh?"

گفت آن زمان که مشتری و مه قران کنند

He said: "That time when Jupiter and the moon conjunction make."

گفتم دعای دولت او ورد حافظ است

I said: "Prayer for his (the Khwaja's) fortune is Hafez's morning exercise."

گفت این دعا ملایک هفت آسمان کنند

He said: "This prayer the angels of the seventh heaven make."

غزل ۱۹۹ ⓞⓓⓔ ①⑨⑨

واعظان کاین جلوه در محراب و منبر می‌کنند

The (outward) admonishers who, in the prayer-arch and the pulpit, grandeur (of exhortation) make,

چون به خلوت می‌روند آن کار دیگر می‌کنند

When into their chamber they go, that work of another kind they make.

مشکلی دارم ز دانشمند مجلس بازپرس

A difficulty, I have. Ask the wisp ones of the assembly, (those ordering penitence)

توبه فرمایان چرا خود توبه کمتر می‌کنند

Why those ordering penitence, themselves penitence seldom make?

گوییا باور نمی‌دارند روز داوری

Thou mayst say, they have no belief in the day of judgment,

کاین همه قلب و دغل در کار داور می‌کنند

That, in the work of the Ruler, (God) a il this fraud and deceit they make.

یا رب این نودولتان را با خر خودشان نشان

O Lord! Place these newly enriched ones upon their own asses: (reward them according to their deeds)

کاین همه ناز از غلام ترک و استر می‌کنند

Because, on account of a Turk slave and a mule, all this arrogance, they make.

ای گدای خانقه برجه که در دیر مغان

O beggar of the monastery! Leap up. For, in the cloister of the Magians!

می‌دهند آبی که دل‌ها را توانگر می‌کنند

They give a little water; (wine of Love for God) and hearts strong make.

حسن بی‌پایان او چندان که عاشق می‌کشد

O heart make void thy house of the idol of lust, and of that other than God that it may become the dwelling of the true Beloved

زمره دیگر به عشق از غیب سر بر می‌کنند

(To the same degree) From the invisible, their head in love, (to God) raised another crowd make. I am the slave of the Pir of the tavern, whose darvishes

بر در میخانه عشق ای ملک تسبیح گوی

O angel! Utter the tasbih[1] at the door of love's tavern

کاندر آن جا طینت آدم مخمر می‌کنند

For within, Adam's clay, dough they make.

صبحدم از عرش می‌آمد خروشی عقل گفت

At dawn, from God's throne, came a shout: wisdom spake:

قدسیان گویی که شعر حافظ از بر می‌کنند

Thou mayst say that chanting of the verse of Hafez, the holy ones (angels) make.

1-Gloria

غزل ۲۰۰ ⓄⒹⒺ ②ⓄⓄ

دانی که چنگ و عود چه تقریر می‌کنند
Thou knowest what tale (it is) that the harp and the lyre (renowned men of piety) make?

پنهان خورید باده که تعزیر می‌کنند
Secretly drink ye wine (of love and reveal it not) that thee precious they may make.

ناموس عشق و رونق عشاق می‌برند
The honor of love and the splendor of lovers, they take:

عیب جوان و سرزنش پیر می‌کنند
The censure of the young; and the reproof of the old, they make.

جز قلب تیره هیچ نشد حاصل و هنوز
Nothing gained but a darken heart, yet,

باطل در این خیال که اکسیر می‌کنند
Wrong in this illusion that someday gold they make.

گویند رمز عشق مگویید و مشنوید
They say: (To any one) Utter ye not love's mystery; (from any one) hear it not

مشکل حکایتیست که تقریر می‌کنند
It is a difficult story, (for the concealing of love is impossible) whereof relation, they make.

ما از برون در شده مغرور صد فریب
Without of the door, we being deceived by a hundred deceits,

تا خود درون پرده چه تدبیر می‌کنند
Let us see, within the screen, what device they make

تشویش وقت پیر مغان می‌دهند باز
Rime's vexation, they give the Pir of the Magians[1]:

این سالکان نگر که چه با پیر می‌کنند
Behold what (sport) with the Pir[2], these holy travelers make!

صد ملک دل به نیم نظر می‌توان خرید
One can purchase a hundred honors with half a glance,

خوبان در این معامله تقصیر می‌کنند
In this act, (of glance – making) deficiency, lovely ones make.

قومی به جد و جهد نهادند وصل دوست
With effort and struggle, a crowd established union with the (true) Beloved

قومی دگر حواله به تقدیر می‌کنند
Reliance on Fate (saying if union be decreed union will be), another crowd make

فی الجمله اعتماد مکن بر ثبات دهر
In short, on Time's permanency, rely not:

کاین کارخانه‌ایست که تغییر می‌کنند
For this (world) is the workshop wherein change they make

می خور که شیخ و حافظ و مفتی و محتسب
Drink wine. For the Shaikh[3], and Hafez, and the Mufti[4] and the Mohtaseb[5]

چون نیک بنگری همه تزویر می‌کنند
All when thou lookest well fraud (openly abstaining from wine, secretly drinking wine) make.

1-The perfect mystic man,
2-A Muslim saint or holy man, Pietist
3-Preacher

4-Lawyer
5-Sheriff

غزل ۲۰۱   ⓄⒹⒺ ②⓪①

شراب بی‌غش و ساقی خوش دو دام رهند
Wine without adulteration and the Saki pleasing are two snares of the Path

که زیرکان جهان از کمندشان نرهند
From whose noose, (even) the wise ones of the world escape not

من ار چه عاشقم و رند و مست و نامه سیاه
Although, lover, profligate, intoxicated and one black of book I am

هزار شکر که یاران شهر بی‌گنهند
(To God) a thousand thanks that the beloved ones of the city sinless are

جفا نه پیشه درویشیست و راهروی
Tyranny is not the way of a dervish and of away-farer

بیار باده که این سالکان نه مرد رهند
Bring wine for the se travellers are not men of the Path

مبین حقیر گدایان عشق را کاین قوم
Regard not contemptible love's beggars.

شهان بی کمر و خسروان بی کلهند
For, these are beltless kings and crown less khusraus.

به هوش باش که هنگام باد استغنا
With sense be for at the time of the wind of in dependence (pride)

هزار خرمن طاعت به نیم جو ننهند
They purchase not for a barley-corn a thousand harvests of devotion.

مکن که کوکبه دلبری شکسته شود
Act not so that the splendour of the Heart-Ravisher (God) be shattered

چو بندگان بگریزند و چاکران بجهند
When His servants flee and His slaves leap upt (o depart)

غلام همت دردی کشان یک رنگم
The slave of resolution, dreg-drinking one of colour, I am

نه آن گروه که ازرق لباس و دل سیهند
Not of that crowd that are blue of garmen (outwardly pious) and black of heart (inwardly impious)

قدم منه به خرابات جز به شرط ادب
Save with the condition of respect, plant not thy foot in the tavern

که سالکان درش محرمان پادشهند
For, the dweller so fit s door are confidants of the king

جناب عشق بلند است همتی حافظ
Hafiz love's rank is lofty. A resolution (make)

که عاشقان ره بی‌همتان به خود ندهند
For to themselves, lover admit not those void of resolution

غزل ۲۰۲   ⓄⒹⒺ ②⓪②

بود آیا که در میکده‌ها بگشایند
(O heart) It may be that the door of the wine-houses, they will open

گره از کار فروبسته ما بگشایند
The knot (of difficulty) of our entangled work they will open

اگر از بهر دل زاهد خودبین بستند

If, for the sake of the Zahid's heart, self-seeing, they closed the door

دل قوی دار که از بهر خدا بگشایند

Strong keep the heart; for, for the sake of God they will open

به صفای دل رندان صبوحی زدگان

By the purity of the heart of profligates, drinkers of them orning cup,

بس در بسته به مفتاح دعا بگشایند

With the key of prayer, many a closed door, they will open.

نامه تعزیت دختر رز بنویسید

Write ye a letter of condolence to the daughter of the vine,

تا همه مغبچگان زلف دوتا بگشایند

So that, the doubled-uptress, all the young Magians will loose.

گیسوی چنگ ببرید به مرگ می ناب

At the death of pure wine, sever the tress (cord) of the harp

تا حریفان همه خون از از مژه‌ها بگشایند

So that, blood, from the eye-lashes, all the companions will loose.

در میخانه ببستند خدایا مپسند

O God they (fate and destiny) closed the door of the wine-house. Approve not

که در خانه تزویر و ریا بگشایند

For, the door of deception and of hyprocrisy, they will

حافظ این خرقه که داری تو ببینی فردا

Hafiz this Khirka that thouhast, tomorrow (the day of resurrection) thou wilt see

که چه زنار ز زیرش به دعا بگشایند

How, with violence, the (religious) cord (of infidelity) from beneath it, they will loose

غزل ۲۰۳ ⓄⒹⒺ ②⓪③

سال‌ها دفتر ما در گرو صهبا بود

Years, in pledge for the wine of the grape, our book (of knowledge and of conduct) was

رونق میکده از درس و دعای ما بود

From our reading and praying, the splendour of the wine-house (the perfect Arif's heart) that was.

نیکی پیر مغان بین که چو ما بدمستان

Be hold the goodness of the Pir of the Magians (the murshid of truth) when we wholly intoxicated (evil-doers, unworthy speakers of love's mysteries, self joy seeker),

هر چه کردیم به چشم کرمش زیبا بود

What eve we did, in his eye of liberality, good was

دفتر دانش ما جمله بشویید به می

Our book of knowledge, wash ye all with wine

که فلک دیدم و در قصد دل دانا بود

For I beheld the sky and, in malice with the sage's heart, it was.

از بتان آن طلب ار حسن شناسی ای دل

O heart seek that (beauty) from idols if thou be beauty-recogniser

کاین کسی گفت که در علم نظر بینا بود

For, that one who spake this, in knowledge of sight, the see-er (the murshid) was

دل چو پرگار به هر سو دورانی می‌کرد

In every direction (in the tavern) like the compass, my heart made a great revolution

و اندر آن دایره سرگشته پابرجا بود

And, standing in that circle, bewildered was

مطرب از درد محبت عملی می‌پرداخت

From love's pain, the minstrel performed a great deed

که حکیمان جهان را مژه خون پالا بود

Such that blood-stained, theeye-lash of the world's sages was.

می‌شکفتم ز طرب زان که چو گل بر لب جوی

With joy, I expanded on that account that, like the rose on the marge of the stream,

بر سرم سایه آن سرو سهی بالا بود

On my head, the shadow of that cypress of straight stature was.

پیر گلرنگ من اندر حق ازرق پوشان

In respect of these blue garment wearers (lovers, fakirs, those possessed of divine knowledge) my Pir (murshid) rose of hue

رخصت خبث نداد ار نه حکایت‌ها بود

Gave no permission to reveal their impurity (in divulging love's mysteries) If not, (in respect to them, many) a late was

قلب اندوده حافظ بر او خرج نشد

The counterfeit gathered by Hafiz was not passed by him (the Pir of the Magians the Murshid the true Beloved)

کاین معامل به همه عیب نهان بینا بود

For the master of business (the Pir) wise as to hidden defect, was.

غزل ۲۰۴ ⓄⒹⒺ ②⓪④

یاد باد آن که نهانت نظری با ما بود

Be memory of that time (O true Beloved) when towards us Thy exceeding glance (of mercy) was.

رقم مهر تو بر چهره ما پیدا بود

(When) evident in our face, the writing of Thy love (mercy) was.

یاد باد آن که چو چشمت به عتابم می‌کشت

Be memory of that time when, me with reproach, Thy eye slew

معجز عیسویت در لب شکرخا بود

(When) in Thy lip, sugar-devouring, the miracle of Isa[1] (life-giving) was.

یاد باد آن که صبوحی زده در مجلس انس

Be memory of that time when, in the assembly of companionship (of the perfect murshid; or of the circle of zikr) we dashed (drained) the morning cup (of wine)

جز من و یار نبودیم و خدا با ما بود

We were not, save I and the friend (the murshid) and, with us, God was

یاد باد آن که رخت شمع طرب می‌افروخت

Be memory of that time when Thy cheek kindled the candle of joy

وین دل سوخته پروانه ناپروا بود

And (its) careless moth, this consumed heart was

1-Name of a prophet

یاد باد آن که در آن بزمگه خلق و ادب
Be memory of that time when, in that banquet-place of courtesy and of manners (the assembly of hal and of zikr)

آن که او خنده مستانه زدی صهبا بود
That which expressed laughter like the intoxicated one, the red morning wine (of Love for God) was

یاد باد آن که چو یاقوت قدح خنده زدی
Be memory of that time, when the ruby (wine) of the goblet expressed laughter (reflected itself, and foamed in tumult)

در میان من و لعل تو حکایت‌ها بود
Between me and thy ruby (lip) many a story was.

یاد باد آن که نگارم چو کمر بربستی
Be memory of that time, when my (lovely) moon used to bind on, a (moon-like, crescent) cap

در رکابش مه نو پیک جهان پیما بود
At her stirrup (in service) the new (crescent) moon, the world-measuring messenger, was.

یاد باد آن که خرابات نشین بودم و مست
Be memory of that time when I was tavern-sitter and intoxicated

وآنچه در مسجدم امروز کم است آن جا بود
And that which (divine knowledge) to-day, in the assembly (of the binding world) is wanting to me; there (in the loosening world) ready was

یاد باد آن که به اصلاح شما می‌شد راست
Be memory of that time when, by your amending, correct became

نظم هر گوهر ناسفته که حافظ را بود
The (lustrous) verse of every unpierced jewel (fresh thought, new melody) that Hafiz's was

غزل ۲۰۵ ⓄⒹⒺ ②⓪⑤

تا ز میخانه و می نام و نشان خواهد بود
As long as name and trace of the tavern' (the existence of the traveller) rand of wine of love shall be,

سر ما خاک ره پیر مغان خواهد بود
The dust of the path of the Pir of the Magians[1] (the murshid of love who is the King of seekers) the our head, shall be

حلقه پیر مغان از ازلم در گوش است
From eternity without beginning, the ring of (obedience of) the Pir of the Magians was in my ear

بر همانیم که بودیم و همان خواهد بود
In this way, we are as we were thus it (the ring) shall be

بر سر تربت ما چون گذری همت خواه
(O Saki of Alast) When, by the head of our tomb thou passest, ask for grace for me

که زیارتگه رندان جهان خواهد بود
For, the pilgrimage –place of the profligates (perfect lovers, comprehenders of the stages of love) of the world, (the tomb of Hafiz) shall be .

برو ای زاهد خودبین که ز چشم من و تو
O Zahid[2], self-seeing go For, from eye of mine and of thine,

راز این پرده نهان است و نهان خواهد بود
Hidden is the mystery of this veil and hidden shall be

1-The perfect mystic man, Fire worshipper   2-Pietist

ترک عاشق کش من مست برون رفت امروز
Today, my Bold one, lover-slayer, went forth intoxicated

تا دگر خون که از دیده روان خواهد بود
Let us see again from whose eye, blood-flowing shall be

چشمم آن دم که ز شوق تو نهد سر به لحد
That night, when, through desire for thee, my eye placeth its desire on the tomb

تا دم صبح قیامت نگران خواهد بود
Till the breath of the moon of resurrection, downward cast it shall

بخت حافظ گر از این گونه مدد خواهد کرد
If, in this way, Hafiz's fortune shall aid (by drawing him into effacement)

زلف معشوقه به دست دگران خواهد بود
In the hand of others, the Beloved's tress (the twist of the vicissitudes of Time, the traitor) shall be

غزل ۲۰۶ ⓄⒹⒺ ②⓪⑥

پیش از اینت بیش از این اندیشه عشاق بود
(O true Beloved) Before this, more than this, thine, thought of (thy) only lover was

مهرورزی تو با ما شهره آفاق بود
Thy (great) love –display to us, the talk of climes was

یاد باد آن صحبت شب‌ها که با نوشین لبان
Be recollection of that society of nights, when with sweet lips

بحث سر عشق و ذکر حلقه عشاق بود
Argument of love's mystery and mention of the lover's circle, was.

پیش از این کاین سقف سبز و طاق مینا برکشند
Before they pluck up this fresh roof and azure arch (the sky)

منظر چشم مرا ابروی جانان طاق بود
The place of sight for my eye, the arch of the true Beloved's eye-brow was

از دم صبح ازل تا آخر شام ابد
From the dawn of the morn of eternity without beginning to the end of the evening of eternity without

دوستی و مهر بر یک عهد و یک میثاق بود
In respect to one covenant and to one agreement, friendship with love

سایه معشوق اگر افتاد بر عاشق چه شد
If the (true) Beloved's shade fell on the lover, what

ما به او محتاج بودیم او به ما مشتاق بود
In need of Him, we are desirous of us, He was.

حسن مه رویان مجلس گر چه دل می‌برد و دین
Although the beauty of those moon of face of the assembly taketh heart and religion

بحث ما در لطف طبع و خوبی اخلاق بود
(Not on outward beauty, but) With the grace of temperament and with the beauty of disposition (of lovers) our love was.

بر در شاهم گدایی نکته‌ای در کار کرد
At the King's door, a beggar made this subtlety in regard to work,

گفت بر هر خوان که بنشستم خدا رزاق بود
He said At every tray, whereat I sate, God, the Provider, was

رشته تسبیح اگر بگسست معذورم بدار

If the cord of the rosary snapped, hold me excused

دستم اندر دامن ساق سیمین ساق بود

On the arm of the Saki of silver leg, my arm was

در شب قدر ار صبوحی کرده‌ام عیبم مکن

On the night of power, if I have drunk a morning draught, censure me not.

سرخوش آمد یار و جامی بر کنار طاق بود

Merry of head, came the Beloved and a cup on the edge of the arch was

شعر حافظ در زمان آدم اندر باغ خلد

God, the Provider, was In Adam's time, in the garden of Paradise, Hafiz's poetry

دفتر نسرین و گل را زینت اوراق بود

The adornment of the leaves of the book of the wild (white) rose and of the red rose

غزل ۲۰۷ ⓞⓓⓔ ②⓪⑦

یاد باد آن که سر کوی توام منزل بود

Mine be recollection of that time when my dwelling the head of thy street was.

دیده را روشنی از خاک درت حاصل بود

(When) from the dust of thy door, to my eye the acquisition of luminosity was

راست چون سوسن و گل از اثر صحبت پاک

From the effects of pure society, up right I became like the lily and the rose

بر زبان بود مرا آن چه تو را در دل بود

On my tongue was, whatever in thy heart was.

دل چو از پیر خرد نقل معانی می‌کرد

When, from the Pir[1] of wisdom, my hear t made transcription of (inquired about) divine significations

عشق می‌گفت به شرح آن چه بر او مشکل بود

in explanation, Love uttered what to him (the Pir of wisdom) difficult was.

آه از آن جور و تطاول که در این دامگه است

Alas, this tyranny and oppression that is in this snare-place (the world)

آه از آن سوز و نیازی که در آن محفل بود

Alas that grace and favour that in that assembly (the world of souls) was

در دلم بود که بی دوست نباشم هرگز

In my heart, it was I will never be without the Friend (God)

چه توان کرد که سعی من و دل باطل بود

What can one do For my effort and the effort of my heart, vain was.

دوش بر یاد حریفان به خرابات شدم

Last night, in recollection of friends (to see them) I went to the tavern

خم می دیدم خون در دل و پا در گل بود

The jar of wine, I be held. In the heart, blood was and, in the clay, (of astonishment) the foot was.

بس بگشتم که بپرسم سبب درد فراق

Much, I wandered to ask the cause of the pain of separation

مفتی عقل در این مسله لایعقل بود

In this matter, void of wisdom, the Mufti[2] of wisdom was.

---

1 -A Muslim saint or holy man, Pietist   2-Lawyer

راستی خاتم فیروزه بواسحاق

The truth of the end of the Abulshak[1] turquoise (is this that)

خوش درخشید ولی دولت مستعجل بود

Well it gleamed; but (it's) the lot of the hastener was

دیدی آن قهقهه کبک خرامان حافظ

Hafiz thou sawest (all) that chatter of the strutting partridge (Amir Abu Is'hak)

که ز سرپنجه شاهین قضا غافل بود

Careless of the grasp of the falcon of Fate, he was.

غزل ۲۰۸ ⓄⒹⒺ ②⓪⑧ ODE 208

خستگان را چو طلب باشد و قوت نبود

Those shattered, when they are in search (of thee) and (theirs) power is not,

گر تو بیداد کنی شرط مروت نبود

If thou vex, the condition of manliness is not.

ما جفا از تو ندیدیم و تو خود نپسندی

From thee, we experienced no tyranny and thou thyself approvest not

آن چه در مذهب ارباب طریقت نبود

What, in the Order of the Shaikh[2] soft he Path, is not

خیره آن دیده که آبش نبرد گریه عشق

Blind that eye, whose water (of lustre) love's fire took not

تیره آن دل که در او شمع محبت نبود

Dark that heart, where in love's light is not

دولت از مرغ همایون طلب و سایه او

From the auspicious bird, (the prosperous one, or the perfect 'Arif) seek fortune and his shadow

زان که با زاغ و زغن شهپر دولت نبود

For the reason that with the (ugly) crow and the (mean) kite, the long wing-feather (of flight) of fortune is not.

گر مدد خواستم از پیر مغان عیب مکن

If, from the wine-house, seek blessing, carp not

شیخ ما گفت که در صومعه همت نبود

Our Pir[3] spake saying In the Christian cloister, blessing is not

چون طهارت نبود کعبه و بتخانه یکیست

When there is no purity (of heart from infidelity) one are the Ka'ba[4] and the idol house

نبود خیر در آن خانه که عصمت نبود

Well, it is not when, in the house (of the heart) chastity is not

حافظا علم و ادب ورز که در مجلس شاه

Hafiz practise knowledge and manners. For, in the king's assembly

هر که را نیست ادب لایق صحبت نبود

Who manners worthy of society hath not is not.

1-King Sheikh Abu Isaac

2-A leader in a Muslim community

3-A Muslim saint or holy man, Pietist

4-Muslims turn at prayer.

غزل ۲۰۹ ODE 209

قتل این خسته به شمشیر تو تقدیر نبود

By the sword (of inclination) of thine, the slaughter of this shattered one decreed, it was not

ور نه هیچ از دل بی‌رحم تو تقصیر نبود

If not, (by the glance of sorcery of) thine, a fault it was not.

من دیوانه چو زلف تو رها می‌کردم

(O true Beloved) When I, distraught, released Thy tress

هیچ لایقترم از حلقه زنجیر نبود

For me, (distraught) more fit than the chain-fetter, aught was not

یا رب این آینه حسن چه جوهر دارد

O Lord! luster how hath Thy beauty's mirror,

که در او آه مرا قوت تاثیر نبود

Where in, to my sigh the power of impression was not.

سر ز حسرت به در میکده‌ها برگردم

Through astonishment, at the door of the wine-house (the world of love and of divine knowledge) I put out of my head

چون شناسای تو در صومعه یک پیر نبود

When, in the cloister, a Pir, a recogniser of thee was

نازنینتر ز قدت در چمن ناز نرست

In the sward of grace, more graceful than Thy stature, aught grew not

خوشتر از نقش تو در عالم تصویر نبود

In the world of picture, more pleasant than thy picture aught was not

تا مگر همچو صبا باز به کوی تو رسم

So that, perchance, like the morning-breeze I may reach Thy tress

حاصلم دوش بجز ناله شبگیر نبود

Last night, my profit save night-weeping, aught was not

آن کشیدم ز تو ای آتش هجران که چو شمع

O fire of separation from thee, that I endured that, candle-like,

جز فنای خودم از دست تو تدبیر نبود

Save self-destruction, by thy hand, a plan for me was none

آیتی بود عذاب انده حافظ بی تو

Hafiz's grief without thee was a mark of torture

که بر هیچ کسش حاجت تفسیر نبود

Of which to any one, need of explanation was (not)

غزل ۲۱۰ ODE 210

دوش در حلقه ما قصه گیسوی تو بود

Last night, in our assembly (of lovers for zikr, formed like a circle) the tale of Thy tress (the path of seekers to the divine world) was.

تا دل شب سخن از سلسله موی تو بود

Until the heart (middle) of the night (which is the season for manifestations) speech regarding the (long) chain of Thy hair was

دل که از ناوک مژگان تو در خون می‌گشت

The heart that (in the world of non – existence) from the point of Thy eye-lash turned to blood

باز مشتاق کمانخانه ابروی تو بود

Again, desirous of the bow-house (wound) of Thy eye-brow was.

هم عفاالله صبا کز تو پیامی می‌داد

(O true Beloved) Pardon the wind, because it brought a message from Thee

ور نه در کس نرسیدیم که از کوی تو بود

And, (if the wind had) not (been, Thy message would not have arrived) for we reached (met with) none, who, from the head of Thy street, was.

عالم از شور و شر عشق خبر هیچ نداشت

Of the tumult and the uproar of love the knowledge of God the world had no news

فتنه انگیز جهان غمزه جادوی تو بود

The calamity-exciter of the world, Thy glance of sorcery absolute love was.

من سرگشته هم از اهل سلامت بودم

(O true Beloved) I, head-bewildered, also was of the people of safety

دام راهم شکن طره هندوی تو بود

The coil of Thy black tress, the snare of my path was.

بگشا بند قبا تا بگشاید دل من

Loose the fastening of Thy coat, so that my hear (in the snare of Thy tress) may expand and rest

که گشادی که مرا بود ز پهلوی تو بود

For the open ness (ease of heart) that was mine, (from sitting and sleeping by) Thy side was.

به وفای تو که بر تربت حافظ بگذر

By Thy fidelity (I adjure Thee) pass by the tomb of Hafiz

کز جهان می‌شد و در آرزوی روی تو بود

Who went from the world and in desire of Thy face was

غزل ۲۱۱ ⓄⒹⒺ ②①①

دوش می‌آمد و رخساره برافروخته بود

Last night, He (the true Beloved) came and His cheek, He had enkindled.

تا کجا باز دل غمزده‌ای سوخته بود

Let us see, the grief-stricken heart (of the lover) how He had consumed

رسم عاشق کشی و شیوه شهرآشوبی

The custom of lover-slaying and the way of city-up setting

جامه‌ای بود که بر قامت او دوخته بود

Was a garment that, on His form, He had stitched

جان عشاق سپند رخ خود می‌دانست

Rue for His own face, He (the true Beloved) regarded the lover's soul

و آتش چهره بدین کار برافروخته بود

And, for this work (of consuming the lover) the (ruddy) the fire of His cheek, had enkindled

گر چه می‌گفت که زارت بکشم می‌دیدم

Although, outwardly, He spake saying: I will cruelly slay thee, I saw

که نهانش نظری با من دلسوخته بود

That secretly towards me, heart-consumed, His glance had been

کفر زلفش ره دین می‌زد و آن سنگین دل

The (black) infidelity of His (dark) tress attacked the path of faith and that one of stony heart,

در پی اش مشعلی از چهره برافروخته بود

In its (faith's) path, a torch (formed) of His ruddy face, had enkindled

دل بسی خون به کف آورد ولی دیده بریخت

To hand, much blood my heart brought; but, my eye (with bloody tears) spilled it

الله الله که تلف کرد و که اندوخته بود

Allah, Allah (this blood) who had expended who had collected

یار مفروش به دنیا که بسی سود نکرد

The (true) Beloved, sell not for the world (and in the world's attachments be not foot – bound) For, much, it profited not

آن که یوسف به زر ناسره بفروخته بود

That one who, for base gold, Yusuf[1], had sold.

گفت و خوش گفت برو خرقه بسوزان حافظ

He spake, and sweetly spake Hafiz go and (burn) the Khirka[2]

یا رب این قلب شناسی ز که آموخته بود

O Lord! from whom, this (power of) base-coin recognising (is it that) He had learned

غزل ۲۱۲ ⓞⓓⓔ ②①②

یک دو جامم دی سحرگه اتفاق افتاده بود

In the morning-time, me the opportunity of drinking one or two cups (of manifestations of glories) had be fallen

و از لب ساقی شرابم در مذاق افتاده بود

And into my palate from the lip of the Saki[3] (whose quality is discourse) wine delight-giving had fallen

از سر مستی دگر با شاهد عهد شباب

With the lovely one of lusty youth's time, again, through intoxication,

رجعتی می‌خواستم لیکن طلاق افتاده بود

I desired restitution of conjugal rights But divorce (from youth's time) had fallen

در مقامات طریقت هر کجا کردیم سیر

In the stages of Tarikat[4], wherever we travelled

عافیت را با نظربازی فراق افتاده بود

In glance-playing, ease, separation had be fallen

ساقیا جام دمادم ده که در سیر طریق

O Saki momently, give the cup. For, in the travelling of the Path

هر که عاشق وش نیامد در نفاق افتاده بود

Who lover-like was not, into hyprocrisy had fallen

ای معبر مژده‌ای فرما که دوشم آفتاب

Interpreter of dreams give glad tidings For, last night, to me, the sun

در شکرخواب صبوحی هم وثاق افتاده بود

In the sweetness of the morning sleep, as an ally had fallen

1-Name of prophet
2-Cloak

3-Tapster
4-Principle, Sufism, religious way

نقش می‌بستم که گیرم گوشه‌ای زان چشم مست

I established the idea saying Apart from that intoxicated eye, I will take the corner (of retirement)

طاقت و صبر از خم ابروش طاق افتاده بود

From the curve of his eye-brow arch (like a terrible bow) my power of patience had fallen.

گر نکردی نصرت دین شاه یحیی از کرم

If, through liberality, the king had not been Yahi Nasratu-d-Din[1]

کار ملک و دین ز نظم و اتساق افتاده بود

From order and peace, the work of the country and of religion had fallen

حافظ آن ساعت که این نظم پریشان می‌نوشت

That moment when Hafiz wrote this agitated verse,

طایر فکرش به دام اشتیاق افتاده بود

Into the snare of longing desire, the bird of his thought had fallen

غزل ۲۱۳ ⓄⒹⒺ ②①③

گوهر مخزن اسرار همان است که بود

Verily the jewel of the treasure of mysteries is a sit was

حقه مهر بدان مهر و نشان است که بود

With that seal and mark, the chest of (our) love is as it was.

عاشقان زمره ارباب امانت باشند

Lovers are the crowd of the Lords of deposit (of love)

لاجرم چشم گهربار همان است که بود

Doubt less, the eye, jewel-raining, is a sit was,

از صبا پرس که ما را همه شب تا دم صبح

(My state) ask the morning-breeze. For all night, up to the breath of morn, our

بوی زلف تو همان مونس جان است که بود

Dear soul-friend, verily the perfume of Thy tress is as it was.

طالب لعل و گهر نیست وگرنه خورشید

The (sincere) seeker of the ruby and of the jewel is none and if not, the sun (the murshid)

همچنان در عمل معدن و کان است که بود

Even so in the work of the mine and of the quarry (wherein jewels are produced) is as it was

کشته غمزه خود را به زیارت دریاب

For the visiting of one slain by Thy own glance, come

زان که بیچاره همان دل‌نگران است که بود

For verily expectant of Thee, the helpless one is a she was

رنگ خون دل ما را که نهان می‌داری

(O true Beloved) the (red) colour of the blood of our heart, which (produced from Thy cheek) Thou concealedst (with Thy fresh down)

همچنان در لب لعل تو عیان است که بود

Even so in Thy ruby lip, visible is as it was

زلف هندوی تو گفتم که دگر ره نزند

(In thought) I spake saying: "Thy Hindu (black) Tress again attacketh not"

سال‌ها رفت و بدان سیرت و سان است که بود

Passed years and (aid) in that way it is as it was.

1-The ruler of Shiraz

حافظا بازنما قصه خونابه چشم
Hafiz again relate the tale of the blood-tears of thy eye
که بر این چشمه همان آب روان است که بود
For in this fountain (eye) verily (blood) water-running is as it was.

غزل ۲۱۴ ⓞⓓⒺ ②①④

دیدم به خواب خوش که به دستم پیاله بود
In a pleasant dream, I be held that in my hand, the cup was
تعبیر رفت و کار به دولت حواله بود
Interpretation passed; and, entrusted to fortune, the work was

چهل سال رنج و غصه کشیدیم و عاقبت
Forty years I endured trouble and vexation (in love's path) In the end,
تدبیر ما به دست شراب دوساله بود
In the power of wine, two years of age (the glorious Kuran, wherein I find every delight I sought) the deliberation of it was.

آن نافه مراد که می‌خواستم ز بخت
That pod of desire that from fortune, I desired
در چین زلف آن بت مشکین کلاله بود
In the tres ode curl of that Idol of musky tresses, was.

از دست برده بود خمار غمم سحر
In the morning, grief's languor had overpowered me
دولت مساعد آمد و می در پیاله بود
Fortune became prosperous in the cup, the wine (of union with the true Beloved wine, life – giving) was

بر آستان میکده خون می‌خورم مدام
Blood, I ever drink on the threshold of the wine-house
روزی ما ز خوان قدر این نواله بود
(As on the first day), this very (blood – drinking) assigned to me was.

هر کو نکاشت مهر و ز خوبی گی نچید
Who planted not love, nor plucked a rose for its loveliness,
در رهگذار باد نگهبان لاله بود
In the wind's path, the tulip's care-taker (ever in trouble) was

بر طرف گلشنم گذر افتاد وقت صبح
By the rose-bed, chanced my passing at morning-time
آن دم که کار مرغ سحر آه و ناله بود
When sigh and wail, the work of the bird of the sward was.

دیدیم شعر دلکش حافظ به مدح شاه
In praise of the king, we saw Hafiz's heart-Alluring verse
یک بیت از این قصیده به از صد رساله بود
Every couple of that book (of verse) better than a hundred letters was

آن شاه تندحمله که خورشید شیرگیر
That king, savage of attack, before whom the sun, lion-seizing
پیشش به روز معرکه کمتر غزاله بود
Less than a fawn, on the day of battle, was.

غزل ۲۱۵ ⓄⒹⒺ ②①⑤

به کوی میکده یا رب سحر چه مشغله بود

O lord in the street of the wine-house (the corner of Hafiz's heart) in the morning (the end of youth, the beginning of old age) what tumult (of zikr) that was

که جوش شاهد و ساقی و شمع و مشعله بود

For, the clamour of the lovely one, and of the Saki[1] (the form of God that, at the beginning of zikr is the spectacle-place of zakirs) and of the candle, and of the fire-grate (the fervour of divine lights, and the descending of endless bounties) was.

حدیث عشق که از حرف و صوت مستغنیست

Love's tale, that is independent of letter or of sound,

به ناله دف و نی در خروش و ولوله بود

With the reverberating drum, and the shrieking reed, and the resounding shout (of the zikr of the zakirs in exceeding desire and delight) was

مباحثی که در آن مجلس جنون می‌رفت

That disputation of hakikat[2] that, in that circle of phrenzy, passed

ورای مدرسه و قال و قیل مسله بود

Beyond (the disputations of the illusory of) the college, and the proposition, (and) the answer, and the question was

دل از کرشمه ساق به شکر بود ولی

From the glance (the glories of manifestations) of (the Saki the adored God) my heart was in thanks but.

ز نامساعدی بختش اندکی گله بود

From want of concordance of fortune, a little complaint mine was.

قیاس کردم و آن چشم جادوانه مست

(Of) that eye, bold, sorcery-displaying, I estimated

هزار ساحر چون سامریش در گله بود

Many a sorcerer, like the (great) Samiri[3], in lamentation of its (sorcery) was.

بگفتمش به لبم بوسه‌ای حوالت کن

To him, Is aid On my lip, place a kiss.

به خنده گفت کی ات با من این معامله بود

With laughter, He spake On my part this thus was.

ز اخترم نظری سعد در ره است که دوش

From thy star, the Auspicious view is in my path For,

میان ماه و رخ یار من مقابله بود

Between the moon and my beloved face, opposition was.

دهان یار که درمان درد حافظ داشت

The beloved's mouth, that Hafiz regarded pain's remedy

فغان که وقت مروت چه تنگ حوصله بود

Ala show little of spirit, the time of manliness was

1-Tapster
2-Truth

3-A person who made a calf in the absence of Prophet Moses and encouraged the Hebrews to worship it

غزل ۲۱۶　ODE 216

آن یار کز او خانه ما جای پری بود
That friend, by whom our house the (happy) dwelling of the Pari[1] was

سر تا قدمش چون پری از عیب بری بود
Head to foot, free from defect, a Pari was

دل گفت فروکش کنم این شهر به بویش
(My) Heart said In hope of her in this city, I will sojourn

بیچاره ندانست که یارش سفری بود
Helpless, it knew not that its friend, a traveler was

تنها نه ز راز دل من پرده برافتاد
Not only from my heart's mystery, fell the screen

تا بود فلک شیوه او پرده دری بود
Since the sky (time) was, screen-rending its habit was

منظور خردمند من آن ماه که او را
Acceptable to the (All) wise of mine (is) that moon For, his,

با حسن ادب شیوه صاحب نظری بود
With beauty of manner, the way of one endowed with vision was.

از چنگ منش اختر بدمهر به دربرد
Out from my grasp, the malignant star plucked her

آری چه کنم دولت دور قمری بود
Yes. What can I do the calamity of the revolution of the moon it was

عذری بنه ای دل که تو درویشی و او را
O heart establish an excuse For thou art a beggar and here

در مملکت حسن سر تاجوری بود
In the kingdom of beauty, the head of a crowned one was

اوقات خوش آن بود که با دوست به سر رفت
Happy were those times which passed with the friend

باقی همه بی‌حاصلی و بی‌خبری بود
All without result and without knowledge, the rest was

خوش بود لب آب و گل و سبزه و نسرین
Sweet was the marge of the water, and the rose and the verdure. But

افسوس که آن گنج روان رهگذری بود
Alas that moving treasure, away-farer was.

خود را بکش ای بلبل از این رشک که گل را
The bulbul[2] (the true lover) slew himself through jealousy of this that, to the rose (the true Beloved)

با باد صبا وقت سحر جلوه گری بود
At morning-time (the last breath of life) With the morning-breeze (the angel of death) splendour (of heavenly messages) was.

هر گنج سعادت که خدا داد به حافظ
Every treasure of happiness that God gave to Hafiz,

از یمن دعای شب و ورد سحری بود
From the auspiciousness of the evening-prayer, and of the morning-supplication, was

---

1-Heaven　　　　　　　　　2-Nightingale

غزل ۲۱۷ ⓄⒹⒺ ②①⑦

مسلمانان مرا وقتی دلی بود
O Muslims (kind of heart) once a heart, mine was

که با وی گفتمی گر مشکلی بود
Where to I used to utter (revelations) if a difficulty was

به گردابی چو می‌افتادم از غم
When, through the eye, I fell into a whirlpool (of calamity)

به تدبیرش امید ساحلی بود
By its deliberation, the hope of a shore (of safety) was.

دلی همدرد و یاری مصلحت بین
A heart, fellow-sufferer, helper, counsel-perceiver

که استظهار هر اهل دلی بود
That, of everyone of heart, the seeker (to aid) was

ز من ضایع شد اندر کوی جانان
In the (true) Beloved's street, it the heart was lost to me,

چه دامنگیر یا رب منزلی بود
O Lord! what a skirt-seizing place it the (true Beloved's street) was,

هنر بی‌عیب حرمان نیست لیکن
Without the drawback of this appointment, is no skill But

ز من محروم‌تر کی سالی بود
More disappointed than I, a beggar when was

بر این جان پریشان رحمت آرید
In this confused intoxication, exercise ye pity (O Muslims)

که وقتی کاردانی کاملی بود
For once a skilful work-knower, (it my heart) was

مرا تا عشق تعلیم سخن کرد
As long as love taught me speech (lustrous verse)

حدیثم نکته هر محفلی بود
The subtle-point of every assembly, my tale (of lustrous verse) was.

مگو دیگر که حافظ نکته‌دان است
Speak not again, saying: "Hafiz knew subtlety"

که ما دیدیم و محکم جاهلی بود
For, we have seen, a confirmed fool he was.

غزل ۲۱۸ ⓄⒹⒺ ②①⑧

در ازل هر که به فیض دولت ارزانی بود
In eternity without beginning, endowed with the bounty of fortune (love for God) whoever is

تا ابد جام مرادش همدم جانی بود
The cup of his desire, to eternity without end, the fellow-companion of his soul is

من همان ساعت که از می خواستم شد توبه کار
That very moment when as to wine I wish ed to be a penitent

گفتم این شاخ ار دهد باری پشیمانی بود
I said If this branch (abstinence from wine) bear a fruit, (the fruit of) repentance it will be.

خود گرفتم کافکنم سجاده چون سوسن به دوش
I grant that like the (pure) lily I cast the prayer-mat on my back

همچو گل بر خرقه رنگ می مسلمانی بود
But, on the religious garment, (can it be that) the colour of wine, (ruddy) like the rose,
fit for a Muslim is

بی چراغ جام در خلوت نمی‌یارم نشست
In Khilvat[1], Without the lamp of the cup (of wine of love for God) I cannot sit

زان که کنج اهل دل باید که نورانی بود
For, it is necessary that illumined, the corner of people of heart should be.

همت عالی طلب جام مرصع گو مباش
Seek lofty resolution. The bejewelled cup (worldy treasure) say Be not

رند را آب عنب یاقوت رمانی بود
To the profligate (the lover of God) the water of the grape (the wine of love) the pomegranate-ruby
(worldly wealth) is

گر چه بی‌سامان نماید کار ما سهلش مبین
Although, disorderly appeareth our work, regard it not easy

کاندر این کشور گدایی رشک سلطانی بود
For, in this realm, the envy of so vereignty, beggary is

نیک نامی خواهی ای دل با بدان صحبت مدار
O heart desirest thou good fame With the bad, associate not

خودپسندی جان من برهان نادانی بود
O my soul approving of the bad, proof of foolishness is

مجلس انس و بهار و بحث شعر اندر میان
In the midst, the assembly of friends, and spring, and the discourse of love

نستدن جام می از جانان گران جانی بود
Not to take the cup of wine from the beloved, slow-souledness is.

دی عزیزی گفت حافظ می‌خورد پنهان شراب
Last night, a dear one (a follower of the shara') said Secretly, Hafiz drinketh wine.

ای عزیز من نه عیب آن به که پنهانی بود
O dear one the sin best that, which a secret is

غزل ۲۱۹ ⓄⒹⒺ ②①⑨

کنون که در چمن آمد گل از عدم به وجود
Now that from non-existence to existence into the sward (the world, the field of this, and of the
next, world) hath come the rose (man)

بنفشه در قدم او نهاد سر به سجود
And at its foot, the violet in homage hath laid its head

بنوش جام صبوحی به ناله دف و چنگ
Drink a cup of morning wine to the throb of the drum and the harp

ببوس غبغب ساقی به نغمه نی و عود
Kiss the Saki'[2]s chin to the melody of the reed and the lyre

---

1-Solitude   2-Tapster

به دور گل منشین بی شراب و شاهد و چنگ

In the rose-season, sit not without wine, and the mistress, and the harp

که همچو روز بقا هفته‌ای بود معدود

For like time, its permanency is marked (only) a week.

شد از خروج ریاحین چو آسمان روشن

From the mansions of odoriferous herbs, luminous like the sky became

زمین به اختر میمون و طالع مسعود

The earth with the auspicious star, and the happy (natal) star

ز دست شاهد نازک عذار عیسی دم

From the hand of a beauty, tender of cheek, 'Isa[1] of breath

شراب نوش و رها کن حدیث عاد و ثمود

Drink wine and give up the tale of Ad[2] and Samud[3]

جهان چو خلد برین شد به دور سوسن و گل

In the season of the lily and of the rose, the world became like highest paradise

ولی چه سود که در وی نه ممکن است خلود

But, what profit since in it no perpetuality is possible

چو گل سوار شود بر هوا سلیمان وار

When the rose becometh, like Sulaiman[4], a rider on the air

سحر که مرغ درآید به نغمه داوود

In the morning when the bird entereth up on the melody of Daud

به باغ تازه کن آیین دین زردشتی

In the garden (of thy existence) renew the usages of the faith of Zardusht

کنون که لاله برافروخت آتش نمرود

Now that the (red) tulip hath kindled the fire of Nimrud

بخواه جام صبوحی به یاد آصف عهد

Demand the brimful cup to the memory of the Asaf[5] of the age

وزیر ملک سلیمان عماد دین محمود

The Vazir[6] of the Land of Sulaiman[7], 'Imadu-d-Din Mahmud.[8]

بود که مجلس حافظ به یمن تربیتش

By the blessing of his instruction, it may be that the assembly of Hafiz

هر آن چه می‌طلبد جمله باشدش موجود

Whatever it may seek, for it all may be ready.

غزل ۲۲۰ ⓞⒹⒺ ②②⓪

از دیده خون دل همه بر روی ما رود

From the eye, all over our face, the heart's blood goeth

بر روی ما ز دیده چه گویم چه‌ها رود

From the eye, against our face, (thou seest not) what (calamity) goeth.

1-Name of a prophet
2-An ancient Arab tribe living on the island of Saudi Arabia
3-One of the ancient Arab tribes that lived between the Levant and the Hejaz around present-day Mosul
4-Name of a prophet

5-Suleiman's minister
6-Minister
7-Name of a prophet
8-Suleiman's minister

ما در درون سینه هوایی نهفته‌ایم
Within the heart, a great desire (for love) we have concealed

بر باد اگر رود دل ما زان هوا رود
If, through that desire, to the wind (of destruction) our heart goeth, it goeth

خورشید خاوری کند از رشک جامه چاک
From envy, the (glorious) eastern sun rendeth his garment

گر ماه مهرپرور من در قبا رود
If, into a coat, my moon (the beloved) love-cherisher, goeth

بر خاک راه یار نهادیم روی خویش
Our face, on the dust of the Friend's path, we placed

بر روی ما رواست اگر آشنا رود
(Dust) on our face is lawful, if the Friend goeth.

سیل است آب دیده و هر کس که بگذرد
The water of (our) eye is a great torrent By whomsoever it passeth,

گر خود دلش ز سنگ بود هم ز جا رود
Though his heart be of stone, from place (senseless and intoxicated) it (the heart) goeth.

ما را به آب دیده شب و روز ماجراست
As to the water of our eye, night and day, ours is the talk,

زان رهگذر که بر سر کویش چرا رود
Of that passage (of tears) that, at the head of His street, why it (the tear) goeth

حافظ به کوی میکده دایم به صدق دل
To the street of the wine-house, ever with purity of heart, Hafiz (dancing and bounding)

چون صوفیان صومعه دار از صفا رود
Like the Sufi (in ecstasy and mystic state) cloister-keeping, with purity goeth

غزل ۲۲۱ ①①① ODE 221

چو دست بر سر زلفش زنم به تاب رود
When I place my hand on the tip of His tress, in wrath He goeth

ور آشتی طلبم با سر عتاب رود
If I seek concord, with a head full of rebuke, He goeth

چو ماه نو ره بیچارگان نظاره
Like the new moon, helpless spectators

زند به گوشه ابرو و در نقاب رود
Heat tacketh with the corner of the eye-brow and, into the veil, goeth

شب شراب خرابم کند به بیداری
On the night of wine, (state of effacement) He maketh me ruined with His wake fulness (effacing)

وگر به روز شکایت کنم به خواب رود
If by day (in sobriety) I relate tales (to friends of the Path) to sleep, He goeth

طریق عشق پرآشوب و فتنه است ای دل
O heart love's path is full of tumult and of strife

بیفتد آن که در این راه با شتاب رود
Falleth that one, who, on this Path, hastily goeth.

گدایی در جانان به سلطنت مفروش

For empire, sell not beggary at the door of the true Beloved

کسی ز سایه این در به آفتاب رود

To the (paltry) sun, from the shadow of this (great) door, (is it that) anyone

سواد نامه موی سیاه چون طی شد

When the black-book of black hair (of youth) this closed,

بیاض کم نشود گر صد انتخاب رود

The white (hair) becometh not less if many an extract (of White hair) goeth.

حباب را چو فتد باد نخوت اندر سر

When, upon the bubble's head, falleth the wind of pride

کلاه داریش اندر سر شراب رود

In the idea of the wine (of pride) its sovereignty (of obstinacy) goeth

حجاب راه تویی حافظ از میان برخیز

Hafiz thou, thy self, art the veil of the Path. From the midst, arise (make negation of thyself so that the veil may be raised)

خوشا کسی که در این راه بی‌حجاب رود

O happy that one, who, on this Path, veil-less goeth.

غزل ۲۲۲ ⓄⒹⒺ ②②②

از سر کوی تو هر کو به ملالت برود

Everyone, who on account of shame, away from the head of Thy street, goeth,

نرود کارش و آخر به خجالت برود

His work proceedeth not and, at last, to shame, he goeth

کاروانی که بود بدرقه‌اش حفظ خدا

The Karvan[1], whose guide is God's grace

به تجمل بنشیند به جلالت برود

In life's enjoyment sitteth (and) to greatness goeth

سالک از نور هدایت ببرد راه به دوست

By the light of guidance (of Muhammad, or of the murshid) the holy traveller seeketh the Path to the (true) Beloved

که به جایی نرسد گر به ضلالت برود

For to place arriveth not he, who, in error, goeth

کام خود آخر عمر از می و معشوق بگیر

At life's end, from wine and the (true) Beloved, take a pledge (of pleasure)

حیف اوقات که یک سر به بطالت برود

Alas, the time that wholly in idleness goeth

ای دلیل دل گمگشته خدا را مددی

O guide (the true Beloved, or the murshid) of the heart-lost for God's sake, a little help

که غریب ار نبرد ره به دلالت ببرد

For if the stranger findeth not the path by the guide, he goeth

---

1-Convoy

حکم مستوری و مستی همه بر خاتم تست
The order of sobriety (piety) and of inebriety (impiety) all is at an end
کس ندانست که آخر به چه حالت برود
None knoweth to what state at last, he goeth.

حافظ از چشمه حکمت به کف آور جامی
Hafiz from the fountain of philosophy, bring to hand a cup (of wisdom)
بو که از لوح دلت نقش جهالت برود
It may be that, from the heart's tablet, the picture of ignorance goeth.

غزل ۲۲۳   ⓄⒹⒺ ②②③

هرگزم نقش تو از لوح دل و جان نرود
From the tablet of my heart and soul, Thy image, ever goeth not
هرگز از یاد من آن سرو خرامان نرود
From my recollection, that proudly moving cypress ever goeth not

از دماغ من سرگشته خیال دهنت
(O true Beloved) From my distraught brain, the image of Thy cheek
به جفای فلک و غصه دوران نرود
By the sky's violence and time's wrath, goeth not

در ازل بست دلم با سر زلفت پیوند
In eternity without beginning, covenant with Thy tres ode tip, my heart established
تا ابد سر نکشد و از سر پیمان نرود
Till eternity without end, it draweth not forth its head and, from the head of the covenant, goeth not

هر چه جز بار غمت بر دل مسکین من است
Save the load of grief for Thee, whatever is in my wretched heart
برود از دل من و از دل من آن نرود
Goeth from my heart; but from my heart that (grief's load) goeth not

آن چنان مهر توام در دل و جان جای گرفت
In my heart and soul, my love for Thee hath taken a place, such
که اگر سر برود از دل و از جان نرود
That (even) if my head (life) goeth, from my soul, (my love for Thee) goeth not

گر رود از پی خوبان دل من معذور است
If for the pursuit of lovely ones, my heart goeth, 'tis excusable
درد دارد چه کند کز پی درمان نرود
It hath (love's) pain. What may it do if, for remedy-sake, it goeth not

هر که خواهد که چو حافظ نشود سرگردان
Whoever head-be wildered like Hafiz, wisheth not to become
دل به خوبان ندهد و از پی ایشان نرود
Giveth not his heart to lovely ones and, in pursuit of them, goeth not

غزل ۲۲۴ ⓄⒹⒺ ②②④

خوشا دلی که مدام از پی نظر نرود

O happy that heart that, ever, after the illusory goeth not,

به هر درش که بخوانند بی‌خبر نرود

To every door where to they call him not, without notice (invitation) he goeth not

طمع در آن لب شیرین نکردنم اولی

Best for me, not to set desire upon that sweet lip

ولی چگونه مگس از پی شکر نرود

But after sugar, 'what kind of fly goeth not

سواد دیده غمدیده‌ام به اشک مشوی

The blackness of grief's eye, I have experienced. Wash it not with

که نقش خال توام هرگز از نظر نرود

For, from my sight, the picture of Thy mole ever goeth not

ز من چو باد صبا بوی خود دریغ مدار

Like the wind, with hold not from me Thy perfume

چراکه بی سر زلف توام به سر نرود

For, to my head, without the desire of Thy tress, it (the perfume) goeth not

دلا مباش چنین هرزه گرد و هرجایی

O heart like this, be not a babbler, and one of every placea (wanderer)

که هیچ کار ز پیشت بدین هنر نرود

For, from before thee, by this (sort of) skill, any work goeth not.

مکن به چشم حقارت نگاه در من مست

(On the sin of) me intoxicated, (put the skirt of Thy pardon)

که آبروی شریعت بدین قدر نرود

For to this (great) degree (of sin) the grace of the shari'at[1] goeth not.

من گدا هوس سروقامتی دارم

It he beggar, desire one of cypres ode stature,

که دست در کمرش جز به سیم و زر نرود

Within whose girdle, save for silver and gold, the hand goeth not.

تو کز مکارم اخلاق عالمی دگری

Thou, who, from the glory of disposition, art of another world,

وفای عهد من از خاطرت به درنرود

Perchance, from Thy heart, fidelity to the covenant with me, goeth not

سیاه نامه‌تر از خود کسی نمی‌بینم

More black of book (sinful) than myself, none I see

چگونه چون قلمم دود دل به سر نرود

To the head, like the reed, the smoke (sigh) of my heart, how (is it that) it goeth not

به تاج هدهدم از ره مبر که باز سفید

By the lapwing's crown, (I conjure thee) take me not from the path. For the (mighty) white falcon,

چو باشه در پی هر صید مختصر نرود

On account of pride, in pursuit of every little prey, goeth not.

1-Religion

بیار باده و اول به دست حافظ ده
Bring wine and to Hafiz's hand first give

به شرط آن که ز مجلس سخن به درنرود
On the condition that, forth from the assembly, them atter (of wine-drinking) goeth not.

غزل ۲۲۵ ⓞⓓⓔ ②②⑤

ساقی حدیث سرو و گل و لاله می‌رود
Saki[1] the tale of the cypress and the rose and the tulip goeth.

وین بحث با ثلاثه غساله می‌رود
And with the three washers (cups of wine) this dispute goeth.

می ده که نوعروس چمن حد حسن یافت
Drink wine for the new bride of the sward hath found beauty's limit (is perfect in beauty)

کار این زمان ز صنعت دلاله می‌رود
Of the trade of the broker, the work of this tale goeth.

شکرشکن شوند همه طوطیان هند
Sugar-shattering (verse of Hafiz devouring) Have Become All The Parrots (Poets) of Hindustan,

زین قند پارسی که به بنگاله می‌رود
On account of this Farsi candy (sweet Persian ode) that (to Bangal) goeth.

طی مکان ببین و زمان در سلوک شعر
In the path of verse, be hold the travelling of place and of time

کاین طفل یک شبه ره یک ساله می‌رود
This child (ode) of one night, the path of (travel of) one year goeth.

آن چشم جادوانه عابدفریب بین
That eye of sorcery (of the beloved) Abid fascinating behold

کش کاروان سحر ز دنباله می‌رود
How, in its rear, the Karvan[2] of sorcery goeth.

از ره مرو به عشوه دنیا که این عجوز
From the path, go not to the world's blandishments. For this old woman

مکاره می‌نشیند و محتاله می‌رود
Sitteth a cheat; and a bawd, she goeth

باد بهار می‌وزد از گلستان شاه
From the king's garden, the spring-wind bloweth

و از ژاله باده در قدح لاله می‌رود
And within the tulip's bowl, wine from dew goeth

حافظ ز شوق مجلس سلطان غیاث دین
Of love for the assembly of the Sultan Ghiyasu-d-Din[3], Hafiz

غافل مشو که کار تو از ناله می‌رود
Be not silent. For, from lamenting, thy work goeth.

1-Tapster
2-Convoy

3-King of India

غزل ۲۲۶ ⓞⓓⓔ ②②⑥

ترسم که اشک در غم ما پرده در شود
I fear lest in respect of our grief the screen render should be

وین راز سر به مهر به عالم سمر شود
And in the world this sealed mystery a (revealed) tale should be

گویند سنگ لعل شود در مقام صبر
They say the stone becometh, in the stage of patience, the (precious) ruby

آری شود ولیک به خون جگر شود
Yes it becometh But (immersed) in blood, the liver should be

خواهم شدن به میکده گریان و دادخواه
Weeping and justice-demanding, I will go to the wine-house

کز دست غم خلاص من آن جا مگر شود
For there, perchance, from grief's power, my release should be.

از هر کرانه تیر دعا کرده‌ام روان
From every side, the arrow of prayer I have sped

باشد کز آن میانه یکی کارگر شود
It may be that out of those (arrows), a work-doer (effective) one should be

ای جان حدیث ما بر دلدار بازگو
O Soul utter our tale to the Heart-Possessor (God)

لیکن چنان مگو که صبا را خبر شود
But do not so that to the breeze, news should be

از کیمیای مهر تو زر گشت روی من
From the alchemy of love for Thee, my (dusty) face became ruddy gold

آری به یمن لطف شما خاک زر شود
Yes by the happiness of Thy grace, dust, gold should be.

در تنگنای حیرتم از نخوت رقیب
From the watcher's pomp, I am in the strait of astonishment

یا رب مباد آن که گدا معتبر شود
O Lord! forbid that revered, the beggar should be.

بس نکته غیر حسن بباید که تا کسی
Besides beauty, many a subtlety is necessary, so that a person

مقبول طبع مردم صاحب نظر شود
Acceptable to the disposition of one possessed of vision, should be

این سرکشی که کنگره کاخ وصل راست
This palace (of empire) whereof (Thou art moon of form),

سرها بر آستانه او خاک در شود
At its threshold, the dust of the door, heads (in supplication) should be.

حافظ چو نافه سر زلفش به دست توست
Hafiz When the musk of His tres ode tip is in thy hand

دم درکش ار نه باد صبا را خبر شود
In-draw thy breath. If not, to the morning breeze,-news should be

غزل ۲۲۷ ⓄⒹⒺ ②②⑦

گر چه بر واعظ شهر این سخن آسان نشود
Although to the city-admonisher, easy this matter becometh not

تا ریا ورزد و سالوس مسلمان نشود
So long as hypocrisy and deceit, hepractiseth, Musulman, he becometh not

رندی آموز و کرم کن که نه چندان هنر است
Learn profligacy and practise liberality For not such a great matter is it,

حیوانی که ننوشد می و انسان نشود
That wine, a mere animal drinketh not and man becometh not

گوهر پاک بباید که شود قابل فیض
That it may be worthy of bounty, the pure essence is necessary

ور نه هر سنگ و گلی لل و مرجان نشود
If not, every (worthless) stone and clod, (the precious); pearl and the coral becometh not.

اسم اعظم بکند کار خود ای دل خوش باش
(The) great name (of God) doeth its work O heart be happy (be not denier of the effects of The great name)

که به تلبیس و حیل دیو مسلمان نشود
For, by fraud and deceit, the (infidel) Div, Musulman, he becometh not.

عشق می‌ورزم و امید که این فن شریف
I teach love and (hence) my hope, that this noble art (of love)

چون هنرهای دگر موجب حرمان نشود
Like other arts, the cause of disappointment (in the attainment of my object) becometh not

دوش می‌گفت که فردا بدهم کام دلت
Last night, He spake saying To-morrow, I give thee thy heart's desire

سبی ساز خدایا که پشیمان نشود
O God devise a means, where by regretful (by breaking his promise) he becometh not

حسن خلقی ز خدا می‌طلبم خوی تو را
From God, I seek a good disposition for thy nature,

تا دگر خاطر ما از تو پریشان نشود
So that again, distressed by thee, our heart becometh not.

ذره را تا نبود همت عالی حافظ
Hafiz So long, as lofty resolution is not the atom's

طالب چشمه خورشید درخشان نشود
Seeker of the fountain of the gleaming sun, it becometh not.

غزل ۲۲۸ ⓄⒹⒺ ②②⑧

گر من از باغ تو یک میوه بچینم چه شود
If, from thy garden, I pluck a rose, what may it be

پیش پایی به چراغ تو ببینم چه شود
(If) by thy lamp (of splendour) I see before my feet what may it

یا رب اندر کنف سایه آن سرو بلند
O Lord! (God) within the border of the shade of that lofty cypress,

گر من سوخته یک دم بنشینم چه شود
If, a moment a tease, I consumed sate, what may it be

آخر ای خاتم جمشید همایون آثار

Oseal-ring of Jamshid[1], auspicious of effort, at last

گر فتد عکس تو بر نقش نگینم چه شود

If, on the ruby of the seal-ring, thy reflection fall what may it be

واعظ شهر چو مهر ملک و شحنه گزید

When the Zahid[2] of the city chose the favour of the King and of the Ruler.

من اگر مهر نگاری بگزینم چه شود

If I choose the love of an idol (an illusory beloved) what may it be

عقلم از خانه به دررفت و گر می این است

Out from the house (of the brain) went my reason and, if wine be this (in effect)

دیدم از پیش که در خانه دینم چه شود

That, from the first, I experienced in the house of my Faith what may it be

صرف شد عمر گران مایه به معشوقه و می

On the (illusory) beloved and on wine, my precious life was expended

تا از آنم چه به پیش آید از اینم چه شود

Let us see, to me, from that (the beloved) what may happen (and) from this (the wine) what may it be

خواجه دانست که من عاشقم و هیچ نگفت

That I was a lover, the Khwaja[3] knew and naught said

حافظ ار نیز بداند که چنینم چه شود

If Hafiz, also, know that I am such (a lover), what may it be

غزل ۲۲۹ ⓞⒹⒺ ②②⑨

بخت از دهان دوست نشانم نمی‌دهد

Trace of the (true) Beloved's mouth, fortune giveth me not.

دولت خبر ز راز نهانم نمی‌دهد

News of the hidden mystery, fortune giveth me not

از بهر بوسه‌ای ز لبش جان همی‌دهم

For a kiss from His lip, I surrender my life

اینم همی‌ستاند و آنم نمی‌دهد

This (my life) He taketh not; and that (the kiss) He giveth me not.

مردم در این فراق و در آن پرده راه نیست

With desire, I died and, within this screen (of divine knowledge) is no path

یا هست و پرده دار نشانم نمی‌دهد

Or (path) the reis and its trace, the screen-holder (the murshid) giveth me not.

زلفش کشید باد صبا چرخ سفله بین

The morning-breeze drew His tress. Be hold the mean sphere

کان جا مجال بادوزانم نمی‌دهد

In that, there, the power of the whirling wind (to draw His tress) it (the sphere) giveth me not

---

1-King
2-Pietist

3-Eunuch, dignitary, vizier, boss, host

چندان که بر کنار چو پرگار می‌شدم

As much as on the border, compass like, I go,

دوران چو نقطه ره به میانم نمی‌دهد

The path to the center, Time like a point giveth me not

شکر به صبر دست دهد عاقبت ولی

In the end, by patience, sugar (of ease) appeareth. But

بدعهدی زمانه زمانم نمی‌دهد

Safety, the bad-faithless ness of Time giveth me not.

گفتم روم به خواب و ببینم جمال دوست

(To myself) I said: "To sleep, I will go; and be hold (in a dream) the beauty of the true Beloved"

حافظ ز آه و ناله امانم نمی‌دهد

(But) With sighing and wailing, sleep, Hafiz giveth me not

غزل ۲۳۰ ⓞⒹⒺ ②③⓪

اگر به باده مشکین دلم کشد شاید

If the heart draw me to musky wine, it be fitteth

که بوی خیر ز زهد ریا نمی‌آید

For, from austerity and hypocrisy, the perfume of goodness cometh not.

جهانیان همه گر منع من کنند از عشق

If all the people of the world forbid me love,

من آن کنم که خداوندگار فرماید

(Yet) that which the Lord commandeth, I shall do.

طمع ز فیض کرامت مبر که خلق کریم

Sever not hope of the bounty of blessing. For the nature of the Merciful (God)

گنه ببخشد و بر عاشقان ببخشاید

Pardoneth sin and lovers' forgiveth

مقیم حلقه ذکر است دل بدان امید

The dweller of the circle of zikr[1], is the heart in the hope

که حلقه‌ای ز سر زلف یار بگشاید

That, the circle (knot) of the Beloved's tres ode tip, it may loose.

تو را که حسن خداداده هست و حجله بخت

For thee, whom God hath given beauty and the chamber of fortune,

چه حاجت است که مشاطه‌ات بیاراید

Is what needth at, thee, the attirer should at tire

چمن خوش است و هوا دلکش است و می بی‌غش

Pleasant is the sward heart-alluring is the air pure is the wine

کنون بجز دل خوش هیچ در نمی‌باید

Now, save the joyous heart, naught is wanting.

جمیله‌ایست عروس جهان ولی هش دار

Beautiful is the bride of the world. But keep sense

که این مخدره در عقد کس نمی‌آید

For, into no one's bond, cometh is young maiden.

1-Orison

به لابه گفتمش ای ماه رخ چه باشد اگر

To her, coaxingly, Is aid O moon of face what will it be if

به یک شکر ز تو دلخسته‌ای بیاساید

With a piece of sugar (a kiss) from thee, a heart shattered one resteth

به خنده گفت که حافظ خدای را مپسند

Laughingly, she spake saying: "Hafiz for God's sake, think not"

که بوسه تو رخ ماه را بیالاید

That, my moon-face, thy kiss shall stain.

غزل ۲۳۱ ①③② ODE 231

گفتم غم تو دارم گفتا غمت سر آید

To (the true Beloved) I said: "Grief for Thee, I have." He said: "To an end (when union is attained) thy grief cometh"

گفتم که ماه من شو گفتا اگر برآید

I spake saying: "Be my moon (make luminous like the moon my eye and bosom) He said (I will be thy moon) if forth, the chance cometh.

گفتم ز مهرورزان رسم وفا بیاموز

I said: "From kind ones (lovers) learn the usage of fidelity."

گفتا ز خوبرویان این کار کمتر آید

He said: "From those moon of face (lovely women) this work of fidelity Seldom cometh."

گفتم که بر خیالت راه نظر بندم

I spake saying: "On Thy image, I bind the path of my vision." (away from the direction of others and glance on naught save) Thee

گفتا که شب رو است او از راه دیگر آید

He spake saying: "The night-prowler is that one, who, by another (unclosed) path, cometh."

گفتم که بوی زلفت گمراه عالمم کرد

I spake saying: "Road-lostin the world, the perfume of Thy tress hath made me."

گفتا اگر بدانی هم اوت رهبر آید

He said: "If thou knowest, thy guide also it the (perfume) becometh."

گفتم خوشا هوایی کز باد صبح خیزد

I said: "O happy the air that, from love's garden, ariseth."

گفتا خنک نسیمی کز کوی دلبر آید

He said: "More pleasant is that breeze that from the heart-ravisher's street cometh."

گفتم که نوش لعلت ما را به آرزو کشت

I spake saying: "With desire, the sweet drink of Thy ruby lip slayeth me."

گفتا تو بندگی کن کو بنده پرور آید

He said: "Perform thou service (of the lip) for He, soul-cherishing cometh."

گفتم دل رحیمت کی عزم صلح دارد

I said: "When hath Thy kind heart the resolution of peace?"

گفتا مگوی با کس تا وقت آن درآید

He said: "To none, speak of this (our violence against thee) till that time (of peace) cometh."

گفتم زمان عشرت دیدی که چون سر آمد

I said: "Thou sawest how quickly the time of ease to an end cometh."

گفتا خموش حافظ کاین غصه هم سر آید

He said: "Hafiz silence. For to an end this grief also cometh."

غزل ۲۳۲ ⓄⒹⒺ ②③②

بر سر آنم که گر ز دست برآید

In desire of that I am that, if, forth from my hand, it come,

دست به کاری زنم که غصه سر آید

I may fix my hand upon a work such that the end of grief may come.

خلوت دل نیست جای صحبت اضداد

The plain of vision of the heart is not a place of society of opponents

دیو چو بیرون رود فرشته درآید

When the demon goeth out, the angel within may come.

صحبت حکام ظلمت شب یلداست

The society of the Ruler is the darkness of night of winter

نور ز خورشید جوی بو که برآید

Ask light of the sun. Possibly, forth it may come.

بر در ارباب بی‌مروت دنیا

At the door of the Lords of the world without manliness,

چند نشینی که خواجه کی به درآید

How long (expectant) sittest thou sayingln, at the door, when will the Khwaja[1] come

ترک گدایی مکن که گنج بیابی

Beggary (seeking the murshid) abandon not. For thou mayst gain treasure

از نظر ره روی که در گذر آید

From the (kind) glance of a (holy) traveller, who, into thy sight, may come.

صالح و طالح متاع خویش نمودند

Salih[2] and Talah[3] displayed (obedience to God)

تا که قبول افتد و که در نظر آید

Let us see to whom acceptance will fall and, into vision, who will come.

بلبل عاشق تو عمر خواه که آخر

O bulbull[4] over ask for life. For, in the end

باغ شود سبز و شاخ گل به بر آید

Green will become the garden and into the bosom, the red rose will come.

غفلت حافظ در این سراچه عجب نیست

In this closet (the world like into the wine-house) Hafiz's careless ness is no wonder

هر که به میخانه رفت بی‌خبر آید

To the wine-house, whoever went, will senseless be come

غزل ۲۳۳ ⓄⒹⒺ ②③③

دست از طلب ندارم تا کام من برآید

From desire (of the beloved) I restrain not my hand until my desire cometh forth

یا تن رسد به جانان یا جان ز تن برآید

Either to the beloved, my body reacheth or, from the body, my soul cometh forth.

1-Eunuch, dignitary, vizier, boss, host
2-Righteous

3-Lecher
4-Nightingale

بگشای تربتم را بعد از وفات و بنگر

(O beloved) after my death, open my tomb and be hold

کز آتش درونم دود از کفن برآید

From the fire of my heart, smoke from the shroud cometh forth.

بنمای رخ که خلقی واله شوند و حیران

Show thy (lovely) face, a whole people go lamenting and wailing (in love for thee)

بگشای لب که فریاد از مرد و زن برآید

Open thy lip (to speak) from man and woman, cry-^cometh forth

جان بر لب است و حسرت در دل که از لبانش

The soul is on the lip (ready to depart) and vexation in the heart. For, from this mouth,

نگرفته هیچ کامی جان از بدن برآید

Not a single desire taken, from the body, the soul cometh forth.

از حسرت دهانش آمد به تنگ جانم

From regret for His mouth, to straits cometh my soul

خود کام تنگدستان کی زان دهن برآید

From that mouth, the self-desire of those short of hand, how cometh forth

گویند ذکر خیرش در خیل عشقبازان

In the crowd of love-players, they make mention for his good

هر جا که نام حافظ در انجمن برآید

Wherever, in the assembly, Hafiz's name cometh forth.

غزل ۲۳۴   ⓄⒹⒺ ②③④

چو آفتاب می از مشرق پیاله برآید

When from the east, the cup (the holy traveller's existence) the sun of wine (of love) cometh up

ز باغ عارض ساقی هزار لاله برآید

From the garden of the cheek, of the Saki (the Murshid) many a tulip of (freshness) cometh up

نسیم در سر گل بشکند کلاله سنبل

On the head of the rose, (the illusory beloved) the gentle perfumed breeze, (lust) shattereth
(and regardeth as naught) the tresses (the decoration) the of the hyacinth,

چو از میان چمن بوی آن کلاله برآید

When, into the midst of the sward (the holy traveller's existence) the perfume of those tresses
(the essence of the true Beloved) cometh up

حکایت شب هجران نه آن حکایت حالیست

Not that tale of the (enraptured) state, is the lament of the nigh t of separation

که شمه‌ای ز بیانش به صد رساله برآید

That, even in a hundred works, a little of its explanation cometh forth.

ز گرد خوان نگون فلک طمع نتوان داشت

(O heart) From the revolving of the sky's in verted tray expect not

که بی ملالت صد غصه یک نواله برآید

That, without reproach (and) a hundred vexations, a morsel cometh forth

به سعی خود نتوان برد پی به گوهر مقصود

To the jewel of desire (union with the true Beloved) one cannot go by one's own effort

خیال باشد کاین کار بی حواله برآید

Mere fancy it is that, without the intermediary, this work, cometh forth

گرت چو نوح نبی صبر هست در غم طوفان
If, like the prophet Nuh, in respect to the deluge of grief, patience be thine,
بلا بگردد و کام هزارساله برآید
Calamity turneth (away) and the desire of a thousand years cometh forth

نسیم زلف تو چون بگذرد به تربت حافظ
If the breeze of Thy grace pass by the tomb of Hafiz,
ز خاک کالبدش صد هزار لاله برآید
From his body's dust, many a shout cometh forth

غزل ۲۳۵ ⓄⒹⒺ ②③⑤

زهی خجسته زمانی که یار بازآید
O how happy the time when the Beloved cometh back.
به کام غمزدگان غمگسار بازآید
When to the desire of the grief-stricken, the grief-consoler cometh back

به پیش خیل خیالش کشیدم ابلق چشم
Before the king of his fancy, the black and the white of the eye, I extended,
بدان امید که آن شهسوار بازآید
In that hope that that imperial horseman might comeback.

اگر نه در خم چوگان او رود سر من
If, in the curve of his chaugan, my head goeth not,
ز سر نگویم و سر خود چه کار بازآید
Of my head what may I say and to what work (is it that) the head itself, cometh back

مقیم بر سر راهش نشسته‌ام چون گرد
Like dust, dweller at the head of His path I have sat,
بدان هوس که بدین رهگذار بازآید
In the desire that, by this way, He may comeback.

دلی که با سر زلفین او قراری داد
That heart, to which the tip of His two tresses gave repose,
گمان مبر که بدان دل قرار بازآید
Think not that, in that heart, rest cometh back.

چه جورها که کشیدند بلبلان از دی
From December, what tyrannies (they were) that the bulbuls[1] endured
به بوی آن که دگر نوبهار بازآید
In the hope that, again, the fresh spring may come back.

ز نقش بند قضا هست امید آن حافظ
Hafiz from the painter of destiny (God) hope of that is
که همچو سرو به دستم نگار بازآید
That, to my hand, like the cypress, the idol may come back

1-Nightingale

غزل ۲۳۶ ⓄⒹⒺ ②③⑥

اگر آن طایر قدسی ز درم بازآید

If, by my door, that holy bird (the true Beloved) comeback

عمر بگذشته به پیرانه سرم بازآید

To me, elderly of head, my passed life may come back.

دارم امید بر این اشک چو باران که دگر

With the se my tears like rain, I hope that

برق دولت که برفت از نظرم بازآید

The lightning of fortune, that departed from my sight, may come back.

آن که تاج سر من خاک کف پایش بود

That one (the true Beloved) the dust of the sole of Whose foot was the crown of my head,

از خدا می‌طلبم تا به سرم بازآید

I will exercise sovereignty, if to me He come back.

خواهم اندر عقبش رفت به یاران عزیز

In pursuit of Him (the Beloved) I will go (and) to dear friends,

شخصم ار بازنیاید خبرم بازآید

If forths (from these troubles) my person come not, news of me may come back.

گر نثار قدم یار گرامی نکنم

If, precious, I make not the scattering of the true Beloved's foot,

گوهر جان به چه کار دگرم بازآید

For what other work, may the jewel of my soul come back

کوس نودولتی از بام سعادت بزنم

From the roof of happiness, I beat the drum of a fresh fortune,

گر ببینم که مه نوسفرم بازآید

If I see that tome, the moon of new journey (the young moon) may come back

مانعش غلغل چنگ است و شکرخواب صبوح

Its preventer is the twang of the harp the (talk of Arifs) and the sweetness of sleep of morning (the carelessness of the careless)

ور نه گر بشنود آه سحرم بازآید

If not, if He hear my morning sigh, He may come back.

آرزومند رخ شاه چو ماهم حافظ

Desirous of the King's face like the moon, I am Hafiz

همتی تا به سلامت ز درم بازآید

A blessing, so that in safety, by my door, He may come back.

غزل ۲۳۷ ⓄⒹⒺ ②③⑦

نفس برآمد و کام از تو بر نمی‌آید

The breath (of life) is sued; and forth from thee, my desire (of union) cometh not

فغان که بخت من از خواب در نمی‌آید

Clamour for, forth from sleep, my fortune cometh not.

صبا به چشم من انداخت خاکی از کویش

Into my eye, the breeze cast a little dust from His street

که آب زندگیم در نظر نمی‌آید

For, into my vision, the water of life cometh not.

قد بلند تو را تا به بر نمی‌گیرم
So long as, into my bosom, I take not Thy lofty stature

درخت کام و مرادم به بر نمی‌آید
To fruit, the time of my desire and purpose cometh not

مگر به روی دلارای یار ما ور نی
Perchance, by (the blessing of) the heart-adorning face of our Beloved (our desire will be ful filled) if not

به هیچ وجه دگر کار بر نمی‌آید
In any way (to accomplishment) another work cometh not

مقیم زلف تو شد دل که خوش سوادی دید
Dweller in Thy tress, became that heart that experienced sweet madness

وز آن غریب بلاکش خبر نمی‌آید
And, from that poor (heart) calamity-endurer, news cometh not.

ز شست صدق گشادم هزار تیر دعا
With the aim of truth, I loosed a thousand arrows of prayer,

ولی چه سود یکی کارگر نمی‌آید
But what profit, effective (even) one cometh not.

بسم حکایت دل هست با نسیم سحر
To the morning-breeze, many are the stories of my heart;

ولی به بخت من امشب سحر نمی‌آید
But, by my fortune, the morning, to night becomenth not

در این خیال به سر شد زمان عمر و هنوز
In this fancy, life's time ended; yet,

بلای زلف سیاهت به سر نمی‌آید
To an end, the calamity of his long tress cometh not.

ز بس که شد دل حافظ رمیده از همه کس
Much affrighted of all men, become the heart of Hafiz

کنون ز حلقه زلفت به در نمی‌آید
Now, forth from the curl of his tress, it cometh not

غزل ۲۳۸ ⓞⓓⓔ ②③⑧

جهان بر ابروی عید از هلال وسمه کشید
On account of the new moon on the eye-brow (of the 'id), the world drew indigo (applied kuhl)

هلال عید در ابروی یار باید دید
On (in) the (curved) eye-brow of the beloved, the new (crescent) moon it is proper to see.

شکسته گشت چو پشت هلال قامت من
Like the (round) back of the new moon, my stature became broken

کمان ابروی یارم چو وسمه بازکشید
Like indigo, my beloved again drew the bow of the eye-brow

مگر نسیم خطت صبح در چمن بگذشت
Perchance, at morn, in the sward, the breeze swept over thy body,

که گل به بوی تو بر تن چو صبح جامه درید
Since, with thy perfume, the garment on its body the rose rent like the morning (rent from night)

نبود چنگ و رباب و نبید و عود که بود

The harp was not, nor the stringed instrument, (the rose) nor wine

گل وجود من آغشته گلاب و نبید

For, stained (with grape – wine) and date-wine, was the rose of my existence

بیا که با تو بگویم غم ملالت دل

Come so that, to thee, I may utter the grief and the distress of my heart

چراکه بی تو ندارم مجال گفت و شنید

For, without thee, power of speaking, or of hearing, I have none

بهای وصل تو گر جان بود خریدارم

(Even) If life be the price of union with thee, the purchaser I am

که جنس خوب مبصر به هر چه دید خرید

For the good thing (union) at whatever price he saw, the penetrating one purchased

چو ماه روی تو در شام زلف می‌دیدم

When the (resplendent) moon of thy face in the (dark) evening of thy tress, I be held

شبم به روی تو روشن چو روز می‌گردید

Luminous like the day, became my (dark) evening by thy (resplendent) face

به لب رسید مرا جان و برنیامد کام

(Ready to depart) My soul reached the lip and yet desire was not accomplished

به سر رسید امید و طلب به سر نرسید

To an end, reached my hope; to an end, reached (fulfilment) not my desire

ز شوق روی تو حافظ نوشت حرفی چند

Some words, through desire of thy face, Hafiz wrote.

بخوان ز نظمش و در گوش کن چو مروارید

In his verse, read (the pearls) and.like pearls, put (the verse) in thy ear.

غزل ۲۳۹ ⓞⓓⓔ ②③⑨

رسید مژده که آمد بهار و سبزه دمید

Arrived the glad news that come hath spring; and up-sprung the verdure

وظیفه گر برسد مصرفش گل است و نبید

If the allowance arrive, its expenditure will be the rose and wine

صفیر مرغ برآمد بط شراب کجاست

Ascendeth the piping of the bird. The leathern flagon of wine is where

فغان فتاد به بلبل نقاب گل که کشید

Falleth clamour upon the bulbuls1 the rose's veil, who drew back.

ز میوه‌های بهشتی چه ذوق دریابد

From the heavenly fruits, what delight gaineth

هر آن که سیب زنخدان شاهدی نگزید

That one who, the apple of a lovely one's chin, tasted (kissed) not.

مکن ز غصه شکایت که در طریق طلب

Complain not of grief. For in the path of search,

به راحتی نرسید آن که زحمتی نکشید

That one who endured not trouble (even) to a little ease, arrived not

---

1-Nightingale

ز روی ساق مه وش گلی بچین امروز

To-day, from the cheek of the moon-like Saki[1] (the Beloved) the pluck a rose

که گرد عارض بستان خط بنفشه دمید

For, around the face of the rose-garden (the cheek) the line of violet (the beard) sprouteth

چنان کرشمه ساق دلم ز دست ببرد

My heart from the hand, the Saki's glance so ravished,

که با کسی دگرم نیست برگ گفت و شنید

That, to any other, power of talking, and of listening, mine is none

من این مرقع رنگین چو گل بخواهم سوخت

This patched religious garment, coloured like the rose, I will burn

که پیر باده فروشش به جرعهای نخرید

For, for even a single draught, the Pir[2], wine-selling, purchaseth it not.

بهار میگذرد دادگسترا دریاب

The spring passeth. O justice-dispenser help

که رفت موسم و حافظ هنوز مینچشید

For, departed hath the sea son and not yet hath Hafiz tasted wine

غزل ۲۴۰ ⓄⒹⒺ ②④⓪

ابرآذاری بر آمد باد نوروزی وزید

Come up hath the cloud azar[3]) and) blown hath the breeze of nau-ruz

وجه می میخواهم و مطرب که میگوید رسید

The way of wine, I desire and the minstrel who singeth hath arrived

شاهدان در جلوه و من شرمسار کیسهام

In splendour (of beauty) the lovely (beloved) ones (are and), ashamed of my empty purse, I am

بار عشق و مفلسی صعب است میباید کشید

O sky! This shamefulness, how long shall I endure?

قحط جود است آبروی خود نمیباید فروخت

'Tis the drought of liberality it is not proper to sell my own honour

باده و گل از بهای خرقه میباید خرید

For the price of the Khirka[4], wine and the rose it is proper to buy.

گویا خواهد گشود از دولتم کاری که دوش

From my fortune, he will probably unfold a great work. For, last night,

من همی کردم دعا و صبح صادق میدمید

I prayed, and the dawn of creation dawned

با لبی و صد هزاران خنده آمد گل به باغ

With a lip and a hundred thous and laughs, the rose came to the garden.

از کریمی گویا در گوشهای بویی شنید

Thou mayst say The perfume of a liberal one in a corner, it perceived

دامنی گر چاک شد در عالم رندی چه باک

If, in the world of profligacy, the skirt became rent, what fear

جامهای در نیک نامی نیز میباید درید

In good name, also, the garment it is necessary to rend

1-Tapster

2-A Muslim saint or holy man

3-The sixth month is the Roman month

4-Cloak

این لطایف کز لب لعل تو من گفتم که گفت
Those graceful words (of praise) that, of thy ruby lip, Is pake, who spake

وین تطاول کز سر زلف تو من دیدم که دید
And that tyranny that, from the tip of thy tress, I experienced who experienced

عدل سلطان گر نپرسد حال مظلومان عشق
If the Sultan's justice asketh not the state of the oppressed ones of love

گوشه گیران را ز آسایش طمع باید برید
For those corner-sitting, I t is necessary to sever love of ease.

تیر عاشق کش ندانم بر دل حافظ که زد
On Hafiz's heart, I know not who cast the arrow, lover-slaying

این قدر دانم که از شعر ترش خون می‌چکید
This much I know that, from his fresh verse, blood dropped

غزل ۲۴۱ ⓞⒹⒺ ②④① ODE 241

معاشران ز حریف شبانه یاد آرید
O dear friends of the friend of the night,-bring ye to mind

حقوق بندگی مخلصانه یاد آرید
The duties of since reservice, bring ye to mind.

به وقت سرخوشی از آه و ناله عشاق
At intoxication's time, of the weeping and the wailing of lovers,

به صوت و نغمه چنگ و چغانه یاد آرید
To the sound (of) the melody of the harp and of the cymbal, bring ye to mind.

چو لطف باده کند جلوه در رخ ساقی
When in the Saki's face, wine's reflection displayeth splendour,

ز عاشقان به سرود و ترانه یاد آرید
Of lovers, with song and melody, bring ye to mind

چو در میان مراد آورید دست امید
When to the object's waist, ye bring the hand of hope,

ز عهد صحبت ما در میانه یاد آرید
Of the covenant of our society in the midst, bring ye to mind

سمند دولت اگر چند سرکشیده رود
If Fortune's bay steed impetuous be, (yet)

ز همرهان به سر تازیانه یاد آرید
At the (time of) desire of whipping (the steed) of fellow-travellers, bring ye to

نمی‌خورید زمانی غم وفاداران
(O beloved ones) a moment, suffer ye no grief for the faithful ones

ز بی‌وفایی دور زمانه یاد آرید
Of the unfaithfulness of Time's revolution, bring ye to mind.

به وجه مرحمت ای ساکنان صدر جلال
O dweller soft he seat of pomp in the way of kindness,

ز روی حافظ و این آستانه یاد آرید
Of Hafiz's face and of that threshold, bring ye to mind

🕭🕭🕭 ODE 242 ٢٤٢ غزل

بیا که رایت منصور پادشاه رسید
Come for the standard of Mansur, the King hath arrived.

نوید فتح و بشارت به مهر و ماه رسید
To the sun and the moon, the joyous news of victory with glad tidings hath arrived

جمال بخت ز روی ظفر نقاب انداخت
The veil from victory's face, the beauty of fortune hath cast.

کمال عدل به فریاد دادخواه رسید
To the complaint of the complainers, the perfection of justice hath arrived.

سپهر دور خوش اکنون کند که ماه آمد
Now, the sky displayeth a sweet revolution for the moon hath come.

جهان به کام دل اکنون رسد که شاه رسید
Now, to the heart's desire, the world arriveth for the King hath arrived

ز قاطعان طریق این زمان شوند ایمن
Safe from the assaulter of the path, at that time go

قوافل دل و دانش که مرد راه رسید
Kafila[1]s of heart and knowledge. For the man of the path hath arrived.

عزیز مصر به رغم برادران غیور
To the vexation of his jealous brothers, the dear one of Egypt (Yusuf)

ز قعر چاه برآمد به اوج ماه رسید
Came forth from the violence of the pit (and) to the Exaltation of the moon, hath arrived

کجاست صوفی دجال فعل ملحدشکل
The Sufi the (hypocrite) Anti-Christ of form, atheist in religion is where

بگو بسوز که مهدی دین پناه رسید
Say: "Consume. For the Mahdi[2], (the murshid) religion-shelter, hath arrived."

صبا بگو که چهها بر سرم در این غم عشق
O morning-breeze tell (the Beloved) the, in this grief of love, over my head, what,

ز آتش دل سوزان و دود آه رسید
From the fire of my consuming heart, and (from) the pain of sigh, hath arrived.

ز شوق روی تو شاها بدین اسیر فراق
O King from the desire of (beholding) Thy face, to this captive to separation

همان رسید کز آتش به برگ کاه رسید
Hath arrived (that consuming) which, from fire to grass hath arrived.

مرو به خواب که حافظ به بارگاه قبول
To sleep, go not. For, at the court of acceptance, Hafiz,

ز ورد نیم شب و درس صبحگاه رسید
From the mid night-prayer, and the morning-reading (of the Kuran) hath arrived

---

1-Convoy   2-King Mansour

غزل ۲۴۳ ⓄⒹⒺ ②④③

بوی خوش تو هر که ز باد صبا شنید

From the morning-breeze, thy pleasant perfume, who perceived

از یار آشنا سخن آشنا شنید

From the dear friend (the breeze) he (true) Beloved's speech (who) heard.

ای شاه حسن چشم به حال گدا فکن

O King of beauty (the true Beloved) cast Thy eye (of mercy) on the state of the beggar (Thy lover)

کاین گوش بس حکایت شاه و گدا شنید

For, many a tale of the King (beggar,-cherishing) and of the beggar this ear heard

خوش می‌کنم به باده مشکین مشام جان

With musky (fragrant) wine, happy I make the perfume-place (the brain) of my soul,

کز دلق پوش صومعه بوی ریا شنید

For, from the ragged garment-wearer (the Sufi – Darvish) of the cloister, the perfume the brain of hypocrisy, it (my soul) perceived.

سر خدا که عارف سالک به کس نگفت

The mystery of God that the Arif[1], the holy traveller, uttered to none,

در حیرتم که باده فروش از کجا شنید

In astonishment I am, whence the wine-seller heard.

یا رب کجاست محرم رازی که یک زمان

O Lord! where is that mystery-confidant, to whom, a moment?

دل شرح آن دهد که چه گفت و چه‌ها شنید

My heart may explain what (of love for God) it said and what (of reproach from the world) it heard.

اینش سزا نبود دل حق گزار من

My heart, thank-offering, for it, this was not fit,

کز غمگسار خود سخن ناسزا شنید

That, from its own grief-consoler, unfit words it heard.

محروم اگر شدم ز سر کوی او چه شد

If, from the head of His street, I am excluded, what matter

از گلشن زمانه که بوی وفا شنید

From the rose-bed of Time, the perfume of fidelity, who perceived

ساقی بیا که عشق ندا می‌کند بلند

Saki come For love maketh high clamour,

کان کس که گفت قصه ما هم ز ما شنید

Saying That one who uttered our tale, even from us heard.

ما باده زیر خرقه نه امروز می‌خوریم

Not to-day, do we drink wine beneath the religious garment

صد بار پیر میکده این ماجرا شنید

This tale, a hundred times, the Pir[2] of the wine-house heard.

ما می به بانگ چنگ نه امروز می‌کشیم

Not to-day, do we drink wine to the harp's sound

بس دور شد که گنبد چرخ این صدا شنید

Many are volution passed since this sound the sphere's do me heard.

1-Mystic   2-A Muslim saint or holy man

پند حکیم محض صواب است و عین خیر
The essence of good and essentially good, is the physician's counsel
فرخنده آن کسی که به سمع رضا شنید
Happy that one's (fortune), who, with the ear of resignation, heard.

حافظ وظیفه تو دعا گفتن است و بس
Hafiz thy office is prayer-uttering to (the true Beloved) and that only
دربند آن مباش که نشنید یا شنید
Be not in the Entanglement of this whether He heard not, or heard

غزل ۲۴۴ ⓄⒹⒺ ②④④

معاشران گره از زلف یار باز کنید
O intimate friends (the crowd of lovers) from the (true) Beloved's (black) tress, the knot (the forbidder of glories) open make ye
شبی خوش است بدین قصه‌اش دراز کنید
Happy is such a night it, with this union (with the tress) long make ye.

حضور خلوت انس است و دوستان جمعند
Tis the court of the assembly of friendship and collected are friends
و ان یکاد بخوانید و در فراز کنید
And to! Those who believe … Read ye; wide the door make ye.

رباب و چنگ به بانگ بلند می‌گویند
(The sound of) the stringed instrument and of the harp (cometh) with shout, speak ye,
که گوش هوش به پیغام اهل راز کنید
Saying: To the message of people of mystery, the ear of sense make ye.

به جان دوست که غم پرده بر شما ندرد
By the Beloved's soul (I swear) that grief rendeth not your screen,
گر اعتماد بر الطاف کارساز کنید
If, on the bounties of the Work-performer (God) reliance make ye

میان عاشق و معشوق فرق بسیار است
Between the lover and the beloved, great is the difference
چو یار ناز نماید شما نیاز کنید
(O lovers) When the beloved showeth disdain, supplication make ye

نخست موعظه پیر صحبت این حرف است
The first counsel of the Pir (Murshid) of the assembly was this world
که از مصاحب ناجنس احتراز کنید
From ignoble associates shunning make ye.

هر آن کسی که در این حلقه نیست زنده به عشق
In this circle, everyone who is not alive with love
بر او نمرده به فتوای من نماز کنید
Over him, not dead, by my decree, prayer for the dead make ye.

وگر طلب کند انعامی از شما حافظ
If from you, Hafiz demand a great reward
حوالتش به لب یار دلنواز کنید
To the lip of the Beloved, heart-cherishing, consignment of him make ye

◈◉◈◈◉◈

ر
The Letter Rā

غزل ۲۴۵ ⓄⒹⒺ ②④⑤

الا ای طوطی گویای اسرار

Ho! O parrot (murshid) thou that art the utterer of the mysteries (of God)

مبادا خالیت شکر ز منقار

Void of sugar (of the mysteries of God) thy beak mouth be not

سرت سبز و دلت خوش باد جاوید

Ever be thy head fresh, and thy heart happy

که خوش نقشی نمودی از خط یار

For of the line (of mysteries) of the (true) Beloved, a happy picture, thou displayedest

سخن سربسته گفتی با حریفان

With the rivals (the Arifs) the thou utteredest speech head-closed (veiled)

خدا را زین معما پرده بردار

For God's sake, uplift the veil of the enigma (of the head-closed speech)

به روی ما زن از ساغر گلابی

(O Saki) On our faces, a cup (of divine truths) of rose-water dash

که خواب آلوده‌ایم ای بخت بیدار

For, wear e sleep-stained, and wakeful of fortune

چه ره بود این که زد در پرده مطرب

In musical (note), what path is this that the minstrel struck,

که می‌رقصند با هم مست و هشیار

That, together, the insensible and the sensible dance

از آن افیون که ساقی در می‌افکند

From this opium (mystery) that the Saki (the murshid) the casteth into wine

حریفان را نه سر ماند نه دستار

To the rivals (the Arifs) remaineth neither head nor turban (so intoxicated on hearing it are they)

سکندر را نمی‌بخشند آبی

To (the great) Sikandar[1], they give not that water (-of – life)

به زور و زر میسر نیست این کار

Attainable neither by force nor by gold (without God's grace) is this matter

بیا و حال اهل درد بشنو

Come and hear the state of the people of pain

به لفظ اندک و معنی بسیار

In word, little in meaning, much.

بت چینی عدوی دین و دل‌هاست

The enemy of our religion, (became) the idol of Chin

خداوندا دل و دینم نگه دار

O Lord! my heart and faith, keep

1-King of Macedonia in ancient Greece

به مستوران مگو اسرار مستی

To those veiled (the illusory beloved ones) utter not the mysteries of intoxication truths

حدیث جان مگو با نقش دیوار

From the (lifeless, senseless) wall-picture, ask not the tale of life

به یمن دولت منصور شاهی

In the fortune of the standard of Mansur Shah

علم شد حافظ اندر نظم اشعار

In the ranks of verse, Hafiz the standard became.

خداوندی به جای بندگان کرد

Towards us slaves, he (our praised one) did the work of a Lord

خداوندا ز آفاتش نگه دار

O Lord! him preserve from calamity

غزل ۲۴۶ Ⓞ Ⓓ Ⓔ Ⓐ Ⓒ Ⓑ

عید است و آخر گل و یاران در انتظار

Tis the' id and, at last, the rose and friends are in expectation

ساقی به روی شاه ببین ماه و می بیار

Saki in the king's (resplendent) face, be hold the (effulgent) moon and bring wine

دل برگرفته بودم از ایام گل ولی

From the spring-season of the rose, I had uplifted my heart (for in the rose-sea-son, I drink no wine wander not about the forbidden and, in the service of the pure, acquire perfection) but,

کاری بکرد همت پاکان روزه دار

(In it) the blessing of the pure ones of the time did no great work (effected little)

دل در جهان مبند و به مستی سال کن

To the world, attach not the heart and of the intoxicated one (the holy traveller) inquire

از فیض جام و قصه جمشید کامگار

Of the bounty of the cup and of the tale of Jamshid

جز نقد جان به دست ندارم شراب کو

Naught have I in hand, save life's cash: the wine is where

کان نیز بر کرشمه ساقی کنم نثار

That it also, on the Saki's glance, I may scatter.

خوش دولتیست خرم و خوش خسروی کریم

Joyous is pleasant fortune and pleasant is the merciful king.

یا رب ز چشم زخم زمانش نگاه دار

O Lord! From time's eye-wound, them preserve.

می خور به شعر بنده که زیی دگر دهد

To the slave's verse, drink wine. For another decoration giveth

جام مرصع تو بدین در شاهوار

Thy bejewelled cup to this royal pearl (the murshid)

گر فوت شد سحور چه نقصان صبوح هست

If the early morning meal (deeds of service and of abstinence) hath vanished, what matter There is (still) the morning wine (deeds of love)

از می کنند روزه گشا طالبان یار

With wine, fast-breaking (keeping back from the world's affluence) the seekers of the true Beloved make

زان جا که پرده پوشی عفو کریم توست
For the reason that Thy merciful disposition is the screen-concealer,

بر قلب ما ببخش که نقدیست کم عیار
On our heart, bestow pardon for it is a little cash of small proof

ترسم که روز حشر عنان بر عنان رود
I fear that, on the day of rising, up, rein on rein (equally) urge

تسبیح شیخ و خرقه رند شرابخوار
The rosary of the holy Shaikh[1], and the Khirka[2] of the profligate, wine-drinker

حافظ چو رفت روزه و گل نیز می‌رود
Hafiz since fasting (austerity and chastity) hath departed and the rose (love's season) also departeth

ناچار باده نوش که از دست رفت کار
Helpless, drink wine (of love) for, from the hand, (the goal of) work Hath departed

غزل ۲۴۷ ⓄⒹⒺ ②④⑦

صبا ز منزل جانان گذر دریغ مدار
O breeze (murshid) thy passing by the dwelling of the (true) Beloved, keep not back

وز او به عاشق بی‌دل خبر دریغ مدار
For the wretched lover (Hafiz) news of Him (the true Beloved) keep not back

به شکر آن که شکفتی به کام بخت ای گل
O rose in thanks that, to thy heart's desire, thou blossomedest,

نسیم وصل ز مرغ سحر دریغ مدار
From the bird of the morning (the nightingale) the breeze of union keep not back

حریف عشق تو بودم چو ماه نو بودی
When thou wast the new moon (in the beginning of youthful beauty) I was thy companion

کنون که ماه تمامی نظر دریغ مدار
Now, that (in beauty) thou art the full moon, (from the state of me foolish) the glance of mercy keep not back,

جهان و هر چه در او هست سهل و مختصر است
Mean small and contracted is the world and all that in it is

ز اهل معرفت این مختصر دریغ مدار
O true Beloved from the people of divine knowledge, this contracted portion keep not back

کنون که چشمه قند است لعل نوشینت
Now, that the fountain of sugar (the water of life) is Thy sweet ruby (lip)

سخن بگوی و ز طوطی شکر دریغ مدار
Utter speech and from the parrot (Hafiz) sugar (the true Beloved) keep not back

مکارم تو به آفاق می‌برد شاعر
To the far horizon, taketh the poet thy deeds (noble and generous):

از او وظیفه و زاد سفر دریغ مدار
From him, allowance and provision for the journey keep not back

چو ذکر خیر طلب می‌کنی سخن این است
(O praised One) Since thou desirest good mention (of thy self) this the matter

که در بهای سخن سیم و زر دریغ مدار
In respect of the price of speech (good mention) silver and gold keep not back

---

1-A leader in a Muslim community   2-cloak

غبار غم برود حال خوش شود حافظ
Hafiz grief's dust departeth better cometh thy state
تو آب دیده از این رهگذر دریغ مدار
From this thoroughfare, the water of thy eye (tears) keep not back

غزل ۲۴۸ ⓄⒹⒺ ②④⑧

ای صبا نکهتی از کوی فلانی به من آر
O breeze from such a one's street, me, a perfume bring.
زار و بیمار غمم راحت جانی به من آر
Weeping and sad of grief, I am me, ease of soul, bring:

قلب بی‌حاصل ما را بزن اکسیر مراد
For our profit less heart, strike out the elixir of purpose
یعنی از خاک در دوست نشانی به من آر
That is From the dust of the Beloved's door (which is indeed an elixir) me, a trace bring.

در کمینگاه نظر با دل خویشم جنگ است
With my own heart, in the ambush-place of vision, is war
ز ابرو و غمزه او تیر و کمانی به من آر
To me, an arrow and a bow (fashioned) from His (curved) eye-brow and (shooting) glance bring

در غریبی و فراق و غم دل پیر شدم
In wandering, and in separation, and in grief of heart (I have spent my life; and now) I
am become old
ساغر می ز کف تازه جوانی به من آر
(So that from the present, freedom, I may obtain; and, for the past, compensation) Me,
a cup of wine from the hand of a youthful one, bring

منکران را هم از این می دو سه ساغر بچشان
Two, or three, cups of this wine, cause the deniers to taste
وگر ایشان نستانند روانی به من آر
And, if they take them not, running (with speed) tome, bring.

ساقیا عشرت امروز به فردا مفکن
O Saki the ease of to-day, to to-morrow, cast not,
یا ز دیوان قضا خط امانی به من آر
Or, from Fate's book, me, the line of safety (that, till to-morrow, I shall live) bring

دلم از دست بشد دوش چو حافظ می‌گفت
Last night, forth from the screen went my heart, when Hafiz said
کای صبا نکهتی از کوی فلانی به من آر
O breeze from such a one's street, me, a perfume bring

غزل ۲۴۹ ⓄⒹⒺ ②④⑨

ای صبا نکهتی از خاک ره یار بیار
O breeze from the dust of the (true) Beloved's path, a perfume bring:
ببر اندوه دل و مژده دلدار بیار
My heart's grief, take; glad tidings of the heart-possessor bring.

نکته‌ای روح فزا از دهن دوست بگو

(O breeze) From the (true) Beloved's mouth, a soul-expanding subtlety utter

نامه‌ای خوش خبر از عالم اسرار بیار

From the world of mysteries, a letter of pleasant news bring.

تا معطر کنم از لطف نسیم تو مشام

So that by the favour of Thy gentle breeze, my perfume-place, I may perfume,

شمه‌ای از نفحات نفس یار بیار

A little of the odours of the Beloved's breath bring.

به وفای تو که خاک ره آن یار عزیز

(O breeze, I conjure thee) by thy fidelity, the dust of the path of that dearly Beloved,

بی غباری که پدید آید از اغیار بیار

Without a particle of dust that from stranger appeareth, bring

گردی از رهگذر دوست به کوری رقیب

From the Friend's thoroughfare, a little dust, for the blindness of the watcher,

بهر آسایش این دیده خونبار بیار

For the assuaging of this my blood-raining eye, bring

خامی و ساده دلی شیوه جانبازان نیست

Immatureness and simple-heartedness is not the way of those life-sporting (who, for the heart-ravisher, play the cash of the heart)

خبری از بر آن دلبر عیار بیار

From that heart-ravisher, sorcerer, (a little) news bring

شکر آن را که تو در عشرتی ای مرغ چمن

O bird of the sward thanks for that thou art in ease,

به اسیران قفس مژده گلزار بیار

To the cage-captives, glad tidings of the rose-bed bring

کام جان تلخ شد از صبر که کردم بی دوست

Bitter became the soul's desire through the patience that I exercised without the Friend

عشوه‌ای زان لب شیرین شکربار بیار

The way of that sweet lip (of the Friend's) sugar-raining bring.

روزگاریست که دل چهره مقصود ندید

Along time it is since that my heart the face of its purpose, be held

ساقیا آن قدح آینه کردار بیار

O Saki that goblet, the mirror of conduct bring

دلق حافظ به چه ارزد به می‌اش رنگین کن

Hafiz's ragged garment, what is it worth Be-colour it with wine

وان گهش مست و خراب از سر بازار بیار

Then, to the head of the market, him Hafiz intoxicated and ruined bring.

غزل ۲۵۰ ⓄⒹⒺ ②⑤⓪

روی بنمای و وجود خودم از یاد ببر

(O beloved) display thy face and my existence from my mind take

خرمن سوختگان را همه گو باد ببر

(And) the harvest of those consumed, (lovers) say O wind all take

ما چو دادیم دل و دیده به طوفان بلا
When to the deluge of calamity, we gave our heart and eye,

گو بیا سیل غم و خانه ز بنیاد ببر
Say: Come grief's torrent, and up, from its foundation, our house take.

زلف چون عنبر خامش که ببوید هیهات
His tress, like pure ambergris, who may smell Alas

ای دل خام طمع این سخن از یاد ببر
O heart raw of greed, from thy memory this matter (of smelling His tress) take

سینه گو شعله آتشکده فارس بکش
Tell the heart (by thy own great fire) slay (quench) the flame of the (great) fire-temple of Fars

دیده گو آب رخ دجله بغداد ببر
Tell the eye (by thy great weeping) luster (from) the face of the mighty Tigris of Baghdad[1] take.

دولت پیر مغان باد که باقی سهل است
Be the fortune (wherein is no decline) of the Pir of the Magians, because the travelling of the rest is easy

دیگری گو برو و نام من از یاد ببر
(If) another (go) say Go and (out) from thy memory (for easy is this) our name, take.

سعی نابرده در این راه به جایی نرسی
In this path (of divine knowledge) effort not borne, (thou) reachest not to place (of rank)

مزد اگر می‌طلبی طاعت استاد ببر
If thou see k the reward, the service of the teacher (the murshid) take.

روز مرگم نفسی وعده دیدار بده
On the day of (my) death, give me, one moment, the promise of seeing (thee)

وان گهم تا به لحد فارغ و آزاد ببر
Then to the tomb me, free and independent, take.

دوش می‌گفت به مژگان درازت بکشم
Last night, He (the Beloved) said With my long dark eye-lashes, I will slay thee

یا رب از خاطرش اندیشه بیداد ببر
O Lord! from His heart, the thought of in justice take.

حافظ اندیشه کن از نازکی خاطر یار
Hafiz think of the delicacy of the (true) Beloved's heart

برو از درگهش این ناله و فریاد ببر
From His court, go and this thy wailing and lamenting, take

غزل ۲۵۱ ⓄⒹⒺ ②⑤①

شب وصل است و طی شد نامه هجر
Tis the night of power; and closed is the book of separation

سلام فیه حتی مطلع الفجر
(On that night, is) safety to the rising of (separation).

دلا در عاشقی ثابت قدم باش
O heart in being a lover, be firm of foot

که در این ره نباشد کار بی اجر
For, in this path, is no work void of reward.

1-The largest city and capital of Iraq

من از رندی نخواهم کرد توبه
Of profligacy, I will not repent me,

و لو آذیتنی بالهجر و الحجر
Although, through stone and separation, thou causest torment to reach me.

برآی ای صبح روشن دل خدا را
O luminous morning of the heart come forth

که بس تاریک می‌بینم شب هجر
For dark indeed, I see the night of separation.

دلم رفت و ندیدم روی دلدار
Went my heart from the hand yet the beloved's face, I saw not

فغان از این تطاول آه از این زجر
Of this tyranny, complaint of this reproof, lamentations

وفا خواهی جفاکش باش حافظ
Hafiz thou desirest fidelity Be endurer of the tyranny (and of the grace of the Beloved)

فان الربح و الخسران فی التجر
Then in traffic, Is the verification of profit and of loss

غزل ۲۵۲ ⊙D̂Ê ②⑤② ODE

گر بود عمر به میخانه رسم بار دگر
If life were, to the wine-house, I would go another time:

بجز از خدمت رندان نکنم کار دگر
Save the service of profligates, I would do no other work.

خرم آن روز که با دیده گریان بروم
Happy that day, when, with weeping eye, I go

تا زنم آب در میکده یک بار دگر
So that, on the wine-house door, water (of tears) I may dash another time

معرفت نیست در این قوم خدا را سببی
In this tribe (with whom, I am captive), divine knowledge is none, O God a little help,

تا برم گوهر خود را به خریدار دگر
Where by, my own jewel of (existence) I may take to another purchaser.

یار اگر رفت و حق صحبت دیرین نشناخت
If the (true) Beloved departed and recognised not the right of ancient society.

حاش لله که روم من ز پی یار دگر
God forbid that I should go in pursuit of another beloved.

گر مساعد شودم دایره چرخ کبود
If my helper be the circle of the azure sphere,

هم به دست آورمش باز به پرگار دگر
Him (the true Beloved) to hand, I will bring with another compass.

عافیت می‌طلبد خاطرم ار بگذارند
Ease seeketh my heart, if permit

غمزه شوخش و آن طره طرار دگر
His bold glance and that cut-purse tress an other (time)

راز سربسته ما بین که به دستان گفتند

Be hold our closed-up mystery that, as a tale, they uttered,

هر زمان با دف و نی بر سر بازار دگر

Momently, with drum and reed, at the head of another bazar (market).

هر دم از درد بنالم که فلک هر ساعت

Momently, with pain, I be wail. For, momently, the sky

کندم قصد دل ریش به آزار دگر

For my wounded heart, maketh device with another torment:

بازگویم نه در این واقعه حافظ تنهاست

Again, I say (Captive) in this matter (of pain) not alone is Hafiz

غرقه گشتند در این بادیه بسیار دگر

In this desert of pain over whelmed, hath become many another person

غزل ۲۵۳ ⓞⓓⓔ ②⑤③

ای خرم از فروغ رخت لاله زار عمر

O thou, from the splendour of whose cheek, is joyous the tulip-bed of life

بازآکه ریخت بی گل رویت بهار عمر

Come back for, without the rose of thy cheek, spilleth the spring of life.

از دیده گر سرشک چو باران چکد رواست

If, like rain, the tear drop from my eye, it is lawful

کاندر غمت چو برق بشد روزگار عمر

For, in grief for thee, like lightning (swiftly in tumult) passed the time of life.

این یک دو دم که مهلت دیدار ممکن است

These moments, one or two, when the fortune of seeing Thee (O Beloved) is possible,

دریاب کار ما که نه پیداست کار عمر

Discover our work (the fortune of seeing Thee) For, not revealed is the work of life

تا کی می صبوح و شکرخواب بامداد

Till when (art thou careless and senseless in) the wine of the morning, and the sweet sleep of dawn

هشیار گرد هان که گذشت اختیار عمر

Ho be wakeful for passed hath the choice of life-

دی در گذار بود و نظر سوی ما نکرد

Yesterday, He (the Beloved) passed and towards me glanced not

بیچاره دل که هیچ ندید از گذار عمر

O helpless heart that saw naught (of profit) from the passing of life.

اندیشه از محیط فنا نیست هر که را

Of the ocean of effacement no thought is his to whom

بر نقطه دهان تو باشد مدار عمر

On the point of thy mouth, (the hidden mystery) is the center of life.

در هر طرف که ز خیل حوادث کمین گهیست

From every quarter (of the world) is the ambuscade of the troop of vicissitudes

زان رو عنان گسسته دواند سوار عمر

In that way of thought, rein-drawn, (impetuously, saying God forbid I should be captive to vicissitude) runneth the horseman of life.

بی عمر زنده‌ام من و این بس عجب مدار
Without life, a live I am. This, esteem no great wonder

روز فراق را که نهد در شمار عمر
The day of separation, who placeth in the reckoning of life

حافظ سخن بگوی که بر صفحه جهان
Hafiz utter speech. For, on earth's surface

این نقش ماند از قلمت یادگار عمر
Of thy eloquence, (only) this picture remaineth, the recollection of life.

غزل ۲۵۴ ⓄⒹⒺ ②⑤④

دیگر ز شاخ سرو سهی بلبل صبور
Again, from the branch of the straight cypress, the patient bulbul[1]

گلبانگ زد که چشم بد از روی گل به دور
Shouted glad tidings, saying From the face of the rose, far be the evil eye

ای گلبشکر آن که تویی پادشاه حسن
O rose (beloved) in thanks that, to thy heart's desire, thou blossomedest

با بلبلان بی‌دل شیدا مکن غرور
With bulbuls the distraught lover, display no pride.

از دست غیبت تو شکایت نمی‌کنم
Against the hand of thy absence, no complaint, I make

تا نیست غیبتی نبود لذت حضور
So long as (long) absence is none, no (great) pleasure giveth the presence (of the beloved)

گر دیگران به عیش و طرب خرمند و شاد
If, joyous and glad some in pleasure and joy others be,

ما را غم نگار بود مایه سرور
For us, the grief (of love) for the idol (the true Beloved) is joy's source.

زاهد اگر به حور و قصور است امیدوار
Hopeful of Hur[2] and of palaces if the Zahid[3] be,

ما را شرابخانه قصور است و یار حور
For us, the wine-house is the palace (above) and the beloved, the Hur.

می خور به بانگ چنگ و مخور غصه ور کسی
To the sound of the harp, drink wine and suffer no grief. If any one

گوید تو را که باده مخور گو هوالغفور
Speak to thee saying: Wine, drink not (for 'tis sin) say: The forgiver is God.

حافظ شکایت از غم هجران چه می‌کنی
Hafiz complaint of grief of separation, why makest thou

در هجر وصل باشد و در ظلمت است نور
In separation, is union in darkness, light

1-Nightingale
2- Heavenly women with black eyes, nymph
3-Pietist

غزل ٢٥٥ ⓄⒹⒺ ②⑤⑤

یوسف گمگشته بازآید به کنعان غم مخور

Back to Kin'an[1], lost Yusuf cometh suffer not grief

کلبه احزان شود روزی گلستان غم مخور

One day, the sorrowful cell becometh the rose-garden suffer not grief.

ای دل غمدیده حالت به شود دل بد مکن

O grief-stricken heart better, becometh thy state; display not the ill-heart:

وین سر شوریده بازآید به سامان غم مخور

Back to reason, cometh this Distraught head suffer not grief.

گر بهار عمر باشد باز بر تخت چمن

If on the sward's throne, again be the spring of life,

چتر گل در سر کشی ای مرغ خوشخوان غم مخور

O bird, night-singing over thy head, thou mayst draw the canopy of the rose suffer not grief

دور گردون گر دو روزی بر مراد ما نرفت

If, for a space of two days, to our desire, the sphere's revolutions turned not

دایما یک سان نباشد حال دوران غم مخور

Ever, in one way, the state of revolution is not suffer not grief.

هان مشو نومید چون واقف نه‌ای از سر غیب

Ho since thou art not acquainted with the hidden mystery, be not hopeless:

باشد اندر پرده بازی‌های پنهان غم مخور

Within the screen, are hidden pastimes suffer not grief.

ای دل ار سیل فنا بنیاد هستی برکند

O heart if the foundation of thy existence, the torrent of passing away (mortality) pluck up

چون تو را نوح است کشتیبان ز طوفان غم مخور

Since Nuh is thy boat-master, of the deluge, suffer not grief

در بیابان گر به شوق کعبه خواهی زد قدم

If, from desire (of pilgrimage) the Ka'ba[2] thou wilt plant thy foot in the desert

سرزنش‌ها گر کند خار مغیلان غم مخور

(Then) If the (mighty) Arabian thorn makere proofs, suffer not grief.

گر چه منزل بس خطرناک است و مقصد بس بعید

Although the stage (of this world) is very fearsome and the purpose hidden,

هیچ راهی نیست کان را نیست پایان غم مخور

There is not a road, whereof is no end suffer not grief

حال ما در فرقت جانان و ابرام رقیب

In separation from the Beloved, and vexing (on the part) of the watcher, our state (of perturbation and confusion)

جمله می‌داند خدای حال گردان غم مخور

All, God, our state causing, knoweth suffer not grief.

حافظا در کنج فقر و خلوت شب‌های تار

In the corner of poverty and in the solitude of dark nights, Hafiz

تا بود وردت دعا و درس قرآن غم مخور

So long as thine are the practice of praying and the reading of the Kuran[3] (wherein is the salvation of the next world) suffer not grief.

1-Ancient regions in southern Syria
2-Muslims turn at prayer.

3-Quran

غزل ۲۵۶ ⓄⒹⒺ ②⑤⑥

نصیحتی کنمت بشنو و بهانه مگیر
A piece of advice, I make thee listen make no excuse

هر آن چه ناصح مشفق بگویدت بپذیر
Whatever the kind admonisher saith to thee, accept.

ز وصل روی جوانان تمتعی بردار
With those of youthful face, the enjoyment of union take up

که در کمینگه عمر است مکر عالم پیر
For, in ambush of life, is the deceit of the old world.

نعیم هر دو جهان پیش عاشقان بجوی
Before lovers (of God) the affluence of both worlds (is) as a barley-corn

که این متاع قلیل است و آن عطای کثیر
For, that (world) is of little merchandise and this (world) of little value

معاشری خوش و رودی بساز می‌خواهم
A pleasant companion, I desire; and some music with an instrument

که درد خویش بگویم به ناله بم و زیر
That, to the wail of bass and of treble, I may utter my pain.

بر آن سرم که ننوشم می و گنه نکنم
On that, I am in tent that I drink no wine, and commit no sin

اگر موافق تدیر من شود تقدیر
If fate be concordant with my desire. (If not, I am helpless)

چو قسمت ازلی بی حضور ما کردند
When, without my presence, they (Fate and Destiny) made God's decree of eternity without beginning,

گر اندکی نه به وفق رضاست خرده مگیر
If a little, not in accordance with fate, be (from me) carp not

چو لاله در قدحم ریز ساقیا می و مشک
O Saki into my cup, (pour) wine like the (ruddy) tulip,

که نقش خال نگارم نمی‌رود ز ضمیر
That, from my mind, depart not the picture of the idol's mole

بیار ساغر در خوشاب ای ساقی
The (ruby) cup of bounty, bring; (and) the pearl of beautiful water (lustrous verse)

حسود گو کرم آصفی ببین و بمیر
Tell the envious one The liberality of an Asaf[1], behold and die

به عزم توبه نهادم قدح ز کف صد بار
A hundred times, with the resolve of repentance, out of my hand the goblet, I put:

ولی کرشمه ساقی نمی‌کند تقصیر
But, desisting from wine, the Saki's glance maketh not.

می دوساله و محبوب چارده ساله
Wine two years old the (Kuran) and the beloved fourteen years old

همین بس است مرا صحبت صغیر و کبیر
For me, this in deed is enough, the society of the small (the two years) and of the great (the fourteen years)

1-Suleiman's minister

دل رمیده ما را که پیش می‌گیرد

Our affrighted heart, who hindereth.

خبر دهید به مجنون خسته از زنجیر

O Majnun, escaped from chains, give ye news.

حدیث توبه در این بزمگه مگو حافظ

Hafiz in this banquet-place, utter not the tale of repentance (as to wine)

که ساقیان کمان ابرویت زنند به تیر

For, thee, with the arrow, the Sakis of bow eye-brow will strik

غزل ۲۵۷ ⓄⒹⒺ ②⑤⑦

روی بنما و مرا گو که ز جان دل برگیر

(O true Beloved) Display Thy face and to me speak, saying: "From life thy heart up take."

پیش شمع آتش پروانه به جان گو درگیر

Say Before the candle, with soul, the fire of the moth kindle

در لب تشنه ما بین و مدار آب دریغ

At our thirsty lip, look and (from it) water with hold not

بر سر کشته خویش آی و ز خاکش برگیر

To the head of thy slain one (thy lover) come; and him, from this dust of (contempt) up take

ترک درویش مگیر ار نبود سیم و زرش

The dervish, a band on not, if his be not silver and gold

در غمت سیم شمار اشک و رخش را زر گیر

In grief for thee, this (crystal) tear, silver reckon and his (ruddy) face, (red) gold take.

چنگ بنواز و بساز ار نبود عود چه باک

Twang the harp and (with it) be content. If aloe-wood (fuel) be not, what fear

آتشم عشق و دلم عود و تنم مجمر گیر

My love, the fire my heart, the aloe-wood (fuel) and my body, the censer, take.

در سماع آی و ز سر خرقه برانداز و برقص

Into sama'[1], come off from thy head, cast the Khirka[2]; and dance

ور نه با گوشه رو و خرقه ما در سر گیر

If not, into the corner (of solitude) go and on thy head, our Khirka of hypocrisy take

صوف برکش ز سر و باده صافی درکش

Off from thy head, draw the wool (garment of beggary) and the wine of purity, drink

سیم درباز و به زر سیمبری در بر گیر

Silver, play (spend money) and, with gold, into thy embrace one of silver bosom (a beloved one) take

دوست گو یار شو و هر دو جهان دشمن باش

Say, the Friend (God) is my friend, then be both worlds my enemy

بخت گو پشت مکن روی زمین لشکر گیر

(Then) say, fortune becometh recreant (and all the men of) and the surface of the land, army taker

میل رفتن مکن ای دوست دمی با ما باش

O friend (the true Beloved) for going away, make no desire with us, a moment be

بر لب جوی طرب جوی و به کف ساغر گیر

On the rivulet's bank (formed of my tears) joy, seekand, in thy hand, the cup take

---

1-Dance   2-Cloak

رفته گیر از برم وز آتش و آب دل و چشم

Gone from my bosom, this fire of love and water of tears of my heart and eye, take

گونه‌ام زرد و لبم خشک و کنارم تر گیر

My hue, yellow (with grief) my lip, dry (with thirst) my bosom wet (with tears) take.

حافظ آراسته کن بزم و بگو واعظ را

Hafiz the banquet, adorned make and to the admonisher, speak,

که ببین مجلسم و ترک سر منبر گیر

Saying: "My assembly be hold and, (the path) of abandoning the pulpit take."

⟨◉⟩⟨◉⟩

ز
The Letter Zā

ⓄⒹⒺ ②⑤⑧ غزل ۲۵۸

هزار شکر که دیدم به کام خویشت باز

Thanks, a thousand, that, again, to my desire, I b held thee,

ز روی صدق و صفا گشته با دلم دمساز

In truth and purity, concordant with myheart, become.

روندگان طریقت ره بلا سپرند

The Path of calamity, tread the travellers of hakikat[1]

رفیق عشق چه غم دارد از نشیب و فراز

Of the descent and of the ascent, reflecteth notThe companion of (the Path tarikat)

غم حبیب نهان به ز گفت و گوی رقیب

Better than search for the watcher, is grief for the hidden Friend (God)

که نیست سینه ارباب کینه محرم راز

For, not the confidant of mystery is the heart of the Lord of malice

اگر چه حسن تو از عشق غیر مستغنیست

Independent of love, though Thy beauty is,

من آن نیم که از این عشقبازی آیم باز

Not that one am I who, from this love-paying, back will turn.

چه گویمت که ز سوز درون چه می‌بینم

To thee, how many I utter what, from the burning of my heart. I behold?

ز اشک پرس حکایت که من نیم غماز

Of my tears, ask the tale; for not the informer am I.

چه فتنه بود که مشاطه قضا انگیخت

What tumult it was that the attire of fate evoked,

که کرد نرگس مستش سیه به سرمه ناز

When, his bold narcissus, he made black with the collyrium of grace.

بدین سپاس که مجلس منور است به دوست

For this thanks that, by the Friend, the assembly is illuminated

گرت چو شمع جفایی رسد بسوز و بساز

If an act of tyranny reach thee, like the candle, consume and be content

غرض کرشمه حسن است ور نه حاجت نیست

The desire of beauty's glance is his If not, is no need

جمال دولت محمود را به زلف ایاز

Of the tress of Ayaz[2] to the beauty of Mahmud[3]'s fortune.

غزل سرایی ناهید صرفه‌ای نبرد

The ghazal-singing of Nahid Venus, the minstrel of the sky taketh not the lead.

در آن مقام که حافظ برآورد آواز

In that place, where forth his voice of song Hafiz bringeth.

1-Truth
2-Slave Sultan Mahmud

3-Sultan Mahmud of Ghazni

غزل ۲۵۹ ⓄⒹⒺ ②⑤⑨

منم که دیده به دیدار دوست کردم باز
Who, for the sight of the (true) Beloved, opened my eye, that one am I

چه شکر گویمت ای کارساز بنده نواز
O work-door, slave cherisher what thanks to Thee, shall I utter

نیازمند بلا گو رخ از غبار مشوی
To the indigent man of calamity, say: From dust, wash not thy face

که کیمیای مراد است خاک کوی نیاز
For the dust of the street of indigency is the alchemy of thy desire.

ز مشکلات طریقت عنان متاب ای دل
O heart from the difficulties of the path, turn not the rein

که مرد راه نیندیشد از نشیب و فراز
For, of descent and of ascent, reflecteth not the man of the Path.

طهارت ار نه به خون جگر کند عاشق
If with the blood of the liver, purification (in love) the lover (of God) make not,

به قول مفتی عشقش درست نیست نماز
By the word of the mufti[1] of love, not true is his prayer.

در این مقام مجازی بجز پیاله مگیر
In this illusory stage, save the cup (of love for God) take naught

در این سراچه بازیچه غیر عشق مباز
In this house (the world) save love, a pastime play not.

به نیم بوسه دعایی بخر ز اهل دلی
With a half kiss purchase a prayer from one of heart

که کید دشمنت از جان و جسم دارد باز
That, from the enemy's malice, thee, soul and body may preserve

فکند زمزمه عشق در حجاز و عراق
Love's murmur, into Hijaz and Irak, casteth

نوای بانگ غزل های حافظ از شیراز
The melody of the strain of the ghazals[2] of Hafiz of Shiraz.

غزل ۲۶۰ ⓄⒹⒺ ②⑥⓪

ای سرو ناز حسن که خوش می‌روی به ناز
O thou dainty cypress of beauty that with grace sweetly movest!

عشاق را به ناز تو هر لحظه صد نیاز
Momently, to lovers, are a hundred needs of Thy grace.

فرخنده باد طلعت خوبت که در ازل
Auspicious be the dress of honour of Thy beauty. For, in eternity without beginning

بریده‌اند بر قد سروت قبای ناز
To thy cypress stature, they (fate and destiny) cut a garment of grace

---

1-Lawyer
2-Sonnet

آن را که بوی عنبر زلف تو آرزوست

Whose is desire for the perfume of the ambergris of thy tress,

چون عود گو بر آتش سودا بسوز و ساز

Say On the consuming fire like the aloe-wood (fuel) consume and be content.

پروانه را ز شمع بود سوز دل ولی

Through the candle, heart-consuming was the moth's (lot)

بی شمع عارض تو دلم را بود گداز

Without the candle of Thy cheek, melting was my heart's (lot)

صوفی که بی تو توبه ز می کرده بود دوش

The Sufi[1] who, last night, without Thee, had repented of wine

بشکست عهد چون در میخانه دید باز

Broke his covenant (of austerity and practised love) when open he be held the door of the wine-house (the stage of love and of divine knowledge)

از طعنه رقیب نگردد عیار من

Through the watcher's reproof, altereth not my proof (of value)

چون زر اگر برند مرا در دهان گاز

If me, like gold, they cut in the mouth of the shears.

دل کز طواف کعبه کویت وقوف یافت

The heart that, from the circuit of (the Ka'ba) of Thy street, gained news

از شوق آن حریم ندارد سر حجاز

Through desire for that sacred fold of Thy street, no wish for Hijaz hath

هر دم به خون دیده چه حاجت وضو چو نیست

Momently, with blood (tears) of the eye, ablution what profit, when there is not

بی طاق ابروی تو نماز مرا جواز

Permitted for me the prayer without the arch of Thy eye-brow

چون باده باز بر سر خم رفت کف زنان

Like the intoxicated cup at the head of the jar, palm-clapping, went

حافظ که دوش از لب ساقی شنید راز

Hafiz who, last night, from the lip of the cup, the mystery (of divine knowledge) heard

غزل ۲۶۱ ÔĎĒ ②⑥①

درآ که در دل خسته توان درآید باز

(O true Beloved) come, so that, in my shattered (and grief-stricken (heart, power may enter

بیا که در تن مرده روان درآید باز

Come so that, in my dead body, life may enter again.

بیا که فرقت تو چشم من چنان در بست

Come for separation from Thee hath closed my eye in such away

که فتح باب وصالت مگر گشاید باز

That, it, (only) the opening of the door of union with Thee may perchance open again.

1-A Muslim ascetic and mystic

غمی که چون سپه زنگ ملک دل بگرفت

That grief, that, like the (black) army of Zang[1] took, (in blood) my heart

ز خیل شادی روم رخت زداید باز

By the troop (of horse) of joyousness of the Rum (the country) of Thy face, will be effaced again

به پیش آینه دل هر آن چه می‌دارم

Before the mirror of the heart, whatever I hold,

بجز خیال جمالت نمی‌نماید باز

Save the image of Thy beauty appeareth not again.

بدان مثل که شب آبستن است روز از تو

By that proverb that the night is pregnant with events, and vicissitudes, far (in separation) from Thee (which is the cause of humiliation),

ستاره می‌شمرم تا که شب چه زاید باز

I count the stars (and am in this fear and danger). Let us see what the night bringeth forth again

بیا که بلبل مطبوع خاطر حافظ

Hafiz come. For the bulbul[2], agreeable of heart

به بوی گلبن وصل تو می‌سراید باز

By the perfume of the rose-bed of union with thee, singeth a gain.

غزل ۲۶۲ ⓄⒹⒺ ②⑥②

حال خونین دلان که گوید باز

The state of bloody hearts, who uttereth again

و از فلک خون خم که جوید باز

From the sky, (revenge for) the blood of Jamshid[3], who seeketh again

شرمش از چشم می پرستان باد

Of the eye of wine-worshippers, shame be its

نرگس مست اگر بروید باز

The intoxicated narcissus, if up it spring again.

جز فلاطون خم نشین شراب

Save Plato, jar-sitter with wine,

سر حکمت به ما که گوید باز

to us, the mystery of philosophy, who uttereth again

هر که چون لاله کاسه گردان شد

Whoever, like the (cup – shaped) tulip became cup-circulator

زین جفا رخ به خون بشوید باز

On account of this tyranny, his face in blood, washeth again.

نگشاید دلم چو غنچه اگر

Like the rose-bud, expandeth my heart, if

ساغری از لبش نبوید باز

The cup of tulip colour, it smell again.

بس که در پرده چنگ گفت سخن

Since, in its notes (the mystery of hakikat the harp the Arif, mystery – revealer) uttered speech (of grief)

ببرش موی تا نموید باز

Its chord, cut; so that it may not moana gain.

1-I used in black and white to mean "light and dark" or "day and night".

2-Nightingale

3-King

گرد بیت الحرام خم حافظ

About the sacred house of the jar of wine (of love) Hafiz.

گر نمیرد به سر بپوید باز

If he can, on his head (swiftly) will run again

غزل ۲۶۳ ⓄⒹⒺ ②⑥③

بیا و کشتی ما در شط شراب انداز

(O true Beloved) Come and, upon the river of wine, our boat (–shaped wine – cup) cast

خروش و ولوله در جان شیخ و شاب انداز

Into the soul of the shaikh[1] (the old) and of the youth, shouting and howling, (in envy thereof) cast.

مرا به کشتی باده درافکن ای ساقی

Saki[2] into my boat, cast wine

که گفتهاند نکویی کن و در آب انداز

For, they have said Goodness, do and upon the water, cast.

کوی میکده برگشتهام ز راه خطا

In mistake, from the street of the wine-house t (he stage of love and of divine knowledge) I wandered

مرا دگر ز کرم با ره صواب انداز

In kindness, in the path of rectitude to (the wine – house) me, again cast.

بیار زان می گلرنگ مشک بو جامی

Of that wine, rose of hue, musk of smell, a cup bring

شرار رشک و حسد در دل گلاب انداز

Into the heart of the rose, sparks of jealousy and of envy cast.

اگر چه مست و خرابم تو نیز لطفی کن

Intoxicated and ruined, though I am, me a little kindness do

نظر بر این دل سرگشته خراب انداز

On this heart, perplexed and ruined, Thy glance (of mercy) cast.

به نیم شب اگرت آفتاب میباید

If at mid night, the sun be necessary for thee

ز روی دختر گلچهر رز نقاب انداز

From (off) the face of the vine's daughter, rose of face, the veil, cast.

مهل که روز وفاتم به خاک بسپارند

Permit not that, on the day of death, they consign me to the dust (of the grave)

مرا به میکده بر در خم شراب انداز

Me, to the wine-house take into the jar of wine, cast

ز جور چرخ چو حافظ به جان رسید دلت

Hafiz when from the sphere's violence, thy heart reacheth to the soul,

به سوی دیو محن ناوک شهاب انداز

At the Dev[3] of calamities, the arrow-point of a falling star cast

---

1-A leader in a Muslim community
2-Tapster

3-Demon

غزل ۲۶۴ ⓄⒹⒺ ②⑥④

خیز و در کاسه زر آب طربناک انداز

(O Saki) Arise and into the cup of gold, joyous water (wine the intoxication of love) cast

پیشتر زان که شود کاسه سر خاک انداز

before that the cap of the head the skull dust becometh cast

عاقبت منزل ما وادی خاموشان است

In the end, our dwelling is the valley of the silent (the place of tombs)

حالیا غلغله در گنبد افلاک انداز

No into the vault of the skies, the (resounding) shout and clamour (of zikr va fikr) cast

چشم آلوده نظر از رخ جانان دور است

Far from the (true) Beloved's face, is the eye stained with sight for other than God

بر رخ او نظر از آینه پاک انداز

On His face, from the pure mirror (of the pure heart) glance cast

به سر سبز تو ای سرو که گر خاک شوم

O cypress (I conjure thee) By thy verdant head, when I become dust

ناز از سر بنه و سایه بر این خاک انداز

Out from thy head, disdain put and, on this my dust, shade cast

دل ما را که ز مار سر زلف تو بخست

For our heart that, from the deadly snake of Thy tress tip, is shattered

از لب خود به شفاخانه تریاک انداز

From Thy own lip to the recovery-house, the antidote of (a kiss) cast

ملک این مزرعه دانی که ثباتی ندهد

The country of this sown-field (the world) thou knowest that it hath no permanency

آتشی از جگر جام در املاک انداز

Into the countries (of the world) from the liver of the wine cup, (the murshid's interior) the a great fire cast.

غسل در اشک زدم کاهل طریقت گویند

In (my own) tears, I bathed. For the people of Tarikat[1] say

پاک شو اول و پس دیده بر آن پاک انداز

First be pure then, on (the beauty of) that Pure One, (the true Beloved) thy eye cast

یا رب آن زاهد خودبین که بجز عیب ندید

O Lord! that Zahid, self-be holding, who, save defect, saw naught,

دود آهیش در آیینه ادراک انداز

Into the mirror of his understanding, (so that he may, no longer, see defect) the smoke of a great sigh cast.

چون گل از نکهت او جامه قبا کن حافظ

Hafiz! like the rose, on account of His perfume make rent thy garment

وین قبا در ره آن قامت چالاک انداز

And, in the path of that form (of the Beloved) swift (for the slaughter of lovers) that (rent) garment cast.

1-Principle, Sufism, religious way

غزل ۲۶۵ ⓄⒹⒺ ②⑥⑤

برنیامد از تمنای لبت کامم هنوز
Through desire of thy lip, forth cometh not my desire yet

بر امید جام لعلت دردی آشامم هنوز
In the hope of the cup of thy ruby (lip) a dreg-drinker am I yet

روز اول رفت دینم در سر زلفین تو
On the first day (the day of Alast) in desire of thy two tresses, departed my faith

تا چه خواهد شد در این سودا سرانجامم هنوز
Let us see, in this phrensy, what my end will be yet.

ساقیا یک جرعه‌ای زان آب آتشگون که من
O Saki (perfect Murshid) of that water, fire of hue, one draught, (give me) For I,

در میان پختگان عشق او خامم هنوز
In the midst of those experienced in His Love, inexperienced am I yet.

از خطا گفتم شبی زلف تو را مشک ختن
One night, in mistake, I called Thy hair the (fragrant) musk of Khutan[1]

می‌زند هر لحظه تیغی مو بر اندامم هنوز
Momently, a sword on my limbs (saying why didst thou liken His glorious hair to contemptible musk) the hair striketh yet

پرتو روی تو تا در خلوتم دید آفتاب
In my khilvat[2], a ray (of splendour) of Thy face, the (resplendent) sun be held

می‌رود چون سایه هر دم بر در و بامم هنوز
Momently, like the shadow, to my door and roof, he (the sun) goeth yet

نام من رفته‌ست روزی بر لب جانان به سهو
One day, in mistake, to the true Beloved's lip, went my name

اهل دل را بوی جان می‌آید از نامم هنوز
To people of heart, from my name the perfume of the soul (of the Beloved) cometh yet

در ازل داده‌ست ما را ساق لعل لبت
To us, in eternity without beginning, the Saki gave the ruby of Thy lip

جرعه جامی که من مدهوش آن جامم هنوز
The draught of a cup, of which cup, senseless am I yet

ای که گفتی جان بده تا باشدت آرام جان
O Thou that saidest: "Give thy soul, that ease of heart may be thine,"

جان به غم‌هایش سپردم نیست آرامم هنوز
In griefs for Him (the true Beloved) my soul, I gave. Mine, not ease, is yet.

در قلم آورد حافظ قصه لعل لبش
The tale of the ruby of Thy lip, Hafiz brought into his pen (writing)

آب حیوان می‌رود هر دم ز اقلامم هنوز
Momently, from my pens, the water of life floweth yet

1-It is a fragrant substance that is from the land of Khotan.   2-Solitude

غزل ۲۶۶ ⓄⒹⒺ ②⑥⑥

دلم رمیده لولی وشیست شورانگیز

Ravished is my heart by one like a singing girl, clamour-exciter

دروغ وعده و قتال وضع و رنگ آمیز

False of promise, slayer by nature, and colour (of deceit) mixer.

فدای پیرهن چاک ماه رویان باد

A ransom for the rent garment of those of moon-face, be

هزار جامه تقوا و خرقه پرهیز

A thousand garments of piety and the Khirka[1] of austerity

خیال خال تو با خود به خاک خواهم برد

Of thy own arm, be not proud; for in record it is:

که تا ز خال تو خاکم شود عبیرآمیز

"In the order of the king-maker a thousand arrayings."

فرشته عشق نداند که چیست ای ساق

The angel does not know what love is, O Saki[2],

بخواه جام و گلابی به خاک آدم ریز

The cup, demand and on Adam's dust, a little water sprinkle

پیاله بر کفنم بند تا سحرگه حشر

In my coffin, put up the cup so that, on the morning of rising,

به می ز دل ببرم هول روز رستاخیز

I may, with wine, take from my heart the terror of the day up-rising and springing.

فقیر و خسته به درگاهت آمدم رحمی

Poor and shattered, to Thy court, I have come. A little pity,

که جز ولای توام نیست هیچ دست آویز

For, save attachment to Thee, attachment, mine is none.

بیا که هاتف میخانه دوش با من گفت

Come for last night, tome, the invisible messenger spake,

که در مقام رضا باش و از قضا مگریز

Saying In contentment's stage, be from destiny, flee not.

میان عاشق و معشوق هیچ حال نیست

Between the lover and the Beloved, veil is none

تو خود حجاب خودی حافظ از میان برخیز

Hafiz thou thyself art thy own veil. From the midst, arise (and attain unto the Beloved).

❮◉❯❮◉❯

1-Cloak   2-Tapster

س
The Letter Sin

غزل ۲۶۷   ODE 267

ای صبا گر بگذری بر ساحل رود ارس

O breeze if by the bank of the river Araxes, thou pass

بوسه زن بر خاک آن وادی و مشکین کن نفس

Upon the dust of that valley, a kiss express and thy breath (from the perfumed dust) musky make

منزل سلمی که بادش هر دم از ما صد سلام

Salma's[1] dwelling to whom, momently, from us, a hundred salutations be,

پرصدای ساربانان بینی و بانگ جرس

Full of the clamour of the camel-driver sand of the crash of the great bell, thou seest.

محمل جانان ببوس آن گه به زاری عرضه دار

The beloved's litter, kiss then, with soft emotion, the request present,

کز فراقت سوختم ای مهربان فریاد رس

Saying O kind one from separation from thee, I consume. Help

من که قول ناصحان را خواندمی قول رباب

I who used to call the counsel of the counsellors (love – forbidding) the empty sound of the stringed instrument

گوشمالی دیدم از هجران که اینم پند بس

(Now, since) I have experienced the ear-rubbing (torment) of separation, enough for me is this counsel

عشرت شبگیر کن می نوش کاندر راه عشق

Night-taking, make pleasure. (without fear) For, in love's city,

شب روان را آشنایی‌هاست با میر عسس

With the chief of the patrol, the night-prowler (the holy traveller) Hath friendship.

عشقبازی کار بازی نیست ای دل سر بباز

O heart not the work of playing is love-playing. Play thy head (life)

زان که گوی عشق نتوان زد به چوگان هوس

(If not) with the chaugan of passion, one cannot strike the ball of (pure) love.

دل به رغبت می‌سپارد جان به چشم مست یار

To the intoxicated eye of the (true) Beloved, Us own soul, my heart with pleasure giveth

گر چه هشیاران ندادند اختیار خود به کس

Although, to none gave sensible ones their own will.

طوطیان در شکرستان کامرانی می‌کنند

In sugar-land, parrots (other disciples) urge their own pleasure (by the aid of the perfect murshid)

و از تحسر دست بر سر می‌زند مسکین مگس

But, through grief, his wings about his head the wretched fly (Hafiz) beateth

نام حافظ گر برآید بر زبان کلک دوست

If to the nib of the friend's reed, the name of Hafiz ascend,

از جناب حضرت شاهم بس است این ملتمس

From His Majesty, the King, this (that is) supplicated is enough.

1-Metaphor of the Beloved

غزل ۲۶۸ ⓄⒹⒺ ②⑥⑧

گلعذاری ز گلستان جهان ما را بس
From the world's rose-garden one rose of cheek is for us enough

زین چمن سایه آن سرو روان ما را بس
From this sward, the shade of that moving cypress the (true Beloved is) for us enough.

من و همصحبتی اهل ریا دورم باد
I and the fellow-companion ship of people of hypocrisy from us be far

از گرانان جهان رطل گران ما را بس
Of the weighty things of the world, the weighty ritl[1], is for us enough.

قصر فردوس به پاداش عمل می‌بخشند
In return for (good) deeds, the palace of paradise, they give

ما که رندیم و گدا دیر مغان ما را بس
We, who are profligate and indigent, the cloister of the Magians[2] (the stage of divine knowledge and of love) is for us enough.

بنشین بر لب جوی و گذر عمر ببین
On the marge of the (passing) stream, sit and the passing of life, be hold

کاین اشارت ز جهان گذران ما را بس
For this example of the passing world is for us enough.

نقد بازار جهان بنگر و آزار جهان
The cash of the world's market, and the world's pain, be hold

گر شما را نه بس این سود و زیان ما را بس
If this profit is not for you enough this loss, for us enough.

یار با ماست چه حاجت که زیادت طلبیم
With us, is the (true) Beloved. That more we should desire, what need

دولت صحبت آن مونس جان ما را بس
The fortune of the society of that dear Friend of the soul, for us enough.

از در خویش خدا را به بهشتم مفرست
For God's sake, from Thy door, send me not to paradise

که سر کوی تو از کون و مکان ما را بس
For of existence and ab ode, the head of Thy street, for us enough.

حافظ از مشرب قسمت گله ناانصافیست
Hafiz void of justice, is the complaint of the watering place of fate (the world)

طبع چون آب و غزل های روان ما را بس
The nature (pure) like water, and the moving ghazal[3]s, (eloquent and sweet are) for us enough

غزل ۲۶۹ ⓄⒹⒺ ②⑥⑨

دلا رفیق سفر بخت نیکخواهت بس
O heart the companion of thy journey, fortune, well-wishing, is for thee enough

نسیم روضه شیراز پیک راهت بس
The footman of the path, the breeze of the garden of Shiraz is for thee enough.

1- large cup or goblet, pound
2-An allusion to ruins and pubs

3-Sonnet

دگر ز منزل جانان سفر مکن درویش

O Dervish from the true Beloved's ab ode, again journey not;

که سیر معنوی و کنج خانقاهت بس

For, the spiritual walk and the cloister-corner (are) for thee enough.

وگر کمین بگشاید غمی ز گوشه دل

If from thy heart's corner, a great grief make ambush,

حریم درگه پیر مغان پناهت بس

The fold of the court of the Pir of the Magians[1] protection is for thee enough.

به صدر مصطبه بنشین و ساغر می‌نوش

On the tavern-settle, sit the cup, drink

که این قدر ز جهان کسب مال و جاهت بس

For, of the world, this degree of acquisition of wealth and of rank is for thee enough.

زیادتی مطلب کار بر خود آسان کن

Excess, seek not easy to thy self, make work

صراحی می لعل و بتی چو ماهت بس

For the flagon of ruby wine and, an idol, (beauteous) as the moon, (are) for thee enough.

فلک به مردم نادان دهد زمام مراد

To the ignorant man, the sky giveth the rein of desire

تو اهل فضلی و دانش همین گناهت بس

A man of excellence and of knowledge, thou art. This very sin is for thee enough.

هوای مسکن مالوف و عهد یار قدیم

The desire for the accustomed dwelling (this world) and the covenant of the ancient Friend (God)

ز ره روان سفرکرده عذرخواهت بس

With way-experienced way-farers, asking pardon on (account of thy refraining from the journey) for thee enough.

به منت دگران خو مکن که در دو جهان

To the favour and (kindness) Of others, accustom not thy self. For, in both worlds,

رضای ایزد و انعام پادشاهت بس

The will of God, and the favour of the king (are) for thee enough

به هیچ ورد دگر نیست حاجت ای حافظ

Hafiz of any other task, no need is thine

دعای نیم شب و درس صبحگاهت بس

The midnight-prayer and the morning-exercise (are) for thee enough.

غزل ۲۷۰ ⓄⒹⒺ ②⑦⓪ ODE 270

درد عشقی کشیده‌ام که مپرس

Love's pain, I have endured to such a degree-that ask not

زهر هجری چشیده‌ام که مپرس

Separation's poison, I have tasted in such away that ask not.

گشته‌ام در جهان و آخر کار

In the world I have wandered (and its good and bad its heat and cold experienced) and at the end of work,

دلبری برگزیده‌ام که مپرس

A heart-ravisher (the true Beloved) I have chosen so peerless that ask not.

1-The perfect mystic man,

آن چنان در هوای خاک درش
In the desire of the dust of His door, in that way,
می‌رود آب دیده‌ام که مپرس
Goeth the water (tears) of my eye that ask not.

من به گوش خود از دهانش دوش
Last night, from His mouth, with my ear,
سخنانی شنیده‌ام که مپرس
Words, I heard such that ask not.

سوی من لب چه می‌گزی که مگوی
Towards me, wherefore bitest thou thy lip, saying Speak not,
لب لعلی گزیده‌ام که مپرس
A ruby lip, I have bitten (kissed) such that ask not

بی تو در کلبه گدایی خویش
In the hu of my own beggary, without Thee
رنج‌هایی کشیده‌ام که مپرس
Sorrows, I have endured such that ask not.

همچو حافظ غریب در ره عشق
In the path of love, like Hafiz the stranger,
به مقامی رسیده‌ام که مپرس
At a stage (of trouble) I have arrived such that ask not.

غزل ۲۷۱ ⓄⒹⒺ ②⑦①

دارم از زلف سیاهش گله چندان که مپرس
Of His black tress (the world) complaint I have to such a degree that ask (not)
که چنان ز او شده‌ام بی سر و سامان که مپرس
For, on account of it, without means and resource, I am become in such a way that ask not

کس به امید وفا ترک دل و دین مکناد
In the hope of its fidelity, let none abandon heart and soul (the being a lover)
که چنانم من از این کرده پشیمان که مپرس
For, of this done, I am penitent to such a degree that ask not.

به یکی جرعه که آزار کسش در پی نیست
For (the sake of) one draught (of wine) wherein is the injury of none.
زحمتی می‌کشم از مردم نادان که مپرس
From the ignorant man, such torment suffer that ask not.

زاهد از ما به سلامت بگذر کاین می لعل
Zahid[1] from us in peace depart for this ruby wine
دل و دین می‌برد از دست بدان سان که مپرس
Taketh from the hand, heart and faith in that way that ask not

گفت‌وگوهاست در این راه که جان بگدازد
In this Path, the talk is that life melteth:
هر کسی عربده‌ای این که مبین آن که مپرس
Everyone the contention of this one is that look not of that one, that ask not

---

1-Pietist

پارسایی و سلامت هوسم بود ولی

Corner (of retirement) taking and safety were my desire.

شیوه‌ای می‌کند آن نرگس فتان که مپرس

That maddening narcissus practiseth a way that ask not

گفتم از گوی فلک صورت حالی پرسم

I said From the ball of the sky, I ask the present state

گفت آن می‌کشم اندر خم چوگان که مپرس

It said In the curve of the chaugan[1], that I endure that ask not

گفتمش زلف به خون که شکستی گفتا

To Him (the true Beloved) I said: By whose malice, dishevelledest Thou Thy tress He said

حافظ این قصه دراز است به قرآن که مپرس

Hafiz long is this tale by the Kuran[2] I conjure thee that ask not

❖◉❖◉❖

---

1 -Game device
2-Quran

ش
The Letter Shin

غزل ۲۷۲ 🔘🔘🔘 272

باز آی و دل تنگ مرا مونس جان باش

(O Murshid) Comeback; and of my straitened heart, the soul's sincere friend be:

وین سوخته را محرم اسرار نهان باش

Of this consumed one (with love) the reposer of hidden mysteries be

زان باده که در میکده عشق فروشند

Of that wine which in the wine-house (the stage) of love, they sell,

ما را دو سه ساغر بده و گو رمضان باش

Me, two or three cups give and say "Ramazan[1], it be."

در خرقه چو آتش زدی ای عارف سالک

O Arif[2], holy traveller when to the Khirka[3] (of hypocrisy) thou settest fire,

جهدی کن و سرحلقه رندان جهان باش

An effort, make and of the circle of profligates (outwardly bad, inwardly good) of the world, chief be.

دلدار که گفتا به توام دل نگران است

That (true) Beloved who said For thee, looker and expecter is My heart

گو می‌رسم اینک به سلامت نگران باش

Say In safety, be hold I arrive expecter be

خون شد دلم از حسرت آن لعل روان بخش

In envy of that ruby lip, life-giving (of the true Beloved) my heart became blood

ای درج محبت به همان مهر و نشان باش

With that very seal and mark, the casket of love the beloved's mouth be

تا بر دلش از غصه غباری ننشیند

So that on His the true Beloved's heart through grief, a particle of dust may not

ای سیل سرشک از عقب نامه روان باش

O torrent of tears following my letter, flowing be

حافظ که هوس می‌کندش جام جهان بین

Hafiz, who maketh his desire the cup, world-displaying (the perfect murshid)

گو در نظر آصف جمشید مکان باش

(To him) Say In sight of Asaf[4] of Jamshid, (his exalted) place be[5].

غزل ۲۷۳ 🔘🔘🔘 273

اگر رفیق شفیقی درست پیمان باش

If thou be the compassionate friend, true of covenant, be:

حریف خانه و گرمابه و گلستان باش

The companion of the closet (in grief) and of the hot bath and of the rose-garden (in ease) be

---

1-The ninth lunar months
2-Mystic
3-Cloak

4-Suleiman's minister
5-Is an allusion to the glory and authority of the ministry under Turanshah

شکنج زلف پریشان به دست باد مده
To the power of wine, the curl of thy dishevelled tress give not (so that its perfume may not agitate lovers)

مگو که خاطر عشاق گو پریشان باش
Speak not saying Say, lovers' hearts agitated be

گرت هواست که با خضر همنشین باشی
If thine be desire to be (in exaltation) fellow-sitter with Khizr[1],

نهان ز چشم سکندر چو آب حیوان باش
Hidden from Sikandar[2]'s eye, like the water of life, be.

زبور عشق نوازی نه کار هر مرغیست
Not the work of every bird is the power of love-playing

بیا و نوگل این بلبل غزل خوان باش
Come and of the bulbul[3], ghazal[4] singing (Hafiz) the new rose (beloved) be.

طریق خدمت و آیین بندگی کردن
The path of service, and the usage of attendance-making

خدای را که رها کن به ما و سلطان باش
For God's sake, let go to us and Sultan be.

دگر به صید حرم تیغ برمکش زنهار
On the prey (the lovers of God) of the sacred fold, again draw not forth the sword. Take care

و از آن که با دل ما کرده‌ای پشیمان باش
Of what thou hast done with our heart, penitent, be.

تو شمع انجمنی یک زبان و یک دل شو
(O true Beloved) The candle of the assembly Thou art one of tongue, one of heart, be

خیال و کوشش پروانه بین و خندان باش
The fancy of the moth's (in sparing not its own life) effort be hold and laughing (consuming like the candle) be

کمال دلبری و حسن در نظربازیست
In glance-playing, is the perfection of heart-ravishingness and beauty (of beloved ones)

به شیوه نظر از نادران دوران باش
Of (the crowd of) the rare ones of the age, in the art of viewing (and comprehending others) be

خموش حافظ و از جور یار ناله مکن
Hafiz silence and of the Beloved's violence, bewail not

تو را که گفت که در روی خوب حیران باش
Who spake to the e saying At the lovely face (of the Beloved) astonied be

غزل ۲۷۴ ⓄⒹⒺ ②⑦④

به دور لاله قدح گیر و بی‌ریا می‌باش
In the (spring) season of the tulip (the murshid) the cup take; and void of hypocrisy be

به بوی گل نفسی همدم صبا می‌باش
With the perfume of the red rose (of 'Irak) moment concordant with the breeze (the murshid) be.

1-Name of prophet
2-King of Macedonia in ancient Greece
3-Nightingale
4-Sonnet

نگویمت که همه ساله می پرستی کن
I say not to thee All the year practise wine worshipping

سه ماه می خور و نه ماه پارسا می‌باش
(Nay) Three (spring) months, wine drink and nine months, austere (and Abid in the world's occupations) be.

چو پیر سالک عشقت به می حواله کند
If the Pir[1], the holy traveller, charge thee with the wine of love

بنوش و منتظر رحمت خدا می‌باش
Drink; and expecter of God's mercy, be

گرت هواست که چون جم به سر غیب رسی
If thine be desire that, like Jamshid[2] (the perfect murshid) thou mayst attain to the mystery of the hidden,

بیا و همدم جام جهان نما می‌باش
Come and, the confidant of this cup, world –displaying (the perfect murshid) be

چو غنچه گر چه فروبستگیست کار جهان
Though like the (closed up) rose-bud, the world's work is a a closed up knot,

تو همچو باد بهاری گره گشا می‌باش
Like the spring-breeze, thou, the knot (bud) opener be.

وفا مجوی ز کس ور سخن نمی‌شنوی
From none, seek fidelity and if, my speech, thou hear not,

به هرزه طالب سیمرغ و کیمیا می‌باش
In foolishness, seeker of the simurg hand of alchemy be.

مرید طاعت بیگانگان مشو حافظ
Hafiz of devotion of strangers, the disciple be not

ولی معاشر رندان پارسا می‌باش
But, of pure profligates, the friend be

غزل ۲۷۵ ⓄⒹⒺ ②⑦⑤

صوفی گلی بچین و مرقع به خار بخش
Sufi[3] a beautiful rose pluck and to the thorn the patched religious garment, give

وین زهد خشک را به می خوشگوار بخش
For pleasant tasting wine, this thy dry austerity, give

طامات و شطح در ره آهنگ چنگ نه
In the path of the harp's melody, put aside idle talk and fraud

تسبیح و طیلسان به می و میگسار بخش
For wine and wine-drinking, the rosary and the dervish-mantle give.

زهد گران که شاهد و ساق نمی‌خرند
Excessive austerity that the lovely one and the Zahid[4] purchase not

در حلقه چمن به نسیم بهار بخش
In the sward's ring (time) to spring's fragrant breeze, give.

1-A Muslim saint or holy man, Pietist 3-A Muslim ascetic and mystic
2-king 4-Pietist

راهم شراب لعل زد ای میر عاشقان
O chief of lovers my path, ruby wine attacked

خون مرا به چاه زنخدان یار بخش
In the pit of the beloved's chin, my blood give.

یا رب به وقت گل گنه بنده عفو کن
O Lord! in the rose-season, pardon the slave's sin

وین ماجرا به سرو لب جویبار بخش
To the cypress of the bank of the stream, this tale gives.

ای آن که ره به مشرب مقصود برده‌ای
O thou that hast travelled to the drinking place of thy desire

زین بحر قطره‌ای به من خاکسار بخش
From this sea (of desire) me dusty, a drop give.

شکرانه را که چشم تو روی بتان ندید
In thanks that the form of idols thy eye be held not,

ما را به عفو و لطف خداوندگار بخش
To us, by the pardon and the favour of the Lord, (work) give.

ساقی چو شاه نوش کند باده صبوح
Saki[1] when the khwaja[2] drinketh the wine of the morning cup

گو جام زر به حافظ شب زنده دار بخش
Tell (him) To Hafiz, night alive keeping, the cup of gold.

غزل ۲۷۶ ⓄⒹⒺ ②⑦⑥

باغبان گر پنج روزی صحبت گل بایدش
The gardener (the holy traveller) if, for a space of five days, (a life – time) the society of the rose (the true Beloved) is necessary for him

بر جفای خار هجران صبر بلبل بایدش
Against the tyranny of the thorn of separation, the (patience) of the patient bulbul[3] is necessary for him.

ای دل اندربند زلفش از پریشانی منال
O heart! in the bond of His tress (the world) regarding perturbation, be wail not,

مرغ زیرک چون به دام افتد تحمل بایدش
When, into the bond, the wise bird falleth, fortitude is necessary for it.

رند عالم سوز را با مصلحت بینی چه کار
To the profligate, world-consuming (who hath abandoned the world's attachments) what business with counsel-considering

کار ملک است آن که تدبیر و تامل بایدش
The land's work is (such) that deliberation and reflection is necessary for it.

تکیه بر تقوا و دانش در طریقت کافریست
In Tarikat[4], reliance on piety and knowledge is in fidelity

راهرو گر صد هنر دارد توکل بایدش
If a hundred kinds of skill, the way-farer have, trust in God is necessary for him.

1-Tapster
3-Eunuch, dignitary, vizier, boss, host

3-Nightingale
4-Principle, Sufism, religious way

با چنین زلف و رخش بادا نظربازی حرام
With tress and face like this of His (the true Beloved) unlawful be glance-playing of (love)
هر که روی یاسمین و جعد سنبل بایدش
To that one, if the jasmine-face, and the hyacinth-curlis necessary for him.

نازها زان نرگس مستانه‌اش باید کشید
The (disdainful) airs of that intoxicated narcissus, it is necessary to endure
این دل شوریده تا آن جعد و کاکل بایدش
O distraught heart since that tress and fore-lock is necessary for it.

ساقیا در گردش ساغر تعلل تا به چند
O Saki[1] in the cup's circulation, delay how long
دور چون با عاشقان افتد تسلسل بایدش
When with lovers, the (cup's) circulation chanceth, successioni (continuity) is necessary for it.

کیست حافظ تا ننوشد باده بی آواز رود
Who is Hafiz since, without the harp's sound, he drinketh not the cup
عاشق مسکین چرا چندین تجمل بایدش
The wretched lover! patience like this, why is necessary for him.

غزل ۲۷۷ ⓄⒹⒺ ②⑦⑦

فکر بلبل همه آن است که گل شد یارش
The thought of the bulbul[2] (the holy traveller) all is that, that the rose (the true Beloved)
his beloved may be
گل در اندیشه که چون عشوه کند در کارش
The rose, in thought how, in her work, grace she may display.

دلربایی همه آن نیست که عاشق بکشند
Not all heart-ravishingness is that that slayeth the lover
خواجه آن است که باشد غم خدمتگارش
Khwaja[3] is he, whose attendant is grief.

جای آن است که خون موج زند در دل لعل
That is a place where into the ruby's heart the wave dasheth blood
زین تغابن که خزف می‌شکند بازارش
With this loss that it's (the ruby's) market-value, the sherd shattereth.

بلبل از فیض گل آموخت سخن ور نه نبود
From the bounty of the rose (the true Beloved) the bulbul (the holy traveller) learned speech and if
not, there had not been
این همه قول و غزل تعبیه در منقارش
In his beak, all this (sweet) speech and song.

ای که در کوچه معشوقه ما می‌گذری
O thou that passest in the street of our Beloved
بر حذر باش که سر می‌شکند دیوارش
Full of caution, befor the head, his wall shattereth

1-Tapster
2-Nightingale
3-Eunuch, dignitary, vizier, boss, host

آن سفرکرده که صد قافله دل همره اوست
That travelled one (the Beloved) whose fellow-traveller is a hundred Kafila[1]s of the heart,

هر کجا هست خدایا به سلامت دارش
O God wherever he be, him, in safety (from the peril of travel) keep.

صحبت عافیتت گر چه خوش افتاد ای دل
O heart although health's company happily falleth to thee

جانب عشق عزیز است فرومگذارش
Precious, is love's quarter it, abandon not.

صوفی سرخوش از این دست که کج کرد کلاه
Merry of head (in toxicated) the Sufi[2] placed his cap aslant

به دو جام دگر آشفته شود دستارش
With two cups (of wine) more, disordered maybe his turban

دل حافظ که به دیدار تو خوگر شده بود
The heart of Hafiz that had become accustomed to the sight of Thee

نازپرورد وصال است مجو آزارش
Is cherished with union. It's (the heart's) torment seek not.

غزل ۲۷۸   ⓄⒹⒺ ②⑦⑧

شراب تلخ می‌خواهم که مردافکن بود زورش
Bitter (strong) wine, whose power is man-over throwing, I desire

که تا یک دم بیاسایم ز دنیا و شر و شورش
Perchance, a moment, from the world and its iniquity and clam our, I'm ay rest.

سماط دهر دون پرور ندارد شهد آسایش
No time of ease, hath time's table cherishing the mean

مذاق حرص و آز ای دل بشو از تلخ و از شورش
O heart from its bitter and salted victuals, wash the palate of greed and of avarice.

بیاور می که نتوان شد ز مکر آسمان ایمن
(O heart) wine (of love) bring. For safe (without) it from the deceit of the sky (the traitor) one cannot go:

به لعب زهره چنگی و مریخ سلحشورش
(Deceit caused) by the sport of Venus, it sharper; and of Mars, its blood-thirsty one.

کمند صید بهرامی بیفکن جام جم بردار
The Bahram hunting[3] noose (lust's desires) let go the cup (of love) of Jamshid, uptake

که من پیمودم این صحرا نه بهرام است و نه گورش
For, this desert (the world) we have traversed. (Visible) Is neither Bahram[4] (sensual desire) Nor his wild ass.

بیا تا در می صافیت راز دهر بنمایم
Come so that, in pure wine, time's mystery, we may show

به شرط آن که ننمایی به کج طبعان دل کورش
On the condition that, to those crooked of disposition (and) blind of heart, thou show it not.

1-Convoy

2-A Muslim ascetic and mystic

3-The irony is from greed for power

4-He is the son of "Yazdgerd

نظر کردن به درویشان منافی بزرگی نیست

To glance at dervishes is not against greatness

سلیمان با چنان حشمت نظرها بود با مورش

With all his pomp, Sulaiman[1], his (mercy) glance was with the (feeble) ant

کمان ابروی جانان نمی‌پیچد سر از حافظ

From Hafiz, turneth not its head the bow of the eye-brow of the (true) Beloved

ولیکن خنده می‌آید بدین بازوی بی زورش

But, at this His arm full of force, (to Hafiz) laughter cometh.

غزل ۲۷۹ ⓄⒹⒺ ②⑦⑨

خوشا شیراز و وضع بی‌مثالش

O happy Shiraz, and its peerless site

خداوندا نگه دار از زوالش

O Lord! it from decline, preserve.

ز رکن آباد ما صد لوحش الله

For our Ruknabad[2], a hundred praises,

که عمر خضر می‌بخشد زلالش

Whose limpid water life to Khizr[3] gave.

میان جعفرآباد و مصلا

Between Ja'farabad[4] and Musalla[5]

عبیرآمیز می‌آید شمالش

Ambergri ode mixing, cometh its cool north wind.

به شیراز آی و فیض روح قدسی

To Shiraz, come; and the bounty of the holy spirit (Jibra.il ')

بجوی از مردم صاحب کمالش

For it, from the man endowed with perfection (Hafiz) ask

که نام قند مصری برد آن جا

Here (in Shiraz) who mentioneth Egyptian candy

که شیرینان ندادند انفعالش

For the sweet ones the (lovely ones, the beloved ones, the utterers of sweet words, of Shiraz) have not given (imputed to) it shame

صبا زان لولی شنگول سرمست

O breeze of that lovely, wholly intoxicated wanton,

چه داری آگهی چون است حالش

News, what hast thou Her state is what

گر آن شیرین پسر خونم بریزد

If that sweet one spill my blood,

دلا چون شیر مادر کن حلالش

O heart it, like mother's milk, lawful hold

1-Name of a prophet

2-An area in Shiraz

3-Name of a prophet

4-Villages near Shiraz

5-An area in Shiraz

مکن از خواب بیدارم خدا را
For God's sake, from this dream, awake me not,

که دارم خلوتی خوش با خیالش
For, in its image, a sweet pleasure I have.

چرا حافظ چو می‌ترسیدی از هجر
Hafiz when of separation, thou art affrighted, why

نکردی شکر ایام وصالش
Offeredest not thou thanks for the time of union with the beloved

غزل ۲۸۰ ⓄⒹⒺ ②⑧⓪

چو برشکست صبا زلف عنبرافشانش
When His (the true Beloved's) tress, ambergri ode diffusing, the breeze (fate and destiny) dishevelled,

به هر شکسته که پیوست تازه شد جانش
Every shattere done, with whom it (the breeze) joined, his life fresh became

کجاست همنفسی تا به شرح عرضه دهم
A fellow-breather is where so that (to him) explanation of, (my grief) I may give

که دل چه می‌کشد از روزگار هجرانش
From the time of separation from Him, what (torments) my heart endureth.

زمانه از ورق گل مثال روی تو بست
Of the leaves of the rose (the limbs of man) time made a token of Thy face O true Beloved

ولی ز شرم تو در غنچه کرد پنهانش
But (on looking – well) through shame of Thee, concealed it (man) in the rose-bud (the closed tomb)

تو خفته‌ای و نشد عشق را کرانه پدید
Thou asleep and no of love limit appeared

تبارک الله از این ره که نیست پایانش
Thanks be to God for this Path (of love) that hath no end

جمال کعبه مگر عذر ره روان خواهد
Perchance, the beauty of the Ka'ba (the true Beloved) desireth excuse (for want of union) of the way-farer (to the Ka'ba)

که جان زنده دلان سوخت در بیابانش
For, in its desert, consumed the soul of those alive of heart (lovers of God)

بدین شکسته بیت الحزن که می‌آرد
To this shattered house of sorrow (the lover's body) who bringeth.

نشان یوسف دل از چه زنخدانش
From the pit of the (true Beloved's) chin trace of the Yusuf of the heart

بگیرم آن سر زلف و به دست خواجه دهم
That tress tip (the world of evidence, or this world) I take and it to the khwaja's hand, I give,

که سوخت حافظ بی‌دل ز مکر و دستانش
That, perchance, my justice from its hand he may take. and, holding me excused, may not drive me away.

غزل ۲۸۱ ⓄⒹⒺ ②⑧①

یا رب این نوگل خندان که سپردی به منش

O Lord! that fresh laughing rose whom to me, Thou entrustedest,

می‌سپارم به تو از چشم حسود چمنش

To Thee, on account of the envious ones of the sward, I entrust.

گر چه از کوی وفا گشت به صد مرحله دور

Although, far to a hundred stages, from the stage of fidelity he hath wandered

دور باد آفت دور فلک از جان و تنش

From his soul and body, far be the calamity of the moon's revolution.

گر به سرمنزل سلمی رسی ای باد صبا

O morning breeze if to the head of the dwelling of Salma[1] thou readiest,

چشم دارم که سلامی برسانی ز منش

A salutation to her from me, i have hope that thou wilt convey.

به ادب نافه گشایی کن از آن زلف سیاه

From that black tress, courteously scatter musk

جای دل‌های عزیز است به هم برمزنش

(For the tress) is the ab ode of clear hearts together heap it not (or our heart will be ruined)

گو دلم حق وفا با خط و خالت دارد

Say To thy down and mole, my heart hath the right of fidelity.

محترم دار در آن طره عنبرشکنش

In that tress, ambergris of coil, it (my heart) sacred keep

در مقامی که به یاد لب او می نوشند

In the stage where, to his lip, they drink wine,

سفله آن مست که باشد خبر از خویشتنش

Mean that intoxicated (unconscious) one to whom is consciousness of himself.

عرض و مال از در میخانه نشاید اندوخت

From the door of the wine-house, not proper is it to gather good sand chattels,

هر که این آب خورد رخت به دریا فکنش

Into the sea, cast the chattels of him who, this water, drinketh

هر که ترسد ز ملال انده عشقش نه حلال

Not true is the love of him, who (in love) feareth distress

سر ما و قدمش یا لب ما و دهنش

(Together, be) our head and his foot or our lip and his mouth

شعر حافظ همه بیت الغزل معرفت است

Hafiz's verse, the couplet of the ghazal[2], all is divine knowledge

آفرین بر نفس دلکش و لطف سخنش

On his heart-alluring soul and grace of verse, Afarin[3]

1-Lover
2-Sonnet, ode

3-Well done

غزل ۲۸۲ ⓞⓓⓔ ②⑧②

بربد از من قرار و طاقت و هوش
From me, tranquillity, power, and sense took,

بت سنگین دل سیمین بناگوش
The idol of stony heart, of silvern lobe of ear

نگاری چابکی شنگی کلهدار
A picture, a beauty, an amorously playful one, Pan-like

ظریفی مه وشی ترکی قباپوش
A subtle one, a moon-like one, a bold one, kaba[1]-wearer (gaily arrayed)

ز تاب آتش سودای عشقش
From the torment of the fire of love's phrenzy for her

به سان دیگ دایم می‌زنم جوش
Ever, tumult, I express like the (seething) caldron.

چو پیراهن شوم آسوده خاطر
Tranquil of heart, like the (close – fitting) garment I should be

گرش همچون قبا گیرم در آغوش
If, her into my embrace, like the kaba, I take.

اگر پوسیده گردد استخوانم
If rotten become my bone (skeleton)

نگردد مهرت از جانم فراموش
Forgotten becometh not, from my soul, the love for her.

دل و دینم دل و دینم ببردهست
My heart and faith my heart and faith have ravished

بر و دوشش بر و دوشش بر و دوش
Her breast and shoulder, her breast and shoulder, her breast and shoulder

دوای تو دوای توست حافظ
Hafiz Thy remedy, thy remedy is

لب نوشش لب نوشش لب نوش
Her sweet lip, her sweet lip, her sweet lip

غزل ۲۸۳ ⓞⓓⓔ ②⑧③

سحر ز هاتف غیبم رسید مژده به گوش
At morn, from the invisible messenger, to my ear reached the glad tidings

که دور شاه شجاع است می دلیر بنوش
Tis the age of Shah[2] Shuja ' (the soul) wine love's (tumult boldly) drink

شد آن که اهل نظر بر کناره می‌رفتند
Gone hath that time when people of vision went aside (fearing all)

هزار گونه سخن در دهان و لب خاموش
In the mouth, a thousand forms of speech and (from fear of the enemy) silent the lip

---

1-Long garment   2-King

به صوت چنگ بگوییم آن حکایت‌ها
To the twang of the harp, those tales (that we have kept concealed) shall we utter

که از نهفتن آن دیگ سینه می‌زد جوش
For, from the concealing of them, seetheth the caldron of the heart.

شراب خانگی ترس محتسب خورده
In fear of the muhtasib[1], the house (secret) wine having drunk

به روی یار بنوشیم و بانگ نوشانوش
(Now, in Shah Shuja's time) To the beloved's face, let us drink and (express) the shout Drink, drink again

ز کوی میکده دوشش به دوش می‌بردند
Last night, from the street of the wine-house, on their back, they carried him,

امام شهر که سجاده می‌کشید به دوش
There vered Imam, who, on his back, the prayer-mat bore.

دلا دلالت خیرت کنم به راه نجات
O heart on the path of salvation, thee, good guidance, I make

مکن به فسق مباهات و زهد هم مفروش
In iniquity, glory not of austerity boast not.

محل نور تجلیست رای انور شاه
The king's luminous opinion is the place of the light of splendour

چو قرب او طلبی در صفای نیت کوش
When propinquity to him, thou desirest, in purity of intention strive

بجز ثنای جلالش مساز ورد ضمیر
Save the praise of his grandeur, aught make not the exercise of the mind

که هست گوش دلش محرم پیام سروش
For the confidant of Surush[2] (Jibra.il) is the ear of his heart.

رموز مصلحت ملک خسروان دانند
Mysteries of the counsel of the empire, kings know

گدای گوشه نشینی تو حافظا مخروش
Hafiz a beggar, a corner-sitter, thou clam our not.

غزل ۲۸۴ ⓄⒹⒺ ②⑧④

هاتفی از گوشه میخانه دوش
Last night from the corner of the wine-house, an invisible messenger

گفت ببخشند گنه می بنوش
Spake Sin, they pardon wine, drink

لطف الهی بکند کار خویش
Its own work, doeth divine pardon

مژده رحمت برساند سروش
The glad tidings of mercy, Surush causeth to arrive.

این خرد خام به میخانه بر
To the wine-house, take this crude wisdom

تا می لعل آوردش خون به جوش
So that to tumult, the ruby wine its blood may bring.

1-Sheriff   2-The unseen angel

گر چه وصالش نه به کوشش دهند
Although, not by effort union with Him, they give
هر قدر ای دل که توانی بکوش
O heart that much that thou canst, strive

لطف خدا بیشتر از جرم ماست
Greater than our sin, is God's grace
نکته سربسته چه دانی خموش
('Tis) a subtlety head closed. What sayest thou Silence

گوش من و حلقه گیسوی یار
(Together are) my ear and the curl of the true Beloved's tress
روی من و خاک در می فروش
(Together are) my face, and the dust of the door of the wine-seller

رندی حافظ نه گناهیست صعب
The profligacy of Hafiz is not a hard perverse sin
با کرم پادشه عیب پوش
In the estimation of mercy of the King, defect-concealing (God)

داور دین شاه شجاع آن که کرد
The Ruler of faith, Shah[1] Shuja',
روح قدس حلقه امرش به گوش
He who, slave to his order, made the holy spirit (Jibra.il)

ای ملک العرش مرادش بده
His desire, give, O angel of the ninth heaven (God's throne)
و از خطر چشم بدش دار گوش
Him, from the evil eye, keep.

غزل ۲۸۵ ⓄⒹⒺ ②⑧⑤

در عهد پادشاه خطابخش جرم پوش
In the age of the king, fault-for giving, crime-covering,
حافظ قرابه کش شد و مفتی پیاله نوش
Flagon-drinker, became Hafiz and cup-drinker, the mufti[2].

صوفی ز کنج صومعه با پای خم نشست
Forth from the cloister-corner, the Sufi[3] sate (drinking) at the wine-jar's foot
تا دید محتسب که سبو می‌کشد به دوش
Since he be held the muhtasib[4] a wine-pitcher on his shoulder bear.

احوال شیخ و قاضی و شرب الیهودشان
The state of the shaikh[5], and of the kazi and of their jew secret drinking,
کردم سال صبحدم از پیر می فروش
I asked, in the morning, of the Pir, the wine-seller.

1-king
2-Lawyer
3-A Muslim ascetic and mystic

4-Sheriff
5-A Muslim ascetic and mystic

گفتا نه گفتنیست سخن گر چه محرمی

He said: "Unfit to be uttered is the matter though thou art a confidant"

درکش زبان و پرده نگه دار و می بنوش

(From slander) thy tongue in draw the screen (of high and of low) preserve and wine (of love) drink

ساقی بهار می‌رسد و وجه می‌نماند

Saki[1] spring arriveth and means of wine (drinking) is none

فکری بکن که خون دل آمد ز غم به جوش

(On getting means) a thought make. For, from grief (of want of means of wine – drinking) into tumult hath come my heart's blood.

عشق است و مفلسی و جوانی و نوبهار

Love and poverty, and youth, and the new spring, (all this) is

عذرم پذیر و جرم به ذیل کرم بپوش

My excuse. It, accept and, in mercy's trail, the crime conceal.

تا چند همچو شمع زبان آوری کنی

Like the (burning) candle, tongue extending (in clamour) how long makest thou

پروانه مراد رسید ای محب خموش

O friend the moth of thy desire hath arrived. Silence

ای پادشاه صورت و معنی که مثل تو

O King, in form and in truth like thee,

نادیده هیچ دیده و نشنیده هیچ گوش

No eye hath seen no ear hath heard

چندان بمان که خرقه ازرق کند قبول

Remain, until the Khirka[2] of hypocrisy, accepteth

بخت جوانت از فلک پیر ژنده پوش

Thy youthful fortune from the old, tattered garment-wearing sky

غزل ۲۸۶ ⓄⒹⒺ ②⑧⑥

دوش با من گفت پنهان کاردانی تیزهوش

Last night, tome, a mystery-knower, keen of sense, secretly spake,

و از شما پنهان نشاید کرد سر می فروش

Saying Concealed from thee, one cannot hold the mystery of the wine-seller

گفت آسان گیر بر خود کارها کز روی طبع

He said To thy self, action easy take. For, from nature's way

سخت می‌گردد جهان بر مردمان سختکوش

On men hard striving, hard the world seizeth.

وان گهم درداد جامی کز فروغش بر فلک

Then, me, he gave a cup, from whose splendour on the heavens

زهره در رقص آمد و بربط زنان می‌گفت نوش

To dancing came Zuhra[3] and the lute-striker (player) kept saying Drink

---

1-Tapster
2-Cloak

3-Refers to the planet Venus, the symbol of the beloved

با دل خونین لب خندان بیاور همچو جام

With the bloody (wounded) heart, bring forth (display) the laughing lip like the cup (laughing with wine's sparkle)

نی گرت زخمی رسد آیی چو چنگ اندر خروش

If, thee, a (cleaving) wound reach, like the (shrieking) reed, into clamour (of grief) come thou not.

تا نگردی آشنا زین پرده رمزی نشنوی

So long as, with this screen (of mystery thou) becomest not acquainted, a hint thou hearest not

گوش نامحرم نباشد جای پیغام سروش

Not the place for Jibrail'[1]s message, is the ear of the unprivileged

گوش کن پند ای پسر و از بهر دنیا غم مخور

O son counsel, hear, grief for the world's sake, suffer not

گفتمت چون در حدیثی گر توانی داشت هوش

To thee, a tale, I utter (lustrous) as a pearl if thou canst, hear.

در حریم عشق نتوان زد دم از گفت و شنید

In love's fold, of talking and of hearing one cannot boast

زان که آن جا جمله اعضا چشم باید بود و گوش

For, there, eye and ear, must be all thy limbs.

بر بساط نکته دانان خودفروشی شرط نیست

On the carpet (stage) of subtlety-knowers, is the condition, no self-selling (boasting)

یا سخن دانسته گو ای مرد عاقل یا خموش

O man of wisdom either words known (understood and weighed) utter or silent be

ساقیا می ده که رندی‌های حافظ فهم کرد

O Saki[2] wine, give. For Hafiz's profligacies, understood

آصف صاحب قران جرم بخش عیب پوش

Asaf[3], the Lord of conjunction, fault-for giving, defect-concealing.

غزل ۲۸۷ ⓄⒹⒺ ②⑧⑦

ای همه شکل تو مطبوع و همه جای تو خوش

(O true Beloved) the form, all of Thine is beautiful and the place all of Thine, happy

دلم از عشوه شیرین شکرخای تو خوش

My heart from the grace of the ruby lip sugar-eating of Thine, happy

همچو گلبرگ طری هست وجود تو لطیف

Gracious is Thy existence like a fresh rose-leaf

همچو سرو چمن خلد سراپای تو خوش

Like the cypress of paradise, head to foot of Thine, happy.

شیوه و ناز تو شیرین خط و خال تو ملیح

Sweet, the way of Thy grace beautiful Thy line (of down) and mole

چشم و ابروی تو زیبا قد و بالای تو خوش

The eye and the eye-brow of Thine, adorned the stature and form of Thine, happy.

1-The name of angel   3-Suleiman's minister
2-Tapster

هم گلستان خیالم ز تو پرنقش و نگار

Both, my fancy the rose-garden full of decoration and adornment of Thine

هم مشام دلم از زلف سمن سای تو خوش

Also, my heart, by the lily-exhaling tress of Thine, happy.

در ره عشق که از سیل بلا نیست گذار

In love's path, where, from calamity's torrent is no passing,

کردهام خاطر خود را به تمنای تو خوش

My own heart, I make by the sight of (the form of) Thine happy

شکر چشم تو چه گویم که بدان بیماری

(O true Beloved before) Thy eye, (I die) For, in that sickness

می کند درد مرا از رخ زیبای تو خوش

Pain maketh me, through the adorned cheek of Thine, happy

در بیابان طلب گر چه ز هر سو خطریست

In the desert of search, although from every side is danger,

می رود حافظ بی دل به تولای تو خوش

Hafiz, heart-bereft, goeth in love of Thine happy

غزل ۲۸۸ ⓄⒹⒺ ②⑧⑧

کنار آب و پای بید و طبع شعر و یاری خوش

The water-bank, and the willow-root and the poetic nature and a friend, happy

معاشر دلبری شیرین و ساقی گلعذاری خوش

A companion, the sweet heart-ravisher, and the Saki, rose of cheek, happy

الا ای دولتی طالع که قدر وقت می دانی

Ho! O fortune of destiny that knoweth (not) the worth of time,

گوارا بادت این عشرت که داری روزگاری خوش

To thee, be this pleasure pleasant for a time, thou hast happy.

هر آن کس را که در خاطر ز عشق دلبری باریست

To whose heart is friendship through the love of a heart-ravisher,

سپندی گو بر آتش نه که دارد کار و باری خوش

Say On the fire, put rue (to dispel the evil eye) for a business, thou hast happy.

عروس طبع را ز زیور ز فکر بکر می بندم

For the bride of nature, with generosity, I bind thought's jewel

بود کز دست ایامم به دست افتد نگاری خوش

It may be, from time's picture, on my hand may fall an idol happy.

شب صحبت غنیمت دان و داد خوشدلی بستان

Plunder, reckon the night of (the Beloved's) the society and do justice to happy-heartedness,

که مهتابی دل افروز است و طرف لاله زاری خوش

For, heart-kindling, is the moon-beam and stream-bank happy.

می ای در کاسه چشم است ساق را بنامیزد

In God's name in the cup of the Saki's eye, is wine

که مستی می کند با عقل و می بخشد خماری خوش

That giveth in toxication with reason and bringeth about a wine-sickness, happy

به غفلت عمر شد حافظ بیا با ما به میخانه

Hafiz in carelessness, went thy life with us, to the wine-house (the stage of love and of divine knowledge) come

که شنگولان خوش باشت بیاموزند کاری خوش

So that the intoxicated lovely ones (perfect Arifs, and the excellent murshid) will teach thee, a work, happy

⊙DⒺ ②⑧⑨ غزل ۲۸۹

مجمع خوبی و لطف است عذار چو مهش

The collection of beauteousness and of gracefulness is his cheek (resplendent) like the moon.

لیکنش مهر و وفا نیست خدایا بدهش

But, love is not his, nor constancy o God (love and constancy) give him.

دلبرم شاهد و طفل است و به بازی روزی

My heart-ravisher is the beloved and is a child in sport, one day

بکشد زارم و در شرع نباشد گنهش

He will cruelly slay me and, in the sharia, no sin is his.

من همان به که از او نیک نگه دارم دل

Verily, best that from him, I guard well my heart

که بد و نیک ندیده‌ست و ندارد نگهش

For, bad and good, he hath not seen and, of them, no knowledge hath (what he wisheth, he doeth)

بوی شیر از لب همچون شکرش می‌آید

From his lip like sugar, cometh a perfume of milk (betokening early childhood)

گر چه خون می‌چکد از شیوه چشم سیهش

Though from the glance of his black eye trickleth blood (betokening, the slayer)

چارده ساله بتی چابک شیرین دارم

Active (and) sweet, fourteen years of age, an idol, I have

که به جان حلقه به گوش است مه چاردهش

Whose slave with soul is the (resplendent full) moon of fourteen days.

از پی آن گل نورسته دل ما یا رب

O Lord! in pursuit of that rose, newly sprung, our heart

خود کجا شد که ندیدیم در این چند گهش

Went where for, in this (place) sometime, it, we havenot seen.

یار دلدار من ار قلب بدین سان شکند

If my beloved, the heart-possessor, in this way shattereth my heart (army)

ببرد زود به جانداری خود پادشهش

Quickly, for his own life-guarding, him, the king will take.

جان به شکرانه کنم صرف گر آن دانه در

Thankfully, I sacrifice my life if that peerless pearl,

صدف سینه حافظ بود آرامگهش

Its place of rest become the shell (the socket) of the eye of Hafiz

غزل ۲۹۰ ⓄⒹⒺ ②⑨Ⓞ

دلم رمیده شد و غافلم من درویش
Affrighted, became my heart; and careless, I, the dervish, am
که آن شکاری سرگشته را چه آمد پیش
As to what hath happened, to that (great) bewildered prey (my heart)

چو بید بر سر ایمان خویش میلرزم
For the head of my own faith, I trembled like the willow
که دل به دست کمان ابروییست کافرکیش
For, in the hand of one of bow eye-brow, Kafir in religion, is my heart.

خیال حوصله بحر میپزد هیهات
(From much weeping) The fancy of the spirit of the (mighty) sea, I (a mere drop) mature. Alas
چههاست در سر این قطره محال اندیش
In the head of this drop, absurd of thought (Hsfiz) are what (crude fancies)

بنازم آن مژه شوخ عافیت کش را
Of that eye-lash, bold, rest-slayer, I boast
که موج میزندش آب نوش بر سر نیش
On the tip of whose point, the wave of the sweet water (of life) dasheth.

ز آستین طبیبان هزار خون بچکد
From the sleeve of a thousand physicians, trickleth blood
گرم به تجربه دستی نهند بر دل ریش
If, for examination, a hand on my wounded heart (drowned in blood, head to foot) they place,

به کوی میکده گریان و سرفکنده روم
In the street of the wine-house (the murshid's threshold) weeping and head cast down, I go
چراکه شرم همیآیدم ز حاصل خویش
Because, of (myempty, vain) produce, ever cometh shame to me

نه عمر خضر بماند نه ملک اسکندر
Remaineth neither the (prolonged) age of Khjzr[1], nor the (great) dominion of Sikandar
نزاع بر سر دنیی دون مکن درویش
Dervish upon the head of the mean world, strife make not

بدان کمر نرسد دست هر گدا حافظ
Hafiz I to that girdle (of the true Beloved) reacheth not every beggar's hand
خزانهای به کف آور ز گنج قارون بیش
The treasury greater than Karun's [2] treasure, to hand bring.

غزل ۲۹۱ ⓄⒹⒺ ②⑨①

ما آزمودهایم در این شهر بخت خویش
In this city, my fortune, I have tried
بیرون کشید باید از این ورطه رخت خویش
From this whirl pool, my chattels't is necessary to draw.

از بس که دست می‌گزم و آه می‌کشم

Since (many a time) I gnaw the hand (of regret) and heave the sigh (from my chest)

آتش زدم چو گل به تن لخت لخت خویش

To my body, piecemeal torn, like the rose leaf shedding (leaf shedding) I set fire.

دوشم ز بلبلی چه خوش آمد که می‌سرود

Last night from a bulbul[1] that sang, how sweetly it came (to me in a place where)

گل گوش پهن کرده ز شاخ درخت خویش

From the branch of its (rose) tree, the rose made wide its ear,

کای دل تو شاد باش که آن یار تندخو

Saying O heart joyful be thou. For that beloved, ill of nature

بسیار تندروی نشیند ز بخت خویش

Long sitteth refractorily on account of his ill fortune.

خواهی که سخت و سست جهان بر تو بگذرد

The world, cruel (in words) and slow (in covenant – keeping) to pass by thee thou wishest

بگذر ز عهد سست و سخن‌های سخت خویش

Thy own slow covenant and cruel words abandon.

وقت است کز فراق تو و ز سوز اندرون

If, upon the lofty sky, vicissitudes Shaitan's temptations wave-mounting, strike their head,

آتش درافکنم به همه رخت و پخت خویش

Yet His chattels and fortune, wet, soiled with Shaitan's snare the Arif[2] maketh not.

ای حافظ ار مراد میسر شدی مدام

O Hafiz! if union had been attainable, ever,

جمشید نیز دور نماندی ز تخت خویش

Far (severed) from bis throne, Jamshid[3] would not have remained.

❖◉❖◉❖

1-Nightingale
2-Mystic

3-King

ع
The Letter Àin

غزل ۲۹۲ ⓞⓓⓔ ②⑨②

قسم به حشمت و جاه و جلال شاه شجاع
By the pomp of glory and of dignity of Shah Shuja'[1] I swear

که نیست با کسم از بهر مال و جاه نزاع
That, for the sake of wealth and of rank, strife is mine with none.

شراب خانگیم بس می مغانه بیار
My house (secret) wine, enough; the Magian wine, bring not

حریف باده رسید ای رفیق توبه وداع
O companion! Arrived hath the companion of the cup: to repentance (of wine) farewell!

خدای را به می‌ام شست و شوی خرقه کنید
For god's sake; with wine, cleansing and cleansing of the Khirka[2], make ye:

که من نمی‌شنوم بوی خیر از این اوضاع
For, from this way, (of khirka-wearing), the perfume of good, I perceive not.

ببین که رقص کنان می‌رود به ناله چنگ
To the harp's twang, behold how dancing goeth,

کسی که رخصه نفرمودی استماع سماع
That one, who for the hearing of sama'[3], permission gave not.

به عاشقان نظری کن به شکر این نعمت
On lovers, cast a glance in thanks for this favour,

که من غلام مطیعم تو پادشاه مطاع
That of thee, the obeyed king, an obedient slave I am.

به فیض جرعه جام تو تشنه‌ایم ولی
Thirsty for the bounty of the draught of the cup, we are But,

نمی‌کنیم دلیری نمی‌دهیم صداع
Boldness, we display not; (of ourselves we take not the cup) thee (through our vexing) pain of head, we give not.

جبین و چهره حافظ خدا جدا مکناد
O God! Separate make not the brow and the face of Hafiz

ز خاک بارگه کبریای شاه شجاع
From the dust of the court of grandeur of Shah Shuja'[4].

غزل ۲۹۳ ⓞⓓⓔ ②⑨③

بامدادان که ز خلوتگه کاخ ابداع
In the dawn, when, from the private chamber of the palace of wonders,

شمع خاور فکند بر همه اطراف شعاع
On all sides, the candle of the east (the sun) casteth splend our-rays

---

1-King   3-Dance
2-Cloak   4-King

برکشد آینه از جیب افق چرخ و در آن
(When) From the pocket of the horizon, the juggler (or the dancer) draweth forth the mirror

بنماید رخ گیتی به هزاران انواع
(And) In a thousand ways, displayeth the world's face

در زوایای طربخانه جمشید فلک
In the recesses of the joy-house of the Jamshid [1] of the sky

ارغنون ساز کند زهره به آهنگ سماع
The organ, to the melody of sama'[2], Zuhra[3] tuneth.

چنگ در غلغله آید که کجا شد منکر
Into twang, cometh the harp, saying: The denier (of love) is where

جام در قهقهه آید که کجا شد مناع
Into juggling (laughing) cometh the cup, saying The forbidder (of wine) is where

وضع دوران بنگر ساغر عشرت برگیر
The way of revolution (of the sphere) of the sphere be hold pleasure's goblet, take (with God's lot, be content)

که به هر حالتی این است بهین اوضاع
For, in every state, the best of ways is this.

طره شاهد دنیی همه بند است و فریب
All snare and deceit, is the tress of the mistress of the world

عارفان بر سر این رشته نجویند نزاع
As to the end of this thread, no strife (of opinion) do Arifs[4] seek.

عمر خسرو طلب ار نفع جهان می‌خواهی
The king's (long) life, seek, if the world's profit thou seek

که وجودیست عطابخش کریم نفاع
For, it is an existence, gift-giver (and) a generous one favour-conferring.

مظهر لطف ازل روشنی چشم امل
The place of evidence of the grace of eternity, the luminosity of hope's eye

جامع علم و عمل جان جهان شاه شجاع
The summation of science (and) action, and the world's soul, (are) Shah Shuja[5].

غزل ۲۹۴ ⓄⒹⒺ ②⑨④

در وفای عشق تو مشهور خوبانم چو شمع
In constancy of love for Thee, renowned of the lovely ones I am like the candle

شب نشین کوی سربازان و رندانم چو شمع
Night-sitter in the street of head (life)-player sand of profligates, I am like the candle.

روز و شب خوابم نمی‌آید به چشم غم پرست
Day and night, to my eye, grief-worshipping, sleep cometh not

بس که در بیماری هجر تو گریانم چو شمع
Since, in sickness of separation from Thee, weeping, I am like the candle

---

1-King
2-Dance

3 -Refers to the planet Venus, the symbol of the beloved
4-Mystic
5-King

رشته صبرم به مقراض غمت ببریده شد

With the shears of grief for Thee, severed became the thread of my patience

همچنان در آتش مهر تو سوزانم چو شمع

So, in fire's separation from Thee, laughing (consuming) I am like the candle.

گر کمیت اشک گلگونم نبودی گرم رو

If hot moving (impetuous) had not been the steed of my rose-hued (bloody) tear,

کی شدی روشن به گیتی راز پنهانم چو شمع

In the world, when would my hidden mystery (love for Thee) have become luminous like the candle.

در میان آب و آتش همچنان سرگرم توست

In the midst of water and of fire, even so ardent of desire for Thee is

این دل زار نزار اشک بارانم چو شمع

This my heart, poor, feeble, tear-raining (guttering) like the candle.

در شب هجران مرا پروانه وصلی فرست

In separation's night, me a letter of union, send

ور نه از دردت جهانی را بسوزانم چو شمع

If not, in grief for Thee, a great world I will cause to consume-like the candle.

بی جمال عالم آرای تو روزم چون شب است

Night is my day without Thy beauty world-adorning

با کمال عشق تو در عین نقصانم چو شمع

With the perfection of love for Thee, in the very essence of loss, (consuming) I am, like the candle.

کوه صبرم نرم شد چون موم در دست غمت

From the power of grief for Thee, soft like wax became the mountain of my patience

تا در آب و آتش عشقت گدازانم چو شمع

Since, in the water and the fire of love for Thee, melting I am like the candle

همچو صبحم یک نفس باقیست با دیدار تو

Like the morning, without a sight of Thee, is left (only) a breath of life

چهره بنما دلبرا تا جان برافشانم چو شمع

O heart-ravisher Thy face, display so that, on Thee, my life I may scatter (in love's consuming) like the candle

سرفرازم کن شبی از وصل خود ای نازنین

O neck-extender (in grandeur) head-exalting make me, one night, by union with Thee

تا منور گردد از دیدارت ایوانم چو شمع

That, by the sight of Thee, luminous may become my hall like the candle

آتش مهر تو را حافظ عجب در سر گرفت

Wonderful in his head, Hafiz caught love's fire for Thee

آتش دل کی به آب دیده بنشانم چو شمع

With the water (tear) of the eye, how may quench the heart's fire like the candle.

❀◉❀◉❀

غ
The Letter Ghàin

﷼ غزل ۲۹۵ ﷼ ⓄⒹⒺ ②⑨⑤

سحر به بوی گلستان دمی شدم در باغ
In the morning for the perfume of the rose, I kept going into the rose-garden;

که تا چو بلبل بیدل کنم علاج دماغ
So that, like the bulbul heart-bereft, remedy for my brain, I might make.

به جلوه گل سوری نگاه میکردم
At the face of a rose, red of hue, I gazed,

که بود در شب تیره به روشنی چو چراغ
That, in the night of darkness, shone with a luminosity like the lamp:

چنان به حسن و جوانی خویشتن مغرور
Of her beauty and youth, so proud,

که داشت از دل بلبل هزار گونه فراغ
That, from the heart of the bulbul of a thousand notes, repose she kept

گشاده نرگس رعنا ز حسرت آب از چشم
In envy, the beautiful narcissus let loose water (night – dew) from her eye

نهاده لاله ز سودا به جان و دل صد داغ
In passion, the tulip planted a hundred streaks (stains) in her soul and heart

زبان کشیده چو تیغی به سرزنش سوسن
In reproof, the lily extended her tongue like a sword

دهان گشاده شقایق چو مردم ایغاغ
Like the man of two women, the anemone opened her mouth.

یکی چو باده پرستان صراحی اندر دست
Sometimes, like the wine-worshipper, in the hand, a goblet:

یکی چو ساق مستان به کف گرفته ایاغ
Sometimes, like the Saki of the intoxicated, taken in the hand, a glass.

نشاط و عیش و جوانی چو گل غنیمت دان
The joy of youthful pleasure, plunder like the rose, reckon

که حافظا نبود بر رسول غیر بلاغ
For, O Hafiz! to the envoy is naught save what is brought (the message)

⟨◉⟩⟨◉⟩

ف
The Letter Fā

غزل ۲۹۶ ⓄⒹⒺ ②⑨⑥

طالع اگر مدد دهد دامنش آورم به کف
If fortune give aid, to my hand I will bring His skirt

گر بکشم زهی طرب ور بکشد زهی شرف
If (the skirt) I draw O great the joy If, me, Heslay great the honour

طرف کرم ز کس نبست این دل پرامید من
How more derived this heart full of hope the advantage of mercy

گر چه سخن همی‌برد قصه من به هر طرف
Though to every quarter, the talk of the day kept taking my tale.

از خم ابروی توام هیچ گشایشی نشد
Mine became no opening from the curve of Thy eye-bro

وه که در این خیال کج عمر عزیز شد تلف
Alas in this crooked fancy, became the destruction of dear life.

ابروی دوست کی شود دست کش خیال من
Leader of me, miserable, when becometh the Friend's eye-brow

کس نزده‌ست از این کمان تیر مراد بر هدف
From this bow, none hath struck the arrow of desire on the target.

چند به ناز پرورم مهر بتان سنگ دل
A while, the love of idols, stone of heart, I cherish

یاد پدر نمی‌کنند این پسران ناخلف
No recollection of the father make these unfavoured sons.

من به خیال زاهدی گوشه نشین و طرفه آنک
In the fancy of being a Zahid[1], corner-sitting I (became) and strange (it is) that,

مغبچه‌ای ز هر طرف می‌زندم به چنگ و دف
From every side, me, with the sound of the harp and the drum, the young Magian proclaimeth.

بی خبرند زاهدان نقش بخوان و لا تقل
Void of knowledge are the Zahids the charm, utter and speak not

مست ریاست محتسب باده بده و لا تخف
Intoxicated is the muhtasib[2]; the cup, drink; and fear not.

صوفی شهر بین که چون لقمه شبهه می‌خورد
Be hold the city-Sufi[3], how a doubtful morsel, he eateth

پاردمش دراز باد آن حیوان خوش علف
Long be his crupper, this animal of good fodder

حافظ اگر قدم زنی در ره خاندان به صدق
Hafiz if, in the path of love's household, thou plant thy foot

بدرقه رهت شود همت شحنه نجف
The guide of thy path shall be the blessing of the watch man of Najaf[4] (Ali)

⟐◉⟐◉⟐

1-Pietist
2-Sheriff

3-Muslim ascetic and mystic
4-Name of a city in Iraq

ق
The Letter Ghāf

غزل ۲۹۷ ⓄⒹⒺ ②⑨⑦

زبان خامه ندارد سر بیان فراق
The reed's tongue hath no desire for the explanation of separation

وگرنه شرح دهم با تو داستان فراق
If not, to thee, I give the explanation of the tale of separation.

دریغ مدت عمرم که بر امید وصال
Alas life's span, in hope of union,

به سر رسید و نیامد به سر زمان فراق
Hath reached to an end and to an end, hath not comethe time of separation

سری که بر سر گردون به فخر می‌سودم
That head that, in glory, one rubbed on the head of the sphere,

به راستان که نهادم بر آستان فراق
(I swear) by the true ones that I (compelled by Fate and Destiny) placed it on the threshold of separation.

چگونه باز کنم بال در هوای وصال
In desire of union, how may I unfold the wing

که ریخت مرغ دلم پر در آشیان فراق
For its feathers, the bird of my heart hath shed on the nest of separation.

کنون چه چاره که در بحر غم به گردابی
Now, what remedy, when, into the great whirl pool of grief's ocean,

فتاد زورق صبرم ز بادبان فراق
The bark of my patience hath fallen on account of the sail of separation.

بسی نماند که کشتی عمر غرقه شود
Not much it wanted that the bark of my life should be overwhelmed,

ز موج شوق تو در بحر بی‌کران فراق
With love's wave from the limit less ocean of separation.

اگر به دست من افتد فراق را بکشم
O lord! Into the world, who brought disjunction and separation.

که روز هجر سیه باد و خان و مان فراق
Dark be the day of disjunction, and the house of separation.

رفیق خیل خیالیم و همنشین شکیب
(O true Beloved) Comrades of the troop of Thy fancy and fellow-riders with patience, are we (lovers of Thee)

قرین آتش هجران و هم قران فراق
The associate of (labour, and of distress) and the companion of separation.

چگونه دعوی وصلت کنم به جان که شده‌ست
Union with Thee, how may (i) claim By my soul (I swear) that hath become

تنم وکیل قضا و دلم ضمان فراق
My heart, the secretary of fate and my body, the pledge of separation.

ز سوز شوق دلم شد کباب دور از یار

Roast-flesh became my heart from the burning of desire (and) far (in separation) from
the (true) Beloved,

مدام خون جگر می‌خورم ز خوان فراق

Ever, the blood of the liver, I drink from the tray of separation.

فلک چو دید سرم را اسیر چنبر عشق

When, captive to love's circle, the sky be held my head

ببست گردن صبرم به ریسمان فراق

The neck of my patience, it bound with the cord of separation.

به پای شوق گر این ره به سر شدی حافظ

Hafiz if, with the foot of desire, this Path (of love) to the end thou hadst gone

به دست هجر ندادی کسی عنان فراق

To the hand of disjunction, none would have given the rein of separation.

غزل ۲۹۸   ⓞⓓⓔ ②⑨⑧

مقام امن و می بی‌غش و رفیق شفیق

The ab ode of peace, unalloyed wine, and the kind companion,

گرت مدام میسر شود زهی توفیق

If ever attainable these be to thee, O excellent the grace of God

جهان و کار جهان جمله هیچ بر هیچ است

The world and the world's work, all naught in naught is

هزار بار من این نکته کرده‌ام تحقیق

The verifying of this matter, a thousand times, I have made.

دریغ و درد که تا این زمان ندانستم

Regret and sorrow that, up to this time, I knew not,

که کیمیای سعادت رفیق بود رفیق

That the alchemy of happiness is the Friend, the Friend

به مأمنی رو و فرصت شمر غنیمت وقت

To, go opportunity, reck on the plunder of time

که در کمینگه عمرند قاطعان طریق

For, in the ambuscades of life, are the highway men of the Path.

بیا که توبه ز لعل نگار و خنده جام

(O Saki) come. For penitence for the ruby lip (of the true Beloved) and for the laughter
(the sparkling) of the cup

حکایتیست که عقلش نمی‌کند تصدیق

Is an imagination, verification whereof reason maketh not.

اگر چه موی میانت به چون منی نرسد

Although, to one contemptible like me, the (slender) hair of thy (small) waist reacheth not,

خوش است خاطرم از فکر این خیال دقیق

From the thought of this subtle matter, happy is my heart.

حلاوتی که تو را در چه زنخدان است

That (darkish) beauty that is in the chin-pit of thine,

به کنه آن نرسد صد هزار فکر عمیق

To its (profound) depth, reach not many at hought profound.

اگر به رنگ عقیقی شد اشک من چه عجب

If, with the colour of red cornelian, my tear be, what wonder

که مهر خاتم لعل تو هست همچو عقیق

For like (red) cornelian, is the seal of the seal-ring of (my eye).

به خنده گفت که حافظ غلام طبع توام

With laughter, he (the Saki) spake, saying Hafiz the servant of thy nature, I am

ببین که تا به چه حدم همی‌کند تحمیق

Behold to what degree, me a fool, he (the Saki) maketh

❖◉❖◉❖

ک
The Letter Kāf

غزل ۲۹۹ ⓄⒹⒺ ②⑨⑨

اگر شراب خوری جرعهای فشان بر خاک

(O murshid) if wine (them) drink, pour a draught on the dust (the sons of dusty Adam)

از آن گناه که نفعی رسد به غیر چه باک

The sin, where in an advantage to the stranger reacheth, what fear.

برو به هر چه تو داری بخور دریغ مخور

With whatever thou hast, go drink (and) regret, suffer not

که بیدریغ زند روزگار تیغ هلاک

For (on thy head) the sword of destruction time pitilessly striketh.

به خاک پای تو ای سرو نازپرور من

O graceful cypress, my cherisher by the dust of Thy foot,

که روز واقعه پا وامگیرم از سر خاک

(I conjure Thee) on the day of events (the day of death) take not off Thy foot from the head of my dust,

چه دوزخی چه بهشتی چه آدمی چه پری

What dweller of hell, what dweller of paradise, what man, what angel

به مذهب همه کفر طریقت است امساک

In the religion of all, infidelity to the path (tarikat) is baseness.

مهندس فلکی راه دیر شش جهتی

The path of the house of six sides (this world) the geometrician of the sky (reason)

چنان ببست که ره نیست زیر دیر مغاک

Established so that, beneath the snare of the pit (this world) is no path (of flight from it)

فریب دختر رز طرفه میزند ره عقل

The path of reason, the deceit of the daughter of the vine wonderfully attacketh

مباد تا به قیامت خراب طارم تاک

Till the judgment-day, ruined be not the vine-trellis

به راه میکده حافظ خوش از جهان رفتی

Hafiz by the path of the wine-house, happily thou wentest,

دعای اهل دلت باد مونس دل پاک

The prayer of one of heart, the consoler of thy pure heart be

غزل ۳۰۰ ⓄⒹⒺ ③⓪⓪

هزار دشمنم ار میکنند قصد هلاک

If design for my destruction, thousands of enemies (Shaitans, intent upon leading one astray) make

گرم تو دوستی از دشمنان ندارم باک

If thou (O perfect murshid) be my friend (and aider) and of enemies, I have no fear

مرا امید وصال تو زنده میدارد

Me, hope of union with Thee keepeth alive

و گر نه هر دمم از هجر توست بیم هلاک

If not, from separation from Thee a hundred ways, fear of destruction is (mine)

نفس نفس اگر از باد نشنوم بویش
Breath (by) breath, if, from the breeze, Thy perfume, I perceive not,
زمان زمان چو گل از غم کنم گریبان چاک
Time (after) time, rent like the rose my collar I make.

رود به خواب دو چشم از خیال تو هیهات
On account of Thy image, go to sleep my two eyes never
بود صبور دل اندر فراق تو حاشاک
In separation from Thee, patient was my heart, 'God forbid

اگر تو زخم زنی به که دیگری مرهم
If a wound, Thou strike, ('tis) better than the plaister of another
وگر تو زهر دهی به که دیگری تریاک
If poison Thou give, better than the antidote of another.

بضرب سیفک قتلی حیاتنا ابدا
My slaughter, by the blow of Thy sword is everlasting life
لان روحی قد طاب ان یکون فداک
For, verily happy is my soul in this that it is a sacrifice for Thee.

عنان مپیچ که گر می‌زنی به شمشیرم
There in, turn not. For if me, Thou strike with the sword,
سپر کنم سر و دستت ندارم از فتراک
My head, the shield I make from the saddle-strap (to bind me as game) Thy hand I keep not back.

تو را چنان که توبی هر نظر کجا بیند
Thee, as Thou art, how may every vision see
به قدر دانش خود هر کسی کند ادراک
To the extent of his vision, everyone understandeth

به چشم خلق عزیز جهان شود حافظ
Indigent Hafiz is the apple of people's eyes.
که بر در تو نهد روی مسکنت بر خاک
At your door, prostrated, your vision espies

غزل ۳۰۱ ⓄⒹⒺ ③⓪① ODE 301

ای دل ریش مرا با لب تو حق نمک
O (beloved) salt rights with thy lip, hath my wounded heart
حق نگه دار که من می‌روم الله معک
The (salt) right, preserve for I depart, (and) thee to God entrust.

توبی آن گوهر پاکیزه که در عالم قدس
(O true Beloved) That pure jewel Thou art that, in the holy world,
ذکر خیر تو بود حاصل تسبیح ملک
The mention of Thee for good is the outcome of the angel's praise

در خلوص منت ار هست شکی تجربه کن
(O beloved) If as to my sincerity doubt be thine, trial make
کس عیار زر خالص نشناسد چو محک
Like the touch-stone, none recogniseth the proof of pure gold.

گفته بودی که شوم مست و دو بوست بدهم

(O true Beloved) Thou spakest saying Intoxicated, I become and will give thee two kisses

وعده از حد بشد و ما نه دو دیدیم و نه یک

Beyond limit, passed the covenant but neither two (kisses) nor one (kiss) have we seen.

بگشا پسته خندان و شکرریزی کن

Thy (small) laughing pistachio (mouth) open, sugar-scattering (speech) make

خلق را از دهن خویش مینداز به شک

In doubt of Thy (having a) mouth, cast not the people

چرخ برهم زنم ار غیر مرادم گردد

The sphere, I will dash together (and destroy) unless to my desire it come

من نه آنم که زبونی کشم از چرخ فلک

Not that one am I, to endure contempt from the sky's sphere

چون بر حافظ خویشش نگذاری باری

Since, access to Hafiz thou allowest him not,

ای رقیب از بر او یک دو قدم دورترک

O watcher (Shaitan) from him, one or two paces farther (go and his society, abandon)

❖◉❖◉❖

ل
The Letter Lām

غزل ۳۰۲ ⓞⒹⒺ ③⓪②

خوش خبر باشی ای نسیم شمال
O (cool) breeze of the north the breeze of good news, thou art,

که به ما می‌رسد زمان وصال
That, us, at union's time, reacheth.

قصه العشق لا انفصام لها
Love's tale, no break is it's

فصمت‌ها هنا لسان القال
Here, speech's tongue is broken.

مالسلمی و من بذی سلم
Salma[1] is where In Zu Salam, is who

این جیراننا وکیف الحال
Our neighbours are where Their state is

عفت الدار بعد عافیه
After safety (from calamity) invisible became the dwelling (of Salma)

فاسالوا حالها عن الاطلال
Of its former state, the ruins ask

فی جمال الکمال نلت منی
In thy beauty of perfection, thou acquiredest hope

صرف الله عنک عین کمال
Far from thee, God keep the eye-wound (of calamity)

یا برید الحمی حماک الله
O messenger of the bird-place God protect thee

مرحبا مرحبا تعال تعال
Welcome welcome Come come

عرصه بزمگاه خالی ماند
Void remaineth the space of the banquet-hall

از حریفان و جام مالامال
Of the companions, and of the brimful ritl[2].

سایه افکند حالیا شب هجر
Now, hath the night of absence cast its shade

تا چه بازند شب روان خیال
Let us see, what (pastime) the night-prowlers (the dreams) of fancy play

ترک ما سوی کس نمی‌نگرد
At none, looketh our saucy one

آه از این کبریا و جاه و جلال
Alas this pride, haughtiness, and disdain

1-Lover   2- large cup or goblet, pound

حافظا عشق و صابری تا چند

O Hafiz! love and patience, how long

ناله عاشقان خوش است بنال

Sweet, is the wail of lovers. Be wail

غزل ۳۰۳ ⓄⒹⒺ ③⓪③

شممت روح وداد و شمت برق وصال

The breeze of love's perfume, I perceived and, expectant of the flashing of the lightning of union, became

بیا که بوی تو را میرم ای نسیم شمال

O (cool) breeze of the north come for, for the perfume of thy body, I die

احادیا بجمال الحبیب قف و انزل

O song-uttering driver of the camels of the Beloved stand, and alight

که نیست صبر جمیلم ز اشتیاق جمال

For, in desire of the Beloved's beauty, no patience is mine

حکایت شب هجران فروگذاشته به

(O heart) The complaint of the night of separation, let go

به شکر آن که برافکند پرده روز وصال

In thanks that the day of union hath up-cast the screen (of the night of separation)

بیا که پرده گریز هفت خانه چشم

(O Friend) come For the seven-fold-rose shedding screen of the eye

کشیده‌ایم به تحریر کارگاه خیال

On the writing of the workshop of (Thy tender) fancy, I have drawn.

چو یار بر سر صلح است و عذر می‌طلبد

When the Beloved is in desire of peace; and excuse asketh

توان گذشت ز جور رقیب در همه حال

In every state, one can pass by (and pardon) the violence of the watcher.

بجز خیال دهان تو نیست در دل تنگ

In my straitened heart, is naught save the fancy of Thy (small) mouth

که کس مباد چو من در پی خیال محال

Like me, in pursuit of vain fancy, be none

قتیل عشق تو شد حافظ غریب ولی

Slain by love for Thee, becamethe stranger, Hafiz, but

به خاک ما گذری کن که خون مات حلال

By our dust, pass for lawful to Thee is our blood

غزل ۳۰۴ ⓄⒹⒺ ③⓪④

دارای جهان نصرت دین خسرو کامل

The world-possessor, defender of the faith perfect sovereign

یحیی بن مظفر ملک عالم عادل

Yahya bin Muzaffar[1], king, just-doer:

1-Shah Yahya was the eldest son of Amir Mobarzaldin

ای درگه اسلام پناه تو گشاده
O thou thy court, the shelter of Islam, hath opened

بر روی زمین روزنه جان و در دل
On the face of the world, the window of the soul, and the door (and) the heart

تعظیم تو بر جان و خرد واجب و لازم
Necessary and proper to the soul and to wisdom, is reverence to thee

انعام تو بر کون و مکان فایض و شامل
To existence and dwelling (the universe) thy reward is a bounding and comprehending

روز ازل از کلک تو یک قطره سیاهی
On the day of eternity without beginning, from thy reed, a drop of blackness (ink)

بر روی مه افتاد که شد حل مسال
That becamethe solver of questions, fell on the face of the moon

خورشید چو آن خال سیه دید به دل گفت
When (on thy face; or on the moon's) the sun beheld that dark mole, to his heart, he said

ای کاج که من بودمی آن هندوی مقبل
Would to heaven that I had been the fortunate slave (the dark mole)

شاها فلک از بزم تو در رقص و سماع است
O king on account of thy banquet, the sky is in dancing and in sama[1]

دست طرب از دامن این زمزمه مگسل
From the skirt of this zamzama[2], thy hand let not go

می نوش و جهان بخش که از زلف کمندت
Drink wine and give the world (be joyous) For, of the tress of thy noose

شد گردن بدخواه گرفتار سلاسل
Captive to chains becamethe neck of thy ill-wisher.

دور فلکی یک سره بر منهج عدل است
(Now) Altogether, in the way of justice, is the sky's revolution

خوش باش که ظالم نبرد راه به منزل
Be happy that the tyrant taketh not the path to the stage (of his object)

حافظ قلم شاه جهان مقسم رزق است
Hafiz (when in) the (power of the) king of the world is the partition of subsistence,

از بهر معیشت مکن اندیشه باطل
For thy livelihood, make no useless thought

غزل ۳۰۵ ⓄⒹⒺ ③⓪⑤

به وقت گل شدم از توبه شراب خجل
(Even as) In the rose-season (the time of manifestations of glories of mysteries) of repentance of (wine) love I became ashamed

که کس مباد ز کردار ناصواب خجل
(So) of un-upright conduct (abandoning wine – drinking) let none be ashamed

---

1-Dance   2-Soft and slow singing

صلاح ما همه دام ره است و من زین بحث

My counsel (the circulation of the cup) is all the snare of the Path and, of the argument

نیم ز شاهد و ساقی به هیچ باب خجل

On account of the lovely one, or of the Saki, in no way am I ashamed.

بود که یار نرنجد ز ما به خلق کریم

It may be that, through His compassionate nature, the (true) Beloved (asketh not) my (sin)

که از سال ملولیم و از جواب خجل

For, of question I am vexed and of answer, a shamed

ز خون که رفت شب دوش از سراچه چشم

Of the blood, that, last night, went (flowing) from the pavilion of the eye

شدیم در نظر ره روان خواب خجل

In the sight of the night-prowlers of sleep (that come upon the path of the eye) we were a shamed.

رواست نرگس مست ار فکند سر در پیش

Lawful it is, if the intoxicated narcissus cast down its head

که شد ز شیوه آن چشم پرعتاب خجل

For, of that (Beloved's) eye full of wrath, it became a shamed

تویی که خوبتری ز آفتاب و شکر خدا

Than the (resplendent) sun, more beauteous of face, thou art. Thanks to God

که نیستم ز تو در روی آفتاب خجل

That, in the sun's face, of thee (o murshid) I am not ashamed

حجاب ظلمت از آن بست آب خضر که گشت

The veil of the Zulmat[1] (darkness) the (gleaming) water (of life) of Khizr[2] established for the reason that it became

ز شعر حافظ و آن طبع همچو آب خجل

Of (the pure) nature of Hafiz and of this (his) poetry (lustrous) like water, ashamed.

غزل ۳۰۶ ⓄⒹⒺ ③⓪⑥ ODE 306

اگر به کوی تو باشد مرا مجال وصول

If, to Thy street, the power of arriving be mine,

رسد به دولت وصل تو کار من به اصول

By the fortune of union with Thee, to foundation arriveth my work.

قرار برده ز من آن دو نرگس رعنا

From me, took rest, those two beauteous hyacinth tresses

فراغ برده ز من آن دو جادوی مکحول

From me, took tranquillity, those two narcissi (eyes) tricked with kuhl.

چو بر در تو من بی‌نوای بی زر و زور

When, at Thy door, without resource, without gold or force,

به هیچ باب ندارم ره خروج و دخول

I have, in no way, the path of egress or of ingress.

کجا روم چه کنم چاره از کجا جویم

I go where I do what (I am) how Remedy, (I make what),

که گشته‌ام ز غم و جور روزگار ملول

For, from grief of time's violence, sorely vexed I am become.

1-Nigritude   2-Name of prophet

من شکسته بدحال زندگی یابم
Battered with ill-fortune, life, I obtain
در آن زمان که به تیغ غمت شوم مقتول
At that moment when, with the sword of grief for Thee, slain I become.

خرابتر ز دل من از غم تو جای نیافت
Worse than my heart, grief for Thee found no place,
که ساخت در دل تنگم قرارگاه نزول
When, in my straitened heart, it made its place of alighting

دل از جواهر مهرت چو صیقلی دارد
Since from the jewel of Thy love, a great polish hath my heart
بود ز زنگ حوادث هر آینه مصقول
Verily, from the rust of vicissitude, polished it was.

چه جرم کرده‌ام ای جان و دل به حضرت تو
O soul and heart (the true Beloved) in Thy presence, what sin have committed,
که طاعت من بی‌دل نمی‌شود مقبول
That, accepted, becometh not the devotion of me, heart-bereft

به درد عشق بساز و خموش کن حافظ
Hafiz with love's pain, be content and be silent
رموز عشق مکن فاش پیش اهل عقول
Love's mysteries, reveal not before people of reason.

غزل ۳۰۷ ⓄⒹⒺ ③⓪⑦ ODE 307

هر نکته‌ای که گفتم در وصف آن شمایل
In praise of those good qualities (of the Beloved or of the murshid) every subtlety that I uttered,
هر کو شنید گفتا لله در قال
Everyone who heard, said The sayer of this, what an excellent speaker is he

تحصیل عشق و رندی آسان نمود اول
At first (on the day of Alast) easy appeared the acquisition of love and of profligacy
آخر بسوخت جانم در کسب این فضایل
In the end, in (attempting) the acquisition of these excellences, the soul consumed.

حلاج بر سر دار این نکته خوش سراید
On the head of the gibbet, this subtlety, sweetly singeth Hallaj[1] (Mansur)
از شافعی نپرسند امثال این مسال
Questions (of love) like these, of the Shafi'[2] (order) ask ye not

گفتم که کی ببخشی بر جان ناتوانم
I spake saying: The powerless soul, Thou pitiest when?
گفت آن زمان که نبود جان در میانه حال
He said: At that time when, between (the lover and the Beloved) life is not the intervener

دل داده‌ام به یاری شوخی کشی نگاری
I have given my heart to a Friend, bold, decorated, arrayed,
مرضیه السجایا محموده الخصال
Agreeable of nature, laudable of disposition

1-Famous mystics

2-One of the Sunni sects

در عین گوشه گیری بودم چو چشم مستت

Like Thy intoxicated (obliquely – looking) eye, I was at the time of corner-taking (retiring to solitude)

و اکنون شدم به مستان چون ابروی تو مایل

Now, like Thy (inclined) eye-brow, I became an incliner to the intoxicated.

از آب دیده صد ره طوفان نوح دیدم

From my tears, a hundred-fold Nuh[1]'s deluge, I be held

و از لوح سینه نقشت هرگز نگشت زایل

Yet, from the heart's tablet, Thy picture ever declined not.

ای دوست دست حافظ تعویذ چشم زخم است

O Beloved Hafiz's hand is the amulet (against) of the (evil) eye-wound

یا رب ببینم آن را در گردنت حمایل

O Lord (grant) that suspended to (circled around) thy neck, it (the hand) I may see

غزل ۳۰۸ ⓄⒹⒺ ③⓪⑧

ای رخت چون خلد و لعلت سلسبیل

O Thou, whose face (is) like paradise, and ruby lip (like) the limpid water of paradise

سلسبیلت کرده جان و دل سبیل

Soul and heart, Thy translucent water hath endowed.

سبزپوشان خطت بر گرد لب

Around Thy lip, Thy fresh-wearing (black) down,

همچو موراند گرد سلسبیل

Is like the (collection of black) ants around the limpid water (Thy resplendent face)

ناوک چشم تو در هر گوشه‌ای

In every corner, the arrow of Thy eye

همچو من افتاده دارد صد قتیل

Hath a hundred slain ones, (lovers) fallen like me.

یا رب این آتش که در جان من است

O lord this (of separation) fire that within my soul is,

سرد کن زان سان که کردی بر خلیل

Make cool (to give me escape from separation and to cause me to attain union with Thee) in that way that to Khalil[2] Thou didst.

من نمی‌یابم مجال ای دوستان

O friends power (of union with Him) I gain not,

گر چه دارد او جمالی بس جمیل

For the reason that exceedingly beauteous beauty, He hath.

پای ما لنگ است و منزل بس دراز

Lame is our foot; (and far distant, is) the stage (like Paradise)

دست ما کوتاه و خرما بر نخیل

Short, is our hand and on the (lofty inaccessible) date-tree, the date.

حافظ از سرپنجه عشق نگار

From the grasp of the love for the idol, Hafiz,

همچو مور افتاده شد در پای پیل

Like the (feeble) ant, at the foot of the (great) elephant, hath fallen.

1-Name of prophet   2-Name of prophet

شاه عالم را بقا و عز و ناز

To the King of the world, permanency and grandeur

باد و هر چیزی که باشد زین قبیل

And everything of this sort that he desireth be

❖◉❖❖◉❖

م
The Letter Mim

غزل ۳۰۹ ⓞⒹⒺ ③⓪⑨

عشقبازی و جوانی و شراب لعل فام

Love-playing and youth fulness and wine of ruby hue (love)

مجلس انس و حریف همدم و شرب مدام

The assembly (of love) kindly, and the companion concordant, and ever the drinking of wine (love's bounties)

ساق شکردهان و مطرب شیرین سخن

The Saki[1] sweet of mouth, and the minstrel sweet of speech (the perfect murshid)

همنشینی نیک کردار و ندیمی نیک نام

Fellow-sitters (friends) of good repute and companions of good fame

شاهدی از لطف و پاکی رشک آب زندگی

The lovely one (the true Beloved who is peerless) with grace and with purity, the envy of the water of

دلبری در حسن و خوبی غیرت ماه تمام

A heart-ravisher, in beauty and goodness, the envy of the full moon

بزمگاهی دل نشان چون قصر فردوس برین

A banquet-place (the assembly of the circle of zikr) heart-alluring, like the palace of loftiest paradise

گلشنی پیرامنش چون روضه دارالسلام

Arose-bed, its borders like the garden of the mansion of peace

صف نشینان نیکخواه و پیشکاران باادب

He tranks of sitters, (the assembly of the circle of zikr) well-wishing (to each other) and the attendants, with respect

دوستداران صاحب اسرار و حریفان دوستکام

Friends possessed of mysteries (and of divine knowledge) and companions friendly of desire

باده گلرنگ تلخ تیز خوش خوار سبک

The cup of rose-hue (true love, that, at first is) very bitter (and) strong (and afterwards) pleasant tasting, light

نقلش از لعل نگار و نقلش از یاقوت خام

Its sweet meat, (the kiss of) the ruby (lip) of the idol its tale, (wine of) the ruby cup

غمزه ساق به یغمای خرد آهخته تیغ

The Saki's glance (the glory, and the splendour, of the true Beloved, that from all things, is manifest) for the plunder of wisdom, sword-drawn

زلف جانان از برای صید دل گسترده دام

The (true) Beloved's tress (the world's strange forms that, from all things make manifest the true Beloved, splendour – kindling) for the capture of the heart snare

نکته دانی بذله گو چون حافظ شیرین سخن

(None is a) subtlety-understander, jest-utterer, like Hafiz sweet of speech

بخشش آموزی جهان افروز چون حاجی قوام

(None is) a liberality-teacher, world-kindling, like Haji Kivam[2]

1-Tapster

2-He is one of the Hafez's close friends

هر که این عشرت نخواهد خوشدلی بر وی تباه

Who, this society desireth not, to him be heart-happiness, ruined

وان که این مجلس نجوید زندگی بر وی حرام

Who, this pleasure seeketh not, to him be life unlawful

غزل ۳۱۰ ⓞⒹⒺ ③①⓪ ODE 310

مرحبا طایر فرخ پی فرخنده پیام

Bird, auspicious of foot, gracious of message, welcome

خیر مقدم چه خبر دوست کجا راه کدام

Happy thy arrival What news of the Friend He (is) (wher) his) path (is) what

یا رب این قافله را لطف ازل بدرقه باد

O Lord! be the grace of eternity without beginning the guide of this kafila[1],

که از او خصم به دام آمد و معشوقه به کام

By (means of) which, to the snare the enemy hath come and to His desire, the Beloved

ماجرای من و معشوق مرا پایان نیست

No limit hath tale of me and of my Beloved

هر چه آغاز ندارد نپذیرد انجام

Whatever no beginning hath, no ending taketh.

گل ز حد برد تنعم نفسی رخ بنما

Grace beyond limit, bringeth the rose (the true Beloved) with generosity, Thy face display

سرو می‌نازد و خوش نیست خدا را بخرام

Elegance, the cypress displayeth; and (in its pride) pleasant is not. For God's sake (so that it may be ashamed) Forth grace fully move

زلف دلدار چو زنار همی‌فرماید

Since the heart-possessing tress keepeth ordering me the zunnar[2] (the mystic cord which is contrary to the khirka)

برو ای شیخ که شد بر تن ما خرقه حرام

O khwaja[3] go for, on our body, unlawful is the Khirka[4].

مرغ روحم که همی‌زد ز سر سدره صفیر

The bird of my soul that, from the summit of the Sidra tree, crieth out

عاقبت دانه خال تو فکندش در دام

It, at last, into the snare (of Thy beauty) the grain of Thy mole cast.

چشم بیمار مرا خواب نه درخور باشد

(For) my blood-raining eye, how is sleep fit

من له یقتل داء دنف کیف ینام

He who hath a grievous malady that slayeth how sleepeth he

تو ترحم نکئی بر من مخلص گفتم

To me, heart-bereft, Thou showest no pity I said

ذاک دعوای و ها انت و تلک الایام

This is my claim (that Thou pity me) and this, Thou art and this is the (opportune) time.

1-Convoy
2-Zunar" is a necklace worn by Christians and Zoroastrians
to distinguish themselves from Muslims.

3-Eunuch, dignitary, vizier, boss, host
4-Cloak

حافظ ار میل به ابروی تو دارد شاید

If inclination for Thy eye-brow, Hafiz have, it is fit

جای در گوشه محراب کنند اهل کلام

In the corner of the prayer-arch, their dwelling, men of eloquence (or men of the Kuran) will make.

غزل ۳۱۱ ⓄⒹⒺ ③①①

عاشق روی جوانی خوش نوخاسته ام

Lover of the face youthful, joyous, newly blossomed (tender of age) am I

و از خدا دولت این غم به دعا خواسته‌ام

From God the joy of this grief (of love) with prayer sought have I.

عاشق و رند و نظربازم و می‌گویم فاش

Lover, profligate, glance-player, I am and it openly, I say

تا بدانی که به چندین هنر آراسته‌ام

That thou mayest know that, with so many excellences, adorned am I.

شرمم از خرقه آلوده خود می‌آید

Cometh shame to me, of the wine-stained Khirka,

که بر او وصله به صد شعبده پیراسته‌ام

Where on, the patch with a hundred arts of hypocrisy, decorated have I.

خوش بسوز از غمش ای شمع که اینک من نیز

O candle for grief for Him, happily consume For (behold) also,

هم بدین کار کمربسته و برخاسته‌ام

In this very work, loin-girt and upstanding am I

با چنین حیرتم از دست بشد صرفه کار

In astonishment like this, went from my hand, my work's gain

در غم افزوده‌ام آنچ از دل و جان کاسته‌ام

In grief, increased have I that which, inrespect of heart and of soul decreased have I.

همچو حافظ به خرابات روم جامه قبا

To the tavern, I go like Hafiz (clad in) the garment of the kaba[1]

بو که در بر کشد آن دلبر آن نوخاسته‌ام

It may be that into His bosom, me, that Heart-ravisher, newly blossomed (youthful) may draw.

غزل ۳۱۲ ⓄⒹⒺ ③①②

بشری اذ السلامه حلت بذی سلم

Glad tidings to (the ab ode of) Zu-Salam, suddenly descended safety (from calamity)

لله حمد معترف غایه النعم

To God praise, (the praise of) the confessor of the greatest blessing

آن خوش خبر کجاست که این فتح مژده داد

That bringer of happy news, who brought the glad tidings of victory, is where

تا جان فشانمش چو زر و سیم در قدم

So that (in joy) my soul (which is dearer than gold and silver) I may scatter on his foot like gold and silver.

1-He is a kind of men's tunic

از بازگشت شاه در این طرفه منزل است

From the King's turning back (what a rare picture established)

آهنگ خصم او به سراپرده عدم

His enemy's resolution in the mansion of non-existence

پیمان شکن هرآینه گردد شکسته حال

Verily, shattered of heart becometh the covenant-breaker

ان العهود عند ملیک النهی ذمم

In the opinion of the Lords of wisdom, sacred charges are covenants.

می‌جست از سحاب امل رحمتی ولی

From hope's cloudlet, he sought a blessing But

جز دیده‌اش معاینه بیرون نداد نم

(To) his seeing eye, (it) gave naught save moisture.

در نیل غم فتاد سپهرش به طنز گفت

Into the (dark) Nil of grief, he (the covenant – breaker) fell to him, in reproach the sky said

ان قد ندمت و ما ینفع الندم

Verily, (now) repentant, thou hast become; and profit from repentance, (thou gainest not).

ساقی چو یار مه رخ و از اهل راز بود

Saki resembled the moon face true beloved and was one of mystery,

حافظ بخورد باده و شیخ و فقیه هم

Hafiz drank wine and so did the sheikh and lawyer.

غزل ۳۱۳ ⓄⒹⒺ ③①③

باز آی ساقیا که هوا خواه خدمتم

Saki (true Beloved) come back; for of Thy service, desirous I am

مشتاق بندگی و دعاگوی دولتم

Of Thy service, and of prayer-uttering for Thy fortune, desirous I am

زان جا که فیض جام سعادت فروغ توست

(O perfect murshid) From that place, where is the (common) bounty of the cup of happiness of thy splendour

بیرون شدی نمای ز ظلمات حیرتم

From the zulmat[1] of astonishment, me the path of going out, show.

هر چند غرق بحر گناهم ز صد جهت

Drowned in the sea of sin from a hundred sides, though I be

تا آشنای عشق شدم ز اهل رحمتم

Since I became love's friend, of the people of mercy am

عیبم مکن به رندی و بدنامی ای حکیم

O Fakih[2] me, for profligacy or for ill-fame, censure not

کاین بود سرنوشت ز دیوان قسمتم

For, from the Court of Fate, pre-ordained was this

می خور که عاشقی نه به کسب است و اختیار

Drink wine. For, neither by acquisition, nor by choice, is the being a lover

این موهبت رسید ز میراث فطرتم

Me, this gift reached from the heritage of creation.

1-Nigritude   2-Lawyer

من کز وطن سفر نگزیدم به عمر خویش
I, who, in my life, chose not travelling from my native land
در عشق دیدن تو هواخواه غربتم
In the love of seeing Thee, desirous of travelling am

دریا و کوه در ره و من خسته و ضعیف
In (love's) path, the (mighty) river and the (lofty) mountain and I, shattered and battered
ای خضر پی خجسته مدد کن به همتم
Khizr auspicious of foot by thy prayer, aid give me

دورم به صورت از در دولتسرای تو
Far from the door of fortune of Thy shelter, apparently am
لیکن به جان و دل ز مقیمان حضرتم
But, with soul and heart, of the (crowd of) dwellers of Thy presence, am I.

حافظ به پیش چشم تو خواهد سپرد جان
Before Thy eye, Hafiz will sacrifice his life
در این خیالم ار بدهد عمر مهلتم
In this fancy, I am, if respite me life will give

غزل ۳۱۴ ⓄⒹⒺ ③①④

دوش بیماری چشم تو ببرد از دستم
Last night, me, from power took (and ruined) the (languishing) sick ness of Thy eye;
لیکن از لطف لبت صورت جان می‌بستم
But, from the bounty of Thy lip, the form of (new) life, I established.

عشق من با خط مشکین تو امروزی نیست
Not of to-day, is my love for Thy musky tress
دیرگاه است کز این جام هلالی مستم
Long time 'tis, since that with this cup, like the new moon, intoxicated I was.

از ثبات خودم این نکته خوش آمد که به جور
From my own constancy, happily came this subtlety: With violence,
در سر کوی تو از پای طلب ننشستم
At the head of Thy street, (down) from the foot of search, I sate not

عافیت چشم مدار از من میخانه نشین
From me, wine-house-sitter, ease expect not
که دم از خدمت رندان زده‌ام تا هستم
For, since I was of the service of profligates, boasted have I.

در ره عشق از آن سوی فنا صد خطر است
In love's path, from that quarter of effacement, are a hundred dangers
تا نگویی که چو عمرم به سر آمد رستم
Take care thou sayest not that, when to an end (in effacement) hath come my life, (from these calamities) I have escaped (Nay before the heart, after death, are a hundred thoughts of danger)

بعد از اینم چه غم از تیر کج انداز حسود
After this, of the arrow of torment of the envious, mine what care,
چون به محبوب کمان ابروی خود پیوستم
When, to my Beloved of bow-eye-brow, joined I am

بوسه بر درج عقیق تو حلال است مرا

Lawful to me, is the kiss on the casket of Thy cornelian (lip)

که به افسوس و جفا مهر وفا نشکستم

For, despite Thy tyranny and oppression, love (and) fidelity, I shattered not.

صنمی لشکریم غارت دل کرد و برفت

My heart, a warrior-idol plundered and departed

آه اگر عاطفت شاه نگیرد دستم

Pity, if the grace of the king (the murshid) take not my hand (and justice give me)

رتبت دانش حافظ به فلک برشده بود

To the (lofty) sky, had ascended the grandeur of Hafiz's knowledge

کرد غمخواری شمشاد بلندت پستم

Me, grieving for Thy lofty box-tree (the true Beloved's stature) made low. made low.

غزل ۳۱۵ ⓞⒹⒺ ③①⑤

به غیر از آن که بشد دین و دانش از دستم

Beyond limit this that from my hand, went religion and knowledge,

بیا بگو که ز عشقت چه طرف بربستم

Come, say what joy from love for Thee, I established

اگر چه خرمن عمرم غم تو داد به باد

Although grief for thee gave to the wind the harvest of my life,

به خاک پای عزیزت که عهد نشکستم

(Falling) In the dust of Thy precious foot, (I displayed fidelity) for the covenant (that I had made) I broke not.

چو ذره گر چه حقیرم ببین به دولت عشق

Contemptible like the atom though I am, Love's wealth, be hold

که در هوای رخت چون به مهر پیوستم

How, in desire of Thy face, joined to love I am.

بیار باده که عمریست تا من از سر امن

Bring wine for 'tis a life-time, since, through desire of safety, I

به کنج عافیت از بهر عیش ننشستم

Sate, in the corner of safety for the sake of ease.

اگر ز مردم هشیاری ای نصیحتگو

O counsel-utterer if (the crowd of) men of sense, thou be,

سخن به خاک میفکن چرا که من مستم

The dust, cast not thy speech (of counsel) for (counsel is useless) intoxicated I am.

چگونه سر ز خجالت برآورم بر دوست

Before the Friend (God) my head forth from shame how may I bring,

که خدمتی به سزا برنیامد از دستم

When, from my hand, a worthy service issueth not

بسوخت حافظ و آن یار دلنواز نگفت

Hafiz consumed; and that Beloved, heart-cherishing, spake not

که مرهمی بفرستم که خاطرش خستم

Saying When his heart, I wounded, a plaister, I sent

غزل ۳۱۶ ⓄⒹⒺ ③①⑥

زلف بر باد مده تا ندهی بر بادم
So that me, to the wind of destruction thou givenot, to the dishevelling breeze, thy tress givenot

ناز بنیاد مکن تا نکنی بنیادم
So that my foundation of life, thou take not, the foundation of disdain, establish not.

می مخور با همه کس تا نخورم خون جگر
So that (in affliction) the blood of my liver, I drinknot, with others, wine drink not

سر مکش تا نکشد سر به فلک فریادم
So that its head to the sky, my plaint draw not, thy head with draw not.

زلف را حلقه مکن تا نکنی دربندم
So that me, in bonds, thou put not thy tress be curlnot

طره را تاب مده تا ندهی بر بادم
So that me, to the wind (of destruction) thou give not, luster to thy face give not.

یار بیگانه مشو تا نبری از خویشم
So that me, from thyself thou take not the friend of the stranger be not

غم اغیار مخور تا نکنی ناشادم
So that me, unhappy thou make not grief for strangers suffer not.

رخ برافروز که فارغ کنی از برگ گلم
So that me, independent of the rose-leaf (perfume) thou mayst make, thy face illumine

قد برافراز که از سرو کنی آزادم
So that me, free of the (lofty) cypress, thou mayst make, thy stature exalt

شمع هر جمع مشو ور نه بسوزی ما را
So that me, thou mayst not consume, the candle of every assembly be not

یاد هر قوم مکن تا نروی از یادم
So that from my remembrance, thou pass not, every tribe remember not

شهره شهر مشو تا ننهم سر در کوه
So that my head (in perturbation) in desire for (the solitude of) the mountain thou put not, the notoriety of the city be not

شور شیرین منما تا نکنی فرهادم
So that me, Farhad[1], thou make not, the disdain of Shirin[2] display not.

رحم کن بر من مسکین و به فریادم رس
On me, miserable, show pity and to my plaint, arrive

تا به خاک در آصف نرسد فریادم
So that, to the dust of the door of Asaf[3], my plaint reach not.

حافظ از جور تو حاشا که بگرداند روی
Of thy tyranny, God forbid that Hafiz should, one day, complain

من از آن روز که دربند توام آزادم
From this day when, in thy bond, I am, free I am.

1-Lover
2-Farhad's mistress

3-Suleiman's minister

غزل ۳۱۷ ⓞⒹⒺ ③①⑦

فاش می‌گویم و از گفته خود دلشادم
Openly, I speak; and of my own utterance, heart-happy am I

بنده عشقم و از هر دو جهان آزادم
Love's slave, I am and of both worlds, free am I.

طایر گلشن قدسم چه دهم شرح فراق
The bird of the holy rose-bed (paradise) am I. Explanation of separation (from paradise)
what shall I give,

که در این دامگه حادثه چون افتادم
(And) Into this disaster's snare-place, how I fell.

من ملک بودم و فردوس برین جایم بود
The angel, I was and loftiest paradise was my a b ode

آدم آورد در این دیر خراب آبادم
Into this ruined cloister (this world) me, Adam brought,

سایه طوبی و دلجویی حور و لب حوض
The shade of the Tuba tree, and the heart-seekingness of the Hur[1], and the marge of
the pool (Kausar)

به هوای سر کوی تو برفت از یادم
(All) In desire of the head of Thy street, passed from my mind.

نیست بر لوح دلم جز الف قامت دوست
On my heart's table t is naught save the (straight) alif of the Friend's stature

چه کنم حرف دگر یاد نداد استادم
What may I do Me, recollection of other letter the teacher (the murshid) thee gave not.

کوکب بخت مرا هیچ منجم نشناخت
Recognised the star of my fortune, astrologer none

یا رب از مادر گیتی به چه طالع زادم
O Lord! of mother-earth, beneath what natal star, born was I

تا شدم حلقه به گوش در میخانه عشق
Since, in love's wine-house, beringed (enslaved) I became,

هر دم آید غمی از نو به مبارک بادم
Momently, cometh anew a great grief (saying) Welcome.

می خورد خون دلم مردمک دیده سزاست
The little man (pupil) of my eye drinketh the heart's blood (in grief) Tis fit

که چرا دل به جگرگوشه مردم دادم
For, to the liver lobe (the darling) of man, why gave I my heart

پاک کن چهره حافظ به سر زلف ز اشک
With the tress tip, pure of tear, make the face of Hafiz

ور نه این سیل دمادم ببرد بنیادم
If not, my foundation, this torrent momently flowing will take.

1-Lover

غزل ۳۱۸ ⓄⒹⒺ ③①⑧

مرا می‌بینی و هر دم زیادت می‌کنی دردم
Me, Thou beholdest; and, in a moment, my pain, greater Thou makest

تو را می‌بینم و میلم زیادت می‌شود هر دم
Thee, I be hold and momently my inclination for Thee greater becometh.

به سامانم نمی‌پرسی نمی‌دانم چه سر داری
As to my state, Thou askest not what mystery Thou hast, I know not

به درمانم نمی‌کوشی نمی‌دانی مگر دردم
For my remedy, Thou strivest not perchance, my pain, Thou knowest not

نه راه است این که بگذاری مرا بر خاک و بگریزی
Not the way is this that me, on the dust, Thou shouldst cast and pass

گذاری آر و بازم پرس تا خاک رهت گردم
Pass by (me) and again my state ask, so that the dust of Thy Path, I may become.

ندارم دست از دامنت بجز در خاک و آن دم هم
From off Thy skirt, I keep not my hand, save in the dust (of the grave) and, that very moment,

که بر خاکم روان گردی به گرد دامنت گردم
When, over my dust (in the grave) Thou passest, Thy skirt, my dust will seize

فرورفت از غم عشقت دمم دم می‌دهی تا کی
From grief of love for Thee, my breath (of life) descended. Breath, Thou givest till when

دمار از من برآوردی نمی‌گویی برآوردم
Forth from me, destruction, Thou takest: Thou sayest not: Breath, Bring forth.

شبی دل را به تاریکی ز زلفت باز می‌جستم
One night, in the darkness, from Thy (dark) tress, my heart Is ought

رخت می‌دیدم و جامی هلالی باز می‌خوردم
Thy face, I be held and a cup of Thy ruby lip, again I drank.

کشیدم در برت ناگاه و شد در تاب گیسویت
Suddenly, Thee, into my bosom, I drew and, into the curl of Thy tress, it (my heart) went

نهادم بر لبت لب را و جان و دل فدا کردم
On Thy lip, my lip I placed and, soul and heart, made sacrifice.

تو خوش می‌باش با حافظ برو گو خصم جان می‌ده
To Hafiz, kind be Thou. To the enemy say Thy life surrender:

چو گرمی از تو می‌بینم چه باک از خصم دم سردم
When on Thy part, warmth I see, of the enemy cold of breath, mine, what fear

غزل ۳۱۹ ⓄⒹⒺ ③①⑨

سال‌ها پیروی مذهب رندان کردم
Years, the pursuit of the service of profligates I made

تا به فتوی خرد حرص به زندان کردم
Until, by wisdom's decree, greed into prison, I put.

من به سرمنزل عنقا نه به خود بردم راه
Not of myself, took I the path to the ab ode of the (inaccessible) Anka[1] (the true Beloved)

قطع این مرحله با مرغ سلیمان کردم
With the bird of Sulaiman[2] (the lapwing) the travelling of the stage, I made.

1-Phoenix   2-Name of prophet

سایه‌ای بر دل ریشم فکن ای گنج روان
O treasure of desire on my heart-wound, thy shade cast

که من این خانه به سودای تو ویران کردم
For, by exceeding desire for thee, this house (the heart) desolate, I made.

توبه کردم که نبوسم لب ساقی و کنون
I repented, saying: The Saki's lip J will not kiss. And now,

می‌گزم لب که چرا گوش به نادان کردم
My lip, I bite because my ear to the (counsel of the) foolish, I placed.

در خلاف آمد عادت بطلب کام که من
Contrary to usage, seek desire. As,

کسب جمعیت از آن زلف پریشان کردم
From that dishevelled tress (of Thine) the acquisition of tranquillity (which is contrary to usage) I made.

نقش مستوری و مستی نه به دست من و توست
Not in my hand, nor in thine, is the picture of abstinence and of intoxication

آن چه سلطان ازل گفت بکن آن کردم
What the Lord of eternity without beginning said Do that, I did.

دارم از لطف ازل جنت فردوس طمع
From (through) the grace of eternity without beginning, paradise, I greedily desire

گر چه دربانی میخانه فراوان کردم
Although, door-keeping of the wine-house, much I did.

این که پیرانه سرم صحبت یوسف بنواخت
This that the society of Yusuf[1] (divine grace) cherisheth my elderly head

اجر صبریست که در کلبه احزان کردم
Is the reward of that patience that, in the sorrowful cell, I made.

صبح خیزی و سلامت طلبی چون حافظ
Morning-rising (open – heartedness) and salvation-seeking, like Hafiz

هر چه کردم همه از دولت قرآن کردم
Whatever I did, all from the fortune of the Kuran[2], I did.

گر به دیوان غزل صدرنشینم چه عجب
If in the Divan of ghazals[3] (the assembly, whereat songs they sing on) the chief seat, I sat, what wonder

سال‌ها بندگی صاحب دیوان کردم
Years, the service of the master of the Divan, I made.

غزل ۳۲۰ ◌۞◌ ODE 320 ◌۞◌

دیشب به سیل اشک ره خواب می‌زدم
Last night, with a torrent of tears, sleep's path, I dashed

نقشی به یاد خط تو بر آب می‌زدم
In memory of Thy down, a (vanishing) picture on water, I dashed.

1-Name of prophet
2-Quran
3-Sonnet, ode

ابروی یار در نظر و خرقه سوخته

In my view, the Friend's eye-brow; and the consumed Khirka[1]

جامی به یاد گوشه محراب می‌زدم

To the memory of the corner of Thy prayer-arch (eye – brow) a cup I dashed.

هر مرغ فکر کز سر شاخ سخن بجست

Every bird of thought, that, from the tip of joy's branch, flew,

بازش ز طره تو به مضراب می‌زدم

Again, to the snare of Thy curl, it, I dashed

روی نگار در نظرم جلوه می‌نمود

In my sight, the form of the idol (the true Beloved) displayed grandeur

وز دور بوسه بر رخ مهتاب می‌زدم

From a far, on the cheek of the moon, a kiss, I dashed.

چشمم به روی ساقی و گوشم به قول چنگ

On the Saki's face, my eye on the harp's wail, my ear

فالی به چشم و گوش در این باب می‌زدم

In this matter, with eye an dear, an omen (of what will be revealed) I dashed

نقش خیال روی تو تا وقت صبحدم

Till morning-dawn, the picture of the fancy of Thy face,

بر کارگاه دیده بی‌خواب می‌زدم

On the workshop of my sleepless eye, I dashed

ساقی به صوت این غزل م کاسه می‌گرفت

To the words of this ghazal, the cup up took my Saki

می‌گفتم این سرود و می ناب می‌زدم

This song, I uttered and pure wine, I dashed.

خوش بود وقت حافظ و فال مراد و کام

Happy, was the time of Hafiz and an omen of object and of desire

بر نام عمر و دولت احباب می‌زدم

In respect of (long) life, and of (great) fortune of friends, I dashed.

غزل ۳۲۱ ⓞⓓⒺ ③②①

هر چند پیر و خسته دل و ناتوان شدم

Although old, shattered of heart, powerless, I have become

هر گه که یاد روی تو کردم جوان شدم

Whenever I recollected Thy face, made, young I became.

شکر خدا که هر چه طلب کردم از خدا

Thanks to God that whatever, from God, I sought,

بر منتهای همت خود کامران شدم

To the limit of my spirit, prosperous I became.

ای گلبن جوان بر دولت بخور که من

O young rose-bush the fruit of fortune enjoy for,

در سایه تو بلبل باغ جهان شدم

Beneath Thy shade, the bulbul[2] of the world's garden I became.

1-Cloak   2-Nightingale

اول ز تحت و فوق وجودم خبر نبود

At first (in eternity without beginning) of (the word and the cry of the world) no news was (mine)

در مکتب غم تو چنین نکته دان شدم

In the school of grief for thee (o murshid) a subtlety-knower like this I became.

قسمت حوالتم به خرابات می‌کند

To the tavern (the stage of divine knowledge) me, fate consigneth (so that, thence, profit and advantage I may reap)

هر چند کاین چنین شدم و آن چنان شدم

As much as like this (a sage) I go and like that (a zahid) I became.

آن روز بر دلم در معنی گشوده شد

To my heart, the door of reality became opened that day

کز ساکنان درگه پیر مغان شدم

When, of the dwellers of Thy court, the Pir of the Magians[1], I became

در شاهراه دولت سرمد به تخت بخت

In eternal fortune's highway to fortune's throne,

با جام می به کام دل دوستان شدم

With the cup of wine, to the desire of the heart of friends I went

از آن زمان که فتنه چشمت به من رسید

From that time when the calamity (wound) of Thy eye reached me,

ایمن ز شر فتنه آخرزمان شدم

From the terrible calamity wound of the end of Time (the last age of this world) safe I became.

من پیر سال و ماه نیم یار بی‌وفاست

Not old in years and months, am I the faithless friend, it was,

بر من چو عمر می‌گذرد پیر از آن شدم

(Who, swiftly), like (swift) life, passeth by me from (grief of) that, old, I became.

دوشم نوید داد عنایت که حافظا

Last night, me, glad tidings, he, (the Pir of the Magians, the perfect murshid) gave, saying Hafiz

بازآکه من به عفو گناهت ضمان شدم

Comeback; for the pardon of thy sins, surety I became.

غزل ۳۲۲ ⓄⒹⒺ ③②②

خیال نقش تو در کارگاه دیده کشیدم

(O true Beloved) On the workshop of the eye, the form of Thy face, I drew

به صورت تو نگاری ندیدم و نشنیدم

An idol in Thy form, not I saw not I heard.

اگر چه در طلبت همعنان باد شمالم

Although in search of Thee, equal in rein (speed) with the (swift) the north breeze I am

به گرد سرو خرامان قامتت نرسیدم

Not (even) the dust of the (swiftly) moving cypress of Thy stature, I reached.

امید در شب زلفت به روز عمر نبستم

Hope in the (dark) night of Thy (dark) tress for the bright day of life, I established not

طمع به دور دهانت ز کام دل ببریدم

From the heart's desire, desire for Thy mouth's round form, I severed

---

1-The perfect mystic man, Fire worshipper

به شوق چشمه نوشت چه قطره‌ها که فشاندم

From desire for Thy sweet fountain, what drops (tears they were) that I scattered

ز لعل باده فروشت چه عشوه‌ها که خریدم

From Thy ruby (lip) wine-selling, what graces I purchased

ز غمزه بر دل ریشم چه تیرها که گشادی

On my wounded heart, what arrows of glances, Thou loosedest

ز غصه بر سر کویت چه بارها که کشیدم

At the head of Thy street, what loads of grief I endured.

ز کوی یار بیار ای نسیم صبح غباری

O breeze of the morning from the (true) Beloved's street, a little dust bring

که بوی خون دل ریش از آن تراب شنیدم

For, from that moist land, the perfume of the blood of the wounded heart I perceived.

گناه چشم سیاه تو بود و گردن دلخواه

The sin (fault) of Thy dark eye, and of Thy heart-alluring neck, it was,

که من چو آهوی وحشی ز آدمی برمیدم

That, like the wild deer, from man I fled.

چو غنچه بر سرم از کوی او گذشت نسیمی

Over my head, from His street, a (fragrant) breeze like (perfumed) the rose-bud passed

که پرده بر دل خونین به بوی او بدریدم

For (obtaining) the perfume of which, the screen over my poor heart, ١ rent.

به خاک پای تو سوگند و نور دیده حافظ

The oath by the dust of Thy foot and by the light of the eye of Hafiz, (I swear) that, without Thy face

که بی رخ تو فروغ از چراغ دیده ندیدم

No splendour from the lamp of the eye, I saw

غزل ٣٢٣ ⓞⓓⓔ ③②③

ز دست کوته خود زیر بارم

Through my short (feeble) arm, beneath grief's load, am I

که از بالابلندان شرمسارم

For, of those of lofty stature ashamed, am I.

مگر زنجیر مویی گیردم دست

Perchance, my hand, the chain of the hair (of Thy tress) will take

وگر نه سر به شیدایی برآرم

If not, in distraughtness, my head I bring forth.

ز چشم من بپرس اوضاع گردون

Of my (sleepless) eye, ask the plane of the spheres

که شب تا روز اختر می‌شمارم

For, night today, the stars, I count

بدین شکرانه می‌بوسم لب جام

Thankfully, the cup of the lip, I kiss for this

که کرد آگه ز راز روزگارم

That, me, it acquainted with time's mystery.

اگر گفتم دعای می فروشان
If, for the wine-sellers, a prayer I uttered,
چه باشد حق نعمت می گزارم
What is it the duty of favour, I offer.

من از بازوی خود دارم بسی شکر
Thanks many, I owe to my (feeble) arm
که زور مردم آزاری ندارم
In that the strength of the man-injurer, I have not.

سری دارم چو حافظ مست لیکن
A head like intoxicated Hafiz, I have But
به لطف آن سری امیدوارم
Hope, in the grace of that chief I have.

غزل ۳۲۴ ⓞⒹⒺ ③②④

گر چه افتاد ز زلفش گرهی در کارم
Although, from His tress, a knot (of difficulty) hath fallen upon my work
همچنان چشم گشاد از کرمش می دارم
Even so, from His liberality, the solution (of it) I expect.

به طرب حمل مکن سرخی رویم که چو جام
To joy, the ruddiness of my face attribute not For, like the cup,
خون دل عکس برون می دهد از رخسارم
Forth from my cheek, the (ruddy) reflection, the heart's blood giveth.

پرده مطربم از دست برون خواهد برد
Me, forth from power will take the melody of the minstrel
آه اگر زان که در این پرده نباشد بارم
Alas, if on that account, within this screen (of the melody) mine, access be none.

پاسبان حرم دل شده ام شب همه شب
Night, all night, the guardian of my heart's fold have I been
تا در این پرده جز اندیشه او نگذارم
So that, into this screen (of dark night) save thought of Him, naught I pass.

منم آن شاعر ساحر که به افسون سخن
That poet-magician am I, who, with the sorcery of speech
از نی کلک همه قند و شکر می بارم
From the reed-pen, all candy and sugar, rain.

دیده بخت به افسانه او شد در خواب
By His tale, to sleep went fortune's eye
کو نسیمی ز عنایت که کند بیدارم
Where, a breeze of favour, that, me, awake may make?

چون تو را در گذر ای یار نمی یارم دید
When, in (the wind's) thorough fare, (Him, my Friend), I see not
با که گویم که بگوید سخنی با یارم
whom, may I speak saying A word to my Friend, utter.

دوش می‌گفت که حافظ همه روی است و ریا

Last night, he kept saying All (double) face and hyprocisy is Hafiz

بجز از خاک درش با که بود بازارم

(Hafiz replied) Save with the dust of Thy door, say in work with whom, am I

غزل ۳۲۵ ⓞⒹⒺ ③②⑤

گر دست دهد خاک کف پای نگارم

If the dust of the sole of my idol's foot give aid

بر لوح بصر خط غباری بنگارم

(With it) On the tablet of vision, a dusty line (whereby my vision may be increased) I will draw

بر بوی کنار تو شدم غرق و امید است

Overwhelmed in desire of Thy embrace I became and my hope is

از موج سرشکم که رساند به کنارم

That, through (the violence of) the wave of my tear, me to reach to the shore, it (the wave) may cause.

پروانه او گر رسدم در طلب جان

If in desire of my life, His order reach me,

چون شمع همان دم به دمی جان بسپارم

That very moment, like the candle, in a moment, my life a (sacrifice for Him) I surrender.

امروز مکش سر ز وفای من و اندیش

To-day, from fidelity to me, turn not away Thy head and think

زان شب که من از غم به دعا دست برآرم

Of that night, when, through grief, my hand in prayer, I up lift.

زلفین سیاه تو به دلداری عشاق

For the consolation of lovers, Thy two tresses

دادند قراری و ببردند قرارم

A great covenant, gave; and my rest, took

ای باد از آن باده نسیمی به من آور

O breeze (murshid) me, a fragrant waft from that cup (of wine of divine love) bring

کان بوی شفابخش بود دفع خمارم

For, (from the grief of) wine-sickness (temptations of the world me) convalescence, that perfume (giveth).

گر قلب دلم را ننهد دوست عیاری

If the Friend establish not the proof of the base-coin of my heart

من نقد روان در دمش از دیده شمارم

From my eye, in His path, current coin (tears) I reckon.

دامن مفشان از من خاکی که پس از من

From me, dusty, shake not (in pride) thy skirt. For, after death

زین در نتواند که برد باد غبارم

From this door, it is not possible that my dust (even) the (whirling) wind can take.

حافظ لب لعلش چو مرا جان عزیز است

Hafiz since His ruby lip is (as) the dear soul to me,

عمری بود آن لحظه که جان را به لب آرم

That moment when to the lip (of the true Beloved) I bring my soul, a (lasting) life (mine) will be.

غزل ۳۲۶ ⓄⒹⒺ ③②⑥

در نهانخانه عشرت صنمی خوش دارم
In the secret house of my ease (the heart) a sweet idol (the true Beloved) I have

کز سر زلف و رخش نعل در آتش دارم
From Whose tress tip and cheek, the horse-shoe (of agitation) in the fire I have

عاشق و رندم و میخواره به آواز بلند
With loud shout, me (they call) lover, profligate, wine-drinker

وین همه منصب از آن حور پریوش دارم
From that Hur[1], like the Pari[2], all I have

گر تو زین دست مرا بی سر و سامان داری
If, in this way, me they call, resource less Thou keep,

من به آه سحرت زلف مشوش دارم
With a morning-sigh, dishevelled, Thy tress, I

گر چنین چهره گشاید خط زنگاری دوست
If the ruddish beard of the Friend display like this its face of splendour

من رخ زرد به خونابه منقش دارم
With bloody water, my yellow (grief – stricken) face painted (ruddy) I have.

گر به کاشانه رندان قدمی خواهی زد
If to the ab ode of profligates, a pace Thou will take,

نقل شعر شکرین و می بیغش دارم
The sweet meat of sweet verse, and unalloyed wine, ruddy I have.

ناوک غمزه بیار و رسن زلف که من
From the path of the tress, bring the arrow of the glance. For

جنگها با دل مجروح بلاکش دارم
With my wounded heart, calamity-enduring, contests I have.

حافظا چون غم و شادی جهان در گذر است
O Hafiz! when avanishing are the world's grief and joy

بهتر آن است که من خاطر خود خوش دارم
That is best that, my own heart, happy I have.

غزل ۳۲۷ ⓄⒹⒺ ③②⑦

مرا عهدیست با جانان که تا جان در بدن دارم
With the true Beloved, a covenant is mine that As long as in body, life I have

هواداران کویش را چو جان خویشتن دارم
The well-wishers of His street, (dear) like my own (precious) life hold.

صفای خلوت خاطر از آن شمع چگل جویم
By that candle of Chigil[3] (the true Beloved) the purity of the khilvat[4] of my heart, I be hold

فروغ چشم و نور دل از آن ماه ختن دارم
From that moon of Khutan[5], the splendour of my eye and the luminosityof heart, I have.

1-Lover
2-Beautiful woman
3-Beautiful beloved

4-Solitude
5-Beautiful beloved

به کام و آرزوی دل چو دارم خلوتی حاصل

When to the desire and wish of my heart, a khilvat, I have gained,

چه فکر از خبث بدگویان میان انجمن دارم

Of the malice of evil-speakers in the assembly, what care (is it that) I have

مرا در خانه سروی هست کاندر سایه قدش

In the house, mine is a cypress (the murshid, perfect and excellent) in the shade of whose (lofty) stature,

فراغ از سرو بستانی و شمشاد چمن دارم

Independence of the cypress of the garden, and of the box tree of the sward I have.

گرم صد لشکر از خوبان به قصد دل کمین سازند

If in design upon my heart, a hundred armies of lovely ones ambush make,

بحمد الله و المنه بتی لشکرشکن دارم

Ba hamd-i-Ilahu va-l-minnat[1], an idol, army-shatterer (the true Beloved) I have.

سزد کز خاتم لعلش زنم لاف سلیمانی

Of the seal-ring of His ruby lip, it is fit that a Sulaiman-like boast I should express

چو اسم اعظمم باشد چه باک از اهرمن دارم

When mine is the ism-i-a'zam[2] (the great name) of Ahriman[3], what fear (is it that) I have.

الا ای پیر فرزانه مکن عیبم ز میخانه

O learned Pir[4] Ho the wine-house, forbid me not

که من در ترک پیمانه دلی پیمان شکن دارم

For, in abandoning the wine-cup, a heart, promise-shattering I have.

خدا را ای رقیب امشب زمانی دیده بر هم نه

O watcher for God's sake, to-night, a while, thy eyes close

که من با لعل خاموشش نهانی صد سخن دارم

For, with His silent ruby lip, a hundred secret words, I have.

چو در گلزار اقبالش خرامانم بحمدالله

When in the rose-bed of his favour, I proudly move Praise be to God

نه میل لاله و نسرین نه برگ نسترن دارم

Inclination neither for the tulip and the wild white rose nor for the narcissus, I have.

به رندی شهره شد حافظ میان همدمان لیکن

(After abstinence like this), notorious for profligacy Hafiz became,

چه غم دارم که در عالم قوام الدین حسن دارم

What grief have I, when (as patron) in the world Aminu-d-Dm Hasan[5], I have.

غزل ۳۲۸ ⓄⒹⒺ ③②⑧

من که باشم که بر آن خاطر عاطر گذرم

Who am I that, over that fragrant (noble) mind, I should pass

لطف‌ها می‌کنی ای خاک درت تاج سرم

Thou doest me favours. O dust of Thy door the crown of my head, be

---

دلبرا بنده نوازیت که آموخت بگو
O heart-ravisher slave-cherishing, taught Thee who Say,

که من این ظن به رقیبان تو هرگز نبرم
For to Thy watchers, this idea never will I impute.

همتم بدرقه راه کن ای طایر قدس
O holy bird (the perfect murshid) thy blessing the guide of my path, make

که دراز است ره مقصد و من نوسفرم
For, to our goal, long is the Path new to journeying, am I.

ای نسیم سحری بندگی من برسان
Morning breeze my service cause to reach (the murshid)

که فراموش مکن وقت دعای سحرم
Saying: Me, at the time of the prayer of morn, forget not.

خرم آن روز کز این مرحله بربندم بار
Happy that day, when, from this stage (this world) my chattels (of existence) I bind

و از سر کوی تو پرسند رفیقان خبرم
And, from the head of Thy street, news of me, the companions ask (saying Where went he)

حافظا شاید اگر در طلب گوهر وصل
O Hafiz! it is fit if, in thy search for the jewel of union,

دیده دریا کنم از اشک و در او غوطه خورم
With tears, my eye I make an ocean and, in it, dive.

پایه نظم بلند است و جهان گیر بگو
Lofty, is the rank of verse and world-captivating. Speak

تا کند پادشه بحر دهان پرگهرم
So that, full of pearls, thy mouth the ocean-king may make.

غزل ۳۲۹ ⓄⒹⒺ ③②⑨

جوزا سحر نهاد حمایل برابرم
In the morning, Jauza (Gemini) placed before me the preservation (the small Kuran)

یعنی غلام شاهم و سوگند می‌خورم
That is The King's slave, I am and the oath, I ate.

ساقی بیا که از مدد بخت کارساز
Saki[1] come for, from effective fortune' said,

کامی که خواستم ز خدا شد میسرم
The desire that I desired became to me, through God attainable.

جامی بده که باز به شادی روی شاه
A cup, give for again in joy of the King's face,

پیرانه سر هوای جوانیست در سرم
Elderly of head, in my head, is desire for a youthful one

راهم مزن به وصف زلال خضر که من
Waylay me not with the description of the limpid water of Khizr[2]

از جام شاه جرعه کش حوض کوثرم
From the King's cup, a draught-drinker of Kausar's[3] fountain, am I.

1-Tapster
2-Name of a prophet

3-Spring head

شاها اگر به عرش رسانم سریر فضل

O King if to the ninth heaven (God's throne) I cause the throne of excellence to reach,

مملوک این جنابم و مسکین این درم

Of this majesty, the purchased slave, am I and of this door, the wretched one.

من جرعه نوش بزم تو بودم هزار سال

A thousand years, draught-drinker of Thy banquet, I was

کی ترک آبخورد کند طبع خوگرم

My disposition, ardent of temperament, water-drinking, how may it abandon

ور باورت نمی‌کند از بنده این حدیث

If, of the slave of this tale, belief be not thine

از گفته کمال دلیلی بیاورم

Of perfect speech, a proof I will bring.

گر برکنم دل از تو و بردارم از تو مهر

If, from thee, I up-pluck my heart and, from thee, up-lift my love,

آن مهر بر که افکنم آن دل کجا برم

On whom, may I cast this love; where, may I taketh at heart

منصور بن مظفر غازیست حرز من

Mansur bin Muhamad Ghazi[1] is my guard

و از این خجسته نام بر اعدا مظفرم

From this auspicious name, victorious over my enemies am I.

عهد الست من همه با عشق شاه بود

All in love for the King, was my covenant of Alast

و از شاهراه عمر بدین عهد بگذرم

From life's highway to this covenant, I pass.

گردون چو کرد نظم ثریا به نام شاه

Since, in the King's name, the sphere framed the Pleiades

من نظم در چرا نکنم از که کمترم

Verse of pearl, where fore make I not Less than who, am I

شاهین صفت چو طعمه چشیدم ز دست شاه

When, from the King's hand, I tasted the victuals like (the mighty) falcon,

کی باشد التفات به صید کبوترم

For the capture of the (mean) pigeon, care how is mine

ای شاه شیرگیر چه کم گردد ار شود

O King, lion-seizer less, how becometh, if becometh

در سایه تو ملک فراغت میسرم

Attainable by me, in thy shadow, the country of ease

شعرم به یمن مدح تو صد ملک دل گشاد

In the felicity of praise of thee, my verse subdued a hundred countries of the heart

گوبی که تیغ توست زبان سخنورم

Thou mayst say that my speaking tongue is thy (cleaving) word.

1-King

بر گلشنی اگر بگذشتم چو باد صبح
If, like the morning breeze, by a rose-bed, I passed,

نی عشق سرو بود و نه شوق صنوبرم
Mine, was neither love for the cypress nor desire for the cone-tree

بوی تو می‌شنیدم و بر یاد روی تو
Thy perfume, I perceived and to the memory of thy face,

دادند ساقیان طرب یک دو ساغرم
The Saki[1]s of joy gave me one or two cups.

مستی به آب یک دو عنب وضع بنده نیست
Not the slave's custom is intoxication with the juice of one or two grapes

من سالخورده پیر خرابات پرورم
Years endured, the Pir[2], tavern-cherisher, am I

با سیر اختر فلکم داوری بسیست
With the revolution of the star (and of) the sky, many a strife is mine

انصاف شاه باد در این قصه یاورم
In this tale, be the King's justice, my ruler

شکر خدا که باز در این اوج بارگاه
Thanks to God, that, again, in this height of court,

طاووس عرش می‌شنود صیت شهپرم
The sound of my long wing-feather (of flight) the peacock of the ninth heaven heareth

نامم ز کارخانه عشاق محو باد
Effaced be my name from the work-shop of the lovers (of God)

گر جز محبت تو بود شغل دیگرم
If mine be other employment save love for Thee.

شبل الاسد به صید دلم حمله کرد و من
For the capture of my heart, the lion's whelp attacked

گر لاغرم وگرنه شکار غضنفرم
Lean, if I be, or if not, the lion's prey I am.

ای عاشقان روی تو از ذره بیشتر
O Thou, the lovers of whose face (are in number) more than the atoms (in the sun – beam)

من کی رسم به وصل تو کز ذره کمترم
To union with Thee, how may reach I who (in capacity) less than an atom, am

بنما به من که منکر حسن رخ تو کیست
Show to me, the denier of the beauty of Thy face, who is he

تا دیده‌اش به گزلک غیرت برآورم
So that, with the dagger of jealousy, his eye I may bring forth.

بر من فتاد سایه خورشید سلطنت
On me, fell the shadow of the (symbolic) sun of empire

و اکنون فراغت است ز خورشید خاورم
Now, (as) to the (material) sun of the east, rest (independence) is mine.

مقصود از این معامله بازارتیزی است
Not brisk is the market of purpose of these deeds:

نی جلوه می‌فروشم و نی عشوه می‌خرم
Neither splendour, do I boast nor ease, do I purchase.

1-Tapster   2-A Muslim saint or holy man

غزل ۳۳۰ ⓄⒹⒺ ③③⓪

تو همچو صبحی و من شمع خلوت سحرم
Like the morning (of laughing forehead) Thou art, and the candle of the chamber of the morning, I am

تبسمی کن و جان بین که چون همی‌سپرم
Smile and be hold how (for Thee) my soul, I surrender

چنین که در دل من داغ زلف سرکش توست
In my heart, the stain of (love for) Thy heart-alluring tress is so (in dwelling) that

بنفشه زار شود تربتم چو درگذرم
When (from this vanishing world) I pass, my tomb becometh the (dark) violet bed.

بر آستان مرادت گشاده‌ام در چشم
On the threshold of hope of Thee, I have opened my eye

که یک نظر فکنی خود فکندی از نظرم
That Thou mayest cast one glance from Thy glance, me Thou Thy self castedest.

چه شکر گویمت ای خیل غم عفاک الله
O crowd of griefs to thee, how may I utter thanks God forgive thee

که روز بی‌کسی آخر نمی‌روی ز سرم
On the day of friendlessness, at last, from my bosom thou goest not.

غلام مردم چشمم که با سیاه دلی
I am the slave of the man of vision, who, notwithstanding his black-hearted-ness,

هزار قطره ببارد چو درد دل شمرم
Raineth a thousand drops (tears) when my heart's pain, I recount.

به هر نظر بت ما جلوه می‌کند لیکن
One very side, our idol (divine bounty) displayeth splendour but,

کس این کرشمه نبیند که من همی‌نگرم
This glance that I keep glancing, none seeth.

به خاک حافظ اگر یار بگذرد چون باد
If the Beloved like the (fragrant) breeze pass to the tomb of Hafiz

ز شوق در دل آن تنگنا کفن بدرم
From desire (of that Beloved) in the heart of that narrow place (the grave) the shroud, I rend.

غزل ۳۳۱ ⓄⒹⒺ ③③①

به تیغم گر کشد دستش نگیرم
If, with the sword (of tyranny) He (the true Beloved) slay me, His hand, I seize not

وگر تیرم زند منت پذیرم
If, upon me, this arrow He strike, obliged I am.

کمان ابرویت را گو بزن تیر
To (the true Beloved) say (At that) our eye brow, Thy arrow strike,

که پیش دست و بازویت بمیرم
That, before Thy hand and arm, I may die.

غم گیتی گر از پایم درآرد
If, me from off my feet, the world's grief bring,

بجز ساغر که باشد دستگیرم
Save the cup, my hand-seizer (helper) is who

برآی ای آفتاب صبح امید

O Sun of the morning of hope (the true Beloved) come forth

که در دست شب هجران اسیرم

For, in the hand of the (dark) night of separation, captive am I

به فریادم رس ای پیر خرابات

O Pir[1] of the tavern (the murshid excellent and perfect) come to my cry (for justice)

به یک جرعه جوانم کن که پیرم

By a draught, me young make for old am I

به گیسوی تو خوردم دوش سوگند

Last night, by thy tress, I ate an oath,

که من از پای تو سر بر نگیرم

That, my head, from off thy foot, I will not take.

بسوز این خرقه تقوا تو حافظ

Hafiz this, thy Khirka[2] of piety, (hard as iron, void of tenderness) consume (with fire)

که گر آتش شوم در وی نگیرم

For (even) if a (consuming) fire I became, I should kindle it not.

غزل ۳۳۲ ODE 332

مزن بر دل ز نوک غمزه تیرم

With the point of Thy arrow-glance, at my heart, strike not

که پیش چشم بیمارت بمیرم

For, before Thy sick (languishing) eye, I die.

نصاب حسن در حد کمال است

Within the limit of excellence, is the (lawful) portion of beauty

زکاتم ده که مسکین و فقیرم

Me, alms give for miserable and fakir[3], I am.

چو طفلان تا کی ای زاهد فریبی

O Zahid[4] like boys, how long (practisest thou towards me) deceitfulness,

به سیب بوستان و شهد و شیرم

With the apple of the garden (of paradise) and the honey, and the milk (of the garden)

چنان پر شد فضای سینه از دوست

With the Friend, my heart's space became full to such a degree,

که فکر خویش گم شد از ضمیرم

That, lost from my mind, became the thought of self.

قدح پر کن که من در دولت عشق

Full, make the goblet for from love's fortune, I

جوان بخت جهانم گر چه پیرم

(Will make) youthful fortune to leap, though old I am.

قراری بسته‌ام با می فروشان

With the wine-sellers, an arrangement I have made,

که روز غم بجز ساغر نگیرم

That, on grief's day, naught save the cup (of love) of I take.

1-A Muslim saint or holy man
2-Cloak

3-Poor
4-Pietist

مبادا جز حساب مطرب و می

Be naught save the account of the minstrel and of wine

اگر نقشی کشد کلک دبیرم

If a word the reed of my secretary write.

در این غوغا که کس کس را نپرسد

In that tumult (of the resurrection) when another's (state) none asketh,

من از پیر مغان منت پذیرم

From the Pir of the Magians (Muhammad) the favour (of acceptance before God) I accept

خوشا آن دم کز استغنای مستی

O happy that moment when in dependence of intoxication,

فراغت باشد از شاه و وزیرم

Me, freedom from dependence on the king and the vazir giveth,

من آن مرغم که هر شام و سحرگاه

I am that bird such that, every evening and morning,

ز بام عرش می‌آید صفیرم

From the roof, the ninth heaven, cometh the cry of mine

چو حافظ گنج او در سینه دارم

In the heart, great treasures I have

اگر چه مدعی بیند حقیرم

Although me, poor (and indigent) the adversary regardeth.

غزل ۳۳۳ ⓄⒹⒺ ③③③

نماز شام غریبان چو گریه آغازم

At the time of the evening-prayer of strangers when weeping I begin,

به مویه‌های غریبانه قصه پردازم

With moans like a stranger, my tale, I compose

به یاد یار و دیار آن چنان بگریم زار

To the memory of the Friend and of my (native) land so bitterly I weep

که از جهان ره و رسم سفر براندازم

That, up from the world, the way and usage of journeying, I cast

من از دیار حبیبم نه از بلاد غریب

From the country of my (true) Beloved I am not from the cities of the stranger

مهیمنا به رفیقان خود رسان بازم

O Divine Protector Me, back to my companions, cause to reach.

خدای را مددی ای رفیق ره تا من

O guide of the Path for God's sake, a little aid (give) so that

به کوی میکده دیگر علم برافرازم

In the street of the wine-house, my banner, again I may exalt

خرد ز پیری من کی حساب برگیرد

Of my being a Pir[1], reckoning how may wisdom take,

که باز با صنمی طفل عشق می‌بازم

When, again, with a child-idol at love I play.

1-A Muslim saint or holy man

بجز صبا و شمالم نمی‌شناسد کس

Save the east morning breeze and the (cool) north wind, me recogniseth none

عزیز من که بجز باد نیست دمسازم

O my friend for, save the (fleeting) wind, my companion is none.

هوای منزل یار آب زندگانی ماست

The air of the Friend's dwelling is our water of life,

صبا بیار نسیمی ز خاک شیرازم

O breeze from the dust of Shiraz, me, a fragrant perfume bring.

سرشکم آمد و عیبم بگفت روی به روی

Forth came my tear and told my crime face to face (publicly)

شکایت از که کنم خانگیست غمازم

Complaint may I make of whom of my house hold, the informer is.

ز چنگ زهره شنیدم که صبحدم می‌گفت

From the harp of Zuhra[1], I heard that, at dawn, it said

غلام حافظ خوش لهجه خوش آوازم

The disciple of Hafiz, sweet of note, sweet of voice I am.

غزل ۳۳۴ ⓄⒹⒺ ③③④

گر دست رسد در سر زلفین تو بازم

IF into the curl of Thy two tresses, my hand again should reach,

چون گوی چه سرها که به چوگان تو بازم

With Thy chaugan, what heads (there are) that like a ball, I shall play.

زلف تو مرا عمر دراز است ولی نیست

Long life to me is Thy (long) tress but there is not

در دست سر مویی از آن عمر درازم

In my hand, a hair-tip of this long life.

پروانه راحت بده ای شمع که امشب

O candle (Beloved) give the order for rest. For, to-night,

از آتش دل پیش تو چون شمع گدازم

From the heart's fire, before Thee, like the consuming candle I melt.

آن دم که به یک خنده دهم جان چو صراحی

That moment when, with a laugh, life I give up like the flagon

مستان تو خواهم که گزارند نمازم

I would that a prayer for me Thy intoxicated ones should offer.

چون نیست نماز من آلوده نمازی

Since the prayer of me stained is not an (acceptable) prayer

در میکده زان کم نشود سوز و گدازم

In the wine-house, on that account less are not my burning and consuming.

در مسجد و میخانه خیالت اگر آید

In the masjid[2] and in the wine-house, if Thy Image come

محراب و کمانچه ز دو ابروی تو سازم

Of Thy two eye-brows, I make the prayer-arch of praying and the lute (of wailing)

1-Refers to the planet Venus, the symbol of the beloved   2-Mosque

گر خلوت ما را شبی از رخ بفروزی

If, one night with Thy face, my khilvat[1], Thou illumine,

چون صبح بر آفاق جهان سر بفرازم

Like the morning in the horizons of the world, my head, I exalt.

محمود بود عاقبت کار در این راه

In this path (of love) laudable is the end of (love's) work

گر سر برود در سر سودای ایازم

If, in desire of passion for Ayaz[2] (the true Beloved) the my head goeth.

حافظ غم دل با که بگویم که در این دور

Hafiz the heart's grief, to whom shall I utter

جز جام نشاید که بود محرم رازم

Not fit is it that, save the cup, the confidant of mystery be mine.

غزل ۳۳۵ ⓄⒹⒺ ③③⑤

در خرابات مغان گر گذر افتد بازم

If again be fall me passing into the tavern of the Magians[3] (the perfect murshid)

حاصل خرقه و سجاده روان دربازم

The produce of the Khirka[4] and of the prayer-mat, running (recklessly) I will play away (and lose)

حلقه توبه گر امروز چو زهاد زنم

If to-day, like the Zahid[5]s, I beat the ring of penitence,

خازن میکده فردا نکند در بازم

To-morrow, open to me the door, the wine-house-guardian maketh not.

ور چو پروانه دهد دست فراغ بالی

If like the moth, freedom from care aid me,

جز بدان عارض شمعی نبود پروازم

Save to that candle-like (luminous) cheek, no flight is mine.

صحبت حور نخواهم که بود عین قصور

The society of the Hur[6], I desire not. For, the essence of defect it is

با خیال تو اگر با دگری پردازم

If, despite the fancy for Thee, with another, I disport.

سر سودای تو در سینه بماندی پنهان

Hidden in my chest would have remained passion's desire for Thee,

چشم تردامن اگر فاش نگردی رازم

If my eye, wet of skirt, the secret had not revealed.

مرغ سان از قفس خاک هوایی گشتم

Like the bird from the cage of dust (the dusty body) I became of the air (flying here and there, and searching)

به هوایی که مگر صید کند شهبازم

In the desire that, perchance, me the falcon (the perfect murshid or the Aril) a prey may make.

1-Solitude

2-Refers to the planet Venus, the symbol of the beloved

3-Fire worshipper

4-Cloak

5-Pietist

6-Lover

همچو چنگ ار به کناری ندهی کام دلم
If like the (cord – slackened) harp, me by reason of the slackness (of its cords) the
heart's desire thou give not,
از لب خویش چو نی یک نفسی بنوازم
(At last With Thy lips, with) a breath, me, like the reed (flute) cherish

ماجرای دل خون گشته نگویم با کس
To none, I utter the circumstances of my heart, blood become
زان که جز تیغ غمت نیست کسی دمسازم
Since that, save the sword of grief for Thee, my fellow-consoler is none.

گر به هر موی سری بر تن حافظ باشد
If, on Hafiz's body, be a head fore very hair.
همچو زلفت همه را در قدمت اندازم
Like Thy (long trailing) tress, all at Thy feet, I cast.

غزل ۳۳۶ ⓞⓓⓔ ③③⑥

مژده وصل تو کو کز سر جان برخیزم
Where, the glad tidings of union with Thee, so that, from desire of life, I may rise
طایر قدسم و از دام جهان برخیزم
The holy bird (of paradise) am I from the world's snare, I rise.

به ولای تو که گر بنده خویشم خوانی
By Thy love (I swear) that, if me, Thy slave, Thou call,
از سر خواجگی کون و مکان برخیزم
Out from desire of lord ship of existence and dwelling (both worlds) I rise.

یا رب از ابر هدایت برسان بارانی
O Lord! from the cloud of guidance, the rain (of mercy) cause to arrive
پیشتر زان که چو گردی ز میان برخیزم
Before that, from the midst, like a (handful of) dust, I rise.

بر سر تربت من با می و مطرب بنشین
(O holy traveller) at the head of my tomb, without wine and the minstrel, sit not
تا به بویت ز لحد رقص کنان برخیزم
So that by thy perfume, dancing, I may rise.

خیز و بالا بنما ای بت شیرین حرکات
O Idol, sweet of motion arise and Thy (lofty, cypress like) stature display
کز سر جان و جهان دست فشان برخیزم
By the sky's tyranny or by time's violence, I rise.

گر چه پیرم تو شبی تنگ در آغوشم کش
Though I am old, one night me, close in Thy embrace take
تا سحرگه ز کنار تو جوان برخیزم
So that, in the morning, from Thy embrace, young I may rise.

روز مرگم نفسی مهلت دیدار بده
Think not that, from the dust of head of thy street,
تا چو حافظ ز سر جان و جهان برخیزم
That, like Hafiz, from desire of life and of the world I may rise

غزل ۳۳۷ ⓄⒹⒺ ③③⑦

چرا نه در پی عزم دیار خود باشم

In the pursuit of the desire of visiting my own (native) Land, why should I not be

چرا نه خاک سر کوی یار خود باشم

The dust of the head of my (true) Beloved's street, why should I not be

غم غریبی و غربت چو بر نمی‌تابم

When the load of grief of being a stranger and the trouble, I bear not,

به شهر خود روم و شهریار خود باشم

To my own city, I go and, my own monarch, I shall be.

ز محرمان سراپرده وصال شوم

Of the confidential ones of the veil of union I shall be

ز بندگان خداوندگار خود باشم

Of the slaves of my own Lord, I shall be.

چو کار عمر نه پیداست باری آن اولی

Since life's work (how it will pass how long it will show fidelity) is unknown, at least that is best

که روز واقعه پیش نگار خود باشم

That, on the day of events (the day of death) before (God) my idol (engaged in zikr and fikr[1]; and, from that exterior to God, turned away) I shall be

ز دست بخت گران خواب و کار بی‌سامان

Of the hand of fortune, heavy with sleep and of resourceless work,

گرم بود گله‌ای رازدار خود باشم

If complaint be mine, my own secret-keeper, I shall be.

همیشه پیشه من عاشقی و رندی بود

The being a lover and a profligate was ever my way

دگر بکوشم و مشغول کار خود باشم

Again, I will strive and engaged in my own work I shall be.

بود که لطف ازل رهنمون شود حافظ

Hafiz perchance, the grace of eternity without beginning may be thy guide

وگرنه تا به ابد شرمسار خود باشم

If not, to eternity without end, ashamed of self, I shall be.

غزل ۳۳۸ ⓄⒹⒺ ③③⑧

من دوستدار روی خوش و موی دلکشم

The friend I am of the sweet face; and of the heart-alluring hair:

مدهوش چشم مست و می صاف بی‌غشم

Distraught with the intoxicated eye, I am and with pure unalloyed wine

گفتی ز سر عهد ازل یک سخن بگو

Thou askedest Of the mystery of the covenant of eternity without beginning, say one word,

آن گه بگویمت که دو پیمانه درکشم

(I reply) That moment when two cups of wine, I drink, I will tell thee.

1- Mention and thought, preoccupation

من آدم بهشتیم اما در این سفر

Adam[1] of paradise, I am but in this journey (through this world)

حالی اسیر عشق جوانان مه وشم

Now, captive to the love of youthful ones (I am).

در عاشقی گزیر نباشد ز ساز و سوز

In being a lover (of God) is no escape from consuming and (yet) being content

استاده‌ام چو شمع مترسان ز آتشم

Like the candle, standing I am me of the fire (of love) affright not

شیراز معدن لب لعل است و کان حسن

The mine of the ruby lip and the quarry of beauty is Shiraz

من جوهری مفلسم ایرا مشوشم

On that account, harassed am I, the poor jeweller.

از بس که چشم مست در این شهر دیده‌ام

From the many intoxicated eyes that in this city (of Shiraz) I have be held,

حقا که می نمی‌خورم اکنون و سرخوشم

O God (I swear) that, now, no wine, I drink and (yet) merry of head I am.

شهریست پر کرشمه حوران ز شش جهت

From six directions, 'tis a city full of the glance of lovely ones

چیزیم نیست ور نه خریدار هر ششم

Not a thing is mine if not of all six, purchaser I be.

بخت ار مدد دهد که کشم رخت سوی دوست

If fortune aid so that, to the Friend, my chattels, I draw (such my dignity will be that)

گیسوی حور گرد فشاند ز مفرشم

The (fragrant) dust from my couch, (even) the (be perfumed) tress of the Hur[2] will wipe

حافظ عروس طبع مرا جلوه آرزوست

Hafiz the bride of my nature desireth splendour

آیینه‌ای ندارم از آن آه می‌کشم

No mirror have I, on that account (being mirrorless) sigh, I heave.

غزل ۳۳۹ ⓄⒹⒺ ③③⑨

خیال روی تو چون بگذرد به گلشن چشم

When to the rose-bed of the eye, passeth the fancy of Thy face,

دل از پی نظر آید به سوی روزن چشم

For the sake of be holding Thee, cometh the heart to the window of the eye

سزای تکیه گهت منظری نمی‌بینم

Fit for Thy resting-place, no place I see.

منم ز عالم و این گوشه معین چشم

Of the world, am I and this established corner of the eye.

بیا که لعل و گهر در نثار مقدم تو

(O Beloved) Come for in scattering for Thy (auspicious) arrival, the ruby (bloody tears) and the jewel (lustrous tears)

ز گنج خانه دل می‌کشم به روزن چشم

From the treasure of the house of the heart, I draw to the treasury of the eye

---

1- Human

2- Heavenly women with black eyes, nymph

سحر سرشک روانم سر خرابی داشت

In the morning, my flowing tears, the thought of my ruin had

گرم نه خون جگر می‌گرفت دامن چشم

If the blood of my liver had not caught the skirt of the eye.

نخست روز که دیدم رخ تو دل می‌گفت

On the first day when I be held Thy face, my heart said

اگر رسد خللی خون من به گردن چشم

If (me) an injury reach (the wrong of shedding), my blood (will be) on the neck of the eye

به بوی مژده وصل تو تا سحر شب دوش

In the hope of the Glad tidings of union with Thee, till morning, last night,

به راه باد نهادم چراغ روشن چشم

On the wind's path, I placed the luminous lamp of the eye.

به مردمی که دل دردمند حافظ را

In manliness (I conjure thee), Hafiz's sorrowful heart,

مزن به ناوک دلدوز مردم افکن چشم

Strike not with the arrow-point, heart-stitching, man-overthrowing of the eye

غزل ۳۴۰ ⓄⒹⒺ ③④⓪

من که از آتش دل چون خم می در جوشم

Although from the heart's fire, like a (foaming) jar of wine, in tumult I am,

مهر بر لب زده خون می‌خورم و خاموشم

The seal (of silence) on my lip pressed, the blood (of grief) I drink and silent I am.

قصد جان است طمع در لب جانان کردن

To show desire for the lip of the (true) Beloved is (to make) an attempt upon (one's own) life

تو مرا بین که در این کار به جان می‌کوشم

Be hold thou me who, in this matter, with soul (strenuously) strive

من کی آزاد شوم از غم دل چون هر دم

Free from the heart's grief, how may I become, when, momently,

هندوی زلف بتی حلقه کند در گوشم

The Hindu of the tress of the idol (the true Beloved) me, beringed (as His slave) maketh

حاش لله که نیم معتقد طاعت خویش

God forbid not trusting to my own devotion, am I

این قدر هست که گه گه قدحی می نوشم

(Only) This is the extent that, sometimes, a goblet of the wine (of love to God) I drink
(and in it strive)

هست امیدم که علیرغم عدو روز جزا

Hope is mine that despite the enemy (shaitan) on the day of requital (resurrection – day)

فیض عفوش ننهد بار گنه بر دوشم

Not, on my back, will the bounty of His pardon place the load of sin.

پدرم روضه رضوان به دو گندم بفروخت

For two wheat-grains, my Father, (Adam) sold the garden of Rizvan (paradise)

من چرا ملک جهان را به جوی نفروشم

(If), for a barley-grain, I sell it not, (un worthy son I shall be).

خرقه پوشی من از غایت دین داری نیست

Not from exceeding religiousness, is my inducing of the Khirka[1]

پرده‌ای بر سر صد عیب نهان می‌پوشم

Over the head of a hundred secret sins, a veil (the khirka) I place

من که خواهم که ننوشم بجز از راوق خم

I who desire not to drink save of the purest wine

چه کنم گر سخن پیر مغان ننیوشم

What shall I do, if the speech of the Pir of the Magians, I hear not

گر از این دست زند مطرب مجلس ره عشق

If with this hand (way) the minstrel of the assembly (the perfect murshid) waylayeth, love (rendering lovers selfless and drawing them into his net)

شعر حافظ ببرد وقت سماع از هوشم

(Even so) At the time of sama'[2], me, from sense, the (lustrous) verse of Hafiz taketh.

غزل ۳۴۱ ⓄⒹⒺ ③④① ODE

گر من از سرزنش مدعیان اندیشم

For the reproof of the adversaries if I care,

شیوه مستی و رندی نرود از پیشم

(Lustre) taketh not (my) way of profligacy and of intoxication.

زهد رندان نوآموخته راهی بدهیست

The austerity of profligates (disciples and seekers of God) path newly learned, is fruitless

من که بدنام جهانم چه صلاح اندیشم

I, who am the ill name of the world, what remedy (for it) may I devise

شاه شوریده سران خوان من بی‌سامان را

Me, resourceless (of wisdom) king of those distraught of head, call

زان که در کم خردی از همه عالم بیشم

On that account that, in being one of little wisdom, greater than all the world I am.

بر جبین نقش کن از خون دل من خالی

(O true Beloved) On Thy forehead with my heart's blood, a great mole depict

تا بدانند که قربان تو کافر کیشم

So that they (men) may know that, sacrifice for Thee, kafir of religion, I am

اعتقادی بنما و بگذر بهر خدا

Trust, display and for God's sake, pass on

تا در این خرقه ندانی که چه نادرویشم

So that thou mayst know, in this Khirka what a no-dervish I am.

شعر خونبار من ای باد بدان یار رسان

O breeze my blood-raining verse utter to the Friend,

که ز مژگان سیه بر رگ جان زد نیشم

Who, me, on life's great vein, with His black eye-lash, lanced

من اگر باده خورم ور نه چه کارم با کس

Whether (I be profligate) or (whether shaikh Pir) to any one my work is what

حافظ راز خود و عارف وقت خویشم

Of my own mystery Hafiz and of my time, the Arif[3], I am.

1-Cloak
2-Dance

3-Mystic

غزل ۳۴۲ ⓞⒹⒺ ③④②

حجاب چهره جان می‌شود غبار تنم

The dust of my body is the veil of the (true) Beloved's face

خوشا دمی که از آن چهره پرده برفکنم

O happy that moment when from off this face, the veil I cast

چنین قفس نه سزای چو من خوش الحانیست

Not fit for a sweet singer like me, is the cage (of the world) like this

روم به گلشن رضوان که مرغ آن چمنم

To Rizvan's rose-bed, I go for the bird of that sward am I

عیان نشد که چرا آمدم کجا رفتم

Manifest, it is not where fore, I have come (into this world) where, I had been

دریغ و درد که غافل ز کار خویشتنم

Regret and sorrow that, of my own work, careless I am

چگونه طوف کنم در فضای عالم قدس

In the expanse of the holy world, my circuit how may I make

که در سراچه ترکیب تخته بند تنم

When, in the mixed a b ode (this dusty world) plank-bound (confined) to a (dusty) body, I am.

اگر ز خون دلم بوی شوق می‌آید

If, from my heart's blood, the perfume of musk issue,

عجب مدار که همدرد نافه ختنم

Have no wonder for fellow-sufferer with the musk-pod of Khutan[1] (the musk – deer) I am.

طراز پیرهن زرکشم مبین چون شمع

(Outwardly) Regard not the embroidery of my gold-thread tunic (resplendent) like the candle,
(saying He is happy)

که سوزهاست نهانی درون پیرهنم

For, within the tunic, hidden consuming sate.

بیا و هستی حافظ ز پیش او بردار

Come and from before him, the existence of Hafiz take up

که با وجود تو کس نشنود ز من که منم

For, with Thy existence, none heareth from me that I am living

غزل ۳۴۳ ⓞⒹⒺ ③④③

چل سال بیش رفت که من لاف می‌زنم

Passed have forty years (and) more since I expressed this boast

کز چاکران پیر مغان کمترین منم

Of the servants of the Pir of the Magians, the least am I.

هرگز به یمن عاطفت پیر می فروش

Ever by the felicity of the favour of the Pir[2], the wine-seller,

ساغر تهی نشد ز می صاف روشنم

Empty of wine, pure (and) luminous, became not the cup of mine.

1-An area of great China   2-A Muslim saint or holy man, Pietist

از جاه عشق و دولت رندان پاکباز

In the majesty of love, and in the fortune of profligates, pure-players,

پیوسته صدر مصطبه‌ها بود مسکنم

Ever the chief seat of the wine-houses was the ab ode of mine.

در شان من به دردکشی ظن بد مبر

For dreg-drinking, bear not an ill opinion of me (Hafiz)

کلوده گشت جامه ولی پاکدامنم

For, (with wine) the Khirka[1] is stained but pure of skirt am I.

شهباز دست پادشهم این چه حالت است

The (mighty) falcon of the King's hand am I.O Lord in what way.

کز یاد برده‌اند هوای نشیمنم

From my recollection, have they taken the desire of the dwelling of mine

حیف است بلبلی چو من اکنون در این قفس

A great bulbul[2] like me, in such a sward, pity' tis,

با این لسان عذب که خامش چو سوسنم

That, with this sweet tongue (verse) silent like the (ten – tongued) lily am I.

آب و هوای فارس عجب سفله پرور است

A wonderful cherisher of the mean is the water and the air of Persia:

کو همرهی که خیمه از این خاک برکنم

A fellow way-farer, where, that, from this land, my tent, up-pluck I may

حافظ به زیر خرقه قدح تا به کی کشی

Hafiz beneath (the guise of) the Khirka[3], how long drinketh thou the goblet

در بزم خواجه پرده ز کارت برافکنم

(God willing) At the Khwaja[4]'s banquet, the veil from thy work (of drinking) upcast will I

تورانشه خجسته که در من یزید فضل

The auspicious Turan King, who, towards me, increased his favour

شد منت مواهب او طوق گردنم

The favour of his gifts became the collar of the neck of mine.

غزل ۳۴۴ ⓄⒹⒺ ③④④

عمریست تا من در طلب هر روز گامی می‌زنم

Tis a life-time since, in search (of good fame) every day, a pace I cast:

دست شفاعت هر زمان در نیک نامی می‌زنم

Every moment, the hand of entreaty on good fame I cast.

بی ماه مهرافروز خود تا بگذرانم روز خود

Without my moon (the Beloved) love-kindling, let me see how my day I pass:

دامی به راهی می‌نهم مرغی به دامی می‌زنم

On a path, a net I lay a fowl in the snare, I cast.

اورنگ کو گلچهر کو نقش وفا و مهر کو

Aurang[5] (the lover) where Gulchihra[6] (the beloved) where The picture of fidelity and of love, where

حالی من اندر عاشقی داو تمامی می‌زنم

Now, in being a lover, complete justice I cast.

1-Cloak
2-Nightingale
3-Cloak

4-Eunuch, dignitary, vizier, boss, host
5-A person who loves Gulchihra
6-Aurang's mistress

تا بو که یابم آگهی از سایه سرو سهی
Since it may be that, of that shade of the straight cypress the Beloved news I may gain,
گلبانگ عشق از هر طرف بر خوش خرامی می‌زنم
From every side, love's clamour in respect of a pleasant strutter (possessed of beauty) I cast.

هر چند کان آرام دل دانم نبخشد کام دل
Although I know that heart's ease giveth not the heart's desire
نقش خیالی می‌کشم فال دوامی می‌زنم
An ideal picture, I draw an omen of immortality, I cast.

دانم سر آرد غصه را رنگین برآرد قصه را
I know grief to an end, it bringeth colour to wine, it bringeth,
این آه خون افشان که من هر صبح و شامی می‌زنم
This sigh, blood-shedding, that every morning and evening, I cast.

با آن که از وی غایبم و از می چو حافظ تایبم
Notwithstanding that, hidden from myself selfless I am; and of wine repenting like Hafiz I am
در مجلس روحانیان گه گاه جامی می‌زنم
In the assembly of souls, sometimes a cup I cast.

غزل ۳۴۵ ⓄⒹⒺ ③④⑤

بی تو ای سرو روان با گل و گلشن چه کنم
O morning cypress without thee, with the rose and the rose-bud, what may I do
زلف سنبل چه کشم عارض سوسن چه کنم
The tress of the hyacinth, how may I draw; (with) the cheek of the lily what may I do

آه کز طعنه بدخواه ندیدم رویت
From the reproach of the ill-wisher, alas I be held not Thy face
نیست چون آینه‌ام روی ز آهن چه کنم
When not mine is the (gleaming) mirror, with (dull) iron what may I do

برو ای ناصح و بر دردکشان خرده مگیر
O admonisher go; and at the dreg-drinkers, carp not:
کارفرمای قدر می‌کند این من چه کنم
This, the work-orderer of Fate doeth what may I do

برق غیرت چو چنین می‌جهد از مکمن غیب
When, like this, from the hidden ambush, leapeth the lightning of jealousy,
تو بفرما که من سوخته خرمن چه کنم
Do thou order for I of consumed harvest, what may I do

شاه ترکان چو پسندید و به چاهم انداخت
When the King of the Turans[1] (Afrasiyab) approved and cast me into the pit,
دستگیر ار نشود لطف تهمتن چه کنم
If the grace of Tahamtan[2] (Rustam) be not hand-seizer to (help) what may I do

مددی گر به چراغی نکند آتش طور
If with a lamp (on the path of travellers) Tur's fire (the perfect murshid) make not a little assistance,
چاره تیره شب وادی ایمن چه کنم
(For) The remedy of the dark night of the Wadi-i-Aiman[3] what may I do

---

1-Afrasiab, here is a metaphor of the beloved
2-It means hero (Rustam)

3-Here is the valley and desert of love that has hundreds of dangers and obstacles.

حافظا خلد برین خانه موروث من است
Hafiz highest paradise is the house of my heritage
اندر این منزل ویرانه نشیمن چه کنم
In this desolate stage (this world) my dwelling, why do I make

غزل ۳۴۶ ⓞⒹⒺ ③④⑥

من نه آن رندم که ترک شاهد و ساغر کنم
Not that profligate am I that abandoning of the (true) Beloved and of the cup I make
محتسب داند که من این کارها کمتر کنم
An act like this, the muhtasib[1] knoweth seldom do I make.

من که عیب توبه کاران کرده باشم بارها
I who, years, censured the repenters (of wine – drinking)
توبه از می وقت گل دیوانه باشم گر کنم
Repentance of drinking wine in the rose-season mad shall I be, if I make.

عشق دردانه‌ست و من غواص و دریا میکده
The (precious) pearl-grain is love I (am) the diver the wine-house (is) the sea
سر فروبردم در آن جا تا کجا سر بر کنم
There, my head, I plunged (it) up-lifted, let us see, where shall I make

لاله ساغرگیر و نرگس مست و بر ما نام فسق
Cup-taker (is) the tulip intoxicated, (is) the narcissus the name of impiety, on me
داوری دارم بسی یا رب که را داور کنم
Many a complaint, I have. O Lord! whom, judge shall I make

بازکش یک دم عنان ای ترک شهرآشوب من
O my bold one, city-up setter (the true Beloved) a moment, the rein draw back,
تا ز اشک و چهره راهت پرزر و گوهر کنم
So that, with my (pearly) tears and (ruddy) face, full of (red) gold and of pearls, Thy path I may make.

من که از یاقوت و لعل اشک دارم گنج‌ها
I, who have treasures of the ruby and of the pearl of tears,
کی نظر در فیض خورشید بلنداختر کنم
Desire for the bounty of the sun, lofty of star, how may I make

چون صبا مجموعه گل را به آب لطف شست
When with the water of grace, the breeze washed the bud of the rose,
کجدلم خوان گر نظر بر صفحه دفتر کنم
Me, crooked of heart, call, if at the page of the book (the world) glance, I make.

عهد و پیمان فلک را نیست چندان اعتبار
The credit of the sky's compact and agreement is not so great
عهد با پیمانه بندم شرط با ساغر کنم
Compact with the goblet, I establish condition (covenant) with the cup I make.

من که دارم در گدایی گنج سلطانی به دست
I who, in beggary, have in hand the imperial treasure,
کی طمع در گردش گردون دون پرور کنم
Greed for the revolution of the sphere, mean-cherishing, how may I make

---

1-Sheriff

گر چه گردآلود فقرم شرم باد از همتم

Dust-stained with poverty though I be, of my spirit, be shame,

گر به آب چشمه خورشید دامن تر کنم

If, with the water (of liberality) of the sun's fountain, my skirt wet I make.

عاشقان را گر در آتش می‌پسندد لطف دوست

If the Friend's grace approve (casting) of lovers into the fire (of hell)

تنگ چشمم گر نظر در چشمه کوثر کنم

Closed of eye, I am (even) if, on the fountain of Kausar[1], glance I make

دوش لعلش عشوه‌ای می‌داد حافظ را ولی

Last night, to Hafiz Thy ruby (lip) kept giving false vows

من نه آنم کز وی این افسانه‌ها باور کنم

Not that one am I that belief in these its idle tales, I make

غزل ۳۴۷ ⓄⒹⒺ ③④⑦ ODE 347

صنما با غم عشق تو چه تدبیر کنم

O idol with grief of love for thee what plaint, shall I make?

تا به کی در غم تو ناله شبگیر کنم

In grief for thee, till when the night-seizing wail shall I make?

دل دیوانه از آن شد که نصیحت شنود

Passed (to the true Beloved) my distraught heart on that account that a Remedy It Might accept

مگرش هم ز سر زلف تو زنجیر کنم

Perchance, with Thy tres ode tip, its chain I may make.

آن چه در مدت هجر تو کشیدم هیهات

In the time of separation from Thee, what I endured alas

در یکی نامه محال است که تحریر کنم

'Tis impossible that, in one letter, writing thereof I should make

با سر زلف تو مجموع پریشانی خود

With (on account) of Thy own tres ode tip (is) all my perturbation

کو مجالی که سراسر همه تقریر کنم

Where the power that, all at once, all the narrative, I should make

آن زمان کرزوی دیدن جانم باشد

That time when the desire of be holding the beloved is mine,

در نظر نقش رخ خوب تو تصویر کنم

In the vision, the picturing of Thy lovely face, imagining I make

گر بدانم که وصال تو بدین دست دهد

If I know that, in this way, union with Thee, aid

دین و دل را همه دربازم و توفیر کنم

Heart and faith, all I will play away (and lose) and (yet) increase (thereof) II will make

دور شو از برم ای واعظ و بیهوده مگوی

O admonisher! far from me go foolishness, utter not

من نه آنم که دگر گوش به تزویر کنم

Not that one am I who, again, the ear (of attention) to thy hypocrisy will put

---

1-It is a spring in heaven

نیست امید صلاحی ز فساد حافظ

O Hafiz! hope of freedom from iniquity is none

چون که تقدیر چنین است چه تدبیر کنم

Since fate is like this, what plan (is it that) I should make

غزل ۳۴۸ ⓄⒹⒺ ③④⑧

دیده دریا کنم و صبر به صحرا فکنم

My eye, an ocean (of weeping) I make to the desert, patience, I cast

و اندر این کار دل خویش به دریا فکنم

And, in this work, my heart into the ocean I cast.

از دل تنگ گنهکار برآرم آهی

From the straitened heart the sinner, I heave such a sigh

کاتش اندر گنه آدم و حوا فکنم

That, into the sin of Adam and of Havva[1], fire I cast.

مایه خوشدلی آن جاست که دلدار آن جاست

There, where is the heart-possessor, is the source of happy-heartedness

می‌کنم جهد که خود را مگر آن جا فکنم

I strive that, perchance there, myself, I may cast.

بگشا بند قبا ای مه خورشیدکلاه

O moon, sun of cap (in effulgence) the fastening of thy coat, loose

تا چو زلفت سر سودازده در پا فکنم

So that like thy (long, trailing) tress at thy feet, my passion-stricken head I may cast

خورده‌ام تیر فلک باده بده تا سرمست

The sky's arrow (of affliction) I have endured wine (of love) give, so that, intoxicated of head,

عقده دربند کمر ترکش جوزا فکنم

Into the girdle of the waist of the quiver of Jauza[2] (Gemini) a knot I may cast

جرعه جام بر این تخت روان افشانم

On this moving throne (the revolving sky) a draught of wine, I pour

غلغل چنگ در این گنبد مینا فکنم

Into this azure vault (the sky) the resounding shout of strife, I cast.

حافظا تکیه بر ایام چو سهو است و خطا

O Hafiz! since reliance on time is error and defect,

من چرا عشرت امروز به فردا فکنم

Then, to to-morrow, the pleasure of to-day why do I cast

غزل ۳۴۹ ⓄⒹⒺ ③④⑨

دوش سودای رخش گفتم ز سر بیرون کنم

Last night, I said Out from my head, the passion for His face I will put

گفت کو زنجیر تا تدبیر این مجنون کنم

He (the true Beloved) said The chain where, that the arrangement (of binding) of this distraught one, I may make

---

1-It is forbidden to eat the fruit that caused them to be expelled from heaven and banished to earth.

2-It is the name of a tower of the twelve constellations of the sky

قامتش را سرو گفتم سر کشید از من به خشم

His stature, I called the (straight, free) cypress. In anger, his head from me, He drew back

دوستان از راست می‌رنجد نگارم چون کنم

O friends with the truth, my idol grieveth. What shall I do?

نکته ناسنجیده گفتم دلبرا معذور دار

O heart-ravisher an un-weighed subtlety, I uttered excuse me

عشوه‌ای فرمای تا من طبع را موزون کنم

Graciousness show that my thought weighed in verse I may make.

زردرویی می‌کشم زان طبع نازک بی‌گناه

For that nature, tender, sinless, I endure yellow (shame)-faced ness,

ساقیا جامی بده تا چهره را گلگون کنم

O Saki[1] a cup give, that my face rose of hue I may make.

ای نسیم منزل لیلی خدا را تا به کی

O breeze of Laila's[2] dwelling for God's sake, how long

ربع را برهم زنم اطلال را جیحون کنم

The fourth (inhabited) part of the world shall lover-turn; (and) the palace-ruins (the waste – places) the river Jaihun shall I make

من که ره بردم به گنج حسن بی‌پایان دوست

I, who took the path to the treasure (of mysteries) of boundless beauty of the Friend,

صد گدای همچو خود را بعد از این قارون کنم

After this, a hundred beggars like myself, (rich as) Karun[3] (with divine knowledge) I make

ای مه صاحب قران از بنده حافظ یاد کن

O moon, Lady of felicity thy slave Hafiz, remember,

تا دعای دولت آن حسن روزافزون کنم

So that, for the fortune of that beauty daily increasing, prayer, I may make.

غزل ۳۵۰ ⓄⒹⒺ ③⑤⓪

به عزم توبه سحر گفتم استخاره کنم

In the morning, with the desire of repentance, (to my heart) I said: "I seek the counsel of God,"

بهار توبه شکن می‌رسد چه چاره کنم

Spring, repentance-shatterer, arriveth what remedy may I make

سخن درست بگویم نمی‌توانم دید

True speech, I utter: I cannot see (that this state is very difficult)

که می خورند حریفان و من نظاره کنم

For the companions drink wine and looking on I make.

چو غنچه با لب خندان به یاد مجلس شاه

To the memory of the King's assembly, like the rose-bud with laughing lip

پیاله گیرم و از شوق جامه پاره کنم

The cup, I take and, through desire, my raiment, rent I make.

1-Tapster
2-Lover

3-Korah, The rich man of the time of Prophet Moses

به دور لاله دماغ مرا علاج کنید
By the cup's circulation, remedy ye my brain
گر از میانه بزم طرب کناره کنم
If, from the midst of the banquet of joy, retirement I make

ز روی دوست مرا چون گل مراد شکفت
Through the Friend's face, blossomed my purpose like the rose
حواله سر دشمن به سنگ خاره کنم
To the hard stone, consignment of the enemy's head (that separation recur not) I make.

گدای میکده‌ام لیک وقت مستی بین
The tavern-beggar am I but at the time of intoxication, be hold
که ناز بر فلک و حکم بر ستاره کنم
Against the (lofty) sky, loftiness; and against the (ordering) star, order, I make

مرا که نیست ره و رسم لقمه پرهیزی
Not mine, is the way and usage of morsel-abstaining For,
چرا ملامت رند شرابخواره کنم
The reprobation of the profligate, the wine-drinker, why do I make

به تخت گل بنشانم بتی چو سلطانی
On the throne of the rose, I place a (beauteous) idol like a Sultan
ز سنبل و سمنش ساز طوق و یاره کنم
With the hyacinth, and the lily, the glory of collar and of bracelet I make.

ز باده خوردن پنهان ملول شد حافظ
Through wine-drinking, distressed became Hafiz
به بانگ بربط و نی رازش آشکاره کنم
With the sound (of the harp) and (with wine), his mystery (of distress) evident I make.

غزل ۳۵۱ ⓞⒹⒺ ③⑤① ODE 351

حاشا که من به موسم گل ترک می کنم
God forbid that, in the rose-season, wine, I should abandon
من لاف عقل می‌زنم این کار کی کنم
Of reason, I boast; this work how should I do

مطرب کجاست تا همه محصول زهد و علم
The minstrel is where? So that all the in-gathering of austerity and of knowledge
در کار چنگ و بربط و آواز نی کنم
In the work of the harp, of the lyre, and of the voice of the reed, I may make.

از قیل و قال مدرسه حالی دلم گرفت
Now, weariness of the (useless) disputation of the (outward) college, hath my heart taken
یک چند نیز خدمت معشوق و می کنم
Once, a while, (only) the service of the beloved (the perfect murshid) and of wine (of love) I will do.

کی بود در زمانه وفا جام می بیار
In time, fidelity was where The cup of wine, bring,
تا من حکایت جم و کاووس کی کنم
That the tale of Jam[1], (and of) Kavus, and of, Kay[2], I may make.

1-Referring to Jamshid, a legendary ruler of ancient Iran   2-king

---

از نامه سیاه نترسم که روز حشر

The black book (of sins) I fear not. for, in the day of assembling,

با فیض لطف او صد از این نامه طی کنم

By the bounty of His grace, a hundred books of this kind, I would close.

کو پیک صبح تا گله‌های شب فراق

The foot-messenger of morn (the breeze from the east) where So that plaints of the night of separation,

با آن خجسته طالع فرخنده پی کنم

To that one, auspicious of fortune, and happy of foot (the murshid) I may make.

این جان عاریت که به حافظ سپرد دوست

This borrowed life, that, to Hafiz, the Friend (God) entrusted;

روزی رخش ببینم و تسلیم وی کنم

His face, one day, I shall see and (to Him) its surrender will make.

غزل ۳۵۲ ⓞⓓⓔ ③⑤②

روزگاری شد که در میخانه خدمت می کنم

For a long time, past, in the tavern (of love, of manifestations, of glories) service (in rue love to God, in manifestations, and in fearful contemplation) I have been doing

در لباس فقر کار اهل دولت می کنم

In the garment of poverty (as a fakir) the work of people of fortune (those joined to God) I keep doing

تا کی اندر دام وصل آرم تذروی خوش خرام

Until that, into union's snare, I bring the partridge (the true Beloved) sweet of gait,

در کمینم و انتظار وقت فرصت می کنم

In my ambush, expectation of time's opportunity, I make.

واعظ ما بوی حق نشنید بشنو کاین سخن

Perceived not truth's perfume, our admonisher. Hear thou for this word (of truth)

در حضورش نیز می‌گویم نه غیبت می کنم

In his presence, do I also utter no calumny, do I make.

با صبا افتان و خیزان می‌روم تا کوی دوست

To the Friend's street, I go like the (swift) breeze, falling and rising,

و از رفیقان ره استمداد همت می کنم

And from (the basil and the rose), prayer for assistance, I make.

خاک کویت زحمت ما برنتابد بیش از این

More than this, our trouble, the dust of Thy street endureth not

لطف‌ها کردی بتا تخفیف زحمت می کنم

O Idol kindnesses, Thou didst: (by going into effacement) the lessening of our trouble (to Thee) I make.

زلف دلبر دام راه و غمزه‌اش تیر بلاست

The snare the Path (tarlkat) is the tress of the Heart-ravisher and the arrow of calamity, His glance

یاد دار ای دل که چندینت نصیحت می کنم

O heart remember the many precepts of counsel that, for thee, I make.

دیده بدبین بپوشان ای کریم عیب پوش

O Merciful One, defect-concealing cover the eye of the ill-see-er,

زین دلیری‌ها که من در کنج خلوت می‌کنم

From these bold deeds, that, in the corner of khilvat, I do.

حافظم در مجلسی دردی کشم در محفلی

In a religious assembly, Hafiz, I am in a convivial assembly, dreg-drinker, I am

بنگر این شوخی که چون با خلق صنعت می‌کنم

This boldness (and expertness) behold how, with (different) people, (different) profession, I make.

غزل ۳۵۳ ⓞⒹⒺ ③⑤③

من ترک عشق شاهد و ساغر نمی‌کنم

Love for the lovely one and for the cup, I abandon not.

صد بار توبه کردم و دیگر نمی‌کنم

A hundred times, repentance, I made, (and broke it) again (repentance) I make not.

باغ بهشت و سایه طوبی و قصر و حور

The garden of paradise, the shade of the Tuba tree, and the palace of the Hur[1]

با خاک کوی دوست برابر نمی‌کنم

Equal (even) to the dust of the Friend's street, 'I make not.

تلقین و درس اهل نظر یک اشارت است

The teaching of the lesson of men of vision is a single hint

گفتم کنایتی و مکرر نمی‌کنم

A hint, I uttered repetition I make not.

هرگز نمی‌شود ز سر خود خبر مرا

Mine, never becometh news of my head (self)

تا در میان میکده سر بر نمی‌کنم

So long as uplifted in the tavern, my head I make not

ناصح به طعن گفت که رو ترک عشق کن

(In wrath the Shaikh[2] the Zahid[3]) said (to me) Go love, abandon

محتاج جنگ نیست برادر نمی‌کنم

Brother wrangling is not necessary (abandoning of love) I make not.

این تقوااام تمام که با شاهدان شهر

This piety is complete (enough) for me. For, with the lovely ones (Zahids) of the city

ناز و کرشمه بر سر منبر نمی‌کنم

At the head of the pulpit, air and glance I make not.

حافظ جناب پیر مغان جای دولت است

Hafiz the court of the Pir of the Magians (the murshid, perfect and excellent) is fortune's place is fortune's place

من ترک خاک بوسی این در نمی‌کنم

The dust-kissing of this door, I abandon not.

1-lover

2-A leader in a Muslim community

3-Pietist

غزل ۳۵۴ ⓄⒹⒺ ③⑤④

به مژگان سیه کردی هزاران رخنه در دینم

A thousand breaches in my faith, with Thy dark eye-lashes, Thou hast made:

بیا کز چشم بیمارت هزاران درد برچینم

Come, so that, out (of my heart) on account of Thy sick (languishing) eye, a thousand pains, (of mine) I may pluck.

الا ای همنشین دل که یارانت برفت از یاد

Ho, O fellow-sitter, of my heart (the true Beloved) from Whose memory, friends (who, in this world of non-existence are Thy companions and slumber in Thy unity) have passed

مرا روزی مباد آن دم که بی یاد تو بنشینم

Not a day be mine, the moment when, void of recollection of Thee, I sit.

جهان پیر است و بی‌بنیاد از این فرهادکش فریاد

Old and foundationless, is the world of this Farhad-slayer, justice

که کرد افسون و نیرنگش ملول از جان شیرینم

Me, vexed with sweet life, its craft and sorcery made.

ز تاب آتش دوری شدم غرق عرق چون گل

Drowned in sweat like the rose, I becameth rough the torment of the fire of separation

بیار ای باد شبگیری نسیمی زان عرق چینم

O breeze, night-seizing (the perfect murshid) a breeze, from the sweat-seizer of mine (the true Beloved) bring

جهان فانی و باقی فدای شاهد و ساقی

The world, transitory and permanent, a ransom for the true Beloved and the Saki (I make)

که سلطانی عالم را طفیل عشق می‌بینم

For, the world's sovereignty, love's humble companion, I deem.

اگر بر جای من غیری گزیند دوست حاکم اوست

If, in my place, the Friend (God) choose a stranger, He is judge

حرامم باد اگر من جان به جای دوست بگزینم

If, in place of the Friend, I choose my life, it, unlawful be

صباح الخیر زد بلبل کجایی ساقیا برخیز

Sabahu-l-khair[1] shouted the bulbul[2]. Saki (murshid) where art thou Arise (bring wine)

که غوغا می‌کند در سر خیال خواب دوشینم

For, in my head, tumult maketh (the intoxication of the wine of) last night (the day of A last)

شب رحلت هم از بستر روم در قصر حورالعین

On the night of departure, I go from the couch to the place of the huru-l'in

اگر در وقت جان دادن تو باشی شمع بالینم

If, at the time of life-surrending, thou be the candle at my pillow.

حدیث آرزومندی که در این نامه ثبت افتاد

The tale of longing that, in this volume, is become verified,

همانا بی‌غلط باشد که حافظ داد تلقینم

Verily is void of error for me, the dictation Hafiz gave

1-Good morning   2-Nightingale

غزل ۳۵۵ ⓄⒹⒺ ③⑤⑤

حالیا مصلحت وقت در آن می‌بینم
Now, the good counsel of the time I see in that

که کشم رخت به میخانه و خوش بنشینم
That, to the wine-house, my chattels I be take and happy sit.

جام می گیرم و از اهل ریا دور شوم
The cup of wine, I take and, from the hypocrite, far I go

یعنی از اهل جهان پاکدلی بگزینم
That is, of the world's creation, (only), pureness of heart, I choose.

جز صراحی و کتابم نبود یار و ندیم
Save the goblet and the book (the Kuran) no companion nor friend may be mine

تا حریفان دغا را به جهان کم بینم
So that the traitor-watchers of the world, seldom, I may see

سر به آزادگی از خلق برآرم چون سرو
Above the people, my head in freedom, like the (lofty) cypress, I uplift,

گر دهد دست که دامن ز جهان درچینم
If it be possible that, away from the world, my skirt, I may pluck.

بس که در خرقه آلوده زدم لاف صلاح
Since, in the stained Khirka[1], rectitude I boasted

شرمسار از رخ ساقی و می رنگینم
A shamed of the Saki[2]s face and of the coloured wine, am I

سینه تنگ من و بار غم او هیهات
My straitened chest and its load of grief. Alas

مرد این بار گران نیست دل مسکینم
Not the man (porter) for this heavy load, is my grieved heart.

من اگر رند خراباتم و گر زاهد شهر
If I be the tavern. profligate or if the city-guardian,

این متاعم که همی‌بینی و کمتر زینم
These, that Thou seest, (I am), and then these, less I am.

بنده آصف عهدم دلم از راه مبر
The slave of the Asaf[3] of the age am I my heart afflicted, keep not

که اگر دم زنم از چرخ بخواهد کینم
For, if I boast of the sphere, revenge it seeketh.

بر دلم گرد ستم‌هاست خدایا مپسند
On my heart is the dust of tyranny. O God! approve not

که مکدر شود آینه مهرآیینم
That dulled should be my love-filled mirror (the heart)

1-Cloak
2-Tapster
3-Suleiman's minister

ODE 356 غزل ۳۵۶

گرم از دست برخیزد که با دلدار بنشینم

If, from my hand, there arise (the chance) that with my heart-possessor I may sit,

ز جام وصل می‌نوشم ز باغ عیش گل چینم

From the cup of fortune (of His face) I drink, (wine and) from the garden of union (with Him) pluck the rose (of profit)

شراب تلخ صوفی سوز بنیادم بخواهد برد

(Not) My foundation (of life) will the bitter (strong) wine (real love) sufi[1]-consuming take

لبم بر لب نه ای ساقی و بستان جان شیرینم

Saki[2] (perfect murshid) on my lip, thy lip, place and my sweet life, take.

مگر دیوانه خواهم شد در این سودا که شب تا روز

(In this vain desire) perchance, distraught I shall become For, (from love of thee) night to day

سخن با ماه می‌گویم پری در خواب می‌بینم

To the moon, (like one distraught) I utter speech in sleep, the Pari[3], I see

لبت شکر به مستان داد و چشمت می به میخواران

To the intoxicated, thy (sweet) lip gave sugar and to the wine-drinkers, thy (intoxicated) eye, wine

منم کز غایت حرمان نه با آنم نه با اینم

Through exceeding disappointment, neither am I with that (the sugar) nor am I with this (the wine Such a one) am I

چو هر خاکی که باد آورد فیضی برد از انعامت

Since every particle of dust that the wind brought was a bounty from Thy grace,

ز حال بنده یاد آور که خدمتگار دیرینم

Thy slave's state remember for an old servant am I.

نه هر کو نقش نظمی زد کلامش دلپذیر افتد

Not pleasing appeared the writing of everyone, who a versified picture, expressed

تذرو طرفه من گیرم که چالاک است شاهینم

A rare partridge (lustrous verse) I take for swift is my royal falcon (the poet's high genius)

اگر باور نمی‌داری رو از صورتگر چین پرس

If belief thou have not, go; ask the painter of Chin (Mani)

که مانی نسخه می‌خواهد ز نوک کلک مشکینم

For, the usage (of word-painting even) the (illustrious painter) Mani desireth from the nib of (my) reed.

وفاداری و حق گویی نه کار هر کسی باشد

Not everyone's work is fidelity and truth-speaking,

غلام آصف ثانی جلال الحق و الدینم

The slave, I am, (of) the Asaf [4]of the age, Jalalu-l-Hakk va-d-Din.

رموز مستی و رندی ز من بشنو نه از واعظ

From me, not from, (Hafiz) hear the mysteries of (love) and (of) intoxication

که با جام و قدح هر دم ندیم ماه و پروینم

For, with the cup and the goblet, every, (night) the companion of the moon and of the Pleiades, am I.

1-A Muslim ascetic and mystic
2-Tapster
3-Beautiful woman
4-Jalaluddin Turanshah's minister

غزل ۳۵۷ ⓄⒹⒺ ③⑤⑦

در خرابات مغان نور خدا می‌بینم
In the tavern of the Magians[1], God's light I see
این عجب بین که چه نوری ز کجا می‌بینم
This wonder be hold what the light (is and) where it, I see.

جلوه بر من مفروش ای ملک الحاج که تو
O King (commander) of the Hajj to me, boast not of dignity. For, thou
خانه می‌بینی و من خانه خدا می‌بینم
Seest the house (the Ka'ba) and God's house, I see.

خواهم از زلف بتان نافه گشایی کردن
From the tress of idols, musk-loosening (perfuming) I will make,
فکر دور است همانا که خطا می‌بینم
Far, is thought (from realisation) verily, Khata[2] (Cathay, a mistake) I see.

سوز دل اشک روان آه سحر ناله شب
(O true Beloved) the heart's consuming, the streaming tears, the night-weeping, the morning-sigh
این همه از نظر لطف شما می‌بینم
All this (calemity of grief) from the sight of Thy grace, I see.

هر دم از روی تو نقشی زندم راه خیال
Momently, my fancy a picture of Thy face way-layeth
با که گویم که در این پرده چه‌ها می‌بینم
To whom, shall I utter what things within this veil (of thought) I see

کس ندیده‌ست ز مشک ختن و نافه چین
Of the musk of Khutan[3] and of the musk-pod of Chin, none hath seen
آن چه من هر سحر از باد صبا می‌بینم
What, from the fragrant morning breeze of (the east) every morning I see.

دوستان عیب نظربازی حافظ مکنید
Friends at Hafiz's glancing, carp not
که من او را ز محبان شما می‌بینم
For, him of (the crowd of) the lovers of God I see.

غزل ۳۵۸ ⓄⒹⒺ ③⑤⑧

غم زمانه که هیچش کران نمی‌بینم
Time's grief whereof limit none, I see
دواش جز می چون ارغوان نمی‌بینم
The remedy (whereof) save wine like this, none, I see.

به ترک خدمت پیر مغان نخواهم گفت
This society of the Pir of the Magians, I will not abandon
چراکه مصلحت خود در آن نمی‌بینم
For in (abandoning) it my own counsel (conducing to welfare) none, I see.

1-It is originally a tribe that belonged to the Medes and the clergy belonged exclusively to them.

2-Mistake

3-It is a fragrant substance

ز آفتاب قدح ارتفاع عیش بگیر

From the sun (cup) of the bowl, the height of pleasure, take

چراکه طالع وقت آن چنان نمی‌بینم

For the fortune of time like that, none, I see.

نشان اهل خدا عاشقیست با خود دار

The mark of one of heart (a sufi) is the being a lover. To thy self, keep

که در مشایخ شهر این نشان نمی‌بینم

For this mark among the city-shaikhs[1], none, I see.

بدین دو دیده حیران من هزار افسوس

For these weeping (blinded) eyes of mine a thousand regrets

که با دو آینه رویش عیان نمی‌بینم

That His face, with the two mirrors (my weeping, blinded, eyes) none, I see

قد تو تا بشد از جویبار دیده من

Since Thy stature went from the stream of my (weeping) eye

به جای سرو جز آب روان نمی‌بینم

In place of the cypress (of Thy stature) save running water, (tears naught) I see.

در این خمار کسم جرعه‌ای نمی‌بخشد

In this wine-sickness, men one giveth a draught (of favour)

ببین که اهل دلی در میان نمی‌بینم

Be hold in the world one of heart, none, I see.

نشان موی میانش که دل در او بستم

The trace of the slender hair of His (the true Beloved's waist) wherein I have fixed my heart,

ز من مپرس که خود در میان نمی‌بینم

Of me, ask not for, in the midst (waist) none, I see.

من و سفینه حافظ که جز در این دریا

(Together are) I and the bark (Divan) of Hafiz. For, save in this ocean (of eloquence)

بضاعت سخن درفشان نمی‌بینم

The capital of speech, heart-placing (comforting) naught, I see

غزل ۳۵۹ ⓄⒹⒺ ③⑤⑨

خرم آن روز کز این منزل ویران بروم

Joyous that day when from this desolate ab ode this world I go

راحت جان طلبم و از پی جانان بروم

The ease of soul the true Beloved I seek and for the sake of the Beloved I go.

گر چه دانم که به جایی نبرد راه غریب

Though I know that to such a place the stranger findeth not the path

من به بوی سر آن زلف پریشان بروم

To the sweet perfume of that dishevelled tress, I go.

دلم از وحشت زندان سکندر بگرفت

From dread of the prison of Sikandar[2] (this fleeting world) my heart took (contraction)

رخت بربندم و تا ملک سلیمان بروم

I bind up my chattels and to the Land of Sulaiman (the lasting world) I go

---

1-A leader in a Muslim community

2-It is an important historical monument in Yazd.

چون صبا با تن بیمار و دل بی‌طاقت

With the sick heart, and powerless body, like the (swift) breeze,

به هواداری آن سرو خرامان بروم

For the love of that moving cypress, I go

در ره او چو قلم گر به سرم باید رفت

In His path, like the pen, if on my head it is necessary to go

با دل زخم کش و دیده گریان بروم

With the heart, wound-enduring and weeping eye, I go.

نذر کردم گر از این غم به درآیم روزی

If of this grief one day come to an end, I have (vowed) that

تا در میکده شادان و غزل خوان بروم

To the wine-house door, joyous and song-singing, I will go

به هواداری او ذره صفت رقص کنان

(That like a mote), in love for Him

تا لب چشمه خورشید درخشان بروم

To the lip of the fountain of the resplendent sun, I will go

تازیان را غم احوال گران باران نیست

Since, to the Arabs those gone before, who rest in proximity to God and who have escaped from time's tumult) grief for (us of) heavy loads is none,

پارسایان مددی تا خوش و آسان بروم

Persians (murshids of the faith guides of the Path of certainty) a little help, that happy and easy (of heart in that Path) I may go.

ور چو حافظ ز بیابان نبرم ره بیرون

And if, out from the desert, I take not the path like Hafiz

همره کوکبه آصف دوران بروم

Along with the constellations of the Asaf[1] of the age I go.

غزل ۳۶۰ ⓞⓓⓔ ③⑥⓪

گر از این منزل ویران به سوی خانه روم

If, from this stage of (this world) travel towards the house (my native land, the next world) I go

دگر آن جا که روم عاقل و فرزانه روم

When there again I go, wise and learned, I go

زین سفر گر به سلامت به وطن بازرسم

If, from this journey, in safety to my native land, I return,

نذر کردم که هم از راه به میخانه روم

I vow that, by the way to the wine-house (of love) I go

تا بگویم که چه کشفم شد از این سیر و سلوک

To utter what became revealed to me, from this travelling and journeying,

به در صومعه با بربط و پیمانه روم

With the harp and the wine-cup, to the door of the wine-house I go.

1- Jalaluddin Turanshah's minister

آشنایان ره عشق گرم خون بخورند

If friends of the Path of love drink my blood,

ناکسم گر به شکایت سوی بیگانه روم

Mean one, am I if, in complaint, to the stranger, I go

بعد از این دست من و زلف چو زنجیر نگار

After this (together are) my hand, and the chain-like tress of the idol (the true Beloved)

چند و چند از پی کام دل دیوانه روم

In pursuit of the desire of my distraught heart, how long, how long do I go

گر ببینم خم ابروی چو محرابش باز

If, again, the curve of His eye-brow Like the prayer-arch I see

سجده شکر کنم و از پی شکرانه روم

Bending in thanks, I make and for the sake of thank ode giving, I go.

خرم آن دم که چو حافظ به تولای وزیر

Happy that moment, when, like Hafiz, in attachment to the vazir[1]

سرخوش از میکده با دوست به کاشانه روم

From the wine-house to my own house (my native land, the next world) happy of head, with the Friend I go

غزل ۳۶۱ ⓄⒹⒺ ③⑥①

آن که پامال جفا کرد چو خاک راهم

That one (the true Beloved, or the murshid) who, like the (trodden) dust of the path, made me trampled of tyranny,

خاک می‌بوسم و عذر قدمش می‌خواهم

The dust (of the path of His foot) I kiss; and for (the trouble of) His approach, pardon beg.

من نه آنم که ز جور تو بنالم حاشا

Not that one am I, who be wail of violence from Thee. God forbids!

بنده معتقد و چاکر دولتخواهم

The faithful servant; and slave, well-wishing, I am.

بسته‌ام در خم گیسوی تو امید دراز

In the curl of (Thy) long tress, my long hope, have I bound

آن مبادا که کند دست طلب کوتاهم

Be it not that my hand of search, short it (the tress) hould make (cut)

ذره خاکم و در کوی توام جای خوش است

An atom of dust, I am and, in Thy street, pleasant, is my time

ترسم ای دوست که بادی ببرد ناگاهم

Friend I fear that suddenly, me, a great wind (of calamity) may take

پیر میخانه سحر جام جهان بینم داد

In the morning, the Pir[2] of the wine-house (the perfect murshid) me, the cup world-viewing (the heart pure of impurity of beholding other than God) gave

و اندر آن آینه از حسن تو کرد آگاهم

And in that (world-viewing cup like a) mirror, me, informed of Thy beauty, made

---

1-Minister   2 -A Muslim saint or holy man, Pietist

صوفی صومعه عالم قدسم لیکن

The Sufi[1] of the (lofty) cloister of the holy world am I But,

حالیا دیر مغان است حوالتگاهم

Now, the (lowly) cloister of the Magians[2] is the charge of mine.

با من راه نشین خیز و سوی میکده آی

With me, the road. sitter, arise and to the wine-house (of love) come

تا در آن حلقه ببینی که چه صاحب جاهم

So that thou mayst see how in that circle (of zikr va fikr) master of rank, am I.

مست بگذشتی و از حافظت اندیشه نبود

Intoxicated, Thou passedest and of Hafiz, no thought was Thine

آه اگر دامن حسن تو بگیرد آهم

Alas if the skirt of Thy beauty, my (morning) sigh should catch (consume)

خوشم آمد که سحر خسرو خاور می‌گفت

Happy to me it came when, in the morning, the Khusrau of the east[3] (the resplendent sun) spake

با همه پادشهی بنده تورانشاهم

Notwithstanding all my sovereignty, the slave of the Turan King am I.

غزل ۳۶۲ ⓄⒹⒺ ③⑥②

دیدار شد میسر و بوس و کنار هم

Obtained was the sight of (the true Beloved) and the kiss, and the embrace also

از بخت شکر دارم و از روزگار هم

To fortune, thanks I owe and to time, also.

زاهد برو که طالع اگر طالع من است

Zahid[4] go (about thy own work and forbid not wine and the lovely one) For if ascendant be my fortune,

جامم به دست باشد و زلف نگار هم

Will be in my hand, the cup and the Beloved's tress also

ما عیب کس به مستی و رندی نمی‌کنیم

For profligacy and intoxication, we ascribe to none defect

لعل بتان خوش است و می خوشگوار هم

Sweet is the ruby (lip) of idols, and pleasant-tasting wine also.

ای دل بشارتی دهمت محتسب نماند

O heart thee, glad tidings, I give The muhtasib[5] is no more

و از می جهان پر است و بت میگسار هم

Full, is the world of wine, and of the wine-drinking idol also

خاطر به دست تفرقه دادن نه زیرکیست

Not wise, is it to give the heart to the power of separation:

مجموعه‌ای بخواه و صراحی بیار هم

Tranquillity (of heart) seek; and a flagon, bring also;

بر خاکیان عشق فشان جرعه لبش

On the dusty ones (lovers) of love, pour a draught of his (Muhammad's) lip,

تا خاک لعل گون شود و مشکبار هم

So that ruby-hue may become the dust; and musk-diffusing also.

آن شد که چشم بد نگران بودی از کمین

Passed hath that time, when from ambush was lurking thee evil-eye

خصم از میان برفت و سرشک از کنار هم

Departed from the midst, hath the enemy (thezahid or the watcher) and, from (the) bosom, the tear also

چون کانات جمله به بوی تو زنده‌اند

(O perfect murshid) since by thy perfume (of hope) all created beings are living,

ای آفتاب سایه ز ما برمدار هم

O (resplendent) sun (the true Beloved) from us, Thy shade of bounty keep not also.

چون آب روی لاله و گل فیض حسن توست

Since the honour (decoration) of the tulip and of the rose is the bounty of thy beauty,

ای ابر لطف بر من خاکی ببار هم

O cloud of grace (Muhammad) on me, dusty (humble, grace) rain also.

حافظ اسیر زلف تو شد از خدا بترس

Captive to thee, became (people of vision) God fear

و از انتصاف آصف جم اقتدار هم

And the obtaining of justice from Asaf[1], powerful as Sulaiman also.

برهان ملک و دین که ز دست وزارتش

Burhan-i-Mulk va Din[2], from whose hand of vazirship

ایام کان یمین شد و دریا یسار هم

(The happy) Time (of the mine) became his right hand and of the ocean, his left also.

بر یاد رای انور او آسمان به صبح

To the memory of his most illumined judgment, in the morning, the sky

جان می‌کند فدا و کواکب نثار هم

Maketh sacrifice of surrendered its own life; and the constellation, scattering also.

گوی زمین ربوده چوگان عدل اوست

Snatched by thy chaugan of justice, is the ball of earth's (sovereignty)

وین برکشیده گنبد نیلی حصار هم

And this up-lifted blue dome of the for tress also.

عزم سبک عنان تو در جنبش آورد

Into motion, thy intention, light of rein, bringeth

این پایدار مرکز عالی مدار هم

This world, firm, lofty of center, also

تا از نتیجه فلک و طور دور اوست

Until that time when, from the effects of the sky; and the way of its revolution, there be

تبدیل ماه و سال و خزان و بهار هم

Change of years, and of month, and of autumn, and of spring also

---

1-Suleiman's minister   2-Minister

خالی مباد کاخ جلالش ز سروران
Void of chiefs, be not thy palace of dignity
و از ساقیان سروقد گلعذار هم
And of Saki[1]s, cypress of stature, rose of cheek also

غزل ۳۶۳ ⓞⒹⒺ ③⑥③ ODE 363

دردم از یار است و درمان نیز هم
From the (true) Beloved, is my pain and my remedy, also
دل فدای او شد و جان نیز هم
A sacrifice for Him, became my heart, and my life, also

این که میگویند آن خوشتر ز حسن
Those that say That (elegance) is better than beauty To them, say
یار ما این دارد و آن نیز هم
This (beauty) hath our Beloved and that (elegance) also

یاد باد آن کو به قصد خون ما
Be memory of that one, who, with desire for our blood,
عهد را بشکست و پیمان نیز هم
Shattered the covenant, and the oath, also.

دوستان در پرده میگویم سخن
Friends within the veil, we utter speech
گفته خواهد شد به دستان نیز هم
It will be uttered with tales, also.

چون سر آمد دولت شبهای وصل
When, to an end, have come the nights of union,
بگذرد ایام هجران نیز هم
Passeth away the time of separation also.

هر دو عالم یک فروغ روی اوست
(Only) One splendour of His face is (the glory of) both worlds, '
گفتمت پیدا و پنهان نیز هم
To thee, I uttered (this matter) evident and hidden, also.

اعتمادی نیست بر کار جهان
Not, on the world's work, is reliance
بلکه بر گردون گردان نیز هم
Nor, on the revolving sphere (whereto is attributed the world's work) also

عاشق از قاضی نترسد می بیار
Not the judge, doth the lover fear, wine, bring
بلکه از یرغوی دیوان نیز هم
Nor the punishment of the Sultan, also.

محتسب داند که حافظ عاشق است
Knoweth that Hafiz is a lover (of God) the muhtasib[2]
و آصف ملک سلیمان نیز هم
And the Asaf[3] of Sulaiman's court, also.

1-Tapster
2-Sheriff

3-Suleiman's minister

غزل ۳۶۴ ⓞⓓⓔ ③⑥④

ما بی غمان مست دل از دست داده‌ایم
Heart given from the hand, (lovers) void of grief, intoxicated, (selfless and powerless) we are

همراز عشق و همنفس جام باده‌ایم
Fellow-associate of love, boon-companions of the cup of wine, we are.

بر ما بسی کمان ملامت کشیده‌اند
On us, the bow of reproach, many have drawn

تا کار خود ز ابروی جانان گشاده‌ایم
Since, from the eye-brow of the (true) Beloved, our work we have loosed.

ای گل تو دوش داغ صبوحی کشیده‌ای
O rose last night, the morning cup thou drankest

ما آن شقایقیم که با داغ زاده‌ایم
That anemone, that (from eternity without beginning) with the stain (of love was) born, we are.

پیر مغان ز توبه ما گر ملول شد
If vexed with our repentance became the Pir of the Magians[1],

گو باده صاف کن که به عذر ایستاده‌ایم
Say Pure, make the wine for with apology (for our conducts) tanding, we are.

کار از تو می‌رود مددی ای دلیل راه
O guide of the path (the perfect murshid) from thee, goeth the work A glance (make)

کانصاف می‌دهیم و ز راه اوفتاده‌ایم
That, me, justice thou mayst give (for) fallen (away) from the Path, we are.

چون لاله می مبین و قدح در میان کار
In the midst of work, be hold not (ruddy) wine like the red-streaked tulip and the goblet

این داغ بین که بر دل خونین نهاده‌ایم
Be hold this stain (of love) that, on our bloody heart, 'we have placed

گفتی که حافظ این همه رنگ و خیال چیست
Thou spakest, saying: "Hafiz all this colour of fancy (imaginary pictures) is what?"

نقش غلط مبین که همان لوح ساده‌ایم
(Hafiz replied) Say not a false picture for, verily, the tablet smooth (like a mirror,
void of picture) we are.

غزل ۳۶۵ ⓞⓓⓔ ③⑥⑤

عمریست تا به راه غمت رو نهاده‌ایم
(A hundred times), before (the dust of Thy foot), our face we have placed

روی و ریای خلق به یک سو نهاده‌ایم
Hypocrisy and dis simulation, aside we have placed

طاق و رواق مدرسه و قال و قیل علم
The arch and the corridor of the College, and the disputation of excellence,

در راه جام و ساقی مه رو نهاده‌ایم
(So that they may go to the wind of destruction) in the path of (ease and of the true Beloved), rose
of face, we have placed.

1-The perfect mystic man,

هم جان بدان دو نرگس جادو سپرده‌ایم

To those two narcissi of the sorcerer, our life we have entrusted

هم دل بدان دو سنبل هندو نهاده‌ایم

In those two Hindu hyacinths (black tresses) also our heart we have placed.

عمری گذشت تا به امید اشارتی

Passed hath a long life, (and) in hopefulness of a glance,

چشمی بدان دو گوشه ابرو نهاده‌ایم

On those two (narcissi of sorcery), an eye (of hope) we have placed.

ما ملک عافیت نه به لشکر گرفته‌ایم

Not with the army, have we taken the country of ease

ما تخت سلطنت نه به بازو نهاده‌ایم

Not with the (powerful) arm, the throne of sovereignty (is it that) we have placed.

تا سحر چشم یار چه بازی کند که باز

Let us see what sport the sorcery of the Friend's eye maketh, for, again,

بنیاد بر کرشمه جادو نهاده‌ایم

On the glance of sorcery, our foundation (of life') we have placed.

بی زلف سرکشش سر سودایی از ملال

Without (the grace of His narcissus), our head of distraughtness from (wine of love)

همچون بنفشه بر سر زانو نهاده‌ایم

Like the dark, mourning violet, on the knee we have placed.

در گوشه امید چو نظارگان ماه

In hope's corner, like (eager) spectators of the (new) moon,

چشم طلب بر آن خم ابرو نهاده‌ایم

On that curve of the eye-brow, hope's eye we have placed.

گفتی که حافظا دل سرگشته‌ات کجاست

Thou spakest saying: "O Hafiz! thy distraugh the artis where?"

در حلقه‌های آن خم گیسو نهاده‌ایم

In the meshes of that curl of the tress, it we have placed.

غزل ۳۶۶ ⓄⒹⒺ ③⑥⑥

ما بدین در نه پی حشمت و جاه آمده‌ایم

Not in pursuit of pomp and of pageant, to this door (of the murshid) we have come

از بد حادثه این جا به پناه آمده‌ایم

For shelter from ill-fortune, here we have come.

ره رو منزل عشقیم و ز سرحد عدم

Way-farers of love's stage are we and from the limits of non-existence,

تا به اقلیم وجود این همه راه آمده‌ایم

Up to the climes of existence, all this way we have come.

سبزه خط تو دیدیم و ز بستان بهشت

The fresh ness of Thy down, we saw and, from the garden of paradise,

به طلبکاری این مهرگیاه آمده‌ایم

In search of this love-grass, we have come.

با چنین گنج که شد خازن او روح امین

With such treasure, whose treasurer is the faithful spirit (Jibra, il)

به گدایی به در خانه شاه آمده‌ایم

In beggary to the door of the King's house we have come.

لنگر حلم تو ای کشتی توفیق کجاست

O bark of grace (the family of Muhammad) thy anchor of patience ('Ali Murtaza) where

که در این بحر کرم غرق گناه آمده‌ایم

For, in this ocean of liberality, immersed in sin we have come.

آبرو می‌رود ای ابر خطاپوش ببار

O cloud, sin-cleansing! honour goeth (mercy) rain

که به دیوان عمل نامه سیاه آمده‌ایم

For in the court of action (as opposed to theory) black of book, we have come,

حافظ این خرقه پشمینه بینداز که ما

Hafiz this woollen Khirka [1] (of outward worship) cast for (with love's consuming and melting)

از پی قافله با آتش آه آمده‌ایم

From behind the kafila[2] with the fire of sighing (and wailing) we have come

غزل ۳۶۷   ⓄⒹⒺ ③⑥⑦

فتوی پیر مغان دارم و قولیست قدیم

The decision of the Pir of the Magians, I have; and an old saying, it is,

که حرام است می آن جا که نه یار است ندیم

That unlawful is wine there, where is neither the friend nor the companion.

چاک خواهم زدن این دلق ریایی چه کنم

This ragged religious garment of hypocrisy I will rend what shall I do

روح را صحبت ناجنس عذابیست الیم

The society of the uncongenial nature is excruciating torment to the soul.

تا مگر جرعه فشاند لب جانان بر من

So that, perchance, on me, the (true) Beloved's lip may scatter a draught

سال‌ها شد که منم بر در میخانه مقیم

For that reason, years dweller I have become at the door of the wine-house (of love)

مگرش خدمت دیرین من از یاد برفت

Perchance, passed from His memory hath my ancient service:

ای نسیم سحری یاد دهش عهد قدیم

O morning breeze Him, recollection of the ancient covenant, give.

بعد صد سال اگر بر سر خاکم گذری

If, after a hundred years, Thy (perfume) blow over my dust,

سر برآرد ز گلم رقص کنان عظم رمیم

Forth from the clay (of the grave) its head the rotten bone dancing bringeth

دلبر از ما به صد امید ستد اول دل

First, from us, with a hundred hopes, the Heart-Ravisher took our heart

ظاهرا عهد فرامش نکند خلق کریم

Apparently, the covenant, His merciful nature forgetteth not.

1-Cloak   2-Convoy

غنچه گو تنگ دل از کار فروبسته مباش

To the rose-bud (the seeker who,) by (not attaining the object of his heart, is strait of heart) speak,
saying: Of thy entangled work, strait of heart be not

کز دم صبح مدد یابی و انفاس نسیم

For, from morn's breath, and from the spirits of the breeze (the perfect murshid) aid thou wilt gain.

فکر بهبود خود ای دل ز دری دیگر کن

O heart thought of thy own welfare make by another door (the door of the true Beloved)

درد عاشق نشود به به مداوای حکیم

By the physician's treatment, better becometh not the lover's pain

گوهر معرفت آموز که با خود بری

The jewel of divine knowledge, a mass, that, it with thyself, (to the next world) thou mayst take

که نصیب دگران است نصاب زر و سیم

For (after thy death) the portion of others is the wealth of gold and of silver.

دام سخت است مگر یار شود لطف خدا

Strong is (the world's) snare (from it, escape is impossible) unless God's grace become thy
friend (ally)

ور نه آدم نبرد صرفه ز شیطان رجیم

If not, over Shaitan[1] whelmed with stones, Adam (man) prevailed not.

حافظ ار سیم و زرت نیست چه شد شاکر باش

Hafiz if silver and gold thine be not, what matter Be grateful.

چه به از دولت لطف سخن و طبع سلیم

Than the fortune of thy grace of speech, and of thy gentle thought, what better (fortune)

غزل ۳۶۸ ⓄⒹⒺ ③⑥⑧

خیز تا از در میخانه گشادی طلبیم

Arise so that by the wine-house door, an opening (of the heart) we may seek.

به ره دوست نشینیم و مرادی طلبیم

In the path of the Friend, may sit; and our purpose seek.

زاد راه حرم وصل نداریم مگر

Road-provisions (for the path of travel) to the Friend's fold, we have not, Perchance

به گدایی ز در میکده زادی طلبیم

By begging, from the wine-house door, road-provisions, we may seek.

اشک آلوده ما گر چه روان است ولی

Though running, are our (blood) stained tears, yet

به رسالت سوی او پاک نهادی طلبیم

For despatching (them) to Him, one of pure nature, we seek

لذت داغ غمت بر دل ما باد حرام

To our heart, forbidden be the taste of the stain of grief for Thee,

اگر از جور غم عشق تو دادی طلبیم

If, for the violence of the grief of love for Thee, justice we seek.

1-Devil

نقطه خال تو بر لوح بصر نتوان زد

On vision's tablet, the point of Thy (dark) mole, one cannot cast,

مگر از مردمک دیده مدادی طلبیم

Unless, from the (dark) pupil of the eye, ink we seek.

عشوه‌ای از لب شیرین تو دل خواست به جان

From Thy sweet lip, my heart with soul sought the way

به شکرخنده لبت گفت مزادی طلبیم

With sweet smile, Thy lip said A purpose, let us seek

تا بود نسخه عطری دل سودازده را

As long as the be perfumed pre scription shall be for the distraught stricken heart,

از خط غالیه سای تو سوادی طلبیم

From Thy perfume-diffusing hair, a passion we seek-

چون غمت را نتوان یافت مگر در دل شاد

Since, save in the joyous heart, one cannot gain grief for Thee

ما به امید غمت خاطر شادی طلبیم

In hope of grief for Thee, a joyous heart, we seek.

بر در مدرسه تا چند نشینی حافظ

Hafiz at the college-doer, how long sittest thou

خیز تا از در میخانه گشادی طلبیم

Arise so that by the wine-house door, an opening (of the heart) we may seek.

غزل ۳۶۹ ①Ⓓ Ⓔ ③⑥⑨

ما ز یاران چشم یاری داشتیم

The eye (of expectation) of friendship from friends we had

خود غلط بود آن چه ما پنداشتیم

Verily, 'twas mistake that which we thought

تا درخت دوستی برگی دهد

Let us see, when fruit, the tree of friend ship will give

حالیا رفتیم و تخمی کاشتیم

Now, we have departed and a seed (zikr va fikr) we have sown.

گفت و گو آیین درویشی نبود

Not the way (usage) of the dervish is discussion (of complaint of the true Beloved, or of the murshid)

ور نه با تو ماجراها داشتیم

If not, (to narrate) passed circumstances to thee we had.

شیوه چشمت فریب جنگ داشت

The way of thy eye, battle's deceit had

ما غلط کردیم و صلح انگاشتیم

(This) We knew not and peace, we sowed.

گلبن حسنت نه خود شد دلفروز

Not of itself, heart-fascinating became the rose-bush of thy beauty

ما دم همت بر او بگماشتیم

On it, the breath of blessing, we established

نکته‌ها رفت و شکایت کس نکرد
Subtleties passed and complaint, none made

جانب حرمت فرونگذاشتیم
Aside, dignity we put not

گفت خود دادی به ما دل حافظا
(The true Beloved) Said Hafiz to Us, thou thyself gavest thy heart

ما محصل بر کسی نگماشتیم
To none, the tax-collector, we sent.

غزل ۳۷۰ ⓞⒹⒺ ③⑦⓪

صلاح از ما چه می‌جویی که مستان را صلا گفتیم
From us, where fore seeketh thou peace, when, to the intoxicated, an invitation we uttered

به دور نرگس مست سلامت را دعا گفتیم
At the revolution of thy intoxicated eye, fare well to safety we uttered.

در میخانه‌ام بگشا که هیچ از خانقه نگشود
Open me the door of the wine-house (of love and drink wine that divine mysteries may be revealed to thee) for, from the monastery, naught is revealed

گرت باور بود ور نه سخن این بود و ما گفتیم
If thine be belief (of my word) if not, this was the speech, we uttered

من از چشم تو ای ساق خراب افتاده‌ام لیکن
O Saki by thy eye, ruined (intoxicated) I have fallen. But

بلایی کز حبیب آید هزارش مرحبا گفتیم
A calamity that cometh from the friend, to it, a thousand welcomes we uttered.

اگر بر من نبخشایی پشیمانی خوری آخر
If me thou for give not, thou wilt at last suffer regret,

به خاطر دار این معنی که در خدمت کجا گفتیم
In thy heart, keep this matter, where (a complaint) in thy service we uttered

قدت گفتم که شمشاد است بس خجلت به بار آورد
We said Thy stature is the (lofty) box-tree much shame it bringeth to fruit

که این نسبت چرا کردیم و این بهتان چرا گفتیم
(To the box – tree) This similarity why made we and this calumny why (is it that) we uttered

جگر چون نافه‌ام خون گشت کم زینم نمی‌باید
Like a (bloody) musk-pod, blood became my liver (and for me) was fit not less than this

جزای آن که با زلفت سخن از چین خطا گفتیم
Its requital because, in comparison with His (glorious, beperfumed) tress the word (of the mean musk) of Chin by mistake, we uttered

تو آتش گشتی ای حافظ ولی با یار درنگرفت
O hafiz! fire (through grief of separation) thou hast become but, with the (true) Beloved, it took no effect

ز بدعهدی گل گویی حکایت با صبا گفتیم
From in fidelity to the covenant of the rose, thou mays t say the tale to the wind we uttered.

غزل ۳۷۱ ⓄⒹⒺ ③⑦①

ما درس سحر در ره میخانه نهادیم
At the head of the wine-house, the morning-lesson (prayer) aside we have laid
محصول دعا در ره جانانه نهادیم
In the path of the true Beloved, the in-gathering of prayer, we have placed.

در خرمن صد زاهد عاقل زند آتش
To the harvest (of existence) of a hundred learned wise ones (Zahids) setteth fire
این داغ که ما بر دل دیوانه نهادیم
This mark (of branding) that, (from love) on our distraught heart, we have placed.

سلطان ازل گنج غم عشق به ما داد
To us, the treasure of love's grief, the Sultan of eternity without beginning (the true Beloved) gave,
تا روی در این منزل ویرانه نهادیم
Since, towards this desolate stage (this world) our face we have placed.

در دل ندهم ره پس از این مهر بتان را
After this to the love of idols, the path into our heart, we give not
مهر لب او بر در این خانه نهادیم
On the door of this house (the heart) the seal of His lip we have placed.

در خرقه از این بیش منافق نتوان بود
More than this, in the Khirka[1] (the garment of austerity) the one cannot be a hypocrite
بنیاد از این شیوه رندانه نهادیم
On account of this, profligately, its (the khirka's) foundation we have placed.

چون می‌رود این کشتی سرگشته که آخر
At last, how goeth this battered bark (the body)
جان در سر آن گوهر یک دانه نهادیم
In desire of which peerless jewel, our life we have placed.

المنه لله که چو ما بی‌دل و دین بود
Thanks to God that like us, without heart and religion, was
آن را که لقب عاقل و فرزانه نهادیم
That one, who mas (as) wisdom-cherisher and learned, we have placed.

قانع به خیالی ز تو بودیم چو حافظ
With (only) an image of Thee, contented we were like Hafiz,
یا رب چه گداهمت و بیگانه نهادیم
O Lord! Whether beggar or friendless one, reliance (on Thee) we have placed.

غزل ۳۷۲ ⓄⒹⒺ ③⑦②

بگذار تا ز شارع میخانه بگذریم
Permit us to pass by the highway of the tavern
کز بهر جرعه‌ای همه محتاج این دریم
For, for a draught, in need of this (tavern)-door, we are all.

1-Cloak

روز نخست چون دم رندی زدیم و عشق
On the first day (of eternity without beginning) when, of profligacy and of love, we boasted,

شرط آن بود که جز ره آن شیوه نسپریم
Its condition was that, no (path) save the Path of this way (of love) we tread.

جایی که تخت و مسند جم می‌رود به باد
The place (this world) where the masnad of Sulaiman[1] goeth to the wind (of destruction)

گر غم خوریم خوش نبود به که می‌خوریم
Pleasant, it is not if we suffer grief Best, that we drink wine.

تا بو که که دست در کمر او توان زدن
Let us see, it may be that, in his girdle, one's hand one can fix

در خون دل نشسته چو یاقوت احمریم
Seated in the heart's blood, like the red ruby, are we.

واعظ مکن نصیحت شوریدگان که ما
Admonisher (to us) make not the counsel of the distraught For we

با خاک کوی دوست به فردوس ننگریم
With (possessing) the (glorious) of the Friend's street, look not at Paradise

چون صوفیان به حالت و رقصند مقتدا
Since (by sama') the Sufis[2] are in the mystic state of the dance

ما نیز هم به شعبده دستی برآوریم
We also by the sorcery (of love – play) a hand uplift (in rapture)

از جرعه تو خاک زمین در و لعل یافت
From thy draught (sprinkling) earth gained (the rank of) the (mighty) ruby

بیچاره ما که پیش تو از خاک کمتریم
Before Thee, less than the dust are we helpless (lovers because, to us Thou inclinest not)

حافظ چو ره به کنگره کاخ وصل نیست
Hafiz when there is no path to the turret of the palace of union

با خاک آستانه این در به سر بریم
Our head, with the dust of the threshold of this door, let us take.

غزل ۳۷۳ ⓄⒹⒺ ③⑦③

خیز تا خرقه صوفی به خرابات بریم
Arise so that to the tavern, the sufi-Khirka[3], we may take

شطح و طامات به بازار خرافات بریم
(So that) To the bazar of idle tales, the ragged religious garment and idle talk, we may take

سوی رندان قلندر به ره آورد سفر
To the path towards the kalandar[4]-profligates, journeying brought us

دلق بسطامی و سجاده طامات بریم
The ragged, religious, garment, (of wool) and the prayer-mat of idle tales, we take

تا همه خلوتیان جام صبوحی گیرند
Since the morning cup, all the khilvat[5] is take,

چنگ صبحی به در پیر مناجات بریم
At the door of the Pir[6] of the tavern, the harp of the morning, we take.

1-Name of prophet
2-A Muslim ascetic and mystic
3-Cloak

4-Sufi
5-Solitude
6-A Muslim saint or holy man, Pietist

با تو آن عهد که در وادی ایمن بستیم

(O true Beloved) That covenant that with Thee, in the Wadi-i-Aiman[1], (eternity without beginning) I established

همچو موسی ارنی گوی به میقات بریم

Like Musa[2], sayer of Let me see, to the appointed (for inducing the ihram) place we take

کوس ناموس تو بر کنگره عرش زنیم

From the turret of the ninth heaven (God's throne) the drum of thy fame, we beat:

علم عشق تو بر بام سماوات بریم

To the roof of (vault) the heavens, the guidons of love from Thee, we take

خاک کوی تو به صحرای قیامت فردا

To-morrow (resurrection – day) in the plain of up-standing-place the glorious the dust of Thy street,

همه بر فرق سر از بهر مباهات بریم

For glorifying, all, on the pate of our head, we take

ور نهد در ره ما خار ملامت زاهد

If, in our path, the thorn of reproach, the Zahid[3] plant,

از گلستانش به زندان مکافات بریم

Into the prison of retribution, him from rose-garden, we take.

شرممان باد ز پشمینه آلوده خویش

Of our stained, woollen, garment, shame be ours,

گر بدین فضل و هنر نام کرامات بریم

If, with this excellence and skill, the reputation of miracles, we take

قدر وقت ار نشناسد دل و کاری نکند

If the value of time, the heart establish not and a work do not,

بس خجالت که از این حاصل اوقات بریم

Great the shame that, from this produce of times, we take

فتنه می‌بارد از این سقف مقرنس برخیز

From this vaulted roof, calamity raineth Arise

تا به میخانه پناه از همه آفات بریم

That, from all calamities, shelter in the wine-house, we may take.

در بیابان فنا گم شدن آخر تا کی

In desire's desert (this ravishing world) to be lost at last how long

ره بپرسیم مگر پی به مهمات بریم

(From the murshid) the path (of escape) we ask; perchance, the foot of (approach) to great deeds we may take

حافظ آب رخ خود بر در هر سفله مریز

Hafiz at the door of every mean one, thy face-luster (reputation) spill not

حاجت آن به که بر قاضی حاجات بریم

To the Kazi[4] of needs (God) best that that need, we take.

1-The desire where the voice of the Almighty reached Moses

2-Name of prophet

3-Pietist

4-Bencher

غزل ۳۷۴ ⓞⒹⒺ ③⑦④

بیا تا گل برافشانیم و می در ساغر اندازیم

(O murshid) come sq that the rose (of ease and of pleasure) we may scatter, and, into the cup (of existence or of the heart) the wine (of love and of divine knowledge) cast,

فلک را سقف بشکافیم و طرحی نو دراندازیم

(By our inward strength) the roof of the sky we rend and (to the height of another heaven) a new way, cast.

اگر غم لشکر انگیزد که خون عاشقان ریزد

If an army, that sheddeth the blood of lovers, grief raise

من و ساقی به هم تازیم و بنیادش براندازیم

Content to get her are I and the Saki[1] and up its foundation, we cast.

شراب ارغوانی را گلاب اندر قدح ریزیم

Into the cup of ruddy wine, rose-water, I pour

نسیم عطرگردان را شکر در مجمر اندازیم

Into the censer of the wind, 'itr[2]-revolving, sugar, I cast.

چو در دست است رودی خوش بزن مطرب سرودی خوش

Minstrel since in thy hand is a sweet instrument, a sweet song sing

که دست افشان غزل خوانیم و پاکوبان سر اندازیم

So that, hand-waving, we may sing the love-song, and dancing, our head down may cast.

صبا خاک وجود ما بدان عالی جناب انداز

O breeze to that lofty quarter of the Beloved, the dust of our existence cast

بود کن شاه خوبان را نظر بر منظر اندازیم

It may be that on the spectacle-place of that king of lovely ones ' (arifs) our glance, we may cast.

یکی از عقل می‌لافد یکی طامات می‌بافد

Of reason, one boasteth another idle talk weaveth

بیا کاین داوری‌ها را به پیش داور اندازیم

Come before the just Ruler (God) these disputes, let us cast.

بهشت عدن اگر خواهی بیا با ما به میخانه

If the paradise of Aden, thou desire, come with us to the tavern (of love and of profligacy)

که از پای خمت روزی به حوض کوثر اندازیم

So that, from the foot of the wine-jar (the murshid of love) thee, at once into the pool of Kausar, we may cast

سخندانی و خوشخوانی نمی‌ورزند در شیراز

In Shiraz, the understanding of verse, and the speaking well, they practise not

بیا حافظ که تا خود را به ملکی دیگر اندازیم

Hafiz come that, into another land, our selves we may cast.

غزل ۳۷۵ ⓞⒹⒺ ③⑦⑤

صوفی بیا که خرقه سالوس برکشیم

O Sufi[3] come the Khirka[4] of hypocrisy, off we will draw

وین نقش زرق را خط بطلان به سر کشیم

On (across) the head of this picture of hypocrisy, the cancelling line, we will draw

---

1-Tapster
2-Fragrance

3-A Muslim ascetic and mystic
4-Cloak

نذر و فتوح صومعه در وجه می‌نهیم

The offering and the alms of the towered building (the monastery) as the price of wine, we place

دلق ریا به آب خرابات برکشیم

In the water of the tavern (of love, from the pollution of self-beholding and of man-displaying, we will wash and) the garment of hypocrisy drawing, we will draw.

فردا اگر نه روضه رضوان به ما دهند

To-morrow (the resurrection day) if to us the garden of Rizvan[1] they give not,

غلمان ز روضه حور ز جنت به درکشیم

Youths from the seventh heaven (ghurfa and) Hur[2] from the garden (jannat) out we draw.

بیرون جهیم سرخوش و از بزم صوفیان

Happy of head, forth (from the world) we (lovers of God) will leap and from the banquet of the rival (the outward worshipper; or the denier of love)

غارت کنیم باده و شاهد به برکشیم

(On the last day) The cup, we plunder; and, to the door, the lovely one we draw.

عشرت کنیم ور نه به حسرت کشندمان

Awork, let us do if not, shame it will bring,

روزی که رخت جان به جهانی دگر کشیم

One day, when to the other world, life's chattels, we draw.

سر خدا که در تتق غیب منزویست

The mystery of fate that, in the veil of the hidden, is hidden,

مستانه‌اش نقاب ز رخسار برکشیم

Intoxicatedly, from off its face, the veil we draw.

کو جلوه‌ای ز ابروی او تا چو ماه نو

From His eye-brow, the glance where, so that, like the new (crescent) moon,

گوی سپهر در خم چوگان زر کشیم

In the chaugan of gold, the ball of the sphere, we may draw.

حافظ نه حد ماست چنین لاف‌ها زدن

Hafiz not our limit is it like this to boast

پای از گلیم خویش چرا بیشتر کشیم

From beyond my blanket, my foot farther why should we draw.

غزل ۳۷۶ ⓄⒹⒺ ③⑦⑥

دوستان وقت گل آن به که به عشرت کوشیم

Friends in the rose-season, that best that for pleasure we strive

سخن اهل دل است این و به جان بنیوشیم

(This) the word of (the Pir of the Magians the murshid) the is With soul, let us listen.

نیست در کس کرم و وقت طرب می‌گذرد

In none, is liberality (that we may have even a groat wherewith to drink wine) passeth joy's time

چاره آن است که سجاده به می بفروشیم

Its remedy is this, for wine, the prayer-mat, we sell.

1-Heaven   2-Heavenly woman

خوش هواییست فرح بخش خدایا بفرست

Tis a pleasant air, joy-giving O God send

نازنینی که به رویش می گلگون نوشیم

One of gracious form, to whose face, wine, rose of hue, we may drink.

ارغنون ساز فلک رهزن اهل هنر است

One of skill (Zuhra) is the organ-player of the sky, highway-robber

چون از این غصه ننالیم و چرا نخروشیم

Of this grief, be wail we not how and clamour we not, why

گل به جوش آمد و از می نزدیمش آبی

Into tumult (of blossom) came the rose and its luster, we dashed not with wine

لاجرم ز آتش حرمان و هوس می‌جوشیم

Therefore, with the fire of regret and of desire, we clamour.

می‌کشیم از قدح لاله شرابی موهوم

From the tulip's cup, illusory wine we draw

چشم بد دور که بی مطرب و می مدهوشیم

Far, the evil eye For without the minstrel and wine, distraught are we.

حافظ این حال عجب با که توان گفت که ما

Hafiz to whom can one uttert his wonderful state For, we

بلبلانیم که در موسم گل خاموشیم

Are bulbuls[1] that, in the rose-season, silent are.

غزل ۳۷۷ ⓄⒹⒺ ③⑦⑦

ما شبی دست برآریم و دعایی بکنیم

One night, our hand we shall up lift and a prayer we shall make.

غم هجران تو را چاره ز جایی بکنیم

For the grief of separation from Thee, a remedy from some place we shall make.

دل بیمار شد از دست رفیقان مددی

Went from the hand, the sick heart. O friends a little help

تا طبیبش به سر آریم و دوایی بکنیم

So that to its head, the physician we may bring and a little remedy we may make.

آن که بی جرم برنجید و به تیغم زد و رفت

He who, without offence (on my part) grieved; and, me, with the sword struck and departed

بازش آرید خدا را که صفایی بکنیم

For God's sake, him bring back, that purity of heart (reconciliation) we may make.

خشک شد بیخ طرب راه خرابات کجاست

Withered, became the root of my joy. The Path to the tavern is where

تا در آن آب و هوا نشو و نمایی بکنیم

So that in that water and air, springing and growing, we may make.

مدد از خاطر رندان طلب ای دل ور نه

O heart aid from the heart of profligates seek if not,

کار صعب است مبادا که خطایی بکنیم

Difficult is the work. God forbid that a fault we should make.

1-Nightingale

سایه طایر کم حوصله کاری نکند
(But) a little work effecteth the shade of the bud of little resolution (the imperfect murshid)

طلب از سایه میمون همای بکنیم
Search for the auspicious shade of the Huma (the murshid, perfect and excel, lent) we shall make

دلم از پرده بشد حافظ خوشگوی کجاست
From the note (of melody) went my heart. Hafiz, sweet of tone, is where

تا به قول و غزل ش ساز نوایی بکنیم
So that, with his words and ghazal[1]s, harmony and melody, we may make.

غزل ۳۷۸ ⓄⒹⒺ ③⑦⑧

ما نگوییم بد و میل به ناحق نکنیم
Evil (of any) we utter not inclination of any to the in justice (of any) we make not

جامه کس سیه و دلق خود ازرق نکنیم
Black, (the face of) any one and blue, our own religious garment, we make not,

عیب درویش و توانگر به کم و بیش بد است
Evil, it is (to show) in deficiency or in excess the defect of the poor man, or of the rich man

کار بد مصلحت آن است که مطلق نکنیم
The counsel is that evil work at all, we do not.

رقم مغلطه بر دفتر دانش نزنیم
On the book of knowledge, fallacious writing (like worldly sages) we write not

سر حق بر ورق شعبده ملحق نکنیم
Confounded with the page of magic, God's mystery, we make not.

شاه اگر جرعه رندان نه به حرمت نوشد
If with dignity, the draught of profligates, the king drink not.

التفاتش به می صاف مروق نکنیم
That to his wine, pure and refined, attention, we make not.

خوش برانیم جهان در نظر راهروان
In the sight of way-farers, we happily urge the world (of our time)

فکر اسب سیه و زین مغرق نکنیم
Thought of the (precious) black steed, or of the golden saddle, we make not,

آسمان کشتی ارباب هنر می‌شکند
The sky shattereth the bark of the Lords of skill

تکیه آن به که بر این بحر معلق نکنیم
Best, that, on this suspended ocean (the sky) reliance we make not

گر بدی گفت حسودی و رفیقی رنجید
If an envious one spake evilness and there on a friend grieved,

گو تو خوش باش که ما گوش به احمق نکنیم
(To the friend) Say Happy, be for to the fool, the ear (of attention) we make not

حافظ ار خصم خطا گفت نگیریم بر او
Hafiz if the enemy utter false hood as regards him, (exception) we take not

ور به حق گفت جدل با سخن حق نکنیم
If, with truth, he spake contention with the speech of truth, we make not

---
1-Sonnet

غزل ۳۷۹ ⓞⒹⒺ ③⑦⑨

سرم خوش است و به بانگ بلند می‌گویم
Happy is my head and with loud shout, I speak
که من نسیم حیات از پیاله می‌جویم
Saying Life's breeze from the cup of (the wine of unity) I seek.

عبوس زهد به وجه خمار ننشیند
On the face of wine sickness, sitteth not the sullenness of austerity
مرید خرقه دردی کشان خوش خویم
The disciple of the Khirka[1], dreg-drinker, pleasant of disposition, (murshid of the age, who hath drunk the pure love of past ones) I am

شدم فسانه به سرگشتگی و ابروی دوست
For head-be wilderedness, notorious I became and the Friend's eye-brow
کشید در خم چوگان خویش چون گویم
Me, like a ball, into the curve of its chaugan[2], drew

گرم نه پیر مغان در به روی بگشاید
If, to us, the Pir of the Magians (the perfect murshid) the open not the door,
کدام در بزنم چاره از کجا جویم
What door, shall I beat What remedy, shall I make

مکن در این چمنم سرزنش به خودرویی
In this sward (the world) rebuke me not for self-growing
چنان که پرورشم می‌دهند می‌رویم
As me, nurture they (Fate and Destiny) give, so I grow.

تو خانقاه و خرابات در میانه مبین
In the midst, be hold not thou the monastery and the tavern
خدا گواه که هر جا که هست با اویم
God is witness, wherever He is with Him, am I

غبار راه طلب کیمیای بهروزیست
The dust of the path of search is the alchemy of well being
غلام دولت آن خاک عنبرین بویم
The slave of the fortune of that dust of ambergri ode perfume am I.

ز شوق نرگس مست بلندبالایی
From desire for one of intoxicated narcissus and of lofty stature,
چو لاله با قدح افتاده بر لب جویم
With the goblet, like the tulip fallen, by the marge of the stream, am I.

بیار می که به فتوی حافظ از دل پاک
Wine, bring that, by Hafiz's decision, (down) from the pure heart,
غبار زرق به فیض قدح فروشویم
Hypocrisy's dust, with the goblet's grace, I may wash.

1-Cloak   2-wicket

غزل ۳۸۰ ⓄⒹⒺ ③⑧⓪

بارها گفته‌ام و بار دگر می‌گویم

Times I have said and again I say,

که من دلشده این ره نه به خود می‌پویم

That, heart bereft, not of myself, have I gone this Path (of love)

در پس آینه طوطی صفتم داشته‌اند

Behind the (pure) mirror me, (of the holy traveller's heart) they have kept like the parrot

آن چه استاد ازل گفت بگو می‌گویم

What the Teacher of eternity without beginning said Say I say.

من اگر خارم و گر گل چمن آرایی هست

Whether I be the thorn, or whether the rose, there is a sward-adorner (God)

که از آن دست که او می‌کشدم می‌رویم

By whose hand, as cherished me, I grew

دوستان عیب من بی‌دل حیران مکنید

O friends me, heart-bereft, astonied, censure not

گوهری دارم و صاحب نظری می‌جویم

A great jewel I have and the master of vision (the jeweller God) I seek.

گر چه با دلق ملمع می گلگون عیب است

Although to (the wearer of) the patched (darvish) garment, (the drinking of) wine, rose of hue, is a sin,

مکنم عیب کز او رنگ ریا می‌شویم

Me, censure not for with it (from off the darvish garment) the colour of hypocrisy, I wash

خنده و گریه عشاق ز جایی دگر است

From another place (cause) is the laughing and the weeping of lovers (of God)

می‌سرایم به شب و وقت سحر می‌مویم

In the night (through union with the Beloved) I sing; in the morning-time (through separation) I moan

حافظم گفت که خاک در میخانه مبوی

Tome, Hafiz spake saying The dust of the tavern-door smell not

گو مکن عیب که من مشک ختن می‌بویم

Say Censure not for the (fragrant) musk of Khutan[1], I smell.

غزل ۳۸۱ ⓄⒹⒺ ③⑧①

گر چه ما بندگان پادشهیم

Although, apparently, the slaves of the King are we,

پادشاهان ملک صبحگهیم

(By weeping and wailing) Kings of the country of the morning (when prayers are answered) are we.

گنج در آستین و کیسه تهی

Treasure in the sleeve and empty, the purse

جام گیتی نما و خاک رهیم

The cup, world-displaying, and the dust of the Path (of tarikat) are we.

1-It is a fragrant substance

هوشیار حضور و مست غرور

Sensible of the presence (of God) and intoxicated with pride

بحر توحید و غرقه گنهیم

The ocean of unity and (yet like the) drowned one of sin are we.

شاهد بخت چون کرشمه کند

The mistress of fortune, when she glanceth,

ماش آیینه رخ چو مهیم

The mirror of her moon-like face are we.

شاه بیدار بخت را هر شب

Every night, of the King of vigilant Fortune

ما نگهبان افسر و کلهیم

The care-taker of the diadem and of the crown are we.

گو غنیمت شمار صحبت ما

Say "Our blessing reck on plunder"

که تو در خواب و ما به دیده گهیم

For in sleep thou (art) and, in the eye (sentry – place) are we.

شاه منصور واقف است که ما

The King, Mansur, is acquainted with this, that we

روی همت به هر کجا که نهیم

Wherever the face of resolution, we place

دشمنان را ز خون کفن سازیم

Make for enemies the shroud of blood (and)

دوستان را قبای فتح دهیم

Give to friends the kaba[1] of victory.

رنگ تزویر پیش ما نبود

Not before us, may be the hue of deceit;

شیر سرخیم و افعی سیهیم

(Either), the ruddy (tawny) lion; or the (black) deadly snake, are we.

وام حافظ بگو که بازدهند

The debt of (due to) Hafiz say that they should give back (to him)

کرده‌ای اعتراف و ما گوهیم

(The debt) Thou hast confessed witnesses, are we.

◆◉◆◆◉◆

1-Long garment

ن
The Letter Nūn

غزل ۳۸۲ ①D̂Ê ③⑧②

فاتحه‌ای چو آمدی بر سر خسته‌ای بخوان
To the shattered one, when thou comest, the Fatiha[1] recite
لب بگشا که می‌دهد لعل لبت به مرده جان
Thy lip, open for life to the dead, the ruby of thy lip giveth.

آن که به پرسش آمد و فاتحه خواند و می‌رود
That one (the holy traveller) who, for inquiry (after my state) came the Fatiha readeth and departeth,
گو نفسی که روح را می‌کنم از پی اش روان
A breath where that my soul after him, I may move (sacrifice)

ای که طبیب خسته‌ای روی زبان من ببین
O thou that art the physician of the shattered my face (and) tongue, be hold
کاین دم و دود سینه‌ام بار دل است بر زبان
For, on the tongue, this breath and sigh of my chest is the heart's load

گر چه تب استخوان من کرد ز مهر گرم و رفت
Though hot with love, fever made my bone, and departed,
همچو تبم نمی‌رود آتش مهر از استخوان
From my bone, like the fever, love's fire departeth not.

حال دلم ز خال تو هست در آتشش وطن
Like (the state of) thy (dark) mole on the ruddy fire of its native land (thy luminous, ruddy, cheek) is the state of my heart
چشمم از آن دو چشم تو خسته شده‌ست و ناتوان
On account of those two eyes of thine (that against me consider tyranny lawful) shattered and powerless my body hath become

بازنشان حرارتم ز آب دو دیده و ببین
With the water of my two eyes, quench my heat (of love's fever) and feel
نبض مرا که می‌دهد هیچ ز زندگی نشان
My pulse whether any trace of life it giveth.

آن که مدام شیشه‌ام از پی عیش داده است
That one (the holy traveller) who, for the sake of rest, me, (the wine of) bottle (the heart) had given,
شیشه‌ام از چه می‌برد پیش طبیب هر زمان
Momently, to the physician, my bottle the heart where fore taketh he

حافظ از آب زندگی شعر تو داد شربتم
Hafiz the draught of the water of life, me, thy verse gave
ترک طبیب کن بیا نسخه شربتم بخوان
The physician, forsake come; the prescription of my draught (sweet verse) read.

1-Assembly convened to pray for the dead

غزل ۳۸۳ ⓄⒹⒺ ③⑧③

چندان که گفتم غم با طبیبان
As much as my grief (of love) to the physicians, I uttered,
درمان نکردند مسکین غریبان
(Me) The wretched stranger they remedied not.

آن گل که هر دم در دست بادیست
That (haughty) rose that, momently, is in the power of a thorn,
گو شرم بادش از عندلیبان
Say Thine be shame of the (poor) nightingale

یا رب امان ده تا بازبیند
O Lord! safety, give so that again may see
چشم محبان روی حبیبان
The eye of lovers, the face of the (beloved) ones.

درج محبت بر مهر خود نیست
Not with its own seal is love's casket
یا رب مبادا کام رقیبان
O Lord! the desire of the watchers, be not

ای منعم آخر بر خوان جودت
O Benefactor beloved at the tray of union with Thee, at last,
تا چند باشیم از بی نصیبان
Of those portionless, how long shall we be

حافظ نگشتی شیدای گیتی
The disgrace of the world, Hafiz would not have been,
گر می‌شنیدی پند ادیبان
If, the counsels of admonishers, he had heard.

غزل ۳۸۴ ⓄⒹⒺ ③⑧④

می‌سوزم از فراقت روی از جفا بگردان
(O beloved) from separation from thee, I consume
هجران بلای ما شد یا رب بلا بگردان
Separation (from the beloved) our (soul)-calamity became O Lord! the calamity, turn.

مه جلوه می‌نماید بر سبز خنگ گردون
On the bay courser of the sky, the moon displayeth splendour:
تا او به سر درآید بر رخش پا بگردان
So that, to an end, it may come, to (mighty) Rakhsh[1], thy foot turn.

مر غول را برافشان یعنی به رغم سنبل
Thy love-lock, dishevel that is, against (the tress – like) hyacinth
گرد چمن بخوری همچون صبا بگردان
About the sward, fragrance like the morning breeze be turn

1-The name of horse

یغمای عقل و دین را بیرون خرام سرمست

Forth for the plunder of reason and of faith, intoxicated gracefully move

در سر کلاه بشکن در بر قبا بگردان

On thy head, aslant (in pride) place the (cap), on the body, the kaba be turn

ای نور چشم مستان در عین انتظارم

O light of the eye of the intoxicated in the essence of expectation, I am

چنگ حزین و جامی بنواز یا بگردان

The wailing harp and the cup, (that one, the harp) play and the (this one, the cup) beturn

دوران همی‌نویسد بر عارضش خطی خوش

When, on thy cheek, time writeth the happy line,

یا رب نوشته بد از یار ما بگردان

O Lord! from our friend, the ill-decree, turn.

حافظ ز خوبرویان بختت جز این قدر نیست

Hafiz from lovely ones, (thy) lot, save that portion (that thou hast) is naught

گر نیستت رضایی حکم قضا بگردان

If (as to it) contentment be not thine, fate's decree, turn.

غزل ۳۸۵ ⓄⒹⒺ ③⑧⑤

یا رب آن آهوی مشکین به ختن بازرسان

O lord that musky (fragrant) deer[1] (my beloved) back to Khutan[2] (safely) cause to reach

وان سهی سرو خرامان به چمن بازرسان

And back to the sward that straight, moving, cypress, cause to reach

دل آزرده ما را به نسیمی بنواز

With a breeze (of kindness) our withered fortune, cherish

یعنی آن جان ز تن رفته به تن بازرسان

That is that soul (the beloved) gone from the body, back to the body cause to reach

ماه و خورشید به منزل چو به امر تو رسند

Since, by Thy order, the moon and the sun reach to their stage

یار مه روی مرا نیز به من بازرسان

Back to me also, my beloved, moon of face, cause to reach

دیده‌ها در طلب لعل یمانی خون شد

In search of the ruby of Yaman[3], blood became our eyes

یا رب آن کوکب رخشان به یمن بازرسان

O Lord! back to Yaman, that gleaming constellation cause to reach.

برو ای طایر میمون همایون آثار

O auspicious bird, auspicious of mien (the murshid) go

پیش عنقا سخن زاغ و زغن بازرسان

Before the (inaccessible) Anka[4] (the true Beloved) the word (message) of the crow and of the kite (disciples) back cause to reach.

سخن این است که ما بی تو نخواهیم حیات

The word (message to the beloved) is this Without thee, life we desire not;

بشنو ای پیک خبرگیر و سخن بازرسان

O foot-messenger, news taker back the word (the message) cause to reach

---

1-An allusion to the beloved
2-An allusion to the city of Shiraz

3-It is a country in the south of the Arabian Peninsula
4-Phoenix

آن که بودی وطنش دیده حافظ یا رب

O Lord! that one (the beloved) whose native land had been the eye of Hafiz,

به مرادش ز غریبی به وطن بازرسان

Her, with desire (fulfilled) back from wandering to her native land cause to reach.

غزل ۳۸۶ ⓄⒹⒺ ③⑧⑥

خدا را کم نشین با خرقه پوشان

(O true Beloved) For God's sake, with Khirka[1]-wearers (hypocrites) little sit

رخ از رندان بیسامان مپوشان

From resource less profligates (inwardly pure and clean) Thy face, conceal not

در این خرقه بسی آلودگی هست

In this Khirka (of the austere zahids) is many a stain

خوشا وقت قبای می فروشان

O happy the time of the kaba[2] of the wine-drinkers (void of stain)

در این صوفی وشان دردی ندیدم

Among these Sufi[3]-like ones, a pain (of love) I see not,

که صافی باد عیش دردنوشان

Pure be the pleasure of the dreg-drinkers

تو نازک طبعی و طاقت نیاری

Thou art of delicate nature and power hast not (to endure)

گرانیهای مشتی دلق پوشان

The hard ship of the handful of ragged garment-wearers.

چو مستم کردهای مستور منشین

When (by shewing Thyself) me, intoxicated Thou hast made, veiled, sit not

چو نوشم دادهای زهرم منوشان

When me, the sweet draught Thou hast given, me, poison cause not to drink

بیا و از غبن این سالوسیان بین

Come and the deceit of these hypocrites, be hold

صراحی خون دل و بربط خروشان

(Like) the flagon, (they have the) heart of blood (ruddy wine like) the harp, (they are a-) twanging.

ز دلگرمی حافظ بر حذر باش

Of the heart-ardency of Hafiz full of caution be

که دارد سینهای چون دیگ جوشان

For a heart like the seething caldron, he hath

غزل ۳۸۷ ⓄⒹⒺ ③⑧⑦

شاه شمشادقدان خسرو شیرین دهنان

The Shah of those box-tree of stature, Khusrau of those sweet of mouth,

که به مژگان شکند قلب همه صف شکنان

Who, with His eye-lash, the center (of an army) all rank-shatterers, shattereth,

---

1-Cloak
2-Long garment

3-A Muslim ascetic and mystic

مست بگذشت و نظر بر من درویش انداخت
Passed intoxicated and, on me, the dervish, a glance cast

گفت ای چشم و چراغ همه شیرین سخنان
(And) Said eye and lamp of those all sweet of speech

تا کی از سیم و زرت کیسه تهی خواهد بود
Void of silver and of gold, thy purse how long will be

بنده من شو و برخور ز همه سیمتنان
My slave, be and, of those all silver of body, the fruit enjoy

کمتر از ذره نه‌ای پست مشو مهر بورز
Not less than an atom (a mote) art thou low, be not love, practise

تا به خلوتگه خورشید رسی چرخ زنان
So that, to the sun's chamber of privacy, whirling, thou mayst reach

بر جهان تکیه مکن ور قدحی می داری
On the world, rely not in that goblet, wine thou hast

شادی زهره جبینان خور و نازک بدنان
The pleasure of those Venus of forehead, and tender of body enjoy

پیر پیمانه کش من که روانش خوش باد
Our Pir[1], the wine-measurer whose soul be happy

گفت پرهیز کن از صحبت پیمان شکنان
Said: The society of covenant-breakers, shun.

دامن دوست به دست آر و ز دشمن بگسل
Into the hand, the Friend's skirt bring; from the enemy break away

مرد یزدان شو و فارغ گذر از اهرمنان
The man oi God, be by Ahriman[2], safely pass.

با صبا در چمن لاله سحر می‌گفتم
In the morning, in the parterre (the red streaked) tulips, to the breeze, I spake,

که شهیدان که‌اند این همه خونین کفنان
Saying Martyrs for whom are these, all of bloody shrouds

گفت حافظ من و تو محرم این راز نه‌ایم
(He the breeze) said Not informed of this mystery are we, I and thou,

از می لعل حکایت کن و شیرین دهنان
The tale of the ruby wine, and (of those silver of chin) mention

غزل ۳۸۸ ⓄⒹⒺ ③⑧⑧

بهار و گل طرب انگیز گشت و توبه شکن
Joy-exciting and repentance-shattering became the spring and the rose

به شادی رخ گل بیخ غم ز دل برکن
With the joy of the face of the rose, grief's root from the heart up-pluck.

رسید باد صبا غنچه در هواداری
Arrived the morning-breeze from passion-possessing (love) the rose-bud,

ز خود برون شد و بر خود درید پیراهن
Out from itself, went and on itself the shirt rent (blossomed)

1-A Muslim saint or holy man, Pietist   2-Devil

طریق صدق بیاموز از آب صافی دل

Heart from water-pureness, the path of truth learn

به راستی طلب آزادگی ز سرو چمن

In up rightness, from the (free) cypress of the sward, freedom seek.

ز دستبرد صبا گرد گل کلاله نگر

Through the breeze's violence, the tresses around the rose, be hold:

شکنج گیسوی سنبل ببین به روی سمن

On the face of the jessamine, the curl of the tress of the hyacinth, behold.

عروس غنچه رسید از حرم به طالع سعد

(With this jewel and sweet) smile, the bride, the rose-bud

به عینه دل و دین می‌برد به وجه حسن

Exactly, in an excellent way, my heart and faith ravished.

صفیر بلبل شوریده و نفیر هزار

The shriek of the distraught bulbul[1], and the scream of the hazar,

برای وصل گل آمد برون ز بیت حزن

For the sake of union with the rose, forth from the sad house (of mourning) came.

حدیث صحبت خوبان و جام باده بگو

Hafiz from the cup, the tale of time story seek

به قول حافظ و فتوی پیر صاحب فن

According to the word of (the minstrel) and to the decision of the Pir[2], possessed of knowledge

غزل ۳۸۹ ⓄⒹⒺ ③⑧⑨

چو گل هر دم به بویت جامه در تن

Like the rose, momently, by thy fragrance, the garment of my body,

کنم چاک از گریبان تا به دامن

Rent, I make from collar to skirt.

تنت را دید گل گویی که در باغ

Thou mayst say The rose in the garden, be held thy body

چو مستان جامه را بدرید بر تن

(Since) Like the intoxicated, the garment on its body, it rent.

من از دست غمت مشکل برم جان

From the power of grief for thee, with difficulty, I bear life

ولی دل را تو آسان بردی از من

But, from me, the heart easily thou tookest.

به قول دشمنان برگشتی از دوست

At the word of enemies (watchers) away from the friends (lovers) thou turnedest;

نگردد هیچ کس دوست دشمن

With the friend, enemy none becometh.

تنت در جامه چون در جام باده

Thy body in the garment, like (sparkling) wine in the cup:

دلت در سینه چون در سیم آهن

Thy head in the chest, like (hard, red) iron in (pure white) silver.

1-Nightingale   2-A Muslim saint or holy man

ببار ای شمع اشک از چشم خونین
O candle from thy eye, rain tears (like the cloud)

که شد سوز دلت بر خلق روشن
For, manifest to the people, hath become the consuming of thy heart

مکن کز سینه‌ام آه جگرسوز
Do not, so that, from my breast, the sigh liver-consuming

برآید همچو دود از راه روزن
May ascend like smoke by way of the window.

دلم را مشکن و در پا مینداز
My heart, shatter not; it, under foot, cast not;

که دارد در سر زلف تو مسکن
For in thy tress tip, its dwelling it hath.

چو دل در زلف تو بسته‌ست حافظ
Since to thy tress, Hafiz hath bound his heart

بدین سان کار او در پا میفکن
In this way, his work under foot, cast not.

غزل ۳۹۰ ⓄⒹⒺ ③⑨⓪

افسر سلطان گل پیدا شد از طرف چمن
Displayed from the garden border hath become the diadem of the Sultan, the rose (the true Beloved)

مقدمش یا رب مبارک باد بر سرو و سمن
O lord to the cypress and the jessamine (disciples and lovers of the Path) its arrival happy be

خوش به جای خویشتن بود این نشست خسروی
In his own (proper) place, happy was this imperial sitting (the Sultan, rose)

تا نشیند هر کسی اکنون به جای خویشتن
Since now in his own (proper) place, everyone sitteth

خاتم جم را بشارت ده به حسن خاتمت
To Sulaiman'[1]s seal-ring, news of the happy conclusion give,

کاسم اعظم کرد از او کوتاه دست اهرمن
Where by, short the hand (of power) of ahriman[2] (the enemy) the ism-i-a'zam made.

تا ابد معمور باد این خانه کز خاک درش
Be prosperous to eternity without end, this house (the world) from the door of which,

هر نفس با بوی رحمان می‌وزد باد یمن
Every moment, with the perfume of mercy, the breeze of felicity (the words of the perfect murshid) bloweth

شوکت پور پشنگ و تیغ عالمگیر او
The majesty of Pashang's[3] son, (Afrasiyab, king of Turan) and his world-seizing sword,

در همه شهنامه‌ها شد داستان انجمن
In all king-chronicles, the tale of the assembly is.

1-The name of prophet   3-Afrasiab's father's name
2-Devil

خنگ چوگانی چرخت رام شد در زیر زین

Obedient to thee, became beneath the saddle, the chaugan-steed of the sphere,

شهسوارا چون به میدان آمدی گویی بزن

O royal horseman since to the field (of sport) thou hast come, the ball strike

جویبار ملک را آب روان شمشیر توست

The stream of the country is the water luster of thy sword

تو درخت عدل بنشان بیخ بدخواهان بکن

The tree of justice, plant thou: the root of ill-wishers, tip-pluck.

بعد از این نشکفت اگر با نکهت خلق خوشت

After this if, despite the perfume of thy sweet nature, it (Iran) blossometh not,

خیزد از صحرای ایذج نافه مشک ختن

From Iran's plain, the musk-pod of the musk of Khutan[1] (the well-being and welfare of Iran) ariseth (and departeth)

گوشه گیران انتظار جلوه خوش می کنند

Expectation of sweets plendour, the corner-takers (recluses) make,

برشکن طرف کلاه و برقع از رخ برفکن

Aslant (in pride) place the cap and, from thy face, the veil up-pluck.

مشورت با عقل کردم گفت حافظ می بنوش

(In love – playing) with (my own) reason, I consulted. He said Hafiz drink wine

ساقیا می ده به قول مستشار متمن

O Saki[2] according to the word of the trusty adviser (reason) wine give.

ای صبا بر ساقی بزم اتابک عرضه دار

O breeze to the Saki of the banquet of Atabak (the praised one) prefer the request,

تا از آن جام زرافشان جرعهای بخشد به من

That, from that cup, gold scattering, me, a draugh the may give

غزل ۳۹۱ ⓄⒹⒺ ③⑨① ODE 391

خوشتر از فکر می و جام چه خواهد بودن

Than the thought of wine and of the cup, more pleasant what will be?

تا ببینم که سرانجام چه خواهد بودن

Let us see the end what will be.

غم دل چند توان خورد که ایام نماند

The heart's grief how can one suffer, when time remaineth not

گو نه دل باش و نه ایام چه خواهد بودن

Say Be neither heart nor time, what will be

مرغ کم حوصله را گو غم خود خور که بر او

To the bird of little spirit, say Thy own grief, suffer For, on it (the bird)

رحم آن کس که نهد دام چه خواهد بودن

The pity of that one who planteth the snare what will be

باده خور غم مخور و پند مقلد منیوش

Wine, drink grief, suffer not the counsel of the imitator (the adviser of the people) hear not

اعتبار سخن عام چه خواهد بودن

To the speech of the (common) people (of this world) credit what will be

---

1-It is a fragrant substance

2-Tapster

دست رنج تو همان به که شود صرف به کام

Verily ('tis) best that thy hand-toil be expended according to desire

دانی آخر که به ناکام چه خواهد بودن

Thou knowest that, at last, to one desire un-attained what will be.

پیر میخانه همی‌خواند معمایی دوش

Last night, the Pir[1] of the tavern (the murshid) kept uttering an enigma

از خط جام که فرجام چه خواهد بودن

Of the line of the cup (of love 'Tis necessary to see) the end, what will be.

بردم از ره دل حافظ به دف و چنگ و غزل

From the Path, Hafiz's heart I took (seduced) with the drum, the harp, and the ghazal

تا جزای من بدنام چه خواهد بودن

Let us see, the requital of me of ill-name what will be.

غزل ۳۹۲ ①ⒹⒺ ③⑨② ODE

دانی که چیست دولت دیدار یار دیدن

Knowest thou what fortune is? 'Tis be holding the sight (true) of the Beloved

در کوی او گدایی بر خسروی گزیدن

In His street, beggary to royalty preferring.

از جان طمع بریدن آسان بود ولیکن

Easy it is to sever desire for life But,

از دوستان جانی مشکل توان بریدن

(Only with) difficulty, (friendship), for friends dear as one's soul, can one sever.

خواهم شدن به بستان چون غنچه با دل تنگ

Like the folded bud, with a straitened heart, to the rose-garden, I will go

وان جا به نیک نامی پیراهنی دریدن

And, there, my garment of good fame, will rend

گه چون نسیم با گل راز نهفته گفتن

Sometimes, like the breeze, hidden mystery with the rose will utter

گه سر عشقبازی از بلبلان شنیدن

Sometimes, from the bulbuls[2], the mystery of love-playing will hear.

بوسیدن لب یار اول ز دست مگذار

First (in this world) from the hand, the kissing of the lip of (true) the Beloved give not up

کخر ملول گردی از دست و لب گزیدن

For, at last (in the next world) thou mayst be distressed (wearied) with the gnawing (in regret) of thy own hand and lip

فرصت شمار صحبت کز این دوراهه منزل

(O heart) The society of friends, opportunity reckon For, from this two-pathed stage (the world)

چون بگذریم دیگر نتوان به هم رسیدن

When (from it) away we pass, (this society) again one cannot reach.

گویی برفت حافظ از یاد شاه یحیی

Thou mayst say From the memory of King Mansur passed Hafiz

یا رب به یادش آور درویش پروریدن

O Lord! to his (Mansur's) memory (thought of) the cherishing the dervish (Hafiz) bring.

1-A Muslim saint or holy man, Pietist 2-Nightingale

غزل ۳۹۳ ⓄⒹⒺ ③⑨③

منم که شهره شهرم به عشق ورزیدن
That one, am I who am renowned for love-playing;

منم که دیده نیالودم به بد دیدن
Not that one, am I who have stained my eye with ill seeing.

وفا کنیم و ملامت کشیم و خوش باشیم
Fidelity, we practise reproach, endure and happy are

که در طریقت ما کافریست رنجیدن
For, in our shari'at[1], in fidelity is grieving.

به پیر میکده گفتم که چیست راه نجات
To the Pir[2] of the wine-house, I spake saying Salvation's path is what

بخواست جام می و گفت عیب پوشیدن
The cup of wine, he demanded and said 'Tis mystery (of love) concealing

مراد دل ز تماشای باغ عالم چیست
From the spectacle of the garden of the (illusory) world, our object is what

به دست مردم چشم از رخ تو گل چیدن
(He said) From thy (ruddy) face, by means of the pupil of the eye, rose-plucking

به می پرستی از آن نقش خود زدم بر آب
For wine-worshipping, the picture of (self-worshipping and self – seeing) on the water I dashed, for the reason,

که تا خراب کنم نقش خود پرستیدن
That I might destroy the picture of self-worshipping.

به رحمت سر زلف تو واثقم ور نه
To the mercy of thy tres ode tip, trusting I am If not

کشش چو نبود از آن سو چه سود کوشیدن
When from that side is no attraction, what profit striving.

عنان به میکده خواهیم تافت زین مجلس
From this assembly of those (without work) to the wine-house (love's stage) the rein will we turn

که وعظ بی عملان واجب است نشنیدن
For the counsel of those without work, improper is the hearing.

ز خط یار بیاموز مهر با رخ خوب
From the down of the friend, love for the lovely cheek (of the Beloved) learn

که گرد عارض خوبان خوش است گردیدن
For, about the cheek of lovely ones, pleasant is wandering.

مبوس جز لب ساقی و جام می حافظ
Hafiz save the lip of the Beloved and the cup of wine, naught kiss

که دست زهدفروشان خطاست بوسیدن
For, the hand of austerity-boasters, sin is kissing.

1-Religion   2-A Muslim saint or holy man, Pietist

غزل ۳۹۴ ODE 394

ای روی ماه منظر تو نوبهار حسن

O Thou, whose face, moon in appearance, (is) the fresh spring of beauty.

خال و خط تو مرکز حسن و مدار حسن

Whose mole and down (are) the center of grace, and the circle of beauty

در چشم پرخمار تو پنهان فسون سحر

Hidden in Thy eye full of intoxication the fascination of sorcery

در زلف بی‌قرار تو پیدا قرار حسن

Revealed on Thy restless (floating) tress, the (calm) rest of beauty

ماهی نتافت همچو تو از برج نیکویی

Not a moon shone like Thee from the mansion of goodness

سروی نخاست چون قدت از جویبار حسن

Not a cypress arose like Thy stature from the stream of

خرم شد از ملاحت تو عهد دلبری

By Thy darkish beauty, joyous became the age of heart-ravishingness;

فرخ شد از لطافت تو روزگار حسن

By Thy grace, expanded became the season of beauty.

از دام زلف و دانه خال تو در جهان

From the snare of Thy tress, and the grain of Thy mole, in the world,

یک مرغ دل نماند نگشته شکار حسن

Not a bird of the heart remaineth, not become the prey of beauty.

دایم به لطف دایه طبع از میان جان

Ever, with grace, from the midst of life nature's nurse,

می‌پرورد به ناز تو را در کنار حسن

Thee, cherisheth with care in the bosom of beauty.

گرد لبت بنفشه از آن تازه و تر است

Fresh and fresh is the (dark) violet (hair) about Thy lip, for that reason,

کب حیات می‌خورد از جویبار حسن

That it keepeth drinking the water of life from the fountain-source of beauty

حافظ طمع برید که بیند نظیر تو

Hafiz severed desire when he seeth Thy equal

دیار نیست جز رخت اندر دیار حسن

There is none save Thy face in the land of beauty.

غزل ۳۹۵ ODE 395

گلبرگ را ز سنبل مشکین نقاب کن

(O Beloved) For Thy rose-leaf (ruddy face) of the musky (fragrant) hyacin (the tress) the veil make

یعنی که رخ بپوش و جهانی خراب کن

That is Thy face conceal and a world ruined make

بفشان عرق ز چهره و اطراف باغ را

The sweat from Thy face, scatter on the borders of the garden

چون شیشه‌های دیده ما پرگلاب کن

As (from seeing Thee) the flagons of our eyes (are full of rose-water, tears) so full of rose-water (the garden) make.

ایام گل چو عمر به رفتن شتاب کرد

Haste for departing, like (swift) life, the rose-season maketh:

ساق به دور باده گلگون شتاب کن

Saki in the circulation of the cup of roseate hue, haste make.

بگشا به شیوه نرگس پرخواب مست را

Thy narcissus, full of sleep, intoxicated, grace fully open

و از رشک چشم نرگس رعنا به خواب کن

And, in envy (of Thy eye) to sleep the eye of the lovely narcissus put.

بوی بنفشه بشنو و زلف نگار گیر

The (dark) violet's perfume, perceive and the (dark) tress of the idol (the true Beloved) take

بنگر به رنگ لاله و عزم شراب کن

At the (want of) colour of the (white) lily, gaze resolution for (the ruddy) wine make

زان جا که رسم و عادت عاشق کشی توست

Since the way and usage of lover-slaying is thine

با دشمنان قدح کش و با ما عتاب کن

With enemies, the goblet drain with us, reproach make.

همچون حباب دیده به روی قدح گشای

On the face of the goblet (the murshid) like (vanishing) bubbles, open thy eye;

وین خانه را قیاس اساس از حباب کن

The foundation of this (world) house from that of (vanishing) bubbles, estimation make.

حافظ وصال می‌طلبد از ره دعا

By the path of prayer, union, Hafiz seeketh

یا رب دعای خسته دلان مستجاب کن

O Lord! the prayer of those heart-broken accepted make.

غزل ۳۹۶ ⊙Ⓓ Ⓔ ③⑨⑥ ODE 396

صبح است ساقیا قدحی پرشراب کن

O Saki[1] 'tis the morn (of youth) full of wine (of divine knowledge) a goblet make

دور فلک درنگ ندارد شتاب کن

The sky's revolution delayeth not haste make

زان پیشتر که عالم فانی شود خراب

Before that ruined this vanishing world becometh,

ما را ز جام باده گلگون خراب کن

With the cup of ruddy wine (true love) us, ruined (intoxicated) make.

خورشید می ز مشرق ساغر طلوع کرد

From the east, the cup (the heart of 'Arifs) the sun of wine (divine knowledge) made appear

گر برگ عیش می‌طلبی ترک خواب کن

If (true) pleasure thou seek, abandoning of the sleep (of carelessness) make.

روزی که چرخ از گل ما کوزه‌ها کند

One day, when out of our clay, pitchers the sky maketh

زنهار کاسه سر ما پرشراب کن

Take care, the cup (skull – pan) of our head full of wine (true love for God) make.

1-Tapster

ما مرد زهد و توبه و طامات نیستیم
Not the man of austerity, nor of penitence, nor of foolish talk are we,
با ما به جام باده صافی خطاب کن
to us, with a cup of pure wine (truth) address make.

کار صواب باده پرستیست حافظا
Hafiz wine-worshipping; (love-playing; divine knowledge – gathering) is the good work
برخیز و عزم جزم به کار صواب کن
Arise to the good work, (the face of) resolution turn

غزل ۳۹۷ ODE 397

ز در درآ و شبستان ما منور کن
(O true Beloved) By the door enter, and our chamber luminous make
هوای مجلس روحانیان معطر کن
The air of the assembly of souls perfumed make.

اگر فقیه نصیحت کند که عشق مباز
If a Fakih[1] advise saying Love practise not
پیاله‌ای بدهش گو دماغ را تر کن
(Him), the cup (of the wine of unity) give say: Thy brain, fresh make.

به چشم و ابروی جانان سپرده‌ام دل و جان
(O true Beloved) To the eye and the eye-brow of the (illusory) beloved, heart and soul, I have entrusted
بیا بیا و تماشای طاق و منظر کن
Come, come and (with the glance of blessing) viewing of the arch (the eye – brow) and of the spectacle-place (the eye) make.

ستاره شب هجران نمی‌فشاند نور
Lights cattereth not the star of the (dark) night of separation the (illusory be – loved)
به بام قصر برآ و چراغ مه برکن
To the palace-roof (the existence of Hafiz) come and the lamp of the moon (the beauty of the true Beloved) uplifted make.

بگو به خازن جنت که خاک این مجلس
To the treasurer of Jannat[2], speak, saying: The dust of this assembly,
به تحفه بر سوی فردوس و عود مجمر کن
As a present to Firdaus[3] take and (it) the aloe-fuel of the censer make.

از این مزوجه و خرقه نیک در تنگم
From this one associated with me (the wife) and the Khirka[4] much in strait I am
به یک کرشمه صوفی وشم قلندر کن
With a glance Sufi-slaying, me Kalandar[5] make.

چو شاهدان چمن زیردست حسن تواند
Since beneath Thy hand (are) the lovely ones (the flowers) of the sward,
کرشمه بر سمن و جلوه بر صنوبر کن
At the jessamine, the glance and towards the cone-tree, grace make

---

1-Lawyer
2-Heaven
3-Heaven

4-Cloak
5-Insouciant

فضول نفس حکایت بسی کند ساقی

O Saki (Murshid) excess of many a tale, the spirit maketh

تو کار خود مده از دست و می به ساغر کن

From the hand, thy own work (the explanation of truths to holy travellers) give not; wine (the delight that surgeth in the traveller's heart) into the cup put.

حجاب دیده ادراک شد شعاع جمال

The splendour-rays of beauty (of illusory love) the veil of the eye of understanding, became

بیا و خرگه خورشید را منور کن

Come the sun's pavilion (the elemental body) effulgent make.

طمع به قند وصال تو حد ما نبود

Not our limit, is desire for the cash of union with Thee

حوالتم به لب لعل همچو شکر کن

With (that) ruby (lip) like sugar, (me a kiss) give

لب پیاله ببوس آنگهی به مستان ده

The lip of the cup, kiss (subtleties of divine knowledge, acquire) then to the intoxicated) holy travellers) give

بدین دقیقه دماغ معاشران تر کن

With this subtlety, (wisdom's train) be perfumed make.

پس از ملازمت عیش و عشق مه رویان

After the service of pleasure and of love, of those moon of face,

ز کارها که کنی شعر حافظ از بر کن

Of deeds that thou doest, the verse of Hafiz exalted make.

غزل ۳۹۸ ⓄⒹⒺ ③⑨⑧

ای نور چشم من سخنی هست گوش کن

O light of my eye (the holy traveller) a matter there is, hear

چون ساغرت پر است بنوشان و نوش کن

Since thy cup (of love for God) is full cause others to drink; and thyself drink.

در راه عشق وسوسه اهرمن بسیست

In love's path, Ahriman's[1] temptations are many

پیش آی و گوش دل به پیام سروش کن

Sense keep and to Surush's[2] message the ear of the heart put.

برگ نوا تبه شد و ساز طرب نماند

Ruined became subsistence remaineth not the means of joy

ای چنگ ناله برکش و ای دف خروش کن

O harp the wail (of grief) draw out O drum exult.

تسبیح و خرقه لذت مستی نبخشدت

Thee, intoxication's delight, the rosary and the Khirka[3] (men of outward forms hypocrites) give not

همت در این عمل طلب از می فروش کن

In this matter, of the wine-seller (the murshid, perfect and excellent) blessing demand.

1-Devil
2-Heavenly Call

3-Cloak

پیران سخن ز تجربه گویند گفتمت
With experience, old men utter words to thee, I said
هان ای پسر که پیر شوی پند گوش کن
Ho O son that old thou mayst become, counsel hear.

بر هوشمند سلسله ننهاد دست عشق
On the sensible one (the philosopher and the man) of reason the chain, love's hand placeth not
خواهی که زلف یار کشی ترک هوش کن
Thou wishest to draw (through thy hand) the tress of the Friend, sense abandon.

با دوستان مضایقه در عمر و مال نیست
In respect to life and property, for friends (lovers of God) need is none
صد جان فدای یار نصیحت نیوش کن
A hundred lives, the ransom for the (true) Beloved (make) counsel hear

ساقی که جامت از می صافی تهی مباد
O Saki[1] (perfect murshid) void of pure wine, be not thy cup
چشم عنایتی به من دردنوش کن
On me, dreg-drinker, an eye (glance) of favour make.

سرمست در قبای زرافشان چو بگذری
When, in the gold scattering kaba[2], thou, intoxicated, passest,
یک بوسه نذر حافظ پشمینه پوش کن
To Hafiz, wool-wearer, (Safi) one kiss, present.

غزل ۳۹۹ ⓄⒹⒺ ③⑨⑨

کرشمه‌ای کن و بازار ساحری بشکن
(O beloved) Glance make and the market of enchantment shatter
به غمزه رونق و ناموس سامری بشکن
With the glance of splendour, the face of the (enchanter) Samiri[3], shatter,

به باد ده سر و دستار عالمی یعنی
To the wind (of destruction) the head (of pride) and the turban (of pomp) of a whole
world give That is
کلاه گوشه به آیین سروری بشکن
In the way of heart-ravishingness, the cap (aslant over) thy ear place

به زلف گوی که آیین دلبری بگذار
To the tress, say The way of arrogance, abandon
به غمزه گوی که قلب ستمگری بشکن
To the glance, say Oppression's army, shatter.

برون خرام و ببر گوی خوبی از همه کس
(O beloved) forth (from thy ab ode) grace fully move and from every one, the ball
(of beauty) take
سزای حور بده رونق پری بشکن
Punishment to (the lovely) Hur[4], give the splendour of beauty of the Pan, shatter.

1-Tapster
2-Long garment

3-A person who made a calf in the absence of Prophet Moses
and encouraged the Hebrews to worship it
4-lover

به آهوان نظر شیر آفتاب بگیر

With thy deer-eyes, take the glance of (captivate) the lion of the sun (the mansion of Leo)

به ابروان دوتا قوس مشتری بشکن

With thy curved eye-brows, the bow of Jupiter the mansion of Sagittarius shatter.

چو عطرسای شود زلف سنبل از دم باد

When, from the breath of the breeze, 'itr-exhaling, becometh the hyacinth,

تو قیمتش به سر زلف عنبری بشکن

Its worth, with the tip of thy be perfumed tress, shatter.

چو عندلیب فصاحت فروشد ای حافظ

O Hafiz! when the bulbul[1] boasteth of eloquence

تو قدر او به سخن گفتن دری بشکن

Its worth, by uttering (the courtly) Dari, do thou shatter.

غزل ۴۰۰ ⊙ⒹⒺ ④⓪⓪ ODE 400

بالا بلند عشوه گر نقش باز من

One lofty of stature, bold, picture-player of mine

کوتاه کرد قصه زهد دراز من

Made short the tale (of renown) of the long austerity of mine.

دیدی دلا که آخر پیری و زهد و علم

O heart thou sawest at the end of old age, of austerity, and of knowledge,

با من چه کرد دیده معشوقه باز من

What, with me, it did, the eye of the beloved of mine

می‌ترسم از خرابی ایمان که می‌برد

The destruction of my faith, I fear. For taketh,

محراب ابروی تو حضور نماز من

The prayer-arch of Thy eyebrow the presence (essence) of prayer of mine

گفتم به دلق زرق بپوشم نشان عشق

(To myself) I said With the garment of hypocrisy, love's trace, I concealed;

غماز بود اشک و عیان کرد راز من

The informer was the tear and made manifest the mystery of mine.

مست است یار و یاد حریفان نمی‌کند

Intoxicated, is the Friend and recollection of rivals (lovers) maketh not

ذکرش به خیر ساقی مسکین نواز من

His mention (be) for good, the Saki, the wretched-cherisher of mine.

یا رب کی آن صبا بوزد کز نسیم آن

O Lord! when bloweth that breeze, from whose fragrant breath

گردد شمامه کرمش کارساز من

A perfume of His mercy becometh the work-doer of mine

نقشی بر آب می‌زنم از گریه حالیا

With weeping, a picture on water I depict Now

تا کی شود قرین حقیقت مجاز من

How long associated becometh the truth with the illusory of mine

---

1-Nightingale

بر خود چو شمع خنده زنان گریه می‌کنم

On myself, like the laughing candle (consuming and melting) I weep,

تا با تو سنگ دل چه کند سوز و ساز من

Till I see what with thee, O heart of stone, maketh (worketh) the consuming of (mine).

زاهد چو از نماز تو کاری نمی‌رود

Zahid (equal are we) when a work (favourably) proceedeth neither by prayer of thine;

هم مستی شبانه و راز و نیاز من

Nor also, (by) the nightly intoxication and (consuming) and supplicating of mine.

حافظ ز گریه سوخت بگو حالش ای صبا

With grief Hafiz burned O breeze his state, say

با شاه دوست پرور دشمن گداز من

To the King, friend-cherisher, enemy-destroyer, of mine.

غزل ۴۰۱ ⓄⒹⒺ ④⓪①

چون شوم خاک رهش دامن بیفشاند ز من

When (to reach His skirt) the dust of His path, I become, His skirt He shaketh from me

ور بگویم دل بگردان رو بگرداند ز من

If I say: (In love) my heart, return, His face, He turneth from me,

روی رنگین را به هر کس می‌نماید همچو گل

To everyone, He displayeth His hued cheek like the red rose,

ور بگویم بازپوشان بازپوشاند ز من

If I say: (Thy face from others) conceal (In grief at that His face) He concealeth from me

چشم خود را گفتم آخر یک نظر سیرش ببین

To my eye, I spake saying At last, Him once fully be hold

گفت می‌خواهی مگر تا جوی خون راند ز من

It (the eye) said Perchance thou wishest that a stream of blood should pour from me.

او به خونم تشنه و من بر لبش تا چون شود

Thirsty for my blood, He and for, (His blood) I So that when it happeneth,

کام بستانم از او یا داد بستاند ز من

My desire I will take from Him; or justice (revenge) He will take from me.

گر چو فرهادم به تلخی جان برآید باک نیست

If, like Farhad, my life in bitterness issueth, there is no fear

بس حکایت‌های شیرین باز می‌ماند ز من

Many sweet tales remain behind of me.

گر چو شمعش پیش میرم بر غمم خندان شود

If before Him, like the candle, I die, at my grief, He laughcth (like the morning)

ور برنجم خاطر نازک برنجاند ز من

If I grieve, His tender heart is grieved against me.

دوستان جان داده‌ام بهر دهانش بنگرید

Friends for His mouth, be hold ye my life, I gave

کو به چیزی مختصر چون باز می‌ماند ز من

Say: How for a trifling matter, He keepeth back from me.

صبر کن حافظ که گر زین دست باشد درس غم

Hafiz (conclude). For, if in this way, love's less on (thou read)

عشق در هر گوشه‌ای افسانه‌ای خواند ز من

In every corner, love uttereth tales of me.

غزل ۴۰۲ ⓞⓓⓔ ④⓪②

نکته‌ای دلکش بگویم خال آن مه رو ببین

A heart-alluring subtlety, I utter, the mole of that one moon of face, be hold.

عقل و جان را بسته زنجیر آن گیسو ببین

Bound with the chain of that tress, my reason and soul be hold

عیب دل کردم که وحشی وضع و هرجایی مباش

My heart, I censured, saying: One of bestial, or one of desert, nature, be not;

گفت چشم شیرگیر و غنج آن آهو ببین

It said The eye (half intoxicated of) the bold one of that deer (the true Beloved) be hold

حلقه زلفش تماشاخانه باد صباست

The ring of His tress is the spectacle-place of the morning breeze

جان صد صاحب دل آن جا بسته یک مو ببین

There, bound by every hair (of His) the soul of a hundred persons possessed of heart, (Sufis) be hold.

عابدان آفتاب از دلبر ما غافلند

Careless of our heart-ravisher, are the Abids[1] (worshippers) of the sun

ای ملامتگو خدا را رو مبین آن رو ببین

O reproach (-utterer) for God's sake, the face (of my true Beloved) be hold (and) not the face (of the sun) be hold.

زلف دل دزدش صبا را بند بر گردن نهاد

The ligature on the wind's neck, His tress, heart-stealing, placed

با هواداران ره رو حیله هندو ببین

Against the desires of the Path, the Hindu's snare (the dark tress) be hold.

این که من در جست و جوی او ز خود فارغ شدم

That one, in whose search, I of myself went astray,

کس ندیده‌ست و نبیند مثلش از هر سو ببین

Like Him, none hath seen, nor will see every quarter be hold.

حافظ ار در گوشه محراب می‌نالد رواست

If, in the corner of the prayer-arch (of the Beloved's eye-brow) Hafiz, (rub his face) it is lawful;

ای نصیحتگو خدا را آن خم ابرو ببین

O reproach-utterer for God's sake, that curve of the eye-brow be hold.

از مراد شاه منصور ای فلک سر برمتاب

O sky away from the purpose of king Mansur, thy face turn not

تیزی شمشیر بنگر قوت بازو ببین

The keenness of his sword, be hold the power of his arm, be hold

---

1-Eremite

غزل ۴۰۳ ⓄⒹⒺ ④⓪③

شراب لعل کش و روی مه جبینان بین

Ruby wine (love for the true Beloved) drink, and the face of those moon of forehead
(Arifs of God) behold

خلاف مذهب آنان جمال اینان بین

Contrary to the religious order of those (Abids, and Zahids, outward worship.pers)
the beauty of these (the Arifs of God) behold.

به زیر دلق ملمع کمندها دارند

Beneath the gilded garment, nooses (of prayer) they (the Arifs and the recognisers of God) have

درازدستی این کوته آستینان بین

(Notwithstanding their poverty) The long-handedness (loftiness of spirit) of these short of sleeve
(the Arifs poor of resource) the be hold

به خرمن دو جهان سر فرو نمی‌آرند

For the harvest of both worlds, their head, they lower not

دماغ و کبر گدایان و خوشه چینان بین

The brain and pride of beggars, corn-gleaners, be hold

بهای نیم کرشمه هزار جان طلبند

The frown from the eye-browfull of frown, the Friend looseneth not:

نیاز اهل دل و ناز نازنینان بین

The need of people of heart, and the grace of the dainty (beloved) ones, behold

حقوق صحبت ما را به باد داد و برفت

From none, the tale of the covenant of love, I hear:

وفای صحبت یاران و همنشینان بین

The non fidelity of the society of friends and of fellow-sitters behold

اسیر عشق شدن چاره خلاص من است

The means of release (from imperious lust) is to become captive to love

ضمیر عاقبت اندیش پیش بینان بین

The fore-seeing mind of the fore-seers behold.

کدورت از دل حافظ ببرد صحبت دوست

(Love's polish, the dust) of Hafiz's heart taketh.

صفای همت پاکان و پاکدینان بین

The purity of (the pure mirror of) those pure of faith behold.

غزل ۴۰۴ ⓄⒹⒺ ④⓪④

می‌فکن بر صف رندان نظری بهتر از این

On the rank of profligates keep casting a glance better than this

بر در میکده می گذری بهتر از این

To the door of the wine-house establish a thorough-fare better than this.

در حق من لبت این لطف که می‌فرماید

This grace that in respect of me, thy Lip displayeth

سخت خوب است ولیکن قدری بهتر از این

Is very good but (make it) a little better than this.

آن که فکرش گره از کار جهان بگشاید

To that one, whose thought looseneth the knot (of difficulty) the world's work,

گو در این کار بفرما نظری بهتر از این

Say In this (subtlety of love) make (reflection) better than this.

ناصحم گفت که جز غم چه هنر دارد عشق

Tome, the admonisher spoke, saying: Save grief, what specialty hath love

برو ای خواجه عاقل هنری بهتر از این

(I said) O wise Khwaja[1] (it hath) ask ill better than this.

دل بدان رود گرامی چه کنم گر ندهم

If to that beautiful youth, my heart I give not, what shall I do

مادر دهر ندارد پسری بهتر از این

Time's mother hath not a youth better than this.

من چو گویم که قدح نوش و لب ساق بوس

Me, who speak, saying: The goblet, take; and in (drinking the cup's) lip kiss

بشنو از من که نگوید دگری بهتر از این

Hear, (O beloved) for, another speaketh not*better than this.

کلک حافظ شکرین میوه نباتیست به چین

The sweetest (branch) of the sugar-cane is Hafiz's reed Pluck

که در این باغ نبینی ثمری بهتر از این

For, in this garden, thou be holdest not a fruit better than this

❖◉❖◉❖

1--Eunuch, dignitary, vizier, boss, host

و
The Letter Wāw

ⓞⓓⓔ ⓐⓞⓢ غزل ۴۰۵

به جان پیر خرابات و حق صحبت او

By the soul of the Pir[1] of the tavern and by my gratitude for the favour of his,

که نیست در سر من جز هوای خدمت او

(I swear) That, in my head, is naught save desire of service of his

بهشت اگر چه نه جای گناهکاران است

Not the place of sinners, though paradise be,

بیار باده که مستظهرم به همت او

(Saki) wine, bring for I am one who imploreth the mercy (i) of His.

چراغ صاعقه آن سحاب روشن باد

Luminous be the lamp of lightning of that cloud

که زد به خرمن ما آتش محبت او

That, to our harvest (of existence) dashed the fire of love of His

بر آستانه میخانه گر سری بینی

If, on the threshold of the wine-house, a head thou see,

مزن به پای که معلوم نیست نیت او

With the foot, kick not. Not known, is the purpose of His

بیا که دوش به مستی سروش عالم غیب

(Saki wine bring.For me) Last night, Surush[2] of the invisible world

نوید داد که عام است فیض رحمت او

Gave news Universal, is the bounty of mercy of His

مکن به چشم حقارت نگاه در من مست

(O Zahid, self – beholding) at me intoxicated look not with the eye of contempt

که نیست معصیت و زهد بی مشیت او

Neither is iniquity nor austerity without the will of His.

نمی‌کند دل من میل زهد و توبه ولی

No inclination to austerity and penitence, maketh my heart But,

به نام خواجه بکوشیم و فر دولت او

For the Khwaja's[3] name, I will strive and for the glory of the fortune of his.

مدام خرقه حافظ به باده در گرو است

Ever in pawn for wine is Hafiz's Khirka[4]

مگر ز خاک خرابات بود فطرت او

Perchance of the tavern-dust, may be the nature of his

1-A Muslim ascetic and mystic

2-Angel

3-A Muslim saint ascetic and mystic

4-Cloak

غزل ۴۰۶ ⓄⒹⒺ ④⓪⑥

گفتا برون شدی به تماشای ماه نو
(The beloved) Said Forth, thou wentest for the spectacle of the new (crescent) moon
از ماه ابروان منت شرم باد رو
Thine, be shame of my (crescent) moon eye-brows (that are more glorious) go

عمریست تا دلت ز اسیران زلف ماست
'Tis a life (time) since, (of the crowd) of captives of our tress, thy heart was
غافل ز حفظ جانب یاران خود مشو
Of keeping the side of thy friends, careless be not

مفروش عطر عقل به هندوی زلف ما
For the blackness of (the friend's) tress, sell not the 'itr[1] of reason
کان جا هزار نافه مشکین به نیم جو
For, there, (they sell) a thousand musk-pods of musk for half abarley-corn.

تخم وفا و مهر در این کهنه کشته زار
In this old sown-place (this world) the seed of fidelity and of love,
آن گه عیان شود که بود موسم درو
At that time becometh manifest when arriveth the time of reaping

ساقی بیار باده که رمزی بگویمت
Saki wine bring for to thee, a mystery, I will tell
از سر اختران کهن سیر و ماه نو
Of the mystery of the old star; (and) of the wandering of the new moon.

شکل هلال هر سر مه می‌دهد نشان
The end of every month, the (waning) form of the moon giveth trace
از افسر سیامک و ترک کلاه زو
Of (the end of) the diadem of Siyamak[2], and of the abandoning of the crown of Zhu[3]

حافظ جناب پیر مغان مامن وفاست
Hafiz the threshold of the Pir[4] of the Magians is the for tress of fidelity
درس حدیث عشق بر او خوان و ز او شنو
To him, read the lesson of love's tale and from him (counsel) hear.

غزل ۴۰۷ ⓄⒹⒺ ④⓪⑦

مزرع سبز فلک دیدم و داس مه نو
The green expanse of sky, I be held and the sickle (the crescent) of the new moon
یادم از کشته خویش آمد و هنگام درو
To me, recollection came of my owns own-field and of the time of reaping (the judgment – day)

گفتم ای بخت بخفتیدی و خورشید دمید
I said fortune thou hast slept and appeared hath the sun
گفت با این همه از سابقه نومید مشو
He said Despite all this, hopeless of the past, be not.

1-Fragrance
2-He was a prince who fought for the salvation of his tribe and the reign of his father and lost his life in the process.

3-Zoo was the son of Tahmaseb after Afrasiab killed Nozar; Zhu reached the throne
4-A Muslim saint or holy man, Pietist

گر روی پاک و مجرد چو مسیحا به فلک

If, like the Masiha[1] (the anointed one) to the sky (heaven) thou go pure and free (of the body)

از چراغ تو به خورشید رسد صد صد پرتو

To the sun, will reach many a ray of thy splendour.

تکیه بر اختر شب دزد مکن کاین عیار

On the star, the (wandering) thief of night, rely not. For this knave

تاج کاووس ببرد و کمر کیخسرو

Took the crown of Kay Kavus[2] and the girdle of Kay Khosrau[3].

گوشوار زر و لعل ار چه گران دارد گوش

Although the ear be heavy (with dull to) the ear-ring of gold and of ruby (profitable counsel)

دور خوبی گذران است نصیحت بشنو

The season of beauteousness (youthfulness) is passing counsel, hear

چشم بد دور ز خال تو که در عرصه حسن

From thy mole, far the evil eye For, on the chess board of beauty,

بیدق راند که برد از مه و خورشید گرو

It (thy mole) moved a pawn that, from the moon and the sun (the moles of the sky) so the bet won.

آسمان گو مفروش این عظمت کاندر عشق

Tell the sky Boast not of this pomp For in love,

خرمن مه به جوی خوشه پروین به دو جو

(They sell) The moon's harvest (the halo) for a barley-corn the (and) cluster of the Pleiades for two barley-corns.

آتش زهد و ریا خرمن دین خواهد سوخت

The fire of hyprocrisy and deceit will consume the harvest of religion

حافظ این خرقه پشمینه بینداز و برو

Hafiz this woollen Khirka, cast away and go.

غزل ۴۰۸ ⓞⓓⓔ ④⓪⑧

ای آفتاب آینه دار جمال تو

O Thou, (that hast) the resplendent sun the mirror-holder of the beauty of Thine

مشک سیاه مجمره گردان خال تو

(And) The musk, (dark fragrant tress) the censer-circulator of the (dark) mole of Thine

صحن سرای دیده بشستم ولی چه سود

The court-yard of the palace of the eye, I washed. But what profit

کاین گوشه نیست درخور خیل خیال تو

Not fit is this retired corner for the troop of the fancy (of love) of Thine

در اوج ناز و نعمتی ای پادشاه حسن

O sun of beauty in the height of grace and graciousness, thou art

یا رب مباد تا به قیامت زوال تو

O Lord! till the up standing (the resurrection) be no decline of Thine

---

1-Jesus Christ

2-Kay Kavus is one of the kings of Kian who came to the kingdom after "Kay Qobad".

3-Kay Khosrau is also one of the sons of Siavash who came to the kingdom after Kay kavus

مطبوعتر ز نقش تو صورت نبست باز

More agreeable than Thy picture, no picture, delineated

طغرانویس ابروی مشکین مثال تو

The Tughra-scribe (God, great and glorious) the musky (dark be perfumed) eye-brow
like (the eye – brow) of Thine

در چین زلفش ای دل مسکین چگونه‌ای

O poor heart in the curl of His tress, how art thou

کشفته گفت باد صبا شرح حال تو

For perturbed, the morning breeze uttered the circumstances of thine

برخاست بوی گل ز در آشتی درآی

(O beloved) Hath risen the perfume, of the rose by the door of friend ship come (and union choose)

ای نوبهار ما رخ فرخنده فال تو

O fresh spring of ours the auspicious face (is) the omen of Thine.

تا آسمان ز حلقه به گوشان ما شود

So that (of the crowd) of our beringed ones (slaves) the sky may be,

کو عشوه‌ای ز ابروی همچون هلال تو

Where, the charm of an eye-brow like the new (crescent) moon of Thine

تا پیش بخت بازروم تهنیت کنان

So that offering congratulation, I may go back to fortune,

کو مژده‌ای ز مقدم عید وصال تو

Where, the glad tidings of the approach of the 'id of the union-of Thine

این نقطه سیاه که آمد مدار نور

This dark spot, that became the center (of) luminosity,

عکسیست در حدیقه بینش ز خال تو

Is in the fold of vision, (only) are flection of the (dark) mole of Thine

در پیش شاه عرض کدامین جفا کنم

Before the Khwaja which hardship shall I represent

شرح نیازمندی خود یا ملال تو

The explanation of my own need (was) the displeasure of Thine.

حافظ در این کمند سر سرکشان بسیست

Hafiz in this noose (the beloved's tress) is the head of many a head strong one;

سودای کج مپز که نباشد مجال تو

Crude passion, indulge not; for it is not the power of thine.

غزل ۴۰۹ ⓄⒹⒺ ④⓪⑨

ای خونبهای نافه چین خاک راه تو

O thou (that hast) the blood-price of the (precious) musk-pod of Chin, the dust of the path of thine

خورشید سایه پرور طرف کلاه تو

(and) The sun, cherished in the shade of the border of the cap of thine

نرگس کرشمه می‌برد از حد برون خرام

(O beloved) Forth beyond limit, the narcissus carrieth her (amorous) glance move forth
(and display thy glance that the narcissus may know thy worth)

ای من فدای شیوه چشم سیاه تو

O soul (be) a sacrifice for the glance of the dark eye of thine

خونم بخور که هیچ ملک با چنان جمال

My blood, drink For, with beauty like this, (even) any angel,

از دل نیایدش که نویسد گناه تو

From his heart, it cometh not to record the sin of thine.

آرام و خواب خلق جهان را سبب توبی

O beloved The cause thou art of the people's ease and the world's slumber

زان شد کنار دیده و دل تکیه گاه تو

On that account, the border of my eye and of my heart became the repose-place of thine.

با هر ستاره‌ای سر و کار است هر شبم

Mine, every night (in recollection of thy effulgent face) with every (gleaming) star is the work (of weeping and wailing)

از حسرت فروغ رخ همچو ماه تو

In envious regret for the splendour of the moon-like (effulgent) face of thine

یاران همنشین همه از هم جدا شدند

From each other separated all are friends, fellow-sitters

ماییم و آستانه دولت پناه تو

(But) together are I and the threshold of the empire-shelter of thine.

حافظ طمع مبر ز عنایت که عاقبت

Hafiz favour, desire not. For, in the end,

آتش زند به خرمن غم دود آه تو

To grief' sharvest, setteth fire the smoke of the sigh of

غزل ۴۱۰ ⓄⒹⒺ ④①⓪

ای قبای پادشاهی راست بر بالای تو

O thou (that hast) the kaba[1] of sovereignty, true to the stature-of thine

زینت تاج و نگین از گوهر والای تو

Decoration (hath) the crown and the seal-ring from the lofty jewel of thine.

آفتاب فتح را هر دم طلوعی می‌دهد

Momently, to the sun of victory, giveth rise,

از کلاه خسروی رخسار مه سیمای تو

From out of the imperial cap, the cheek of moon form of thine.

جلوه گاه طایر اقبال باشد هر کجا

The splendour-place of the bird of fortune is wherever,

سایه‌اندازد همای چتر گردون سای تو

(its) Shadow casteth the Huma of the canopy, sphere-scraping of thine.

از رسوم شرع و حکمت با هزاران اختلاف

(O perfect murshid) Notwithstanding a thousand diversities of the ways of the shara'[2], and of philosophy (divine knowledge)

نکته‌ای هرگز نشد فوت از دل دانای تو

Never a point (of the lofty shara') passed unexplained from the wise heart of thine.

1-Long garment   2-Principle, Sufism, religious way

آب حیوانش ز منقار بلاغت می‌چکد

From its beak of eloquence droppeth the water of life

طوطی خوش لهجه یعنی کلک شکرخای تو

The parrot sweet of note that is, (O king) the sugar-devouring reed of thine.

گر چه خورشید فلک چشم و چراغ عالم است

Although the sun of the sky is the eye and the lamp of the world

روشنایی بخش چشم اوست خاک پای تو

The light-giving of its eye is (only) the dust of the foot of thine

آن چه اسکندر طلب کرد و ندادش روزگار

What Sikandar [1] desired and him, time gave not

جرعه‌ای بود از زلال جام جان افزای تو

Was a draught of pure water of the cup, life-refreshing, of thine

عرض حاجت در حریم حضرتت محتاج نیست

Not in the fold of thy majesty is need of the representation of need

راز کس مخفی نماند با فروغ رای تو

Concealed is the secret of none to the splendour of the judgment of thine

خسروا پیرانه سر حافظ جوانی می‌کند

O Khusrau[2]! Youthfulness putteth the elderly head of Hafiz

بر امید عفو جان بخش گنه فرسای تو

In hope of the pardon, life-giving, sin-forgiving of thine.

غزل ۴۱۱ ⓄⒹⒺ ④①①

تاب بنفشه می‌دهد طره مشک سای تو

Torment (of envy) to the violet, giveth the musk-exhaling tress of thine.

پرده غنچه می‌درد خنده دلگشای تو

The fold of the rose-bud, rendeth the heart-alluring laughter of thine.

ای گل خوش نسیم من بلبل خویش را مسوز

O my rose, sweet of perfume (the beloved) thy bulbul[3] (thy lover, in separation) consume not

کز سر صدق می‌کند شب همه شب دعای تو

For, night, all night, with the essence of sincerity, it makfth prayer for (the welfare of) thine.

من که ملول گشتمی از نفس فرشتگان

I who, with the breathing (murmuring) of angels used to be vexed (so delicate was my nature)

قال و مقال عالمی می‌کشم از برای تو

(Now) The disputation of a whole world (high and low) I endure for the sake of Thee

دولت عشق بین که چون از سر فقر و افتخار

Love's fortune be hold, how, for the desire of pomp and glory,

گوشه تاج سلطنت می‌شکند گدای تو

The corner of the crown of sovereignty aslant placeth, the beggar of Thine

خرقه زهد و جام می گر چه نه درخور همند

Though not fitted matched together are the Khirka[4] of austerity, and the cup of wine,

این همه نقش می‌زنم از جهت رضای تو

All this picture, I paint trick I play for the sake of the will of Thine

---

1-King of Macedonia in ancient Greece 3-Nightingale
2-King 4-Cloak

شور شراب عشق تو آن نفسم رود ز سر

Goeth from my head, wine's clamouring (and) love's (consuming) at that moment

کاین سر پرهوس شود خاک در سرای تو

When this head full of passion becometh the dust of the door of the ab ode of Thine.

شاهنشین چشم من تکیه گه خیال توست

My eye's king-seat is the resting-place of Thy image

جای دعاست شاه من بی تو مباد جای تو

A place of prayer it is. O my sovereign, without thee, be not the place of Thine

خوش چمنیست عارضت خاصه که در بهار حسن

A pleasant sward is Thy cheek, especially when in the spring of beauty,

حافظ خوش کلام شد مرغ سخنسرای تو

Hafiz, sweet of speech, became the bird, song-singing, 'of Thine,

غزل ۴۱۲ ⓄⒹⒺ ④①②

مرا چشمیست خون افشان ز دست آن کمان ابرو

Mine is an eye, blood-shedding on account of the eye of that bow eye-brow

جهان بس فتنه خواهد دید از آن چشم و از آن ابرو

Full of tumult will be comethe world on account of that eye, and of that eye-brow.

غلام چشم آن ترکم که در خواب خوش مستی

The slave of the eye I am of that saucy one (such) that, in the sweet sleep of intoxication,

نگارین گلشنش روی است و مشکین سایبان ابرو

The adorned rose-bed is her face and the musky canopy, her eye brow

هلالی شد تنم زین غم که با طغرای ابرویش

Through this grief, my body became (lean and slender like) a crescent moon. For, notwithstanding (her musky) dark (fragrant) writing (the decorated eyebrow)

که باشد مه که بنماید ز طاق آسمان ابرو

Where is the moon that, from the arch of sky will (dare) show its eye-brow.

رقیبان غافل و ما را از آن چشم و جبین هر دم

The watchers careless, (unacquainted with my secrets and) momently, from that eye and forehead, ours

هزاران گونه پیغام است و حاجب در میان ابرو

Are a thousand kinds of message and, the curtain between (them is) the eye-brow.

روان گوشه گیران را جبینش طرفه گلزاریست

To the soul of the corner-sitters, (the beauty of) the rose-bed (is only a little of his beauty)

که بر طرف سمن زارش همی‌گردد چمان ابرو

On the border of whose sward, a saunter becometh the eye-brow

دگر حور و پری را کس نگوید با چنین حسنی

Notwithstanding such beauty, again none speaketh of the Hur and the Pari[1]

که این را این چنین چشم است و آن را آن چنان ابرو

Saying: "Of this (the Hur) is like this, the eye; and of that (the Pari) like that, the eye-brow."

تو کافردل نمی‌بندی نقاب زلف و می‌ترسم

Thou, Kafir of heart, bindest not the veil of thy tress. I fear

که محرابم بگرداند خم آن دلستان ابرو

That my prayer-arch will turn, the curve of that heart-ravishing eye-brow.

1-Angel and the black-eyed woman of heaven

اگر چه مرغ زیرک بود حافظ در هواداری

Although, in possessing fidelity, Hafiz is the wise bird (yet)

به تیر غمزه صیدش کرد چشم آن کمان ابرو

Him, with the arrow of the glance, prey made, the eye of that bow eye-brow

غزل ۴۱۳   ⓞⓓⓔ ④①③

خط عذار یار که بگرفت ماه از او

The down (the world's up – springing) of the true Beloved's cheek, eclipsed is the moon by which,

خوش حلقهایست لیک به در نیست راه از او

Is a joyous ring; but path is none out from it.

ابروی دوست گوشه محراب دولت است

The eye-brow (the world, the stage of acquisition of love) of the Friend (God) is the corner (stone) of the prayer-arch of fortune

آن جا بمال چهره و حاجت بخواه از او

There, thy face rub thy need (the degrees of the first and the last world and the ladders of loftiest stages) ask from Him.

ای جرعه نوش مجلس جم سینه پاک دار

O thou (that art) the draught-drinker (the holy traveller) of the assembly of Jamshid[1] (the murshid, perfect and excellent) thy heart keep pure

کیینهایست جام جهان بین که آه از او

For a mirror this is the cup world-viewing (the heart of the murshid) Alas for it.

کردار اهل صومعهام کرد می پرست

The (hypocritical) conduct of the men of the monastery (abids and the austere ones, who for deceiving men, made wailing) me, a wine-worshipper, made.

این دود بین که نامه من شد سیاه از او

Be hold this smoke (of their hypocritical wailing and sighing) black (with wine-worshipping) became my book by which

سلطان غم هر آن چه تواند بگو بکن

To the Shaitan of grief, whatever is possible say (and) do

من بردهام به باده فروشان پناه از او

With the wine-sellers to whom no access is hisI have taken shelter from him.

ساقی چراغ می به ره آفتاب دار

Saki[2] the luminous lamp of wine on the sun's path keep

گو برفروز مشعله صبحگاه از او

Say: the torch of the morning enkindle from it.

آبی به روزنامه اعمال ما فشان

(O murshid) On the day-record of our deeds, a (little) water (of thy kindness) scatter

باشد توان سترد حروف گناه از او

Perchance, the letters of sin, one can efface with it

حافظ که ساز مطرب عشاق ساز کرد

Hafiz, who, the arrangement of the assembly of the lovers straight made,

خالی مباد عرصه این بزمگاه از او

The space of this banquet-place be not void of him

1-king   2-Tapster

آیا در این خیال که دارد گدای شهر

In this fancy, that a city-beggar hath,

روزی بود که یاد کند پادشاه از او

May it be that, one day, the king may make recollection of him

غزل ۴۱۴ ⊙ⒹⒺ ④①④

گلبن عیش می‌دمد ساقی گلعذار کو

Pleasure's rose-bush blossometh the Saki, rose of cheek, where

باد بهار می‌وزد باده خوشگوار کو

Bloweth the spring breeze the pleasant tasting wine, where

هر گل نو ز گلرخی یاد همی‌کند ولی

Recollection of one rose of cheek (the beloved) keepeth giving every fresh rose But,

گوش سخن شنو کجا دیده اعتبار کو

The ear, speech (of counsel) hearing where The eye of caution (to see) where

مجلس بزم عیش را غالیه مراد نیست

For the assembly of pleasure's banquet, is no perfumed ball of desire

ای دم صبح خوش نفس نافه زلف یار کو

O breath of morn, sweet of soul the musk-pod of the Friend's tress where

حسن فروشی گلم نیست تحمل ای صبا

O breeze not mine is endurance of the beauty-boasting of the rose

دست زدم به خون دل بهر خدا نگار کو

In the heart's blood, my hand I dashed For God's sake, the beauteous one where

شمع سحرگهی اگر لاف ز عارض تو زد

(With malevolence) The candle of the morn boasted of (having) thy (ruddy) cheek

خصم زبان دراز شد خنجر آبدار کو

Long of tongue became the enemy the dagger, luster-possessing where

گفت مگر ز لعل من بوسه نداری آرزو

He (the Beloved) said Per chance, the kiss of My ruby (lip) thou desireth not.

مردم از این هوس ولی قدرت و اختیار کو

Through this desire (for a kiss) I died; but, (mine) the power and the will where

حافظ اگر چه در سخن خازن گنج حکمت است

Though in speech, the treasurer of the treasure of wisdom is Hafiz,

از غم روزگار دون طبع سخن گزار کو

Of the grief of time, mean of nature, the speech-utterer where

غزل ۴۱۵ ⊙ⒹⒺ ④①⑤

ای پیک راستان خبر یار ما بگو

Messenger of the true ones! (sincere lovers) news of our Beloved utter:

احوال گل به بلبل دستان سرا بگو

To the bulbul[1], song-singing (the lover) the state of the rose (the Beloved) utter.

1-Nightingale

ما محرمان خلوت انسیم غم مخور

Confidants (lovers) of the chamber of affection, are we grief, suffer not

با یار آشنا سخن آشنا بگو

To the kind friend, mention of the Friend (the Beloved) make.

برهم چو می‌زد آن سر زلفین مشکبار

When those two tres ode tips dashed together

با ما سر چه داشت ز بهر خدا بگو

O breeze! Come, what mystery those two tress tips had, utter.

هر کس که گفت خاک در دوست توتیاست

Everyone who said The dust of the Friend's door is kuhl

گو این سخن معاینه در چشم ما بگو

(To him) Say Exhibited in our eye, this matter (was this, to another) say

آن کس که منع ما ز خرابات می‌کند

(The Sufi), who prohibiteth us the tavern,

گو در حضور پیر من این ماجرا بگو

Say In the presence of my Pir[1], this matter, utter.

گر دیگرت بر آن در دولت گذر بود

If, again, by that door of fortune, passing be thine,

بعد از ادای خدمت و عرض دعا بگو

After the service of attendance, and the presentation of prayer, say

هر چند ما بدیم تو ما را بدان مگیر

Though we be bad, us, bad regard not

شاهانه ماجرای گناه گدا بگو

Sovereign-like, the tale of the beggar's sin utter.

بر این فقیر نامه آن محتشم بخوان

To this fakir[2], the letter of that great one, read

با این گدا حکایت آن پادشا بگو

To this beggar, the tale of that King, utter

جان‌ها ز دام زلف چو بر خاک می‌فشاند

When, from the snare of His tress, He scattered hearts on the dust,

بر آن غریب ما چه گذشت ای صبا بگو

To that our miserable (heart) what chanced, (out by way of love), utter.

جان پرور است قصه ارباب معرفت

Soul-cherishing, is the tale of the Lords of ma'rifat[3]

رمزی برو بپرس حدیثی بیا بگو

(In respect of it), a mystery ask (and) a tale, come (and) utter.

حافظ گرت به مجلس او راه می‌دهند

Hafiz if to His assembly thee, the path (of access) they give,

می نوش و ترک زرق ز بهر خدا بگو

Wine, drink and, for God's sake, the abandoning of hypocrisy utter

◈ ◉ ◈ ◉ ◈

1-A Muslim saint ascetic and mystic   3-Wise
2-poor

ه

The Letter Hā

غزل ۴۱۶ ⓄⒹⒺ ④①⑥

خنک نسیم معنبر شمامهای دلخواه

Happy (is) the breeze, ambergris be-perfumed, a perfumed pastile, desired of heart,

که در هوای تو برخاست بامداد پگاه

That, in desire of thee, a rose early the morning

دلیل راه شو ای طایر خجسته لقا

O bird of auspicious face (the murshid, perfect, excellent) the road-guide be

که دیده آب شد از شوق خاک آن درگاه

For, from desire of the dust of that court (of God) water hath become my eye.

به یاد شخص نزارم که غرق خون دل است

In recollection of my slender person, that is immersed in the blood (of grief) of the heart,

هلال را ز کنار افق کنید نگاه

The new (slender crescent) moon, from the quarter of the (ruddy) crepuscule, they regard.

منم که بی تو نفس میکشم زهی خجلت

That one am I who, without thee, breathe. What shame!

مگر تو عفو کنی ور نه چیست عذر گناه

Perchance, thou mayst pardon If not, the excuse for sin is what?

ز دوستان تو آموخت در طریقت مهر

In love's path, from thy friends, learned

سپیده دم که صبا چاک زد شعار سیاه

The dawn, that (desire) rent the black (under)-garment.

به عشق روی تو روزی که از جهان بروم

In love for thy (roseate) face, one day when, from this world, I depart

ز تربتم بدمد سرخ گل به جای گیاه

From my tomb, the red rose in place of green herbage, shall blossom

مده به خاطر نازک ملالت از من زود

For me (Hafiz) give not grief (access) to thy tender heart

که حافظ تو خود این لحظه گفت بسم الله

For, this moment, thy Hafiz himself uttered bismi-llah (and in death departed)

غزل ۴۱۷ ⓄⒹⒺ ④①⑦

عیشم مدام است از لعل دلخواه

From the heart-desiring ruby (lip of the true Beloved) ever is my ease

کارم به کام است الحمدلله

(And) My work to desire, alhamdu-l-illah

ای بخت سرکش تنگش به بر کش

O obstinate fortune Him, to thy bosom, tightly draw

گه جام زر کش گه لعل دلخواه

Drink, sometimes, the cup of gold sometimes, the heart-desiring ruby (lip)

ما را به رندی افسانه کردند

Us, in intoxication, tales told,

پیران جاهل شیخان گمراه

The ignorant Pirs[1] (and) road-lost Shaikhs[2]

از دست زاهد کردیم توبه

Of the Zahid's[3] word, we repented

و از فعل عابد استغفرالله

And of the abid's deed, we seek the pardon of God.

جانا چه گویم شرح فراقت

O soul the explanation of separation, how shall I utter

چشمی و صد نم جانی و صد آه

(Together are) An eye and a hundred humidities (tears) a (stricken) a soul and a hundred sighs

کافر مبیناد این غم که دیدهست

Let not the Kafir see (experience) this grief that hath seen (experienced)

از قامتت سرو از عارضت ماه

The cypress from thy (lofty) stature (and) the moon from thy (luminous) cheek.

شوق لبت برد از یاد حافظ

From Hafiz's memory, the desire of Thy face took (made forgotten)

درس شبانه ورد سحرگاه

The prayer (of) the night-time (and) the lesson of the morning-time.

غزل ۴۱۸ ⓞⒹⒺ ④①⑧

گر تیغ بارد در کوی آن ماه

If, in the street of that moon (the true Beloved) the sword of calamity rain

گردن نهادیم الحکم لله

(Beneath it) The neck, we have placed. The order is of God.

آیین تقوا ما نیز دانیم

There gulation of piety, we also k now

لیکن چه چاره با بخت گمراه

But, with (our) road-lost fortune, remedy (is) what

ما شیخ و واعظ کمتر شناسیم

The shaikh[4] and the admonisher, we seldom recognise

یا جام باده یا قصه کوتاه

Either (give) the cup of wine or (make) the tale short.

من رند و عاشق در موسم گل

I profligate and lover (then repentance)

آن گاه توبه استغفرالله

(seek pardon from God) from God, I seek pardon

مهر تو عکسی بر ما نیفکند

Upon us, not a reflection (the glory of manifestations from) the sun of Thy face fell:

آیینه رویا آه از دلت آه

O mirror of (face) Alas Thy (hard) heart, alas

1-A Muslim saint ascetic and mystic   3-Pietist
2-A leader in a Muslim community   4-A leader in a Muslim community

الصبر مر و العمر فان
Bitter, is patience fleeting is life

یا لیت شعری حتام القاه
(This being doomed to live) how long shall I experience

حافظ چه نالی گر وصل خواهی
Hafiz why complaineth thou, if union thou desirest

خون بایدت خورد در گاه و بی‌گاه
In season and out of season, it is necessary for thee to drink the blood (of grief)

غزل ۴۱۹   ⓄⒹⒺ ④①⑨

وصال او ز عمر جاودان به
Union with (the Beloved) than ever lasting life, better

خداوندا مرا آن ده که آن به
O Lord! me that (union) give for that (is) best.

به شمشیرم زد و با کس نگفتم
Me, with the sword, He struck and to none, I spake

که راز دوست از دشمن نهان به
For, concealed from the enemy, the Beloved's mystery best.

به داغ بندگی مردن بر این در
With the mark of service, at this door (of the Beloved) to die

به جان او که از ملک جهان به
By His soul (I swear) that, than the region of the (whole) world, (it is) better

خدا را از طبیب من بپرسید
For God's sake, ask my physician, (the Beloved)

که آخر کی شود این ناتوان به
Saying: "At last, when (by the remedy of union) becometh this powerless one (through separation) better."

گلی کان پایمال سرو ما گشت
That rose, that foot-trodden of our cypress (the Beloved) becometh

بود خاکش ز خون ارغوان به
Its dust (trampled leaf) than The blood of the (ruddy) arghavan[1], better

به خلدم دعوت ای زاهد مفرما
O Zahid[2] me, to paradise invite not

که این سیب زنخ زان بوستان به
For this apple of the chin (dimple of the Beloved) than that garden (of paradise) better.

دلا دایم گدای کوی او باش
O heart be ever a beggar of His street

به حکم آن که دولت جاودان به
By the decree Perpetual fortune best

جوانا سر متاب از پند پیران
O youth from the counsel of old men, turn not thy head

که رای پیر از بخت جوان به
For, the old man's counsel than youthful fortune, better.

1-Flower   2-Pietist

شبی می‌گفت چشم کس ندیده‌ست
One night He said My eye hath seen none

ز مروارید گوشم در جهان به
In the world, than the pearl of my ear better.

اگر چه زنده رود آب حیات است
Although the Zinda river (of Isfahan) is the water of life

ولی شیراز ما از اصفهان به
Yet our Shlraz than Is fahan, better

سخن اندر دهان دوست شکر
In the Beloved's mouth, speech (is) the jewel

ولیکن گفته حافظ از آن به
But, Hafiz's utterance than that, better.

غزل ۴۲۰ ۞ ODE 420 ۞

ناگهان پرده برانداخته‌ای یعنی چه
(O beloved) suddenly, thy veil thou up-castedest. This is what?

مست از خانه برون تاخته‌ای یعنی چه
Intoxicated, forth from the house, thou hastenedest. This is what?

زلف در دست صبا گوش به فرمان رقیب
In the power of the breeze, thy tress (thou hast given) to the order of the watcher,
thy ear (thou hast placed)

این چنین با همه درساخته‌ای یعنی چه
Thus, with all thou hast contented thy self. This is what

شاه خوبانی و منظور گدایان شده‌ای
The king of the lovely ones, thou art and the accepted of beggars, thou hast become

قدر این مرتبه نشناخته‌ای یعنی چه
The degree of this rank, thou hast not recognised. This is what

نه سر زلف خود اول تو به دستم دادی
Fresh, to my hand, thy tress tip, gavest thou not

بازم از پای درانداخته‌ای یعنی چه
Then, down from my foot (powerless) me thou castedest. This is what

سخنت رمز دهان گفت و کمر سر میان
The mystery of thy mouth, thy speech told the mystery of thy waist, thy girdle

و از میان تیغ به ما آخته‌ای یعنی چه
Yet, from the girdle, against me, the sword thou hast drawn. This is what

هر کس از مهره مهر تو به نقشی مشغول
(Intently) engaged with the die of love, everyone

عاقبت با همه کج باخته‌ای یعنی چه
In the end, with all, crookedly, thou hast played. This is what

حافظا در دل تنگت چو فرود آمد یار
Hafiz when, in thy straitened heart, the beloved alighted

خانه از غیر نپرداخته‌ای یعنی چه
The house void of the stranger, (why) madest thou not This is what

غزل ۴۲۱ ⓄⒹⒺ ④②①

در سرای مغان رفته بود و آب زده
The door (threshold) of the Magians' house was swept and water-sprinkled

نشسته پیر و صلایی به شیخ و شاب زده
(At the door) The Pir sat, and to old and to young, salutation gave

سبوکشان همه در بندگیش بسته کمر
In his service, the cup-lifters (topers) all loin-girt

ولی ز ترک کله چتر بر سحاب زده
But, with the cap-crown, the canopy above the cloud was fixed.

شعاع جام و قدح نور ماه پوشیده
The splendour of the cup and the goblet (holy travellers, possessed of excellence) concealed the light of the moon (the qualities of the young magians, Sakis of the tavern)

عذار مغبچگان راه آفتاب زده
The path of the young Magians to the sun (the splendour of the glory of unity) the cheeks (of the holy travellers, possessed of excellence, joined with the qualities of God) waylaid.

عروس بخت در آن حجله با هزاران ناز
In that chamber of privacy, notwithstanding all her graces, the bride of fortune

شکسته کسمه و بر برگ گل گلاب زده
Placed indigo and, on the tress of dark, fragrant musk, musk shed.

گرفته ساغر عشرت فرشته رحمت
The angel of mercy (the perfect murshid) took the cup of delight (ma'rifat)

ز جرعه بر رخ حور و پری گلاب زده
(And) From the dregs, on the face of Hur and of Pari (seekers of God) rose-water, dashed.

ز شور و عربده شاهدان شیرین کار
From the grace and the strife, (in state of restlessness of) the Sakis (the seekers possessed of excellence) sweet of work,

شکر شکسته سمن ریخته رباب زده
Sugar broke a sunder; (its petals) the lily shed (its cords) the harp snapped

سلام کردم و با من به روی خندان گفت
(To the bride of fortune) salutation, I made and, with laughing face, she spake

که ای خمارکش مفلس شراب زده
Saying O sufferer of wine-sickness, poor, wine stricken

که این کند که تو کردی به ضعف همت و رای
Who doeth this that thou, with weak judgment and reason, hast done

ز گنج خانه شده خیمه بر خراب زده
From the treasure wine-house, thou hast gone and thy tent on the waste hast pitched.

وصال دولت بیدار ترسمت ندهند
Thee, union with wakeful fortune, I fear that they (fate and destiny) will not give;

که خفته‌ای تو در آغوش بخت خواب زده
For thou art asleep in the embrace of fortune, sleep stricken

بیا به میکده حافظ که بر تو عرضه کنم
Hafiz to the wine-house, come that to thee, I may present

هزار صف ز دعاهای مستجاب زده
Of those whose prayers are answered a hundred ranks arrayed

فلک جنیبه کش شاه نصره الدین است

The sky is the led-horse leader of king Nasratu-d-Din

بیا ببین ملکش دست در رکاب زده

Come; his hand in his stirrup, be hold the angel hath fixed.

خرد که ملهم غیب است بهر کسب شرف

For the sake of gaining honour, wisdom, that is in spired of the Hidden,

ز بام عرش صدش بوسه بر جناب زده

From the vault of the ninth heaven, a hundred kisses on his majesty cast

غزل ۴۲۲ ⓄⒹⒺ ④②②

ای که با سلسله زلف دراز آمدهای

O thou that, with the long trailing tress, hast come

فرصتت باد که دیوانه نواز آمدهای

Thine be leisure for, (with love) pitying the distraught, thou hast come.

ساعتی ناز مفرما و بگردان عادت

One moment, disdain display not thy custom (so that by thee, they may be prosperous) alter

چون به پرسیدن ارباب نیاز آمدهای

For, for inquiring (after the state) of the Lords of need thou hast come

پیش بالای تو میرم چه به صلح و چه به جنگ

Before thy (cypress) stature, (I boast) whether (thou be) in peace or in war;

چون به هر حال برازنده ناز آمدهای

Because, in every state, (as) the up lifter (the taker away) of disdain thou hast come.

آب و آتش به هم آمیختهای از لب لعل

(O beloved) Out of that lip of ruby, thou hast evoked water and fire

چشم بد دور که بس شعبده بازآمدهای

Far (be) the evil eye for the sweet magic-player (strangely mixing water and fire) thou hast come.

آفرین بر دل نرم تو که از بهر ثواب

Afarin[1] on thy tender heart, for the sake of good,

کشته غمزه خود را به نماز آمدهای

To him slain by thy glance, in prayer, thou hast come.

زهد من با تو چه سنجد که به یغمای دلم

With thee, what weigheth my austerity For the plundering-of my heart

مست و آشفته به خلوتگه راز آمدهای

Intoxicated and perturbed, to the khilvat[2]-place of mystery, thou hast come.

گفت حافظ دگرت خرقه شراب آلودهست

Hafiz said Again, wine-stained is thy Khirka[3]

مگر از مذهب این طایفه بازآمدهای

Perchance, back from this religious order of this band zahids and sufis thou hast come

---

1-Well done
2-Solitude

3-Cloak

غزل ۴۲۳ ⓄⒹⒺ ④②③

دوش رفتم به در میکده خواب آلوده
Last night, to the door of the wine-house, I went, sleep stained
خرقه تر دامن و سجاده شراب آلوده
The Khirka wet of skirt, and the prayer-mat, wine stained

آمد افسوس کنان مغبچه باده فروش
Them again boy of the wine-seller, cry-making, came
گفت بیدار شو ای ره رو خواب آلوده
He said Awake, O way farer, sleep stained.

شست و شویی کن و آن گه به خرابات خرام
Washing and washing, do then, to the tavern, proudly move
تا نگردد ز تو این دیر خراب آلوده
So that, by thee, this ruined cloister become not' stained

به هوای لب شیرین پسران چند کنی
In desire for (those) sweet of mouth (beloved ones) how long makest thou
جوهر روح به یاقوت مذاب آلوده
The jewel of thy soul with the melted ruby (the bloody tear) stained

به طهارت گذران منزل پیری و مکن
In purity, pass the stage of old age and make not,
خلعت شیب چو تشریف شباب آلوده
The honour-robe of old age, with the splendid dress of youth, stained.

پاک و صافی شو و از چاه طبیعت به درآی
Pure And clean, be and, from nature's well, come forth
که صفایی ندهد آب تراب آلوده
Giveth not purity water, earth stained.

گفتم ای جان جهان دفتر گل عیبی نیست
I said O soul of the world not a defect is it, the rose-book
که شود فصل بهار از می ناب آلوده
(If) In the spring season, it become with pure (ruddy) wine be stained

آشنایان ره عشق در این بحر عمیق
In this deep sea (of love) those acquainted with love's path,
غرقه گشتند و نگشتند به آب آلوده
Were drowned and were not with water stained.

گفت حافظ لغز و نکته به یاران مفروش
He said: Hafiz to friends, thy jest and subtlety boast not;
آه از این لطف به انواع عتاب آلوده
Alas for this (thy) grace, with varied forms of reproach be stained.

غزل ۴۲۴ ⓄⒹⒺ ④②④

از من جدا مشو که توام نور دیده‌ای
(O beloved) separate from me, be not for, the light of my eye thou art
آرام جان و مونس قلب رمیده‌ای
The ease of soul and the friend of the heart-distraught one

از دامن تو دست ندارند عاشقان
Off from thy skirt, (restless) lovers keep not their hand
پیراهن صبوری ایشان دریده‌ای
Their garment of patience, thou hast rent

از چشم بخت خویش مبادت گزند از آنک
From the (evil) eye-, (wound of the people) no injury be thine (for).
در دلبری به غایت خوبی رسیده‌ای
To exceeding beauty in heart-ravishing ness, thou hast attained

منعم مکن ز عشق وی ای مفتی زمان
Their garment of patience, thou hast rent
معذور دارمت که تو او را ندیده‌ای
I hold the excused for her thou hast not seen.

آن سرزنش که کرد تو را دوست حافظا
Hafiz this reproach that the friend made thee,
بیش از گلیم خویش مگر پا کشیده‌ای
Perchance, out from the blanket, thy foot thou hast drawn.

غزل ۴۲۵ ⓄⒹⒺ ④②⑤

دامن کشان همی‌شد در شرب زرکشیده
The skirt-trailer (damsel) kept moving in cloth, gold-embroidered,
صد ماه رو ز رشکش جیب قصب دریده
In envy of her, a hundred moon-of-face, the collar of hempen cloth rent

از تاب آتش می بر گرد عارضش خوی
From the heat of the fire of wine, round about her cheek, sweat
چون قطره‌های شبنم بر برگ گل چکیده
Like drops of night-dew on the rose-leaf dropped.

لفظی فصیح شیرین قدی بلند چابک
A pronunciation, eloquent (and) sweet a stature, tall (and) beautiful
رویی لطیف زیبا چشمی خوش کشیده
A face, gracious and (heart)-alluring; the eye (in a bow) sweetly drawn.

یاقوت جان فزایش از آب لطف زاده
Her soul refreshing ruby (lip) of the water of grace born
شمشاد خوش خرامش در ناز پروریده
The boxtree (stature) sweetly moving, in daintiness cherished.

آن لعل دلکشش بین وان خنده دل آشوب
That heart-alluring ruby (lip) of hers, be hold and that laughter (full of ripple)
وان رفتن خوشش بین وان گام آرمیده
That sweet moving of hers, be hold and that gait reposed

آن آهوی سیه چشم از دام ما برون شد
Forth from our snare, that mistress, dark of eye, hath gone
یاران چه چاره سازم با این دل رمیده
Friends what remedy may I make with this heart affrighted

زنهار تا توانی اهل نظر میازار

Take care so far as thou canst, injure not people of vision

دنیا وفا ندارد ای نور هر دو دیده

No fidelity, hath the world. O light of both eyes

تا کی کشم عتیبت از چشم دلفریبت

On account of that heart-fascinating eye, reproach how long shall I endure

روزی کرشمه‌ای کن ای ای یار برگزیده

One day, glance, O friend well chosen

گر خاطر شریفت رنجیده شد ز حافظ

If, on account of Hafiz thy noble heart be grieved,

بازآ که توبه کردیم از گفته و شنیده

Comeback. For repentance, we have made of that uttered and heard.

بس شکر بازگویم در بندگی خواجه

On account of the Khwaja's[1] service, many the thanks that I shall utter,

گر اوفتد به دستم آن میوه رسیده

If to my hand fall that

غزل ۴۲۶   ⓞⒹⒺ ④②⑥

از خون دل نوشتم نزدیک دوست نامه

With my heart's blood, a letter to the friend, I wrote

انی رایت دهرا من هجرک القیامه

Verily, through separation from thee, I experience the torment of the resurrection.

دارم من از فراقش در دیده صد علامت

A hundred signs of separation from thee, in my (weeping) eye, I have

لیست دموع عینی هذا لنا العلامه

Not alone, (are) our signs, these tears of our eye.

هر چند کزمودم از وی نبود سودم

Though I tried, no boon from him was mine

من جرب المجرب حلت به الندامه

Who ever tried the tried, will repent having tried.

پرسیدم از طبیبی احوال دوست گفتا

Of a physician, I asked the friend's state. He said

فی بعدها عذاب فی قربها السلامه

In being near, (the beloved) is torture in being far, safety

گفتم ملامت آید گر گرد دوست گردم

I said: If, about, (thy street) I wander, reproach it bringeth

و الله ما راینا حبا بلا ملامه

By God (I swear) that love, without reproach (to the lover coming from his be – loved) never have we seen.

حافظ چو طالب آمد جامی به جان شیرین

Since Hafiz hath become the seeker (of thee) him, (give) a cup (in exchange) for his sweet life,

حتی یذوق منه کاسا من الکرامه

So that, thereof, a cup of honour he may taste

1-Eunuch, dignitary, vizier, boss, host

غزل ۴۲۷ ODE 427

چراغ روی تو را شمع گشت پروانه
The moth of the lamp of thy (resplendent) face became the candle.
مرا ز حال تو با حال خویش پروانه
On account of thy mole, care for my own state, mine none

خرد که قید مجانین عشق می‌فرمود
Wisdom, who bound those love-distraught;
به بوی سنبل زلف تو گشت دیوانه
By the perfume of the curl of thy tress, became distraught.

به بوی زلف تو گر جان به باد رفت چه شد
If by the perfume of thy tress, my soul went to the wind, (of destruction) what matter?
هزار جان گرامی فدای جانانه
The ransom for the beloved is a thousand precious souls.

من رمیده ز غیرت ز پا فتادم دوش
Last night, through jealousy, affrighted, I fell from my feet,
نگار خویش چو دیدم به دست بیگانه
When, in the stranger's hand, my idol I beheld.

چه نقشه‌ها که برانگیختیم و سود نداشت
What plan we evoked and (none) had profit,
فسون ما بر او گشته است افسانه
On her, our sorcery (of words) a (mere) a tale became.

بر آتش رخ زیبای او به جای سپند
On the fire (ruddy radiance) of her adorned (flushed cheek, in place of me,
به غیر خال سیاهش که دید به دانه
The grain better than her dark mole, who saw?

به مژده جان به صبا داد شمع در نفسی
At the glad tiding, in a moment, its life to breeze, the candle gave,
ز شمع روی تواش چون رسید پروانه
When, a message to it, from the candle of thy face, it conveyed.

مرا به دور لب دوست هست پیمانی
By the round from of the friend's lip, a covenant is mine,
که بر زبان نبرم جز حدیث پیمانه
That, on the tongue, I take naught save the tale of cup.

حدیث مدرسه و خانقه مگوی که باز
The tale of the college and the cloister utter not. For, again,
فتاد در سر حافظ هوای میخانه
Into Hafiz's head, fell the desire for the wine-house.

غزل ۴۲۸ ODE 428

سحرگاهان که مخمور شبانه
In the early morn, when intoxicated with the night's wine,
گرفتم باده با چنگ و چغانه
The cup, I took, with the harp and the flute

نهادم عقل را ره توشه از می

For (the sake of) wisdom, I placed road-provisions with wine

ز شهر هستیش کردم روانه

Him (wisdom) to the city of intoxication, I sent travelling.

نگار می فروشم عشوه‌ای داد

Me, the form of the wine-seller (the murshid) gave a look

که ایمن گشتم از مکر زمانه

That safe, from time's deceit, I became.

ز ساقی کمان ابرو شنیدم

From the Saki[1] of bow eye-brow, I heard

که ای تیر ملامت را نشانه

O butt of the arrow of reproach!

نبندی زان میان طرفی کمروار

Like the girdle, profit from that waist thou gainest not

اگر خود را ببینی در میانه

If within, (only) thy self thou seest

برو این دام بر مرغی دگر نه

Go (about thy own work) over another bird, this net place

که عنقا را بلند است آشیانه

For lofty (inaccessible) is the Anka's[2] nest.

که بندد طرف وصل از حسن شاهی

Who gaineth (good) profit from union (with a lovely one)

که با خود عشق بازد جاودانه

Who, at love with her self ever playeth

ندیم و مطرب و ساقی همه اوست

All He is the companion, the minstrel, and the Saki

خیال آب و گل در ره بهانه

As pretence (is) the fancy (the illusory form) of water and clay (the form of man)

بده کشتی می تا خوش برانیم

(O perfect murshid) The bark of the wine (of ma'rifat) [3] give, that happily I may come out

از این دریای ناپیداکرانه

From this stream (the world of bodies) shore unseen.

وجود ما معماییست حافظ

Hafiz our existence is an enigma

که تحقیقش فسون است و فسانه

The investigating whereof is fable and enchantment.

❦◉❧ ❦◉❧

1-Tapster
2-Phoenix

3-Insight

ی
The Letter Yā

غزل ۴۲۹ ⓄⒹⒺ ④②⑨

ساقی بیا که شد قدح لاله پر ز می
Saki[1] come for the goblet of the tulip hath become full of wine

طامات تا به چند و خرافات تا به کی
Mutterings, how long raving words till when

بگذر ز کبر و ناز که دیدهست روزگار
Pride and disdain, abandon for time hath seen

چین قبای قیصر و طرف کلاه کی
The wrinkling (in decay) of the robe of the Kaisar[2] and the abandoning (in death) of the crown of Kay.

هشیار شو که مرغ چمن مست گشت هان
Sensible be (drink wine) For the bird of the sward became intoxicated (with love for the rose) Ho

بیدار شو که خواب عدم در پی است هی
Vigilant be, for the sleep of non-existence is in pursuit Alas

خوش نازکانه میچمی ای شاخ نوبهار
O branch of fresh spring gracefully thou wavest;

کشفتگی مبادت از آشوب باد دی
Be it not that distress (be) thine from the torment of the wind of December

بر مهر چرخ و شیوه او اعتماد نیست
On the kindness of the sphere, and its way, reliance is none

ای وای بر کسی که شد ایمن ز مکر وی
O woe to that one who became safe (careless) of its deceit

فردا شراب کوثر و حور از برای ماست
(O Zahids) Tomorrow (after death) the wine of Kausar[3] is for us and the hur;

و امروز نیز ساق مه روی و جام می
Today (before death) the Saki (the murshid) moon of face and the cup of wine (of love)

باد صبا ز عهد صبی یاد میدهد
Recollection of the covenant of youth, the morning breeze giveth

جان دارویی که غم ببرد درده ای صبی
O kind youth me, the life-elixir that pain taketh, give.

حشمت مبین و سلطنت گل که بسپرد
The pomp and the sovereignty of the rose, regard not For scattereth

فراش باد هر ورقش را به زیر پی
The chamberlain of the breeze every leaf of it beneath the foot.

درده به یاد حاتم طی جام یک منی
To the memory of Hatim Tai[4] (the perfect murshid) the give the cup of one "man'" (two gallons)

تا نامه سیاه بخیلان کنیم طی
So that we may fold up the black book of the misers (void of God's bounty, ignorant of His love)

1-Tapster
2-An allusion to glory
3-A river in heaven

4-He was one of the great Arab men, a gentleman, and a benefactor

زان می که داد حسن و لطافت به ارغوان

That wine that, to the ruddy Arghavan[1], gave colour and grace,

بیرون فکند لطف مزاج از رخش به خوی

Casteth out in sweat from His face the grace of His nature.

مسند به باغ بر که به خدمت چو بندگان

To the garden, take the cushion For in service like attendants,

استاده است سرو و کمر بسته است نی

The cypress is standing and loin-girt is the reed.

حافظ حدیث سحرفریب خوشت رسید

Hafiz the tale of magic of thy sweet deceit (thy lustrous verse) hath reached

تا حد مصر و چین و به اطراف روم و ری

To the limits of Egypt and of Chin, and to the boundaries of Rum and of Rai.

غزل ۴۳۰ ⓄⒹⒺ ④③⓪

به صوت بلبل و قمری اگر ننوشی می

If to the voice of the bulbul[2] and of the turtle-dove, wine thou drink not;

علاج کی کنمت آخرالدواء الکی

Thee, how may I cure The last remedy is the cautery.

ذخیره‌ای بنه از رنگ و بوی فصل بهار

Of the colour and perfume of the spring season, lay up

که می‌رسند ز پی رهزنان بهمن و دی

For keep arriving in pursuit the highway men, autumn and winter

چو گل نقاب برافکند و مرغ زد هوهو

When (in spring – time) her veil the roseup-lifted; and the bird shouted "hu, hu!"

منه ز دست پیاله چه می‌کنی هی هی

From the hand, the cup put not. Where fore makest thou (the reproachful cry) "hai, hai?"

شکوه سلطنت و حسن کی ثباتی داد

The pomp of sovereignty and of command, how hath it stability

ز تخت جم سخنی مانده است و افسر کی

Of the throne of Jamshid[3] and of the diadem of Kay[4], only a word hath remained.

خزینه داری میراث خوارگان کفر است

Treasure-possessing, by the inheritors is kufr

به قول مطرب و ساقی به فتوی دف و نی

According to the word of the minstrel, of the Saki[5] and to the decision of the drum (and) of the pipe.

زمانه هیچ نبخشد که بازنستاند

Time giveth naught that, back again, it taketh not

مجو ز سفله مروت که شیه لا شی

From the mean, generosity seek not; for his existence is no thing (worthless)

1-Flower
2-Nightingale
3-king

4-Kay Qobad
5-Tapster

نوشته‌اند بر ایوان جنه الماوی

On the hall of the garden of the Abode (the threshold of the perfect murshid) they have written

که هر که عشوه دنی خرید وای به وی

Who purchased the world's favour, to him, woe

سخا نماند سخن طی کنم شراب کجاست

Generosity remained not; my word (of counsel) I close; wine is where

بده به شادی روح و روان حاتم طی

To the joy of the soul and the spirit of Hatim Tai[1], it give.

بخیل بوی خدا نشنود بیا حافظ

God's perfume (of liberality) the miser perceiveth not Hafiz come

پیاله گیر و کرم ورز و الضمان علی

The cup take liberality, practise on me, the responsibility (that saved thou shall be)

غزل ۴۳۱ ODE 431

لبش می‌بوسم و در می‌کشم می

His lip, I kiss and down drink its wine

به آب زندگانی برده‌ام پی

To the water of life I have taken my foot.

نه رازش می‌توانم گفت با کس

Neither His mystery can I utter to any

نه کس را می‌توانم دید با وی

Nor anyone can I see (in comparison) with Him.

لبش می‌بوسد و خون می‌خورد جام

O Saki The cup keepeth kissing his ruby lip and drinking blood

رخش می‌بیند و گل می‌کند خوی

The red (rose) keepeth seeing his (ruddy) face, and maketh sweat.

بده جام می و از جم مکن یاد

(O Saki) The cup of wine, give and recollection of Jamshid[2], make not

که می‌داند که جم کی بود و کی کی

Who knoweth when Jams hid was or when Kay[3]

بزن در پرده چنگ ای ماه مطرب

O moon-minstrel on the harp, (thy hand) extend

رگش بخراش تا بخروشم از وی

Its veins (cords) touch, so that with them I may exult

گل از خلوت به باغ آورد مسند

From retirement to the garden, the rose brought its throne

بساط زهد همچون غنچه کن طی

(O Zahid) Like the (folded) rose-bud, the carpet of austerity, make folded

چو چشمش مست را مخمور مگذار

Like his (intoxicated) eye, let not the intoxicated be intoxicated

به یاد لعلش ای ساق بده می

Saki to the memory of his ruby (lip) give wine.

1-He was one of the great Arab men, a gentleman, and a benefactor

2-king

3 -The title of Kiani kings like key khosrau

نجوید جان از آن قالب جدایی
Separation, the soul seeketh not from that body,

که باشد خون جامش در رگ و پی
In whose veins and body, the blood of the cup is.

زبانت درکش ای حافظ زمانی
Hafiz thy tongue in draw a while

حدیث بی زبانان بشنو از نی
The tongue (language) of the tongue less, hear from the (tongueless) reed (pipe)

غزل ۴۳۲ ⓄⒹⒺ ④③②

مخمور جام عشقم ساقی بده شرابی
O Saki intoxicated with love's cup, I am; give a little wine.

پر کن قدح که بی می مجلس ندارد آبی
Full, make the goblet for, without wine, the assembly hath not (even) a little luster

وصف رخ چو ماهش در پرده راست ناید
(Love for) His face like the moon, cometh not truly within the screen

مطرب بزن نوایی ساقی بده شرابی
Minstrel a melody, strike up Saki give a little wine.

شد حلقه قامت من تا بعد از این رقیبت
(At Thy door, curved like) The ring, became my stature so that, after this, the watcher

زین در دگر نراند ما را به هیچ بابی
May not drive us again from this door to another door.

در انتظار رویت ما و امیدواری
(Together are) In expectation of Thy face, we and hopefulness

در عشوه وصالت ما و خیال و خوابی
(Together are) In the deceit (vain hope) of union, we and vain fancy, and a vain dream

مخمور آن دو چشمم آیا کجاست جامی
Intoxicated with those two eyes (of Thine) I am, (in the end) less than an (empty) question

بیمار آن دو لعلم آخر کم از جوابی
Languishing for those two ruby (lips of Thine) I am in the end, (less than a vain dream).

حافظ چه می‌نهی دل تو در خیال خوبان
Hafiz in the fancy for lovely ones, thy heart wherefore placest thou

کی تشنه سیر گردد از لمعه سرابی
When becometh sated the thirsty one, from the flashing of a mirage.

غزل ۴۳۳ ⓄⒹⒺ ④③③

ای که بر ماه از خط مشکین نقاب انداختی
O thou that, on the moon (of thy radiant face) the veil of musky hair castest,

لطف کردی سایه‌ای بر آفتاب انداختی
Kindness, thou didst on the sun (thy effulgent face, so that from love's fire, lovers should not consume) a shade thou castest.

تا چه خواهد کرد با ما آب و رنگ عارضت

With us, the water (lustre of) colour of thy cheek, what will it do?

حالیا نیرنگ نقشی خوش بر آب انداختی

Now, on water, the picture of thy own sorcery, thou castest.

گوی خوبی بردی از خوبان خلخ شاد باش

From the lovely ones of the world, the ball of loveliness thou tookest. Be joyful

جام کیخسرو طلب کافراسیاب انداختی

The (world – viewing) cup of Kay Khusrau[1] seek for Afrasiyab[2], down thou castest.

هر کسی با شمع رخسارت به وجهی عشق باخت

In a different way, with the (luminous) candle of thy face, love everyone played

زان میان پروانه را در اضطراب انداختی

Out from the midst, into trepidation, the moth, (the lover) thou castest.

گنج عشق خود نهادی در دل ویران ما

In our desolate heart, the treasure of thy own love, thou placedest

سایه دولت بر این کنج خراب انداختی

On this ruined treasure, mercy's shadow thou castest

زینهار از آب آن عارض که شیران را از آن

Shelter from the water (luster) of, (thy flashing sword) by which lions

تشنه لب کردی و گردان را در آب انداختی

Thirsty (with wounds) thou madest and heroes into water (of shame) thou castest

خواب بیداران ببستی وان گه از نقش خیال

The sleep of the wakeful, thou boundest (preventedest) then from the picture of fancy

تهمتی بر شب روان خیل خواب انداختی

On the night-prowlers of the troop of sleep, a suspicion, thoucastest.

پرده از رخ برفکندی یک نظر در جلوه گاه

(For the sake of) One glance, thy veil thou up-castest in the place-of-splend our

و از حیا حور و پری را در حجاب انداختی

And into the veil, through shame, Hur and Pari[3] thou castest.

باده نوش از جام عالم بین که بر اورنگ جم

From the cup, world-viewing, wine drink for, on Jamshid's throne,

شاهد مقصود را از رخ نقاب انداختی

From the face of the desired Beloved, the veil (down) thou castest.

از فریب نرگس مخمور و لعل می پرست

From (the desire for) intoxicated narcissus (eye) and for the ruby (lip) wine-worshipping,

حافظ خلوت نشین را در شراب انداختی

Into wine, Hafiz sitting in khilvat[4], thou easiest.

و از برای صید دل در گردنم زنجیر زلف

For the sake of capturing the heart, on his neck, the chain of thy tress,

چون کمند خسرو مالک رقاب انداختی

Like the (mighty) noose of Khusrau[5], the master of necks, thou castest.

1-king

2-The mythical king of Turan is the son of Peshang in Shahnameh

3-Angel and the black-eyed woman of heaven

4-Solitude

5-king

داور دارا شکوه‌ای آن که تاج آفتاب

The Ruler, Dara of pomp, (O thou), who, the sun's crown,

از سر تعظیم بر خاک جناب انداختی

From the height of mightiness, on the dust of the door-post, thou castest

نصره الدین شاه یحیی آن که خصم ملک را

Nusratu-d-Din Shah Yahiya[1], (O thou) who, the enemy's land

از دم شمشیر چون آتش در آب انداختی

Into water, with the foam of thy (flashing) sword, like fire, thou castest

غزل ۴۳۴ ⓞⓓⓔ ④③④

ای دل مباش یک دم خالی ز عشق و مستی

O heart a moment, void of love and of intoxication, be not

وان گه برو که رستی از نیستی و هستی

At that time, go when, from non-existence to existence, thou escapedest.

گر جان به تن ببینی مشغول کار او شو

If (the Khirka[2]-wearer), thou see, engaged in thy own work be

هر قبله‌ای که بینی بهتر ز خودپرستی

Every kibla[3] that (is) better than self-worshiping (is)

با ضعف و ناتوانی همچون نسیم خوش باش

Notwithstanding weakness and powerlessness, like the pleasant breeze be:

بیماری اندر این ره بهتر ز تندرستی

In this path, more pleasant than body-soundness is sickness.

در مذهب طریقت خامی نشان کفر است

In the religious order of Tarikat[4] (love) immatureness is kufr

آری طریق دولت چالاکی است و چستی

Yes, the path of (profligacy) is expertness and quickness

تا فضل و عقل بینی بی‌معرفت نشینی

As long as (in thyself) the wisdom of excellence thou seest (and, of that wisdom, art proud) thou sittest void of divine knowledge

یک نکته‌ات بگویم خود را مبین که رستی

To thee, one word I say: Thy self, be hold not, so that (in safety) thou mayst escape.

در آستان جانان از آسمان میندیش

At the threshold of the beloved, of the lofty sky think not:

کز اوج سربلندی افتی به خاک پستی

That from summit of loftiness to the dust of lowliness, thou shouldest fall!!

خار ار چه جان بکاهد گل عذر آن بخواهد

Although the thorn diminisheth life, pardon for it the rose seeketh,

سهل است تلخی می در جنب ذوق مستی

By the side of intoxication's delight, easy is the bitterness of wine.

1-The nickname of King Yahya
2-Cloak

3-Temple
4-Principle, Sufism, religious way

صوفی پیاله پیما حافظ قرابه پرهیز

Sufi[1]! The cup, drink; Hafiz! The great flagon prepares,

ای کوته آستینان تا کی درازدستی

O ye short of sleeve, how long long-handedness?

غزل ۴۳۵ ⓄⒹⒺ ④③⑤

با مدعی مگویید اسرار عشق و مستی

To the adversary, utter not the mysteries of love and of intoxication,

تا بی‌خبر بمیرد در درد خودپرستی

So that, without knowledge (of love) in pain of self-worshipping, he may die

عاشق شو ار نه روزی کار جهان سر آید

(O Zahid) The lover (of the true Beloved) be if not, one day, the world's work endeth

ناخوانده نقش مقصود از کارگاه هستی

(And) from the workshop of existence (the world) the picture of thy purpose unread
(unattained, thou shall die)

دوش آن صنم چه خوش گفت در مجلس مغانم

Last night, in the assembly of the Magians, to me how well said that idol:

با کافران چه کارت گر بت نمی‌پرستی

"If the idol, thou worship not, with the kafirs, what work thine?"

سلطان من خدا را زلفت شکست ما را

On my Sultan! For God's sake, us, thy tress bath shattered,

تا کی کند سیاهی چندین درازدستی

Long-handedness like this, how long malceth the black?

در گوشه سلامت مستور چون توان بود

Veiled in the corner of safety, how can one be,

تا نرگس تو با ما گوید رموز مستی

As long as, to me, the mysteries of intoxication thy narcissus (eye) uttereth

آن روز دیده بودم این فتنه‌ها که برخاست

These calamities that have arisen I had seen that day,

کز سرکشی زمانی با ما نمی‌نشستی

When, awhile with us, through perverseness, thou satest not.

عشقت به دست طوفان خواهد سپرد حافظ

From the Path, Hafiz gazed till he beheld thy lovely tress;

چون برق از این کشاکش پنداشتی که جستی

Notwithstanding his loftiness, trodden in lowliness (truly humble), he became.

غزل ۴۳۶ ⓄⒹⒺ ④③⑥

آن غالیه خط گر سوی ما نامه نوشتی

If to us a letter, that perfumed hair (the beloved) had written,

گردون ورق هستی ما درننوشتی

The leaf of our existence, the sphere would not have folded up.

1-A Muslim ascetic and mystic.

هر چند که هجران ثمر وصل برآرد
Although separation bringeth forth the fruit of union,

دهقان جهان کاش که این تخم نکشتی
Would to (God) that this seed, the villager of the world (God) had not sown.

آمرزش نقد است کسی را که در این جا
Forgiveness is the cash of that one to whom, here,

یاریست چو حوری و سرایی چو بهشتی
Is a Friend like a huri[1] and an ab ode like a paradise.

در مصطبه عشق تنعم نتوان کرد
In love's inn, one cannot make happiness

چون بالش زر نیست بسازیم به خشتی
When the pillow is golden, with a brick, I am content

مفروش به باغ ارم و نخوت شداد
For the garden of Iram, and the power of Shudad[2], sell not

یک شیشه می و نوش لبی و لب کشتی
A bottle of wine (of love) and a sweet lip (of the murshid) and the border of a field

تا کی غم دنیای دنی ای دل دانا
O wise heart grief for a mean world, how long

حیف است ز خوبی که شود عاشق زشتی
Alas it is that with beauteousness, it (the heart) became the lover of hideousness

آلودگی خرقه خرابی جهان است
The stain of the Khirka is the ruin of the world

کو راهروی اهل دلی پاک سرشتی
Away-farer, one of heart, one pure of nature where

از دست چرا هشت سر زلف تو حافظ
From his hand, Thy tres ode tip why did Hafiz let go

تقدیر چنین بود چه کردی که نهشتی
Thus, was fate. What would he have done, (if) he had not let go

غزل ۴۳۷ ODE 437

ای قصه بهشت ز کویت حکایتی
O thou, of whose street, (only) a tale is the tale of paradise

شرح جمال حور ز رویت روایتی
(And) of whose face, (only) a sign is the description of the beauty of the Hur.

انفاس عیسی از لب لعلت لطیفه‌ای
From thy ruby lip, (only) a jest is (the life-giving) breathing of' Isa

آب خضر ز نوش لبانت کنایتی
(And), from, thy sweet mouth, only asign is the water of life.

هر پاره از دل من و از غصه قصه‌ای
(Together are) every fragment of my heart and a tale of grief

هر سطری از خصال تو و از رحمت آیتی
(Together are) every line of thy qualities, and a verse of mercy.

1-Lover

2-He was believed to be the king of the lost Arabian city of Iram of the Pillars

کی عطرسای مجلس روحانیان شدی
'Itr-diffuser of the assembly of souls, when would it (the rose) have been,
گل را اگر نه بوی تو کردی رعایتی
If, to the rose, thy perfume, thou hadst not entrusted

در آرزوی خاک در یار سوختیم
In desire of the dust of the Friend's path, I consumed,
یاد آور ای صبا که نکردی حمایتی
O morning breeze bring to mind that even a little protection thou gavest not.

ای دل به هرزه دانش و عمرت به باد رفت
O heart in absurd knowledge (thou wast) and, (from the hand) life passed
صد مایه داشتی و نکردی کفایتی
A hundred sources (of capital) thou hadst and a sufficiency, thou madest not.

بوی دل کباب من آفاق را گرفت
Took the horizons (of the world) the perfume of my roasted (grief – stricken) heart
این آتش درون بکند هم سرایتی
This consuming of my heart, (into the beloved's heart) may penetrate.

در آتش ار خیال رخش دست می‌دهد
If, in the fire, appear the form of thy (lovely) face
ساقی بیا که نیست ز دوزخ شکایتی
Saki come (and give wine) for (even) of hell, no complaint (then) is mine.

دانی مراد حافظ از این درد و غصه چیست
From this (lesson of) grief, Hafiz's desire, what it is, thou knowest
از تو کرشمه‌ای و ز خسرو عنایتی
From thee (O murshid) [1] a glance (of kindness) and from the Khusrau (God) the bounty (of pardon)

غزل ۴۳۸ ⓄⒹⒺ ④③⑧

سبت سلمی بصدغیها فوادی
By her two tresses, Salma[2] bound my heart
و روحی کل یوم لی ینادی
Yet, every day, my soul crieth to me (Come and die)

نگارا بر من بی‌دل ببخشای
For God's sake on me, heart-bereft, bestow pity
و واصلنی علی رغم الاعادی
Me, despite the hate of enemies, cause to reach to (the beloved).

حبیبا در غم سودای عشقت
O idol in grief of love's passion for Thee
توکلنا علی رب العباد
On the Lord (God) of slaves, is our reliance.

امن انکرتنی عن عشق سلمی
O thou who despisedest me for my love for Salma
تزاول آن روی نهکو بوادی
Her face, thou shouldst at first have clearly seen.

1-Guru   2-Lover

که همچون مت به بوتن دل و ای ره
(To the true Beloved) Wholly and completely, (surrender), like me, thy heart,

غریق العشق فی بحر الوداد
O drowned in love in the sea of friendship

به پی ماچان غرامت بسپریمن
Subsequently, (to thee, our soul), we shall have to (advance)

غرت یک وی روشتی از امادی
For, stubbornly, hast thou fought with lovers and their heart taken

غم این دل بواتت خورد ناچار
Grief for (Thee wholly) devoured this heart, help less Me, the news of the good fortune of my verse deceiveth

و غر نه او بنی آنچت نشادی
Me, the news of the good fortune of my verse deceiveth.

دل حافظ شد اندر چین زلفت
Within the curl of Thy tress, went Hafiz

بلیل مظلم و الله هادی
In the dark night and God is the guide.

غزل ۴۳۹ ⓄⒹⒺ ④③⑨

دیدم به خواب دوش که ماهی برآمدی
Last night, in sleep, I saw that forth, a great moon had come

کز عکس روی او شب هجران سر آمدی
From the reflection of the face whereof, to an end, the night of separation had come.

تعبیر رفت یار سفرکرده می‌رسد
The explanation is what The much journeyed Friend (the true Beloved) arriveth

ای کاج هر چه زودتر از در درآمدی
O would (that) by my door, He, (splendour-giving, adorned), had come

ذکرش به خیر ساقی فرخنده فال من
My Saki[1], auspicious of omen whose mention be for good

کز در مدام با قدح و ساغر آمدی
Ever, by my door, with the goblet and the cup, he used to come

خوش بودی ار به خواب بدیدی دیار خویش
Happy, had it been if, in sleep, his native land he had seen

تا یاد صحبتش سوی ما رهبر آمدی
So that the guide to us, the recollection of its association would have come.

فیض ازل به زور و زر ار آمدی به دست
If, with force and gold, to our hand, the bounty of eternity without beginning (union with the true Beloved) had come

آب خضر نصیبه اسکندر آمدی
The water of life of Khizr[2] Sikandar's[3] portion would have come.

1-Tapster
2-Name of prophet

3-Was the king of Macedonia in ancient Greece

آن عهد یاد باد که از بام و در مرا

O true Beloved wherefore fleest Thou be memory of that time, when, from roof and door, to me,

هر دم پیام یار و خط دلبر آمدی

The message of the Beloved and the letter of the Heart-ravisher, used to come.

کی یافتی رقیب تو چندین مجال ظلم

Such power of tyranny, Thy watcher where would have obtained,

مظلومی ار شبی به در داور آمدی

If, one night, to the Ruler's door, an oppressed one had come

خامان ره نرفته چه دانند ذوق عشق

Love's desire, how know the immature ones of the Path

دریادلی بجوی دلیری سرآمدی

One of ocean-heart (generous) seek (and) a bold one (who is) a chief.

آن کو تو را به سنگ دلی کرد رهنمون

That one who, thee, road-guide to stone-heartedness, made,

ای کاشکی که پاش به سنگی برآمدی

O would that against a stone (so that he might fall) his foot had come.

گر دیگری به شیوه حافظ زدی رقم

If, in Hafiz's way, another had written,

مقبول طبع شاه هنرپرور آمدی

Agreeably to the nature of the king, skill-cherishing, it would have come

غزل ۴۴۰ ⓄⒹⒺ ④④Ⓞ

سحر با باد می‌گفتم حدیث آرزومندی

In the morning, to the breeze, I uttered the tale of my longing

خطاب آمد که واثق شو به الطاف خداوندی

The address (of reply) came saying: "A relier be on the favours of Lordship."

دعای صبح و آه شب کلید گنج مقصود است

(O darvish) The key of the treasure of purpose is the prayer of the morning, and the sigh of the evening

بدین راه و روش می‌رو که با دلدار پیوندی

By this path and way, go; so that, with the Heart-possess (God) thou mayst join.

قلم را آن زبان نبود که سر عشق گوید باز

Not that tongue is the reed's that love's (great) mystery it may unfold

ورای حد تقریر است شرح آرزومندی

Beyond the limit of narration, is the explanation of longing.

الا ای یوسف مصری که کردت سلطنت مغرور

Ho O Yusuf of Egypt (the beloved) whom sovereignty (of Egypt) kept engaged

پدر را بازپرس آخر کجا شد مهر فرزندی

Ask the father, (Yfckub) where went at last filial

جهان پیر رعنا را ترحم در جبلت نیست

In the nature of the beautiful, old world, compassion is none

ز مهر او چه می‌پرسی در او همت چه می‌بندی

From its love, what seekest thou In it, what desire attachest thou

همایی چون تو عالی قدر حرص استخوان تا کی
A Huma[1] like thee, lofty of rank, (and) greed for the (rotten) bone how long
دریغ آن سایه همت که بر نااهل افکندی
Alas that shadow of fortune, that, on the mean, thou castest.

در این بازار اگر سودیست با درویش خرسند است
In this market (of the world) if a profit There Be. 'tis with the happy dervish:
خدایا منعمم گردان به درویشی و خرسندی
O God me, happy make with dervish ness, and with happiness.

به شعر حافظ شیراز می‌رقصند و می‌نازند
To the verse of Hafiz of Shiraz, dance and whirl
سیه چشمان کشمیری و ترکان سمرقندی
Those dark of eye of Kashmir[2], and the saucy ones of Samarkand[3].

غزل ۴۴۱ ⓄⒹⒺ ④④①

چه بودی ار دل آن ماه مهربان بودی
If, kind (on our state) the heart of that (Beloved) had been, how well it would have been
که حال ما نه چنین بودی ار چنان بودی
For, if (kind) like that, He had been, not like this our state would have been

بگفتمی که چه ارزد نسیم طره دوست
I would have said The breeze of the Friend's tress, what is it worth
گرم به هر سر مویی هزار جان بودی
If, for every hair-tip, mine a thousand lives had been.

برات خوشدلی ما چه کم شدی یا رب
O Lord! the order of our heart-happiness, less how would it have been,
گرش نشان امان از بد زمان بودی
If, from the evil of time, it's the mark of safety had been

گرم زمانه سرافراز داشتی و عزیز
If, me, head exalting and dear, time had kept,
سریر عزتم آن خاک آستان بودی
That dust of His threshold, my throne of honour would have been.

ز پرده کاش برون آمدی چو قطره اشک
Would to God forth from the screen, like a tear-drop, He had come,
که بر دو دیده ما حکم او روان بودی
So that, on my two eyes, His order current would have been.

اگر نه دایره عشق راه بربستی
If the Path, love's circle had not closed,
چو نقطه حافظ سرگشته در میان بودی
(Not) Like a point, in the midst, heart-bereft Hafiz would have been.

1-It is a bird of the carnivorous genus and resembles a hawk
2-Kashmir is a region in the northwest of the Indian subcontinent

3-The second largest city of Uzbekistan

غزل ۴۴۲ ODE 442

به جان او که گرم دسترس به جان بودی
By His (the true Beloved's) soul I swear that if power of (sacrificing) my life had been,

کمینه پیشکش بندگانش آن بودی
The humble offering of His slave, it would have been.

بگفتمی که بها چیست خاک پایش را
The dust of His foot, what its price is, manifest would have been,

اگر حیات گران مایه جاودان بودی
If perpetual, precious life had been.

به بندگی قدش سرو معترف گشتی
Confessor, in service to His stature, the (tongueless) cypress would have been,

گرش چو سوسن آزاده ده زبان بودی
If, to it, like the noble (ten – tongued) lily, tongue had been.

به خواب نیز نمی‌بینمش چه جای وصال
Him, even in sleep, I see not. What room for (speaking of) union

چو این نبود و ندیدیم باری آن بودی
When this (union) might not be, (Him) we saw not. Would to God that (the beholding of Him in sleep) had been

اگر دلم نشدی پایبند طره او
If foot-bound to His tress, my heart had not been,

کی اش قرار در این تیره خاکدان بودی
In this dark dust-heap (this world) rest mine, how would have been

به رخ چو مهر فلک بی‌نظیر آفاق است
In face like the (resplendent) sun of the sky, peerless of climes is He

به دل دریغ که یک ذره مهربان بودی
In heart, alas, that (only) a little kind He should have been.

درآمدی ز درم کاشکی چو لمعه نور
Would to God by my door, like a flash of light, he had entered,

که بر دو دیده ما حکم او روان بودی
So that, on my two eyes his order current had been

ز پرده ناله حافظ برون کی افتادی
Forth from the screen, when would have fallen Hafiz's wail (of lustrous verse)

اگر نه همدم مرغان صبح خوان بودی
If not fellow-companion of the birds, morning-singing, he had been

غزل ۴۴۳ ODE 443

چو سرو اگر بخرامی دمی به گلزاری
If, like the (lofty) cypress, a moment thou move in arose-garden,

خورد ز غیرت روی تو هر گلی خاری
In envy of thy face, every rose suffereth a thorn.

ز کفر زلف تو هر حلقه‌ای و آشوبی
On account of the infidelity of thy tress, (together are) every assembly and a great tumult

ز سحر چشم تو هر گوشه‌ای و بیماری
On account of the sorcery of thy eye, (together are) every corner and a sick one

مرو چو بخت من ای چشم مست یار به خواب

O intoxicated eye of the beloved to sleep, like my fortune, go not

که در پی است ز هر سویت آه بیداری

For, in pursuit, from every direction, is the sigh of a wakeful one

نثار خاک رهت نقد جان من هر چند

The scattering of Thy Path's dust is my soul's cash, although

که نیست نقد روان را بر تو مقداری

On Thy part the soul's cash hath not (even) a little value.

دلا همیشه مزن لاف زلف دلبندان

O heart ever, a (malignant) opinion of the tress of heart-enslavers, express not

چو تیره رای شوی کی گشایدت کاری

When malignant of opinion thou becomest, how openeth to thee a work

سرم برفت و زمانی به سر نرفت این کار

(Separate from the body) went my head and, a while, this work ended not

دلم گرفت و نبودت غم گرفتاری

My heart caught (grief of love) and Thine, was no grief for a captive

چو نقطه گفتمش اندر میان دایره آی

To him, I said Like the (centre) point enter into the midst of the circle of (desirous ones)

به خنده گفت که ای حافظ این چه پرگری

With laughter, he spake, saying Hafiz in what compass, art thou

غزل ۴۴۴ ⓄⒹⒺ ④④④

شهریست پر ظریفان و از هر طرف نگاری

'Tis a city full of graceful ones and, one very side, an idol.

یاران صلای عشق است گر می کنید کاری

O friends' tis love's salutation, if ye make a bargain.

چشم فلک نبیند زین طرفه‌تر جوانی

More fresh than this, the sky's eye seeth not a youth

در دست کس نیفتد زین خوبتر نگاری

In the hand, none be held more beautiful than this an idol.

هرگز که دیده باشد جسمی ز جان مرکب

Created of soul, who shall have seen a body

بر دامنش مبادا زین خاکیان غباری

On this skirt, of these dusty ones be not a particle of dust

چون من شکسته‌ای را از پیش خود چه رانی

The shattered one like me, from before thy self wherefore drivest thou

کم غایت توقع بوسیست یا کناری

For great expectation is mine, of a kiss, or of an embrace.

می بی‌غش است دریاب وقتی خوش است بشتاب

Know the wine is without alloy haste the time is opportune

سال دگر که دارد امید نوبهاری

Another year, who hath hope of a new spring

در بوستان حریفان مانند لاله و گل
In the garden, companions like the tulip and the rose
هر یک گرفته جامی بر یاد روی یاری
Each a cup taken to the memory of the face of a friend

چون این گره گشایم وین راز چون نمایم
This knot, how may I loose This mystery, how may I unfold
دردی و سخت دردی کاری و صعب کاری
A pain, and a severe pain a work, and a difficult work.

هر تار موی حافظ در دست زلف شوخی
In the hand of the tress, of a saucy one, is every thread of Hafiz's hair
مشکل توان نشستن در این چنین دیاری
It is difficult to dwell in a land like this.

غزل ۴۴۵ ⓄⒹⒺ ④④⑤

تو را که هر چه مراد است در جهان داری
(O Beloved) Thou whose purpose in the world whatever it be, Thou hast;
چه غم ز حال ضعیفان ناتوان داری
Of the state of the feeble (and of) the powerless, what grief (is it that) Thou hast

بخواه جان و دل از بنده و روان بستان
From Thy slave, life and heart, demand the soul, take
که حکم بر سر آزادگان روان داری
For over the free, the current order Thou hast

میان نداری و دارم عجب که هر ساعت
No waist, hast Thouand momently I wonder how,
میان مجمع خوبان کنی میانداری
In the midst of the assembly of lovely ones, thou displayest exaltation

بیاض روی تو را نیست نقش درخور از آنک
Fit, is no picture for the whiteness of Thy face because,
سوادی از خط مشکین بر ارغوان داری
From the musky (dark) line (of down) blackness, upon the ruddy arghavan (the ruddy cheek) Thou hast.

بنوش می که سبکروحی و لطیف مدام
O graceful one ever drink wine, for light of soul thou art
علی الخصوص در آن دم که سرگران داری
Especially, at this moment, when the heavy head (through wine) thou hast.

مکن عتاب از این بیش و جور بر دل ما
More than this, against my heart, make neither reproach, nor violence
مکن هر آن چه توانی که جای آن داری
Do whatever thou canst, when room (occasion) for it,-thou hast.

به اختیارت اگر صد هزار تیر جفاست
If, in thy power, be a hundred thousand arrows of violence,
به قصد جان من خسته در کمان داری
(Them) with the in tention of (taking) the life of me, shattered, (thou hast).

بکش جفای رقیبان مدام و جور حسود

The tyranny of the watchers, ever endure; (happy of heart, be);

که سهل باشد اگر یار مهربان داری

For' tis easy, if the kind Beloved thou hast.

به وصل دوست گرت دست می‌دهد یک دم

If, one moment, to thy hand, union with the Friend reacheth,

برو که هر چه مراد است در جهان داری

Go (do thy work) For, whatever desire is in the world, thou hast.

چو گل به دامن از این باغ می‌بری حافظ

Hafiz when, in the border of this garden, thou takest the rose,

چه غم ز ناله و فریاد باغبان داری

Of the weeping and the lamenting of the gardener, what grief hast thou

غزل ۴۴۶ ⓄⒹⒺ ④④⑥

صبا تو نکهت آن زلف مشک بو داری

O breeze the perfume of that musk-scented tress thou hast

به یادگار بمانی که بوی او داری

As the token, thou stayest for its perfume thou hast.

دلم که گوهر اسرار حسن و عشق در اوست

My heart, where in is the jewel of the mysteries of beauty and of love,

توان به دست تو دادن گرش نکو داری

To thy hand, one can give, if it, well thou keepest.

در آن شمایل مطبوع هیچ نتوان گفت

In respect of those pleasant innate qualities (of thine) one cannot speak at all,

جز این قدر که رقیبان تندخو داری

Save this, that watchers, austere of nature, thou hast.

نوای بلبلت ای گل کجا پسند افتد

O rose (the beloved) agreeable to thee how falleth the melody of the bulbul[1] (the lover)

که گوش و هوش به مرغان هرزه گو داری

When, to the birds (the watchers) nonsense-uttering, thy ear thou hast

به جرعه تو سرم مست گشت نوشت باد

Distraught, became my head by thy draught. Sweet be It to thee

خود از کدام خم است این که در سبو داری

Of what wine is this in deed that in the pitcher, thou hast

به سرکشی خود ای سرو جویبار مناز

O cypress of the rivulet of thy arrogance, boast not

که گر بدو رسی از شرم سر فروداری

For, if to him thou reach, low with shame thy head, thou wilt have

دم از ممالک خوبی چو آفتاب زدن

Of kingdoms of beauteousness like the sun, to boast

تو را رسد که غلامان ماه رو داری

Reacheth (befitteth) thee (for) slaves, moon of face, thou hast.

1-Nightingale

قبای حسن فروشی تو را برازد و بس

(O beloved) Befitteth thee a kaba, beauty-boasting and that only,

که همچو گل همه آیین رنگ و بو داری

For, like the rose, all the way of colour and of perfume, thou hast.

ز کنج صومعه حافظ مجوی گوهر عشق

Hafiz from (the cloister)-corner, seek not love's jewel

قدم برون نه اگر میل جست و جو داری

Outside the cloister plant thy foot, if inclination for search, thou hast.

غزل ۴۴۷ ⓄⒹⒺ ④④⑦

بیا با ما مورز این کینه داری

(O beloved) Come towards us this hatred exercise not

که حق صحبت دیرینه داری

For the light of ancient society, thou hast.

نصیحت گوش کن کاین در بسی به

My counsel hear for this pearl (of counsel) much better is

از آن گوهر که در گنجینه داری

Than that jewel that, in the treasury, thou hast.

ولیکن کی نمایی رخ به رندان

But, to the profligates, thy face how mayst thou show,

تو کز خورشید و مه آیینه داری

Thou who, the mirror of the sun and of the moon, thou hast

بد رندان مگو ای شیخ و هش دار

O Shaikh[1] sense, keep against the profligates speak not

که با حکم خدایی کینه داری

(Lest) That with God's love hate thou have.

نمی‌ترسی ز آه آتشینم

(O Zahid) Fearest thou not my fiery (burning) sigh

تو دانی خرقه پشمینه داری

Thou knowest, the woollen Khirka[2], (easily consumed) thou hast.

به فریاد خمار مفلسان رس

(O Saki) [3] to the cry of the poor wine-drinkers come. (Them, give wine)

خدا را گر می‌دوشینه داری

For God's sake, if the wine of last night thou hast.

ندیدم خوشتر از شعر تو حافظ

Hafiz I have not (seen) verse more beautiful than thy verse,

به قرآنی که اندر سینه داری

Which, in thy heart, by the great Kuran (I swear) thou hast

1-A Muslim saint ascetic and mystic in a Muslim community   3-Tapster
2-Cloak

غزل ۴۴۸ ⓄⒹⒺ ④④⑧

ای که در کوی خرابات مقامی داری

O thou that, in the tavern-street, thy dwelling hast

جم وقت خودی ار دست به جامی داری

The Jamshid[1] of thy own time, thou art, if, on the cup, thy hand thou hast

ای که با زلف و رخ یار گذاری شب و روز

O thou that, night and day, with the tress and the face of the Beloved, passest

فرصتت باد که خوش صبحی و شامی داری

Be opportunity thine, so that a happy morning and evening thou mayst have.

ای صبا سوختگان بر سر ره منتظرند

O morning breeze at the head of thy path, those consumed (with love), are expectant,

گر از آن یار سفرکرده پیامی داری

Whether, from that (true) Beloved (many a) journey made, a message thou hast.

خال سرسبز تو خوش دانه عیشیست ولی

Thy (dark) mole, fresh of head, is a pleasant grain of pleasure. But

بر کنار چمنش وه که چه دامی داری

On the border of its sward (face) alas what a snare (the tress) thou hast

بوی جان از لب خندان قدح می‌شنوم

From the laughing lip of the goblet, the soul's perfume, I perceive

بشنو ای خواجه اگر زان که مشامی داری

O Khwaja[2] smell if, for that, a perfume-place thou hast.

چون به هنگام وفا هیچ ثباتیت نبود

(O true Beloved) Though, at the time of fidelity, stability (constancy) is not thine

می‌کنم شکر که بر جور دوامی داری

Thanks, I offer that, against violence, stability thou hast.

نام نیک ار طلبد از تو غریبی چه شود

If, from thee, a name a stranger seek, what (a wonder) it will be,

تویی امروز در این شهر که نامی داری

To-day, in this city, thou art one, who a great name hast.

بس دعای سحرت مونس جان خواهد بود

The guardian of thy soul will be many a prayer of dawn

تو که چون حافظ شبخیز غلامی داری

For, like Hafiz, night-rising, a slave thou hast.

غزل ۴۴۹ ⓄⒹⒺ ④④⑨

ای که مهجوری عشاق روا می‌داری

O thou that lawful, the separation of lovers holdest

عاشقان را ز بر خویش جدا می‌داری

(And) apart from thy bosom, lovers holdest

1-king   2-Eunuch, dignitary, vizier, boss, host

تشنه بادیه را هم به زلالی دریاب

With a little water, the thirsty one of the desert, aid

به امیدی که در این ره به خدا میداری

By reason of that hope that, in this Path to God, thou holdest.

دل ببردی و بحل کردمت ای جان لیکن

O soul my heart, thou ravishedest and thee, I forgave. But

به از این دار نگاهش که مرا میداری

Guard of it, keep better than this (guard) that of me thou keepest.

ساغر ما که حریفان دگر مینوشند

Our cup that the other adversaries drink

ما تحمل نکنیم ار تو روا میداری

It we endure, if, lawful, thou holdest.

ای مگس حضرت سیمرغ نه جولانگه توست

O (contemptible) fly the presence of the (mighty) Simurgh[1] is not thy place of display

عرض خود میبری و زحمت ما میداری

Thy own honour, thou takest and, our trouble, thou causest.

تو به تقصیر خود افتادی از این در محروم

Excluded from this door (of the true Beloved) by thy own fault, thou fellest,

از که مینالی و فریاد چرا میداری

Of whom, be wailest thou complaint, where fore (is it that) thou hast

حافظ از پادشهان پایه به خدمت طلبند

Hafiz from kings, shelter in service they seek

سعی نابرده چه امید عطا میداری

Work not done, hope of gift what (is it that) thou holdest

غزل ۴۵۰ ⓄⒹⒺ ④⑤⓪

روزگاریست که ما را نگران میداری

Tis a time when expectant, us thou keepest;

مخلصان را نه به وضع دگران میداری

Not in the way of others, thy slaves, thou keepest.

گوشه چشم رضایی به منت باز نشد

Not opened towards me became the corner of the eye of thy satisfaction

این چنین عزت صاحب نظران میداری

Like this, the honour of those possessed of vision thou keepest

ساعد آن به که بپوشی تو چو از بهر نگار

Best that Thou cover up that arm when, for the sake of colouring

دست در خون دل پرهنران میداری

In the heart's blood of those full of skill, Thy hand Thou keepest.

نه گل از دست غمت رست و نه بلبل در باغ

(O true Beloved) From the stain of grief (of separation) from Thee, escaped neither the rose nor the bulbul[2] in the garden

همه را نعره زنان جامه دران میداری

All clamouring, garment-of the Sufi rending, Thou keepest

1-Phoenix   2-Nightingale

ای که در دلق ملمع طلبی نقد حضور

O thou that, in the coloured tattered garment (of the Sufi[1]) seekest the delight of the presence (of God it, how mayst thou obtain)

چشم سری عجب از بی‌خبران می‌داری

Wonderful by those voids of knowledge, hope of satiation thou keepest.

چون توپی نرگس باغ نظر ای چشم و چراغ

O eye and lamp since the narcissus of the garden of vision thou art,

سر چرا بر من دلخسته گران می‌داری

With me, heart shattered, the head heavy where fore (is it that) thou keepest

گوهر جام جم از کان جهانی دگر است

From the mine of the other world, is the jewel of (world – viewing) the cup of Jamshid[2]; (the Arif acquainted with m'arifat)

تو تمنا ز گل کوزه گران می‌داری

From the clay of the pitcher-makers (dry zahids) desire (for this jewel vainly) Thou keepest

پدر تجربه ای دل توپی آخر ز چه روی

O heart the father of experience of the end, thou art. Wherefore, (is it that)

طمع مهر و وفا زین پسران می‌داری

Desire for the love and the fidelity of these youths thou keepest

کیسه سیم و زرت پاک بباید پرداخت

You must play for this your last pot of silver and gold.

این طمع‌ها که تو از سیمبران می‌داری

Why beg this thief that gold and silver returns?

گر چه رندی و خرابی گنه ماست ولی

Though, (profligacy and depravity) are our sin, yet,

عاشقی گفت که تو بنده بر آن می‌داری

A lover spake, saying: On them profligacy and depravity the slave Thou keepest

مگذران روز سلامت به ملامت حافظ

Hafiz in reproach, abandon not the day of safety

چه توقع ز جهان گذران می‌داری

From the passing world, what expectation (is it that) thou keepest

غزل ۴۵۱ ⓄⒹⒺ ④⑤①

خوش کرد یاوری فلکت روز داوری

On the day of judgment, thee the sky happily aided

تا شکر چون کنی و چه شکرانه آوری

Let us see thanks, how thou mayst offer; in thanks, what thou mayst bring.

آن کس که اوفتاد خدایش گرفت دست

That one who fell and whose hand, God seized,

گو بر تو باد تا غم افتادگان خوری

Say (So that thy hand, God may seize) on thee, be it that the grief of the fallen thou mayst suffer.

1-A Muslim saint or holy man, Pietist   2-king

در کوی عشق شوکت شاهی نمی‌خرند
In love's street, kingly rank they purchase not
اقرار بندگی کن و اظهار چاکری
(Here) Make confession of service and claim of attendance

ساقی به مژدگانی عیش از درم درآی
Saki with the reward for tidings of joy enter by my door,
تا یک دم از دلم غم دنیا به دربری
So that, one moment, forth from my heart, grief thou mayst take.

در شاهراه جاه و بزرگی خطر بسیست
In the highway of rank and of lord ship is many a danger,
آن به که از این گریوه سبکبار بگذری
That is best that by this acclivity, light of burden, thou pass.

سلطان و فکر لشکر و سودای تاج و گنج
(Together are) The Sultan and the thought of the army, and the passion for treasure,
and the pomp of the crown
درویش و امن خاطر و کنج قلندری
(Together are) The dervish, and tranquillity of heart, and the corner of kalandardom

یک حرف صوفیانه بگویم اجازت است
One sufi[1]-istic word, I will utter permission is there
ای نور دیده صلح به از جنگ و داوری
O light of the eye peace is better than war and dominion.

نیل مراد بر حسب فکر و همت است
To the limit of thought and spirit is the success of desire
از شاه نذر خیر و ز توفیق یاوری
From the king, the liberal gift from the grace of (God), aid

حافظ غبار فقر و قناعت ز رخ مشوی
Hafiz from thy face, the dust of poverty and of contentment wash not
کاین خاک بهتر از عمل کیمیاگری
For, better (is) this dust than the work of alchemy

غزل ۴۵۲ ⓄⒹⒺ ④⑤②

طفیل هستی عشقند آدمی و پری
For the sake of love's existence are man and Pari[2],
ارادتی بنما تا سعادتی ببری
A little (pure) desire, show, so that a great happiness (in attaining to true love) thou mayst achieve.

بکوش خواجه و از عشق بی‌نصیب مباش
Khwaja[3] strive portion less of love be not
که بنده را نخرد کس به عیب بی‌هنری
For none buy eth the slave with the defect of being void of skill.

1-A Muslim saint or holy man, Pietist   3-Eunuch, dignitary, vizier, boss, host
2-Pari-Beautiful woman

می صبوح و شکرخواب صبحدم تا چند

The wine of the morning draught, and the sweet sleep of dawn, how long

به عذر نیم شبی کوش و گریه سحری

(For pardon) Strive by the supplication of mid-night; and, with the weeping of the morning.

تو خود چه لعبتی ای شهسوار شیرین کار

O dainty one, sorcery-player what doll art thou thy self

که در برابر چشمی و غایب از نظری

(Neither) In front of the eye art thou (nor) hidden from vision art thou.

هزار جان مقدس بسوخت زین غیرت

A thousand holy souls consumed on account of this jealousy,

که هر صباح و مسا شمع مجلس دگری

For, every morning and evening, the candle of another assembly Thou art

ز من به حضرت آصف که می‌برد پیغام

The message from me to His Highness Asaf[1], who taketh,

که یاد گیر دو مصرع ز من به نظم دری

Saying Recollect two hemistiches of mine in Dan verse

بیا که وضع جهان را چنان که من دیدم

Come, so that, even so, the world's way I may be hold

گر امتحان بکنی می خوری و غم نخوری

If, examination, thou wilt make, wine, thou drinkest and grief, sufferest not.

کلاه سروریت کج مباد بر سر حسن

On thy head of beauty, aslant (in pride) be not the crown of sovereignty

که زیب بخت و سزاوار ملک و تاج سری

For, the beauty of fortune, and worthy of throne and of the crown of gold, thou art.

به بوی زلف و رخت می‌روند و می‌آیند

By the perfume of Thy tress and Thy cheek, go and come

صبا به غالیه سایی و گل به جلوه گری

The morning breeze for (acquiring from Thy tress the power of) perfume-diffusing, and the rose for (acquiring from Thy cheek) splendour

چو مستعد نظر نیستی وصال مجوی

Since, prepared of vision, thou art not, union, seek not,

که جام جم نکند سود وقت بی‌بصری

For, no good doeth (the world – viewing) cup of Jamshid at the time of being without vision.

دعای گوشه نشینان بلا بگرداند

Turneth calamity the prayer of the corner-sitters

چرا به گوشه چشمی به ما نمی‌نگری

With a corner of thy eye, at us (corner – sitters) where fore lookest thou not

بیا و سلطنت از ما بخر به مایه حسن

(O beloved) Come and, from us, with the capital of thy beauty, sovereignty purchase

و از این معامله غافل مشو که حیف خوری

Careless of this matter, be not, lest sorrow thou suffer.

1-Suleiman's minister

طریق عشق طریقی عجب خطرناک است

Love's Path is a path wonder fully dangerous,

نعوذبالله اگر ره به مقصدی نبری

We seek refuge in God If to a place of safety, the path thou take not

به یمن همت حافظ امید هست که باز

By the blessing of (the prayer of) Hafiz, is hope that again

اری اسامر لیلای لیله القمر

I may see the traces (of glories) of my Laila (the true Beloved in the path of) the night, luminous with the moon.

غزل ۴۵۳ ⊙ⒹⒺ ④⑤③ ODE

ای که دایم به خویش مغروری

O thou that art ever proud of thy self

گر تو را عشق نیست معذوری

If love be not thine, excused thou art.

گرد دیوانگان عشق مگرد

Around those distraught of love, wander not

که به عقل عقیله مشهوری

For, for the best wisdom, renowned thou art.

مستی عشق نیست در سر تو

(O father of lust) Not in thy head is love's intoxication

رو که تو مست آب انگوری

Go (no access to me is thine) for, with the wine of the grape, intoxicated thou art.

روی زرد است و آه دردآلود

The yellow (grief-stricken) face, and the grief-stained sigh are

عاشقان را دوای رنجوری

For lovers, the evidence of affliction.

بگذر از نام و ننگ خود حافظ

Hafiz thy own name and fame, abandon

ساغر می‌طلب که مخموری

The cup of wine, seek for wine-sick, thou art.

غزل ۴۵۴ ⊙ⒹⒺ ④⑤④ ODE

ز کوی یار می‌آید نسیم باد نوروزی

From the street of the friend (the perfect murshid) came the fragrant breeze of the nau-ruz (guidance in the Path to God)

از این باد ار مدد خواهی چراغ دل برافروزی

From this breeze, if thou desire aid, the lamp of the heart, thou mayest kindle.

چو گل گر خرده‌ای داری خدا را صرف عشرت کن

If, like the red rose, a particle of (red gold) thou hast, for God's sake, expend it in pleasure

که قارون را غلط‌ها داد سودای زراندوزی

For caused Karun's[1] errors, the passion for gold-gathering.

1-Korah, A wealthy man from the Hebrews

ز جام گل دگر بلبل چنان مست می لعل است

I have the wine that's as pure as the soul and yet the Sufi criticizes it:

که زد بر چرخ فیروزه صفیر تخت فیروزی

O God may an unhappy fate not fall for a day, on one wise and right.

به صحرا رو که از دامن غبار غم بیفشانی

To the assembly, come; so that from Hafiz, ghazal-singing, thou mayst learn.

به گلزار آی کز بلبل غزل گفتن بیاموزی

To the garden, go that, from the bulbul, love's mysteries thou mayst take to mind;

طریق کام بخشی چیست ترک کام خود کردن

Seeking the path of (the true Beloved's) desire is what' Tis the abandoning of our own desire

کلاه سروری آن است کز این ترک بردوزی

The crown of sovereignty is that which from this abandoning, thou stitchest.

سخن در پرده می‌گویم چو گل از غنچه بیرون آی

Within the screen, speech I utter forth from (thyself), like the rose-bud (from the bud) come

که بیش از پنج روزی نیست حکم میر نوروزی

For, not more than a space of five days, is the order of the chief of a nau-ruz

ندانم نوحه قمری به طرف جویباران چیست

The lament of the turtle-dove by the marge of the stream, I know not where-fore it is

مگر او نیز همچون من غمی دارد شبانروزی

Perchance, like me, a grief it hath night and day

می‌ای دارم چو جان صافی و صوفی می‌کند عیبش

A wine like the pure soul, I have yet its detraction, the Sufi [1]maketh

خدایا هیچ عاقل را مبادا بخت بد روزی

O God let not ill fortune be the sage's portion (even one day)

جدا شد یار شیرینت کنون تنها نشین ای شمع

Separated became thy sweet friend (the murshid)[2] candle now, sit alone

که حکم آسمان این است اگر سازی و گر سوزی

For this the sky's decree is whether thou be content; or whether thou consume

به عجب علم نتوان شد ز اسباب طرب محروم

Excluded from the means of joy, in wonder of knowledge, one cannot be

بیا ساقی که جاهل را هنی تر می‌رسد روزی

Saki[3] come; to the fool arriveth the largest victual-portion.

به بستان شو که از بلبل رموز عشق گیری یاد

To the garden, go that, from the bulbul[4], love's mysteries thou mayst take to mind.

به مجلس آی کز حافظ غزل گفتن بیاموزی

To the assembly, come; so that from Hafiz, ghazal-singing, thou mayst learn.

غزل ۴۵۵ ⓄⒹⒺ ④⑤⑤

عمر بگذشت به بی‌حاصلی و بوالهوسی

In fruitlessness (and) lust fulness, passed my life

ای پسر جام می‌ام ده که به پیری برسی

O son! me, the cup of wine, give, so that to old age thou mayst reach.

1-A Muslim ascetic and mystic   3 -Tapster
2-Guru   4 -Nightingale

چه شکرهاست در این شهر که قانع شده‌اند

In this city, what sugars that became contented,

شاهبازان طریقت به مقام مگسی

The (mighty) falcons of tarikat[1] with the stage of a pitiful fly

دوش در خیل غلامان درش می‌رفتم

Last night, in the crowd of slaves of His door, I went,

گفت ای عاشق بیچاره تو باری چه کسی

He spake saying O (friendless), remediless, one the load of what person art thou

با دل خون شده چون نافه خوشش باید بود

Despite the heart become blood (in grief) to be like the (pleasant) fragrant musk-pod, is necessary for him

هر که مشهور جهان گشت به مشکین نفسی

Who became world-renowned for a fragrant breath (of excellence)

لمع البرق من الطور و آنست به

From the direction of Tar, lightning flashed; to it, I inclined (in love)

فلعلی لک آت بشهاب قبس

Perchance, thee, a brand of bright flame, I may bring

کاروان رفت و تو در خواب و بیابان در پیش

Departed (in death) hath the Karvan[2] (of friends) and, (in the ambush – place) thou in sleep

وه که بس بی‌خبر از غلغل چندین جرسی

(Arise prepare the requisites of the end) Alas of so many crashes of the great bell (of death) wholly void of knowledge, (thou art).

بال بگشا و صفیر از شجر طوبی زن

(O bird of my soul) Thy pinion, spread and, from lofty Tuba tree, the shout of praise in recollection of Thy Creator raise

حیف باشد چو تو مرغی که اسیر قفسی

Woe is it that a glorious bird like thee captive of the cage (of worldly delights that befit thee not) thou art

تا چو مجمر نفسی دامن جانان گیرم

So that, like the censer, a moment, we may take the skirt of the beloved

جان نهادیم بر آتش ز پی خوش نفسی

We placed our heart on the fire, for the sake of a pleasant breath.

چند پوید به هوای تو ز هر سو حافظ

In desire of Thee, in every direction, Hafiz runneth how much

یسر الله طریقا بک یا ملتمسی

O object of desire to thee, easy the path, may God make.

غزل ۴۵۶ ⓄⒹⒺ ④⑤⑥

نوبهار است در آن کوش که خوشدل باشی

'Tis the fresh spring. In this strive that joyous of heart thou mayst be

که بسی گل بدمد باز و تو در گل باشی

For, again, blossometh many a rose when in the clay (of the grave) thou shall be

---

1-Principle, Sufism, religious way   2-Convoy

من نگویم که کنون با که نشین و چه بنوش
I say not now, with whom, sit what drink

که تو خود دانی اگر زیرک و عاقل باشی
For thou knowest, if wise and learned thou be

چنگ در پرده همین می‌دهدت پند ولی
Within the veil, thee, the harp keepeth giving counsel But

وعظت آن گاه کند سود که قابل باشی
Thee, counsel profiteth at that time when worthy thou mayst be.

در چمن هر ورق دفتر حالی دگر است
In the sward, every leaf is a book of a different state

حیف باشد که ز کار همه غافل باشی
Woe is it if, careless of the state of all, thou be

نقد عمرت ببرد غصه دنیا به گزاف
In excess, the world's anguish taketh life's cash,

گر شب و روز در این قصه مشکل باشی
If, night and day, in this difficult tale, (of journeying to the Friend) thou be

گر چه راهیست پر از بیم ز ما تا بر دوست
Though, from us to the Friend, is a Path full (the path of ma'rifat) of fear,

رفتن آسان بود ار واقف منزل باشی
Easy is the going, if acquainted with the stage (the Shaikh) [1] thou be.

حافظا گر مدد از بخت بلندت باشد
O Hafiz! if, from lofty fortune, aid be thine,

صید آن شاهد مطبوع شمایل باشی
The prey of that (true) Beloved, impressed with excellences, thou shalt be

غزل ۴۵۷ ⓄⒹⒺ ④⑤⑦

هزار جهد بکردم که یار من باشی
Efforts, a thousand, I made that my (true) Beloved, thou shouldst be.

مرادبخش دل بی‌قرار من باشی
(That) The desire-giver of my sorrowful heart, Thou shouldst be.

چراغ دیده شب زنده دار من گردی
(O true Beloved since) The lamp of my eye, Thou madest night a live keeper (watchful)

انیس خاطر امیدوار من باشی
The consoler of my hopeful heart, Thou shalt be.

چو خسروان ملاحت به بندگان نازند
When to slaves, Khusraus[2] of darkish beauty be have kindly,

تو در میانه خداوندگار من باشی
in the midst, the Lord of my work thou shouldst be.

از آن عقیق که خونین دلم ز عشوه او
By that cornelian (mouth) by the way whereof, bloody of heart, I am,

اگر کنم گله‌ای غمگسار من باشی
If complaint, I make, my mystery-keeper, thou shalt be

1-A leader in a Muslim community   2-king

در آن چمن که بتان دست عاشقان گیرند

In that sward where idols (beloved ones) the hand of lovers take,

گرت ز دست برآید نگار من باشی

If, from thy hand, (this hand-taking) take place, my idol, thou shall be.

شبی به کلبه احزان عاشقان آیی

And a night, the consoling friend of my sorrowful heart, Thou shouldst be

دمی انیس دل سوکوار من باشی

(That) a moment into the hut of sorrow full overs, Thou shouldst come

شود غزاله خورشید صید لاغر من

My slender prey becometh the rays of the sun,

گر آهویی چو تو یک دم شکار من باشی

If, a moment, a deer like thee, my prey thou be.

سه بوسه کز دو لبت کرده‌ای وظیفه من

The three kisses that of Thy two lips, my portion Thou hast made,

اگر ادا نکنی قرض دار من باشی

If Thou give not, my debtor, Thou shalt be.

من این مراد ببینم به خود که نیم شبی

In (sleep of) midnight, this desire I see

به جای اشک روان در کنار من باشی

In place of streaming tears, in my embrace, thou shalt be.

من ار چه حافظ شهرم جوی نمی‌ارزم

Though I am the Hafiz (the guardian) of the city, not worth a barley-corn I am

مگر تو از کرم خویش یار من باشی

Perchance, out of thy own liberality, my beloved, thou shalt be.

غزل ۴۵۸ ⓄⒹⒺ ④⑤⑧

ای دل آن دم که خراب از می گلگون باشی

O heart that moment when, intoxicated with wine rose of hue, thou art

بی زر و گنج به صد حشمت قارون باشی

Without gold and treasure, with a hundred pomps of Karun[1] thou art

در مقامی که صدارت به فقیران بخشند

In the stage where to fakirs[2] the seat of wazirship, they give,

چشم دارم که به جاه از همه افزون باشی

I expect that above all in rank thou art.

در ره منزل لیلی که خطرهاست در آن

In the path to the Abode of Laila[3] (the true Beloved) where in are dangers,

شرط اول قدم آن است که مجنون باشی

The first condition of its step is, that Majnun[4] (the perfect lover) the thou be.

نقطه عشق نمودم به تو هان سهو مکن

Thee, love's center I showed. Ho! mistake make not

ور نه چون بنگری از دایره بیرون باشی

If not, when thou lookest outside of the circle (of lovers) thou art

---

1-Korah, The rich man of the time of Prophet Moses   3-Lover
2-Poor   4-Lily famous and legendary lover

کاروان رفت و تو در خواب و بیابان در پیش

Departed, the karvan[1] (of thy fellow-travellers) and, in sleep, thou, (art) and the desert (is) in front

کی روی ره ز که پرسی چه کنی چون باشی

(O heart I know not) How thou goest from whom, the path thou askest what thou doest how (in this desert, ignorant of the path, alone) thou art

تاج شاهی طلبی گوهر ذاتی بنمای

The kingly crown, thou seekest the essence (perfection) of thy own nature, display

ور خود از تخمه جمشید و فریدون باشی

If, indeed, of the essence (the race) the of Jamshid[2] and of Firidun[3] thou be.

ساغری نوش کن و جرعه بر افلاک فشان

A cup, drink and on the skies, a draught, cast

چند و چند از غم ایام جگرخون باشی

On account of time's grief, the liver of blood (of grief) how long, how long art thou

حافظ از فقر مکن ناله که گر شعر این است

Hafiz of poverty, be wail not For if this be thy poetry,

هیچ خوشدل نپسندد که تو محزون باشی

Appeareth no one happy of heart, that sorrowful thou shouldst be

غزل ۴۵۹ ⓄⒹⒺ ④⑤⑨

زین خوش رقم که بر گل رخسار می‌کشی

With this beauteous writing that on the rose of thy cheek thou drawest,

خط بر صحیفه گل و گلزار می‌کشی

On the page (leaf) of the rose, and of the rose-bed, the line of (effacement) thou drawest

اشک حرم نشین نهانخانه مرا

My tear, sitting in the fold of the hidden house,

زان سوی هفت پرده به بازار می‌کشی

From within the seven screens to the market (of renown) Thou drawest.

کاهل روی چو باد صبا را به بوی زلف

By the perfume of thy tress, the sluggish mover like the (soft) morning breeze,

هر دم به قید سلسله در کار می‌کشی

Momently, in bond (and) chain into (swift) action, Thou drawest

هر دم به یاد آن لب میگون و چشم مست

Momently, in recollection of that lip, wine of hue and of that intoxicated eye

از خلوتم به خانه خمار می‌کشی

Me, from khilvat[4] to the vintner's house, Thou drawest.

گفتی سر تو بسته فتراک ما شود

(O true Beloved) Thou saidest Thy head bound to our saddle-strap is fit

سهل است اگر تو زحمت این بار می‌کشی

'Tis easy (here is my head) if the trouble of this load, Thou endurest.

1-Convoy
2-king

3-king
4-Solitude

با چشم و ابروی تو چه تدبیر دل کنم

With (against) Thy eye and eye-brow, what deliberation of heart may I make

وه زین کمان که بر من بیمار می‌کشی

Alas this bow that, against me miserable, Thou drawest

بازآ که چشم بد ز رخت دفع می‌کند

Come back so that, with Thy cheek, far I may put the evil-eye,

ای تازه گل که دامن از این خار می‌کشی

O fresh rose, that, from this thorn (Hafiz, possessed of imperious lust) Thy skirt Thou drawest.

حافظ دگر چه می‌طلبی از نعیم دهر

Hafiz from the favour of time, what more seekest thou

می می‌خوری و طره دلدار می‌کشی

Wine thou tastest and (through the hand) the heart-possessor's tress thou drawest

غزل ۴۶۰ ⓞⒹⒺ ④⑥⓪

سلیمی منذ حلت بالعراق

Since my Sulaima[1] went to' Irak.

الاقی من نواها ما الاقی

Through love for her, I meet (with) what I meet with, (the pain of separation)

الا ای ساروان منزل دوست

Ho camel-driver of the friend's litter

الی رکبانکم طال اشتیاقی

Towards your riders of the camels of the karvan great hath become my longing.

خرد در زنده رود انداز و می نوش

Into the Zinda stream (of Isfahan) cast thy wisdom wine, drink,

به گلبانگ جوانان عراقی

To the shout of youths of' Irak

ربیع العمر فی مرعی حماکم

The spring of life is passed in the sward of thy care

حماک الله یا عهد التلاقی

O time of union God protect thee.

بیا ساقی بده رطل گرانم

Saki come me, the heavy ritl[2] give

سقاک الله من کاس دهاق

God give thee to drink from a full cup

جوانی باز می‌آرد به یادم

Back to my recollection, youthfulness bring

سماع چنگ و دست افشان ساقی

The sound of the harp and the hand-waiving of the Saki.

می باقی بده تا مست و خوشدل

The remaining wine, give, so that, intoxicated and happy of heart,

به یاران برفشانم عمر باقی

My remaining life, I may scatter (as a sacrifice) on friends.

1-Lover   2- large cup or goblet, pound

درونم خون شد از نادیدن دوست

From not seeing the beloved, blood became my heart

الا تعسا لایام الفراق

Now (evil) be fall the days of separation

دموعی بعدکم لا تحقروها

My (scanty) tears after (separation from) you, regard not mean

فکم بحر عمیق من سواقی

For, from (small) streams, many a (great) sea is collected

دمی با نیکخواهان متفق باش

A moment, with well-wishers, be concordant

غنیمت دان امور اتفاقی

Affairs of concord, plunder reckon.

بساز ای مطرب خوشخوان خوشگو

O minstrel, sweet singer, sweet speaker prepare

به شعر فارسی صوت عراقی

An 'Irak note in Persian verse.

عروسی بس خوشی ای دختر رز

O daughter of the vine the pleasant bride, thou art

ولی گه گه سزاوار طلاقی

But, sometimes, worthy of divorce, thou art.

مسیحای مجرد را برازد

The lonely (un-married) Masiha[1], it suiteth

که با خورشید سازد هم وثاقی

That, fellow ship with the sun, he should make.

وصال دوستان روزی ما نیست

Not our lot, is the union of friends

بخوان حافظ غزل های فراقی

Hafiz ghazals[2] of 'Irak, utter

غزل ۴۶۱ ⓄⒹⒺ ④⑥① ODE 461

کتبت قصه شوق و مدمعی باکی

The tale of my desire, I wrote, and weeping was my eye:

بیا که بی تو به جان آمدم ز غمناکی

Come for, through sorrow fulness without thee, I am ready to die.

بسا که گفته‌ام از شوق با دو دیده خود

Through desire, to my two eyes, much I have said

ایا منازل سلمی فاین سلماک

O dwellings of Salma![3] thy Salma is where.

عجیب واقعه‌ای و غریب حادثه‌ای

Tis a strange event and a wonderful occurrence this,

انا اصطبرت قتیلا و قاتلی شاکی

Afflicted, was I and (in the palpitating, quivering, fluttering state of one slain. Yet, against me the slayer was complainer).

1-Jesus Christ
2-Sonnet

3-Lover

که را رسد که کند عیب دامن پاکت

Reacheth to whom (the power) that, at thy pure skirt, he should carp

که همچو قطره که بر برگ گل چکد پاکی

For, like the (dew)-drop that, on the rose-leaf droppeth, pure thou art.

ز خاک پای تو داد آب روی لاله و گل

From the dust of thy foot, it gave honour to the tulip and to the rose,

چو کلک صنع رقم زد به آبی و خاکی

When creation's reed wrote the decree on the watery and the dusty.

صبا عبیرفشان گشت ساقیا برخیز

O Saki[1] arise ambergri ode scattering, hath become the breeze

و هات شمسه کرم مطیب زاکی

Bring the juice of the grape, wine perfumed and pure the antidote of the lover's poison

دع التکاسل تغنم فقد جری مثل

(Idleness) Abandon successful, (thou shalt be. For) the proverb is

که زاد راهروان چستی است و چالاکی

The road-provision of wayfarers is alertness and expertness.

اثر نماند ز من ز بی شمایلت آری

Without (seeing) thy praised qualities, trace of me remaineth not. Yes.

اری مثر محیای من محیاک

From thy face (O Salma) I be hold the traces of life.

ز وصف حسن تو حافظ چگونه نطق زند

Of the description of thy beauty, how may Hafiz speak

که همچو صنع خدایی ورای ادراکی

For, like the divine qualities, beyond comprehension, thou art.

غزل ۴۶۲ ⓄⒹⒺ ④⑥②

یا مبسما یحاکی درجا من اللالی

O mouth, thou resembleth a casket of pearls

یا رب چه درخور آمد گردش خط هلالی

Lord around thy face, how fit became the line of a new moon

حالی خیال وصلت خوش میدهد فریبم

Now, me, the (vain) fancy of union with Thee pleasantly deceiveth

تا خود چه نقش بازد این صورت خیالی

Let us see what picture, sporteth this form of a (vain) fancy.

می ده که گر چه گشتم نامه سیاه عالم

Wine, give. For, though black of book of the world, I became

نومید کی توان بود از لطف لایزالی

Hopeless of the grace of the Eternal, when can one be

ساقی بیار جامی و از خلوتم برون کش

Saki a cup bring and, me, forth from khilvat[2] put

تا در به در بگردم قلاش و لاابالی

So that, crafty and nothing-earning, door to door, I may wander.

1-Tapster   2-Solitude

از چار چیز مگذر گر عاقلی و زیرک
If learned and wise thou be, let not go four things
امن و شراب بی‌غش معشوق و جای خالی
Safety, wine void of alloy, the Beloved, and the void place (the desert of solitude)

چون نیست نقش دوران در هیچ حال ثابت
Since time's picture is in no way fixed,
حافظ مکن شکایت تا می خوریم حالی
Hafiz complaint, make not wine, let us drink.

صافیست جام خاطر در دور آصف عهد
Pure is the cup of the heart in the time of the Asaf[1] of the age,
قم فاسقنی رحیقا اصفی من الزلال
Arise and cause me to drink of a cup of wine purer than limpid water.

الملک قد تباهی من جده و جده
Verily, the country boasteth of him and of his efforts
یا رب که جاودان باد این قدر و این معالی
Lord ever be this rank and this sublimity

مسندفروز دولت کان شکوه و شوکت
The seat-kindler of the fortune of the mine of pomp and of grandeur,
برهان ملک و ملت بونصر بوالمعالی
The proof of the country and of religion, (is) Abu Nasr Abu-l-Mu'ali[2].

غزل ۴۶۳ ⓄⒹⒺ ④⑥③

سلام الله ما کر اللیالی
The salutation of God as long as nights recur (till the judgment day)
و جاوبت المثانی و المثالی
And as long as the lutes of two, or three, strings respond (to each other or to the singer)

علی وادی الاراک و من علیها
On the valley of Arak, and on him who is the rein
و دار باللوی فوق الرمال
(On) My dwelling on the bend of the hill above the sands

دعاگوی غریبان جهانم
The prayer-utterer for travellers of the world, I am
و ادعو بالتواتر و التوالی
Constantly and perpetually, I pray.

به هر منزل که رو آرد خدا را
O God in every stage whereto he turneth his face
نگه دارش به لطف لایزالی
Him, in Thy eternal protection, keep.

منال ای دل که در زنجیر زلفش
O heart be wail not. For, in the chain of His tress
همه جمعیت است آشفته حالی
The distraught state is all collectedness (tranquillity)

1-Suleiman's minister   2-He was a Judge

ز خطت صد جمال دیگر افزود

From Thy down, a hundred other beauties increase

که عمرت باد صد سال جلالی

Be Thy life a hundred illustrious years

تو می‌باید که باشی ور نه سهل است

That thou be is necessary If not, easy is

زیان مایه جاهی و مالی

The loss of capital, of rank, and of wealth

بر آن نقاش قدرت آفرین باد

Afarin be on that Painter of power

که گرد مه کشد خط هلالی

Who, around the (full) moon, draweth the line of a crescent (a new moon)

فحبک راحتی فی کل حین

For, at all times, love for Thee is my rest

و ذکرک مونسی فی کل حال

In every state, remembrance of Thee is my consoler

سویدای دل من تا قیامت

Till the judgment-day, the black point of my heart

مباد از شوق و سودای تو خالی

Be it not void of consuming and of distraughtness for Thee

کجا یابم وصال چون تو شاهی

Union with a King like Thee, how may gain,

من بدنام رند لاابالی

I, bad of name, profligate, careless

خدا داند که حافظ را غرض چیست

God knoweth Hafiz's intention

و علم الله حسبی من سالی

God's knowledge (of my wants) is sufficient for me without my asking

غزل ۴۶۴ ⓞⓓⓔ ④⑥④

بگرفت کار حسنت چون عشق من کمالی

As my love (so) the work of Thy beauty took a great perfection

خوش باش زان که نبود این هر دو را زوالی

Happy be on this account that, this (beauty of love and of form) hath not (even) a little decline.

در وهم می‌نگنجد کاندر تصور عقل

In my imagination, it cometh not that in the (vain) imaginings of wisdom,

آید به هیچ معنی زین خوبتر مثالی

In any way, should come more beautiful than this a form.

شد حظ عمر حاصل گر زان که با تو ما را

Life's delight would have been gained, if, with Thee, for us,

هرگز به عمر روزی روزی شود وصالی

Ever in life (only) one day had been the lot of a great union.

آن دم که با تو باشم یک سال هست روزی

That moment when, with Thee, I may be, the space of one (long) year is (only) a short day

وان دم که بی تو باشم یک لحظه هست سالی

That moment when, without Thee, I may be (the momentary twinkling of the eye) is a long year.

چون من خیال رویت جانا به خواب بینم

O beloved in sleep, the image of thy face how may I be hold,

کز خواب می‌نبیند چشمم بجز خیالی

Because, out of sleep, my eye seeth naught save an image

رحم آر بر دل من کز مهر روی خوبت

On my heart, bestow pity. For, from love for the lovely face,

شد شخص ناتوانم باریک چون هلالی

My powerless body became slender (and wan) like a new (crescent) moon.

حافظ مکن شکایت گر وصل دوست خواهی

Hafiz if thou desire union with the Beloved, make no complaint

زین بیشتر بباید بر هجرت احتمالی

For thee, on account of separation, is necessary greater than this a load.

غزل ۴۶۵ ⒪⒟⒠ ④⑥⑤

رفتم به باغ صبحدمی تا چنم گلی

One morning to the garden I went a rose to pluck

آمد به گوش ناگهم آواز بلبلی

Suddenly, came to my ear the clam our of a bulbul[1].

مسکین چو من به عشق گلی گشته مبتلا

Like me, wretched, in love for a rose, entangled he was

و اندر چمن فکنده ز فریاد غلغلی

And into the sward, by his plaint, cast a clamour.

می‌گشتم اندر آن چمن و باغ دم به دم

Momently, in that garden-sward, I sauntered

می‌کردم اندر آن گل و بلبل تاملی

On that rose and bulbul, I kept a-musing

گل یار حسن گشته و بلبل قرین عشق

The rose became the lover of (the thorn) and the bulbul, the associate of love (and its pain)

آن را تفضلی نه و این را تبدلی

Not a change to this (the rose) nor to that (the bulbul) a change.

چون کرد در دلم اثر آواز عندلیب

When, in my heart, the bulbul's voice impression made,

گشتم چنان که هیچ نماندم تحملی

Is o became that mine remained not a particle of patience

بس گل شکفته می‌شود این باغ را ولی

Of this garden, many a rose keepeth blossoming. But

کس بی بلای خار نچیده‌ست از او گلی

From it, without the calamity of the thorn, none plucked a rose.

1-Nightingale

حافظ مدار امید فرج از مدار چرخ
Hafiz of this center-place of existence, have no hope

دارد هزار عیب و ندارد تفضلی
A thousand defects, it hath it hath not a single excellence.

غزل ۴۶۶ ⓄⒹⒺ ④⑥⑥

این خرقه که من دارم در رهن شراب اولی
This Khirka[1] that I have in pledge for wine best

وین دفتر بی‌معنی غرق می ناب اولی
This meaning less book immersed in pure wine (of ma'rifat) best.

چون عمر تبه کردم چندان که نگه کردم
My life, how I ruined as much as I gazed,

در کنج خراباتی افتاده خراب اولی
In the tavern-corner, fallen in toxicated, best.

چون مصلحت اندیشی دور است ز درویشی
Since, from poverty, far is counsel-considering,

هم سینه پر از آتش هم دیده پرآب اولی
Both my heart full of fire best; and my eye full of water, best.

من حالت زاهد را با خلق نخواهم گفت
To the people, the state of the Zahid[2], I will not utter,

این قصه اگر گویم با چنگ و رباب اولی
For this state, if I utter, with the harp and the ribab best

تا بی سر و پا باشد اوضاع فلک زین دست
Since, in this way, headless and footless (fickle) are the sky's motions,

در سر هوس ساقی در دست شراب اولی
In the head, desire for the Saki; in the hand, wine best.

از همچو تو دلداری دل برنکنم آری
From a heart-possessor like thee, the heart up I pluck not. Yes

چون تاب کشم باری زان زلف به تاب اولی
If I endure torment, at least in the curl of that tress, best

چون پیر شدی حافظ از میکده بیرون آی
Hafiz since old thou hast become, forth from the tavern, come

رندی و هوسناکی در عهد شباب اولی
In youth's season, profligacy and desire best.

غزل ۴۶۷ ⓄⒹⒺ ④⑥⑦

زان می عشق کز او پخته شود هر خامی
(O Saki) of that (pure) wine of love (for God) whereby matured become the very immature one

گر چه ماه رمضان است بیاور جامی
Although it is the month of Ramazan[3] (so that I may escape-from this immatureness and to matureness, attain) bring a great cup

---

1-Cloak
2-Pietist

3-The nineth lunar months

روزها رفت که دست من مسکین نگرفت

Passed days, since the hand of me miserable clasped not

زلف شمشادقدی ساعد سیم اندامی

The leg of one box-tree of stature the arm of one silver of limb.

روزه هر چند که مهمان عزیز است ای دل

O heart though the fast of (Ramazan) be the dear guest,

صحبتش موهبتی دان و شدن انعامی

Regard its society a gift; it's going a favour.

مرغ زیرک به در خانقه اکنون نپرد

Now (in the Ramazan) to the cloister-door fleeth not the wise bird,

که نهادهست به هر مجلس وعظی دامی

For, at every assembly of exhortation, is placed a snare

گله از زاهد بدخو نکنم رسم این است

No complaint, do I make of the Zahids[1], ill of nature. The way is this

که چو صبحی بدمد در پی اش افتد شامی

That, when a (bright) morning dawneth, in its pursuit falleth a (dark) evening.

یار من چون بخرامد به تماشای چمن

When, to the spectacle of the sward, my Friend moveth,

برسانش ز من ای پیک صبا پیغامی

O foot man of the breeze from me to him, convey a message

آن حریفی که شب و روز می صاف کشد

A companion, who night and day drinketh pure wine, (where)

بود آیا که کند یاد ز دردآشامی

Is it that he maketh recollection of a dreg-drinker

حافظا گر ندهد داد دلت آصف عهد

O Hafiz! if the justice of the heart, thee the Asaf[2] of the age give not,

کام دشوار به دست آوری از خودکامی

With difficulty, thou bringest to hand thy desire through a great selfishness.

غزل ۴۶۸ ⓞⓓⓔ ④⑥⑧

که برد به نزد شاهان ز من گدا پیامی

From me, the beggar, to kings, who taketh a message,

که به کوی می فروشان دو هزار جم به جامی

Saying: "In the street of the wine-sellers, (they sell) two thousand (mighty) Jamshids for a single cup of wine."

شدهام خراب و بدنام و هنوز امیدوارم

Ruined and ill of fame, I have become yet, hope I have

که به همت عزیزان برسم به نیک نامی

That, by the blessing of dear ones (those of good name) I may (escape from ill-fame and) reach to good-fame

---

1-Pietist   2-Suleiman's minister

تو که کیمیافروشی نظری به قلب ما کن
Thou that sellest alchemy, at our impure gold (heart) cast a glance (of alchemy)
که بضاعتی نداریم و فکندهایم دامی
For, a great capital (in trade) we have not and a snare (to captivate the true murshid) we have cast

عجب از وفای جانان که عنایتی نفرمود
The fidelity of the Beloved, wonder that He made not an inquiry,
نه به نامه پیامی نه به خامه سلامی
Neither by the reed, a salutation nor by letter, a message.

اگر این شراب خام است اگر آن حریف پخته
If this wine be immature, (and) this companion matured,
به هزار بار بهتر ز هزار پخته خامی
By a thousand times, than a thousand matured ones better (is) an immature one

ز رهم میفکن ای شیخ به دانههای تسبیح
O Shaikh[1] by the beads of the rosary, (I beseech thee) cast me not from the Path
که چو مرغ زیرک افتد نفتد به هیچ دامی
For, when (once) the wise bird falleth, he falleth not (again) into any snare.

سر خدمت تو دارم بخرم به لطف و مفروش
Desire for Thy service, I have; in kindness, me, purchase and sell not
که چو بنده کمتر افتد به مبارکی غلامی
For, into good fortune, seldom falleth, like (me) the slave a slave.

به کجا برم شکایت به که گویم این حکایت
My plaint, I take to where. This tale, I utter to whom
که لبت حیات ما بود و نداشتی دوامی
For thy lip was our life and, Thou hadst not (even) a little permanency.

بگشای تیر مژگان و بریز خون حافظ
(O true Beloved) The arrow of Thy eye-lash, loose and the blood of Hafiz, spill
که چنان کشندهای را نکند کس انتقامی
For, in respect of such as layer, none maketh (even) a little revenge.

غزل ۴۶۹ ⓄⒹⒺ ④⑥⑨

انت رواح رند الحمی و زاد غرامی
Came the breeze giving fragrance of Hima; and my desire increased
فدای خاک در دوست باد جان گرامی
Be my precious life a ransom for the dust of the Friend's door.

پیام دوست شنیدن سعادت است و سلامت
The hearing of the Friend's message is felicity and safety
من المبلغ عنی الی سعاد سلامی
From me to Su'ad greeting, who will convey

بیا به شام غریبان و آب دیده من بین
To the evening (shelter) of strangers, come, and (the bloody) water of our eye, behold,
به سان باده صافی در آبگینه شامی
Like pure (red) wine in Damascus glass.

1-A leader in a Muslim community

اذا تغرد عن ذی الاراک طار خیر

If, in praise of the dweller of Arak (the beloved) the bird of happiness warbleth,

فلا تفرد عن روضها انین حمامی

From its gardens, the moaning of my pigeons (in desire of the possessor of Arak) will not be separated.

بسی نماند که روز فراق یار سر آید

Not much remaineth when to an end cometh the dayof separation from the beloved

رایت من هضبات الحمی قباب خیام

From the hills of Hima (the beloved's ab ode) I almost be held the removing of tents.

خوشا دمی که درآیی و گویمت به سلامت

O happy that moment when thou enterest, and to thee I say: In safety

قدمت خیر قدوم نزلت خیر مقام

Happy arrival in the best of a bodes, thou hast a lighted.

بعدت منک و قد صرت ذابا کهلال

Being far from thee, I have become slender (lean) as the new (crescent) moon

اگر چه روی چو ماهت ندیدهام به تمامی

Although thy face like the moon, in its fulness, I have not seen.

و ان دعیت بخلد و صرت ناقض عهد

If, to paradise, I inclined and became a covenant-breaker,

فما تطیب نفسی و ما استطاب منامی

Be neither my sleep agreeable, nor my sleeping place tranquil

امید هست که زودت به بخت نیک ببینم

Hope is that, by good fortune, thee I may quickly see

تو شاد گشته به فرماندهی و من به غلامی

Thou being joyous in order-giving; and I, in slavery.

چو سلک در خوشاب است شعر نغز تو حافظ

Hafiz like the string of pearls of good water is thy pure lustrous verse

که گاه لطف سبق میبرد ز نظم نظامی

For in the place of grace it surpasseth the verse of Nizami[1]

غزل **۴۷۰** ⓄⒹⒺ ④⑦⓪

سینه مالامال درد است ای دریغا مرهمی

Alas full, full of pain is my heart, a plaister

دل ز تنهایی به جان آمد خدا را همدمی

God through loneliness, to (giving up) life my heart hath come; a companion

چشم آسایش که دارد از سپهر تیزرو

From the swift moving sky, hope of ease, hath who

ساقیا جامی به من ده تا بیاسایم دمی

O Saki[2] a cup bring, so that I may rest a while.

زیرکی را گفتم این احوال بین خندید و گفت

To a wit, I said Be hold these circumstances. He laughed and said

صعب روزی بوالعجب کاری پریشان عالمی

A work, difficult a state, the father of wonders perturbed, a world.

1-Poet   2-Tapster

سوختم در چاه صبر از بهر آن شمع چگل

In the pit of patience, for that candle of Chigil, I consumed

شاه ترکان فارغ است از حال ما کو رستمی

Of our state, the King of the Turkans[1] (Turans) is careless. Where a Rustam?

در طریق عشقبازی امن و آسایش بلاست

In the Path of love-play, calamity is safety and ease

ریش باد آن دل که با درد تو خواهد مرهمی

Wounded be that heart that with (on account of) pain desireth a plaister

اهل کام و ناز را در کوی رندی راه نیست

No path, into the street of profligates, is for the man of desire and indulgence

ره روی باید جهان سوزی نه خامی بی‌غمی

A way farer is necessary, a world-consumer not a raw one, without a grief

آدمی در عالم خاکی نمی‌آید به دست

In this dusty world, to hand cometh not a man

عالمی دیگر بباید ساخت و از نو آدمی

It is necessary to make another world, and a new a man.

خیز تا خاطر بدان ترک سمرقندی دهیم

Arise. To the saucy ones of Samarkand[2], let us give our heart

کز نسیمش بوی جوی مولیان آید همی

For, from its breeze, the fragrance of the river Mulian[3] (the Oxus) cometh anon.

گریه حافظ چه سنجد پیش استغنای عشق

Hafiz before (in comparison with) love's in dependence what weigheth thy weeping

کاندر این دریا نماید هفت دریا شبنمی

For, in this deluge, the seven (all the) seas (of the world) appear (only) a little night-dew

غزل ۴۷۱ ①ⒹⒺ ④⑦① ODE 471

ز دلبرم که رساند نوازش قلمی

To me, from the heart-ravisher who will convey the kindness (of a letter) of a pen

کجاست پیک صبا گر همی‌کند کرمی

The foot-man of the wind is where, if he still doeth a kindness

قیاس کردم و تدبیر عقل در ره عشق

In love's path, I considered that the deliberation of wisdom

چو شبنمی است که بر بحر می‌کشد رقمی

Is like a little night-dew, that, on the sea, draweth a mark (wrinkle)

بیا که خرقه من گر چه رهن میکده‌هاست

Come for, though my Khirka[4] is the endowment of the wine-house,

ز مال وقف نبینی به نام من درمی

Of the property of endowment, thou seest not to my name (even) a diram.

حدیث چون و چرا درد سر دهد ای دل

O heart (Saki) head-pain giveth the tale of how and why

پیاله گیر و بیاسا ز عمر خویش دمی

The cup (of pure wine) take and, from (the care of) thy own life, rest a moment.

1-Afrasiab,
2-Was the king of Macedonia in ancient Greece

3 -The name of a river in Bukhara
4-Cloak

طبیب راه نشین درد عشق نشناسد

Love's pain knoweth not the road-sitting physician (the dry zahid; the sufi, void of wisdom)

برو به دست کن ای مرده دل مسیح دمی

O one dead of heart got o hand get a Masih-breath.

دلم گرفت ز سالوس و طبل زیر گلیم

From hypocrisy, my heart took (flight) and the drum (was) beneath the blanket

به آن که بر در میخانه برکشم علمی

Come, so that at the wine-house door, I may up-lift a great standard.

بیا که وقت شناسان دو کون بفروشند

Come (and drink wine) For the time-recogniser selleth two worlds (this and the next)

به یک پیاله می صاف و صحبت صنمی

For one cup of pure wine; and for the society of a lovely idol

دوام عیش و تنعم نه شیوه عشق است

Not love's way is ever pleasure and ease

اگر معاشر مایی بنوش نیش غمی

If, our companion, thou be, drink the poison of a great grief.

نمی‌کنم گله‌ای لیک ابر رحمت دوست

No complaint (only mention) I make But the cloud of mercy of the Friend,

به کشته زار جگرتشنگان نداد نمی

To the field of liver-thirsty ones, gave not (even) a little dew.

چرا به یک نی قندش نمی‌خرند آن کس

For one reed of his candy, why purchase they not that one (Hafiz)

که کرد صد شکرافشانی از نی قلمی

Who, a hundred sugar-scatterings, made from the reed of a single pen

سزای قدر تو شاها به دست حافظ نیست

O king in Hafiz's hand is naught worthy of thy value

جز از دعای شبی و نیاز صبحدمی

Save the supplication of a night and the prayer of a morning.

غزل ۴۷۲ ⓄⒹⒺ ④⑦②

احمد الله علی معدله السلطان

God, I praise for the justice of the great Sultan

احمد شیخ اویس حسن ایلخانی

Ahmad (bin) Shaikh Uvais (bin) Hasan Ilkhani.[1]

خان بن خان و شهنشاه شهنشاه نژاد

Khan bin Khan, Shahinshah of Shahin-shah-descent;

آن که می‌زیبد اگر جان جهانش خوانی

That one, whom, if thou call the soul of the world. 'tis well.

دیده نادیده به اقبال تو ایمان آورد

Confidence in thy fortune bringeth he who hath seen and he who hath not seen;

مرحبا ای به چنین لطف خدا ارزانی

Excellent! O thou (that art) worthy of such grace of God.

1-Baghdad Ilkhanid dynasty

ماه اگر بی تو برآید به دو نیمش بزنند
If, without thee, the moon ascend, it in two halves they dash

دولت احمدی و معجزه سبحانی
The fortune of Ahmad (Muhammad), and the miracle of a Holy one (God),

جلوه بخت تو دل می‌برد از شاه و گدا
Heart from king and beggar, the splendour of thy fortune ravisheth;

چشم بد دور که هم جانی و هم جانانی
Far be the evil-eye, for both soul thou art, and also the beloved thou art.

برشکن کاکل ترکانه که در طالع توست
Turk-like, the forelock arrange. For, in thy fortune, is

بخشش و کوشش خاقانی و چنگزخانی
The liberality of a Khakan; and the energy of a Chingiz Khan.

گر چه دوریم به یاد تو قدح می‌گیریم
Though (apparently) far, we are, to thy recollection the goblet, we drink;

بعد منزل نبود در سفر روحانی
For, in the spiritual journey, distance of stage is none.

از گل پارسیم غنچه عیشی نشکفت
Not a rose-bud of ease blossomed from my Persian clay;

حبذا دجله بغداد و می ریحانی
Excellent! the Tigris of Baghdad; and the fragrant wine.

سر عاشق که نه خاک در معشوق بود
The lover's head that was not the dust of the Beloved's door,

کی خلاصش بود از محنت سرگردانی
From the labour of head-revolvingness, when is freedom his?

ای نسیم سحری خاک در یار بیار
O morning breeze! the dust of the Beloved's path, bring;

که کند حافظ از او دیده دل نورانی
That, luminous with it, the eye of his heart, Hafiz may make.

غزل ۴۷۳ ⓄⒹⒺ ④⑦③

وقت را غنیمت دان آن قدر که بتوانی
Time consider plunder to that degree that thou canst

حاصل از حیات ای جان این دم است تا دانی
O soul the out-come of life is (only) this moment if thou knowest.

کام بخشی گردون عمر در عوض دارد
The desire-giving of the sphere hath life in barter,

جهد کن که از دولت داد عیش بستانی
Strive that, from fortune, the justice of ease thou mayst take.

باغبان چو من زین جا بگذرم حرامت باد
Gardener when hence I pass, be it unlawful to thee,

گر به جای من سروی غیر دوست بنشانی
If, in my place, a cypress other than the beloved thou plant

زاهد پشیمان را ذوق باده خواهد کشت

The wine's delight will slay the penitent Zahid[1]

عاقلا مکن کاری کورد پشیمانی

O sage do not a deed, that bringeth penitence.

محتسب نمی‌داند این قدر که صوفی را

The jar-shatterer knoweth not this value that to the Sufi[2],

جنس خانگی باشد همچو لعل رمانی

Is a household chattel like a pomegranate ruby.

با دعای شبخیزان ای شکردهان مستیز

O sweet mouth with the prayer of the night-risers, strive not

در پناه یک اسم است خاتم سلیمانی

In the shelter of the one (ineffable) name (of God) is the seal having the quality of a Sulaiman[3].

پند عاشقان بشنو و از در طرب بازآ

The counsel of lovers, hear and out from the door of joy come

کاین همه نمی‌ارزد شغل عالم فانی

For all this is not worth the occupation of a transitory world.

یوسف عزیزم رفت ای برادران رحمی

O brothers compassion Went my precious Yusuf[4],

کز غمش عجب بینم حال پیر کنعانی

For grief for whom, wonderful (in wretchedness) I be held the state of the old man
(Y'akub) of Kin'an[5]

پیش زاهد از رندی دم مزن که نتوان گفت

Before the Zahid, boast not of profligacy For one cannot utter

با طبیب نامحرم حال درد پنهانی

To the physician, not the confidant, the state of a hidden pain

می‌روی و مژگانت خون خلق می‌ریزد

Thou goest and, the people's blood, thy eye-lashes shed

تیز می‌روی جانا ترسمت فرومانی

O soul fiercely (impetuously) thou goest fear is, behind, thou wilt remain

دل ز ناوک چشمت گوش داشتم لیکن

Aside from the glance of Thy eye, my heart, I kept But,

ابروی کماندارت می‌برد به پیشانی

Thy eye brow, bow-possessor, taketh (the heart) by its forehead.

جمع کن به احسانی حافظ پریشان را

With kindness, tranquillise Hafiz's heart

ای شکنج گیسویت مجمع پریشانی

O Thou, whose (beauteous) tress coil (is) the assembly-place (perfection) of dispersion

گر تو فارغی از ما ای نگار سنگین دل

O idol, stony of heart if of me careless thou be

حال خود بخواهم گفت پیش آصف ثانی

My own state, I will utter before Asaf[6] the second

1-Pietist
2-A Muslim ascetic and mystic
3-king

4-Name of a prophet
5-Jacob, the father of the Prophet Joseph
6-Touranshah's minister

غزل ۴۷۴ ⓄⒹⒺ ④⑦④

هواخواه توام جانا و می‌دانم که می‌دانی
O (true) Beloved Thy well-wisher, I am, and (this) I know that Thou knowest

که هم نادیده می‌بینی و هم ننوشته می‌خوانی
For, both the un-seen, Thou seest; and also the un-written (by fate) Thou readest.

ملامتگو چه دریابد میان عاشق و معشوق
Of the mystery of the lover and of the Beloved, what gaineth the reproacher

نبیند چشم نابینا خصوص اسرار پنهانی
The non-seeing eye especially seeth not a secret mystery.

بیفشان زلف و صوفی را به پابازی و رقص آور
(O true Beloved) Dishevel Thy tress and, to sport and to dancing, bring the Sufi[1] (people of the world)

که از هر رقعه دلقش هزاران بت بیفشانی
That, from every patch of his ragged garment, thousands of idols (of hypocrisy) Thou mayst scatter.

گشاد کار مشتاقان در آن ابروی دلبند است
The solving of the work of desirous ones is in that heart-binding eye-brow

خدا را یک نفس بنشین گره بگشا ز پیشانی
For God's sake, a moment (with towards us) unloose the knot frown from thy forehead

ملک در سجده آدم زمین بوس تو نیت کرد
In the adoration of Adam[2], the angel made resolve of thy ground-kiss,

که در حسن تو لطفی دید بیش از حد انسانی
For, in Thy beauty, (something) he found more than the way, human.

چراغ افروز چشم ما نسیم زلف جانان است
The lamp-kindler of our eye is the breeze of the tress of lovely ones

مباد این جمع را یا رب غم از باد پریشانی
Lord to this gathering (smoo.th state of the tress) be not grief for the breeze of dispersion

دریغا عیش شبگیری که در خواب سحر بگذشت
Alas that pleasure of night-sitting (up) that passed (swiftly like the) morning (breeze)

ندانی قدر وقت ای دل مگر وقتی که درمانی
O heart the value of union, thou knowest, (only) when behind in separation thou remainest.

ملول از همرهان بودن طریق کاردانی نیست
To be vexed with fellow way-farers, is not the action of a work-knower

بکش دشواری منزل به یاد عهد آسانی
The difficulty of the stage, endure in memory of a time of ease

خیال چنبر زلفش فریبت می‌دهد حافظ
Hafiz thee, the fancy of the yoke of His tress fascinates

نگر تا حلقه اقبال ناممکن نجنبانی
See, so that the ring of impossible fortune, thou shake not.

1-A Muslim ascetic and mystic   2-Human

غزل ۴۷۵ ⓄⒹⒺ ④⑦⑤

گفتند خلایق که تویی یوسف ثانی

People spake, saying (in beauty) a second Yusuf thou art

چون نیک بدیدم به حقیقت به از آنی

When, well, I looked, verily better than that (I had heard) thou art.

شیرینتر از آنی به شکرخنده که گویم

Sweeter than that which, with sweet smile, they say thou art

ای خسرو خوبان که تو شیرین زمانی

Khusrau of the lovely ones for, the Shirin of the age, thou art.

تشبیه دهانت نتوان کرد به غنچه

To the (folded) rose-bud, thy mouth, one cannot compare

هرگز نبود غنچه بدین تنگ دهانی

Never is the rose-bud with this narrow-mouthness.

صد بار بگفتی که دهم زان دهنت کام

A hundred times Thou saidest: From this mouth, thy desire I give

چون سوسن آزاده چرا جمله زبانی

Like the noble (ten – tongued) lily, why art Thou all a tongue

گویی بدهم کامت و جانت بستانم

Thou saidest Thy desire, I will give thy life, I will take

ترسم ندهی کامم و جانم بستانی

If ear my desire, Thou givest not and my life Thou wilt take.

چشم تو خدنگ از سپر جان گذراند

Through the shield of my life, Thy (sick, languishing) eye causeth to pass the poplar (arrow)

بیمار که دیدهست بدین سخت کمانی

(The eye) sick, who hath seen with so strong a bow

چون اشک بیندازیش از دیده مردم

(O true Beloved) Like the (worthless) tear from the eye of man, him Thou easiest,

آن را که دمی از نظر خویش برانی

Him, whom a moment, away from Thy sight, Thou drivest.

غزل ۴۷۶ ⓄⒹⒺ ④⑦⑥

نسیم صبح سعادت بدان نشان که تو دانی

Breeze of the morning of happiness for that trace that thou knowest,

گذر به کوی فلان کن در آن زمان که تو دانی

To a certain one's street, pass at that time that thou knowest.

تو پیک خلوت رازی و دیده بر سر راهت

The footman of the chamber of mystery, thou art and on the head of the Path, is my eye

به مردمی نه به فرمان چنان بران که تو دانی

By manliness, hot by order, urge in that way, that thou knowest.

بگو که جان عزیزم ز دست رفت خدا را

Say: From my hand passed my feeble soul For God's sake,

ز لعل روح فزایش ببخش آن که تو دانی

From Thy ruby (lip) soul-refreshing, give that that Thou knowest.

من این حروف نوشتم چنان که غیر ندانست

(O true Beloved) These (few) words I wrote, in such a way that the stranger hath not known

تو هم ز روی کرامت چنان بخوان که تو دانی

(Them) by way of kindness, do Thou also read in such a way that Thou knowest

خیال تیغ تو با ما حدیث تشنه و آب است

With us, the image of Thy (slaying) sword is the tale of the thirsty one and of water
(whereto he desireth to reach)

اسیر خویش گرفتی بکش چنان که تو دانی

Thy own captive, Thou seizest. Slay in such a way that Thou knowest.

امید در کمر زرکشت چگونه ببندم

On Thy girdle, gold-woven, hope how may I note stablish

دقیقه‌ایست نگارا در آن میان که تو دانی

O idol in that waist, is a subtlety that Thou knowest.

یکیست ترکی و تازی در این معامله حافظ

Hafiz in this matter, one are Turki and Tazi (Arabian)

حدیث عشق بیان کن بدان زبان که تو دانی

Love's tale, relate in every tongue (language) that thou knowest

غزل ۴۷۷ ⓄⒹⒺ ④⑦⑦

دو یار زیرک و از باده کهن دومنی

Two friends (holy travellers) good of understanding, and of old wine a quantity, two "mans",

فراغتی و کتابی و گوشه چمنی

A little leisure, and a book, and a sward-corner.

من این مقام به دنیا و آخرت ندهم

For (this), and (the next, world) I give not this state

اگر چه در پی ام افتند هر دم انجمنی

Though, (of carpers) momently, fall up on me

هر آن که کنج قناعت به گنج دنیا داد

Everyone who, for the world's treasure, gave the treasure of contentment,

فروخت یوسف مصری به کمترین ثمنی

Sold, (the precious) Yusuf of Egypt for a very paltry sum.

بیا که رونق این کارخانه کم نشود

Come; for not less becometh the amplitude of this workshop (the world)

به زهد همچو توبی یا به فسق همچو منی

By the austerity of one like thee or, by the profligacy of one like me.

ز تندباد حوادث نمی‌توان دیدن

From the fierce wind of vicissitude, one cannot see,

در این چمن که گلی بوده است یا سمنی

That, in this sward, hath been (even) a red rose, or a wild white rose.

ببین در آینه جام نقش بندی غیب

In the mirror of the Picture-establisher (God) the hidden (form), be hold

که کس به یاد ندارد چنین عجب زمنی

If, for thee out of the country of contentment, desire maketh a native land.

از این سموم که بر طرف بوستان بگذشت

From this simum (blast of lust) that, by the garden-borders, passed

عجب که بوی گلی هست و رنگ نسترنی

Wonder that (from the heart of love's lust) the colour of a rose remaineth, or the perfume of a jessamine.

به صبر کوش تو ای دل که حق رها نکند

O heart strive thou for patience. For God delivereth not

چنین عزیز نگینی به دست اهرمنی

A seal-ring so precious (as patience) to the hand of an evil one.

مزاج دهر تبه شد در این بلا حافظ

Hafiz in this calamity, ruined became time's temper

کجاست فکر حکیمی و رای برهمنی

Where is the thought of a physician or the judgment of a Barhaman[1]?

غزل ۴۷۸ ⓞⓓⓔ ④⑦⑧

نوش کن جام شراب یک منی

Drink the cup of the wine of unity of a man

تا بدان بیخ غم از دل برکنی

So that, by it grief's root, up from the heart, thou mayst pluck.

دل گشاده دار چون جام شراب

Expanded, keep the heart, like the cup of wine

سر گرفته چند چون خم دنی

Head closed how long like a large jar

چون ز جام بیخودی رطلی کشی

When, from the jar of selflessness, a ritl[2] thou drinkest,

کم زنی از خویشتن لاف منی

Less of thy self (voluntarily) thou boastest of self

سنگسان شو در قدم نی همچو آب

Like (the humble and worthless) stone at thy foot be, not like the water (of the cloud glorying in sublimity)

جمله رنگ آمیزی و تردامنی

All colour (of deceit), thou mixest and wet of skirt (lust – stained) thou art

دل به می دربند تا مردانه وار

To wine, bind the heart, so that, like a man,

گردن سالوس و تقوا بشکنی

The neck of hypocrisy and of piety thou mayst shatter.

خیز و جهدی کن چو حافظ تا مگر

Arise, and, like Hafiz, an effort (in the service of the Pir of tarikat) make so that, perchance

خویشتن در پای معشوق افکنی

Thyself, at the true Beloved's foot, thou mayest cast.

1-An allusion to the scientist   2- large cup or goblet, pound

غزل ۴۷۹ ⓄⒹⒺ ④⑦⑨

صبح است و ژاله می‌چکد از ابر بهمنی
It's morning; and droppeth hail from the cloud of (the winter-month) Bahman

برگ صبوح ساز و بده جام یک منی
The morning cup, prepare and give a cup of one' man.

در بحر مایی و منی افتاده‌ام بیار
Into the sea of self and self-praise, I am fallen Bring

می تا خلاص بخشدم از مایی و منی
Wine, so that freedom from self and self-praise me, it may give.

خون پیاله خور که حلال است خون او
The blood (red wine) of the cup, drink for lawful is its blood

در کار یار باش که کاریست کردنی
In the work of the cup, (engaged) be; for' tis a work fit to bed one

ساقی به دست باش که غم در کمین ماست
Saki[1] at hand (to give the cup) be for, in ambush for us, is grief

مطرب نگاه دار همین ره که می‌زنی
Minstrel (so that grief may not reach us) keep this very path (of song) that thou singest.

می ده که سر به گوش من آورد چنگ و گفت
Give wine for, the secret to my ear, the harp hath brought and said

خوش بگذران و بشنو از این پیر منحنی
Happily pass (life) and, heart his bowed Pir[2] (the harp)

ساقی به بی‌نیازی رندان که می بده
Hafiz by the in dependence of profligates, drink, (I conjure thee) wine,

تا بشنوی ز صوت مغنی هوالغنی
So that, thou mayst heart he song of the Singer, God the Independent One.

غزل ۴۸۰ ⓄⒹⒺ ④⑧⓪

ای که در کشتن ما هیچ مدارا نکنی
O thou who, in our slaughter, mercy exercisest not

سود و سرمایه بسوزی و محابا نکنی
Profit and capital, thou consumest manliness, thou showest not.

دردمندان بلا زهر هلاهل دارند
Deadly poison, the sorrowful ones of calamity (lovers, sorrowful through separation from thee) drink

قصد این قوم خطا باشد هان تا نکنی
The design of (slaying) this tribe (of lovers) is dangerous. Take care that it, thou doest not

رنج ما را که توان برد به یک گوشه چشم
Since, with a corner of thy eye, our grief it is possible to take

شرط انصاف نباشد که مداوا نکنی
The part of justice it is not, that our remedy (for freedom from grief) thou makest not.

1-Tapster   2-A Muslim saint or holy man, Pietist

دیده ما چو به امید تو دریاست چرا

Since, in hope of thee, our eye is the ocean (through weeping) why (is it that)

به تفرج گذری بر لب دریا نکنی

On the ocean-shore, in recreation, passing thou makest not

نقل هر جور که از خلق کریمت کردند

The tale of every violence that, of thy gentle nature, they made,

قول صاحب غرضان است تو آنها نکنی

Is the word of the interested (and is therefore discredited) Those deeds (of violence) thou doest not.

بر تو گر جلوه کند شاهد ما ای زاهد

O Zahid[1] if our beloved display splendour to thee (by visiting thee)

از خدا جز می و معشوق تمنا نکنی

God, save wine and the beloved, a wish thou makest not.

حافظا سجده به ابروی چو محرابش بر

O Hafiz! adoration of his eyebrow (curved) like the prayer-arch, make

که دعایی ز سر صدق جز آن جا نکنی

For save here, a prayer from sincerity's source thou makest not.

غزل ۴۸۱ ⓄⒹⒺ ④⑧①

بشنو این نکته که خود را ز غم آزاده کنی

This my subtlety, hear that, free from grief, thyself thou mayst make

خون خوری گر طلب روزی ننهاده کنی

Blood (of grief) thou drinkest, if search for victuals, not placed (intended for thee) thou makest.

آخرالامر گل کوزه گران خواهی شد

In the end, the clay of the goglet-maker (potters) thou wilt become;

حالیا فکر سبو کن که پر از باده کنی

Now, think of the pitcher (of thy heart) that, it, full of wine (of ma'rifat and of love) thou mayst make

گر از آن آدمیانی که بهشتت هوس است

If, of those men thou be, whose desire is paradise,

عیش با آدمی ای چند پری زاده کنی

O Pari-born[2] ease with man, how long (is it that) thou makest

تکیه بر جای بزرگان نتوان زد به گزاف

On the (sitting)-place of the great, boastingly it is impossible to lean,

مگر اسباب بزرگی همه آماده کنی

Unless, the chattels of greatness, all prepared, thou makest.

اجرها باشدت ای خسرو شیرین دهنان

O Khusrau[3] of those sweet of mouth (Hafiz) rewards are thine,

گر نگاهی سوی فرهاد دل افتاده کنی

If, to Farhad, heart-fallen, a glance thou makest.

خاطرت کی رقم فیض پذیرد هیهات

The writing of (God's) bounty, how taketh away thy heart (stuffed with sensual claims and ideas of impurity)

مگر از نقش پراگنده ورق ساده کنی

Unless pure of the stuffed picture, the leaf (of thy heart) thou makest

---

1-Pietist
2-An allusion to the beautiful
3-king

کار خود گر به کرم بازگذاری حافظ
Hafiz if back to the Merciful, thy own work thou pass,
ای بسا عیش که با بخت خداداده کنی
O great the pleasure that with fortune God-given, thou makest.

ای صبا بندگی خواجه جلال الدین کن
O breeze the service of Khwaja Jallalu-d-Din[1] do,
که جهان پرسمن و سوسن آزاده کنی
Till, full of the lily of the valley and of the noble lily, the world thou makest.

غزل ۴۸۲ ⓄⒹⒺ ④⑧②

ای دل به کوی عشق گذاری نمی کنی
O heart in the Beloved's street, passing thou makest not
اسباب جمع داری و کاری نمی کنی
The chattels of conjunction, thou hast and a work thou doest not.

چوگان حکم در کف و گویی نمی زنی
In the hand, the chaugan of desire yet the ball thou strikest not
باز ظفر به دست و شکاری نمی کنی
In the hand, a game (like this) and a prey thou makest not.

این خون که موج می زند اندر جگر تو را
This (red) blood that, into thy liver, waveth,
در کار رنگ و بوی نگاری نمی کنی
For the work (use) of (thy face)-colour, a point (why is it that) thou makest not

مشکین از آن نشد دم خلقت که چون صبا
Musky (fragrant) becometh not creation's breath; because (swiftly) like the wind,
بر خاک کوی دوست گذاری نمی کنی
On the dust of the Beloved's street, passing, thou makest not.

ترسم کز این چمن نبری آستین گل
From this sward (the world) I fear that thou takest not the sleeve of the rose (ma'rifat)
کز گلشنش تحمل خاری نمی کنی
For, the endurance of at horn from its rose-bed, thou sufferest not.

در آستین جان تو صد نافه مدرج است
Enclosed in the sleeve of thy soul, are a hundred musk-pods
وان را فدای طره یاری نمی کنی
Them, a sacrifice for the Beloved' stress, thou makest not.

ساغر لطیف و دلکش و می افکنی به خاک
To the dust thou castest, the cup joyous and (full of wine) and wine
و اندیشه از بلای خماری نمی کنی
And of the calamity of wine-sickness, thought thou makest not.

حافظ برو که بندگی پادشاه وقت
Hafiz go. For the service of the Friend's court,
گر جمله می کنند تو باری نمی کنی
If all do, once thou doest not.

1-Minister with the competence of the brave king, a close
friend of Hafez

غزل ۴۸۳ ⓞⓓⓔ ④⑧③

سحرگه ره روی در سرزمینی
In the morning time, a way-farer, on the confines of a land,

همی‌گفت این معما با قرینی
Kept saying this enigma to a companion:

که ای صوفی شراب آن گه شود صاف
"O Sufi[1]! pure, becometh wine at that time,

که در شیشه برآرد اربعینی
"When, in bottle, it bringeth forth (accomplisheth) a forty days' space."

خدا زان خرقه بیزار است صد بار
A hundred times, vexed is God with that Khirka[2],

که صد بت باشدش در آستینی
Whereof, a hundred idols (of hypocrisy) are in a sleeve.

مروت گر چه نامی بی‌نشان است
Though (only) a name, without trace (of reality), is generosity,

نیازی عرضه کن بر نازنینی
(Yet) Thy need present to a noble one?

ثوابت باشد ای دارای خرمن
O Lord! of the harvest! recompense shall be thine,

اگر رحمی کنی بر خوشه چینی
If, a little pity, thou show to a (poor) corn-gleaner.

نمی‌بینم نشاط عیش در کس
In none, I see pleasure (and) ease

نه درمان دلی نه درد دینی
Neither, the remedy for a heart nor, the pain of (working for) a faith.

درون‌ها تیره شد باشد که از غیب
Dark became the inward parts. It may be that, from the hidden,

چراغی برکند خلوت نشینی
A lamp may uplift a khilvat[3]-sitter.

گر انگشت سلیمانی نباشد
If the finger of a Sulaiman[4] be not, (to wear it)

چه خاصیت دهد نقش نگینی
What special excellence giveth the engraving of a seal stone?

اگر چه رسم خوبان تندخویست
Although the way of lovely ones is cruel (haughty) of nature,

چه باشد گر بسازد با غمینی
What will it be if thou be content with a (sad humble) one?

ره میخانه بنما تا بپرسم
The wine-house-door (the threshold of the perfect murshid) show so that I may inquire,

مال خویش را از پیش بینی
My own end from a fore-see-er.

1-A Muslim ascetic and mystic   3-Solitude
2-Cloak   4-Name of the prophet

نه حافظ را حضور درس خلوت
Neither for Hafiz, present reading and (the Kuran and) khilvat;
نه دانشمند را علم الیقینی
Nor for the sage, a knowledge of certainty.

ⓄⒹⒺ ④⑧④ ۴۸۴ غزل

تو مگر بر لب آبی به هوس بنشینی
Perchance, with desire (of khilvat) by the marge of a pool, thou sittest (not),
ور نه هر فتنه که بینی همه از خود بینی
If not, every calamity, that (thou experiencest), all thou experiences from self-seeingness.

به خدایی که تویی بنده بگزیده او
(I conjure thee) by God, Whose chosen slave, thou art,
که بر این چاکر دیرینه کسی نگزینی
That, to this ancient slave, none thou choose (prefer)

گر امانت به سلامت ببرم باکی نیست
If, in safety, (love's) deposit I take, there is no fear
بی دلی سهل بود گر نبود بی‌دینی
Easy is the state of being void of heart (heart – bereft) if be not the state of being void of faith infidelity)

ادب و شرم تو را خسرو مه رویان کرد
Thee, the Khusrau[1] of those moon of face, respect and shame did
آفرین بر تو که شایسته صد چندینی
Afarin[2] on thee for, worthy of a hundred such thou art.

عجب از لطف تو ای گل که نشستی با خار
O rose (beloved) wonderful, with (all) thy grace thou sittest with the thorn (the watcher)
ظاهرا مصلحت وقت در آن می‌بینی
Apparently, in it, the good counsel of thy welfare thou seest

صبر بر جور رقیبت چه کنم گر نکنم
If, as to the watcher's tyranny patience I exercise not, what may I do
عاشقان را نبود چاره بجز مسکینی
To wretched lovers, is no remedy save wretchedness.

باد صبحی به هوایت ز گلستان برخاست
From the rose-garden, a rose a morning breeze in desire of thee
که تو خوشتر ز گل و تازه‌تر از نسرینی
For, more pleasant than the red rose and more fresh than the wild white rose, thou art.

شیشه بازی سرشکم نگری از چپ و راست
From left and right, the bottle-play of my (bloody) tears thou seest
گر بر این منظر بینش نفسی بنشینی
If a moment, on this spectacle-place of my vision, thou sittest.

سخنی بی‌غرض از بنده مخلص بشنو
From thy sincere slave, a disinterested word, hear
ای که منظور بزرگان حقیقت بینی
O thou that, the cynosure of great ones, truth be holding, art

1-king   2-Well done!

نازنینی چو تو پاکیزه دل و پاک نهاد
A dainty one like thee, pure of heart, pure of nature,
بهتر آن است که با مردم بد ننشینی
That is best that, with evil men, thou sit not.

سیل این اشک روان صبر و دل حافظ برد
Taketh the patience (of) the heart of Hafiz, the torrent of these streaming tears
بلغ الطاقه یا مقله عینی بینی
O pupil of my eye come (to my aid)

تو بدین نازکی و سرکشی ای شمع چگل
O candle of Chigil with this delicacy, and heart-alluring ness thou art
لایق بندگی خواجه جلال الدینی
Worthy of the banquet-place of Khwaja[1] Jalalu-d-Din[2], thou art.

غزل ۴۸۵ ⓄⒹⒺ ④⑧⑤ ODE 485

ساقیا سایه ابر است و بهار و لب جوی
O Saki[3]' tis the shade of the cloud, and spring, and the stream-bank
من نگویم چه کن ار اهل دلی خود تو بگوی
I say not, do what. Of the men of heart (Sufis) [4] thou art Do thou thy self say.

بوی یک رنگی از این نقش نمی‌آید خیز
From this picture (of outward Sufis) cometh not the perfume of one colouredness (constancy) Arise
دلق آلوده صوفی به می ناب بشوی
With pure wine, the (deceit)-stained (and) tattered garment of the Sufi, wash.

سفله طبع است جهان بر کرمش تکیه مکن
Mean of nature, is the world on its generosity, rely not
ای جهان دیده ثبات قدم از سفله مجوی
O world-experienced one from the mean, stability of foot do not thou-seek.

دو نصیحت کنمت بشنو و صد گنج بر
Thee, two counsels I make, Hear; and a hundred treasures bear away:
از در عیش درآ و به ره عیب مپوی
By the door of pleasure, enter in the path of defect, do not strive.

شکر آن را که دگربار رسیدی به بهار
For thanks for that, that again to spring thou hast reached,
بیخ نیکی بنشان و ره تحقیق بجوی
The root of goodness, plant; (the rose of the grace of God smell).

روی جانان طلبی آینه را قابل ساز
The true Beloved's (face), th'ou seekest Fit, the mirror (of the heart) make;
ور نه هرگز گل و نسرین ندمد ز آهن و روی
If not, ever blossometh not the (red) rose and the wild (white) rose from (hard) iron and from (base) brass.

1-Eunuch, dignitary, vizier, boss, host
2-Minister with the competence of the brave king, a close friend of Hafez

3-Tapster
4-A Muslim ascetic and mystic

گوش بگشای که بلبل به فغان می‌گوید

Thy ear open for, (this) lament, the bulbul[1] saith

خواجه تقصیر مفرما گل توفیق ببوی

Khwaja deficiency commit not; the rose of the grace (of God) smell

گفتی از حافظ ما بوی ریا می‌آید

Thou saidest From our Hafiz, cometh the perfume of hypocrisy

آفرین بر نفست باد که خوش بردی بوی

Afarin[2] be on the breath for well thou broughtest a great perfume

غزل ۴۸۶ ⓄⒹⒺ ④⑧⑥

بلبل ز شاخ سرو به گلبانگ پهلوی

From the cypress hough, in Pahlavi shout, the bulbul,

می‌خواند دوش درس مقامات معنوی

Last night, the lesson of the stages of spirituality (the Masnavl of Jalalu-d-Din Rumi) kept saying

یعنی بیا که آتش موسی نمود گل

Come, for the rose hath displayed the fire of Musa[3],

تا از درخت نکته توحید بشنوی

So that, from the (fiery) bush, the subtlety of the unity (of God) thou mayst hear

مرغان باغ قافیه سنجند و بذله گوی

Melody-measuring and jest-uttering, are the birds of the garden,

تا خواجه می خورد به غزل های پهلوی

So that, to Pahlavi ghazals[4] (and Persian subtleties) wine the khwaja[5] may drink.

جمشید جز حکایت جام از جهان نبرد

Naught from the world took Jamshid, save the (world – viewing) cup;

زنهار دل مبند بر اسباب دنیوی

Ho on worldly chattels, bind not thy heart

این قصه عجب شنو از بخت واژگون

This tale of wonder of inverted fortune, hear

ما را بکشت یار به انفاس عیسوی

Us, the beloved, with the revivifying breath of 'Isa[6], slew.

خوش وقت بوریا و گدایی و خواب امن

Happy the time the (quiet) mat (of) beggary; and the sleep (thereon) Of tranquillity,

کاین عیش نیست درخور اورنگ خسروی

For, not be fitting the khusravi[7] crown is this ease

چشمت به غمزه خانه مردم خراب کرد

Man's house with the glance, thy eye hath darkened

مخموریت مباد که خوش مست می‌روی

Thine, be no wine-sickness For, intoxicated, happy thou goest.

1-Nightingale
2-Well done!
3-Prophet
4-Sonnet

5-Eunuch, dignitary, vizier, boss, host
6-Name of prophet
7-king

دهقان سالخورده چه خوش گفت با پسر

To his son, the years endured (old) villager spake how well,

کای نور چشم من بجز از کشته ندروی

Saying: O light of my eye save that sown, thou reapest naught

ساقی مگر وظیفه حافظ زیاده داد

Perchance, more (than his due) Hafiz's allowance (of wine) the Saki[1] gave,

کشفته گشت طره دستار مولوی

That disarranged became the Maulavi's turban-tassel

غزل ۴۸۷ ⓄⒹⒺ ④⑧⑦

ای بی‌خبر بکوش که صاحب خبر شوی

O thou void of news (of love) strive that the master of news, thou mayst be

تا راهرو نباشی کی راهبر شوی

So long as way-farer thou art not, road-guide how (is it that) thou mayst be

در مکتب حقایق پیش ادیب عشق

In the school of truths (and of ma'rifat) [2] before love's master (the murshid, perfect and excellent)

هان ای پسر بکوش که روزی پدر شوی

Ho O son strive that, one day (worthy to be) father old thou mayst be.

دست از مس وجود چو مردان ره بشوی

From the copper of thy existence, like men of the Path (Tarikat) [3] thy handwash,

تا کیمیای عشق بیابی و زر شوی

So that love's alchemy, thou mayst obtain and gold thou mayst be.

خواب و خورت ز مرتبه خویش دور کرد

Far from love's degree, thee, sleeping and eating put

آن گه رسی به خویش که بی خواب و خور شوی

To love, thou attainest at that time when sleepless and foodless thou shalt be.

گر نور عشق حق به دل و جانت اوفتد

When, on thy heart and soul, the light of God's love falleth,

بالله کز آفتاب فلک خوبتر شوی

By God (I swear) that fairer than the sky's (resplendent) sun thou shalt be

یک دم غریق بحر خدا شو گمان مبر

A moment, immersed in God's sea, be; think not,

کز آب هفت بحر به یک موی تر شوی

That, to the extent of a single hair, with the water of seven (all the) seas (of the world) wet, thou shalt be.

از پای تا سرت همه نور خدا شود

From head to foot, thine all God's light shall be,

در راه ذوالجلال چو بی پا و سر شوی

When footless and headless the world's chattels and (ease abandoned) in the Path of Him possessed of majesty, thou shalt be

---

1-Tapster
2-knowledge

3-Principle, Sufism, religious way

وجه خدا اگر شودت منظر نظر

If the face of God be the spectacle-place of thy vision

زین پس شکی نماند که صاحب نظر شوی

After this, not a doubt remaineth that the possessor of vision, thou shalt be.

بنیاد هستی تو چو زیر و زبر شود

It, below and above (ruined) the foundation of thy existence be

در دل مدار هیچ که زیر و زبر شوی

Think not in thy heart that, below and above, thou mayst be.

گر در سرت هوای وصال است حافظا

Hafiz if in thy head be desire of union (with the true Beloved)

باید که خاک درگه اهل هنر شوی

It is necessary that the dust of the court of (Him possessed of vision) thou shouldest be.

غزل ۴۸۸ ⓄⒹⒺ ④⑧⑧

سحرم هاتف میخانه به دولتخواهی

In the morning, the invisible speaker of the wine-house with fortune-wishing,

گفت بازآی که دیرینه این درگاهی

Said (O Hafiz)! come back for an old friend of this court thou art

همچو جم جرعه ما کش که ز سر دو جهان

Like Jamshid[1], a draught of wine, drink, so that, of the mystery of (the angels),

پرتو جام جهان بین دهدت آگاهی

Thee, the ray of the cup, world-viewing, may give news.

بر در میکده رندان قلندر باشند

At the wine-house door, are Kalandar[2]-profligates,

که ستانند و دهند افسر شاهنشاهی

Who take (away) and give the imperial diadem

خشت زیر سر و بر تارک هفت اختر پای

Beneath the head, the brick and the foot on the summit of the seven stars (Pleiades)

دست قدرت نگر و منصب صاحب جاهی

Be hold the hand of power and the dignity of (one) possessed of dignity

سر ما و در میخانه که طرف بامش

(Together are) Our head and the door of the wine-house, the side of the vault whereof

به فلک بر شد و دیوار بدین کوتاهی

(Is) up lifted to the sky, (though) the wall be of this low liness.

قطع این مرحله بی همرهی خضر مکن

Without the road-fellow ship of Khizr[3], this path travel not

ظلمات است بترس از خطر گمراهی

Tis the zulmat[4] fear the danger of road-losing.

اگرت سلطنت فقر ببخشند ای دل

O heart if thee, the kingdom of poverty, they give,

کمترین ملک تو از ماه بود تا ماهی

Thy least territory will be from the moon (above) to the fish (beneath supporting the earth)

1-king   3-Name of prophet
2-Released from bondage   4-Darkness

تو دم فقر ندانی زدن از دست مده

The door of poverty, thou knowest not (how) to beat. From the hand, let not go,

مسند خواجگی و مجلس تورانشاهی

These at of Lord ship, and the royal assembly of Turan.

حافظ خام طمع شرمی از این قصه بدار

Hafiz, crude of greed of this tale, have shame

عملت چیست که فردوس برین میخواهی

What is thy work, (reward) for (which two worlds) thou desirest

غزل ۴۸۹   ⓄⒹⒺ ④⑧⑨

ای در رخ تو پیدا انوار پادشاهی

O them, in whose face (are) revealed the splendours of sovereignty.

در فکرت تو پنهان صد حکمت الهی

(And) In whose thought, (are) concealed divine philosophies

کلک تو بارک الله بر ملک و دین گشاده

In the country (of) faith, thy reed it, may God bless

صد چشمه آب حیوان از قطره سیاهی

A hundred fountains of the (limpid) water of life from a small ink-drop opened

بر اهرمن نتابد انوار اسم اعظم

On Ahriman, shine not the splendours of the ism-i-a'zam[1],

ملک آن توست و خاتم فرمای هر چه خواهی

Thine, is the country and these al-ring What thou wishest, order.

در حکمت سلیمان هر کس که شک نماید

Doubt in Sulaiman's pomp, whoever displayeth

بر عقل و دانش او خندند مرغ و ماهی

On his wisdom and knowledge, (even) the bird and the fish will (in mockery) laugh.

باز ار چه گاه گاهی بر سر نهد کلاهی

Though, sometimes, on his head, the cap of sovereignty, the hawk putteth,

مرغان قاف دانند آیین پادشاهی

The usage of sovereignty, the birds of (the mountain of) the Kaf[2] (well) know

تیغی که آسمانش از فیض خود دهد آب

That sword, to which, out of its own bounty, the sky giveth luster,

تنها جهان بگیرد بی منت سپاهی

Alone, without the aid of an army, will sever the world.

کلک تو خوش نویسد در شان یار و اغیار

In respect of the friend and of the enemy, pleasantly writeth (in the magic figure) thy reed

تعویذ جان فزایی افسون عمر کاهی

The amulet, life-increasing (for the friend) sorcery, life-decreasing (for the enemy)

ای عنصر تو مخلوق از کیمیای عزت

O them, whose element s (are) created of the alchemy of honour

و ای دولت تو ایمن از وصمت تباهی

And thou, whose fortune (is) safe from the disaster of ruin

1-Blessed name of God

2-In the legends, the mountain that was thought to be Simorgh had a nest on top of it.

ساق بیار آبی از چشمه خرابات

Saki[1] (Murshid) [2] from the fountain of the tavern (of ma'rifat) a little water bring,

تا خرقه‌ها بشوییم از عجب خانقاهی

So that, from the wonder of the monastery (pride of our own devotion) the Khirkas[3], we may wash (and, in supplication and in submission to God, engage)

عمریست پادشاها کز می تهیست جامم

O King tis a life (time) since void of wine was my cup

اینک ز بنده دعوی و از محتسب گواهی

Be hold (thereof) from the slave, a claim; and, from the muhtasib[4], testimony

گر پرتوی ز تیغت بر کان و معدن افتد

If, on quarry and mine, a flash of thy sword fall,

یاقوت سرخ رو را بخشند رنگ کاهی

To the ruby, red of face, it giveth the hue of withe red (yellow) grass.

دانم دلت ببخشد بر عجز شب نشینان

The weakness of the night-sitters, I know, thy heart will pity

گر حال بنده پرسی از باد صبحگاهی

If, of the breeze of the morning-time, my state thou ask

جایی که برق عصیان بر آدم صفی زد

When, on (the sin of pure) Adam, lightning flashed,

ما را چگونه زیبد دعوی بی گناهی

Us, the claim to sinlessness how adorneth (befitteth)?

حافظ چو پادشاهت گه گاه می‌برد نام

Hafiz since, sometimes, thy name the King taketh (mentioneth)

رنجش ز بخت منما بازآ به عذرخواهی

To him, grief on account of fortune display not in pardon-seeking, come back

غزل ۴۹۰ ⓞⓓⓔ ④⑨⓪

در همه دیر مغان نیست چو من شیدایی

Not, in all the cloisters of the Magians, is like me a distraught one

خرقه جایی گرو باده و دفتر جایی

(in) one place, the khirka[5] (my existence is) the pledge for wine the book (the heart in) a not her place.

دل که آیینه شاهیست غباری دارد

The heart, which is a royal mirror, hath (by worldly affairs and by the dross of sin) a great dust, (the prohibitor of divine bounty)

از خدا می‌طلبم صحبت روشن رایی

From God, I seek the society of one, luminous of opinion.

کرده‌ام توبه به دست صنم باده فروش

By the hand of an idol, wine-selling, repentance I have made

که دگر می نخورم بی رخ بزم آرایی

That again, wine I drink not without the face of a banquet-adorner.

1-Tapster
2-Guru
3-Cloak

4-Sheriff
5-Cloak

نرگس ار لاف زد از شیوه چشم تو مرنج
If of the way of its (beauteous) eye, the narcissus boasted, grieve not (for, vision, it hath not)
نروند اهل نظر از بی نابینایی
The man of vision goeth not in pursuit of anon-see-er.

شرح این قصه مگر شمع برآرد به زبان
The mystery of this subtlety, perchance, the candle will bring to its tongue
ور نه پروانه ندارد به سخن پروایی
If not, for speech, the moth hath not (even) a little solicitude.

جوی‌ها بسته‌ام از دیده به دامان که مگر
From my eye to the skirt, I have established streams (of tears) so that, per chance,
در کنارم بنشانند سهی بالایی
In my bosom, they may place one, straight of stature.

کشتی باده بیاور که مرا بی رخ دوست
The bark (shaped) cup, bring for, without the Beloved's face,
گشت هر گوشه چشم از غم دل دریایی
From the heart's grief, every corner of the eye hath become a great ocean (of tears)

سخن غیر مگو با من معشوقه پرست
To me, mistress worshipping, speak not (of) aught (beside)
کز وی و جام می‌ام نیست به کس پروایی
For, beyond her and the cup of wine, for none is mine, (even) a little solicitude.

این حدیثم چه خوش آمد که سحرگه می‌گفت
How pleasantly to me came this tale when in the morning time, said,
بر در میکده‌ای با دف و نی ترسایی
At the door of the wine-house, with drum and reed, a Christian

گر مسلمانی از این است که حافظ دارد
If the being a musulman be of this sort that Hafiz is,
آه اگر از پی امروز بود فردایی
Alas, if, after to-day, be a to-morrow.

غزل ۴۹۱ ⓄⒹⒺ ④⑨① ODE 491

به چشم کرده‌ام ابروی ماه سیمایی
In my eye, the eye-brow of one moon of form, I have made
خیال سبزخطی نقش بسته‌ام جایی
The fancy of one fresh of down, I have pictured a place.

امید هست که منشور عشقبازی من
The hope is that the order of my love-play
از آن کمانچه ابرو رسد به طغرایی
May reach from that bow-eye-brow to the rank of a (beautiful) Tughra1.

سرم ز دست بشد چشم از انتظار بسوخت
From the hand, went my head frome xpectation, my eye consumed
در آرزوی سر و چشم مجلس آرایی
In desire of the head and of the eye of an assembly-adorner.

1-Decree

مکدر است دل آتش به خرقه خواهم زد

(From separation) Perturbed is my heart; fire to the Khirka[1], I will set (and, from this, escape)

بیا ببین که که را می‌کند تماشایی

Come, (come) for, (glorious), it will make aspectacle

به روز واقعه تابوت ما ز سرو کنید

In the day of events (of death) make ye our coffin of the (lofty) cypress,

که می‌رویم به داغ بلندبالایی

For, we go with the mark of a lofty one.

زمام دل به کسی داده‌ام من درویش

My heart's rein I, the darvIsh, have given to that one (God)

که نیستش به کس از تاج و تخت پروایی

To whom, for any one's crown, or throne, is not (even) a little solicitude.

در آن مقام که خوبان ز غمزه تیغ زنند

In that place where, with a glance, the lovely ones strike the sword,

عجب مدار سری اوفتاده در پایی

Wonder not, at a head which, hath fallen (severed) at a foot

مرا که از رخ او ماه در شبستان است

Since, from His, (the true Beloved's) face the (effulgent) moon in the bedchamber is mine,

کجا بود به فروغ ستاره پروایی

For the twinkling of the star (the illusory beloved) where is (even) a little solicitude

فراق و وصل چه باشد رضای دوست طلب

Separation or union what martereth it The Friend's will, seek

که حیف باشد از او غیر او تمنایی

For, from Him, (aught) beside (union with) Him, vain is a wish

درر ز شوق برآرند ماهیان به نثار

For scattering (on Hafiz) through exceeding desire the fishers bring forth pearls,

اگر سفینه حافظ رسد به دریایی

If Hafiz's bark should reach a sea.

غزل ۴۹۲ ⓄⒹⒺ ④⑨②

سلامی چو بوی خوش آشنایی

A salutation, like the pleasant perfume of friendship

بدان مردم دیده روشنایی

To that man of the eye of light

درودی چو نور دل پارسایان

A salutation, like the light of the heart of the pious

بدان شمع خلوتگه پارسایی

To that candle of the khilvat[2]-place of piety

نمی‌بینم از همدمان هیچ بر جای

None of my fellow-companion sin his place, I see

دلم خون شد از غصه ساقی کجایی

With grief, my heart is become blood. Saki[3] (the murshid) where art thou

---

1-Cloak   3-Tapster
2-Solitude

زکوی مغان رخ مگردان که آن جا
Thy face, away from the street of the Magians[1], turn not. For, there
فروشند مفتاح مشکل گشایی
They sell the key of the opening of difficulty.

عروس جهان گر چه در حد حسن است
Although within limit, the bride of the world hath beauty,
ز حد می‌برد شیوه بی‌وفایی
Beyond limit, she taketh the way of unfaithfulness

دل خسته من گرش همتی هست
My shattered heart if it's be a desire,
نخواهد ز سنگین دلان مومیایی
Desireth not, from those stone of heart, a mumiyai[2].

می صوفی افکن کجا می‌فروشند
The wine, Sufi[3]-overthrowing, they sell where
که در تابم از دست زهد ریایی
For, in torment, I am from the hand of austerity of hypocrisy.

رفیقان چنان عهد صحبت شکستند
The covenant of society, the companion shave so shattered,
که گویی نبوده‌ست خود آشنایی
That thou mayst say Verily, hath not been friendship.

مرا گر تو بگذاری ای نفس طامع
O lust of greed if thou leave me,
بسی پادشایی کنم در گدایی
Great sovereignty (contentment) I will make in beggary

بیاموزمت کیمیای سعادت
Thee, the chemistry of happiness, I will teach
ز همصحبت بد جدایی جدایی
From bad fellow ship, separation, separation

مکن حافظ از جور دوران شکایت
Hafiz of time's violence, complain not
چه دانی تو ای بنده کار خدایی
O slave what knowest thou divine work

غزل ۴۹۳ ⓄⒹⒺ ④⑨③

ای پادشه خوبان داد از غم تنهایی
O king of the lovely (the beloved) ones of the world for grief of being alone, justice
دل بی تو به جان آمد است وقت که بازآیی
Without Thee, to the soul, my heart hath come. Tis the time when thou shouldst come back (and me safety, give).

1-They were originally a tribe of the Medes to whom the position of clergy belonged exclusively

2-The name of a black medicine like bitumen that was used for fractures in Persia.
3-A Muslim ascetic and mystic

دایم گل این بستان شاداب نمی‌ماند

(O Beloved) Ever joyous, remaineth not the rose of this garden (of the world).

دریاب ضعیفان را در وقت توانایی

At the time of power fulness (perfection of beauty) the feeble one aid (and their state, pity)

دیشب گله زلفش با باد همی‌کردم

Last night, to the morning breeze, complaint of His tress, I uttered

گفتا غلطی بگذر زین فکرت سودایی

(The breeze) Said A mistake This thy distraught thought, abandon (of Him complain not; whatever He wisheth, He doeth)

صد باد صبا این جا با سلسله می‌رقصند

Here with the chain (of His tress) a hundred morning breezes keep dancing

این است حریف ای دل تا باد نپیمایی

O heart so long as thou measurest not the wind (a thing impossible to do) this is thy companion.

مشتاق و مهجوری دور از تو چنانم کرد

Me, so far from Thee desirousness and farness made

کز دست بخواهد شد پایان شکیبایی

That, from the hand, will depart the power of patience

یا رب به که شاید گفت این نکته که در عالم

O Lord! to whom is it fit to utter this subtlety that, in the world

رخساره به کس ننمود آن شاهد هرجایی

That lovely one of every place the true Beloved His face displayed not.

ساقی چمن گل را بی روی تو رنگی نیست

Saki[1] not a colour (of decoration hath) the sward of the rose without thy face

شمشاد خرامان کن تا باغ بیارایی

Moving make thy box-tree stature so that the garden thou mayst adorn

ای درد توام درمان در بستر ناکامی

O (Beloved) the pain of (love for) Thee (is) my remedy on the couch of unfulfilled desire

و ای یاد توام مونس در گوشه تنهایی

And O (Beloved) Thy memory, my consoler in the corner of solitude

در دایره قسمت ما نقطه تسلیمیم

In the compass of our fate, the point of the compass, are we

لطف آن چه تو اندیشی حکم آن چه تو فرمایی

The favour is whatever Thou thinkest the order, whatever Thou orderest

فکر خود و رای خود در عالم رندی نیست

In the world of profligacy (of being a lover of God) is neither thought of self, nor opinion of self:

کفر است در این مذهب خودبینی و خودرایی

In this religious order, Kufr[2] is self-seeing and self-opinioning.

زین دایره مینا خونین جگرم می ده

On account of this blue circle (the sky) bloody of liver I am give wine

تا حل کنم این مشکل در ساغر مینایی

So that, in the enamel-cup, this difficulty I may solve

1-Tapster   2-Profanity

حافظ شب هجران شد بوی خوش وصل آمد

Hafiz departed hath the night of separation come hath the sweet fragrance of morn

شادیت مبارک باد ای عاشق شیدایی

O lover of distraughtness auspicious be thy gladness

غزل ۴۹۴ ⓞⓓⒺ ④⑨④

ای دل گر از آن چاه زنخدان به درآیی

O heart if, from that pit of the chin (of the true Beloved) thou comest forth,

هر جا که روی زود پشیمان به درآیی

Everywhere that thou goest, quickly regretful, thou comest forth.

هش دار که گر وسوسه عقل کنی گوش

Sense keep for if lust's temptation thou heed

آدم صفت از روضه رضوان به درآیی

From the garden of Rizvan[1], like Adam, thou comest forth.

شاید که به آبی فلکت دست نگیرد

It is possible that (even) with a little water thee, the sky may not aid

گر تشنه لب از چشمه حیوان به درآیی

If, thirsty of lip, (and hopeless) from the fountain of life thou comest forth

جان می‌دهم از حسرت دیدار تو چون صبح

In desire of seeing thee, like the (radiant) morning, my soul I surrender;

باشد که چو خورشید درخشان به درآیی

Possibly, like the gleaming sun, thou mayest come forth.

چندان چو صبا بر تو گمارم دم همت

Like the breeze, on thee, the breath of blessing I send to such a degree

کز غنچه چو گل خرم و خندان به درآیی

That, from the rose-bud, like the rose, joyous and laughing thou comest forth

در تیره شب هجر تو جانم به لب آمد

In the dark night of separation from thee, to the lip (ready to depart) came my soul

وقت است که همچون مه تابان به درآیی

'Tis the time when like the shining moon, thou comest forth.

بر رهگذرت بسته‌ام از دیده دو صد جوی

From my two eyes, on the dust of thy door, I have established a hundred streams

تا بو که تو چون سرو خرامان به درآیی

It may be that, like the moving cypress thou mayest come forth

حافظ مکن اندیشه که آن یوسف مه رو

Hafiz think not that that Yusuf[2], moon of face (the Beloved)

بازآید و از کلبه احزان به درآیی

Again cometh (to thee) and that, from the hut of sorrow, thou comest forth.

1-Heaven   2-Name of the prophet

غزل ۴۹۵ ⓄⒹⒺ ④⑨⑤

می خواه و گل افشان کن از دهر چه می‌جویی

"Wine, demand; rose-scattering, make; from time, what seekest thou?"

این گفت سحرگه گل بلبل تو چه می‌گویی

Thus, at morn, to the bulbul[1] spake the rose. What sayest thou?

مسند به گلستان بر تا شاهد و ساقی را

To the rose-garden, the cushion take; so that of the lovely one and of the Saki[2],

لب گیری و رخ بوسی می نوشی و گل بویی

The lip, thou mayst take, and the cheek, kiss; (so that) wine thou mayst drink and the rose, smell.

شمشاد خرامان کن و آهنگ گلستان کن

(O beloved) The box-tree (of thy stature) proudly move; and, the resolution of (sauntering in) the garden, make;

تا سرو بیاموزد از قد تو دلجویی

So that, from thy stature, (the lofty, straight) the cypress may learn heart-seeking.

تا غنچه خندانت دولت به که خواهد داد

Let us see, in whose fortune will be thy laughing rose-bud:

ای شاخ گل رعنا از بهر که می‌رویی

O bough of the rose ra'na[3]! for whose sake, growest thou?

امروز که بازارت پرجوش خریدار است

To-day, when full of tumult of the purchaser is thy market,

دریاب و بنه گنجی از مایه نیکویی

Get, and establish a little road-provision out of the capital of goodness.

چون شمع نکورویی در رهگذر باد است

As, in the thoroughfare of the breeze, is the (flaming) candle, (so is thy good going 'tis profitless)

طرف هنری بربند از شمع نکورویی

A little profit of skill derive out of the capital of goodness.

آن طره که هر جعدش صد نافه چین ارزد

That tress, every ringlet whereof is worth a hundred musk-pods of Chin,

خوش بودی اگر بودی بوییش ز خوش خویی

Happy had it been if had been its perfume from happy disposition!

هر مرغ به دستانی در گلشن شاه آمد

In the king's rose-bed, cometh every bird singing:

بلبل به نواسازی حافظ به غزل گویی

The bulbul[4] to melody-making; Hafiz to prayer-uttering.

⟨◉⟩⟨◉⟩

1-Nightingale
2-Tapster

3-The irony is that the lover is young
4-Nightingale

حافظ شیرازی

خواجه شمس‌الدّین محمّد شیرازی متخلص به "حافظ" مشهور به لِسانُ الْغِیْب، تَرجُمانُ الْاَسرار، بلبل شیراز، خواجه عرفان، کاشف الحقایق، مجذوب سالک، غزل سرای بزرگ و از خداوندان شعر و ادب پارسی سده‌ی هشتم هجری قمری شیراز است. او در دوران جوانی بر تمام علوم مذهبی و ادبی تسلط یافت و قرآن را حفظ نمود و در دهه بیست زندگی به یکی از مشاهیر علم و ادب دیار خود تبدل شد و اشعار او به مناطقی دور دست همچون هند هم راه یافت. برخی گفته‌اند وجه تخلص و شهرت او به حافظ، آن است که او، حافظ قرآن بوده و بسیاری از ابیات او ترجمان مفاهیم قرآنی است.

نام پدر وی، بها الدین و مادرش اهل کازرون بوده است. در خانواده‌ای از نظر مالی در حد متوسط جامعه‌ی زمان خویش متولد شده است. او فقط یک بار ازدواج کرده و همسرش در همان سال‌های اول ازدواج، پسری به دنیا آورده که تنها فرزند حافظ است و در دوران جوانی در راه سفر نیمه کاره به هند (همراه پدرش)، فوت می شود.گروهی نام همسر حافظ را شاخ نبات و گروهی دیگر بر این باور هستند که نام همسر حافظ، نسرین بوده و حافظ شیرین زبانی معشوقش را به شاخ نبات تشبیه کرده است.

در دوران امارات شاه شیخ ابواسحاق به دربار راه پیدا کرده و علاوه بر شاه اسحاق در دربار شاهان آل مظفر به نام شاه مبارزالدین، شاه شجاع، شاه منصور و شاه یحیی راه داشته است.

دیوان اشعار او شامل غزل یات و چند قصیده، چند مثنوی، قطعات، رباعیات است. موضوع اشعار او بیشتر عرفانی و با موضوع وحدت وجود می باشد نوآوری اصلی حافظ در تک بیت‌های درخشان، مستقل و خوش مضمون است. موضوع غزل وصف معشوق، می، و مغازله است و غزل سرایی را باید هنری دانست ادبی، که درخور سرود و غنا و ترانه پردازی است. موضوع اشعار حافظ بسیار متنوع بوده و از شعرهای او در موسیقی سنتی ایرانی، هنرهای تجسمی و خوشنویسی استفاده می شود.

از آن جایی که حافظ تنها در لحظاتی که خاص و الهام بخش بود به سرودن اشعارش می پرداخت، به طور متوسط در هر سال فقط ۱۰ غزل و دیوان خود را در طول ۵۰ سال سروده و تمرکز او خلق اثری شایسته مقام واقعی معشوق بوده است. تعداد نسخه‌های خطّی ساده یا تذهیب شده آن در کتابخانه های ایران، افغانستان، هند، پاکستان، ترکیه و حتی کشورهای غربی از هر دیوان فارسی دیگری بیشتر است. تاکنون بیش از چهارصد بار به اشکال مختلف به زبان فارسی و به چندین زبان از جمله انگلیسی، فرانسوی، روسی، عربی، اردو، پنجابی، سندی، هندی، پشتو و بلوچی در دنیا به چاپ رسیده است.نکته خاصی که در دیوان حافظ وجود دارد، کثرت نسخه هایی با مفردات و واژه های گوناگون است که این ویژگی سبب بروز تصحیحات متعدد و گاه متناقض هم در بین مصححان می شود.

وی‌به سال ۷۹۲ هجری قمری در شیراز درگذشت. آرامگاه او در شهر شیراز و در منطقه ی حافظیه، زیارتگاه صاحبنظران و عاشقان شعر و ادب پارسی است. هر ساله در تاریخ بیستم مهرماه مراسم بزرگداشت حافظ در محل آرامگاه او در شیراز با حضور پژوهشگران ایرانی و خارجی برگزار می شود.

اسکناس های هزار ریالی ایران از سال ۱۳۴۱ تا سال ۱۳۵۸ با نمایی از آرامگاه حافظ چاپ می شده است که نشان دهنده بالا بودن ارزش این شاعر در میان ایرانیان می باشد. تفأل به شعر حافظ ریشه‌ای دیرینه در فرهنگ ایران دارد. ولی آنچه از قراین پیداست، فال گرفتن با دیوان حافظ احتمالا سال‌ها پس از درگذشت او مرسوم شده است.

Persian Learning Center

We are the Persian Learning Center and we have been teaching Farsi and writing Farsi book here in Dallas, TX since 2016. We believe a simple way to stay sharp throughout our lives is learning a second language, because we neglect to train our brains. you can learn and speak Persian language with our method quickly and easily, even if you found it impossible before. We started teaching and learning Farsi, because some of the next generation of population who immigrated, need to know the legacy of last generation. Also, we are looking forward teaching the learners that have related to Persia culture. I would like to personally invite you to call and have a free session with us.

دیوان حافظ

شمس الدّین محمد حافظ شیرازی

با ترجمه انگلیسی: هنری ویلبرت فورس کلارک

گردآوری: حمید اسلامیان

Printed in Great Britain
by Amazon

39351437R00256